NINETEENTH-CENTURY ENGLISH VERSE DRAMA

Other books by **Gerald** B. Kauvar
    The Other Poetry of Keats
    The Victorian Mind (Coeditor with Gerald C. Sorensen)

Other books by **Gerald C.** Sorensen
    The Victorian Mind (Coeditor with Gerald B. Kauvar)

Nineteenth-Century English Verse Drama

with Introductions and Edited
by Gerald B. Kauvar and Gerald C. Sorensen

Rutherford • *Madison* • *Teaneck*
Fairleigh Dickinson University Press

© 1973 by Associated University Presses, Inc.

Associated University Presses, Inc.
Cranbury, New Jersey 08512

Library of Congress Cataloging in Publication Data

Kauvar, Gerald B   comp.
Nineteenth-century English verse drama.

   CONTENTS: General introduction, by G. B. Kauvar.—W. Wordsworth's
The borderers.—S. T. Coleridge's Remorse. [etc.]
1. English drama—19th century.   I. Sorensen, Gerald C., joint comp.
II. Title.
PR1271.K3   822'.7'09   79-146163
ISBN 0-8386-7631-6

Printed in the United States of America

CONTENTS

General Introduction   7
    by Gerald B. Kauvar

1   William Wordsworth's *The Borderers*   13
    Introduction by Gerald B. Kauvar
    The Borderers   21

2   Samuel Taylor Coleridge's *Remorse*   59
    Introduction by Gerald B. Kauvar
    Remorse   65

3   George Gordon, Lord Byron's *Manfred*   97
    Introduction by Gerald B. Kauvar
    Manfred   105

4   Percy Bysshe Shelley's *The Cenci*   125
    Introduction by Gerald B. Kauvar
    The Cenci   132

5   John Keats's *Otho The Great*   169
    Introduction by Gerald B. Kauvar
    Otho The Great   175

6   Matthew Arnold's *Empedocles on Etna*   203
    Introduction by Gerald C. Sorensen
    Empedocles on Etna   208

7   Robert Browning's *King Victor and King Charles*   223
    Introduction by Gerald C. Sorensen
    King Victor and King Charles   229

8   Alfred, Lord Tennyson's *Becket*   255
    Introduction by Gerald C. Sorensen
    Becket   260

9   Algernon Charles Swinburne's *Atalanta in Calydon*   309
    Introduction by Gerald C. Sorensen
    Atalanta in Calydon   314

Bibliography   353

GENERAL INTRODUCTION

For an analysis of what went wrong with nineteenth-century verse tragedy, one might well raid Ezra Pound: for ninety years out of key with their times, we could say, its authors "strove to resuscitate the dead art / Of poetry; to maintain 'the sublime'/In the old sense." Like Pound's E.P., it is not our poets who were wrong; the age demanded and got something more appropriate to its needs, and most recent scholarly activity in the area of nineteenth-century drama has been concerned to account for, justify, and applaud the rise of the melodrama. Scholars are now concerned with elucidating "the psychological and sociological significance of a genre that brought drama into a completely new relationship with its audience and thereby, for the first time in human history, made play-watching a major public amusement of the people, created the entertainment industry, and then established the indulgence of visual fantasy as the greatest single leisure occupation of a technological society."[1] Richard Corrigan, arguing that melodrama was "the dominant modality of all nineteenth-century British life and thought," defends its anti-intellectualism and ethical simplicity on the grounds of its "capacity to give direct objective form to our irrational fears," inasmuch as "it deals with the kind of external conflict typical of our daily lives and anxieties."[2]

But is it merely a wish to escape such anxieties that makes Lamb reminisce about "The Artificial Comedy of the Last Century"?

> We have been spoiled with—not sentimental comedy—but a tyrant far more pernicious to our pleasures which has succeeded to it, the exclusive and all-devouring drama of common life; where the moral point is everything; where, instead of the fictitious half-believed personages of the stage (the phantoms of old comedy), we recognize ourselves, our brothers, aunts, kinsfolk, allies, patrons, enemies,— the same as in life, — with an interest in what is going on so hearty and substantial, that we cannot afford our moral judgment, in its deepest and most vital results, to compromise or slumber for a moment. What is *there* transacting, by no modification is made to affect us in any other manner than the same events and characters would do in our relationships of life. We carry our fire-side concerns to the theatre with us. We do not go thither, like our ancestors, to escape from the pressure of reality, so much as to confirm our experience of it; to make assurance double, and take a bond of fate. We must live our toilsome lives twice over, as it was the mournful privilege of Ulysses to descend twice to the shades.

If we take Lamb without discount for irony, and if we read "escape" without recognizing the implicit "transcend" that we—Platonist or Aristotelian—attribute to the realm of art, especially poetic tragedy, then we can with calm of mind continue our resuscitation of melodrama and continue to neglect those dramas selected for inclusion in this collection—dramas which are in seriousness, magnitude, and completeness a significant portion of the canons of nine of the most important

7

nineteenth-century poets. No neglected masterpieces are so widely known and, with two or three exceptions, so little studied—or read. Our knowledge of them tends to organize itself around the poets' need for money, for popular acclaim, or their attempts to emulate Elizabethan predecessors. Or we study this drama and its lack of success in terms of the economics of the theater, the power of the two major playhouses and their managers, or the impositions of the star system. Seldom do we look for value in the work of art itself. As one reviewer has put it, we tend to deplore available criticism without thinking very well of the dramas themselves, which are not championed but patronized.[3] To be sure, this anonymous reviewer limited his comments to the Romantic drama, for this is the concern of the work he reviews; nonetheless, the criticism is equally pertinent to the Victorian dramas in this collection and, for the most part, to their critics.

Of course, it is easy to devalue the dramatic efforts of these poets, for it is not wholly without reason that their plays are so largely ignored; yet, we ignore them at our peril. First of all, as suggested earlier, these are major works in each man's canon. Second, as is shown in the critical introductions, these plays often succeed in literary and dramatic terms far beyond our expectations. Moreover, when they fail, the reasons for their collapse are instructive: they are members of that too frequently maligned genre: "interesting failures." For one thing, they are interesting in terms of their relationships with the remainder of their author's *œuvres*; often their themes, motifs, symbols, and strategies provide significant counter-truths to more popular works. For another, as the introductions demonstrate, the majority of these dramas have an intrinsic interest and value beyond that ordinarily attributed to them. They are not only works of important artists; they are works of art that have something interesting and important to express about the human condition.

For too long we have dismissed these dramas without studying them except as they contribute to our gossipy knowledge of the lives of the poets or the life of the theater. Each of us can, unreflectingly, utter the critical commonplace that the plays are failures as dramas because their authors' gifts are primarily lyrical, not dramatic. Yet much of the recent criticism of many of these authors has emphasized the radically dramatic nature of individual works and of the canons themselves. We are tending more and more to read works like these plays as expressionist dramas, the various characters revealing moods of one mind. And again, there is the tendency to use the label "closet drama," which applies to many of these works, as if it were normative as well as descriptive. Surely there are some superior closet dramas and some inferior ones.

It is true that, despite their expressionist cum lyric centers, these dramas occasionally attempt to achieve the operatic and spectacular effects appropriate to the contemporary theaters and their stars. Still, if these plays are failures in some senses, they are failures of an extraordinary kind. They are not merely unwatched potboilers, and the introductions in this volume are designed to reveal their genuine literary and dramatic merits.

Ignorance of the theater is another charge frequently laid against these dramatists; the consequence, naturally, is an ill-wrought play. In the recently edited "Reminiscences" of the Reverend Alexander Dyce we are given an illuminating instance:

> James Wallack was present among the other actors in the Green-room of Drurylane Theatre when Coleridge read them his tragedy of *Remorse*, and gave them particular directions how certain passages were to be delivered. His reading was a sort of high musical chant; and his ideas of stage-effects were so exquisitely ridiculous, that the actors had great difficulty in listening to him without bursting out into laughter.[4]

Unfortunately, we do not have the reverse of the coin. Among Coleridge's unborn works is the one referred to in his 1813 Preface to *Remorse*:

I defer all answers to the different criticisms on the Piece to an essay, which I am about to publish immediately, on Dramatic Poetry, relatively to the present state of the Metropolitan Theatres.

That the then-present (and undoubtedly deplorable) state of the theaters made them generally indifferent to verse tragedy is largely true. But it must also be recognized that some such dramas, like *Remorse* itself, did succeed, and it must also be recognized that " 'the sublime'/In the old sense" was uncongenial both to the poets' capacities and to the times. Writing of Beddoes's "Death's Jest-Book," Northrop Frye corrects our authors and us:

> before we assign Beddoes to that unhappy, obsessed, and somewhat masochistic band of modern poets who have tried to "revive poetic drama," we should glance at the courage and common sense with which he defines his attitude:
>> I am convinced that the man who is to awaken the drama must be a bold trampling fellow . . . [w]ith the greatest reverence for all the antiquities of the drama, I still think we had better beget than revive—attempt to give the literature of this age an idiosyncrasy and spirit of its own, and only raise a ghost to gaze on, not to live with.[5]

In this effort, Beddoes and our nine authors failed. But their verse dramas are not failures. Lest the current craze for nineteenth-century melodrama bury them deeper, this volume presents nine ghosts to gaze on and nine introductions that attempt to provide us with some terms on which we may be able to begin living with them. For these verse dramas are, if not central jewels in, at least adjuncts to, "the Muse's diadem."

G. B. K.

1. Gary J. Scrimgeour, "Nineteenth-Century Drama," *Victorian Studies* (Sept. 1968), p. 94.
2. Quoted in *ibid*.
3. Anon. rev. of *English Romantic Drama*, by Richard Fletcher. *Yale Review* 57 (Winter, 1968): xvi.
4. Ed. Sam Schoenbaum. *TLS* (22 Jan. 71), p. 101.
5. *A Study of English Romanticism* (New York: 1968), pp. 59–60.

NINETEENTH-CENTURY ENGLISH VERSE DRAMA

WILLIAM WORDSWORTH'S *THE BORDERERS*

Wordsworth chose two couplets from Pope's "Moral Essays: Epistle 1" to close his preface to *The Borderers:*

> Of human actions reason though you can,
> It may be Reason, but it is not Man;
> His principle of action once explore,
> That instant 'tis his principle no more.

This warning about the tangled roots of human motivation follows Wordsworth's long and complex analysis of Oswald's character, an analysis which, though penetrating, is lifeless, much as Pope warned in the succeeding couplet:

> Like following life through creatures you dissect,
> You lose it in the moment you detect.

Wordsworth's aim in *The Borderers* was not to dissect; rather, as he told Isabella Fenwick, "My care was almost exclusively given to the passions and the characters, and the position in which the persons in the Drama stood relatively to each other, that the reader (for I had then no thought of the Stage) might be moved, and to a degree instructed, by lights penetrating somewhat into the depths of our nature." To this explanation can be added the following paragraph of Wordsworth's preface, the paragraph immediately preceding the quotation from Pope.

> We are too apt to apply our own moral sentiments as a measure of the conduct of others. We insensibly suppose that a criminal action assumes the same form to the agent as to ourselves. We forget that his feelings and his reason are equally busy in contracting its dimensions and pleading for its necessity.

A more dramatic aim is not easy to conceive, and, expressed in this way, Wordsworth's intention shares much with those of Shelley and Keats. The Romantic recognition and celebration of each man's unique personality were defended by Shelley as tending in literature to strengthen our moral organ, the imagination, and Keats's quest for negative capability, insofar as it seeks a Shakespearean negation of the poet's own personality, complements Shelley's ideas. Wordsworth, often considered the most egotistical of the Romantics in obtruding his personality, his morality, his ideas into his poetry, shares with his contemporaries a dramatic impulse that achieves expression in a powerful and impressive, if not wholly successful, verse drama.

Written at Racedown in 1795–1797, revised for possible theater production in 1797, and slightly corrected in the year of its publication, 1842, *The Borderers* is a theme-ridden play; commentators have found in it not only a reaction against the extremes of Godwinian rationalism,[1] but, more significantly, one of the first literary presentations of modern man's intellectual divorce from nature. Geoffrey Hartman has stated this case with great persuasiveness. *The Borderers,* he argues "projects, in fact, a myth of the birth of modern intellectual consciousness, and explores the question of whether that can ever have a moral function."[2] Hartman finds that "Its real value is as a drama revealing the perils of the soul in its passage towards individuation, or from a morality based on 'nature' to one based on the autonomous self."[3] That Wordsworth was unable to find answers to the questions or alternatives posed in the play is a belief shared by many of its students. A supposed lack of literary structure and depth is another frequently encountered criticism.

This substantive lack is not one of a merely technical nature, though Wordsworth himself was conscious of *The Borderers'* weakness as drama. He told Isabella Fenwick that had the play "been the work of a later period of life, the plot would have been something more complex, and a greater variety of characters introduced to relieve the mind from the pressure of incidents so mournful." Still, Meyer's judgments that *The Borderers* is "all but unintelligible," and "a work almost devoid of artistic merit" are not warranted.[4] It is true that, with the exception of Marmaduke and Oswald, the characters are flat and static. Even Oswald does not develop; he is merely revealed, and Marmaduke's progress is more nearly a jerky succession of conflicting attitudes than the reciprocal ambivalences of a tormented soul. Added to this, the frequent changes of scene and the long, almost expository, philosophical and psychological speeches of Oswald and Marmaduke tend to corroborate Wordsworth's disclaimer that *The Borderers* was not intended for the stage but rather for the closet.

Yet *The Borderers* was sent late in 1797 to the manager of Covent Garden, after revisions were made at the suggestion of "one of the principle actors" of the house. Coleridge's approbation had buoyed Wordsworth's hopes. Calling the play "absolutely wonderful," Coleridge continued: "There are in the piece those *profound* touches of the human heart which I find three or four times in 'The Robbers' of Schiller, and often in Shakespeare, but in Wordsworth there are no inequalities." Despite the curtailment of the original version, and despite the justice of Coleridge's attribution of profundity, the play was rejected. The following year Wordsworth wrote, "If ever I attempt another drama, it shall be written either purposely for the closet, or purposely for the stage. There is no middle way."

The dramatic elements in *The Borderers* are threefold. First, the fate of Herbert, constantly in jeopardy, is not resolved until Act V. Second, the revelation of Oswald's character is not complete until Act IV, when, believing that Marmaduke has slain Herbert, Oswald narrates his history. Third, and in many ways the most important, the description of Marmaduke's psychological state and his changing relationship with Oswald are not completed until the end of the drama. Only then, having confessed his guilt and challenged that mystical sympathy with Oswald so often referred to by the latter, does he choose to endure, to "wander on— / A man by pain and thought compelled to live, / Yet loathing

1. See G. W. Meyer's *Wordsworth's Formative Years,* University of Michigan Publications in Language and Literature 20 (Ann Arbor, 1943) : 174 ff.
2. *Wordsworth's Poetry: 1787–1814,* (New Haven, 1964) , p. 126.
3. *Ibid.,* p. 129.
4. Meyer, p. 153. John Jones calls the play "almost unreadable." *The Egotistical Sublime* (London, 1964) , p. 54.

life." Not until the end of the play does Marmaduke achieve an understanding of his own tormented nature. Only then, with the burden of Herbert's Christian forgiveness, can Marmaduke abjure the morality thrust upon him by Oswald and choose to wander until Mercy allows him to die.

The soul of Marmaduke in torment is the true subject of Wordsworth's drama. Regardless of the relationships between the play and the life of the poet in France and his feelings about the putative desertion of Annette Vallon,[5] his dramatic portrayal of "the mind of man upturned" is compelling. The villainy of Oswald (over-determined by his history, as elaborated by Wordsworth's long psychological discussion in the preface) lies not so much in Godwinian rationalism, a denial of benevolence,[6] as it does in the curiously Hawthornesque nature of his manipulation of Marmaduke's soul. In Hawthorne's works, elevating the head over the heart is an unpardonable sin and the sort of rationalism Hawthorne condemned is often accompanied in his characters by a quasi-scientific manipulation of one human being, such as Dimmesdale, by another, such as Chillingworth. The experimentation, the apparently dispassionate, clinical dissection, is equally repugnant to Wordsworth. What is dissected is the natural bond of thought and feeling, of head and heart, of man and nature. This violent separation is, as Pope warned, life-stifling. Yet it is this sort of endeavor in which Oswald is engaged:

> This Stripling's mind
> Is shaken till the dregs float on the surface;
> And, in the storm and anguish of the heart,
> He talks of a transition in his Soul,
> And dreams that he is happy. We dissect
> The senseless body, and why not the mind?—
> These are strange sights—the mind of man, upturned,
> Is in all natures a strange spectacle;
> In some a hideous one.
>
> (III.1.28–36)

Salvation can be achieved only if the links are restored—but this is a grace beyond the reach of science. Once made, the breach between head and heart, man and nature, can be bridged only by nature. The finer impulses, residing in our benevolent feelings and communicated directly to the soul by the senses, constitute nature's healing power in much of Wordsworth's poetry, as they do in *The Borderers*. That unaided reason is insufficient to chart mankind's voyage through life is a familiar Romantic dictum, though, to be sure, the bootless remorse condemned by Oswald, and the evidence available in the play that "the world is poisoned at the heart" may lead us to agree with Hartman that "Wordsworth may have been of his [Oswald's] party (and Nietzsche's) without knowing it."[7]

Dissatisfaction with the substance of the play has at its intellectual core neither a simple rejection of the pessimism in the drama nor a disappointment with Marmaduke's choice of exile. Rather, it is charged that Wordsworth failed to posit an ethic that could provide a unifying principle. *The Borderers*, as G. Wilson Knight writes, was published late in Wordsworth's life, a life which is "one long attempt to modify his sight of the nakedly spectral powers into a more positive doctrine of nature and human existence."[8] Corollary to this are John

---

5. See, for example, Mary Moorman, *William Wordsworth: A Biography* (London, 1957), Vol. 1, pp. 303–4, and O. J. Campbell and P. Mueschke, "The Borderers as a Document in the History of Wordsworth's Aesthetic Development," *Modern Philology* 23, no. 26: 465–82.

6. On this point see Carl Woodring, *Wordsworth* (Boston: Houghton Mifflin, 1965), pp. 16–17.

7. Hartman, p. 129.

8. G. W. Knight, *The Starlit Dome* (New York, 1941), p. 36.

Jones's observations about the lack of Shakespearean resonance in a drama echoing so much of *Othello, Macbeth, Hamlet,* and *Lear.* There are, Jones points out, fine statements about maturity, patience, and the cyclical nature of things, "but because they have not the massive structure of Lear behind them, they sound in their context ghostly thin."[9] So, for all its intellectual density, resulting in charges of unintelligibility, *The Borderers* is said to lack a consistent profundity; the philosophy and psychology ring hollow in a drama without rounded, dynamic characters and a centripetal vision.

Yet there is evidence of an attempt to provide a unifying ethical principle. Throughout the play Marmaduke's attempts to bring Herbert to "Justice" are thwarted by the moral power residing in the physical beauty shared by Herbert and Idonea. And just as Marmaduke seems ready to murder Herbert, the beauty of a single star thwarts him. This latent ethic achieves clearer expression in other places in Wordsworth's poetry, and it is worth exploring a few such instances now for the help they can give us in understanding *The Borderers.* The following familiar lines from "Expostulation and Reply" are relevant here:

> The eye—it cannot choose but see:
> We cannot bid the ear be still;
> Our bodies feel where'er they be,
> Against or with our will.

And in the companion piece to this poem we learn that

> One impulse from a vernal wood
> May teach you more of man,
> Of moral evil and of good,
> Than all the sages can.
>
> Sweet is the lore which Nature brings;
> Our meddling intellect
> Mis-shapes the beauteous forms of things—
> We murder to dissect.

In Book XI of *The Prelude* we learn more about souls tormented like Marmaduke's (and like Wordsworth's at the time he composed *The Borderers*) :

> I summoned my best skill, and toiled, intent
> To *anatomise* the frame of social life,
> Yea, the whole body of society
> Searched to its heart. Share with me, Friend! the wish
> That some *dramatic tale,* endued with shapes
> Livelier, and flinging out less guarded words
> Than suit the work we fashion, might set forth
> What then I learned, or think I learned, of truth,
> And the errors into which I fell, betrayed
> By present objects, and by reasonings false
> From their beginnings, inasmuch as drawn
> Out of a heart that had been turned aside
> From Nature's way by outward accidents,
> And which was thus confounded, more and more
> Misguided, and misguiding. So I fared,
> Dragging all precepts, judgments, maxims, creeds,
> Like culprits to the bar; calling the mind,
> Suspiciously, to establish in plain day

---

9. Jones, p. 58.

> Her titles and her honours; now believing,
> Now disbelieving; endlessly perplexed
> With impulse, motive, right and wrong, the ground
> Of obligation, what the rule and whence
> The sanction; till, demanding formal *proof,*
> And seeking it in every thing, I lost
> All feeling of conviction, and, in fine,
> Sick, wearied out with contrarieties,
> Yielded up moral questions in despair.
>
> (279–305)

This sounds a good deal like the mental process and tortures undergone by Oswald as he describes them at the opening of Act III. His doubts about the efficacy of proof and passion, and his anatomizing of society are elaborated here. His praise of unaided reason and his congratulation to Marmaduke for having

> obeyed the only law that sense
> Submits to recognize; the immediate law
> From the clear light of circumstance, flashed
> Upon an independent intellect
>
> (III.359–62)

culminate in the expressed belief that he is future's darling.

The French Revolution as a movement inspired by ideas had given the young Wordsworth similar feelings of hope and elation, untainted by Oswald's personal motives.

> But speaking more in charity, the dream
> Flattered the young, pleased with extremes, nor least
> With that which makes our Reason's naked self
> The object of its fervour. What delight!
> How glorious! in self-knowledge and self-rule,
> To look through all the frailties of the world,
> And, with a resolute mastery shaking off
> Infirmity of nature, time, and place,
> Build social upon personal liberty,
> Which, to the blind restraints of general laws
> Superior, majestically adopts
> One guide, the light of circumstances flashed
> Upon an independent intellect.
>
> (*Prelude* XI.232–44)

As we have seen in the first quoted passage, the Revolution was a disappointment, and as a result, the young Wordsworth's soul was in crisis, yielding up moral questions in despair and "Deeming our blessed reason of least use / Where wanted most."

Dorothy and Coleridge offered him the hope that "brightness would return" and an "office upon earth," but primarily,

> Nature's self,
> By all varieties of human love
> Assisted, led me back through opening day
> To those sweet counsels between head and heart
> Where grows that genuine knowledge, fraught with peace,
> Which, through the latter sinkings of this cause,
> Hath still upheld me and upholds me now.
>
> (*Prelude* XI.350–56)

To Marmaduke such counsel was interdicted by Oswald; yet, as we suggested, the possibilities for "one impulse from the vernal wood" to gain access through the senses were present throughout the first four acts. It is worth scrutinizing these in detail for the light they shed on that supposed lack of a unifying ethical ethos in the drama.

Oswald, as a champion of Reason, is blind to the salutary visitations of feeling and is alert only to pernicious or sentimental effects. Although his motives for making an "equal" of Marmaduke are prompted more by feeling than reason, Oswald thinks he has purged himself of such weaknesses.

> The insult bred
> More of contempt than hatred; both are flown;
> That either e'er existed is my shame:
> 'Twas a dull spark—a most unnatural fire
> That died the moment the air breathed upon it,
> —These fools of feeling are mere birds of winter
> That haunt some barren island of the north
> Where, if a famishing man stretch forth his hand,
> They think it is to feed them.
>
> (II.3–11)

Many of Oswald's observations are not contemptible: his ideas on the debilitating effects of remorse have attracted much sympathetic comment. His condemnation of the sort of open-heartedness which finds consolation and ease in finding someone to share its pain, which purchases a "puling sympathy" is an equally vigorous and admirable part of his code. Yet Oswald's blindness to the truths of the heart is his undoing. Having found an apparently successful way of coping with his history, Oswald overgeneralizes and attempts to elevate strategy into principle. Unaware of the extent to which his feelings direct his actions, he is blind and deaf to those natural impulses which at least temporarily prevent Marmaduke from committing an outrageous crime.

Despite Oswald's efforts to turn him against Herbert, Marmaduke's natural compassion is a powerful hedge against action: "Ne'er may I own the heart / That cannot feel for one, helpless as he is." (I.67–68)

Oswald, urging Marmaduke to *feel* Herbert's crimes, is thwarted by Marmaduke's recollection of his early, spontaneous love for the man (I. 87 ff.). The reciprocal part of Oswald's plan—the fear of Marmaduke he has implanted in Herbert, is argued against by Idonea, and the arguments she uses are worthy of special note:

> O could you hear his voice:
> Alas! you do not know him. He is one
>
> .   .   .   .
>
> All gentleness and love. His face bespeaks
> A deep and simple meekness: And that Soul,
> Which, with the motion of a virtuous act
> Flashes a look of terror upon guilt,
> Is, after conflict, quiet as the ocean.
>
> (I.165–66, 168–72)

With a similar argument Idonea continues to oppose her father: "Oh, could you *hear* his voice!" (I.210)

The moral force of beauty (a theme increasingly important to the action of the drama) is connected in the play to Idonea and to her resemblance to her father. Idonea is aware of her power: she rejects the host's offer of a guide by telling her father

Why if a wolf should leap out from a thicket,
A look of mine would send him scouring back
Unless I differ from the thing I am
When you are by my side.

(I.317–20)

From the beggar woman hired by Oswald to tell Marmaduke a false story, we learn again of the moral force of Idonea's beauty, though here used perversely for authenticity: "I cast a look upon the girl, and felt / As if my heart would burst."

Marmaduke's tormented soul is preyed upon by Oswald, who urges "the wholesome ministry of pain and evil" as the ally of benevolence, but Marmaduke retains a respect for natural feelings and believes he can separate magnanimity from weakness:

You are a man—and therefore, if compassion,
Which to our kind is natural as life,
Be known unto you, you will love this Woman,
Even as I do; but I should loathe the light,
If I could think one weak or partial feeling.

(II.76–80)

Marmaduke, attempting to murder Herbert, is unable to act, again checked by preternatural sympathy: "I look at him and tremble like a child." Then, in talking with his intended victim, Marmaduke's natural reluctance is reinforced by Herbert's description of how Idonea's "looks won pity" from an unsympathetic world. Oswald, learning that Marmaduke has failed to act, sneers, "Verily, when he said / How his old heart would leap to hear her steps / You thought his voice the echo of Idonea's," to which Marmaduke replies, "And never heard a sound so terrible." When Marmaduke reascends from the dungeon, having failed again to commit murder, he explains to Oswald the reasons for his hesitation. One of them is Herbert's resemblance to Idonea, even though

'Twas dark—dark as the grave; yet did I see,
Saw him—his face turned toward me; and I tell thee
Idonea's filial countenance was there
To baffle me—it put me to my prayers.
Upwards I cast my eyes, and through a crevice,
Beheld a star twinkling above my head,
And, by the living God, I could not do it.

(II.434–40)

This miraculous vision is similar to one given to the blind Herbert. An old pilgrim describes the scene to Idonea:

O Lady, you have need to love your Father.
His voice—me thinks I hear it now, his voice
When, after a broad flash that filled the cave,
He said to me that he had seen his Child,
A face (no cherub's face more beautiful)
Revealed by lustre brought with it from heaven.

(II.163–68)

Other instances of the power of looks and voices abound in the play, but it seems to me that, in conjunction with the intervention of the star, this instance functions to reveal the existence of a sustaining ethic in the play. The association of beauty and virtue, natural and human, is no accident or contrivance; behind it lies a philosophy of some profundity. In Thomas Taylor's essay "Concerning the Beautiful," the following exposition is made: "Thus, to the good man, virtue shining forth in youth is lovely, because consonant to true virtue, which lies deep in the soul. . . . Again, the music of the voice rouses the harmony latent in the soul, and opens her eye to the perception of beauty."[10]

The moral power of feeling, of our sensuous response to beauty that echoes the divine order of the universe, is sufficient to destroy the sophistical philosophy advocated by Oswald. At the end of the third act, this is made explicit. Idonea, explaining to Marmaduke the reason for choosing duty rather than personal happiness, asks for forgiveness if she has erred. Marmaduke responds:

> M.   I *do* forgive thee.
> I.   But take me to your arms—this breast, alas!
>   It throbs and you have a heart that does not feel it.
> M.   She is innocent.
> O.   Were I a moralist
>   I should make a wondrous revolution here;
>   It were a quaint experiment to show
>   The beauty of truth.
>
>   (III.484–90)

This is precisely what has been shown and it is the ethic sustaining the play. The inner beauty of the soul, reflected on the face and in the voice, like the beauty and peace of nature represented by the twinkling star, blasts Oswald's deification of reason. These twin powers are a source of consolation and a promise that, though powerfully constricting, the earth's provocations, men's musty laws, will not prevail. The beauty of truth, as particularized by Idonea, triumphs over the flimsy philosophical generalizations Oswald rationalized out of his own suffering. The permanent order of the universe overwhelms our more temporary discomforts.

Pope's *Moral Essay*, from which Wordsworth chose his epigraph, reminds us that

> God and Nature only are the same:
> In man, the judgment shoots at flying game,
> A bird of passage! gone as soon as found,
> Now in the Moon perhaps now under ground.

Had Marmaduke allowed himself to yield to these influxes of beauty—the beauty of the star and of Idonea's face, reinforced by a host of minor instances in the play; had his soul not been dissected by Oswald's meddling; had he not "cast off the chains of feeling" that, according to Oswald, fettered his "nobility of mind" and delivered "heart and head" to that villain, Marmaduke would not be the tragic character that he is. Though he is able to choose exile as expiation, his story is not, in its entirety, optimistic. That Marmaduke fails to achieve the salvation implicit in the drama makes his fate even more tragic.

                                                                           G.B.K.

---

10. *Thomas Taylor, the Platonist: Selected Writings,* ed. Kathleen Raine and G. M. Harper (Princeton, N.J., 1969), p. 149. For Wordsworth's knowledge of Taylor, see Raine's introduction, p. 8.

The Borderers

A TRAGEDY

1795–96. 1842

DRAMATIS PERSONÆ

MARMADUKE
OSWALD
WALLACE } *Of the Band of Borderers.*
LACY
LENNOX
HERBERT.
WILFRED, *Servant to Marmaduke.*
Host.
Forester.
ELDRED, *a Peasant.*
Peasant, Pilgrims, etc.
IDONEA.
Female Beggar.
ELEANOR, *Wife to Eldred.*
   SCENE — *Borders of England and Scotland.*
   TIME — *The Reign of Henry III.*

Readers already acquainted with my Poems will recognise, in the following composition, some eight or ten lines which I have not scrupled to retain in the places where they originally stood. It is proper, however, to add, that they would not have been used elsewhere, if I had foreseen the time when I might be induced to publish this Tragedy.

February 28, 1842.

ACT I

   SCENE — *Road in a Wood*
     WALLACE *and* LACY

Lacy. The troop will be impatient ; let us hie
Back to our post, and strip the Scottish Foray

Of their rich Spoil, ere they recross the Border.
— Pity that our young Chief will have no part
In this good service.
   Wal.   Rather let us grieve
That, in the undertaking which has caused
His absence, he hath sought, whate'er his aim,
Companionship with One of crooked ways,
From whose perverted soul can come no good
To our confiding, open-hearted, leader. 10
   Lacy. True ; and, remembering how the Band have proved
That Oswald finds small favour in our sight,
Well may we wonder he has gained such power
Over our much-loved Captain.
   Wal.   I have heard
Of some dark deed to which in early life
His passion drove him — then a Voyager
Upon the midland Sea. You knew his bearing
In Palestine ?
   Lacy.   Where he despised alike
Mahommedan and Christian. But enough ;
Let us begone — the Band may else be foiled.   [*Exeunt.*
   Enter MARMADUKE *and* WILFRED.
   Wil. Be cautious, my dear Master !
   Mar.   I perceive 21
That fear is like a cloak which old men huddle
About their love, as if to keep it warm.
   Wil. Nay, but I grieve that we should

part. This Stranger,
For such he is ——
   Mar.   Your busy fancies, Wilfred,
Might tempt me to a smile ; but what of
   him ?
   Wil. You know that you have saved his
   life.
   Mar.   I know it.
   Wil. And that he hates you ! — Pardon
   me, perhaps
That word was hasty.
   Mar.   Fy ! no more of it.
   Wil. Dear Master ! gratitude 's a heavy
   burden   30
To a proud Soul. — Nobody loves this
   Oswald —
Yourself, you do not love him.
   Mar.   I do more,
I honour him. Strong feelings to his heart
Are natural ; and from no one can be
   learnt
More of man's thoughts and ways than his
   experience
Has given him power to teach: and then
   for courage
And enterprise — what perils hath he
   shunned ?
What obstacles hath he failed to over-
   come ?
Answer these questions, from our common
   knowledge,
And be at rest.
   Wil.   Oh, Sir !
   Mar.   Peace, my good Wilfred;
Repair to Liddesdale, and tell the Band 41
I shall be with them in two days, at
   farthest.
   Wil. May He whose eye is over all pro-
   tect you !   [*Exit.*
Enter OSWALD (*a bunch of plants in his*
   hand).
   Osw. This wood is rich in plants and
   curious simples.
   Mar. (*looking at them*). The wild rose,
   and the poppy and the nightshade :
Which is your favourite, Oswald ?
   Osw.   That which, while it is
Strong to destroy, is also strong to heal —
                 [*Looking forward.*
Not yet in sight ! — We'll saunter here
   awhile ;
They cannot mount the hill, by us unseen.
   Mar. (*a letter in his hand*). It is no com-
   mon thing when one like you   50
Performs these delicate services, and there-
   fore
I feel myself much bounden to you,
   Oswald ;
'Tis a strange letter this ! — You saw her

write it ?
   Osw. And saw the tears with which she
   blotted it.
   Mar. And nothing less would satisfy
   him ?
   Osw.   No less ;
For that another in his Child's affection
Should hold a place, as if 't were robbery,
He seemed to quarrel with the very
   thought.
Besides, I know not what strange prejudice
Is rooted in his mind ; this Band of ours, 60
Which you 've collected for the noblest
   ends,
Along the confines of the Esk and Tweed
To guard the Innocent — he calls us " Out-
   laws " ;
And, for yourself, in plain terms he asserts
This garb was taken up that indolence
Might want no cover, and rapacity
Be better fed.
   Mar.   Ne'er may I own the heart
That cannot feel for one, helpless as he is.
   Osw.   Thou know'st me for a Man not
   easily moved,
Yet was I grievously provoked to think 70
Of what I witnessed.
   Mar.   This day will suffice
To end her wrongs.
   Osw.   But if the blind Man's tale
Should *yet* be true ?
   Mar.   Would it were possible !
Did not the soldier tell thee that himself,
And others who survived the wreck, beheld
The Baron Herbert perish in the waves
Upon the coast of Cyprus ?
   Osw.   Yes, even so,
And I had heard the like before : in sooth
The tale of this his quondam Barony
Is cunningly devised ; and, on the back 80
Of his forlorn appearance, could not fail
To make the proud and vain his tribu-
   taries,
And stir the pulse of lazy charity.
The seignories of Herbert are in Devon ;
We, neighbors of the Esk and Tweed: 't is
   much
The Arch-Impostor ——
   Mar.   Treat him gently, Oswald ;
Though I have never seen his face, me-
   thinks,
There cannot come a day when I shall
   cease
To love him. I remember, when a Boy
Of scarcely seven years' growth, beneath
   the Elm   90
That casts its shade over our village school,
'T was my delight to sit and hear Idonea
Repeat her Father's terrible adventures,

Till all the band of playmates wept to-
gether ;
And that was the beginning of my love.
And, through all converse of our later
years,
An image of this old Man still was present,
When I had been most happy. Pardon me
If this be idly spoken.
 Osw.   See, they come, 99
Two Travellers !
 Mar. (points). The woman is Idonea.
 Osw. And leading Herbert.
 Mar.   We must let them pass —
This thicket will conceal us.
      [They step aside.
Enter IDONEA, *leading* HERBERT *blind.*
 Idon. Dear Father, you sigh deeply ;
ever since
We left the willow shade by the brook-side,
Your natural breathing has been troubled.
 Her.   Nay,
You are too fearful ; yet must I confess,
Our march of yesterday had better suited
A firmer step than mine.
 Idon.   That dismal Moor —
In spite of all the larks that cheered our
path,
I never can forgive it : but how steadily
You paced along, when the bewildering
moonlight   111
Mocked me with many a strange fantastic
shape ! —
I thought the Convent never would ap-
pear ;
It seemed to move away from us : and yet,
That you are thus the fault is mine ; for
the air
Was soft and warm, no dew lay on the
grass,
And midway on the waste ere night had
fallen
I spied a Covert walled and roofed with
sods —
A miniature ; belike some Shepherd-
boy,
Who might have found a nothing-doing
hour   120
Heavier than work, raised it : within that
hut
We might have made a kindly bed of heath
And thankfully there rested side by side
Wrapped in our cloaks, and, with re-
cruited strength,
Have hailed the morning sun. But cheerily,
Father, —
That staff of yours, I could almost have
heart
To fling 't away from you : you make no
use

Of me, or of my strength ; — come, let me
feel
That you do press upon me. There — in-
deed
You are quite exhausted. Let us rest
awhile   130
On this green bank.   *[He sits down.*
 Her. (after some time). Idonea, you are
silent,
And I divine the cause.
 Idon.   Do not reproach me :
I pondered patiently your wish and will
When I gave way to your request ; and
now,
When I behold the ruins of that face,
Those eyeballs dark — dark beyond hope
of light,
And think that they were blasted for my
sake,
The name of Marmaduke is blown away :
Father, I would not change that sacred
feeling   139
For all this world can give.
 Her.   Nay, be composed :
Few minutes gone a faintness overspread
My frame, and I bethought me of two
things
I ne'er had heart to separate — my grave,
And thee, my Child !
 Idon.   Believe me, honoured Sire !
'T is weariness that breeds these gloomy
fancies,
And you mistake the cause : you hear the
woods
Resound with music, could you see the
sun,
And look upon the pleasant face of Na-
ture ——
 Her. I comprehend thee — I should be
as cheerful
As if we two were twins ; two songsters
bred   150
In the same nest, my spring-time one with
thine.
My fancies, fancies if they be, are such
As come, dear Child ! from a far deeper
source
Than bodily weariness. While here we sit
I feel my strength returning. — The be-
quest
Of thy kind Patroness, which to receive
We have thus far adventured, will suffice
To save thee from the extreme of penury ;
But when thy Father must lie down and
die
How wilt thou stand alone ?
 Idon.   Is he not strong ?
Is he not valiant ?
 Her.   Am I then so soon 161

Forgotten ? have my warnings passed so
    quickly
Out of thy mind ? My dear, my only,
    Child ;
Thou wouldst be leaning on a broken
    reed —
This Marmaduke ——
    Idon.   O could you hear his voice :
Alas ! you do not know him. He is one
(I wot not what ill tongue has wronged
    him with you)
All gentleness and love. His face bespeaks
A deep and simple meekness : and that
    Soul,
Which with the motion of a virtuous act
Flashes a look of terror upon guilt,   171
Is, after conflict, quiet as the ocean,
By a miraculous finger, stilled at once.
    Her. Unhappy Woman !
    Idon.   Nay, it was my duty
Thus much to speak ; but think not I for-
    get —
Dear Father ! how *could* I forget and
    live —
You and the story of that doleful night
When, Antioch blazing to her topmost
    towers,
You rushed into the murderous flames, re-
    turned
Blind as the grave, but, as you oft have
    told me,   180
Clasping your infant Daughter to your
    heart.
    Her. Thy Mother too ! — scarce had I
    gained the door,
I caught her voice ; she threw herself upon
    me,
I felt thy infant brother in her arms ;
She saw my blasted face — a tide of sol-
    diers
That instant rushed between us, and I
    heard
Her last death-shriek, distinct among a
    thousand.
    Idon. Nay, Father, stop not ; let me hear
    it all.
    Her. Dear Daughter ! precious relic of
    that time —
For my old age, it doth remain with thee
To make it what thou wilt. Thou hast
    been told,   191
That when, on our return from Palestine,
I found how my domains had been
    usurped,
I took thee in my arms, and we began
Our wanderings together. Providence
At length conducted us to Rossland, —
    there,

Our melancholy story moved a Stranger
To take thee to her home — and for myself,
Soon after, the good Abbot of St. Cuth-
    bert's
Supplied my helplessness with food and
    raiment,   200
And, as thou know'st, gave me that hum-
    ble Cot
Where now we dwell. — For many years I
    bore
Thy absence, till old age and fresh infirmi-
    ties
Exacted thy return, and our reunion.
I did not think that, during that long ab-
    sence,
My Child, forgetful of the name of Her-
    bert,
Had given her love to a wild Freebooter,
Who here, upon the borders of the Tweed,
Doth prey alike on two distracted Coun-
    tries,   209
Traitor to both.
    Idon.   Oh, could you hear his voice !
I will not call on Heaven to vouch for me,
But let this kiss speak what is in my heart.
            Enter a PEASANT.
    Pea. Good morrow, Strangers ! If you
    want a Guide,
Let me have a leave to serve you !
    Idon.   My Companion
Hath need of rest ; the sight of Hut or
    Hostel
Would be most welcome.
    Pea.   Yon white hawthorn gained,
You will look down into a dell, and there
Will see an ash from which a sign-board
    hangs ;
The house is hidden by the shade. Old
    Man,
You seem worn out with travel — shall I
    support you ?   220
    Her. I thank you ; but, a resting-place
    so near,
'T were wrong to trouble you.
    Pea.   God speed you both.
                    [*Exit* Peasant.
    Her. Idonea, we must part. Be not
    alarmed —
'T is but for a few days — a thought has
    struck me.
    Idon. That I should leave you at this
    house, and thence
Proceed alone. It shall be so ; for strength
Would fail you ere our journey's end be
    reached.
        [*Exit* Herbert *supported by* Idonea.
    Re-enter MARMADUKE *and* OSWALD.
    Mar. This instant will we stop him ——

Osw.   Be not hasty,
For, sometimes, in despite of my conviction,
He tempted me to think the Story true ; 230
'T is plain he loves the Maid, and what he said
That savoured of aversion to thy name
Appeared the genuine colour of his soul —
Anxiety lest mischief should befall her
After his death.
    Mar.   I have been much deceived.
    Osw. But sure he loves the Maiden, and never love
Could find delight to nurse itself so strangely,
Thus to torment her with *inventions !* — death —
There must be truth in this.
    Mar.   Truth in his story !
He must have felt it then, known what it was,   240
And in such wise to rack her gentle heart
Had been a tenfold cruelty.
    Osw.   Strange pleasures
Do we poor mortals cater for ourselves !
To see him thus provoke her tenderness
With tales of weakness and infirmity !
I'd wager on his life for twenty years.
    Mar. We will not waste an hour in such a cause.
    Osw. Why, this is noble ! shake her off at once.
    Mar. Her virtues are his instruments. —
A Man
Who has so practised on the world's cold sense,   250
May well deceive his Child — what ! leave her thus,
A prey to a deceiver ? — no — no — no —
'T is but a word and then ——
    Osw.   Something is here
More than we see, or whence this strong aversion ?
Marmaduke ! I suspect unworthy tales
Have reached his ear — you have had enemies.
    Mar. Enemies ! — of his own coinage.
    Osw.   That may be,
But wherefore slight protection such as you
Have power to yield ? perhaps he looks elsewhere, —
I am perplexed.
    Mar.   What hast thou heard or seen ?
    Osw. No — no — the thing stands clear of mystery ;   261
(As you have said) he coins himself the slander

With which he taints her ear ; — for a plain reason ;
He dreads the presence of a virtuous man
Like you ; he knows your eye would search his heart,
Your justice stamp upon his evil deeds
The punishment they merit. All is plain :
It cannot be ——
    Mar.   What cannot be ?
    Osw.   Yet that a Father
Should in his love admit no rivalship,
And torture thus the heart of his own Child ——   270
    Mar. Nay, you abuse my friendship !
    Osw.   Heaven forbid ! —
There was a circumstance, trifling indeed —
It struck me at the time — yet I believe
I never should have thought of it again
But for the scene which we by chance have witnessed.
    Mar. What is your meaning ?
    Osw.   Two days gone I saw,
Though at a distance and he was disguised,
Hovering round Herbert's door, a man whose figure
Resembled much that cold voluptuary,
The villain, Clifford. He hates you, and he knows   280
Where he can stab you deepest.
    Mar.   Clifford never
Would stoop to skulk about a Cottage door —
It could not be.
    Osw.   And yet I now remember,
That, when your praise was warm upon my tongue,
And the blind Man was told how you had rescued
A maiden from the ruffian violence
Of this same Clifford, he became impatient
And would not hear me.
    Mar.   No — it cannot be —
I dare not trust myself with such a thought —
Yet whence this strange aversion ? You are a man   290
Not used to rash conjectures ——
    Osw.   If you deem it
A thing worth further notice, we must act
With caution, sift the matter artfully.
        [*Exeunt* Marmaduke *and* Oswald.

Scene — *The Door of the Hostel*

Herbert, Idonea, *and* Host.

Her. (*seated*) . As I am dear to you, re-

member, Child !
This last request.

Idon.   You know me, Sire ; farewell !

Her. And are you going then ? Come,
come, Idonea,
We must not part, — I have measured
many a league
When these old limbs had need of rest, —
and now
I will not play the sluggard.

Idon.   Nay, sit down.
                    [*Turning to* Host.
Good Host, such tendance as you would
expect   300
From your own Children, if yourself were
sick,
Let this old Man find at your hands ;
poor Leader,   [*Looking at the dog*
We soon shall meet again. If thou neglect
This charge of thine, then ill befall thee !
— Look,
The little fool is loth to stay behind.
Sir Host ! by all the love you bear to cour-
tesy,
Take care of him, and feed the truant
well.

Host. Fear not, I will obey you ; — but
One so young,
And One so fair, it goes against my heart
That you should travel unattended,
Lady ! —   310
I have a palfrey and a groom: the lad
Shall squire you, (would it not be better,
Sir ?)
And for less fee than I would let him run
For any lady I have seen this twelvemonth.

Idon. You know, Sir, I have been too
long your guard
Not to have learnt to laugh at little fears.
Why, if a wolf should leap from out a
thicket,
A look of mine would send him scouring
back,
Unless I differ from the thing I am   319
When you are by my side.

Her.   Idonea, wolves
Are not the enemies that move my fears.

Idon. No more, I pray, of this. Three
days at farthest
Will bring me back — protect him, Saints
— farewell !   [*Exit* Idonea.

Host. 'T is never drought with us — St.
Cuthbert and his Pilgrims,
Thanks to them, are to us a stream of com-
fort :
Pity the Maiden did not wait a while ;
She could not, Sir, have failed of company.

Her. Now she is gone, I fain would call
her back.

Host (calling). Holla !

Her.   No, no, the business must be
done. —
What means this riotous noise ?

Host.   The villagers
Are flocking in — a wedding festival — 331
That's all — God save you, Sir.

Enter OSWALD.

Osw.   Ha ! as I live,
The Baron Herbert.

Host.   Mercy, the Baron Herbert !

Osw. So far into your journey ! on my
life,
You are a lusty Traveller. But how fare
you ?

Her. Well as the wreck I am permits.
And you, Sir ?

Osw. I do not see Idonea.

Her.   Dutiful Girl,
She is gone before, to spare my weariness.
But what has brought you hither ?

Osw.   A slight affair,
That will be soon despatched.

Her.   Did Marmaduke
Receive that letter ?

Osw.   Be at peace. — The tie 341
Is broken, you will hear no more of *him*.

Her. This is true comfort, thanks a thou-
sand times ! —
That noise ! — would I had gone with her
as far
As the Lord Clifford's Castle : I have heard
That, in his milder moods, he has ex-
pressed
Compassion for me. His influence is great
With Henry, our good King ; — the Baron
might
Have heard my suit, and urged my plea at
Court.
No matter — he 's a dangerous Man. —
That noise ! —   850
'T is too disorderly for sleep or rest.
Idonea would have fears for me, — the
Convent
Will give me quiet lodging. You have a
boy, good Host,
And he must lead me back.

Osw.   You are most lucky ;
I have been waiting in the wood hard by
For a companion — here he comes ; our
journey

Enter MARMADUKE.

Lies on your way ; accept us as your
Guides.

Her. Alas ! I creep so slowly.

Osw. Never fear;
We 'll not complain of that.
  Her. My limbs are stiff
And need repose. Could you but wait an
  hour ?   360
  Osw. Most willingly ! — Come, let me
  lead you in,
And, while you take your rest, think not
  of us ;
We 'll stroll into the wood ; lean on my
  arm.
    [*Conducts* Herbert *into the house.
    Exit* Marmaduke.

                Enter Villagers.

  Osw. (*to himself coming out of the
                         Hostel*).
      I have prepared a most apt Instru-
      ment —
  The Vagrant must, no doubt, be loitering
    somewhere
  About this ground ; she hath a tongue
    well skilled,
  By mingling natural matter of her own
  With all the daring fictions I have taught
    her,
  To win belief, such as my plot requires.
                         [*Exit* Oswald.

Enter more Villagers, *a* Musician *among
                them.*

  Host (*to them*). Into the court, my
    Friend, and perch yourself   370
Aloft upon the elm-tree. Pretty Maids,
Garlands and flowers, and cakes and
    merry thoughts,
Are here, to send the sun into the west
More speedily than you belike would
    wish.

SCENE *changes to the Wood adjoining the
                Hostel*

MARMADUKE *and* OSWALD *entering.*

  Mar. I would fain hope that we deceive
    ourselves ;
When first I saw him sitting there, alone,
It struck upon my heart I know not how.
  Osw. To-day will clear up all. — You
    marked a Cottage,
That ragged Dwelling, close beneath a
    rock   379
By the brook-side : it is the abode of One,
A Maiden innocent till ensnared by Clif-
    ford,

Who soon grew weary of her ; but, alas !
What she had seen and suffered turned
    her brain.
Cast off by her Betrayer, she dwells alone,
Nor moves her hands to any needful work :
She eats her food which every day the
    peasants
Bring to her hut ; and so the Wretch has
    lived
Ten years ; and no one ever heard her
    voice ;
But every night at the first stroke of twelve
She quits her house, and, in the neigh-
    bouring Churchyard   390
Upon the self-same spot, in rain or storm,
She paces out the hour 'twixt twelve and
    one —
She paces round and round an Infant's
    grave,
And in the churchyard sod her feet have
    worn
A hollow ring ; they say it is knee-deep ——
Ah ! what is here ?
    [*A female* Beggar *rises up, rubbing
    her eyes as if in sleep — a* Child *in
    her arms.*
  Beg. Oh ! Gentlemen, I thank you ;
I 've had the saddest dream that ever
    troubled
The heart of living creature. — My poor
    Babe
Was crying, as I thought, crying for bread
When I had none to give him ; where-
    upon,   400
I put a slip of foxglove in his hand,
Which pleased him so, that he was hushed
    at once :
When, into one of those same spotted
    bells
A bee came darting, which the Child with
    joy
Imprisoned there, and held it to his ear,
And suddenly grew black, as he would die.
  Mar. We have no time for this, my
    babbling Gossip ;
Here's what will comfort you.
                         [*Gives her money.*
  Beg.   The Saints reward you
For this good deed ! — Well, Sirs, this
    passed away ;
And afterwards I fancied, a strange dog,
Trotting alone along the beaten road, 411
Came to my child as by my side he slept
And, fondling, licked his face, then on a
    sudden
Snapped fierce to make a morsel of his
    head ;
But here he is (*kissing the Child*) it must
    have been a dream.

Osw. When next inclined to sleep, take
    my advice,
And put your head, good Woman, under
    cover.
    Beg. Oh, sir, you would not talk thus, if
        you knew
What life is this of ours, how sleep will
    master
The weary-worn. — You gentlefolk have
    got   420
Warm chambers to your wish. I 'd rather
    be
A stone than what I am. — But two nights
    gone,
The darkness overtook me — wind and rain
Beat hard upon my head — and yet I saw
A glow-worm, through the covert of the
    furze,
Shine calmly as if nothing ailed the sky :
At which I half accused the God in
    Heaven —
You must forgive me.
    Osw.   Ay, and if you think
The Fairies are to blame, and you should
    chide
Your favourite saint — no matter — this
    good day   430
Has made amends.
    Beg.   Thanks to you both ; but, O sir !
How would you like to travel on whole
    hours
As I have done, my eyes upon the ground,
Expecting still, I knew not how, to find
A piece of money glittering through the
    dust.
    Mar. This woman is a prater. Pray,
        good Lady !
Do you tell fortunes ?
    Beg.   Oh, Sir, you are like the rest.
This Little-one — it cuts me to the heart —
Well ! they might turn a beggar from their
    doors,
But there are Mothers who can see the
    Babe   440
Here at my breast, and ask me where I
    bought it :
This they can do, and look upon my face —
But you, Sir, should be kinder.
    Mar.   Come hither, Fathers,
And learn what nature is from this poor
    Wretch !
    Beg. Ay, Sir, there 's nobody that feels
        for us.
Why now — but yesterday I overtook
A blind old Greybeard and accosted him,
I' th' name of all the Saints, and by the
    Mass
He should have used me better ! — Char-
    ity !

If you can melt a rock, he is your man ;
But I 'll be even with him — here again 451
Have I been waiting for him.
    Osw.   Well, but softly,
Who is it that hath wronged you ?
    Beg.   Mark you me ;
I 'll point him out ; — a Maiden is his
    guide,
Lovely as Spring's first rose ; a little dog,
Tied by a woollen cord, moves on before
With look as sad as he were dumb ; the
    cur,
I owe him no ill will, but in good sooth
He does his Master credit.
    Mar.   As I live,   459
'T is Herbert and no other !
    Beg.   'T is a feast to see him,
Lank as a ghost and tall, his shoulders
    bent,
And long beard white with age — yet
    evermore,
As if he were the only Saint on earth,
He turns his face to heaven.
    Osw.   But why so violent
Against this venerable Man ?
    Beg.   I 'll tell you :
He has the very hardest heart on earth ;
I had as lief turn to the Friars' school
And knock for entrance, in mid holiday.
    Mar. But to your story.
    Beg.   I was saying, Sir —
Well ! — he has often spurned me like a
    toad,   470
But yesterday was worse than all ; — at last
I overtook him, Sirs, my Babe and I,
And begged a little aid for charity :
But he was snappish as a cottage cur.
Well then, says I — I 'll out with it ; at
    which
I cast a look upon the Girl, and felt
As if my heart would burst ; and so I left
    him.
    Osw. I think, good Woman, you are the
        very person
Whom, but some few days past, I saw in
    Eskdale,   479
At Herbert's door.
    Beg.   Ay ; and if truth were known
I have good business there.
    Osw.   I met you at the threshold,
And he seemed angry.
    Beg.   Angry ! well he might ;
And long as I can stir I 'll dog him. —
    Yesterday,
To serve me so, and knowing that he owes
The best of all he has to me and mine.
But 't is all over now. — That good old
    Lady
Has left a power of riches ; and, I say it,

If there's a lawyer in the land, the knave
Shall give me half.
    Osw. What's this? — I fear, good Wom-
      an,   489
You have been insolent.
    Beg.   And there's the Baron,
I spied him skulking in his peasant's dress.
    Osw. How say you? in disguise? —
    Mar.   But what's your business
With Herbert or his Daughter?
    Beg.   Daughter! truly —
But how's the day? — I fear, my little
    Boy,
We've overslept ourselves. — Sirs, have you
    seen him?   [*Offers to go.*
    Mar. I must have more of this; — you
    shall not stir
An inch, till I am answered. Know you
    aught
That doth concern this Herbert?
    Beg.   You are provoked,
And will misuse me, Sir?   499
    Mar.   No trifling, Woman!
    Osw. You are as safe as in a sanctuary;
Speak.
    Mar. Speak!
    Beg.   He is a most hard-hearted Man.
    Mar. Your life is at my mercy.
    Beg.   Do not harm me,
And I will tell you all! — You know not,
    Sir,
What strong temptations press upon the
    Poor.
    Osw. Speak out.
    Beg.   Oh Sir, I've been a wicked
    Woman.
    Osw. Nay, but speak out!
    Beg.   He flattered me, and said
What harvest it would bring us both; and
    so,
I parted with the Child.
    Mar.   Parted with whom?
    Beg. Idonea, as he calls her; but the
    Girl
Is mine.
    Mar. Yours, Woman! are you Herbert's
    wife?   510
    Beg. Wife, Sir! his wife — not I; my
    husband, Sir,
Was of Kirkoswald — many a snowy winter
We've weathered out together. My poor
    Gilfred!
He has been two years in his grave.
    Mar.   Enough.
    Osw. We've solved the riddle — Mis-
    creant!
    Mar.   Do you,
Good Dame, repair to Liddesdale and wait
For my return; be sure you shall have

justice.
    Osw. A lucky woman! go, you have
    done good service.   [*Aside.*
    Mar. (*to himself*). Eternal praises on the
    power that saved her! —
    Osw. (*gives her money*). Here's for your
    little boy — and when you christen
    him   520
I'll be his Godfather.
    Beg.   Oh Sir, you are merry with me.
In grange or farm this Hundred scarcely
    owns
A dog that does not know me. — These
    good Folks,
For love of God, I must not pass their
    doors;
But I'll be back with my best speed: for
    you —
God bless and thank you both, my gentle
    Masters.   [*Exit* Beggar.
    Mar. (*to himself*). The cruel Viper! —
    Poor devoted Maid,
Now I *do* love thee.
    Osw.   I am thunderstruck.
    Mar. Where is she — holla!
    [*Calling to the* Beggar, *who returns;
    he looks at her stedfastly.*
            You are Idonea's mother? —
Nay, be not terrified — it does me good 530
To look upon you.
    Osw. (*interrupting*). In a peasant's dress
You saw, who was it?
    Beg.   Nay, I dare not speak;
He is a man, if it should come to his ears
I never shall be heard of more.
    Osw.   Lord Clifford?
    Beg. What can I do? believe me, gentle
    Sirs,
I love her, though I dare not call her
    daughter.
    Osw. Lord Clifford — did you see him
    talk with Herbert?
    Beg. Yes, to my sorrow — under the
    great oak
At Herbert's door — and when he stood
    beside
The blind Man — at the silent Girl he
    looked   540
With such a look — it makes me tremble,
    Sir,
To think of it.
    Osw.   Enough! you may depart.
    Mar. (*to himself*). Father! — to God
    himself we cannot give
A holier name; and, under such a mask,
To lead a Spirit, spotless as the blessed,
To that abhorrèd den of brutish vice! —
Oswald, the firm foundation of my life
Is going from under me; these strange

discoveries —
Looked at from every point of fear or
hope,
Duty, or love — involve, I feel, my ruin.

ACT II

SCENE — *A Chamber in the Hostel*

OSWALD *alone, rising from a Table on
which he had been writing.*

Osw. They chose *him* for their Chief ! —
what covert part
He, in the preference, modest Youth,
might take,
I neither know nor care. The insult bred
More of contempt than hatred ; both are
flown ;
That either e'er existed is my shame :
'T was a dull spark — a most unnatural fire
That died the moment the air breathed
upon it.
— These fools of feeling are mere birds of
winter
That haunt some barren island of the
north,
Where, if a famishing man stretch forth
his hand,   10
They think it is to feed them. I have left
him
To solitary meditation ; — now
For a few swelling phrases, and a flash
Of truth, enough to dazzle and to blind,
And he is mine for ever — here he comes.

Enter MARMADUKE.

Mar. These ten years she has moved
her lips all day
And never speaks !
Osw.   Who is it ?
Mar.   I have seen her.
Osw. Oh ! the poor tenant of that ragged
homestead,
Her whom the Monster, Clifford, drove to
madness.
Mar. I met a peasant near the spot ; he
told me,   20
These ten years she had sate all day alone
Within those empty walls.
Osw.   I too have seen her ;
Chancing to pass this way some six months
gone,
At midnight, I betook me to the Church-
yard :
The moon shone clear, the air was still,
so still

The trees were silent as the graves be-
neath them.
Long did I watch, and saw her pacing
round
Upon the self-same spot, still round and
round,
Her lips for ever moving.
Mar.   At her door
Rooted I stood ; for, looking at the woman,
I thought I saw the skeleton of Idonea.   31
Osw. But the pretended Father ——
Mar.   Earthly law
Measures not crimes like his.
Osw.   *We* rank not, happily,
With those who take the spirit of their
rule
From that soft class of devotees who feel
Reverence for life so deeply, that they
spare
The verminous brood, and cherish what
they spare
While feeding on their bodies. Would that
Idonea
Were present, to the end that we might
hear
What she can urge in his defence ; she
loves him.   40
Mar. Yes, loves him ; 't is a truth that
multiplies
His guilt a thousand-fold.
Osw.   'T is most perplexing :
What must be done ?
Mar.   We will conduct her hither ;
These walls shall witness it — from first to
last
He shall reveal himself.
Osw.   Happy are we,
Who live in these disputed tracts, that own
No law but what each man makes for
himself ;
Here justice has indeed a field of triumph.
Mar. Let us be gone and bring her
hither ; — here
The truth shall be laid open, his guilt
proved   50
Before her face. The rest be left to me.
Osw. You will be firm : but though we
well may trust
The issue to the justice of the cause,
Caution must not be flung aside ; remem-
ber,
Yours is no common life. Self-stationed
here
Upon these savage confines, we have seen
you
Stand like an isthmus 'twixt two stormy
seas
That oft have checked their fury at your
bidding.

Mid the deep holds of Solway's mossy
   waste,
Your single virtue has transformed a
   Band   60
Of fierce barbarians into Ministers
Of peace and order. Aged men with tears
Have blessed their steps, the fatherless re-
   tire
For shelter to their banners. But it is,
As you must needs have deeply felt, it is
In darkness and in tempest that we seek
The majesty of Him who rules the world.
Benevolence, that has not heart to use
The wholesome ministry of pain and evil,
Becomes at last weak and contemptible. 70
Your generous qualities have won due
   praise,
But vigorous Spirits look for something
   more
Than Youth's spontaneous products; and
   to-day
You will not disappoint them; and here-
   after ——
  Mar. You are wasting words; hear me
   then, once for all:
You are a Man — and therefore, if com-
   passion,
Which to our kind is natural as life,
Be known unto you, you will love this
   Woman,
Even as I do; but I should loathe the
   light,
If I could think one weak or partial feel-
   ing ——   80
  Osw. You will forgive me ——
  Mar.   If I ever knew
My heart, could penetrate its inmost core,
'T is at this moment. — Oswald, I have
   loved
To be the friend and father of the op-
   pressed,
A comforter of sorrow; — there is some-
   thing
Which looks like a transition in my soul,
And yet it is not. — Let us lead him
   hither.
  Osw. Stoop for a moment; 't is an act
   of justice;
And where 's the triumph if the delegate
Must fall in the execution of his office ? 90
The deed is done — if you will have it so —
Here where we stand — that tribe of vul-
   gar wretches
(You saw them gathering for the festival)
Rush in — the villains seize us ——
  Mar.   Seize !
  Osw.   Yes, they —
Men who are little given to sift and
   weigh —

Would wreak on us the passion of the
   moment.
  Mar. The cloud will soon disperse —
   farewell — but stay.
Thou wilt relate the story.
  Osw.   Am I neither
To bear a part in this Man's punishment,
Nor be its witness ?
  Mar.   I had many hopes 100
That were most dear to me, and some
   will bear
To be transferred to thee.
  Osw.   When I 'm dishonoured !
  Mar. I would preserve thee. How may
   this be done ?
  Osw. By showing that you look beyond
   the instant.
A few leagues hence we shall have open
   ground,
And nowhere upon earth is place so fit
To look upon the deed. Before we enter
The barren Moor, hangs from a beetling
   rock
The shattered Castle in which Clifford oft
Has held infernal orgies — with the gloom,
And very superstition of the place,   111
Seasoning his wickedness. The Debauchee
Would there perhaps have gathered the
   first fruits
Of this mock Father's guilt.

     Enter Host *conducting* Herbert.

  Host.   The Baron Herbert
Attends your pleasure.
  Osw. (*to* Host).   We are ready —
            (*To* Herbert) Sir !
I hope you are refreshed. — I have just
   written
A notice for your Daughter, that she may
   know
What is become of you. — You 'll sit down
   and sign it;
'T will glad her heart to see her father's
   signature.
     [*Gives the letter he had written*
  Her. Thanks for your care.
     [*Sits down and writes.*   *Exit* Host
  Osw. (*aside to* Marmaduke). Perhaps it
   would be useful   120
That you too should subscribe your name.
  [Marmaduke *overlooks* Herbert — *then*
   writes — examines the letter eagerly.
  Mar. I cannot leave this paper.
     [*He puts it up, agitated.*
  Osw. (*aside*).   Dastard ! Come.
  [Marmaduke *goes towards* Herbert
   and supports him — Marmaduke
   tremblingly beckons Oswald *to take*

his place.

Mar. (as he quits Herbert). There is a palsy in his limbs — he shakes.

[*Exeunt* Oswald *and* Herbert — Marmaduke *following.*

SCENE *changes to a Wood*

A group of Pilgrims, IDONEA *with them.*

First Pil. A grove of darker and more lofty shade
I never saw.

Second Pil. The music of the birds
Drops deadened from a roof so thick with leaves.

Old Pil. This news ! It made my heart leap up with joy.

Idon. I scarcely can believe it.

Old Pil.   Myself, I heard
The Sheriff read, in open Court, a letter   129
Which purported it was the royal pleasure
The Baron Herbert, who, as was supposed,
Had taken refuge in this neighbourhood,
Should be forthwith restored. The hearing, Lady,
Filled my dim eyes with tears. — When I returned
From Palestine, and brought with me a heart,
Though rich in heavenly, poor in earthly, comfort,
I met your Father, then a wandering Outcast :
He had a Guide, a Shepherd's boy ; but grieved
He was that One so young should pass his youth
In such sad service ; and he parted with him.   140
We joined our tales of wretchedness together,
And begged our daily bread from door to door.
I talk familiarly to you, sweet Lady !
For once you loved me.

Idon.   You shall back with me
And see your Friend again. The good old Man
Will be rejoiced to greet you.

Old Pil.   It seems but yesterday
That a fierce storm o'ertook us, worn with travel,
In a deep wood remote from any town.
A cave that opened to the road presented
A friendly shelter, and we entered in.   150

Idon. And I was with you ?

Old Pil.   If indeed 't was you —

But you were then a tottering Little-one —
We sate us down. The sky grew dark and darker :
I struck my flint, and built up a small fire
With rotten boughs and leaves, such as the winds
Of many autumns in the cave had piled.
Meanwhile the storm fell heavy on the woods ;
Our little fire sent forth a cheering warmth
And we were comforted, and talked of comfort ;
But 't was an angry night, and o'er our heads   160
The thunder rolled in peals that would have made
A sleeping man uneasy in his bed.
O Lady, you have need to love your Father.
His voice — methinks I hear it now, his voice
When, after a broad flash that filled the cave,
He said to me, that he had seen his Child,
A face (no cherub's face more beautiful)
Revealed by lustre brought with it from Heaven ;
And it was you, dear Lady !

Idon.   God be praised,
That I have been his comforter till now !   170
And will be so through every change of fortune
And every sacrifice his peace requires. —
Let us be gone with speed, that he may hear
These joyful tidings from no lips but mine.

[*Exeunt* Idonea *and* Pilgrims.

SCENE — *The Area of a half-ruined Castle — on one side the entrance to a dungeon*

OSWALD *and* MARMADUKE *pacing backwards and forwards.*

Mar. 'T is a wild night.

Osw.   I 'd give my cloak and bonnet
For sight of a warm fire.

Mar.   The wind blows keen ;
My hands are numb.

Osw.   Ha! ha! 't is nipping cold.
[*Blowing his fingers.*
I long for news of our brave Comrades ; Lacy
Would drive those Scottish Rovers to their dens

If once they blew a horn this side the
Tweed.   180
   Mar. I think I see a second range of
Towers ;
This castle has another Area — come,
Let us examine it.
   Osw.   'T is a bitter night ;
I hope Idonea is well housed. That horse-
man,
Who at full speed swept by us where the
wood
Roared in the tempest, was within an ace
Of sending to his grave our precious
Charge :
That would have been a vile mischance.
   Mar.   It would.
   Osw. Justice had been most cruelly de-
frauded.
   Mar. Most cruelly.
   Osw.   As up the steep we clomb,
I saw a distant fire in the north-east ;   191
I took it for the blaze of Cheviot Beacon :
With proper speed our quarters may be
gained
To-morrow evening.
   [*Looks restlessly towards the mouth of
the dungeon.*
   Mar.   When, upon the plank,
I had led him 'cross the torrent, his voice
blessed me :
You could not hear, for the foam beat the
rocks
With deafening noise, — the benediction
fell
Back on himself ; but changed into a curse.
   Osw. As well indeed it might.
   Mar.   And this you deem
The fittest place ?
   Osw. (*aside*). He is growing pitiful.   200
   Mar. (*listening*). What an odd moaning
that is ! —
   Osw.   Mighty odd
The wind should pipe a little, while we
stand
Cooling our heels in this way ! — I 'll
begin
And count the stars.
   Mar. (*still listening*). That dog of his,
you are sure,
Could not come after us — he *must* have
perished ;
The torrent would have dashed an oak to
splinters.
You said you did not like his looks — that
he
Would trouble us ; if he were here again,
I swear the sight of him would quail me
more
Than twenty armies.

   Osw.   How ?
   Mar.   The old blind Man,
When you had told him the mischance,
was troubled   211
Even to the shedding of some natural
tears
Into the torrent over which he hung,
Listening in vain.
   Osw.   He has a tender heart !
   [*Oswald offers to go down into the
dungeon.*
   Mar. How now, what mean you ?
   Osw.   Truly, I was going
To waken our stray Baron. Were there not
A farm or dwelling-house within five
leagues,
We should deserve to wear a cap and bells,
Three good round years, for playing the
fool here
In such a night as this.
   Mar.   Stop, stop.
   Osw.   Perhaps,
You 'd better like we should descend to-
gether,   221
And lie down by his side — what say you
to it ?
Three of us — we should keep each other
warm :
I 'll answer for it that our four-legged
friend
Shall not disturb us ; further I 'll not en-
gage ;
Come, come, for manhood's sake !
   Mar.   These drowsy shiverings,
This mortal stupor which is creeping over
me,
What do they mean ? were this my single
body
Opposed to armies, not a nerve would
tremble :
Why do I tremble now ? — Is not the depth
Of this Man's crimes beyond the reach of
thought ?   231
And yet, in plumbing the abyss for judg-
ment,
Something I strike upon which turns my
mind
Back on herself, I think, again — my breast
Concentres all the terrors of the Universe :
I look at him and tremble like a child.
   Osw. Is it possible ?
   Mar.   One thing you noticed not :
Just as we left the glen a clap of thunder
Burst on the mountains with hell-rousing
force.
This is a time, said he, when guilt may
shudder ;   240
But there 's a Providence for them who
walk

In helplessness, when innocence is with
them.
At this audacious blasphemy, I thought
The spirit of vengeance seemed to ride
the air.
    Osw. Why are you not the man you
were that moment?
    [*He draws* Marmaduke *to the dun-
geon.*
    Mar. You say he was asleep, — look at
this arm,
And tell me if 't is fit for such a work.
Oswald, Oswald!   [*Leans upon* Oswald.
    Osw.   This is some sudden seizure!
    Mar. A most strange faintness, — will
you hunt me out   249
A draught of water?
    Osw.   Nay, to see you thus
Moves me beyond my bearing. — I will try
To gain the torrent's brink. [*Exit* Oswald.
    Mar. (*after a pause*).   It seems an age
Since that Man left me. — No, I am not
lost.
    Her. (*at the mouth of the dungeon*).
Give me your hand; where are you,
Friends? and tell me
How goes the night.
    Mar.   'T is hard to measure time,
In such a weary night, and such a place.
    Her. I do not hear the voice of my
friend Oswald.
    Mar. A minute past, he went to fetch a
draught
Of water from the torrent. 'T is, you 'll say,
A cheerless beverage.
    Her.   How good it was in you
To stay behind! — Hearing at first no an-
swer,   261
I was alarmed.
    Mar.   No wonder; this is a place
That well may put some fears into *your*
heart.
    Her. Why so? a roofless rock had been
a comfort,
Storm-beaten and bewildered as we were;
And in a night like this, to lend your
cloaks
To make a bed for me! — My Girl will
weep
When she is told of it.
    Mar.   This Daughter of yours
Is very dear to you.
    Her.   Oh! but you are young;
Over your head twice twenty years must
roll,   270
With all their natural weight of sorrow
and pain,
Ere can be known to you how much a
Father

May love his Child.
    Mar.   Thank you, old Man, for this!
    [*Aside.*
    Her. Fallen am I, and worn out, a use-
less Man;
Kindly have you protected me to-night,
And no return have I to make but prayers;
May you in age be blest with such a
daughter! —
When from the Holy Land I had returned
Sightless, and from my heritage was driven,
A wretched Outcast — but this strain of
thought   280
Would lead me to talk fondly.
    Mar.   Do not fear;
Your words are precious to my ears; go on.
    Her. You will forgive me, but my heart
runs over.
When my old Leader slipped into the
flood
And perished, what a piercing outcry you
Sent after him. I have loved you ever since.
You start — where are we?
    Mar.   Oh, there is no danger;
The cold blast struck me.
    Her.   'T was a foolish question.
    Mar. But when you were an Outcast? —
Heaven is just;
Your piety would not miss its due reward;
The little Orphan then would be your
succour,   291
And do good service, though she knew it
not.
    Her. I turned me from the dwellings of
my Fathers,
Where none but those who trampled on
my rights
Seemed to remember me. To the wide
world
I bore her, in my arms; her looks won
pity;
She was my Raven in the wilderness,
And brought me food. Have I not cause
to love her?   298
    Mar. Yes.
    Her. More than ever Parent loved a
Child?
    Mar. Yes, yes.
    Her. I will not murmur, merciful God!
I will not murmur; blasted as I have been,
Thou hast left me ears to hear my Daugh-
ter's voice,
And arms to fold her to my heart. Sub-
missively
Thee I adore, and find my rest in faith.

        Enter OSWALD

    Osw. Herbert! — confusion!   (*Aside.*)

Here it is, my Friend,

[*Presents the Horn.*

A charming beverage for you to carouse,
This bitter night.

Her. Ha ! Oswald ! ten bright crosses
I would have given, not many minutes
    gone,
To have heard your voice.

Osw. Your couch, I fear, good Baron,
Has been but comfortless ; and yet that
    place, 310
When the tempestuous wind first drove
    us hither,
Felt warm as a wren's nest. You 'd better
    turn
And under covert rest till break of day,
Or till the storm abate.

(*To* Marmaduke *aside.*) He has restored
    you.
No doubt you have been nobly enter-
    tained ?
But soft ! — how came he forth ? The
    Night-mare Conscience
Has driven him out of harbour ?

Mar. I believe
You have guessed right.

Her. The trees renew their murmur.
Come, let us house together.

[Oswald *conducts him to the dungeon.*

Osw. (*returns*). Had I not
Esteemed you worthy to conduct the affair
To its most fit conclusion, do you think 321
I would so long have struggled with my
    Nature,
And smothered all that 's man in me ? —
    away ! —

[*Looking towards the dungeon.*

This man 's the property of him who best
Can feel his crimes. I have resigned a
    privilege ;
It now becomes my duty to resume it.

Mar. Touch not a finger ——

Osw. What then must be done ?

Mar. Which way soe'er I turn, I am
    perplexed.

Osw. Now, on my life, I grieve for you.
    The misery
Of doubt is insupportable. Pity, the facts
Did not admit of stronger evidence ; 331
Twelve honest men, plain men, would set
    us right ;
Their verdict would abolish these weak
    scruples.

Mar. Weak ! I am weak — there does my
    torment lie,
Feeding itself.

Osw. Verily, when he said
How his old heart would leap to hear her
    steps,

You thought his voice the echo of Idonea's.

Mar. And never heard a sound so ter-
    rible.

Osw. Perchance you think so now ?

Mar. I cannot do it :
Twice did I spring to grasp his withered
    throat, 340
When such a sudden weakness fell upon
    me,
I could have dropped asleep upon his
    breast.

Osw. Justice — is there not thunder in
    the word ?
Shall it be law to stab the petty robber
Who aims but at our purse ; and shall this
    Parricide —
Worse is he far, far worse (if foul dis-
    honour
Be worse than death) to that confiding
    Creature
Whom he to more than filial love and duty
Hath falsely trained — shall he fulfil his
    purpose ? 349
But you are fallen.

Mar. Fallen should I be indeed —
Murder — perhaps asleep, blind, old, alone,
Betrayed, in darkness ! Here to strike the
    blow —
Away ! away ! ——

[*Flings away his sword.*

Osw. Nay, I have done with you :
We 'll lead him to the Convent. He shall
    live,
And she shall love him. With unquestioned
    title
He shall be seated in his Barony,
And we too chant the praise of his good
    deeds.
I now perceive we do mistake our masters,
And most despise the men who best can
    teach us :
Henceforth it shall be said that bad men
    only 360
Are brave : Clifford is brave ; and that old
    Man
Is brave.

[*Taking* Marmaduke's *sword and giving
    it to him.*

To Clifford's arms he would have led
His Victim — haply to this desolate house.

Mar. (*advancing to the dungeon*). It
    must be ended ! —

Osw. Softly ; do not rouse him ;
He will deny it to the last. He lies
Within the Vault, a spear's length to the
    left.

[Marmaduke *descends to the dungeon.*

(*Alone.*) The Villains rose in mutiny to
    destroy me ;

I could have quelled the Cowards, but this
    Stripling
Must needs step in, and save my life. The
    look
With which he gave the boon — I see it
    now !   370
The same that tempted me to loathe the
    gift. —
For this old venerable Greybeard — faith
'T is his own fault if he hath got a face
Which doth play tricks with them that
    look on it :
'T was this that put it in my thoughts —
    that countenance —
His staff — his figure — Murder ! — what,
    of whom ?
We kill a worn-out horse, and who but
    women
Sigh at the deed ? Hew down a withered
    tree,
And none look grave but dotards. He may
    live
To thank me for this service. Rainbow
    arches,   380
Highways of dreaming passion, have too
    long,
Young as he is, diverted wish and hope
From the unpretending ground we mortals
    tread ; —
Then shatter the delusion, break it up
And set him free. What follows ? I have
    learned
That things will work to ends the slaves o'
    the world
Do never dream of. I *have* been what he —
This Boy — when he comes forth with
    bloody hands —
Might envy, and am now, — but he shall
    know   389
What I am now —
    [*Goes and listens at the dungeon.*
        Praying or parleying ? — tut !
Is he not eyeless ? He has been half-dead
These fifteen years ——
Enter female Beggar *with two or three of
    her Companions.*
(*Turning abruptly.*) *Ha ! speak* — what
    Thing art thou ?
(*Recognizes her.*) Heavens ! my good
    Friend !   [*To her.*
  Beg.   Forgive me, gracious Sir ! —
  Osw. (*to her companions*) . Begone, ye
    Slaves, or I will raise a whirlwind
And send ye dancing to the clouds, like
    leaves.   [*They retire affrighted.*
  Beg. Indeed we meant no harm ; we
    lodge sometimes
In this deserted Castle — *I repent me.*
    [*Oswald goes to the dungeon — listens —*

returns to the Beggar.
  Osw. Woman, thou hast a helpless In-
    fant — keep
Thy secret for its sake, or verily
That wretched life of thine shall be the
    forfeit.   400
  Beg. I *do* repent me, Sir ; I fear the curse
Of that blind Man. 'T was not your
    money, sir ——
  Osw. Begone !
  Beg. (*going*). There is some wicked deed
    in hand :   [*Aside.*
Would I could find the old Man and his
    Daughter.   [*Exit Beggar.*
MARMADUKE (*re-enters from the dungeon*).
  Osw. It is all over then ; — your foolish
    fears
Are hushed to sleep, by your own act and
    deed,
Made quiet as he is.
  Mar.   Why came you down ?
And when I felt your hand upon my arm
And spake to you, why did you give no
    answer ?
Feared you to waken him ? he must have
    been   410
In a deep sleep. I whispered to him thrice.
There are the strangest echoes in that
    place !
  Osw. Tut ! let them gabble till the day
    of doom.
  Mar. Scarcely, by groping, had I reached
    the Spot,
When round my wrist I felt a cord drawn
    tight,
As if the blind Man's dog were pulling at
    it.
  Osw. But after that ?
  Mar.   The features of Idonea
Lurked in his face ——
  Osw.   Psha ! Never to these eyes
Will retribution show itself again   419
With aspect so inviting. Why forbid me
To share your triumph ?
  Mar.   Yes, her very look,
Smiling in sleep ——
  Osw.   A pretty feat of Fancy !
  Mar. Though but a glimpse, it sent me
    to my prayers.
  Osw. Is he alive ?
  Mar.   What mean you ? who alive ?
  Osw. Herbert ! since you will have it,
    Baron Herbert ;
He who will gain his Seignory when Idonea
Hath become Clifford's harlot — is *he* liv-
    ing ?
  Mar. The old Man in that dungeon *is*
    alive.
  Osw. Henceforth, then, will I never in

camp or field
Obey you more. Your weakness, to the
   Band   430
Shall be proclaimed : brave Men, they all
   shall hear it.
You a protector of humanity !
Avenger you of outraged innocence !
   Mar. 'T was dark — dark as the grave :
   yet did I see,
Saw him — his face turned toward me ; and
   I tell thee
Idonea's filial countenance was there
To baffle me — it put me to my prayers.
Upwards I cast my eyes, and, through a
   crevice,
Beheld a star twinkling above my head,
And, by the living God, I could not do
   it.   [*Sinks exhausted.*
   Osw. (*to himself*). Now may I perish if
   this turn do more   441
Than make me change my course.
(*To* Marmaduke.)   Dear Marmaduke,
My words were rashly spoken ; I recall
   them :
I feel my error ; shedding human blood
Is a most serious thing.
   Mar.   Not I alone,
Thou too art deep in guilt.
   Osw.   We have indeed
Been most presumptuous. There *is* guilt in
   this,
Else could so strong a mind have ever
   known
These trepidations ?   Plain it is that
   Heaven
Has marked out this foul Wretch as one
   whose crimes   450
Must never come before a mortal judg-
   ment-seat,
Or be chastised by mortal instruments.
   Mar. A thought that 's worth a thousand
   worlds ! [*Goes towards the dungeon.*
   Osw.   I grieve
That, in my zeal, I have caused you so
   much pain.
   Mar. Think not of that ! 't is over — we
   are safe.
   Osw. (*as if to himself, yet speaking
   aloud*).
      The truth is hideous, but how stifle
   it ? [*Turning to* Marmaduke.
Give me your sword — nay, here are stones
   and fragments,
The least of which would beat out a man's
   brains ;
Or you might drive your head against that
   wall.   459
No ! this is not the place to hear the tale :
It should be told you pinioned in your

bed,
Or on some vast and solitary plain,
Blown to you from a trumpet.
   Mar.   Why talk thus ?
Whate'er the monster brooding in your
   breast
I care not : fear I have none, and cannot
   fear ——
        [*The sound of a horn is heard.*
That horn again — 'T is some one of our
   Troop ;
What do they here ? Listen !
   Osw.   What ! dogged like thieves !
    Enter WALLACE *and* LACY, etc.
   Lacy. You are found at last, thanks to
   the vagrant Troop
For not misleading us.
   Osw. (*looking at* Wallace). That subtle
   Greybeard —
I 'd rather see my father's ghost.   470
   Lacy (*to* Marmaduke).   My Captain,
We come by order of the Band. Belike
You have not heard that Henry has at
   last
Dissolved the Barons' League, and sent
   abroad
His Sheriffs with fit force to reinstate
The genuine owners of such Lands and
   Baronies
As, in these long commotions, have been
   seized.
His Power is this way tending. It befits us
To stand upon our guard, and with our
   swords
Defend the innocent.
   Mar.   Lacy ! we look
But at the surfaces of things ; we hear   480
Of towns in flames, fields ravaged, young
   and old
Driven out in troops to want and naked-
   ness ;
Then grasp our swords and rush upon a
   cure
That flatters us, because it asks not
   thought :
The deeper malady is better hid ;
The world is poisoned at the heart.
   Lacy.   What mean you ?
   Wal. (*whose eye has been fixed suspi-
   ciously upon* Oswald).   Ay, what is
   it you mean ?
   Mar.   Hark'e, my Friends ; —
               [*Appearing gay.*
Were there a Man who, being weak and
   helpless
And most forlorn, should bribe a Mother,
   pressed
By penury, to yield him up her Daughter,
A little Infant, and instruct the Babe,   491

Prattling upon his knee, to call him
    Father ——
  Lacy. Why, if his heart be tender, that
    offence
I could forgive him.
    Mar. (*going on*). And should he make
    the Child
An instrument of falsehood, should he
    teach her
To stretch her arms, and dim the gladsome
    light
Of infant playfulness with piteous looks
Of misery that was not ——
  Lacy.   Troth, 't is hard —
But in a world like ours ——
    Mar. (*changing his tone*). This selfsame
    Man —
Even while he printed kisses on the cheek
Of this poor Babe, and taught its innocent
    tongue   501
To lisp the name of Father — could he look
To the unnatural harvest of that time
When he should give her up, a Woman
    grown,
To him who bid the highest in the market
Of foul pollution ——
  Lacy.   The whole visible world
Contains not such a Monster !
    Mar.   For this purpose
Should he resolve to taint her Soul by
    means
Which bathe the limbs in sweat to think
    of them ;
Should he, by tales which would draw
    tears from iron,   510
Work on her nature, and so turn compas-
    sion
And gratitude to ministers of vice,
And make the spotless spirit of filial love
Prime mover in a plot to damn his Victim
Both soul and body ——
  Wal.   'T is too horrible ;
Oswald, what say you to it ?
  Lacy.   Hew him down,
And fling him to the ravens.
    Mar.   But his aspect
It is so meek, his countenance so venerable.
  Wal. (*with an appearance of mistrust*).
    But how, what say you, Oswald ?
  Lacy (*at the same moment*). Stab him,
    were it
Before the Altar.
    Mar.   What, if he were sick,
Tottering upon the very verge of life, 521
And old, and blind ——
  Lacy.   Blind, say you ?
  Osw. (*coming forward*). Are we Men,
Or own we baby Spirits ? Genuine cour-
    age

Is not an accidental quality,
A thing dependent for its casual birth
On opposition and impediment.
Wisdom, if justice speak the word, beats
    down
The giant's strength ; and, at the voice of
    Justice,
Spares not the worm. The giant and the
    worm —
She weighs them in one scale. The wiles
    of woman,   530
And craft of age, seducing reason, first
Made weakness a protection, and obscured
The moral shapes of things. His tender
    cries
And helpless innocence — do they protect
The infant lamb ? and shall the infirmities,
Which have enabled this enormous Culprit
To perpetrate his crimes, serve as a Sanc-
    tuary
To cover him from punishment ? Shame !
    — Justice,
Admitting no resistance, bends alike
The feeble and the strong. She needs not
    here   540
Her bonds and chains, which make the
    mighty feeble.
— We recognize in this old Man a victim
Prepared already for the sacrifice.
  Lacy. By heaven, his words are reason !
  Osw.   Yes, my Friends,
His countenance is meek and venerable ;
And, by the Mass, to see him at his
    prayers ! —
I am of flesh and blood, and may I perish
When my heart does not ache to think of
    it ! —
Poor Victim ! not a virtue under heaven
But what was made an engine to ensnare
    thee ;   550
But yet I trust, Idonea, thou art safe.
  Lacy. Idonea !
  Wal.   How ! what ? your Idonea ?
                (*To* Marmaduke.)
  Mar.   Mine !
But now no longer mine. You know Lord
    Clifford ;
He is the Man to whom the Maiden —
    pure
As beautiful, and gentle and benign,
And in her ample heart loving even me —
Was to be yielded up.
  Lacy.   Now, by the head
Of my own child, this Man must die ; my
    hand,
A worthier wanting, shall itself entwine
In his grey hairs ! —
    Mar. (*to* Lacy). I love the Father in
    thee.   560

You know me, Friends; I have a heart to
feel,
And I have felt, more than perhaps be-
comes me
Or duty sanctions.
    Lacy.   We will have ample justice.
Who are we, Friends? Do we not live on
ground
Where Souls are self-defended, free to
grow
Like mountain oaks rocked by the stormy
wind.
Mark the Almighty Wisdom, which de-
creed
This monstrous crime to be laid open —
here,
Where Reason has an eye that she can use,
And Men alone are Umpires. To the
Camp   570
He shall be led, and there, the Country
round
All gathered to the spot, in open day
Shall Nature be avenged.
    Osw.   'T is nobly thought;
His death will be a monument for ages.
    Mar. (*to* Lacy). I thank you for that
hint. He shall be brought
Before the Camp, and would that best and
wisest
Of every country might be present. There,
His crime shall be proclaimed; and for
the rest
It shall be done as Wisdom shall decide:
Meanwhile, do you two hasten back and
see   580
That all is well prepared.
    Wal.   We will obey you.
(*Aside.*) But softly! we must look a little
nearer.
    Mar. Tell where you found us. At some
future time
I will explain the cause.   [*Exeunt.*

ACT III

SCENE — *The Door of the Hostel*

A group of Pilgrims *as before;* IDONEA *and
the* HOST *among them.*

    Host. Lady, you 'll find your Father at
the Convent
As I have told you: He left us yesterday
With two Companions; one of them, as
seemed,
His most familiar Friend. (*Going.*) There
was a letter

Of which I heard them speak, but that I
fancy
Has been forgotten.
    Idon. (*to* Host). Farewell!
    Host.   Gentle pilgrims,
St. Cuthbert speed you on your holy errand.
            [*Exeunt* Idonea *and* Pilgrims.

SCENE — *A desolate Moor*

OSWALD (*alone*).

    Osw. Carry him to the Camp! Yes, to
the Camp.
Oh, Wisdom! a most wise resolve! and
then,
That half a word should blow it to the
winds!   10
This last device must end my work. — Me-
thinks
It were a pleasant pastime to construct
A scale and table of belief — as thus —
Two columns, one for passion, one for
proof;
Each rises as the other falls: and first,
Passion a unit and *against* us — proof —
Nay, we must travel in another path,
Or we 're stuck fast for ever; — passion,
then,
Shall be a unit *for* us; proof — no, pas-
sion!
We 'll not insult thy majesty by time,   20
Person, and place — the where, the when,
the how,
And all particulars that dull brains require
To constitute the spiritless shape of Fact,
They bow to, calling the idol, Demon-
stration.
A whipping to the Moralists who preach
That misery is a sacred thing: for me,
I know no cheaper engine to degrade a
man,
Nor any half so sure. This Stripling's
mind
Is shaken till the dregs float on the sur-
face;
And, in the storm and anguish of the
heart,   30
He talks of a transition in his Soul,
And dreams that he is happy. We dissect
The senseless body, and why not the
mind? —
These are strange sights — the mind of
man, upturned,
Is in all natures a strange spectacle;
In some a hideous one — hem! shall I
stop?
No. — Thoughts and feelings will sink

deep, but then
They have no substance. Pass but a few
    minutes,
And something shall be done which Mem-
    ory
May touch, whene'er her Vassals are at
    work.   40

Enter MARMADUKE, *from behind.*

Osw. (*turning to meet him*). But listen,
    for my peace ——
Mar.   Why, I *believe* you.
Osw. But hear the proofs ——
Mar.   Ay, prove that when two peas
Lie snugly in a pod, the pod must then
Be larger than the peas — prove this —
    't were matter
Worthy the hearing. Fool was I to dream
It ever could be otherwise!
Osw.   Last night
When I returned with water from the
    brook,
I overheard the Villains — every word
Like red-hot iron burnt into my heart.
Said one, " It is agreed on. The blind
    Man   50
Shall feign a sudden illness, and the Girl,
Who on her journey must proceed alone,
Under pretence of violence, be seized.
She is," continued the detested Slave,
" She is right willing — strange if she were
    not ! —
They say, Lord Clifford is a savage man ;
But, faith, to see him in his silken tunic,
Fitting his low voice to the minstrel's
    harp,
There's witchery in 't. I never knew a
    maid
That could withstand it. True," continued
    he,   60
" When we arranged the affair, she wept a
    little
(Not the less welcome to my Lord for
    that)
And said, ' My Father he will have it so. ' "
Mar. I am your hearer.
Osw.   This I caught, and more
That may not be retold to any ear.
The obstinate bolt of a small iron door
Detained them near the gateway of the
    Castle.
By a dim lantern's light I saw that wreaths
Of flowers were in their hands, as if de-
    signed
For festive decoration ; and they said,   70
With brutal laughter and most foul allu-
    sion,
That they should share the banquet with

their Lord
And his new Favourite.
Mar.   Misery ! —
Osw.   I knew
How you would be disturbed by this dire
    news,
And therefore chose this solitary Moor,
Here to impart the tale, of which, last
    night,
I strove to ease my mind, when our two
    Comrades,
Commissioned by the Band, burst in upon
    us.
Mar. Last night, when moved to lift the
    avenging steel,
I did believe all things were shadows —
    yea,   80
Living or dead all things were bodiless,
Or but the mutual mockeries of body,
Till that same star summoned me back
    again.
Now I could laugh till my ribs ached. Oh
    Fool !
To let a creed, built in the heart of things,
Dissolve before a twinkling atom ! — Os-
    wald,
I could fetch lessons out of wiser schools
Than you have entered, were it worth the
    pains.
Young as I am, I might go forth a teacher,
And you should see how deeply I could
    reason   90
Of love in all its shapes, beginnings, ends ;
Of moral qualities in their diverse aspects ;
Of actions, and their laws and tendencies.
Osw. You take it as it merits ——
Mar.   One a King,
General or Cham, Sultan or Emperor,
Strews twenty acres of good meadow-
    ground
With carcases, in lineament and shape
And substance nothing differing from his
    own,
But that they cannot stand up of them-
    selves ;
Another sits i' th' sun, and by the hour 100
Floats kingcups in the brook — a Hero one
We call, and scorn the other as Time's
    spendthrift ;
But have they not a world of common
    ground
To occupy — both fools, or wise alike,
Each in his way ?
Osw.   Troth, I begin to think so.
Mar. Now for the corner-stone of my
    philosophy :
I would not give a denier for the man
Who, on such provocation as this earth
Yields, could not chuck his babe beneath

the chin,
And send it with a fillip to its grave.   110
Osw. Nay, you leave me behind.
Mar.   That such a One,
So pious in demeanour ! in his look
So saintly and so pure ! —— Hark'e, my
    Friend,
I 'll plant myself before Lord Clifford's
    Castle,
A surly mastiff kennels at the gate,
And he shall howl and I will laugh, a
    medley
Most tunable.
Osw.   In faith, a pleasant scheme ;
But take your sword along with you, for
    that
Might in such neighbourhood find seemly
    use. —
But first, how wash our hands of this old
    Man ?   120
Mar. Oh yes, that mole, that viper in
    the path ;
Plague on my memory, him I had forgot-
    ten.
Osw. You know we left him sitting —
    see him yonder.
Mar. Ha ! ha ! —
Osw. As 't will be but a moment's work,
I will stroll on ; you follow when 't is done.
                            [*Exeunt.*

SCENE *changes to another part of the Moor
    at a short distance*

HERBERT *is discovered seated on a stone.*

Her. A sound of laughter, too ! — 't is
    well — I feared,
The Stranger had some pitiable sorrow
Pressing upon his solitary heart.
Hush ! — 't is the feeble and earth-loving
    wind
That creeps along the bells of the crisp
    heather.   130
Alas ! 't is cold — I shiver in the sunshine —
What can this mean ? There is a psalm
    that speaks
Of God's parental mercies — with Idonea
I used to sing it. — Listen ! — what foot is
    there ?

Enter MARMADUKE

Mar. (*aside — looking at* Herbert). And
    I have loved this Man ! and *she* hath
    loved him !
And I loved her, and she loves the Lord
    Clifford !
And there it ends ; — if this be not enough

To make mankind merry for evermore,
Then plain it is as day, that eyes were
    made
For a wise purpose — verily to weep with !
                        [*Looking round.*
A pretty prospect this, a masterpiece   141
Of Nature, finished with most curious
    skill !
(*To* Herbert.) Good Baron, have you ever
    practised tillage ?
Pray tell me what this land is worth by
    the acre ?
Her. How glad I am to hear your voice !
    I know not
Wherein I have offended you ; — last night
I found in you the kindest of Protectors ;
This morning, when I spoke of weariness,
You from my shoulder took my scrip and
    threw it
About your own ; but for these two hours
    past   150
Once only have you spoken, when the lark
Whirred from among the fern beneath our
    feet,
And I, no coward in my better days,
Was almost terrified.
Mar.   That 's excellent ! —
So, you bethought you of the many ways
In which a man may come to his end,
    whose crimes
Have roused all Nature up against him —
    pshaw ! —
Her. For mercy's sake, is nobody in
    sight ?
No traveller, peasant, herdsman ?
Mar.   Not a soul :
Here is a tree, ragged, and bent, and
    bare,   160
That turns its goat's-beard flakes of pea-
    green moss
From the stern breathing of the rough sea-
    wind ;
This have we, but no other company :
Commend me to the place. If a man
    should die
And leave his body here, it were all one
As he were twenty fathoms underground.
Her. Where is our common Friend ?
Mar.   A ghost, methinks —
The Spirit of a murdered man, for in-
    stance —
Might have fine room to ramble about
    here,
A grand domain to squeak and gibber
    in.   170
Her. Lost Man ! if thou have any close-
    pent guilt
Pressing upon thy heart, and this the hour
Of visitation ——

Mar. A bold word from *you!*

Her. Restore him, Heaven!

Mar. The desperate Wretch! — A Flower,

Fairest of all flowers, was she once, but now

They have snapped her from the stem —
Poh! let her lie

Besoiled with mire, and let the houseless snail

Feed on her leaves. You knew her well —
ay, there, 178

Old Man! you were a very Lynx, you knew

The worm was in her —

Her. Mercy! Sir, what mean you?

Mar. You have a Daughter!

Her. Oh that she were here! —

She hath an eye that sinks into all hearts,

And if I have in aught offended you,

Soon would her gentle voice make peace between us.

Mar. (aside). I do believe he weeps —
I could weep too

There is a vein of her voice that runs through his:

Even such a Man my fancy bodied forth

From the first moment that I loved the Maid;

And for his sake I loved her more: these tears —

I did not think that aught was left in me 190

Of what I have been — yes, I thank thee, Heaven!

One happy thought has passed across my mind.

— It may not be — I am cut off from man;

No more shall I be man — no more shall I

Have human feelings! — (*To* Herbert) —
Now, for a little more

About your Daughter!

Her. Troops of armed men,

Met in the roads, would bless us; little children,

Rushing along in the full tide of play,

Stood silent as we passed them! I have heard

The boisterous carman, in the miry road,

Check his loud whip and hail us with mild voice, 201

And speak with milder voice to his poor beasts.

Mar. And whither were you going?

Her. Learn, young Man,

To fear the virtuous, and reverence misery,

Whether too much for patience, or, like mine,

Softened till it becomes a gift of mercy.

Mar. Now, this is as it should be!

Her. I am weak! —

My Daughter does not know how weak I am;

And, as thou see'st, under the arch of heaven

Here do I stand, alone, to helplessness, 210

By the good God, our common Father, doomed! —

But I had once a spirit and an arm ——

Mar. Now, for a word about your Barony:

I fancy when you left the Holy Land,

And came to — what's your title — eh?
your claims

Were undisputed!

Her. Like a mendicant,

Whom no one comes to meet, I stood alone; —

I murmured — but, remembering Him who feeds

The pelican and ostrich of the desert,

From my own threshold I looked up to Heaven 220

And did not want glimmerings of quiet hope.

So, from the court I passed, and down the brook,

Led by its murmur, to the ancient oak

I came; and when I felt its cooling shade,

I sate me down, and cannot but believe —

While in my lap I held my little Babe

And clasped her to my heart, my heart that ached

More with delight than grief — I heard a voice

Such as by Cherith on Elijah called;

It said, "I will be with thee." A little boy, 230

A shepherd-lad, ere yet my trance was gone,

Hailed us as if he had been sent from heaven,

And said, with tears, that he would be our guide:

I had a better guide — that innocent Babe —

Her, who hath saved me, to this hour, from harm,

From cold, from hunger, penury, and death;

To whom I owe the best of all the good

I have, or wish for, upon earth — and more

And higher far than lies within earth's bounds:

Therefore I bless her: when I think of Man, 240

I bless her with sad spirit, — when of God,

I bless her in the fulness of my joy!

Mar. The name of daughter in his

mouth, he prays!
With nerves so steady, that the very flies
Sit unmolested on his staff. — Innocent! —
If he were innocent — then he would
    tremble
And be disturbed, as I am. (*Turning aside.*)
    I have read
In Story, what men now alive have wit-
    nessed,
How, when the People's mind was racked
    with doubt,
Appeal was made to the great Judge : the
    Accused   250
With naked feet walked over burning
    ploughshares.
Here is a Man by Nature's hand prepared
For a like trial, but more merciful.
Why else have I been led to this bleak
    Waste?
Bare is it, without house or track, and
    destitute
Of obvious shelter, as a shipless sea.
Here will I leave him — here — All-seeing
    God!
Such as *he* is, and sore perplexed as I am,
I will commit him to this final *Ordeal!* —
He heard a voice — a shepherd-lad came to
    him   260
And was his guide; if once, why not again,
And in this desert? If never — then the
    whole
Of what he says, and looks, and does, and
    is,
Makes up one damning falsehood. Leave
    him here
To cold and hunger! — Pain is of the
    heart,
And what are a few throes of bodily suf-
    fering
If they can waken one pang of remorse?
                    [*Goes up to* Herbert.
Old Man! my wrath is as a flame burnt
    out,
It cannot be rekindled. Thou art here
Led by my hand to save thee from per-
    dition;   270
Thou wilt have time to breathe and
    think ——
    Her.   Oh, Mercy!
    Mar. I know the need that all men have
        of mercy,
And therefore leave thee to a righteous
    judgment.
    Her. My Child, my blessèd Child!
    Mar.   No more of that;
Thou wilt have many guides if thou art
    innocent;
Yea, from the utmost corners of the earth,
That Woman will come o'er this Waste to

save thee.
        [*He pauses and looks at* Herbert's *staff.*
Ha! what is here? and carved by her own
    hand!   [*Reads upon the staff.*
" I am eyes to the blind, saith the Lord.
He that puts his trust in me shall not
    fail!"   280
Yes, be it so; — repent and be forgiven —
God and that staff are now thy only guides.
        [*He leaves* Herbert *on the Moor.*

SCENE — *An eminence, a Beacon on the
        summit*

LACY, WALLACE, LENNOX, etc, etc.

    Several of the Band (*confusedly*). But
        patience!
    One of the Band. Curses on that Traitor,
        Oswald! —
Our Captain made a prey to foul device! —
    Len. (*to* Wal.). His tool, the wandering
        Beggar, made last night
A plain confession, such as leaves no
    doubt,
Knowing what otherwise we know too well,
That she revealed the truth. Stand by me
    now;
For rather would I have a nest of vipers
Between my breast-plate and my skin, than
    make   290
Oswald my special enemy, if you
Deny me your support.
    Lacy.   We have been fooled —
But for the motive?
    Wal.   Natures such as his
Spin motives out of their own bowels,
    Lacy!
I learned this when I was a Confessor.
I know him well; there needs no other
    motive
Than that most strange incontinence in
    crime
Which haunts this Oswald. Power is life
    to him
And breath and being; where he cannot
    govern,
He will destroy.
    Lacy.   To have been trapped like
        moles! —   300
Yes, you are right, we need not hunt for
    motives:
There is no crime from which this man
    would shrink;
He recks not human law; and I have
    noticed
That often when the name of God is
    uttered,
A sudden blankness overspreads his face.

Len. Yet, reasoner as he is, his pride has built

Some uncouth superstition of its own.

Wal. I have seen traces of it.

Len.   Once he headed

A band of Pirates in the Norway seas;

And when the King of Denmark summoned him   310

To the oath of fealty, I well remember,

'T was a strange answer that he made; he said,

"I hold of Spirits, and the Sun in heaven."

Lacy. He is no madman.

Wal.   A most subtle doctor

Were that man, who could draw the line that parts

Pride and her daughter, Cruelty, from Madness,

That should be scourged, not pitied. Restless Minds,

Such Minds as find amid their fellow-men

No heart that loves them, none that they can love,

Will turn perforce and seek for sympathy

In dim relation to imagined Beings.   321

One of the Band. What if he mean to offer up our Captain

An expiation and a sacrifice

To those infernal fiends!

Wal.   Now, if the event

Should be as Lennox has foretold, then swear,

My Friends, his heart shall have as many wounds

As there are daggers here.

Lacy.   What need of swearing!

One of the Band. Let us away!

Another.   Away!

A third.   Hark! how the horns

Of those Scotch Rovers echo through the vale.

Lacy. Stay you behind; and when the sun is down,   330

Light up this beacon.

One of the Band. You shall be obeyed.

                        [*They go out together.*

SCENE — *The Wood on the edge of the Moor*

MARMADUKE (*alone*).

Mar. Deep, deep and vast, vast beyond human thought,

Yet calm. — I could believe, that there was here

The only quiet heart on earth. In terror,

Remembered terror, there is peace and rest.

Enter OSWALD

Osw. Ha! my dear Captain.

Mar.   A later meeting, Oswald,

Would have been better timed.

Osw.   Alone, I see;

You have done your duty. I had hopes, which now

I feel that you will justify.

Mar.   I had fears,

From which I have freed myself — but 't is my wish   340

To be alone, and therefore we must part.

Osw. Nay, then — I am mistaken. There 's a weakness

About you still; you talk of solitude —

I am your friend.

Mar.   What need of this assurance

At any time? and why given now?

Osw.   Because

You are now in truth my Master; you have taught me

What there is not another living man

Had strength to teach; — and therefore gratitude

Is bold, and would relieve itself by praise.

Mar. Wherefore press this on me?

Osw.   Because I feel

That you have shown, and by a signal instance,   351

How they who would be just must seek the rule

By diving for it into their own bosoms.

To-day you have thrown off a tyranny

That lives but in the torpid acquiescence

Of our emasculated souls, the tyranny

Of the world's masters, with the musty rules

By which they uphold their craft from age to age:

You have obeyed the only law that sense

Submits to recognise; the immediate law,   360

From the clear light of circumstances, flashed

Upon an independent Intellect.

Henceforth new prospects open on your path;

Your faculties should grow with the demand;

I still will be your friend, will cleave to you

Through good and evil, obloquy and scorn,

Oft as they dare to follow on your steps.

Mar. I would be left alone.

Osw. (*exultingly*). I know your motives!

I am not of the world's presumptuous judges,

Who damn where they can neither see nor
   feel,   370
With a hard-hearted ignorance ; your
   struggles
I witnessed, and now hail your victory.
  Mar. Spare me awhile that greeting.
  Osw.   It may be,
That some there are, squeamish half-think-
   ing cowards,
Who will turn pale upon you, call you
   murderer,
And you will walk in solitude among them.
A mighty evil for a strong-built mind ! —
Join twenty tapers of unequal height
And light them joined, and you will see
   the less
How 't will burn down the taller ; and
   they all   380
Shall prey upon the tallest. Solitude ! —
The Eagle lives in Solitude.
  Mar.   Even so,
The Sparrow so on the housetop, and I,
The weakest of God's creatures, stand re-
   solved
To abide the issue of my act, alone.
  Osw. Now would you ? and for ever ? —
   My young Friend,
As time advances either we become
The prey or masters of our own past deeds.
Fellowship we *must* have, willing or no ;
And if good Angels fail, slack in their
   duty,   390
Substitutes, turn our faces where we may,
Are still forthcoming ; some which, though
   they bear
Ill names, can render no ill services,
In recompense for what themselves re-
   quired.
So meet extremes in this mysterious world,
And opposites thus melt into each other.
  Mar. Time, since Man first drew breath,
   has never moved
With such a weight upon his wings as
   now ;
But they will soon be lightened.
  Osw.   Ay, look up —
Cast round you your mind's eye, and you
   will learn   400
Fortitude is the child of Enterprise :
Great actions move our admiration, chiefly
Because they carry in themselves an ear-
   nest
That we can suffer greatly.
  Mar.   Very true.
  Osw. Action is transitory — a step, a
   blow,
The motion of a muscle — this way or
   that —
'T is done, and in the after-vacancy

We wonder at ourselves like men be-
   trayed :
Suffering is permanent, obscure and dark,
And shares the nature of infinity.   410
  Mar. Truth — and I feel it.
  Osw.   What ! if you had bid
Eternal farewell to unmingled joy
And the light dancing of the thoughtless
   heart ;
It is the toy of fools, and little fit
For such a world as this. The wise abjure
All thoughts whose idle composition lives
In the entire forgetfulness of pain.
— I see I have disturbed you.
  Mar.   By no means.
  Osw. Compassion ! — pity ! — pride can
   do without them ;
And what if you should never know them
   more ! —   420
He is a puny soul who, feeling pain,
Finds ease because another feels it too.
If e'er I open out this heart of mine
It shall be for a nobler end — to teach
And not to purchase puling sympathy.
— Nay, you are pale.
  Mar.   It may be so.
  Osw.   Remorse —
It cannot live with thought ; think on,
   think on,
And it will die. What ! in this universe,
Where the least things control the great-
   est, where
The faintest breath that breathes can move
   a world ;   430
What ! feel remorse, where, if a cat had
   sneezed,
A leaf had fallen, the thing had never been
Whose very shadow gnaws us to the vitals.
  Mar. Now, whither are you wandering ?
   That a man
So used to suit his language to the time,
Should thus so widely differ from himself —
It is most strange.
  Osw. Murder ! — what 's in the word ! —
I have no cases by me ready made
To fit all deeds. Carry him to the Camp ! —
A shallow project ; — you of late have seen
More deeply, taught us that the institutes
Of Nature, by a cunning usurpation   442
Banished from human intercourse, exist
Only in our relations to the brutes
That make the fields their dwelling. If a
   snake
Crawl from beneath our feet we do not
   ask
A license to destroy him : our good gov-
   ernors
Hedge in the life of every pest and plague
That bears the shape of man ; and for

what purpose,
But to protect themselves from extirpa-
    tion ? —   450
This flimsy barrier you have overleaped.
    Mar. My Office is fulfilled — the Man is
    now
Delivered to the Judge of all things.
    Osw.   Dead !
    Mar. I have borne my burthen to its
    destined end.
    Osw. This instant we 'll return to our
    companions —
Oh how I long to see their faces again !

Enter Idonea, *with* Pilgrims *who continue
    their journey.*

    Idon. (*after some time*). What, Marma-
    duke ! now thou art mine for ever.
And Oswald, too ! (*To* Marmaduke.) On
    will we to my Father
With the glad tidings which this day hath
    brought ;
We 'll go together, and, such proof re-
    ceived   460
Of his own rights restored, his gratitude
To God above will make him feel for ours.
    Osw. I interrupt you ?
    Idon.   Think not so.
    Mar.   Idonea,
That I should ever live to see this mo-
    ment !
    Idon. Forgive me. — Oswald knows it all
    — he knows,
Each word of that unhappy letter fell
As a blood drop from my heart.
    Osw.   'T was even so.
    Mar. I have much to say, but for whose
    ear ? — not thine.
    Idon. Ill can I bear that look — Plead
    for me, Oswald !
You are my Father's Friend.
(*To* Marmaduke.)   Alas, you know not,
And never *can* you know, how much he
    loved me.   471
Twice had he been to me a father, twice
Had given me breath, and was I not to be
His daughter, once his daughter ? could
    I withstand
His pleading face, and feel his clasping
    arms,
And hear his prayer that I would not for-
    sake him
In his old age ——   [*Hides her face.*
    Mar.   Patience — Heaven grant me
    patience ! —
She weeps, she weeps — *my* brain shall
    burn for hours
Ere *I* can shed a tear

Idon.   I was a woman ;
And, balancing the hopes that are the
    dearest   480
To womankind with duty to my Father,
I yielded up those precious hopes, which
    nought
On earth could else have wrested from
    me ; — if erring,
Oh let me be forgiven !
    Mar.   I *do* forgive thee.
    Idon. But take me to your arms — this
    breast, alas !
It throbs, and you have a heart that does
    not feel it.
    Mar. (*exultingly*). She is innocent.
                        [*He embraces her.*
    Osw. (*aside*).   Were I a Moralist,
I should make wondrous revolution here ;
It were a quaint experiment to show   489
The beauty of truth — [*Addressing them.*
                    I see I interrupt you ;
I shall have business with you, Marma-
    duke ;
Follow me to the Hostel.   [*Exit* Oswald.
    Idon.   Marmaduke,
This is a happy day. My Father soon
Shall sun himself before his native doors ;
The lame, the hungry, will be welcome
    there.
No more shall he complain of wasted
    strength,
Of thoughts that fail, and a decaying
    heart ;
His good works will be balm and life
    to him.
    Mar. This is most strange ! — I know
    not what it was,
But there was something which most
    plainly said,   500
That thou wert innocent.
    Idon.   How innocent ! —
Oh heavens ! you 've been deceived.
    Mar.   Thou art a Woman,
To bring perdition on the universe.
    Idon. Already I 've been punished to the
    height
Of my offence.   [*Smiling affectionately.*
                    I see you love me still,
The labours of my hand are still your
    joy ;
Bethink you of the hour when on your
    shoulder
I hung this belt.
    [*Pointing to the belt on which was
    suspended* Herbert's *scrip.*
    Mar. Mercy of Heaven !   [*Sinks.*
    Idon.   What ails you ! [*Distractedly.*
    Mar. The scrip that held his food, and
    I forgot

To give it back again!

Idon.　　　　What mean your words?

Mar. I know not what I said — all may
　　be well.　　　　　　　　　　　**511**

Idon. That smile hath life in it!

Mar.　　　　This road is perilous;
I will attend you to a Hut that stands
Near the wood's edge — rest there to-night,
　　I pray you:
For me, I have business, as you heard,
　　with Oswald,
But will return to you by break of day.
　　　　　　　　　　　　[*Exeunt.*

ACT IV

SCENE — *A desolate prospect — a ridge of
rocks — a Chapel on the summit of one
— Moon behind the rocks — night
stormy — irregular sound of a Bell*

HERBERT *enters exhausted.*

Her. That Chapel-bell in mercy seemed
　　to guide me,
But now it mocks my steps; its fitful
　　stroke
Can scarcely be the work of human hands.
Hear me, ye Men, upon the cliffs, if such
There be who pray nightly before the
　　Altar.
Oh that I had but strength to reach the
　　place!
My Child — my child — dark — dark — I
　　faint — this wind —
These stifling blasts — God help me!

Enter ELDRED.

Eld.　　　　　Better this bare rock,
Though it were tottering over a man's
　　head,
Than a tight case of dungeon walls for
　　shelter　　　　　　　　　　　10
From such rough dealing.
　　　　　　[*A moaning voice is heard.*
　　　　　　Ha! what sound is that?
Trees creaking in the wind (but none are
　　here)
Send forth such noises — and that weary
　　bell!
Surely some evil Spirit abroad to-night
Is ringing it — 't would stop a Saint in
　　prayer,
And that — what is it? never was sound
　　so like
A human groan. Ha! what is here? Poor
　　Man —

Murdered! alas! speak — speak, I am your
　　friend:
No answer — hush — lost wretch, he lifts
　　his hand
And lays it to his heart — (*Kneels to him*).
　　I pray you speak!　　　　　　20
What has befallen you?

Her. (*feebly*). A stranger has done this,
And in the arms of a stranger I must die.

Eld. Nay, think not so; come, let me
　　raise you up;　　　[*Raises him.*
This is a dismal place — well — that is
　　well —
I was too fearful — take me for your guide
And your support — my hut is not far off.
　　　　　[*Draws him gently off the stage.*

SCENE — *A room in the Hostel*

MARMADUKE *and* OSWALD.

Mar. But for Idonea! — I have cause to
　　think
That she is innocent.

Osw.　　　　Leave that thought awhile,
As one of those beliefs, which in their
　　hearts
Lovers lock up as pearls, though oft no
　　better　　　　　　　　　　　30
Than feathers clinging to their points of
　　passion.
This day's event has laid on me the duty
Of opening out my story; you must hear
　　it,
And without further preface. — In my
　　youth,
Except for that abatement which is paid
By envy as a tribute to desert,
I was the pleasure of all hearts, the
　　darling
Of every tongue — as you are now. You 've
　　heard
That I embarked for Syria. On our voyage
Was hatched among the crew a foul Con-
　　spiracy　　　　　　　　　　　40
Against my honour, in the which our Cap-
　　tain
Was, I believed, prime Agent. The wind
　　fell;
We lay becalmed week after week, until
The water of the vessel was exhausted;
I felt a double fever in my veins,
Yet rage suppressed itself; — to a deep
　　stillness
Did my pride tame my pride; — for many
　　days,
On a dead sea under a burning sky,
I brooded o'er my injuries, deserted

By man and nature ; — if a breeze had
   blown,   50
It might have found its way into my heart,
And I had been — no matter — do you
   mark me ?
   Mar. Quick — to the point — if any un-
   told crime
Doth haunt your memory.
   Osw.   Patience, hear me further ! —
One day in silence did we drift at noon
By a bare rock, narrow, and white, and
   bare ;
No food was there, no drink, no grass, no
   shade,
No tree, nor jutting eminence, nor form
Inanimate large as the body of man,
Nor any living thing whose lot of life 60
Might stretch beyond the measure of one
   moon.
To dig for water on the spot, the Captain
Landed with a small troop, myself being
   one :
There I reproached him with his treachery.
Imperious at all times, his temper rose ;
He struck me ; and that instant had I
   killed him,
And put an end to his insolence, but my
   Comrades
Rushed in between us : then did I insist
(All hated him, and I was stung to mad-
   ness)
That we should leave him there, alive ! —
   we did so.   70
   Mar. And he was famished ?
   Osw.   Naked was the spot ;
Methinks I see it now — how in the sun
Its stony surface glittered like a shield ;
And in that miserable place we left him,
Alone but for a swarm of minute creatures
Not one of which could help him while
   alive,
Or mourn him dead.
   Mar.   A man by men cast off.
Left without burial ! nay, not dead nor
   dying,
But standing, walking, stretching forth his
   arms,
In all things like ourselves, but in the
   agony   80
With which he called for mercy ; and —
   even so —
He was forsaken ?
   Osw.   There is a power in sounds :
The cries he uttered might have stopped
   the boat
That bore us through the water — —
   Mar.   You returned
Upon that dismal hearing — did you not ?

   Osw. Some scoffed at him with hellish
   mockery,
And laughed so loud it seemed that the
   smooth sea
Did from some distant region echo us.
   Mar. We all are of one blood, our veins
   are filled   89
At the same poisonous fountain !
   Osw.   'T was an island
Only by sufferance of the winds and waves,
Which with their foam could cover it at
   will.
I know not how he perished ; but the
   calm,
The same dead calm, continued many
   days.
   Mar. But his own crime had brought on
   him this doom,
His wickedness prepared it ; these expe-
   dients
Are terrible, yet ours is not the fault.
   Osw. The man was famished, and was
   innocent !
   Mar. Impossible !
   Osw. The man had never wronged me.
   Mar. Banish the thought, crush it, and
   be at peace.   100
His guilt was marked — these things could
   never be
Were there not eyes that see, and for good
   ends,
Where ours are baffled.
   Osw.   I had been deceived.
   Mar. And from that hour the miserable
   man
No more was heard of ?
   Osw.   I had been betrayed.
   Mar. And he found no deliverance !
   Osw.   The Crew
Gave me a hearty welcome ; they had laid
The plot to rid themselves, at any cost,
Of a tyrannic Master whom they loathed.
So we pursued our voyage : when we
   landed,   110
The tale was spread abroad ; my power at
   once
Shrunk from me ; plans and schemes, and
   lofty hopes —
All vanished. I gave way — do you attend ?
   Mar. The Crew deceived you ?
   Osw.   Nay, command yourself.
   Mar. It is a dismal night — how the wind
   howls !
   Osw. I hid my head within a Convent,
   there
Lay passive as a dormouse in mid-winter.
That was no life for me — I was o'er-
   thrown,

But not destroyed.

Mar.   The proofs — you ought to have
      seen
The guilt — have touched it — felt it at
      your heart —   120
As I have done.

Osw.   A fresh tide of Crusaders
Drove by the place of my retreat; three
      nights
Did constant meditation dry my blood;
Three sleepless nights I passed in sound-
      ing on,
Through words and things, a dim and
      perilous way;
And, wheresoe'er I turned me, I beheld
A slavery compared to which the dungeon
And clanking chains are perfect liberty.
You understand me — I was comforted;
I saw that every possible shape of action
Might lead to good — I saw it and burst
      forth   131
Thirsting for some of those exploits that
      fill
The earth for sure redemption of lost
      peace.
      [*Marking* Marmaduke's *countenance.*
Nay, you have had the worst. Ferocity
Subsided in a moment, like a wind
That drops down dead out of a sky it
      vexed.
And yet I had within me evermore
A salient spring of energy; I mounted
From action up to action with a mind
That never rested — without meat or drink
Have I lived many days — my sleep was
      bound   141
To purposes of reason — not a dream
But had a continuity and substance
That waking life had never power to give.

Mar. O wretched Human-kind! — Until
      the mystery
Of all this world is solved, well may we
      envy
The worm, that, underneath a stone whose
      weight
Would crush the lion's paw with mortal
      anguish,
Doth lodge, and feed, and coil, and sleep,
      in safety.
Fell not the wrath of Heaven upon those
      traitors?   150

Osw. Give not to them a thought. From
      Palestine
We marched to Syria: oft I left the Camp,
When all that multitude of hearts was
      still,
And followed on, through woods of gloomy
      cedar,

Into deep chasms troubled by roaring
      streams;
Or from the top of Lebanon surveyed
The moonlight desert, and the moonlight
      sea:
In these my lonely wanderings I perceived
What mighty objects do impress their
      forms
To elevate our intellectual being;   160
And felt, if aught on earth deserves a
      curse,
'T is that worst principle of ill which
      dooms
A thing so great to perish self-consumed.
— So much for my remorse!

Mar.   Unhappy Man!

Osw. When from these forms I turned
      to contemplate
The World's opinions and her usages,
I seemed a Being who had passed alone
Into a region of futurity,
Whose natural element was freedom ——

Mar.   Stop —
I may not, cannot, follow thee.

Osw.   You must.
I had been nourished by the sickly food 171
Of popular applause. I now perceived
That we are praised, only as men in us
Do recognise some image of themselves,
An abject counterpart of what they are,
Or the empty thing that they would wish
      to be.
I felt that merit has no surer test
Than obloquy; that, if we wish to serve
The world in substance, not deceive by
      show,
We must become obnoxious to its hate, 180
Or fear disguised in simulated scorn.

Mar. I pity, can forgive, you; but those
      wretches —
That monstrous perfidy!

Osw.   Keep down your wrath.
False Shame discarded, spurious Fame de-
      spised,
Twin sisters both of Ignorance, I found
Life stretched before me smooth as some
      broad way
Cleared for a monarch's progress. Priests
      might spin
Their veil, but not for me — 't was in fit
      place
Among its kindred cobwebs. I had been,
And in that dream had left my native
      land,   190
One of Love's simple bondsmen — the soft
      chain
Was off for ever; and the men, from
      whom

This liberation came, you would destroy :
Join me in thanks for their blind services.
   Mar. 'T is a strange aching that, when
    we would curse
And cannot. — You have betrayed me — I
    have done —
I am content — I know that he is guilt-
    less —
That both are guiltless, without spot or
    stain,
Mutually consecrated. Poor old Man !
And I had heart for this, because thou
    lovedst   200
Her who from very infancy had been
Light to thy path, warmth to thy blood ! —
    Together   [*Turning to* Oswald.
We propped his steps, he leaned upon us
    both.
   Osw. Ay, we are coupled by a chain of
    adamant ;
Let us be fellow-labourers, then, to enlarge
Man's intellectual empire. We subsist
In slavery ; all is slavery ; we receive
Laws, but we ask not whence those laws
    have come ;
We need an inward sting to goad us on.
   Mar. Have you betrayed me ? Speak
    to that.
   Osw.   The mask,   210
Which for a season I have stooped to wear,
Must be cast off. — Know then that I was
    urged,
(For other impulse let it pass) was driven,
To seek for sympathy, because I saw
In you a mirror of my youthful self ;
I would have made us equal once again,
But that was a vain hope. You have struck
    home,
With a few drops of blood cut short the
    business ;
Therein for ever you must yield to me.
But what is done will save you from the
    blank   220
Of living without knowledge that you live :
Now you are suffering — for the future
    day,
'T is his who will command it. — Think of
    my story —
Herbert is *innocent.*
   Mar. (*in a faint voice, and doubtingly*).
          You do but echo
My own wild words ?
   Osw.   Young Man, the seed must lie
Hid in the earth, or there can be no har-
    vest ;
'Tis Nature's law. What I have done in
    darkness
I will avow before the face of day.

Herbert *is* innocent.
   Mar.   What fiend could prompt
This action ? Innocent ! — oh, breaking
    heart ! —   230
Alive or dead, I'll find him.   [*Exit.*
   Osw.   Alive — perdition !   [*Exit.*

    SCENE — *The inside of a poor Cottage*

    ELEANOR *and* IDONEA *seated.*

   Idon. The storm beats hard — Mercy
    for poor or rich,
Whose heads are shelterless in such a
    night !
   A Voice without. Holla ! to bed, good
    Folks, within !
   Elea.   O save us !
   Idon. What can this mean ?
   Elea.   Alas, for my poor husband ! —
We'll have a counting of our flocks to-
    morrow ;
The wolf keeps festival these stormy
    nights :
Be calm, sweet Lady, they are wassailers
    [*The voices die away in the distance.*
Returning from their Feast — my heart
    beats so —
A noise at midnight does *so* frighten
    me.   240
   Idon. Hush !   [*Listening.*
   Elea.   They are gone.   On such a
    night my husband,
Dragged from his bed, was cast into a dun-
    geon,
Where, hid from me, he counted many
    years,
A criminal in no one's eyes but theirs —
Not even in theirs — whose brutal violence
So dealt with him.
   Idon.   I have a noble Friend
First among youths of knightly breeding,
    One
Who lives but to protect the weak or
    injured.
There again !   [*Listening.*
   Elea. 'T is my husband's foot. Good
    Eldred
Has a kind heart ; but his imprisonment 250
Has made him fearful, and he 'll never be
The man he was.
   Idon.   I will retire ; — good night !
        [*She goes within.*
    Enter ELDRED (*hides a bundle*).
   Eld. Not yet in bed, Eleanor ! — there
are stains in that frock which must be
washed out.

Elea. What has befallen you?

Eld. I am belated, and you must know the cause — (*speaking low*) that is the blood of an unhappy Man.

Elea. Oh! we are undone for ever. 260

Eld. Heaven forbid that I should lift my hand against any man. Eleanor, I have shed tears to-night, and it comforts me to think of it.

Elea. Where, where is he?

Eld. I have done him no harm, but —— it will be forgiven me; it would not have been so once.

Elea. You have not *buried* anything? You are no richer than when you left me? 271

Eld. Be at peace; I am innocent.

Elea. Then God be thanked —

[*A short pause; she falls upon his neck.*

Eld. To-night I met with an old Man lying stretched upon the ground — a sad spectacle: I raised him up with a hope that we might shelter and restore him.

Elea. (*as if ready to run*). Where is he? You were not able to bring him *all* the way with you; let us return, I can help you.   [Eldred *shakes his head.* 281

Eld. He did not seem to wish for life: as I was struggling on, by the light of the moon I saw the stains of blood upon my clothes — he waved his hand, as if it were all useless; and I let him sink again to the ground.

Elea. Oh that I had been by your side!

Eld. I tell you his hands and his body were cold — how could I disturb his last moments? he strove to turn from me as if he wished to settle into sleep. 292

Elea. But, for the stains of blood —

Eld. He must have fallen, I fancy, for his head was cut; but I think his malady was cold and hunger.

Elea. Oh, Eldred, I shall never be able to look up at this roof in storm or fair but I shall tremble. 299

Eld. Is it not enough that my ill stars have kept me abroad to-night till this hour? I come home, and this is my comfort!

Elea. But did he say nothing which might have set you at ease?

Eld. I thought he grasped my hand while he was muttering something about his Child — his Daughter — (*starting as if he heard a noise*). What is that?

Elea. Eldred, you are a father.

Eld. God knows what was in my heart, and will not curse my son for my sake. 311

Elea. But you prayed by him? you waited the hour of his release?

Eld. The night was wasting fast; I have no friend; I am spited by the world — his wound terrified me — if I had brought him along with me, and he had died in my arms! —— I am sure I heard something breathing — and this chair! 319

Elea. Oh, Eldred, you will die alone. You will have nobody to close your eyes — no hand to grasp your dying hand — I shall be in my grave. A curse will attend us all.

Eld. Have you forgot your own troubles when I was in the dungeon?

Elea. And you left him alive?

Eld. Alive! — the damps of death were upon him — he could not have survived an hour.

Elea. In the cold, cold night. 330

Eld. (*in a savage tone*). Ay, and his head was bare; I suppose you would have had me lend my bonnet to cover it. — You will never rest till I am brought to a felon's end.

Elea. Is there nothing to be done? cannot we go to the Convent?

Eld. Ay, and say at once that I murdered him! 339

Elea. Eldred, I know that ours is the only house upon the Waste; let us take heart; this Man may be rich; and could he be saved by our means, his gratitude may reward us.

Eld. 'T is all in vain.

Elea. But let us make the attempt. This old Man may have a wife, and he may have children — let us return to the spot; we may restore him, and his eyes may yet open upon those that love him. 350

Eld. He will never open them more; even when he spoke to me, he kept them firmly sealed as if he had been blind.

Idon. (*rushing out*). It is, it is, my Father —

Eld. We are betrayed (*looking at Idonea*).

Elea. His Daughter! — God have mercy! (*turning to Idonea*).

Idon. (*sinking down*). Oh! lift me up and carry me to the place. 360
You are safe; the whole world shall not harm you.

Elea. This Lady is his Daughter.

Eld. (*moved*). I'll lead you to the spot.

Idon. (*springing up*). Alive! — you heard him breathe? quick, quick —
[*Exeunt.*

ACT V

SCENE — *A wood on the edge of the Waste*

Enter Oswald *and a* Forester.

For. He leaned upon the bridge that
    spans the glen,
And down into the bottom cast his eye,
That fastened there, as it would check the
    current.
    Osw. He listened too ; did you not say
    he listened ?
    For. As if there came such moaning
    from the flood
As is heard often after stormy nights.
    Osw. But did he utter nothing ?
    For.   See him there !

MARMADUKE *appearing.*

    Mar. Buzz, buzz, ye black and winged
    freebooters ;
That is no substance which ye settle on !
    For. His senses play him false ; and see,
    his arms   10
Outspread, as if to save himself from fall-
    ing ! —
Some terrible phantom I believe is now
Passing before him, such as God will not
Permit to visit any but a man
Who has been guilty of some horrid crime.
            [Marmaduke *disappears.*
    Osw. The game is up ! —
    For.   If it be needful, Sir,
I will assist you to lay hands upon
    him.
    Osw. No, no, my Friend, you may pursue
    your business —
'T is a poor wretch of an unsettled mind,
Who has a trick of straying from his keep-
    ers ;   20
We must be gentle. Leave him to my
    care.   [*Exit* Forester.
If his own eyes play false with him, these
    freaks
Of fancy shall be quickly tamed by mine ;
The goal is reached. My Master shall be-
    come
A shadow of myself — made by myself.

SCENE — *The edge of the Moor*

MARMADUKE *and* ELDRED *enter from
opposite sides.*
    Mar. (raising *his eyes and perceiving*
    Eldred). In any corner of this
    savage Waste,

Have you, good Peasant, seen a blind old
    Man ?
    Eld. I heard ——
    Mar.   You heard him, where ? when
    heard him ?
    Eld.   As you know,
The first hours of last night were rough
    with storm :   29
I had been out in search of a stray heifer ;
Returning late, I heard a moaning sound ;
Then, thinking that my fancy had deceived
    me,
I hurried on, when straight a second moan,
A human voice distinct, struck on my ear,
So guided, distant a few steps, I found
An aged Man, and such as you describe.
    Mar. You heard ! — he called you to
    him ? Of all men
The best and kindest ! — but where is he ?
    guide me,
That I may see him.
    Eld.   On a ridge of rocks
A lonesome Chapel stands, deserted now :
The bell is left, which no one dares re-
    move ;   41
And, when the stormy wind blows o'er the
    peak,
It rings, as if a human hand were there
To pull the cord. I guess he must have
    heard it ;
And it had led him towards the precipice,
To climb up to the spot whence the sound
    came ;
But he had failed through weakness. From
    his hand
His staff had dropped, and close upon the
    brink
Of a small pool of water he was laid,
As if he had stooped to drink, and so re-
    mained   50
Without the strength to rise.
    Mar.   Well, well, he lives,
And all is safe : what said he ?
    Eld.   But few words :
He only spake to me of a dear Daughter,
Who, so he feared, would never see him
    more ;
And of a Stranger to him, One by whom
He had been sore misused ; but he forgave
The wrong and the wrong-doer. You are
    troubled —
Perhaps you are his son ?
    Mar.   The All-seeing knows,
I did not think he had a living Child. —
But whither did you carry him ?
    Eld.   He was torn,
His head was bruised, and there was blood
    about him ——   61
    Mar. That was no work of mine.

Eld.   Nor was it mine.
Mar. But had he strength to walk ? I
could have borne him
A thousand miles.
Eld. .   I am in poverty,
And know how busy are the tongues of
men ;
My heart was willing, Sir, but I am one
Whose good deeds will not stand by their
own light ;
And, though it smote me more than words
can tell,
I left him.
Mar. I believe that there are phantoms,
That in the shape of man do cross our
path   70
On evil instigation, to make sport
Of our distress — and thou art one of
them !
But things substantial have so pressed on
me ——
Eld. My wife and children came into my
mind.
Mar. Oh Monster ! Monster ! there are
three of us,
And we shall howl together.
        [*After a pause and in a feeble voice.*
                              I am deserted
At my worst need, my crimes have in a net
(*Pointing to* Eldred) Entangled this poor
man. — Where was it ? where ?
                        [*Dragging him along.*
Eld. 'T is needless ; spare your violence.
His Daughter ——
Mar. Ay, in the word a thousand scor-
pions lodge   80
This old man *had* a Daughter.
Eld.   To the spot
I hurried back with her. — O save me, Sir,
From such a journey ! —— there was a black
tree,
A single tree ; she thought it was her
Father. —
Oh Sir, I would not see that hour again
For twenty lives. The daylight dawned,
and now —
Nay ; hear my tale, 't is fit that you should
hear it —
As we approached, a solitary crow
Rose from the spot ; — the Daughter
clapped her hands,
And then I heard a shriek so terrible   90
        [*Marmaduke shrinks back.*
The startled bird quivered upon the wing.
Mar. Dead, dead ! —
Eld. (*after a pause*). A dismal matter,
Sir, for me,
And seems the like for you ; if 't is your
wish,

I'll lead you to his Daughter ; but 't were
best
That she should be prepared ; I'll go be-
fore.
Mar. There will be need of preparation.
                        [Eldred *goes off.*
Elea. (*enters*).   Master !
Your limbs sink under you, shall I support
you ?
Mar. (*taking her arm*). Woman, I 've
lent my body to the service
Which now thou tak'st upon thee. God
forbid
That thou shouldst ever meet a like occa-
sion   100
With such a purpose in thine heart as
mine was.
Elea. Oh, why have I to do with things
like these ?   [*Exeunt.*

SCENE *changes to the door of* ELDRED's
cottage

IDONEA *seated — enter* ELDRED.

Eld. Your Father, Lady, from a wilful
hand
Has met unkindness ; so indeed he told
me,
And you remember such was my report :
From what has just befallen me I have
cause
To fear the very worst.
Idon   My Father is dead ;
Why dost thou come to me with words like
these ?
Eld. A wicked Man should answer for
his crimes.   109
Idon. Thou seest me what I am.
Eld.   It was most heinous,
And doth call out for vengeance.
Idon.   Do not add,
I prithee, to the harm thou 'st done al-
ready.
Eld. Hereafter you will thank me for
this service.
Hard by, a Man I met, who, from plain
proofs
Of interfering Heaven, I have no doubt,
Laid hands upon your Father. Fit it were
You should prepare to meet him.
Idon.   I have nothing
To do with others ; help me to my Father
        [*She turns and sees* Marmaduke
        leaning on Eleanor — *throws herself
        upon his neck, and after some time,*
In joy I met thee, but a few hours past ;
And thus we meet again ; one human stay
Is left me still in thee. Nay, shake not so.

Mar. In such a wilderness — to see no
    thing,   122
No, not the pitying moon !
   Idon.   And perish so.
Mar. Without a dog to moan for him.
   Idon.   Think not of it,
But enter there and see him how he sleeps,
Tranquil as he had died in his own bed.
   Mar. Tranquil — why not ?
   Idon.   Oh, peace !
   Mar.   He is at peace ;
His body is at rest : there was a plot,
A hideous plot, against the soul of man :
It took effect — and yet I baffled it,   130
In *some* degree.
   Idon.   Between us stood, I thought,
A cup of consolation, filled from Heaven
For both our needs ; must I, and in thy
    presence,
Alone partake of it ? — Belovèd Marma-
    duke !
   Mar. Give me a reason why the wisest
    thing
That the earth owns shall never choose to
    die,
But some one must be near to count his
    groans.
The wounded deer retires to solitude,
And dies in solitude : all things but man,
All die in solitude.
        [*Moving towards the cottage door.*
            Mysterious God,   140
If she had never lived I had not done it ! —
   Idon. Alas, the thought of such a cruel
    death
Has overwhelmed him. — I must follow.
   Eld.   Lady !
You will do well ; (*she goes*) unjust sus-
    picion may
Cleave to this Stranger : if, upon his en-
    tering,
The dead Man heave a groan, or from his
    side
Uplift his hand — that would be evidence.
   Elea. Shame ! Eldred, shame !
   Mar. (*both returning*). The dead have
    but one face (*to himself*).
And such a Man — so meek and unoffend-
    ing —   149
Helpless and harmless as a babe ; a Man,
By obvious signal to the world's protection,
Solemnly dedicated — to decoy him ! —
   Idon. Oh, had you seen him living ! —
   Mar.   I (so filled
With horror is this world) am unto thee
The thing most precious, that it now con-
    tains :
Therefore through me alone must be re-
    vealed

By whom thy Parent was destroyed, Ido-
    nea !
I have the proofs ! —
   Idon.   O miserable Father !
Thou didst command me to bless all man-
    kind ;
Nor to this moment, have I ever wished 160
Evil to any living thing ; but hear me,
Hear me, ye Heavens ! — (*kneeling*) — may
    vengeance haunt the fiend
For this most cruel murder : let him live
And move in terror of the elements ;
The thunder send him on his knees to
    prayer
In the open streets, and let him think he
    sees,
If e'er he entereth the house of God,
The roof, self-moved, unsettling o'er his
    head ;
And let him, when he would lie down at
    night,
Point to his wife the blood-drops on his
    pillow !   170
   Mar. My voice was silent, but my heart
    hath joined thee.
   Idon. (*leaning on* Marmaduke). Left to
    the mercy of that savage Man !
How could he call upon his Child ! — O
    Friend !   [*Turns to* Marmaduke.
My faithful true and only Comforter.
   Mar. Ay, come to me and weep. (*He
    kisses her.*) (*To* Eldred.) Yes, Var-
    let, look,
The devils at such sights do clap their
    hands.
        [Eldred *retires alarmed.*
   Idon. Thy vest is torn, thy cheek is dead-
    ly pale ;
Hast thou pursued the monster ?
   Mar.   I have found him. —
Oh ! would that thou hadst perished in the
    flames !
   Idon. Here art thou, then can I be deso-
    late ? —   180
   Mar. There was a time, when this pro-
    tecting hand
Availed against the mighty ; never more
Shall blessings wait upon a deed of mine.
   Idon. Wild words for me to hear, for
    me, an orphan
Committed to thy guardianship by Heav-
    en ;
And, if thou hast forgiven me, let me
    hope,
In this deep sorrow, trust, that I am thine
For closer care ; — here, is no malady.
        [*Taking his arm.*
   Mar. There, *is* a malady —
(*Striking his heart and forehead*). And

here, and here,
A mortal malady. — I am accurst :   190
All nature curses me, and in my heart
Thy curse is fixed ; the truth must be laid
bare.
It must be told, and borne. I am the man,
(Abused, betrayed, but how it matters not)
Presumptuous above all that ever breathed,
Who, casting as I thought a guilty Person
Upon Heaven's righteous judgment, did
become
An instrument of Fiends. Through me,
through me
Thy Father perished.
    Idon.   Perished — by what mischance ?
    Mar. Belovèd ! — if I dared, so would I
    call thee —   200
Conflict must cease, and, in thy frozen
heart,
The extremes of suffering meet in absolute
    peace.   [*He gives her a letter.*
    Idon. (*reads*). "Be not surprised if you
hear that some signal judgment has befallen the man who calls himself your father ; he is now with me, as his signature will
shew : abstain from conjecture till you
see me.

               "Herbert.
               "Marmaduke."

The writing Oswald's ; the signature my
Father's :
(*Looks steadily at the paper*). And here is
    yours. — or do my eyes deceive me ?
You have then seen my Father ?
    Mar.   He has leaned
Upon this arm.
    Idon. You led him towards the Convent ?
    Mar. That Convent was Stone-Arthur
    Castle. Thither   212
We were his guides. I on that night re-
solved
That he should wait thy coming till the
day
Of resurrection.
    Idon.   Miserable Woman,
Too quickly moved, too easily giving way,
I put denial on thy suit, and hence,
With the disastrous issue of last night,
Thy perturbation, and these frantic words.
Be calm, I pray thee !
    Mar.   Oswald ——
    Idon.   Name him not.

      Enter female Beggar.

    Beg. And he is dead ! — that Moor —
    how shall I cross it ?   221
By night, by day, never shall I be able
To travel half a mile alone. — Good Lady !

Forgive me ! — Saints forgive me. Had I
thought
It would have come to this ! —
    Idon. What brings you hither ? speak !
    Beg. (*pointing to* Marmaduke). This in-
nocent Gentleman. Sweet heavens !
I told him
Such tales of your dead Father ! — God is
my judge,
I thought there was no harm : but that bad
Man,
He bribed me with his gold, and looked so
fierce.
Mercy ! I said I know not what — oh pity
me —   230
I said, sweet Lady, you were not his
Daughter —
Pity me, I am haunted ; — thrice this day
My conscience made me wish to be struck
blind ;
And then I would have prayed, and had
no voice.
    Idon. (*to* Marmaduke). Was it my Fa-
ther ? — no, no, no, for he
Was meek and patient, feeble, old and
blind,
Helpless, and loved me dearer than his life.
— But hear me. For *one* question, I have
a heart
That will sustain me. Did you murder
him ?
    Mar. No, not by stroke of arm. But
    learn the process :   240
Proof after proof was pressed upon me ;
guilt
Made evident, as seemed, by blacker guilt,
Whose impious folds enwrapped even
thee ; and truth
And innocence, embodied in his looks,
His words and tones and gestures, did but
serve
With me to aggravate his crimes, and
heaped
Ruin upon the cause for which they
pleaded.
Then pity crossed the path of my resolve :
Confounded, I looked up to Heaven, and
cast,
Idonea ! thy blind Father, on the Or-
deal   250
Of the bleak Waste — left him — and so he
died ! —
    [Idonea *sinks senseless ;* Beggar, Elea-
    nor, *etc., crowd round, and bear her
    off.*
Why may we speak these things, and do
no more ;
Why should a thrust of the arm have such
a power,

And words that tell these things be heard
    in vain ?
She is not dead. Why ! — if I loved this
    Woman,
I would take care she never woke again ;
But she WILL wake, and she will weep for
    me,
And say, no blame was mine — and so,
    poor fool,
Will waste her curses on another name.
            [*He walks about distractedly.*

Enter OSWALD.

Osw. (*to himself*). Strong to o'erturn,
    strong also to build up.   260
                [*To* Marmaduke.
The starts and sallies of our last encounter
Were natural enough ; but that, I trust,
Is all gone by. You have cast off the chains
That fettered your nobility of mind —
Delivered heart and head !
                Let us to Palestine ;
This is a paltry field for enterprise.
Mar. Ay, what shall we encounter next ?
    This issue —
'T was nothing more than darkness deep-
    ening darkness,
And weakness crowned with the impotence
    of death ! —
Your pupil is, you see, an apt proficient.
    (*Ironically.*)   270
Start not ! — Here is another face hard by ;
Come, let us take a peep at both together,
And, with a voice at which the dead will
    quake,
Resound the praise of your morality —
Of this too much.
        [*Drawing* Oswald *towards the Cottage
        — stops short at the door.*
            Men are there, millions, Oswald,
Who with bare hands would have plucked
    out thy heart
And flung it to the dogs : but I am raised
Above, or sunk below, all further sense
Of provocation. Leave me, with the weight
Of that old Man's forgiveness on thy
    heart,   280
Pressing as heavily as it doth on mine.
Coward I have been ; know, there lies not
    now
Within the compass of a mortal thought,
A deed that I would shrink from ; — but
    to endure,
That is my destiny. May it be thine :
Thy office, thy ambition, be henceforth
To feed remorse, to welcome every sting
Of penitential anguish, yea with tears.

When seas and continents shall lie be-
    tween us —
The wider space the better — we may
    find   290
In such a course fit links of sympathy,
An incommunicable rivalship
Maintained, for peaceful ends beyond our
    view.
    [*Confused voices — several of the band
    enter — rush upon* Oswald, *and seize
    him.*
    One of them. I would have dogged him
    to the jaws of hell —
Osw. Ha ! is it so ! — That vagrant Hag !
    — this comes
Of having left a thing like her alive !
                [*Aside.*
Several voices. Despatch him !
Osw.   If I pass beneath a rock
And shout, and, with the echo of my voice,
Bring down a heap of rubbish, and it
    crush me,   299
I die without dishonour. Famished, starved,
A Fool and Coward blended to my wish !
    [*Smiles scornfully and exultingly at*
    Marmaduke.
Wal. 'T is done ! (*Stabs him*).
Another of the Band. The ruthless
    Traitor !
Mar.   A rash deed ! —
With that reproof I do resign a station
Of which I have been proud.
    Wil. (*approaching* Marmaduke). O my
    poor Master !
Mar. Discerning Monitor, my faithful
    Wilfred,
Why art thou here ? [*Turning to* Wallace.
            Wallace, upon these Borders,
Many there be whose eyes will not want
    cause
To weep that I am gone. Brothers in
    arms !
Raise on that dreary Waste a monument
That may record my story : nor let words —
Few must they be, and delicate in their
    touch   311
As light itself — be these withheld from
    Her
Who, through most wicked arts, was made
    an orphan
By One who would have died a thousand
    times,
To shield her from a moment's harm. To
    you,
Wallace and Wilfred, I commend the
    Lady,
By lowly nature reared, as if to make her
In all things worthier of that noble birth,

Whose long-suspended rights are now on
   the eve   319
Of restoration : with your tenderest care
Watch over her, I pray — sustain her ——
   Several of the Band (eagerly) . Captain !
   Mar. No more of that ; in silence hear
   my doom :
A hermitage has furnished fit relief
To some offenders : other penitents,
Less patient in their wretchedness, have
   fallen,
Like the old Roman, on their own sword's
   point.
They had their choice : a wanderer *must*
   I go,

The Spectre of that innocent Man, my
   guide.
No human ear shall ever hear me speak ;
No human dwelling ever give me food, 330
Or sleep, or rest : but, over waste and
   wild,
In search of nothing, that this earth can
   give,
But expiation, will I wander on —
A Man by pain and thought compelled to
   live
Yet loathing life — till anger is appeased
In Heaven, and Mercy gives me leave to
   die.

SAMUEL TAYLOR COLERIDGE'S *REMORSE*

By the time Coleridge's tragedy *Remorse* enjoyed its remarkably successful run of twenty nights (beginning 23 January 1813), the drama, and its themes, characters, and constructions, had been part of his life for sixteen years. On 13 February 1813 Coleridge wrote to Thomas Poole: "No grocer's apprentice, after his first month's permitted riot, was ever sicker of figs and raisins than I of hearing about the 'Remorse.'" Coleridge continues: "From what I myself saw, and from what an intelligent friend, more solicitous about it than myself has told me, the 'Remorse' has succeeded in spite of bad scenes, execrable acting, and newspaper calumny."

Richard Brinsley Sheridan's shabby dealing with a play whose composition he urged and an author to whom both the money and public acceptance were important is an affair whose history can be traced in Coleridge's letters. Sheridan's assertion that the play, originally "Osorio," needed revision and that Coleridge was obstinate in refusing to alter it is given the lie by the extensive revisions evident in the text of *Remorse*. Most notable are the revisions in structure; there is little doubt that Coleridge was aiming at successful public performance, that he was aware of the necessary differences in structure between a closet drama and a drama that will play well, and when we measure his achievement we must remember that *Remorse* is the only Romantic drama in this volume to have achieved contemporary success on the stage.

Coleridge's awareness of the defects of the play goes beyond the general and, for the most part, nonliterary comments in the letter to Poole. Writing in January 1816 of his new tragedy, *Zapolya*, he thought it "will not be as interesting in the Closet, as the Remorse—I mean, that it is less a Poem—but I hope it will be proportionally more on the stage." Three months earlier he was more specific about the distinction in a letter to Byron. There he writes of a new tragedy "in which I have endeavored to avoid the faults and deficiencies of The Remorse, by a better subordination of the characters by avoiding a duplicity of interest, by a greater clearness of the Plot, and by a deeper Pathos. Above all, I have labored to render the Poem more tragic and dramatic." And it can be argued that *Zapolya* succeeds in these ways; yet it was rejected and few today would elevate it over its older rival. Another strand in the skein of ironies attending *Remorse* is that despite the fact of its wholeness, it has not been the object of much critical attention: lamenting Coleridge's failure to bring to completion so many projects, we continue to ignore one of his most sustained performances.

And, in some ways, rightly so. The magnitude of achievement in *Remorse* is not that of the major poetic works. Yet it may be of the same order as that in the conversation poems, our recent critical discovery. Coleridge's criticisms of his drama are well taken. It is more suited to the closet than the stage because of a kind of Euripidean fussiness. The small portrait of Teresa, which looms so large in Alvar's mind as evidence of her faithlessness, is one whose history the theater audience would have to be extraordinarily acute to follow. The details of the action prior to the opening scene are not given in a condensed exposition: a degree of participation is required if the audience is to understand the springs of the developing action. But contrasting with this subtlety is the gothic opera of Act III, scene i: off-stage voices, music from a glass or metal instrument, necromancy, a huge painting of the assassination attempt engulfed in flames. More important than this disjunction may be the lack of focus implicit in Coleridge's other comments to Byron. Tragedy is not the effect achieved, perhaps because our sympathetic identification must be spread too thin. Ordonio is not the focus of our interest—the play is not about him. His death is not a tragic one for he has demonstrated no depth or nobility of character; he is neither misguided nor, in fact, truly evil. As Coleridge wrote in a manuscript note, "In the character of Osorio (Don Ordonio in the later version) I wished to represent a man who from his childhood had mistaken constitutional abstinence from vices for strength of character—thro' his pride duped into guilt & the endeavoring to shield himself from the reproaches of his own mind by misanthropy." And in another note Coleridge comments that "the growth of Osorio's character is nowhere explained."

Our interest is primarily centered on Don Alvar, whose role is that of benevolent avenging detective: he will root out guilt, implant remorse, and cultivate forgiveness. His plans miscarry: he is imprisoned following the Hamletian play-within-a-play. The picture of the assassination attempt succeeds in convincing his father of his death. His desire to induce remorse and repentance in his brother is defeated by Alhadra's revenge. We have, in sum, the elements of melodrama, not of tragedy.

Still, we have an intricate and often subtle melodrama. There is a fluidity of movement in, for example, Act I, scene ii, that is clearly theatrical in the best sense. There is the affecting realism of Alhadra's speech on imprisonment. The psychology of Isidor, especially as understood by Alhadra and manipulated by Ordonio, is intricate, yet plain. The almost Greek detailing of Isidor's death, seen in prospect, actuality, and retrospect, is forceful and painfully intense. Again we see the acuteness of Coleridge's criticisms: our interest in the conflicts and personalities of secondary characters because they are lifelike, reduces the impact of the drama as a whole as it would appear on the stage, though we must say at once that it enhances its richness in the closet.

Thus the diffuseness and richness of the play are located in the same structures and effects. Tensions in the play between Moslem and Christian are as much political as theological, although the conflicts between Moslem and Christian characters are profoundly psychological in origin. The ironic way in which the retributive Moresco is the real Christian (the play is set during the time of the Spanish Inquisition) does not seem didactic: it springs naturally from the history and psychology of the characters. Even in this conflict there is haziness: there are so many tensions and plots—or, rather, problematic personal and intellectual relationships—that here too the drama lacks a focus. Yet this defect is also a source of the strength that does reside in the play. The abundance of problems overwhelms us in *Remorse* in the same way as it does in life, leaving us weary of the eternal strife of contraries, yearning for an unambivalent feeling, an unequivocal choice. Coleridge resists the temptation to arrange, to categorize, to petrify life. The play is resolved by affirming a continuing dialectic, the process itself being both beneficent and malignant in its form and in its workings.

These workings, the thematic ambiguities and psychological ambivalences in *Remorse,* have their counterparts elsewhere in Coleridge, as in the following lines from "The Pains of Sleep":

> Such punishments I said were due,
> To natures deepliest stained with sin,—
> For aye entempesting anew
> The unfathomable hell within,
> The horror of their deeds to view,
> To know and loathe, yet wish and do.

The amalgam of attraction and repulsion, and the implied debate between suffering and acting, are important themes in *Remorse.* Ordonio, talking of himself and his crime, tells Isidore:

> With his human hand
> He gave a substance and reality
> To that wild fancy of a possible thing.
> (IV.1.124–26)

The punishment fit for Ordonio's crimes is also a matter of contention. Alvar believes that his picture of the attempt on his life will be the agent to awaken remorse, the alter ego of conscience and harbinger of forgiveness, in his brother:

> That worst bad man shall find
> A picture, which will wake the hell within him,
> And rouse a fiery whirlwind in his conscience.
> (II.ii.176–78)

Alhadra, wife of the Moor Isidore, the suborned assassin who spared Alvar's life, thinks differently:

> Know you not,
> What nature makes you mourn she bids you heal?
> Great evils ask great passions to redress them,
> And whirlwinds fitliest scatter pestilence.
> (I.ii.228–31)

Alvar would forgive Ordonio; Alhadra kill him. No subtler retribution, such as Alvar's wish that Ordonio feel remorse, will do.
Alvar had prayed

> That Remorse might fasten on their hearts,
> And cling with poisonous tooth, inextricable
> As the gored lion's bite.
> (I.ii.310–12)

Alhadra asks whether no more active revenge was contemplated; Alvar says no. The Christians Alhadra has known "never pardon" (I.ii.200)—their persecution of her fellow Morescos had proved this to her. Hence, her desire for revenge and action is, ironically, Christian. Because the play takes place at the time of the Inquisition, there can be little doubt that she is correct.
Ordonio himself envisions an eternal justice stalking him:

> Let the Eternal Justice
> Prepare my punishment in the obscure world—

> I will not bear to live—to live—O Agony!
> And be myself alone my own sore torment!
>
> (V.i.225–28)

In an earlier death wish, Ordonio construed this torment as an inward day of conscience or consciousness:

> For while we live—
> An inward day that never, never sets,
> Glares round the soul, and mocks the closing eyelids!

Then Ordonio, recognizing that Alvar's earlier description of remorse is correct, chooses death rather than life—the act of dying rather than the more difficult nonaction of continuing to live. In a typically fitful way, he attempts suicide after Teresa stops him from killing Alvar.

Again in a sudden reversal, he defies Alhadra's band. Teresa senses that "Some secret poison / Drinks up his spirit!" (V.i.123–24). The poison is described early in the play by Zulimez in a speech that stands as the motto on the title page of the first edition.

> Remorse is as the heart in which it grows:
> If that be gentle, it drops balmy dews
> Of true repentance; but if proud and gloomy,
> It is a poison-tree, that pierced to the inmost
> Weeps only tears of poison.
>
> (I.i.20–24)

In Act III, scene i, Alvar describes Ordonio as swollen-hearted, proud, misanthropic, yet afraid of conscience:

> What, if his very virtues
> Had pamper'd his swoln heart and made him proud?
> And what if pride had duped him into guilt?
> Yet still he stalk'd a self-created God,
> Not very bold, but exquisitely cunning
>
> . . . .
>
> Yea, and it gives fierce merriment to the damn'd,
> To see these most proud men, that loathe mankind,
> At every stir and buzz of coward conscience,
> Trick, cant, and lie, most whining hypocrites!
>
> (102–6; 110–13)

Ordonio, speaking of himself to Isidore, says: "He was a man different from other men, / And he despised them, yet revered himself" (IV.i.101–2). Earlier, in Act III, scene ii, Ordonio uttered misanthropic sentiments to Valdez, his father, and earlier still, again talking to Isidore, he attempted to rationalize his behavior by characterizing himself as the naturalistic victim of a blind determinism:

> What have I done but that which Nature destined,
> Or the blind elements stirr'd up within me?
> If good were meant, why were we made these beings?
> And if not meant—
>
> (II.i.130–33)

These feelings lead to misanthropy, and finally to a seemingly careless attitude, as though he were unsentient: speaking to Alvar, whom he still thinks of as a Moorish necromancer, he says,

> Thou hast conspired against my life and honour,
> Hast trick'd me fully; yet I hate thee not.
> Why should I hate thee? This same world of ours,
> 'Tis but a pool amid a storm of rain,
> And we the air-bladders that course up and down,
> And joust and tilt in merry tournament;
> And when one bubble runs foul of another,
> The weaker needs must break.
>
> (V.i.109–16)

Alvar recognizes that this is sham, that poisonous remorse is nourishing Ordonio's attitudes:

> Thou blind self-worshipper! Thy pride, thy cunning,
> Thy faith in universal villany,
> Thy shallow sophisms, thy pretended scorn
> For all thy human brethren—out upon them!
> What have they done for thee? have they given thee peace?
> Cured thee of starting in thy sleep? or made
> The darkness pleasant when thou wakest at midnight?
>
> (V.i.157–63)

Coleridge tells us that the poison tree, like the one in Blake's *Songs of Experience*, grows in the human brain, nurtured by hypocrisy.

That Alhadra kills Ordonio to revenge Isidore's death is true, yet the play is a remorse melodrama, not a revenge tragedy. The essential relationship is not the one between Alhadra and Ordonio; rather, it is that between Alvar and Ordonio—Alvar, who would forgive Ordonio if he saw in him signs of a genuine remorse. Yet in a larger sense, the play is about acting and suffering, the punishment fit for Ordonio's crime or his criminal nature. Alvar, the true Christian who defends the religious liberty of the Moors, argues at the end for the efficacy of the unfathomable hell within. He sees conscience and remorse as Heaven's twin voices, the one offering salvation, the other exacting retribution. Alhadra's creed, however, is psychologically as apt: "Extremes bring their own cure" (V.i.266), or, as she stated earlier, "Great evils ask great passions to redress them" (I.ii.230).

In "Osorio" Alhadra has the last word. Recognizing that

>   misery, which makes the oppressed man
> Regardless of his own life, makes him too
> Lord of the oppressor's
>
> (V.i.267–69)

she calls for political warfare of an apocalyptic kind. Coleridge's change from a political-psychological to a theological-psychological ending for the revised drama is an important change of direction. The second ending is more didactic and excrescent than the first. But in its opening it is solidly linked with an important theme ignored in the original conclusion:

> Turn not thy face that way, my father! hide
> O hide it from his eye! O let thy joy
> Flow in unmingled stream through thy first blessing.
>
> (V.i.280–82)

Then Alvar sees a lesson in the mingled presence of delight (his father blessing his refound son and his half-sister fiancée), and grief (for his dead brother). Unmingled delights, his last words tell us, are ominous, because they are false to the nature of human experience, which must teach us of both conscience and dire remorse.

Earlier in the drama Alvar had wished to escape the ambivalences of life—perhaps reflecting Coleridge's own love-hate relationship with his brother Frank (which identifies him with Ordonio, as well as with Alvar, as is usually thought). At any rate, in his first speech, returning to his birthplace, Alvar asks to forget his anguish, for "If aught on earth demand an unmix'd feeling, / 'Tis surely this" (I.i.4–5). And at the end of the act, he argues with himself that Teresa cannot be faithless. So

> I will die believing
> That I shall meet her where no evil is,
> No treachery, no cup dash'd from the lips.
> (I.ii.158–60)

By Act II, scene ii Alvar recognizes that in this tangled web of affections there can be no single, pure, uncontaminated act: an unmingled though horrible pang would be the result of Ordonio's death, but its effects on Valdez and Teresa would lead to his own death for he "could not survive the complicated ruin" (II.ii.139).

Teresa wished to recapture the blessed days of their courtship when they "saw nought but beauty" (IV.ii.101), but the speech continues with a recognition of the brighter half of the strife of contraries:

> O we have listen'd, even till high-wrought pleasure
> Hath half assumed the countenance of grief,
> And the deep sigh seemed to heave up a weight
> Of bliss that press'd too heavy on the heart.
> (IV.ii.104–7)

By the end of the play, Alvar has recognized and accepted the human necessity that delight be alloyed with grief, even as Alhadra has learned again that extremes bring their own cure. Together with Teresa's brighter knowledge, Alvar's recognition of the darker half of the dialectic process of human life is a Coleridgean affirmation of human life in all its continuing complexity. As at the end of "This Lime-Tree Bower My Prison" we learn that "no sound is dissonant which tells of life," so too *Remorse,* by refusing to solve the insoluble and by focusing attention on all its themes and characters, makes swans of all its geese.

G.B.K.

Remorse

A TRAGEDY IN FIVE ACTS

DRAMATIS PERSONAE

1797.	1813–1834.
VELEZ	= MARQUIS VALDEZ, *Father to the two brothers, and Doña Teresa's Guardian.*
ALBERT	= DON ALVAR, *the eldest son.*
OSORIO	= DON ORDONIO, *the youngest son.*
FRANCESCO	= MONVIEDRO, *a Dominican and Inquisitor.*
MAURICE	= ZULIMEZ, *the faithful attendant on Alvar.*
FERDINAND	= ISIDORE, *a Moresco Chieftain, ostensibly a Christian. Familiars of the Inquisition.*
NAOMI	= NAOMI.
	Moors, Servants, &c.
MARIA	= DOÑA TERESA, *an Orphan Heiress.*
ALHADRA, *wife* of FERDINAND,	= ALHADRA, *Wife of Isidore.*

FAMILIARS OF THE INQUISITION.
MOORS, SERVANTS, &c.

Time. The reign of Philip II., just at the close of the civil wars against the Moors, and during the heat of the persecution which raged against them, shortly after the edict which forbade the wearing of Moresco apparel under pain of death.

ACT I

SCENE I

The Sea Shore on the Coast of Granada.

DON ALVAR, *wrapt in a Boat cloak, and* ZULIMEZ (*a Moresco*), *both as just landed.*

Zulimez. No sound, no face of joy to
welcome us!
Alvar. My faithful Zulimez, for one brief
moment
Let me forget my anguish and their
crimes.
If aught on earth demand an unmix'd
feeling,
'Tis surely this — after long years of
exile,   5
To step forth on firm land, and gazing
round us,
To hail at once our country, and our
birth-place.
Hail, Spain! Granada, hail! once more
I press
Thy sands with filial awe, land of my
fathers!
 Zulimez. Then claim your rights in it!
O, revered Don Alvar,   10
Yet, yet give up your all too gentle purpose.
It is too hazardous! reveal yourself,
And let the guilty meet the doom of guilt!
 Alvar. Remember, Zulimez! I am his
brother,
Injured indeed! O deeply injured! yet   15
Ordonio's brother.
 Zulimez. Nobly-minded Alvar!
This sure but gives his guilt a blacker dye.
 Alvar. The more behoves it I should
rouse within him
Remorse! that I should save him from
himself.
 Zulimez. Remorse is as the heart in
which it grows: 20
If that be gentle, it drops balmy dews
Of true repentance; but if proud and
gloomy,

65

It is a poison-tree, that pierced to the
  inmost
Weeps only tears of poison !
  Alvar.   And of a brother,
Dare I hold this, unproved ? nor make one
  effort   25
To save him ? — Hear me, friend ! I have
  yet to tell thee,
That this same life, which he conspired
  to take,
Himself once rescued from the angry flood,
And at the imminent hazard of his own.
Add too my oath —
  Zulimez.   You have thrice told
  already   30
The years of absence and of secrecy,
To which a forced oath bound you ; if in
  truth
A suborned murderer have the power to
  dictate
A binding oath —
  Alvar.   My long captivity
Left me no choice : the very wish too
  languished   35
With the fond hope that nursed it ; the
  sick babe
Drooped at the bosom of its famished
  mother.
But (more than all) Teresa's perfidy ;
The assassin's strong assurance, when no
  interest,
No motive could have tempted him to
  falsehood :   40
In the first pangs of his awaken'd con-
  science,
When with abhorrence of his own black
  purpose
The murderous weapon, pointed at my
  breast,
Fell from his palsied hand —
  Zulimez.   Heavy presumption !
  Alvar. It weighed not with me — Hark !
  I will tell thee all ;   45
As we passed by, I bade thee mark the
  base
Of yonder cliff —
  Zulimez.   That rocky seat you mean,
Shaped by the billows ? —
  Alvar.   There Teresa met me
The morning of the day of my departure.
We were alone : the purple hue of dawn 50
Fell from the kindling east aslant upon us,
And blending with the blushes on her
  cheek,
Suffused the tear-drops there with rosy
  light.
There seemed a glory round us, and
  Teresa
The angel of the vision !

            Had'st thou seen 55
How in each motion her most innocent
  soul
Beamed forth and brightened, thou thy-
  self would'st tell me,
Guilt is a thing impossible in her !
She must be innocent!
  Zulimez.   Proceed, my lord !
  Alvar. A portrait which she had pro-
  cured by stealth,   60
(For even then it seems her heart fore-
  boded
Or knew Ordonio's moody rivalry)
A portrait of herself with thrilling hand
She tied around my neck, conjuring me,
With earnest prayers, that I would keep
  it sacred   65
To my own knowledge : nor did she desist,
Till she had won a solemn promise from
  me,
That (save my own) no eye should e'er
  behold it
Till my return. Yet this the assassin knew,
Knew that which none but she could have
  disclosed.   70
  Zulimez. A damning proof !
  Alvar.   My own life wearied me !
And but for the imperative voice within,
With mine own hand I had thrown off
  the burthen.
That voice, which quelled me, calmed me :
  and I sought
The Belgic states : there joined the better
  cause ;   75
And there too fought as one that courted
  death !
Wounded, I fell among the dead and
  dying,
In death-like trance : a long imprisonment
  followed.
The fulness of my anguish by degrees
Waned to a meditative melancholy ;   80
And still the more I mused, my soul be-
  came
More doubtful, more perplexed ; and still
  Teresa,
Night after night, she visited my sleep,
Now as a saintly sufferer, wan and tearful,
Now as a saint in glory beckoning to
  me !   85
Yes, still as in contempt of proof and
  reason,
I cherish the fond faith that she is guilt-
  less !
Hear then my fix'd resolve : I'll linger here
In the disguise of a Moresco chieftain. —
The Moorish robes ? —
  Zulimez.   All, all are in the sea-
  cave,   90

Some furlong hence. I bade our mariners
Secrete the boat there.
Alvar.   Above all, the picture
Of the assassination —
Zulimez.   Be assured
That it remains uninjured.
Alvar.   Thus disguised
I will first seek to meet Ordonio's —
    wife !   95
If possible, alone too. This was her wonted
    walk,
And this the hour ; her words, her very
    looks
Will acquit her or convict.
Zulimez. Will they not know you ?
Alvar. With your aid, friend, I shall un-
    fearingly   100
Trust the disguise ; and as to my com-
    plexion,
My long imprisonment, the scanty food,
This scar — and toil beneath a burning
    sun,
Have done already half the business for us.
Add too my youth ; since last we saw each
    other,   105
Manhood has swoln my chest, and taught
    my voice
A hoarser note — Besides, they think me
    dead :
And what the mind believes impossible,
The bodily sense is slow to recognize.
Zulimez. 'Tis yours, sir, to command,
    mine to obey.   110
Now to the cave beneath the vaulted rock,
Where having shaped you to a Moorish
    chieftain,
I'll seek our mariners ; and in the dusk
Transport whate'er we need to the small
    dell
In the Alpujarras — there where Zagri
    lived.   115
Alvar. I know it well : it is the obscur-
    est haunt
Of all the mountains —
                [Both stand listening.
                Voices at a distance !
Let us away !   *[Exeunt.*

SCENE II

Enter TERESA *and* VALDEZ.

Teresa. I hold Ordonio dear ; he is your
    son
And Alvar's brother.
Valdez.   Love him for himself,
Nor make the living wretched for the dead.
Teresa. I mourn that you should plead
    in vain, Lord Valdez,
But heaven hath heard my vow, and I

remain   5
Faithful to Alvar, be he dead or living.
Valdez. Heaven knows with what de-
    light I saw your loves,
And could my heart's blood give him back
    to thee
I would die smiling. But these are idle
    thoughts !
Thy dying father comes upon my soul 10
With that same look, with which he gave
    thee to me ;
I held thee in my arms a powerless babe,
While thy poor mother with a mute en-
    treaty
Fixed her faint eyes on mine. Ah not for
    this,
That I should let thee feed thy soul with
    gloom,   15
And with slow anguish wear away thy life,
The victim of a useless constancy.
I must not see thee wretched.
Teresa.   There are woes
Ill bartered for the garishness of joy !
If it be wretched with an untired eye 20
To watch those skiey tints, and this green
    ocean ;
Or in the sultry hour beneath some rock,
My hair dishevelled by the pleasant sea
    breeze,
To shape sweet visions, and live o'er again
All past hours of delight ! If it be
    wretched   25
To watch some bark, and fancy Alvar
    there,
To go through each minutest circumstance
Of the blest meeting, and to frame ad-
    ventures
Most terrible and strange, and hear him
    tell them ;
(As once I knew a crazy Moorish maid 30
Who drest her in her buried lover's
    clothes,
And o'er the smooth spring in the moun-
    tain cleft
Hung with her lute, and played the self-
    same tune
He used to play, and listened to the
    shadow
Herself had made) — if this be wretched-
    ness,   35
And if indeed it be a wretched thing
To trick out mine own death-bed, and
    imagine
That I had died, died just ere his return !
Then see him listening to my constancy,
Or hover round, as he at midnight oft 40
Sits on my grave and gazes at the moon ;
Or haply in some more fantastic mood,
To be in Paradise, and with choice flowers

Build up a bower where he and I might
    dwell,
And there to wait his coming! O my
    sire!   45
My Alvar's sire! if this be wretchedness
That eats away the life, what were it,
    think you,
If in a most assured reality
He should return, and see a brother's
    infant
Smile at him from my arms?   50
Oh what a thought!
    Valdez. A thought? even so! mere
    thought! an empty thought.
The very week he promised his return ——
    Teresa. Was it not then a busy joy?
    to see him,
After those three years' travels! we had no
    fears —   55
The frequent tidings, the ne'er failing
    letter,
Almost endeared his absence! Yet the
    gladness,
The tumult of our joy! What then if
    now ——
    Valdez. O power of youth to feed on
    pleasant thoughts,
Spite of conviction! I am old and heart-
    less!   60
Yes, I am old — I have no pleasant fan-
    cies —
Hectic and unrefreshed with rest —
    Teresa.   My father!
    Valdez. The sober truth is all too much
    for me!
I see no sail which brings not to my mind
The home-bound bark in which my son
    was captured   65
By the Algerine — to perish with his cap-
    tors!
    Teresa. Oh no! he did not!
    Valdez.   Captured in sight of land!
From yon hill point, nay, from our castle
    watch-tower
We might have seen ——
    Teresa.   His capture, not his death.
    Valdez. Alas! how aptly thou forget'st
    a tale   70
Thou ne'er didst wish to learn! my brave
    Ordonio
Saw both the pirate and his prize go down,
In the same storm that baffled his own
    valour,
And thus twice snatched a brother from
    his hopes:
Gallant Ordonio! O beloved Teresa,   75
Would'st thou best prove thy faith to
    generous Alvar,
And most delight his spirit, go, make thou

His brother happy, make his aged father
Sink to the grave in joy.
    Teresa.   For mercy's sake
Press me no more! I have no power to
    love him.   80
His proud forbidding eye, and his dark
    brow,
Chill me like dew-damps of the unwhole-
    some night:
My love, a timorous and tender flower,
Closes beneath his touch.
    Valdez.   You wrong him, maiden!
You wrong him, by my soul! Nor was it
    well   85
To character by such unkindly phrases
The stir and workings of that love for you
Which he has toiled to smother. 'Twas
    not well,
Nor is it grateful in you to forget
His wounds and perilous voyages, and
    how   90
With an heroic fearlessness of danger
He roam'd the coast of Afric for your
    Alvar.
It was not well — You have moved me
    even to tears.
    Teresa. Oh pardon me, Lord Valdez!
    pardon me!
It was a foolish and ungrateful speech, 95
A most ungrateful speech! But I am
    hurried
Beyond myself, if I but hear of one
Who aims to rival Alvar. Were we not
Born in one day, like twins of the same
    parent?
Nursed in one cradle? Pardon me, my
    father!   100
A six years' absence is a heavy thing,
Yet still the hope survives ——
    Valdez (looking forward). Hush! 'tis
    Monviedro.
    Teresa. The Inquisitor! on what new
    scent of blood?

Enter MONVIEDRO *with* ALHADRA.

Monviedro. Peace and the truth be with
    you! Good my Lord,   105
My present need is with your son.
We have hit the time. Here comes he!
    Yes, 'tis he.

Enter from the opposite side
DON ORDONIO.

My Lord Ordonio, this Moresco woman
(Alhadra is her name) asks audience of
    you.
    Ordonio. Hail, reverend father! what

may be the business ? 110
Monviedro. My lord, on strong suspicion of relapse
To his false creed, so recently abjured,
The secret servants of the Inquisition
Have seized her husband, and at my command
To the supreme tribunal would have led him, 115
But that he made appeal to you, my lord,
As surety for his soundness in the faith.
Though lessoned by experience what small trust
The asseverations of these Moors deserve,
Yet still the deference to Ordonio's name, 120
Nor less the wish to prove, with what high honour
The Holy Church regards her faithful soldiers,
Thus far prevailed with me that ——
Ordonio. Reverend father,
I am much beholden to your high opinion,
Which so o'erprizes my light services.
[*Then to* ALHADRA.
I would that I could serve you ; but in truth 126
Your face is new to me.
Monviedro. My mind foretold me
That such would be the event. In truth, Lord Valdez,
'Twas little probable, that Don Ordonio,
That your illustrious son, who fought so bravely 130
Some four years since to quell these rebel Moors,
Should prove the patron of this infidel !
The warranter of a Moresco's faith !
Now I return.
Alhadra. My Lord, my husband's name 135
Is Isidore. (ORDONIO *starts.*) You may remember it :
Three years ago, three years this very week,
You left him at Almeria.
Monviedro. Palpably false !
This very week, three years ago, my lord,
(You needs must recollect it by your wound) 140
You were at sea, and there engaged the pirates,
The murderers doubtless of your brother Alvar !
What, is he ill, my Lord ? how strange he looks !
Valdez. You pressed upon him too abruptly, father !

The fate of one, on whom, you know, he doted. 145
Ordonio. O Heavens ! I ? — I doted ?
Yes ! I doted on him.
[ORDONIO *walks to the end of the stage,* VALDEZ *follows.*
Teresa. I do not, can not, love him. Is my heart hard ?
Is my heart hard ? that even now the thought
Should force itself upon me ? — Yet I feel it ! 150
Monviedro. The drops did start and stand upon his forehead !
I will return. In very truth, I grieve
To have been the occasion. Ho ! attend me, woman !
Alhadra (*to Teresa*). O gentle lady ! make the father stay,
Until my lord recover. I am sure, 155
That he will say he is my husband's friend.
Teresa. Stay, father ! stay ! my lord will soon recover.
Ordonio (*as they return, to Valdez*).
Strange, that this Monviedro
Should have the power so to distemper me !
Valdez. Nay, 'twas an amiable weakness, son ! 160
Monviedro. My lord, I truly grieve ——
Ordonio. Tut ! name it not.
A sudden seizure, father ! think not of it.
As to this woman's husband, I do know him.
I know him well, and that he is a Christian.
Monviedro. I hope, my lord, your merely human pity 165
Doth not prevail ——
Ordonio. 'Tis certain that he was a catholic ;
What changes may have happened in three years,
I can not say ; but grant me this, good father ;
Myself I'll sift him : if I find him sound, 170
You'll grant me your authority and name
To liberate his house.
Monviedro. Your zeal, my lord,
And your late merits in this holy warfare
Would authorize an ampler trust — you have it.
Ordonio. I will attend you home within an hour. 175
Valdez. Meantime return with us and take refreshment.
Alhadra. Not till my husband 's free ! I

may not do it.
I will stay here.
   Teresa (*aside*). Who is this Isidore ?
   Valdez.   Daughter !
   Teresa. With your permission, my dear
     lord,   180
I'll loiter yet awhile t' enjoy the sea breeze.
[*Exeunt* VALDEZ, MONVIEDRO *and* ORDONIO.
   Alhadra. Hah ! there he goes ! a bitter
     curse go with him,
A scathing curse !
You hate him, don't you, lady ?
   Teresa. Oh fear not me ! my heart is sad
     for you.   185
   Alhadra. These fell inquisitors ! these
     sons of blood !
As I came on, his face so maddened me,
That ever and anon I clutched my dagger
And half unsheathed it ——
   Teresa.   Be more calm, I pray you.
   Alhadra. And as he walked along the
     narrow path   190
Close by the mountain's edge, my soul
   grew eager ;
'Twas with hard toil I made myself re-
   member
That his Familiars held my babes and hus-
   band.
To have leapt upon him with a tiger's
   plunge,
And hurl'd him down the rugged preci-
   pice,   195
O, it had been most sweet !
   Teresa.   Hush ! hush for shame !
Where is your woman's heart ?
   Alhadra.   O gentle lady !
You have no skill to guess my many
   wrongs,
Many and strange ! Besides, I am a Chris-
   tian,
And Christians never pardon — 'tis their
   faith !   200
   Teresa. Shame fall on those who so have
     shewn it to thee !
   Alhadra. I know that man ; 'tis well he
     knows not me.
Five years ago (and he was the prime
   agent),
Five years ago the holy brethren seized me.
   Teresa. What might your crime be ?
   Alhadra.   I was a Moresco !
They cast me, then a young and nursing
   mother,   206
Into a dungeon of their prison house,
Where was no bed, no fire, no ray of light,
No touch, no sound of comfort ! The
   black air,
It was a toil to breathe it ! when the
   door,   210

Slow opening at the appointed hour, dis-
   closed
One human countenance, the lamp's red
   flame
Cowered as it entered, and at once sank
   down.
Oh miserable ! by that lamp to see
My infant quarrelling with the coarse hard
   bread   215
Brought daily ; for the little wretch was
   sickly —
My rage had dried away its natural food.
In darkness I remained — the dull bell
   counting,
Which haply told me, that the all-cheering
   sun
Was rising on our garden. When I
   dozed,   220
My infant's moanings mingled with my
   slumbers
And waked me. — If you were a mother,
   lady,
I should scarce dare to tell you, that its
   noises
And peevish cries so fretted on my brain
That I have struck the innocent babe in
   anger.   225
   Teresa. O Heaven ! it is too horrible to
     hear.
   Alhadra. What was it then to suffer ?
     'Tis most right
That such as you should hear it. — Know
   you not,
What nature makes you mourn, she bids
   you heal ?
Great evils ask great passions to redress
   them,   230
And whirlwinds fitliest scatter pestilence.
   Teresa. You were at length released ?
   Alhadra.   Yes, at length
I saw the blessed arch of the whole
   heaven !
'Twas the first time my infant smiled.
   No more —
For if I dwell upon that moment,
   Lady,   235
A trance comes on which makes me o'er
   again
All I then was — my knees hang loose and
   drag,
And my lip falls with such an idiot laugh,
That you would start and shudder !
   Teresa.   But your husband —
   Alhadra. A month's imprisonment would
     kill him, Lady.   240
   Teresa. Alas, poor man !
   Alhadra.   He hath a lion's
     courage,
Fearless in act, but feeble in endurance ;

Unfit for boisterous times, with gentle
  heart
He worships nature in the hill and valley,
Not knowing what he loves, but loves it
  all —   245
  Enter ALVAR *disguised as a Moresco, and
  in Moorish garments.*
  Teresa. Know you that stately Moor ?
  Alhadra.   I know him not :
But doubt not he is some Moresco chief-
  tain,
Who hides himself among the Alpujarras.
  Teresa. The Alpujarras ? Does he know
  his danger,
So near this seat ?
  Alhadra.   He wears the Moorish robes
  too,   250
As in defiance of the royal edict.
  [ALHADRA *advances to* ALVAR, *who has
  walked to the back of the stage, near
  the rocks.* TERESA *drops her veil.*
  Alhadra. Gallant Moresco ! An inquisi-
  tor,
Monviedro, of known hatred to our
  race ——
  Alvar. You have mistaken me. I am a
  Christian.
  Alhadra. He deems, that we are plotting
  to ensnare him :   255
Speak to him, Lady — none can hear you
  speak,
And not believe you innocent of guile.
  Teresa. If aught enforce you to con-
  cealment, Sir —
  Alhadra. He trembles strangely.
  [ALVAR *sinks down and hides his
  face in his robe.*
  Teresa.   See, we have disturbed him.
  [*Approaches nearer to him.*
I pray you, think us friends — uncowl your
  face,   260
For you seem faint, and the night-breeze
  blows healing.
I pray you, think us friends !
  Alvar (*raising his head*). Calm, very
  calm !
'Tis all too tranquil for reality !
And she spoke to me with her innocent
  voice,   265
That voice, that innocent voice ! She is no
  traitress !
  Teresa. Let us retire (*haughtily to Al-
  hadra*).
  Alhadra. He is indeed a Christian.
  Alvar (*aside*). She deems me dead, yet
  wears no mourning garment !
Why should my brother's — wife — wear
  mourning garments ?   270
  [*To* TERESA.

Your pardon, noble dame ! that I dis-
  turbed you :
I had just started from a frightful dream.
  Teresa. Dreams tell but of the past, and
  yet, 'tis said,
They prophesy —
  Alvar.   The Past lives o'er again
In its effects, and to the guilty spirit   275
The ever-frowning Present is its image.
  Teresa. Traitress !   (*Then aside.*)
  What sudden spell o'ermasters me ?
Why seeks he me, shunning the Moorish
  woman ?
  Alvar. I dreamt I had a friend, on whom
  I leant
With blindest trust, and a betrothéd
  maid,   280
Whom I was wont to call not mine, but
  me :
For mine own self seem'd nothing, lacking
  her.
This maid so idolized, that trusted friend
Dishonoured in my absence, soul and
  body !
Fear, following guilt, tempted to blacker
  guilt,   285
And murderers were suborned against my
  life.
But by my looks, and most impassioned
  words,
I roused the virtues that are dead in no
  man,
Even in the assassins' hearts ! they made
  their terms,
And thanked me for redeeming them
  from murder.   290
  Alhadra. You are lost in thought : hear
  him no more, sweet Lady !
  Teresa. From morn to night I am my-
  self a dreamer,
And slight things bring on me the idle
  mood !
Well sir, what happened then ?
  Alvar.   On a rude rock,
A rock, methought, fast by a grove of
  firs,   295
Whose thready leaves to the low-breathing
  gale
Made a soft sound most like the distant
  ocean,
I stayed, as though the hour of death
  were passed,
And I were sitting in the world of spirits —
For all things seemed unreal ! There I
  sate —   300
The dews fell clammy, and the night
  descended,
Black, sultry, close ! and ere the midnight
  hour

A storm came on, mingling all sounds of
    fear,
That woods, and sky, and mountains,
    seemed one havock.
The second flash of lightning shewed a
    tree   305
Hard by me, newly scathed. I rose tumul-
    tuous:
My soul worked high, I bared my head
    to the storm,
And with loud voice and clamorous agony,
Kneeling I prayed to the great Spirit that
    made me,
Prayed, that Remorse might fasten on their
    hearts,   310
And cling with poisonous tooth, inextrica-
    ble
As the gored lion's bite!
    Teresa.   A fearful curse!
    Alhadra. But dreamt you not that you
      returned and killed them?
Dreamt you of no revenge?
    Alvar.   She would have died
Died in her guilt — perchance by her own
    hands!   315
And bending o'er her self-inflicted wounds,
I might have met the evil glance of frenzy,
And leapt myself into an unblest grave!
I prayed for the punishment that cleanses
    hearts:
For still I loved her!
    Alhadra. And you dreamt all this?   320
    Teresa. My soul is full of visions all as
      wild!
    Alhadra. There is no room in this heart
      for puling love-tales.
    Teresa (lifts up her veil, and advances
      to Alvar). Stranger, farewell! I
      guess not who you are,
Nor why you so addressed your tale to me.
Your mien is noble, and, I own, perplexed
    me,   325
With obscure memory of something past,
Which still escaped my efforts, or pre-
    sented
Tricks of a fancy pampered with long
    wishing.
If, as it sometimes happens, our rude
    startling,
Whilst your full heart was shaping out its
    dream,   330
Drove you to this, your not ungentle, wild-
    ness —
You have my sympathy, and so farewell!
But if some undiscovered wrongs oppress
    you,
And you need strength to drag them into
    light,
The generous Valdez, and my Lord Or-
    donio,   335

Have arm and will to aid a noble sufferer,
Nor shall you want my favourable plead-
    ing.
         [*Exeunt* TERESA *and* ALHADRA.
    Alvar (alone). 'Tis strange! It cannot
      be! my Lord Ordonio!
Her Lord Ordonio! Nay, I will not do it!
I cursed him once — and one curse is
    enough!   340
How sad she looked, and pale! but not
    like guilt —
And her calm tones — sweet as a song of
    mercy!
If the bad spirit retain'd his angel's voice,
Hell scarce were Hell. And why not inno-
    cent?
Who meant to murder me, might well
    cheat her?   345
But ere she married him, he had stained
    her honour;
Ah! there I am hampered. What if this
    were a lie
Framed by the assassin? Who should tell
    it him,
If it were truth? Ordonio would not tell
    him.
Yet why one lie? all else, I know, was
    truth.   350
No start, no jealousy of stirring conscience!
And she referred to me — fondly, me-
    thought!
Could she walk here if she had been a
    traitress?
Here where we played together in our
    childhood?
Here where we plighted vows? where her
    cold cheek   355
Received my last kiss, when with sup-
    pressed feelings
She had fainted in my arms? It cannot be!
'Tis not in nature! I will die believing,
That I shall meet her where no evil is,
No treachery, no cup dashed from the
    lips.   360
I'll haunt this scene no more! live she in
    peace!
Her husband — aye her husband! May this
    angel
New mould his canker'd heart! Assist me,
    heaven,
That I may pray for my poor guilty
    brother!   [*Exit.*

ACT II

SCENE I

A wild and mountainous country. ORDO-
NIO *and* ISIDORE *are discovered, supposed
at a little distance from* ISIDORE's *house.*

Ordonio. Here we may stop : your house distinct in view,
Yet we secured from listeners.

Isidore.   Now indeed
My house ! and it looks cheerful as the clusters
Basking in sunshine on yon vine-clad rock,
That over-brows it ! Patron ! Friend ! Preserver !   5
Thrice have you saved my life. Once in the battle
You gave it me : next rescued me from suicide
When for my follies I was made to wander,
With mouths to feed, and not a morsel for them :
Now but for you, a dungeon's slimy stones   10
Had been my bed and pillow.

Ordonio.   Good Isidore !
Why this to me ? It is enough, you know it.

Isidore. A common trick of gratitude, my lord,
Seeking to ease her own full heart ——

Ordonio.   Enough !
A debt repaid ceases to be a debt.   15
You have it in your power to serve me greatly.

Isidore. And how, my lord ? I pray you to name the thing.
I would climb up an ice-glazed precipice
To pluck a weed you fancied !

Ordonio.   Why — that — Lady —

Isidore. 'Tis now three years, my lord, since last I saw you :   20
Have you a son, my lord ?

Ordonio.   O miserable —   [*Aside.*
Isidore ! you are a man, and know mankind.
I told you what I wished — now for the truth —
She loved the man you kill'd.

Isidore.   You jest, my lord ?

Ordonio. And till his death is proved she will not wed me.

Isidore. You sport with me, my lord ?

Ordonio.   Come, come ! this foolery 26
Lives only in thy looks, thy heart disowns it !

Isidore. I can bear this, and any thing more grievous
From you, my lord — but how can I serve you here ?

Ordonio. Why, you can utter with a solemn gesture   30
Oracular sentences of deep no-meaning,
Wear a quaint garment, make mysterious antics —

Isidore. I am dull, my lord ! I do not comprehend you.

Ordonio. In blunt terms, you can play the sorcerer.
She hath no faith in Holy Church, 'tis true :   35
Her lover schooled her in some newer nonsense !
Yet still a tale of spirits works upon her.
She is a lone enthusiast, sensitive,
Shivers, and can not keep the tears in her eye :
And such do love the marvellous too well   40
Not to believe it. We will wind up her fancy
With a strange music, that she knows not of —
With fumes of frankincense, and mummery,
Then leave, as one sure token of his death,
That portrait, which from off the dead man's neck   45
I bade thee take, the trophy of thy conquest.

Isidore. Will that be a sure sign ?

Ordonio.   Beyond suspicion.
Fondly caressing him, her favour'd lover,
(By some base spell he had bewitched her senses)
She whispered such dark fears of me forsooth,   50
As made this heart pour gall into my veins.
And as she coyly bound it round his neck
She made him promise silence ; and now holds
The secret of the existence of this portrait
Known only to her lover and herself.   55
But I had traced her, stolen unnotic'd on them,
And unsuspected saw and heard the whole.

Isidore. But now I should have cursed the man who told me
You could ask aught, my lord, and I refuse —
But this I can not do.

Ordonio.   Where lies your scruple ? 60

Isidore. Why — why, my lord !
You know you told me that the lady lov'd you,
Had loved you with incautious tenderness ;
That if the young man, her betrothéd husband,
Returned, yourself, and she, and the honour of both   65
Must perish. Now though with no tenderer scruples
Than those which being native to the heart,
Than those, my lord, which merely being

a man —
Ordonio. This fellow is a Man — he killed for hire
One whom he knew not, yet has tender scruples !   70
          [*Then turning to* ISIDORE.
These doubts, these fears, thy whine, thy stammering —
Pish, fool ! thou blunder'st through the book of guilt,
Spelling thy villainy.
     Isidore.   My lord — my lord,
I can bear much — yes, very much from you !
But there's a point where sufferance is meanness :   75
I am no villain — never kill'd for hire —
My gratitude ——
Ordonio.   O aye — your gratitude !
'Twas a well-sounding word — what have you done with it ?
     Isidore. Who proffers his past favours for my virtue —
Ordonio.   Virtue ——
Isidore. Tries to o'erreach me — is a very sharper,   80
And should not speak of gratitude, my lord.
I knew not 'twas your brother !
     Ordonio.   And who told you ?
Isidore. He himself told me.
Ordonio.   Ha ! you talk'd with him !
And those, the two Morescoes who were with you ?
     Isidore. Both fell in a night brawl at Malaga.   85
Ordonio (*in a low voice*). My brother —
Isidore.   Yes, my lord, I could not tell you !
I thrust away the thought — it drove me wild.
But listen to me now — I pray you listen ——
Ordonio. Villain ! no more. I'll hear no more of it.
Isidore. My lord, it much imports your future safety   90
That you should hear it.
Ordonio (*turning off from Isidore*). Am not I a man !
'Tis as it should be ! tut — the deed itself
Was idle, and these after-pangs still idler !
     Isidore. We met him in the very place you mentioned.
Hard by a grove of firs —
     Ordonio.   Enough — enough —   95
Isidore. He fought us valiantly, and wounded all ;
In fine, compelled a parley.

Ordonio.   Alvar ! brother !
Isidore. He offered me his purse —
Ordonio.   Yes ?
Isidore.   Yes — I spurned it. —
He promised us I know not what — in vain !
Then with a look and voice that overawed me,   100
He said, What mean you, friends ? My life is dear :
I have a brother and a promised wife,
Who make life dear to me — and if I fall,
That brother will roam earth and hell for vengeance.
There was a likeness in his face to yours ;   105
I asked his brother's name : he said — Ordonio,
Son of Lord Valdez ! I had well nigh fainted.
At length I said (if that indeed I said it,
And that no Spirit made my tongue its organ,)
That woman is dishonoured by that brother,   110
And he the man who sent us to destroy you.
He drove a thrust at me in rage. I told him
He wore her portrait round his neck. He look'd
As he had been made of the rock that propt his back —
Aye, just as you look now — only less ghastly !   115
At length recovering from his trance, he threw
His sword away, and bade us take his life,
It was not worth his keeping.
     Ordonio.   And you kill'd him ?
Oh blood hounds ! may eternal wrath flame round you !
He was his Maker's Image undefac'd !   120
It seizes me — by Hell I will go on !
What — would'st thou stop, man ? thy pale looks won't save thee !
Oh cold — cold — cold ! shot through with icy cold !
Isidore (*aside*). Were he alive he had returned ere now.
The consequence the same — dead through his plotting !   125
Ordonio. O this unutterable dying away — here —
This sickness of the heart !
               What if I went
And liv'd in a hollow tomb, and fed on weeds ?
Aye ! that's the road to heaven ! O fool ! fool ! fool !

What have I done but that which nature
 destined,   130
Or the blind elements stirred up within
 me ?
If good were meant, why were we made
 these beings ?
And if not meant —
 Isidore. You are disturbed, my lord !
 Ordonio (starts). A gust of the soul !
  i'faith it overset me.
O 'twas all folly — all ! idle as laugh-
 ter !   135
Now, Isidore ! I swear that thou shalt aid
 me.
 Isidore (in a low voice). I'll perish first !
 Ordonio. What dost thou mutter of ?
 Isidore. Some of your servants know
  me, I am certain.
 Ordonio. There 's some sense in that
  scruple ; but we'll mask you.
 Isidore. They'll know my gait : but
  stay ! last night I watched 140
A stranger near the ruin in the wood,
Who as it seemed was gathering herbs
 and wild flowers.
I had followed him at distance, seen him
 scale
Its western wall, and by an easier entrance
Stole after him unnoticed. There I
 marked,   145
That mid the chequer work of light and
 shade
With curious choice he plucked no other
 flowers,
But those on which the moonlight fell :
 and once
I heard him muttering o'er the plant. A
 wizard —
Some gaunt slave prowling here for dark
 employment.   150
 Ordonio. Doubtless you question'd him ?
 Isidore.   'Twas my intention,
Having first traced him homeward to his
 haunt.
But lo ! the stern Dominican, whose spies
Lurk every where, already (as it seemed)
Had given commission to his apt famil-
 iar   155
To seek and sound the Moor ; who now
 returning,
Was by this trusty agent stopped midway.
I, dreading fresh suspicion if found near
 him
In that lone place, again concealed my-
 self :
Yet within hearing. So the Moor was
 question'd,   160
And in your name, as lord of this domain,
Proudly he answered, 'Say to the Lord

Ordonio,
He that can bring the dead to life again ! '
 Ordonio. A strange reply !
 Isidore. Aye, all of him is strange.
He called himself a Christian, yet he
 wears   165
The Moorish robes, as if he courted death.
 Ordonio. Where does this wizard live ?
 Isidore (pointing to the distance). You
  see that brooklet ?
Trace its course backward : through a nar-
 row opening
It leads you to the place.
 Ordonio.   How shall I know it ?
 Isidore. You cannot err. It is a small
  green dell   170
Built all around with high off-sloping hills,
And from its shape our peasants aptly
 call it
The Giant's Cradle. There 's a lake in
 the midst,
And round its banks tall wood that
 branches over,
And makes a kind of faery forest grow 175
Down in the water. At the further end
A puny cataract falls on the lake ;
And there, a curious sight ! you see its
 shadow
For ever curling, like a wreath of smoke,
Up through the foliage of those faery
 trees.   180
His cot stands opposite. You cannot miss
 it.
 *Ordonio (in retiring stops suddenly at
  the edge of the scene, and then
  turning round to Isidore).* Ha ! —
  Who lurks there ! Have we been
  overheard ?
There where the smooth high wall of
 slate-rock glitters ——
 Isidore. 'Neath those tall stones, which
  propping each the other,
Form a mock portal with their pointed
 arch ?   185
Pardon my smiles ! 'Tis a poor idiot boy,
Who sits in the sun, and twirls a bough
 about,
His weak eyes seeth'd in most unmeaning
 tears.
And so he sits, swaying his cone-like head,
And staring at his bough from morn to
 sun-set,   190
See-saws his voice in inarticulate noises.
 Ordonio. 'Tis well, and now for this
  same wizard's lair.
 Isidore. Some three strides up the hill,
  a mountain ash
Stretches its lower boughs and scarlet clus-
 ters

O'er the old thatch.
    Ordonio.   I shall not fail to find it. 195
      [*Exeunt* ORDONIO *and* ISIDORE.

SCENE II

The inside of a Cottage, around which flowers and plants of various kinds are seen. Discovers ALVAR, ZULIMEZ *and* ALHADRA, *as on the point of leaving.*

    Alhadra (*addressing Alvar.*) Farewell then! and though many thoughts perplex me,
Aught evil or ignoble never can I
Suspect of thee! If what thou seem'st thou art,
The oppressed brethren of thy blood have need
Of such a leader.
    Alvar.   Nobly-minded woman! 5
Long time against oppression have I fought,
And for the native liberty of faith
Have bled and suffered bonds. Of this be certain :
Time, as he courses onward, still unrolls
The volume of concealment. In the future, 10
As in the optician's glassy cylinder,
The indistinguishable blots and colours
Of the dim past collect and shape themselves,
Upstarting in their own completed image
To scare or to reward.
              I sought the guilty, 15
And what I sought I found : but ere the spear
Flew from my hand, there rose an angel form
Betwixt me and my aim. With baffled purpose
To the Avenger I leave vengeance, and depart !
Whate'er betide, if aught my arm may aid, 20
Or power protect, my word is pledged to thee :
For many are thy wrongs, and thy soul noble.
Once more, farewell.   [*Exit* ALHADRA.
            Yes, to the Belgic states
We will return. These robes, this stained complexion,
Akin to falsehood, weigh upon my spirit. 25
Whate'er befall us, the heroic Maurice
Will grant us an asylum, in remembrance
Of our past services.
    Zulimez. And all the wealth, power, in-

fluence which is yours,
You let a murderer hold ?
    Alvar.   O faithful Zulimez! 30
That my return involved Ordonio's death,
I trust, would give me an unmingled pang,
Yet bearable : — but when I see my father
Strewing his scant grey hairs, e'en on the ground,
Which soon must be his grave, and my Teresa — 35
Her husband proved a murderer, and her infants
His infants — poor Teresa ! — all would perish,
All perish — all ! and I (nay bear with me)
Could not survive the complicated ruin !
    Zulimez. Nay now ! I have distress'd you — you well know, 40
I ne'er will quit your fortunes. True, 'tis tiresome !
You are a painter, one of many fancies !
You can call up past deeds, and make them live
On the blank canvas ! and each little herb,
That grows on mountain bleak, or tangled forest, 45
You have learnt to name —
    Hark ! heard you not some footsteps ?
    Alvar. What if it were my brother coming onwards ?
I sent a most mysterious message to him.

Enter ORDONIO

    Alvar. It is he !
    Ordonio (*to himself as he enters*). If I distinguish'd right her gait and stature, 50
It was the Moorish woman, Isidore's wife,
That passed me as I entered. A lit taper,
In the night air, doth not more naturally
Attract the night-flies round it, than a conjuror
Draws round him the whole female neighbourhood. 55
             [*Addressing* ALVAR.
You know my name, I guess, if not my person.
I am Ordonio, son of the Lord Valdez.
    Alvar. The Son of Valdez !
    [ORDONIO *walks leisurely round the room, and looks attentively at the plants.*
    Zulimez (*to Alvar*) . Why, what ails you now ?
How your hand trembles ! Alvar, speak ! what wish you ?
    Alvar. To fall upon his neck and weep forgiveness ! 60

Ordonio (returning, and aloud).
    Plucked in the moonlight from a
    ruined abbey —
Those only, which the pale rays visited !
O the unintelligible power of weeds,
When a few odd prayers have been mut-
    tered o'er them :
Then they work miracles ! I warrant
    you,   65
There's not a leaf, but underneath it lurks
Some serviceable imp.
                There's one of you
Hath sent me a strange message.
    Alvar.   I am he.
    Ordonio. With you, then, I am to speak :
    [*Haughtily waving his hand to* ZULIMEZ.
And mark you, alone.   [*Exit* ZULIMEZ.
'He that can bring the dead to life
    again !' —   71
Such was your message, Sir ! You are no
    dullard,
But one that strips the outward rind of
    things !
    Alvar. 'Tis fabled there are fruits with
    tempting rinds,
That are all dust and rottenness within. 75
Would'st thou I should strip such ?
    Ordonio.   Thou quibbling fool,
What dost thou mean ? Think'st thou I
    journeyed hither
To sport with thee ?
    Alvar.   O no, my lord ! to sport
Best suits the gaiety of innocence.
    Ordonio (aside). O what a thing is
    man ! the wisest heart   80
A fool ! a fool that laughs at it own folly,
Yet still a fool ! [*Looks round the cottage*.
                You are poor !
    Alvar. What follows thence ?
    Ordonio. That you would fain be richer.
The inquisition, too — You comprehend
    me ?
You are poor, in peril. I have wealth and
    power,   85
Can quench the flames, and cure your
    poverty :
And for the boon I ask of you but this,
That you should serve me — once — for a
    few hours.
    Alvar. Thou art the son of Valdez !
    would to Heaven
That I could truly and for ever serve
    thee.   90
    Ordonio. The slave begins to soften.
                    [*Aside*.
              You are my friend,
'He that can bring the dead to life again,'
Nay, no defence to me ! The holy brethren
Believe these calumnies — I know thee

better.
Thou art a man, and as a man I'll trust
    thee !   95
    Alvar (aside). Alas ! this hollow mirth —
    Declare your business.
    Ordonio. I love a lady, and she would
    love me
But for an idle and fantastic scruple.
Have you no servants here, no listeners ?
           [ORDONIO *steps to the door*.
    Alvar. What, faithless too ? False to his
    angel wife ?   100
To such a wife ? Well might'st thou look
    so wan,
Ill-starr'd Teresa ! —— Wretch ! my softer
    soul
Is pass'd away, and I will probe his con-
    science !
    Ordonio. In truth this lady lov'd an-
    other man,
But he has perish'd.
    Alvar. What ! you kill'd him ? hey ? 105
    Ordonio. I'll dash thee to the earth, if
    thou but think'st it !
Insolent slave ! how dar'dst thou —
    [*Turns abruptly from* ALVAR, *and then
    to himself*.
                Why ! what's this ?
'Twas idiotcy ! I'll tie myself to an aspen,
And wear a fool's cap —
    Alvar.   Fare thee well —
I pity thee, Ordonio, even to anguish.
              [ALVAR *is retiring*.
    Ordonio. Ho !   [*Calling to* ALVAR.
    Alvar.   Be brief, what wish you ? 111
    Ordonio. You are deep at bartering —
    You charge yourself
At a round sum. Come, come, I spake
    unwisely.
    Alvar. I listen to you.
    Ordonio.   In a sudden tempest
Did Alvar perish — he, I mean — the
    lover —   115
The fellow ——
    Alvar.   Nay, speak out ! 'twill ease
    your heart
To call him villain ! — Why stand'st thou
    aghast ?
Men think it natural to hate their rivals.
    Ordonio. Now, till she knows him dead,
    she will not wed me.
    Alvar. Are you not wedded, then ? Mer-
    ciful Heaven !   120
Not wedded to Teresa ?
    Ordonio.   Why, what ails thee ?
What, art thou mad ? why look'st thou up-
    ward so ?
Dost pray to Lucifer, Prince of the Air ?
    Alvar. Proceed. I shall be silent.

Ordonio.   To Teresa ?
Politic wizard ! ere you sent that mes-
    sage,   125
You had conn'd your lesson, made your-
    self proficient
In all my fortunes. Hah ! you prophesied
A golden crop ! Well, you have not mis-
    taken —
Be faithful to me and I'll pay thee nobly.
    Alvar. Well ! and this lady !   130
    Ordonio. If we could make her certain
    of his death,
She needs must wed me. Ere her lover
    left her,
She tied a little portrait round his neck,
Entreating him to wear it.
    Alvar.   Yes ! he did so !
    Ordonio. Why no : he was afraid of
    accidents,   135
Of robberies, and shipwrecks, and the like.
In secrecy he gave it me to keep,
Till his return.
    Alvar. What ! he was your friend then ?
    Ordonio. I was his friend. —
                    Now that he gave it me, 140
This lady knows not. You are a mighty
    wizard —
Can call the dead man up — he will not
    come. —
He is in heaven then — there you have no
    influence.
Still there are tokens — and your imps may
    bring you
Something he wore about him when he
    died.   145
And when the smoke of the incense on
    the altar
Is pass'd, your spirits will have left this
    picture.
What say you now ?
    Alvar.   Ordonio, I will do it.
    Ordonio. We'll hazard no delay. Be it
    to-night,
In the early evening. Ask for the Lord
    Valdez.   150
I will prepare him. Music too, and in-
    cense,
(For I have arranged it — music, altar,
    incense)
All shall be ready. Here is this same pic-
    ture,
And here, what you will value more, a
    purse.
Come early for your magic ceremonies. 155
    Alvar. I will not fail to meet you.
    Ordonio. Till next we meet, farewell !
                            [*Exit* ORDONIO.
*Alvar (alone, indignantly flings the purse
    away and gazes passionately at the*

portrait).   And I did curse thee !
At midnight ! on my knees ! and I be-
    lieved
Thee perjur'd, thee a traitress ! thee dis-
    honour'd !
O blind and credulous fool ! O guilt of
    folly !   160
Should not thy inarticulate fondnesses,
Thy infant loves — should not thy maiden
    vows
Have come upon my heart ? And this
    sweet Image
Tied round my neck with many a chaste
    endearment,
And thrilling hands, that made me weep
    and tremble —   165
Ah, coward dupe ! to yield it to the mis-
    creant,
Who spake pollution of thee ! barter for
    life
This farewell pledge, which with impas-
    sioned vow
I had sworn that I would grasp — ev'n in
    my Death-pang !

I am unworthy of thy love, Teresa,   170
Of that unearthly smile upon those lips,
Which ever smiled on me ! Yet do not
    scorn me —
I lisp'd thy name, ere I had learnt my
    mother's.

Dear portrait ! rescued from a traitor's
    keeping,
I will not now profane thee, holy
    image,   175
To a dark trick. That worst bad man
    shall find
A picture, which will wake the hell within
    him,
And rouse a fiery whirlwind in his con-
    science.

ACT III

SCENE I

*A Hall of Armory, with an Altar at the
back of the Stage. Soft Music from an
        instrument of Glass or Steel.*
VALDEZ, ORDONIO, *and* ALVAR *in a Sorcer-
        er's robe, are discovered.*
    Ordonio. This was too melancholy,
    Father.
Valdez.   Nay,
My Alvar lov'd sad music from a child.
Once he was lost ; and after weary search
We found him in an open place in the

wood,
To which spot he had followed a blind
  boy, 5
Who breath'd into a pipe of sycamore
Some strangely moving notes : and these,
  he said,
Were taught him in a dream. Him we
  first saw
Stretch'd on the broad top of a sunny
  heath-bank :
And lower down poor Alvar, fast asleep, 10
His head upon the blind boy's dog. It
  pleas'd me
To mark how he had fasten'd round the
  pipe
A silver toy his grandam had late given
  him.
Methinks I see him now as he then
  look'd —
Even so ! — He had outgrown his infant
  dress, 15
Yet still he wore it.
  Alvar (aside). My tears must not flow !
I must not clasp his knees, and cry, My
  father !

Enter Teresa *and* Attendants.

Teresa. Lord Valdez, you have asked my
  presence here,
And I submit ; but (Heaven bear witness
  for me)
My heart approves it not ! 'tis mockery. 20
  Ordonio. Believe you then no preter-
  natural influence :
Believe you not that spirits throng around
  us ?
  Teresa. Say rather that I have imagined
  it
A possible thing : and it has sooth'd my
  soul
As other fancies have ; but ne'er seduced
  me 25
To traffic with the black and frenzied hope
That the dead hear the voice of witch or
  wizard. [*To* Alvar.
Stranger, I mourn and blush to see you
  here,
On such employment ! With far other
  thoughts
I left you. 30
  Ordonio (aside). Ha ! he has been tam-
  pering with her ?
  Alvar. O high-soul'd Maiden ! and more
  dear to me
Than suits the stranger's name ! —
          I swear to thee
I will uncover all concealéd guilt.
Doubt, but decide not ! Stand ye from
  the altar. 35

[*Here a strain of music is heard from
  behind the scene.*
  Alvar. With no irreverent voice or un-
  couth charm
I call up the departed !
            Soul of Alvar !
Hear our soft suit, and heed my milder
  spell :
So may the gates of Paradise, unbarr'd,
Cease thy swift toils ! Since haply thou
  art one 40
Of that innumerable company
Who in broad circle, lovelier than the
  rainbow,
Girdle this round earth in a dizzy motion,
With noise too vast and constant to be
  heard :
Fitliest unheard ! For oh, ye numberless, 45
And rapid travellers ! what ear unstunn'd,
What sense unmadden'd, might bear up
  against
The rushing of your congregated wings ?
                 [*Music.*
Even now your living wheel turns o'er my
  head !
Ye, as ye pass, toss high the desert sands, 50
That roar and whiten, like a burst of
  waters,
A sweet appearance, but a dread illusion
To the parch'd caravan that roams by
  night !
And ye upbuild on the becalmed waves
That whirling pillar, which from earth
  to heaven 55
Stands vast, and moves in blackness ! Ye
  too split
The ice mount ! and with fragments many
  and huge
Tempest the new-thaw'd sea, whose sud-
  den gulfs
Suck in, perchance, some Lapland wizard's
  skiff !
Then round and round the whirlpool's
  marge ye dance, 60
Till from the blue swoln corse the soul
  toils out,
And joins your mighty army.
  [*Here behind the scenes a voice sings
  the three words, 'Hear, Sweet Spirit.'*
                 Soul of Alvar !
Hear the mild spell, and tempt no blacker
  charm !
By sighs unquiet, and the sickly pang
Of a half-dead, yet still undying hope, 65
Pass visible before our mortal sense !
So shall the Church's cleansing rites be
  thine,
Her knells and masses that redeem the
  dead !

SONG

*Behind the Scenes, accompanied by the
same Instrument as before.*

Hear, sweet spirit, hear the spell,
Lest a blacker charm compel !   70
So shall the midnight breezes swell
With thy deep long-lingering knell.

And at evening evermore,
In a chapel on the shore,
Shall the chaunter, sad and saintly,   75
Yellow tapers burning faintly,
Doleful masses chaunt for thee,
Miserere Domine !

Hark ! the cadence dies away
    On the quiet moonlight sea :   80
The boatmen rest their oars and say,
    Miserere Domine !   [*A long pause.*

Ordonio. The innocent obey nor charm
    nor spell !
My brother is in heaven. Thou sainted
    spirit,
Burst on our sight, a passing visitant !   85
Once more to hear thy voice, once more
    to see thee,
O 'twere a joy to me !
    Alvar.   A joy to thee !
What if thou heard'st him now ? What if
    his spirit
Re-enter'd its cold corse, and came upon
    thee
With many a stab from many a mur-
    derer's poniard ?   90
What (if his stedfast eye still beaming pity
And brother's love) he turn'd his head
    aside,
Lest he should look at thee, and with one
    look
Hurl thee beyond all power of penitence ?
Valdez. These are unholy fancies !
Ordonio.   Yes, my father,   95
He is in Heaven !
    Alvar (*still to Ordonio*). But what if he
    had a brother,
Who had lived even so, that at his dying
    hour,
The name of Heaven would have con-
    vulsed his face,
More than the death-pang ?
    Valdez.   Idly prating man !
Thou hast guess'd ill : Don Alvar's only
    brother   100
Stands here before thee — a father's bless-
    ing on him !
He is most virtuous.
    Alvar (*still to Ordonio*). What, if his
    very virtues

Had pampered his swoln heart and made
    him proud ?
And what if pride had duped him into
    guilt ?
Yet still he stalked a self-created god,   105
Not very bold, but exquisitely cunning :
And one that at his mother's looking-glass
Would force his features to a frowning
    sternness ?
Young Lord ! I tell thee, that there are
    such beings —
Yea, and it gives fierce merriment to the
    damn'd,   110
To see these most proud men, that loath
    mankind,
At every stir and buzz of coward con-
    science,
Trick, cant, and lie, most whining hypo-
    crites !
Away, away ! Now let me hear more music.
          [*Music again.*
    Teresa. 'Tis strange, I tremble at my
    own conjectures !   115
But whatsoe'er it mean, I dare no longer
Be present at these lawless mysteries,
This dark provoking of the hidden Pow-
    ers !
Already I affront — if not high Heaven —
Yet Alvar's memory ! — Hark ! I make ap-
    peal   120
Against the unholy rite, and hasten hence
To bend before a lawful shrine, and seek
That voice which whispers, when the still
    heart listens,
Comfort and faithful hope ! Let us retire.
    Alvar (*to Teresa*). O full of faith and
    guileless love, thy Spirit   125
Still prompts thee wisely. Let the pangs
    of guilt
Surprise the guilty : thou art innocent !
        [*Exeunt* TERESA *and* Attendant. *Music
        as before.*
The spell is mutter'd — Come, thou wan-
    dering shape,
Who own'st no master in a human eye,
Whate'er be this man's doom, fair be it,
    or foul,   130
If he be dead, O come ! and bring with
    thee
That which he grasp'd in death ! But if
    he live,
Some token of his obscure perilous life.
      [*The whole Music clashes into a Chorus.*

CHORUS

Wandering demons, hear the spell !
Lest a blacker charm compel —   135
    [*The incense on the altar takes fire
    suddenly, and an illuminated picture*

of ALVAR's *assassination is discovered,
and having remained a few seconds
is then hidden by ascending flames.*

Ordonio (*starting*). Duped! duped!
duped! — the traitor Isidore!

[*At this instant the doors are forced
open,* MONVIEDRO *and the* Familiars
*of the Inquisition, Servants, &c., en-
ter and fill the stage.*

Monviedro. First seize the sorcerer! suf-
fer him not to speak!
The holy judges of the Inquisition
Shall hear his first words. — Look you pale,
Lord Valdez?
Plain evidence have we here of most foul
sorcery.   140
There is a dungeon underneath this castle,
And as you hope for mild interpretation,
Surrender instantly the keys and charge
of it.

Ordonio (*recovering himself as from
stupor, to Servants*). Why haste you
not? Off with him to the dungeon!

[*All rush out in tumult.*

SCENE II

*Interior of a Chapel, with painted
Windows.*

Enter TERESA.

Teresa. When first I entered this pure
spot, forebodings
Press'd heavy on my heart: but as I knelt,
Such calm unwonted bliss possess'd my
spirit,
A trance so cloudless, that those sounds,
hard by,
Of trampling uproar fell upon mine ear 5
As alien and unnoticed as the rain-storm
Beats on the roof of some fair banquet-
room,
While sweetest melodies are warbling ——

Enter VALDEZ.

Valdez. Ye pitying saints, forgive a fa-
ther's blindness,
And extricate us from this net of peril! 10
Teresa. Who wakes anew my fears, and
speaks of peril?
Valdez. O best Teresa, wisely wert thou
prompted!
This was no feat of mortal agency!
That picture — Oh, that picture tells me
all!
With a flash of light it came, in flames it
vanished,   15

Self-kindled, self-consum'd: bright as thy
life,
Sudden and unexpected as thy fate,
Alvar! My son! My son! — The Inquisi-
tor —
Teresa. Torture me not! But Alvar —
Oh of Alvar?
Valdez. How often would he plead for
these Morescoes!   20
The brood accurst! remorseless, coward
murderers!
Teresa. So? so? — I comprehend you —
He is ——
Valdez.   He is no more!
Teresa. O sorrow! that a father's voice
should say this,
A Father's Heart believe it!
Valdez.   A worse sorrow
Are fancy's wild hopes to a heart de-
spairing!   25
Teresa. These rays that slant in through
those gorgeous windows,
From yon bright orb — though coloured as
they pass,
Are they not light? — Even so that voice,
Lord Valdez!
Which whispers to my soul, though haply
varied
By many a fancy, many a wishful hope, 30
Speaks yet the truth: and Alvar lives for
me!
Valdez. Yes, for three wasting years, thus
and no other,
He has lived for thee — a spirit for thy
spirit!
My child, we must not give religious faith
To every voice which makes the heart a
listener   35
To its own wish.
Teresa.   I breath'd to the Unerring
Permitted prayers. Must those remain un-
answer'd,
Yet impious sorcery, that holds no com-
mune
Save with the lying spirit, claim belief?
Valdez. O not to-day, not now for the
first time   40
Was Alvar lost to thee —
                        Accurst assassins!
Disarmed, o'erpowered, despairing of de-
fence,
At his bared breast he seem'd to grasp
some relique
More dear than was his life ——
Teresa.   O Heavens! my portrait!
And he did grasp it in his death pang!
                        Off, false demon,
That beat'st thy black wings close above
my head!   46

[ORDONIO *enters with the keys of the dungeon in his hand.*

Hush ! who comes here ? The wizard Moor's employer !
Moors were his murderers, you say ? Saints shield us
From wicked thoughts ——

[VALDEZ *moves towards the back of the stage to meet* ORDONIO, *and dur- the concluding lines of* TERESA'S *speech appears as eagerly conversing with him.*

Is Alvar dead ? what then ?
The nuptial rites and funeral shall be one !   50
Here 's no abiding-place for thee, Tere-sa. —
Away ! they see me not — Thou seest me, Alvar !
To thee I bend my course. — But first one question,
One question to Ordonio. — My limbs tremble —
There I may sit unmark'd — a moment will restore me.   55

[*Retires out of sight.*

Ordonio (as he advances with Valdez).
These are the dungeon keys. Mon-viedro knew not,
That I too had received the wizard's mes-sage,
' He that can bring the dead to life again. '
But now he is satisfied, I plann'd this scheme
To work a full conviction on the cul-prit,   60
And he entrusts him wholly to my keeping.
Valdez. 'Tis well, my son ! But have you yet discovered
(Where is Teresa ?) what those speeches meant —
Pride, and hypocrisy, and guilt, and cun-ning ?
Then when the wizard fix'd his eye on you,   65
And you, I know not why, look'd pale and trembled —
Why — why, what ails you now ? —
Ordonio.   Me ? what ails me ?
A pricking of the blood — It might have happen'd
At any other time.— Why scan you me ?
Valdez. His speech about the corse, and stabs and murderers,   70
Bore reference to the assassins ——
Ordonio.   Dup'd ! dup'd ! dup'd !
The traitor, Isidore ! [*A pause, then wildly.*
I tell thee, my dear father !
I am most glad of this.

Valdez.   True — sorcery
Merits its doom ; and this perchance may guide us
To the discovery of the murderers.   75
I have their statures and their several faces
So present to me, that but once to meet them
Would be to recognize.
Ordonio.   Yes ! yes ! we recognize them.
I was benumb'd, and staggered up and down
Through darkness without light — dark — dark — dark !   80
My flesh crept chill, my limbs felt man-acled
As had a snake coil'd round them ! — Now 'tis sunshine,
And the blood dances freely through its channels !

[*Then to himself.*

This is my virtuous, grateful Isadore !

[*Then mimicking* ISIDORE'S *manner and voice.*

' A common trick of gratitude, my lord ! '   85
Old Gratitude ! a dagger would dissect
His ' own full heart ' — 'twere good to see its colour.
Valdez. These magic sights ! O that I ne'er had yielded
To your entreaties ! Neither had I yielded,
But that in spite of your own seeming faith   90
I held it for some innocent stratagem,
Which love had prompted, to remove the doubts
Of wild Teresa — by fancies quelling fan-cies !
Ordonio. Love ! love ! and then we hate ! and what ? and wherefore ?
Hatred and love ! fancies opposed by fan-cies !   95
What ? if one reptile sting another rep-tile ?
Where is the crime ? The goodly face of nature
Hath one disfeaturing stain the less upon it.
Are we not all predestined transiency,
And cold dishonour ? Grant it, that this hand   100
Had given a morsel to the hungry worms
Somewhat too early — Where 's the crime of this ?
That this must needs bring on the idiotcy
Of moist-eyed penitence — 'tis like a dream !
Valdez. Wild talk, my son ! But thy ex-

cess of feeling —— 105
Almost I fear it hath unhinged his brain.

Ordonio (*Teresa reappears and advances slowly*). Say, I had laid a body in the sun!

Well! in a month there swarm forth from the corse
A thousand, nay, ten thousand sentient beings
In place of that one man. — Say, I had kill'd him! 110

[TERESA *stops listening.*
Yet who shall tell me, that each one and all
Of these ten thousand lives is not as happy,
As that one life, which being push'd aside,
Made room for these unnumber'd ——

Valdez. O mere madness!

[TERESA *moves hastily forwards, and places herself directly before* ORDONIO.

Ordonio. Teresa? or the phantom of Teresa? 115

Teresa. Alas! the phantom, only, if in truth
The substance of her being, her life's life,
Have ta'en its flight through Alvar's death-wound — [*A pause.*
Where —
(Even coward murder grants the dead a grave)
O tell me, Valdez! — answer me, Ordonio! 120
Where lies the corse of my betrothéd husband?

Ordonio. There, where Ordonio likewise would fain lie!
In the sleep-compelling earth, in unpierc'd darkness!
For while we live —
An inward day that never, never sets, 125
Glares round the soul, and mocks the closing eyelids!

Over his rocky grave the fir-grove sighs
A lulling ceaseless dirge! 'Tis well with him.

[*Strides off towards the altar, but returns as* VALDEZ *is speaking.*

Teresa. The rock! the fir-grove! [*To* VALDEZ
Did'st thou hear him say it?
Hush! I will ask him!

Valdez. Urge him not — not now! 130
This we beheld. Nor he nor I know more,
Than what the magic imagery revealed.
The assassin, who pressed foremost of the three ——

Ordonio. A tender-hearted, scrupulous, grateful villain,
Whom I will strangle!

Valdez. While his two companions —— 135

Ordonio. Dead! dead already! what care we for the dead?

Valdez (*to Teresa*). Pity him! soothe him! disenchant his spirit!
These supernatural shews, this strange disclosure,
And this too fond affection, which still broods
O'er Alvar's fate, and still burns to avenge it — 140
These, struggling with his hopeless love for you,
Distemper him, and give reality
To the creatures of his fancy.

Ordonio. Is it so?
Yes! yes! even like a child, that too abruptly
Roused by a glare of light from deepest sleep 145
Starts up bewildered and talks idly.
Father!
What if the Moors that made my brother's grave,
Even now were digging ours? What if the bolt,
Though aim'd, I doubt not, at the son of Valdez,
Yet miss'd its true aim when it fell on Alvar? 150

Valdez. Alvar ne'er fought against the Moors, — say rather,
He was their advocate; but you had march'd
With fire and desolation through their villages. —
Yet he by chance was captured.

Ordonio. Unknown, perhaps,
Captured, yet as the son of Valdez, murdered. 155
Leave all to me. Nay, whither, gentle lady?

Valdez. What seek you now?

Teresa. A better, surer light
To guide me ——

Both Valdez and Ordonio. Whither?

Teresa. To the only place
Where life yet dwells for me, and ease of heart.
These walls seem threatening to fall in upon me! 160
Detain me not! a dim power drives me hence,
And that will be my guide.

Valdez. To find a lover !
Suits that a high-born maiden's modesty ?
O folly and shame ! Tempt not my rage,
    Teresa !
  Teresa. Hopeless, I fear no human be-
    ing's rage. 165
And am I hastening to the arms —— O
    Heaven !
I haste but to the grave of my belov'd !
      [*Exit,* VALDEZ *following after her.*
  Ordonio. This, then, is my reward ! and
    I must love her ?
Scorn'd ! shudder'd at ! yet love her still ?
    yes ! yes !
By the deep feelings of revenge and
    hate 170
I will still love her — woo her — win her
    too ! [*A pause.*
Isidore safe and silent, and the portrait
Found on the wizard — he, belike, self-
    poison'd
To escape the crueller flames —— My soul
    shouts triumph !
The mine is undermined ! blood ! blood !
    blood ! 175
They thirst for thy blood ! thy blood,
    Ordonio ! [*A pause.*
The hunt is up ! and in the midnight
    wood
With lights to dazzle and with nets they
    seek
A timid prey : and lo ! the tiger's eye
Glares in the red flame of his hunter's
    torch ! 180

To Isidore I will dispatch a message,
And lure him to the cavern ! aye, that
    cavern !
He cannot fail to find it. Thither I'll lure
    him,
Whence he shall never, never more re-
    turn !
      [*Looks through the side window.*
A rim of the sun lies yet upon the sea, 185
And now 'tis gone ! All shall be done to-
    night. [*Exit.*

ACT IV

SCENE I

A cavern, dark, except where a gleam of
    moonlight is seen on one side at
    the further end of it ; supposed to
    be cast on it from a crevice in a
    part of the cavern out of sight. ISI-
    DORE *alone, an extinguished torch*
    in his hand

  Isadore. Faith 'twas a moving letter —
    very moving !
' His life in danger, no place safe but this !
'Twas his turn now to talk of gratitude. '
And yet — but no ! there can't be such a
    villain.
It can not be !
    Thanks to that little crevice, 5
Which lets the moonlight in ! I'll go and
    sit by it.
To peep at a tree, or see a he-goat's beard,
Or hear a cow or two breathe loud in
    their sleep —
Any thing but this crash of water drops !
These dull abortive sounds that fret the
    silence 10
With puny thwartings and mock opposi-
    tion !
So beats the death-watch to a sick man's
    ear.
      [*He goes out of sight, opposite to*
        the patch of moonlight : and
        returns.
A hellish pit ! The very same I dreamt of !
I was just in — and those damn'd fingers of
    ice
Which clutch'd my hair up ! Ha ! — what 's
    that — it mov'd. 15
      [ISIDORE *stands staring at another*
        recess in the cavern. In the
        mean time ORDONIO *enters with*
        a torch, and halloes to ISIDORE.
  Isidore. I swear that I saw something
    moving there !
The moonshine came and went like a flash
    of lightning ——
I swear, I saw it move.
  Ordonio (goes into the recess, then re-
    turns).
        A jutting clay stone
Drops on the long lank weed, that grows
    beneath :
And the weed nods and drips.
  Isidore. A jest to laugh at ! 20
It was not that which scar'd me, good my
    lord.
  Ordonio. What scar'd you, then ?
  Isidore. You see that little rift ?
But first permit me !
      [*Lights his torch at* ORDONIO'S, *and*
        while lighting it.
      (A lighted torch in the hand
Is no unpleasant object here — one's
    breath
Floats round the flame, and makes as many
    colours 25
As the thin clouds that travel near the
    moon.)
You see that crevice there ?

My torch extinguished by these water-
    drops
And marking that the moonlight came
    from thence,
I stept in to it, meaning to sit there ;   30
But scarcely had I measured twenty
    paces —
My body bending forward, yea, o'er-
    balanced
Almost beyond recoil, on the dim brink
Of a huge chasm I stept. The shadowy
    moonshine
Filling the void so counterfeited sub-
    stance,   35
That my foot hung aslant adown the edge.
Was it my own fear ?
               Fear too hath its instincts !
(And yet such dens as these are wildly
    told of,
And there are beings that live, yet not for
    the eye)
An arm of frost above and from behind
    me   40
Pluck'd up and snatched me backward.
    Merciful Heaven !
You smile ! alas, even smiles look ghastly
    here !
My lord, I pray you, go yourself and view
    it.
    Ordonio. It must have shot some pleas-
    ant feelings through you.
    Isidore. If every atom of a dead man's
    flesh   45
Should creep, each one with a particular
    life,
Yet all as cold as ever — 'twas just so !
Or had it drizzled needle-points of frost
Upon a feverish head made suddenly
    bald —
    Ordonio.   Why, Isidore,
I blush for thy cowardice. It might have
    startled,   50
I grant you, even a brave man for a
    moment —
But such a panic —
    Isidore.   When a boy, my lord !
I could have sate whole hours beside that
    chasm,
Push'd in huge stones and heard them
    strike and rattle
Against its horrid sides : then hung my
    head   55
Low down, and listened till the heavy
    fragments
Sank with faint crash in that still groan-
    ing well,
Which never thirsty pilgrim blest, which
    never
A living thing came near — unless, per-
    chance,
Some blind-worm battens on the ropy
    mould   60
Close at its edge.
    Ordonio.   Art thou more coward now ?
    Isidore. Call him, that fears his fellow-
    man, a coward !
I fear not man — but this inhuman cavern,
It were too bad a prison-house for goblins.
Beside, (you'll smile, my lord) but true it
    is,   65
My last night's sleep was very sorely
    haunted
By what had passed between us in the
    morning.
O sleep of horrors ! Now run down and
    stared at
By forms so hideous that they mock re-
    membrance —
Now seeing nothing and imagining noth-
    ing,   70
But only being afraid — stifled with fear !
While every goodly or familiar form
Had a strange power of breathing terror
    round me !
I saw you in a thousand fearful shapes ;
And, I entreat your lordship to believe
    me,   75
In my last dream ——
    Ordonio.   Well ?
    Ordonio.   I was in the act
Of falling down that chasm, when Alhadra
Wak'd me : she heard my heart beat.
    Ordonio.   Strange enough !
Had you been here before ?
    Isidore.   Never, my lord !
But mine eyes do not see it now more
    clearly,   80
Than in my dream I saw — that very
    chasm.
    Ordonio (*after a pause*). I know not
    why it should be ! yet it is —
    Isidore. What is, my lord ?
    Ordonio.   Abhorrent from our nature
To kill a man. —
    Isidore.   Except in self-defence.
    Ordonio. Why that's my case ; and yet
    the soul recoils from it —   85
'Tis so with me at least. But you, perhaps,
Have sterner feelings ?
    Isidore.   Something troubles you.
How shall I serve you ? By the life you
    gave me,
By all that makes that life of value to me,
My wife, my babes, my honour, I swear to
    you,   90
Name it, and I will toil to do the thing,
If it be innocent ! But this, my lord !
Is not a place where you could perpetrate,

No, nor propose a wicked thing. The darkness,
When ten strides off we know 'tis cheer-ful moonlight,   95
Collects the guilt, and crowds it round the heart.
It must be innocent.
 Ordonio. Thyself be judge.
One of our family knew this place well.
 Isidore. Who ? when ? my lord ?
 Ordonio. What boots it, who or when ?
Hang up thy torch — I'll tell his tale to thee.   100
  [*They hang up their torches on some ridge in the cavern.*
He was a man different from other men,
And he despised them, yet revered him-self.
 Isidore (aside). He ? He despised ?
  Thou'rt speaking of thyself !
I am on my guard, however : no surprise.
   [*Then to* ORDONIO.
What, he was mad ?
 Ordonio. All men seemed mad to him !   105
Nature had made him for some other planet,
And pressed his soul into a human shape
By accident or malice. In this world
He found no fit companion.
 Isidore. Of himself he speaks. [*Aside.*
  Alas ! poor wretch !   110
Mad men are mostly proud.
 Ordonio. He walked alone,
And phantom thoughts unsought-for trou-bled him.
Something within would still be shadow-ing out
All possibilities ; and with these shadows
His mind held dalliance. Once, as so it happened,   115
A fancy crossed him wilder than the rest :
To this in moody murmur and low voice
He yielded utterance, as some talk in sleep :
The man who heard him. —
  Why did'st thou look round ?
 Isidore. I have a prattler three years old, my lord !   120
In truth he is my darling. As I went
From forth my door, he made a moan in sleep —
But I am talking idly — pray proceed !
And what did this man ?
 Ordonio. With this human hand
He gave a substance and reality   125
To that wild fancy of a possible thing. —
Well it was done !
  Why babblest thou of guilt ?

The deed was done, and it passed fairly off.
And he whose tale I tell thee — dost thou listen ?
 Isidore. I would, my lord, you were by my fire-side,   130
I'd listen to you with an eager eye,
Though you began this cloudy tale at midnight,
But I do listen — pray proceed, my lord.
 Ordonio. Where was I ?
 Isidore. He of whom you tell the tale —
 Ordonio. Surveying all things with a quiet scorn,   135
Tamed himself down to living purposes,
The occupations and the semblances
Of ordinary men — and such he seemed !
But that same over ready agent — he —
 Isidore. Ah ! what of him, my lord ?
 Ordonio. He proved a traitor,   140
Betrayed the mystery to a brother-traitor,
And they between them hatch'd a damnéd plot
To hunt him down to infamy and death.
What did the Valdez ? I am proud of the name
Since he dared do it. —
  [ORDONIO *grasps his sword, and turns off from* ISIDORE, *then after a pause returns.*
   Our links burn dimly.   145
 Isidore. A dark tale darkly finished !
  Nay, my lord !
Tell what he did.
 Ordonio. That which his wisdom prompted —
He made the traitor meet him in this cavern,
And here he kill'd the traitor.
 Isidore. No ! the fool !   150
He had not wit enough to be a traitor.
Poor thick-eyed beetle ! not to have fore-seen
That he who gulled thee with a whim-pered lie
To murder his own brother, would not scruple
To murder thee, if e'er his guilt grew jealous,   155
And he could steal upon thee in the dark !
 Ordonio. Thou would'st not then have come, if —
 Isidore. Oh yes, my lord !
I would have met him arm'd, and scar'd the coward.
  [ISIDORE *throws off his robe ; shews himself armed, and draws his sword.*

Ordonio. Now this is excellent and
    warms the blood !   160
My heart was drawing back, drawing me
    back
With weak and womanish scruples. Now
    my vengeance
Beckons me onwards with a warrior's
    mien,
And claims that life, my pity robb'd her
    of —
Now will I kill thee, thankless slave, and
    count it   165
Among my comfortable thoughts hereafter.
    Isidore. And all my little ones father-
    less —
                    Die thou first.
    [*They fight,* ORDONIO *disarms* ISI-
    DORE, *and in disarming him
    throws his sword up that recess
    opposite to which they were
    standing.* ISIDORE *hurries into
    the recess with his torch,* OR-
    DONIO *follows him; a loud cry
    of 'Traitor! Monster!' is heard
    from the cavern, and in a mo-
    ment* ORDONIO *returns alone.*
Ordonio. I have hurl'd him down the
    chasm ! treason for treason.
He dreamt of it : henceforward let him
    sleep,
A dreamless sleep, from which no wife
    can wake him.   170
His dream too is made out — Now for his
    friend.
                  [*Exit* ORDONIO.

SCENE II

*The interior Court of a Saracenic or
Gothic Castle, with the Iron Gate of a
Dungeon visible.*
Teresa. Heart-chilling superstition ! thou
    canst glaze
Ev'n pity's eye with her own frozen tear.
In vain I urge the tortures that await him ;
Even Selma, reverend guardian of my
    childhood,
My second mother, shuts her heart against
    me !   5
Well, I have won from her what most
    imports
The present need, this secret of the dun-
    geon
Known only to herself. — A Moor ! a Sor-
    cerer !
No, I have faith, that Nature ne'er per-
    mitted
Baseness to wear a form so noble. True, 10
I doubt not that Ordonio had suborned
    him
To act some part in some unholy fraud ;

As little doubt, that for some unknown
    purpose
He hath baffled his suborner, terror-struck
    him,
And that Ordonio meditates revenge !   15
But my resolve is fixed ! myself will rescue
    him,
And learn if haply he knew aught of
    Alvar.

Enter VALDEZ.

Valdez. Still sad ? — and gazing at the
    massive door
Of that fell dungeon which thou ne'er
    had'st sight of,
Save what, perchance, thy infant fancy
    shap'd it   20
When the nurse still'd thy cries with un-
    meant threats.
Now by my faith, girl ! this same wizard
    haunts thee !
A stately man, and eloquent and tender —
Who then need wonder if a lady sighs
Even at the thought of what these stern
    Dominicans —   25
    Teresa. The horror of their ghastly pun-
    ishments
Doth so o'ertop the height of all com-
    passion,
That I should feel too little for mine
    enemy,
If it were possible I could feel more,
Even though the dearest inmates of our
    household   30
Were doom'd to suffer them. That such
    things are —
    Valdez. Hush, thoughtless woman !
    Teresa.   Nay, it wakes within me
More than a woman's spirit.
    Valdez.   No more of this —
What if Monviedro or his creatures hear
    us !
I dare not listen to you.
    Teresa.   My honoured lord, 35
These were my Alvar's lessons, and
    whene'er
I bend me o'er his portrait, I repeat them,
As if to give a voice to the mute image.
    Valdez. ——We have mourned for Alvar.
Of his sad fate there now remains no
    doubt.   40
Have I no other son ?
    Teresa.   Speak not of him !
That low imposture ! That mysterious pic-
    ture !
If this be madness, must I wed a madman ?
And if not madness, there is mystery,
And guilt doth lurk behind it.
    Valdez.   Is this well ? 45

Teresa. Yes, it is truth : saw you his countenance ?

How rage, remorse, and scorn, and stupid fear

Displaced each other with swift interchanges ?

O that I had indeed the sorcerer's power. ——

I would call up before thine eyes the image   50

Of my betrothéd Alvar, of thy first-born !

His own fair countenance, his kingly forehead,

His tender smiles, love's day-dawn on his lips !

That spiritual and almost heavenly light

In his commanding eye — his mien heroic,   55

Virtue's own native heraldry ! to man

Genial, and pleasant to his guardian angel.

Whene'er he gladden'd, how the gladness spread

Wide round him ! and when oft with swelling tears,

Flash'd through by indignation, he bewail'd   60

The wrongs of Belgium's martyr'd patriots,

Oh, what a grief was there — for joy to envy,

Or gaze upon enamour'd !

                O my father !

Recall that morning when we knelt together,

And thou didst bless our loves ! O even now,   65

Even now, my sire ! to thy mind's eye present him,

As at that moment he rose up before thee,

Stately, with beaming look ! Place, place beside him

Ordonio's dark perturbéd countenance !

Then bid me (Oh thou could'st not) bid me turn   70

From him, the joy, the triumph of our kind !

To take in exchange that brooding man, who never

Lifts up his eye from the earth, unless to scowl.

    Valdez. Ungrateful woman ! I have tried to stifle

An old man's passion ! was it not enough,   75

That thou hast made my son a restless man,

Banish'd his health, and half unhing'd his reason ;

But that thou wilt insult him with suspicion ?

And toil to blast his honour ? I am old,

A comfortless old man !

    Teresa.   O grief ! to hear   80

Hateful entreaties from a voice we love !

Enter a Peasant *and presents a letter to* VALDEZ.

    Valdez (reading it). ' He dares not venture hither ! ' Why, what can this mean ?

' Lest the Familiars of the Inquisition,

That watch around my gates, should intercept him ;

But he conjures me, that without delay   85

I hasten to him — for my own sake entreats me

To guard from danger him I hold imprison'd —

He will reveal a secret, the joy of which

Will even outweigh the sorrow.' — Why what can this be ?

Perchance it is some Moorish stratagem,   90

To have in me a hostage for his safety.

Nay, that they dare not ! Ho ! collect my servants !

I will go thither — let them arm themselves.   [*Exit* VALDEZ.

    Teresa (alone). The moon is high in heaven, and all is hush'd.

Yet anxious listener ! I have seem'd to hear   95

A low dead thunder mutter thro' the night,

As 'twere a giant angry in his sleep.

O Alvar ! Alvar ! that they could return,

Those blessed days that imitated heaven,

When we two wont to walk at eventide ;   100

When we saw nought but beauty ; when we heard

The voice of that Almighty One who loved us

In every gale that breathed, and wave that murmur'd !

O we have listen'd, even till high-wrought pleasure

Hath half assumed the countenance of grief,   105

And the deep sigh seemed to heave up a weight

Of bliss, that pressed tóo heavy on the heart.   [*A pause.*

And this majestic Moor, seems he not one

Who oft and long communing with my Alvar

Hath drunk in kindred lustre from his presence,   110

And guides me to him with reflected light ?

What if in yon dark dungeon coward treachery

Be groping for him with envenomed
   poniard —
Hence, womanish fears, traitors to love
   and duty —
I'll free him.   [*Exit* TERESA.

SCENE III

The mountains by moonlight. ALHADRA
   alone in a Moorish dress.

   Alhadra. Yon hanging woods, that
   touch'd by autumn seem
As they were blossoming hues of fire and
   gold
The flower-like woods, most lovely in
   decay,
The many clouds, the sea, the rock, the
   sands,
Lie in the silent moonshine : and the
   owl,   5
(Strange ! very strange !) the screech-owl
   only wakes !
Sole voice, sole eye of all this world of
   beauty !
Unless, perhaps, she sing her screeching
   song
To a herd of wolves, that skulk athirst for
   blood.
Why such a thing am I ? — Where are
   these men ?   10
I need the sympathy of human faces,
To beat away this deep contempt for all
   things,
Which quenches my revenge. O ! would
   to Alla,
The raven, or the sea-mew, were appointed
To bring me food ! or rather that my
   soul   15
Could drink in life from the universal air !
It were a lot divine in some small skiff
Along some Ocean's boundless solitude,
To float for ever with a careless course,
And think myself the only being alive ! 20

My children ! — Isidore's children ! — Son
   of Valdez,
This hath new strung mine arm. Thou
   coward tyrant !
To stupify a woman's heart with anguish
Till she forgot — even that she was a
   mother !
   [*She fixes her eye on the earth. Then
   drop in one after another, from different parts of the stage, a consider-
   able number of* Morescoes, *all in
   Moorish garments and Moorish ar-
   mour. They form a circle at a distance round* ALHADRA, *and remain

silent till* NAOMI *enters.*
   Naomi. Woman ! May Alla and the
   Prophet bless thee !   25
We have obeyed thy call. Where is our
   chief ?
And why didst thou enjoin these Moorish
   garments ?
   *Alhadra (raising her eyes, and looking
   round on the circle).* Warriors of
   Mahomet ! faithful in the battle !
My countrymen ! Come ye prepared to
   work
An honourable deed ? And would ye work
   it   30
In the slave's garb ? Curse on those Chris-
   tian robes !
They are spell-blasted : and whoever wears
   them,
His arm shrinks wither'd, his heart melts
   away,
And his bones soften.
   Naomi.   Where is Isidore ?
   Alhadra. This night I went from forth
   my house, and left   35
His children all asleep : and he was liv-
   ing !
And I return'd and found them still asleep,
But he had perished ——
   All Morescoes.   Perished ?
   Alhadra.   He had perished !
Sleep on, poor babes ! not one of you
   doth know
That he is fatherless — a desolate or-
   phan !   40
Why should we wake them ? Can an in-
   fant's arm
Revenge his murder ?
   One Moresco (to another). Did she say
   his murder ?
   Naomi. Murder ? Not murdered ?
   Alhadra.   Murdered by a Christian !
   [*They all at once draw their sabres.*
   *Alhadra (to Naomi, who advances from
   the circle).* Brother of Zagri ! fling
   away thy sword ;
This is thy chieftain's !
                [*He steps forward to take it.*
                Dost thou dare receive it ? 45
For I have sworn by Alla and the Prophet,
No tear shall dim these eyes, this woman's
   heart
Shall heave no groan, till I have seen that
   sword
Wet with the life-blood of the son of
   Valdez !   [*A pause.*
Ordonio was your chieftain's murderer ! 50
   Naomi. He dies, by Alla !
   All (kneeling).   By Alla !
   Alhadra. This night your chieftain

armed himself,
And hurried from me. But I followed him
At distance, till I saw him enter — there !
  Naomi. The cavern ?
  Alhadra.   Yes, the mouth of yonder
    cavern   55
After a while I saw the son of Valdez
Rush by with flaring torch ; he likewise
    entered.
There was another and a longer pause ;
And once, methought I heard the clash
    of swords !
And soon the son of Valdez re-ap-
    peared :   60
He flung his torch towards the moon in
    sport,
And seemed as he were mirthful ! I stood
    listening,
Impatient for the footsteps of my hus-
    band !
  Naomi. Thou called'st him ?
  Alhadra.   I crept into the cavern —
'Twas dark and very silent.
                    What said'st thou ? 65
No ! no ! I did not dare call, Isidore,
Lest I should hear no answer ! A brief
    while,
Belike, I lost all thought and memory
Of that for which I came ! After that
    pause,
O Heaven ! I heard a groan, and followed
    it :   70
And yet another groan, which guided me
Into a strange recess — and there was light,
A hideous light ! his torch lay on the
    ground ;
Its flame burnt dimly o'er a chasm's brink :
I spake ; and whilst I spake, a feeble
    groan   75
Came from that chasm ! it was his last !
    his death-groan !
  Naomi. Comfort her, Alla !
  Alhadra. I stood in unimaginable trance
And agony that cannot be remembered,
Listening with horrid hope to hear a
    groan !   80
But I had heard his last : my husband's
    death-groan !
  Naomi. Haste ! let us onward.
  Alhadra.   I looked far down the pit —
My sight was bounded by a jutting frag-
    ment :
And it was stained with blood. Then first
    I shrieked,
My eye-balls burnt, my brain grew hot as
    fire,   85
And all the hanging drops of the wet roof
Turned into blood — I saw them turn to
    blood !

And I was leaping wildly down the chasm,
When on the farther brink I saw his
    sword,
And it said, Vengeance ! — Curses on my
    tongue !   90
The moon hath moved in Heaven, and I
    am here,
And he hath not had vengeance ! Isidore !
Spirit of Isidore ! thy murderer lives !
Away ! away !
  All.   Away ! away !
    [*She rushes off, all following her.*

ACT V

SCENE I

A Dungeon.

ALVAR (*alone*) *rises slowly from a bed of
    reeds.*

  Alvar. And this place my forefathers
    made for man !
This is the process of our love and wisdom
To each poor brother who offends against
    us —
Most innocent, perhaps — and what if
    guilty ?
Is this the only cure ? Merciful God !   5
Each pore and natural outlet shrivelled up
By ignorance and parching poverty,
His energies roll back upon his heart,
And stagnate and corrupt, till, chang'd to
    poison,
They break out on him, like a loathsome
    plague-spot !   10
Then we call in our pampered mounte-
    banks :
And this is their best cure ! uncomforted
And friendless solitude, groaning and
    tears,
And savage faces, at the clanking hour,
Seen through the steam and vapours of
    his dungeon   15
By the lamp's dismal twilight ! So he lies
Circled with evil, till his very soul
Unmoulds its essence, hopelessly deformed
By sights of evermore deformity !
With other ministrations thou, O Na-
    ture !   20
Healest thy wandering and distempered
    child :
Thou pourest on him thy soft influences,
Thy sunny hues, fair forms, and breathing
    sweets ;
Thy melodies of woods, and winds, and
    waters !

Till he relent, and can no more endure 25
To be a jarring and a dissonant thing
Amid this general dance and minstrelsy ;
But, bursting into tears, wins back his
way,
His angry spirit healed and harmonized
By the benignant touch of love and
beauty. 30

I am chill and weary ! Yon rude bench of
stone,
In that dark angle, the sole resting-place !
But the self-approving mind is its own
light
And life's best warmth still radiates from
the heart
Where love sits brooding, and an honest
purpose. 35

[*Retires out of sight.*

Enter TERESA *with a taper.*

Teresa. It has chilled my very life — my
own voice scares me ;
Yet when I hear it not I seem to lose
The substance of my being — my strongest
grasp
Sends inwards but weak witness that I am.
I seek to cheat the echo. — How the half
sounds 40
Blend with this strangled light ! Is he not
here —

[*Looking round.*

O for one human face here — but to see
One human face here to sustain me. —
Courage !
It is but my own fear ! The life within me,
It sinks and wavers like this cone of
flame, 45
Beyond which I scarce dare look onward !
Oh !
If I faint ? If this inhuman den should be
At once my death-bed and my burial
vault ?

[*Faintly screams as* ALVAR *emerges
from the recess.*

Alvar (*rushes towards her, and catches
her as she is falling*). O gracious
heaven ! it is, it is Teresa !
Shall I reveal myself ? The sudden shock 50
Of rapture will blow out this spark of life,
And joy complete what terror has begun.
O ye impetuous beatings here, be still !
Teresa, best beloved ! pale, pale, and cold !
Her pulse doth flutter ! Teresa ! my
Teresa ! 55

Teresa (*recovering*). I heard a voice ;
but often in my dreams
I hear that voice ! and wake and try —
and try —

To hear it waking ! but I never could —
And 'tis so now — even so ! Well ! he is
dead —
Murdered perhaps ! and I am faint, and
feel 60
As if it were no painful thing to die !
Alvar. Believe it not, sweet maid ! Be-
lieve it not,
Belovéd woman ! 'Twas a low imposture
Framed by a guilty wretch.
Teresa. Ha ! Who art thou ?
Alvar. Suborned by his brother —
Teresa. Didst thou murder him ?
And dost thou now repent ? Poor troubled
man, 66
I do forgive thee, and may Heaven for-
give thee !
Alvar. Ordonio — he —
Teresa. If thou didst murder him —
His spirit ever at the throne of God
Asks mercy for thee : prays for mercy for
thee, 70
With tears in Heaven !
Alvar. Alvar was not murdered.
Be calm ! Be calm, sweet maid !
Teresa. Nay, nay, but tell me !

[*A pause.*

O 'tis lost again !
This dull confuséd pain — [*A pause.*
Mysterious man !
Methinks I can not fear thee : for thine
eye 75
Doth swim with love and pity — Well !
Ordonio —
Oh my foreboding heart ! And he sub-
orned thee,
And thou didst spare his life ? Blessings
shower on thee,
As many as the drops twice counted o'er
In the fond faithful heart of his Teresa ! 80
Alvar. I can endure no more. The
Moorish sorcerer
Exists but in the stain upon his face.
That picture —
Teresa. Ha ! speak on !
Alvar. Beloved Teresa !
It told but half the truth. O let this por-
trait
Tell all — that Alvar lives — that he is
here ! 85
Thy much deceived but ever faithful
Alvar.

[*Takes her portrait from his neck,
and gives it her.*

Teresa (*receiving the portrait*). The
same — it is the same ! Ah ! Who
art thou ?
Nay, I will call thee, Alvar !

[*She falls on his neck.*

Alvar.   O joy unutterable!
But hark! a sound as of removing bars
At the dungeon's outer door. A brief,
    brief while   90
Conceal thyself, my love! It is Ordonio.
For the honour of our race, for our dear
    father;
O for himself too (he is still my brother)
Let me recall him to his nobler nature,
That he may wake as from a dream of
    murder!   95
O let me reconcile him to himself,
Open the sacred source of penitent tears,
And be once more his own beloved Alvar.
   Teresa. O my all virtuous love! I fear
    to leave thee
With that obdurate man.
   Alvar.   Thou dost not leave me! 100
But a brief while retire into the darkness:
O that my joy could spread its sunshine
    round thee!
   Teresa. The sound of thy voice shall be
    my music!
Alvar! my Alvar! am I sure I hold thee?
Is it no dream? thee in my arms, my
    Alvar!   [*Exit.*   105
   [*A noise at the Dungeon door. It
   opens, and* ORDONIO *enters, with a
   goblet in his hand.*
   Ordonio. Hail, potent wizard! in my
    gayer mood
I poured forth a libation to old Pluto,
And as I brimmed the bowl, I thought
    on thee.
Thou hast conspired against my life and
    honour,
Hast tricked me foully; yet I hate thee
    not.   110
Why should I hate thee? this same world
    of ours,
'Tis but a pool amid a storm of rain,
And we the air-bladders that course up
    and down,
And joust and tilt in merry tournament;
And when one bubble runs foul of an-
    other,   115
The weaker needs must break.
   Alvar.   I see thy heart!
There is a frightful glitter in thine eye
Which doth betray thee. Inly-tortured
    man,
This is the revelry of a drunken anguish,
Which fain would scoff away the pang of
    guilt,   120
And quell each human feeling.
   Ordonio.   Feeling! feeling!
The death of a man — the breaking of a
    bubble —
Tis true I cannot sob for such misfor-
    tunes;
But faintness, cold and hunger — curses
    on me
If willingly I e'er inflicted them!   125
Come, take the beverage; this chill place
    demands it.
        [ORDONIO *proffers the goblet.*
   Alvar. Yon insect on the wall,
Which moves this way and that its hun-
    dred limbs,
Were it a toy of mere mechanic craft,
It were an infinitely curious thing!   130
But it has life, Ordonio! life, enjoyment!
And by the power of its miraculous will
Wields all the complex movements of its
    frame
Unerringly to pleasurable ends!
Saw I that insect on this goblet's brim   135
I would remove it with an anxious pity!
   Ordonio. What meanest thou?
   Alvar.   There's poison in the wine.
   Ordonio. Thou hast guessed right;
    there's poison in the wine.
There's poison in't — which of us two
    shall drink it?
For one of us must die!
   Alvar.   Whom dost thou think me? 140
   Ordonio. The accomplice and sworn
    friend of Isidore.
   Alvar. I know him not.
And yet methinks, I have heard the name
    but lately.
Means he the husband of the Moorish
    woman?
Isidore? Isidore?   145
   Ordonio. Good! good! that lie! by
    heaven it has restored me.
Now I am thy master! — Villain! thou
    shalt drink it,
Or die a bitterer death.
   Alvar.   What strange solution
Hast thou found out to satisfy thy fears,
And drug them to unnatural sleep?
   [ALVAR *takes the goblet, and throws
   it to the ground.*
               My master! 150
   Ordonio. Thou mountebank!
   Alvar.   Mountebank and villain!
What then art thou? For shame, put up
    thy sword!
What boots a weapon in a withered arm?
I fix mine eye upon thee, and thou trem-
    blest!
I speak, and fear and wonder crush thy
    rage,   155
And turn it to a motionless distraction!
Thou blind self-worshipper! thy pride, thy
    cunning,
Thy faith in universal villainy,

Thy shallow sophisms, thy pretended scorn
For all thy human brethren — out upon
    them !   160
What have they done for thee ? have they
    given thee peace ?
Cured thee of starting in thy sleep ? or
    made
The darkness pleasant when thou wak'st
    at midnight ?
Art happy when alone ? Can'st walk by
    thyself
With even step and quiet cheerfulness ? 165
Yet, yet thou may'st be saved ——
    Ordonio.   Saved ? saved ?
    Alvar.   One pang !
Could I call up one pang of true re-
    morse !
    Ordonio. He told me of the babes that
    prattled to him,
His fatherless little ones ! remorse ! re-
    morse !
Where got'st thou that fool's word ? Curse
    on remorse !   170
Can it give up the dead, or recompact
A mangled body ? mangled — dashed to
    atoms !
Not all the blessings of a host of angels
Can blow away a desolate widow's curse !
And though thou spill thy heart's blood
    for atonement,   175
It will not weigh against an orphan's
    tear !
    Alvar. But Alvar ——
    Ordonio.   Ha ! it chokes thee in the
    throat,
Even thee ; and yet I pray thee speak
    it out.
Still Alvar ! — Alvar ! — howl it in mine
    ear !
Heap it like coals of fire upon my
    heart,   180
And shoot it hissing through my brain !
    Alvar.   Alas !
That day when thou didst leap from off
    the rock
Into the waves, and grasped thy sinking
    brother,
And bore him to the strand ; then, son of
    Valdez,
How sweet and musical the name of
    Alvar !   185
Then, then, Ordonio, he was dear to thee,
And thou wert dear to him : heaven only
    knows
How very dear thou wert ! Why did'st
    thou hate him !
O heaven ! how he would fall upon thy
    neck,
And weep forgiveness !

    Ordonio.   Spirit of the dead ! 190
Methinks I know thee ! ha ! my brain
    turns wild
At its own dreams ! — off — off, fantastic
    shadow !
    Alvar. I fain would tell thee what I am,
    but dare not !
    Ordonio. Cheat ! villain ! traitor ! what-
    soever thou be —
I fear thee, man !
    Teresa (rushing out and falling on Al-
    var's neck). Ordonio ! 'tis thy
    brother !   195
    [Ordonio *runs upon* Alvar *with his*
    sword. Teresa *flings herself on* Or-
    donio *and arrests his arm.*
            Stop, madman, stop !
    Alvar. Does then this thin disguise im-
    penetrably
Hide Alvar from thee ? Toil and painful
    wounds
And long imprisonment in unwholesome
    dungeons,
Have marred perhaps all trait and linea-
    ment   200
Of what I was ! But chiefly, chiefly,
    brother,
My anguish for thy guilt !
            Ordonio — Brother !
Nay, nay, thou shalt embrace me.
    Ordonio (drawing back, and gazing at
    Alvar). Touch me not !
Touch not pollution, Alvar ! I will die.
    [*He attempts to fall on his sword,*
    Alvar *and* Teresa *prevent him.*
    Alvar. We will find means to save your
    honour. Live,   205
Oh live, Ordonio ! for our father's sake !
Spare his grey hairs !
    Teresa.   And you may yet be happy.
    Ordonio. O horror ! not a thousand
    years in heaven
Could recompose this miserable heart,
Or make it capable of one brief joy ! 210
Live ! live ! Why yes ! 'Twere well to live
    with you :
For is it fit a villain should be proud ?
My brother ! I will kneel to you, my
    brother !   [*Kneeling.*
Forgive me, Alvar ! —— Curse me with for-
    giveness !
    Alvar. Call back thy soul, Ordonio, and
    look round thee !   215
Now is the time for greatness ! Think
    that heaven —
    Teresa. O mark his eye ! he hears not
    what you say.
    Ordonio. Yes, mark his eye ! there 's
    fascination in it !

Thou said'st thou did'st not know him —
    That is he!
He comes upon me!
    Alvar.   Heal, O heal him, heaven! 220
    Ordonio. Nearer and nearer! and I can
    not stir!
Will no one hear these stifled groans, and
    wake me?
He would have died to save me, and I
    killed him —
A husband and a father! —
    Teresa.   Some secret poison
Drinks up his spirits!
    Ordonio.   Let the eternal justice 225
Prepare my punishment in the obscure
    world —
I will not bear to live — to live — O agony!
And be myself alone my own sore tor-
    ment!
    [*The doors of the dungeon are broken
    open, and in rush* ALHADRA, *and the
    band of* Morescoes.
    Alhadra. Seize first that man!
        [ALVAR *presses onward to defend*
        ORDONIO.
    Ordonio. Off, ruffians! I have flung
    away my sword.   230
Woman, my life is thine! to thee I give it!
Off! he that touches me with his hand
    of flesh,
I'll rend his limbs asunder! I have
    strength
With this bare arm to scatter you like
    ashes.
    Alhadra. My husband —
    Ordonio.   Yes, I murdered him most
    foully.   235
    Alvar and Teresa. O horrible!
    Alhadra.   Why did'st thou leave his
    children?
Demon, thou should'st have sent thy dogs
    of hell
To lap their blood. Then, then I might
    have hardened
My soul in misery, and have had comfort.
I would have stood far off, quiet though
    dark,   240
And bade the race of men raise up a
    mourning
For a deep horror of desolation,
Too great to be one soul's particular lot!
Brother of Zagri! let me lean upon thee.
The time is not yet come for woman's
    anguish,   245
I have not seen his blood — Within an
    hour
Those little ones will crowd around and
    ask me,
Where is our father? I shall curse thee

then!
Wert thou in heaven, my curse would
    pluck thee thence!
    Teresa. He doth repent! See, see, I
    kneel to thee!   250
O let him live! That agéd man, his
    father ——
    Alhadra. Why had he such a son?
    [*Shouts from the distance of* Rescue!
    Rescue! Alvar! Alvar! *and the voice
    of* VALDEZ *heard.*
Rescue? — and Isidore's spirit unavenged?
— The deed be mine!
            [*Suddenly stabs* ORDONIO.
            Now take my life!
    Ordonio (staggering from the wound).
    Atonement!
    *Alvar (while with Teresa supporting
    Ordonio).* Arm of avenging Heav-
    en   255
Thou hast snatched from me my most
    cherished hope —
But go! my word was pledged to thee.
    Ordonio.   Away!
Brave not my Father's rage! I thank thee!
    Thou —
    [*Then turning his eyes languidly
    to* ALVAR.
She hath avenged the blood of Isidore!
I stood in silence like a slave before her 260
That I might taste the wormwood and the
    gall,
And satiate this self-accusing heart
With bitterer agonies than death can give.
Forgive me, Alvar!
            Oh! — could'st thou forget me!
                        [*Dies.*
    [ALVAR *and* TERESA *bend over the
    body of* ORDONIO.
    Alhadra (to the Moors). I thank thee,
    Heaven! thou hast ordained it
    wisely,   265
That still extremes bring their own cure.
    That point
In misery, which makes the oppressed Man
Regardless of his own life, makes him too
Lord of the Oppressor's — Knew I a hun-
    dred men
Despairing, but not palsied by despair, 270
This arm should shake the kingdoms of
    the world;
The deep foundations of iniquity
Should sink away, earth groaning from
    beneath them;
The strongholds of the cruel men should
    fall,
Their temples and their mountainous tow-
    ers should fall;   275
Till   desolation   seemed   a   beautiful

thing,
And all that were and had the spirit of
.life,
Sang a new song to her who had gone
forth,
Conquering and still to conquer!

[ALHADRA *hurries off with the* Moors;
the stage fills with armed Peasants,
and Servants, ZULIMEZ *and* VALDEZ
at their head. VALDEZ *rushes into* AL-
VAR'S *arms.*

Alvar. Turn not thy face that way, my
father! hide,   280
Oh hide it from his eye! Oh let thy joy
Flow in unmingled stream through thy
first blessing.

[*Both kneel to* VALDEZ.

Valdez. My Son! My Alvar! bless, Oh
bless him, heaven!

Teresa. Me too, my Father?

Valdez. Bless, Oh bless my children!

[*Both rise.*

Alvar. Delights so full, if unalloyed with
grief,   285
Were ominous. In these strange dread
events
Just Heaven instructs us with an awful
voice,
That Conscience rules us e'en against our
choice.
Our inward Monitress to guide or warn,
If listened to; but if repelled with
scorn,   290
At length as dire Remorse, she reappears,
Works in our guilty hopes, and selfish
fears!
Still bids, Remember! and still cries, Too
late!
And while she scares us, goads us to our
fate.

APPENDIX

The following Scene, as unfit for the
stage, was taken from the tragedy, in the
year 1797, and published in the Lyrical
Ballads.

Enter Teresa and Selma.

Teresa. 'Tis said, he spake of you familiarly,
As mine and Alvar's common foster-
mother.

Selma. Now blessings on the man, who-
e'er he be
That joined your names with mine! O
my sweet Lady,
As often as I think of those dear times, 5
When you two little ones would stand,
at eve,
On each side of my chair, and make me
learn
All you had learnt in the day; and how
to talk
In gentle phrase; then bid me sing to
you —
'Tis more like heaven to come, than what
has been!   10

Teresa. But that entrance, Selma?

Selma.   Can no one hear? It is
a perilous tale!

Teresa. No one.

Selma.   My husband's father told it me,
Poor old Sesina — angels rest his soul;
He was a woodman, and could fell and saw
With lusty arm. You know that huge
round beam   15
Which props the hanging wall of the old
chapel?
Beneath that tree, while yet it was a tree,
He found a baby wrapt in mosses, lined
With thistle-beards, and such small locks
of wool
As hang on brambles. Well, he brought
him home,   20
And reared him at the then Lord Valdez'
cost.
And so the babe grew up a pretty boy,
A pretty boy, but most unteachable —
And never learn'd a prayer, nor told a
bead,
But knew the names of birds, and mocked
their notes,   25
And whistled, as he were a bird himself.
And all the autumn 'twas his only play
To gather seeds of wild flowers, and to
plant them
With earth and water on the stumps of
trees.
A Friar, who gathered simples in the
wood,   30
A grey-haired man, he loved this little
boy:
The boy loved him, and, when the friar
taught him,
He soon could write with the pen; and
from that time
Lived chiefly at the convent or the castle.
So he became a rare and learned youth: 35
But O! poor wretch! he read, and read,
and read,
Till his brain turned; and ere his twen-
tieth year
He had unlawful thoughts of many
things:
And though he prayed, he never loved to
pray

With holy men, nor in a holy place.   40
But yet his speech, it was so soft and sweet,
The late Lord Valdez ne'er was wearied
    with him.
And once, as by the north side of the
    chapel
They stood together chained in deep dis-
    course,
The earth heaved under them with such
    a groan,   45
That the wall tottered, and had well nigh
    fallen
Right on their heads. My Lord was sorely
    frightened ;
A fever seized him, and he made confession
Of all the heretical and lawless talk
Which brought this judgment : so the
    youth was seized,   50
And cast into that hole. My husband's
    father
Sobbed like a child — it almost broke his
    heart :
And once he was working near this dun-
    geon,
He heard a voice distinctly ; 'twas the
    youth's,
Who sung a doleful song about green
    fields,   55
How sweet it were on lake or wide savanna

To hunt for food, and be a naked man,
And wander up and down at liberty.
He always doted on the youth, and now
His love grew desperate ; and defying
    death,   60
He made that cunning entrance I de-
    scribed,
And the young man escaped.
    Teresa.   'Tis a sweet tale :
Such as would lull a listening child to
    sleep,
His rosy face besoiled with unwiped tears.
And what became of him ?
    Selma.   He went on shipboard 65
With those bold voyagers who made dis-
    covery
Of golden lands. Sesina's younger brother
Went likewise, and when he returned to
    Spain,
He told Sesina, that the poor mad youth,
Soon after they arrived in that new
    world,   70
In spite of his dissuasion, seized a boat,
And all alone set sail by silent moonlight
Up a great river, great as any sea,
And ne'er was heard of more : but 'tis
    supposed,
He lived and died among the savage
    men.   75

3

GEORGE GORDON, LORD BYRON'S *MANFRED*

Of all Byron's dramas the one least a play, of all Byron's plays the one most like his poetry, *Manfred* best fits Byron's own appellation, "a dramatic poem." A drama in form, ostensibly a closet drama, *Manfred's* lyric intensity is like that in Shelley's *Prometheus Unbound,* for the characters are profitably understood as expressionistic manifestations of the mind of the eponymous hero.[1] This attempt to discover reality by objectifying different voices to express different attitudes or the various constituents of the personality is generally characteristic of Byron's work, considered piece by piece. It is found in the various voices within *Childe Harold* and *Don Juan,*[2] but it is rare to find it so neatly delineated as it is in *Manfred.* Manfred's conflicting psychological, intellectual, and spiritual needs are in tumult. Further frustrated by man's limited ability to cope with, reconcile, or satisfy most of these needs, Manfred is, like Cain, possessed "by the rage and fury of the inadequacy of his state to his conceptions."[3]

In Byron's explanation of Cain's motivation we may find not only a philosophic foundation for *Cain,* but also one for *Manfred,* and, to a large extent, one for most of Byron's work. Without claiming that dualism or Manichaeanism lies at the heart of the conflict, we can find throughout Byron's work this thematic note from the letter to Murray. Man's twin needs, to participate in the world and to outsoar it, have no single radical: the network of roots includes psychological, intellectual, and spiritual quests for certainty, knowledge, and happiness. While it may be true that in poems like *Don Juan* and *Beppo* Byron was able to make comedy of the disparity between man's state and his conceptions,[4] we cannot forget that it is in *Don Juan* that we learn:

> And if I laugh at any mortal thing,
> 　'Tis that I may not weep; and if I weep,
> 'Tis that our nature cannot always bring
> 　Itself to apathy, for we must steep
> Our hearts first in the depths of Lethe's spring,
> 　Ere what we least wish to behold will sleep:
> Thetis baptized her mortal son in Styx;
> A mortal mother would on Lethe fix.
>
> 　　　　　　　　　　　　(IV.v)

In this stanza there are two clear links to *Manfred.* The first is the theme of

---

1. E. J. Lovell, "Irony and Image in *Don Juan,*" in the *Major English Romantic Poets,* ed. C. D. Thorpe, et al. (Carbondale, Ill., 1964), p. 130.
2. Especially in the recent books by Robert Gleckner and W. Paul Elledge.
3. Byron's letter to Murray of 3 November 1821.
4. E. E. Bostetter, *The Romantic Ventriloquists* (Seattle, Wash., 1963), p. 6.

forgetfulness—the boon for which Manfred originally asks. The second link lies concealed in the phrase "any mortal thing," for, as recent criticism has emphasized, Manfred is in many respects representative of humanity's quest to fulfill its conception of its possibilities. Not the least of the ways in which Manfred is representative is his inability to transcend himself, to escape the inadequacy of his state. Like other literary characters who challenge the limitations, internal and external, clipping man's wings—Ahab, Prometheus, Ulysses, Lucifer—he is the more representative for being imperfect, for our various quests are in conflict not only with the external order of things but often with themselves and with each other. And Manfred's triumph is not over these conflicts within and without; it lies rather in his acceptance of his common humanity, in the poignancy of his last speech and gesture. After defying the Spirit and enunciating the superiority of man's unaided abilities and strengths, Manfred stretches forth his hand to the old Abbot saying, "Old man! 'tis not so difficult to die." And even though his hand is "cold—even to the heart," Manfred has reaffirmed his connection with the rest of suffering mankind. His quest was ours, his success and failure ours too. It is not so much that "in the vacuum of Manfred's self-hood, our traditional interpretations of 'triumph' and 'defeat' are altogether meaningless";[5] nor is it so much that Manfred "is not in any sense a representative or champion of mankind,"[6] as it is that, because the paradoxes, conflicts, and contradictions of the world and ourselves remain unsurmounted and unresolved, he, albeit undeliberately, represents us.

This latter point is one explored in Robert Hume's penetrating article on the differences between the Gothic and the Romantic. "Byron," according to Hume, "seems closer to the Gothic camp than to the romantics" because in his work the conflicts remain unresolved: there are no resolutions offered.[7] Pursuing Hume's valuable distinctions, we will discover that Manfred is both "terror" gothic and "horror" gothic. It is "terror" gothic inasmuch as we are responding to suspense (we are not told the precise nature of Manfred's secret) and therefore our imaginations are stretched and we become participants in the action. But Manfred is also "horror" gothic because we do sense his secret and become involved with the psychologically consistent actions of a villain-hero protagonist. I am suggesting, then, that we both know and do not know Manfred's secret: I believe this to be true, but fuller explanation must wait until later in this introduction where I try to reconcile Manfred's weak dramatic structure with its continuing power and fascination. But now the dual perspective can be related to another explanation Hume offers. In analyzing the components of the gothic he reminds us that "although the reader is to be immersed in an extraordinary world, he must not feel that its psychological (as distinct from its factual) bounds are utterly foreign to him. If he does, then the story loses its immediacy for him; any application to his own mind is ruled out."[8]

I believe it can be shown that Manfred derives its excellence as poetic drama and its continuing popularity from the same source. The ways in which it is both terror and horror gothic and the ways in which the dramatic treatment of Manfred's secret reveal man's conflicting needs are gothic in the best sense—the sense in which they are the product of what Hume calls a serious fancy. As suggested earlier, recent critics have tended to read Manfred as a declaration of independence for the human spirit, although there is debate about whether this particular individual is a success or a failure. Without ignoring this broad,

---

5. W. Paul Elledge, *Byron and the Dynamics of Metaphor* (Nashville, Tenn., 1969), p. 94.
6. Andrew Rutherford, *Byron: A Critical Study* (Palo Alto, Calif., 1965), p. 88.
7. Robert Hume, "Gothic versus Romantic: A revaluation of the Gothic Novel," *PMLA* 84 (March 1969): 209.
8. *Ibid.*, p. 287.

symbolic meaning, I believe it is worth exploring the psychological necessity of the particular dramatic quest, for such an explanation will reveal the common humanity of the play.

In much the same way as Byron's description, "a dramatic poem," provides us a way to understand the form of *Manfred,* so his choice of epigraph will illuminate the ways in which the play involves us in its issues and emotions.

> There are more things in heaven and earth, Horatio
> Than are dreamt of in your philosophy.

We can interpret the relationship between these lines and the entire play in several ways. First, we might consider that "Philosophy" is rejected as a possible source of consolation to those who, like Manfred,

> Must mourn the deepest o'er the fatal truth–
> The Tree of Knowledge is not that of Life.
> Philosophy and Science, and the springs
> Of Wonder, and the wisdom of the World
> I have essayed, and in my mind there is
> A Power to make these subject to itself—
> But they avail not.
>
> I.i.11–17

In this we learn that Manfred has mastered and subjugated all philosophic and scientific knowledge, and, in addition, has an equivalent comprehension of knowledge ordinarily beyond human ken, "the springs of Wonder." Moreover, this knowledge is not merely abstruse but includes "the wisdom of the World"; that is, Manfred's knowledge is coupled with judgment. But all this avails him not; he cannot lose himself in abstractions and forget "that all nameless hour" (I.i.24).

In the final act of the drama, Manfred, having learned that he is spending his last day on earth, has attained from this awareness a calm of mind and spirit.

> There is a calm upon me–
> Inexplicable stillness! which till now
> Did not belong to what I knew of life
> If that I did not know Philosophy
> To be of all our vanities the motliest,
> The merest word that ever fooled the ear
> From out the schoolman's jargon, I should deem
> The golden secret, the sought "Kalon," found,
> And seated in my soul.
>
> III.i.6–14

The "Philosophy" Manfred describes as unsuccessful in this speech does not seem to me quite the same as that described in Act I. The philosophy that is the motliest of our vanities is, I think, of a more religious nature, as evidenced by the word "vanities." This, too, places *Manfred* squarely in the gothic tradition, whose "writers simply cannot find in religion acceptable answers to the fundamentally psychological questions of good and evil which they were posing."[9] Also, the notion of a "golden secret" in the universe which would have served as an anodyne or consolation, bringing calm to Manfred's spirit, differs from the previous use of philosophy as a refuge, an escape, a realm where his mind could be distracted by abstractions from brooding on its agonies.

So Manfred's rejection of two kinds of "philosophy" is a rejection whose occurrence and importance are adumbrated in the epigraph.

---

9. *Ibid.*

Pursuing further the significance of the epigraph, we should next consider that Hamlet's comment to Horatio apparently concerns the appearance of the ghost of Hamlet's father and its intervention in human lives. *Manfred* is populated largely by supernatural figures: Nemesis, Arimines, the Witch of the Alps, and assorted Spirits and Destinies; the epigraph may also serve as their introduction. But looking once again at Hamlet's remark to Horatio, we would have to agree that it is heavily ironic. Not only is the appearance of the ghost strange, what he has to tell is stranger still. The violence of fratricide and the incestuous marriage of Hamlet's mother are aspects of the ghost's story that it is unlikely Horatio, a loyal but rather unprofound fellow, would have conceived of.

The point in *Hamlet* needs to be followed yet a little further. Ernest Jones and Freud have shown convincingly how the motif of repressed incest accounts not only for Hamlet's behavior but also for the continuing popularity of a play which has seemed to many readers highly melodramatic, where far more credence must be given to what is told than to what is shown, especially insofar as the credibility of the behavior and personality of the main character is concerned.

Objections to *Manfred* as drama have taken a similar form. Like much of Byron, it seems melodramatic: the amount of emotion expressed, even evoked, appears to exceed that inherent in the chain of events portrayed upon the stage. The dramatic structure is said inadequately to project the villainy and the nobility of Manfred. As Andrew Rutherford has put the case, in *Manfred*, "as in almost all his 'romantic' works, Byron seems to demand more sympathy and admiration for the hero than he shows him to deserve."[10]

Manfred's crime or sin, committed in "that all nameless hour" (I.i.24), a deed whose nature he knows but whose name he cannot utter, is a deed of guilty blood:

> I say 'tis blood—my blood! the pure warm stream
> Which ran in the veins of my fathers, and in ours
> When we were in our youth, and had one heart,
> And loved each other as we should not love,
> And this was shed.
>
> II.i.24–28

Manfred can bear, asleep or awake, "What others could not brook to dream,/ But perish in their slumber" (II.i.78–79), the knowledge that his "embrace was fatal" (II.i.87). From Manfred's confession to the Witch of the Alps we learn that he loved and destroyed one who

> was like me in her lineaments—her eyes—
> Her hair—her features—all, to the very tone
> Even of her voice, they said was like to mine
> II.ii.105–7

When the spirit of Astarte is raised by Nemesis, Manfred cries:

> Hear me, hear me—
> Astarte! my beloved! speak to me:
> I have so much endured—so much endure—
> Look on me! the grave has not changed thee more
> Than I am changed for thee. Thou lovedst me
> Too much, as I loved thee: we were not made
> To torture thus each other—though it were
> The deadliest sin to love as we have loved.
>
> II.iv.116–23

---

10. Rutherford, p. 89.

Manfred pleads for Astarte's forgiveness, though for what sin is not explicitly clear. However, that close familial ties link the lovers is stressed again in the speech of Manuel, the old family servant, who describes an event which occurred on a nearly identical night some years before:

> Count Manfred was, as now, within his tower,—
> How occupied we knew not, but with him
> The sole companion of his wanderings
> And watchings—her, whom of all earthly things
> That lived, the only thing he seemed to love,—
> As he, indeed, by blood was bound to do
> The Lady Astarte, his—
>
> III.iii.41–47

Early in the drama Manfred asks for oblivion, forgetfulness, and of Astarte he asks forgiveness. For what? Not merely for the incestuous love implicit in the material I have been quoting, but for having led Astarte to the path of suicide. He tells the Witch he destroyed Astarte

> Not with my hand, but heart, which broke her heart;
> It gazed on mine and withered. I have shed
> Blood, but not hers—and yet her blood was shed;
> I saw—and could not staunch it.
>
> II.ii.118–21

And later Manfred describes Astarte as "One without a tomb" (II.iv.82) —a suicide—and Nemesis, in calling up Astarte from the dead, ends by saying: "Who sent thee there requires thee here" (II.iv.97).

We can conjecture that Astarte's feelings of guilt about her incestuous relationship with Manfred led her to suicide. Such a reaction is not difficult to understand, for many of society's most stringent taboos are reserved for incest, as Freud comments in the twenty-first lecture of *A General Introduction to Psychoanalysis*.

> What has not been invented for this purpose! We are told that sexual attraction is diverted from the members of the opposite sex in one family owing to their living together from early childhood; or that a biological tendency against inbreeding has a mental equivalent in the horror of incest! Whereby it is entirely overlooked that no such rigorous prohibitions in law and custom would be required if any trust-worthy natural barriers against the temptation to incest existed. The opposite is the truth. The first choice of object in mankind is regularly an incestuous one, directed to the mother and sister of men, and the most stringent prohibitions are required to prevent this sustained infantile tendency from being carried into effect.[11]

No wonder, then, that Astarte is a suicide, and Manfred feels that

> There is no future pang
> Can deal that justice on the self-condemned
> He deals on his own soul.
>
> III.i.76–78

A commonplace of Byron criticism is that our interest in Byron the man sustains our interest in his poems. Byron remarks in a letter to Thomas Moore that he wrote *Manfred* "for the sake of introducing the Alpine scenery in description," and in a letter to John Murray he remarks of an early version of

---

11. (New York, 1953), p. 344.

the drama, "I have no great opinion of this piece of phantasy." Yet critics have found disingenuous these attempts to disconnect his life from the themes in the work. Andrew Rutherford writes:

> As one might expect, Byron's own feelings are the ultimate source for the poem . . . not his domestic circumstances this time, but his relations, real or imagined, with Augusta, and their psychological aftermath.[12]

The precise extent of Byron's incestuous relationship with his half-sister Augusta, the daughter of his father's first wife, is yet to be disclosed; that it existed is today regarded as beyond doubt. Also beyond doubt is that the taboos against this sort of incest are no less strong than those against the guilty love of Claudius and Gertrude. Claudius usurped the role Hamlet unconsciously yearned to fulfill, and there is, in Manfred, a hint that his role is one he has taken from his father. Hamlet's problem is not in the stars but in himself; Manfred's, though foreshadowed by a star, is in his blood and in his father's blood. We expect the male parent to desire such an incestuous relationship with his daughter. Ernest Jones has explained the psychodynamics of the situation as follows:

> The characteristics of the father-daughter complex are also found in a similar one, the brother-sister complex. As analytic work shows every day, this also, like the former one, is a derivative of the fundamental Oedipus complex. When the incest barrier develops early in the life of the young boy it begins first in regard to his relationship with the mother, and only later sets in with the sister as well; indeed, erotic experiences between brother and sister early in childhood are exceedingly common. The sister is usually the first replacement of the mother as an erotic object.[13]

There is some symbolic evidence in the poem which bears out the implicit suggestions of an incestuous relationship. Upon reading for the first time the lines that tell us Manfred and Astarte shared one blood which was shed, it is not unlikely that we might have thought of hymenal blood, especially when we recall that Manfred has just descended from the summit of the Jungfrau mountain. Mountains are, of course, symbolic of female breasts, and *Jungfrau*, in German, means virgin. Emile Gutheil, in *The Handbook of Dream Analysis*, points out that "in the dream, having intercourse may mean climbing a mountain."[14] We have learned from the Chamois Hunter who rescued Manfred, that Manfred

> hath reached
> A height which none even of our mountaineers,
> Save our best hunters, may attain.
>
> I.ii.60–62

The mention of dreams in *Manfred* is particularly revealing. Twice in the first act we learn that even when asleep Manfred cannot achieve forgetfulness:

> My slumbers—if I slumber—are not sleep,
> But a continuance of enduring thought
> Which then I can resist not: in my heart
> There is a vigil, and these eyes but close
> To look within.
>
> I.i.3–7

The operative word is "then." In the dream Manfred cannot beguile his thoughts:

---

12. Rutherford, pp. 77–78.
13. *Hamlet and Oedipus* (New York, 1949), p. 157.
14. (New York, 1960), p. 154.

they will be represented, symbolically, and evidently escape severe transformation by the censor.

Near the end of the act, a voice intones a curse over the senseless Manfred:

> Though thy slumber may be deep,
> Yet thy spirit shall not sleep;
> These are shades which will not vanish,
> These are thoughts thou canst not banish.
>
> I.1.202–5

The punishment is invoked by a mysterious agency, identified only as "a voice." This voice may be seen to be an externalization of Manfred's super-ego—which is an internalization of society's restrictions. As was stated earlier, *Manfred* has long been considered an interior drama; the characters other than Manfred are most readily conceived of as parts of Manfred's mind. The voice of the super-ego is heard when Manfred falls senseless after the appearance of Astarte in Act I. The same voice continues by describing a Manfred whom we never see during the play, but to whose evil, unprincipled actions we are probably willing to give credence because of the taboos against incest and our personal unwillingness to accept such desires as normal.

> From thy false tears I did distill
> An essence which hath strength to kill;
> From thy own heart I then did wring
> The black blood in its blackest spring;
> From thy own smile I snatched the snake,
> For there it coiled as in a brake;
> From thy own lip I drew the charm
> Which gave all those their chiefest harm;
> In proving every poison known,
> I found the strongest was thine own.
>
> By thy cold breast and serpent smile,
> By thy unfathomed gulfs of guile,
> By that most seeming virtuous eye,
> By thy shut soul's hypocrisy;
> By the perfection of thine art
> Which passed for human thine own heart:
> By thy delight in other's pain,
> And by the brotherhood of Cain,
> I call upon thee! and compel
> Thyself to be thy proper hell.
>
> I.i.231–51

So there are more things in heaven and earth than are dreamed of in Horatio's philosophy, not the least of which is incest. As implied earlier, the incest theme may be one of the reasons Byron selected the lines from *Hamlet* as an epigraph for *Manfred*. Furthermore, the undeniable power and fascination Byron's drama has had, despite its weak dramatic structure which presents only a "falling action," are attributable not only to the power of the poet's own feelings but to our unconscious sharing in the incestuous sexual quest. Freud's explanation of the dynamics of our attraction to *Oedipus Rex* is also applicable to Byron's *Manfred*.

If *Oedipus Rex* moves a modern audience no less than it did the contemporary Greek one, the explanation can only be that its effect does not lie in the contrast between destiny and human will, but is to be looked for in the particular nature of the material on which that contrast is exemplified. . . . His destiny moves us only because it might have been ours—because the oracle laid the same curse upon us before our birth as upon him. It is the fate of us all, perhaps, to direct our first sexual impulse against our mother. . . . Here is one in whom the primaeval wishes of our childhood have been fulfilled, and we shrink back from him with the whole force of the repression by which those wishes have since that time been held down within us. While the poet, as he unravels the past, brings to light the guilt of Oedipus, he is at the same time compelling us to recognize our own inner minds, in which the same impulses, though suppressed, are still to be found.[15]

That incest is never specified may be, as Bertrand Evans suggests,[16] a mechanism for making heroic the villainous, but it is surely as much a psychological as a dramatic necessity.[17] It must be suggested, not revealed, both for the purpose of enlarging the symbolic meaning of Manfred's cosmic defiance and for the purpose of gaining the sympathy of the audience—or, rather, for evoking pity and terror for an act it could have committed. In this way, the melodrama works to affect us, not because of the power of the author's emotions,[18] but because it awakens in us corresponding feelings, long repressed but still vital. And, as Paul West suggests, "a steady look at the demons heals better than any exorcizing homily."[19]

Thus M. K. Joseph's observation, "his incest (if it is such) is too much of a special case; Manfred's real guilt is that he is a member of the human race,"[20] is too neat an exclusion. It is precisely this special case that connects Manfred to humanity and to us. It is through both the terrible compulsion and the terrible taboo connected to incest that Byron particularizes the conflicts between our state and our conceptions. That need not and does not mean that the abstract nature of the theme is subordinate to its particular expression in *Manfred.* The incest motif is the vehicle for the broadly symbolic meanings. Through *Manfred* and by means of this astonishingly apt vehicle, we can look at our demons, and we can objectify, confront, and perhaps understand our all-too-human conflicts and contradictions—the paradox within.

G. B. K.

---

15. *The Interpretation of Dreams,* trans. James Strachey (New York, 1960) pp. 262–63.
16. "Manfred's Remorse and Dramatic Tradition," *PMLA* 62 (Sept. 1947) : 752–73.
17. For a perceptive comment on the dramatic necessity of the incest theme as an objectification of the quest for forbidden knowledge, see the article by Richard Van Der Beets, "A Note on Dramatic Necessity and the Incest Motif in Manfred," *N & Q* 211 (Jan. 1964) : 26–28.
18. Lovell takes this position in "Irony and Image in *Don Juan,*" pp. 129–48.
19. *Byron and the Spoiler's Art* (New York, 1960) , p. 120.
20. M. K. Joseph. *Byron the Poet* (London, 1964) , p. 106.

Manfred

A DRAMATIC POEM

"There are more things in heaven and
    earth, Horatio,
Than are dreamt of in your philosophy."

DRAMATIS PERSONÆ

MANFRED

CHAMOIS HUNTER

ABBOT OF ST. MAURICE

MANUEL

HERMAN

WITCH OF THE ALPS

ARIMANES

NEMESIS

THE DESTINIES

SPIRITS, ETC.

*The Scene of the Drama is amongst the
Higher Alps — partly in the Castle of
Manfred, and partly in the Mountains.*

ACT I

SCENE I

MANFRED *alone. — Scene, a Gothic Gallery.
Time, Midnight.*

MANFRED. The lamp must be replen-
    ished, but even then
It will not burn so long as I must watch :
My slumbers — if I slumber — are not
    sleep,
But a continuance of enduring thought,
Which then I can resist not : in my heart
There is a vigil, and these eyes but close
To look within ; and yet I live, and bear
The aspect and the form of breathing men.
But grief should be the instructor of the
    wise ;

Sorrow is knowledge : they who know the
    most   10
Must mourn the deepest o'er the fatal
    truth,
The tree of knowledge is not that of life.
Philosophy and science, and the springs
Of wonder, and the wisdom of the world,
I have essayed, and in my mind there is
A power to make these subject to itself —
But they avail not : I have done men
    good,
And I have met with good even among
    men —
But this availed not : I have had my foes,
And none have baffled, many fallen before
    me —   20
But this availed not : — Good, or evil, life,
Powers, passions, all I see in other beings,
Have been to me as rain unto the sands,
Since that all-nameless hour. I have no
    dread,
And feel the curse to have no natural fear,
Nor fluttering throb, that beats with hopes
    or wishes,
Or lurking love of something on the earth.
Now to my task. —
                    Mysterious agency !
Ye spirits of the unbounded universe !
Whom I have sought in darkness and in
    light —   30
Ye, who do compass earth about, and
    dwell
In subtler essence — ye, to whom the tops
Of mountains inaccessible are haunts,
And earth's and ocean's caves familiar
    things —
I call upon ye by the written charm
Which gives me power upon you — Rise !
    Appear !
            [*A pause.*]
They come not yet. — Now by the voice of
    him
Who is the first among you — by this sign,

Which makes you tremble — by the claims
   of him
Who is undying, — Rise ! Appear —— Ap-
   pear !   40
           [*A pause.*]
If it be so — Spirits of earth and air,
Ye shall not thus elude me : by a power,
Deeper than all yet urged, a tyrant-spell,
Which had its birthplace in a star con-
   demned,
The burning wreck of a demolished world,
A wandering hell in the eternal space;
By the strong curse which is upon my
   soul,
The thought which is within me and
   around me,
I do compel ye to my will — Appear !

[*A star is seen at the darker end of the
gallery : it is stationary ; and a voice
is heard singing.*]

FIRST SPIRIT

Mortal ! to thy bidding bowed,   50
From my mansion in the cloud,
Which the breath of twilight builds
And the summer's sunset gilds
With the azure and vermilion,
Which is mixed for my pavilion,
Though thy quest may be forbidden,
On a star-beam I have ridden :
To thine adjuration bowed,
Mortal — be thy wish avowed !

VOICE OF THE SECOND SPIRIT

Mont Blanc is the monarch of moun-
   tains ;   60
   They crowned him long ago
On a throne of rocks, in a robe of clouds,
   With a diadem of snow.
Around his waist are forests braced,
   The avalanche in his hand ;
But ere it fall, that thundering ball
   Must pause for my command.
The glacier's cold and restless mass
   Moves onward day by day ;
But I am he who bids it pass,   70
   Or with its ice delay.
I am the spirit of the place,
   Could make the mountain bow
And quiver to his caverned base —
   And what with me would *thou* ?

VOICE OF THE THIRD SPIRIT

In the blue depth of the waters,

Where the wave hath no strife,
Where the wind is a stranger,
   And the sea-snake hath life,
Where the mermaid is decking   80
   Her green hair with shells,
Like the storm on the surface
   Came the sound of thy spells ;
O'er my calm Hall of Coral
   The deep echo rolled —
To the Spirit of Ocean
   Thy wishes unfold !

FOURTH SPIRIT

Where the slumbering earthquake
   Lies pillowed on fire,
And the lakes of bitumen   90
   Rise boilingly higher ;
Where the roots of the Andes
   Strike deep in the earth,
As their summits to heaven
   Shoot soaringly forth ;
I have quitted my birthplace
   Thy bidding to bide —
Thy spell hath subdued me,
   Thy will be my guide !

FIFTH SPIRIT

I am the rider of the wind,   100
   The stirrer of the storm ;
The hurricane I left behind
   Is yet with lightning warm ;
To speed to thee, o'er shore and sea
   I swept upon the blast :
The fleet I met sailed well, and yet
   'Twill sink ere night be past.

SIXTH SPIRIT

My dwelling is the shadow of the night,
Why doth thy magic torture me with
   light ?

SEVENTH SPIRIT

The star which rules thy destiny   110
Was ruled, ere earth began, by me :
It was a world as fresh and fair
As e'er revolved round sun in air ;
Its course was free and regular,
Space bosomed not a lovelier star.
The hour arrived — and it became
A wandering mass of shapeless flame,
A pathless comet, and a curse,
The menace of the universe ;
Still rolling on with innate force,   120
Without a sphere, without a course,

A bright deformity on high,
The monster of the upper sky!
And thou! beneath its influence born —
Thou worm! whom I obey and scorn —
Forced by a power (which is not thine,
And lent thee but to make thee mine)
For this brief moment to descend,
Where these weak spirits round thee bend
And parley with a thing like thee —— 130
What wouldst thou, child of clay! with
   me?

THE SEVEN SPIRITS

Earth, ocean, air, night, mountains, winds,
   thy star,
   Are at thy beck and bidding, child of
      clay!
Before thee at thy quest their spirits are —
   What wouldst thou with us, son of mor-
      tals — say?
MAN. Forgetfulness —
FIRST SPIRIT. Of what — of whom — and
   why?
MAN. Of that which is within me; read
   it there —
Ye know it, and I cannot utter it.
   SPIRIT. We can but give thee that which
      we possess: 140
Ask of us subjects, sovereignty, the
   power
O'er earth — the whole, or portion — or a
   sign
Which shall control the elements, whereof
We are the dominators, — each and all,
These shall be thine.
   MAN.   Oblivion, self-oblivion.
Can ye not wring from out the hidden
   realms
Ye offer so profusely what I ask?
   SPIRIT. It is not in our essence, in our
      skill;
But — thou may'st die.
   MAN.   Will death bestow it on me?
   SPIRIT. We are immortal, and do not
      forget;   150
We are eternal; and to us the past
Is, as the future, present. Art thou an-
   swered?
   MAN. Ye mock me — but the power
      which brought ye here
Hath made you mine. Slaves, scoff not at
   my will!
The mind, the spirit, the Promethean
   spark,
The lightning of my being, is as bright,
Pervading, and far darting as your own,
And shall not yield to yours, though
   cooped in clay!

Answer, or I will teach you what I am.
   SPIRIT. We answer as we answered; our
      reply   160
Is even in thine own words.
   MAN.   Why say ye so?
   SPIRIT. If, as thou say'st, thine essence be
      as ours,
We have replied in telling thee, the thing
Mortals call death hath naught to do with
   us.
   MAN. I then have called ye from your
      realms in vain;
Ye cannot, or ye will not, aid me.
   SPIRIT.   Say,
What we possess we offer; it is thine:
Bethink ere thou dismiss us; ask again —
Kingdom, and sway, and strength, and
   length of days —
   MAN. Accursed! what have I to do with
      days?   170
They are too long already. — Hence — be-
   gone!
   SPIRIT. Yet pause: being here, our will
      would do thee service;
Bethink thee, is there then no other gift
Which we can make not worthless in thine
   eyes?
   MAN. No, none: yet stay — one moment,
      ere we part,
I would behold ye face to face. I hear
Your voices, sweet and melancholy sounds,
As music on the waters; and I see
The steady aspect of a clear large star;
But nothing more. Approach me as ye
   are,   180
Or one, or all, in your accustomed forms.
   SPIRIT. We have no forms, beyond the
      elements
Of which we are the mind and principle:
But choose a form — in that we will ap-
   pear.
   MAN. I have no choice; there is no form
      on earth
Hideous or beautiful to me. Let him,
Who is most powerful of ye, take such
   aspect
As unto him may seem most fitting —
   Come!
   SEVENTH SPIRIT (*appearing in the shape
      of a beautiful female figure*). Be-
      hold!
   MAN. Oh God! if it be thus, and *thou*
Art not a madness and a mockery,   190
I yet might be most happy, I will clasp
   thee,
And we again will be —
      [*The figure vanishes.*]
            My heart is crushed!
   [MANFRED *falls senseless.*]

*(A voice is heard in the Incantation which
follows.)*

When the moon is on the wave,
  And the glow-worm in the grass,
And the meteor on the grave,
  And the wisp on the morass;
When the falling stars are shooting,
And the answered owls are hooting,
And the silent leaves are still
In the shadow of the hill,   200
Shall my soul be upon thine,
With a power and with a sign.

Though thy slumber may be deep,
Yet thy spirit shall not sleep;
There are shades that will not vanish,
There are thoughts thou canst not banish;
By a power to thee unknown,
Thou canst never be alone;
Thou art wrapt as with a shroud,
Thou art gathered in a cloud;   210
And forever shalt thou dwell
In the spirit of this spell.

Though thou seest me not pass by,
Thou shalt feel me with thine eye
As a thing that, though unseen,
Must be near thee, and hath been;
And when in that secret dread
Thou hast turned around thy head,
Thou shalt marvel I am not
As thy shadow on the spot,   220
And the power which thou dost feel
Shall be what thou must conceal.

And a magic voice and verse
Hath baptized thee with a curse;
And a spirit of the air
Hath begirt thee with a snare;
In the wind there is a voice
Shall forbid thee to rejoice;
And to thee shall night deny
All the quiet of her sky;   230
And the day shall have a sun,
Which shall make thee wish it done.

From thy false tears I did distil
An essence which hath strength to kill;
From thy own heart I then did wring
The black blood in its blackest spring;
From thy own smile I snatched the snake,
For there it coiled as in a brake;
From thy own lip I drew the charm
Which gave all these their chiefest
    harm;   240
In proving every poison known,
I found the strongest was thine own.
By thy cold breast and serpent smile,

By thy unfathomed gulfs of guile,
By that most seeming virtuous eye,
By thy shut soul's hypocrisy;
By the perfection of thine art
Which passed for human thine own heart;
By thy delight in others' pain,
And by thy brotherhood of Cain,   250
I call upon thee! and compel
Thyself to be thy proper hell!

And on thy head I pour the vial
Which doth devote thee to this trial;
Nor to slumber, nor to die,
Shall be in thy destiny;
Though thy death shall still seem near
To thy wish, but as a fear;
Lo! the spell now works around thee,
And the clankless chain hath bound
    thee;   260
O'er thy heart and brain together
Hath the word been passed — now wither!

SCENE II

*The Mountain of the Jungfrau. — Time,
Morning. —*

MANFRED *alone upon the Cliffs.*

MAN. The spirits I have raised abandon
    me,
The spells which I have studied baffle me,
The remedy I recked of tortured me;
I lean no more on superhuman aid;
It hath no power upon the past, and for
The future, till the past be gulfed in dark-
    ness,
It is not of my search. — My mother earth!
And thou fresh breaking day, and you, ye
    mountains,
Why are ye beautiful? I cannot love ye.
And thou, the bright eye of the uni-
    verse,   10
That openest over all, and unto all
Art a delight — thou shin'st not on my
    heart.
And you, ye crags, upon whose extreme
    edge
I stand, and on the torrent's brink be-
    neath
Behold the tall pines dwindled as to
    shrubs
In dizziness of distance; when a leap,
A stir, a motion, even a breath, would
    bring
My breast upon its rocky bosom's bed
To rest forever — wherefore do I pause?
I feel the impulse — yet I do not
    plunge;   20

I see the peril — yet do not recede ;
And my brain reels — and yet my foot is
   firm :
There is a power upon me which with-
   holds,
And makes it my fatality to live ;
If it be life to wear within myself
This barrenness of spirit, and to be
My own soul's sepulchre, for I have ceased
To justify my deeds unto myself —
The last infirmity of evil. Ay,
Thou winged and cloud-cleaving minis-
   ter,   30

        [*An eagle passes.*]

Whose happy flight is highest into heaven,
Well may'st thou swoop so near me — I
   should be
Thy prey, and gorge thine eaglets ; thou
   art gone
Where the eye cannot follow thee ; but
   thine
Yet pierces downward, onward, or above,
With a pervading vision. — Beautiful !
How beautiful is all this visible world !
How glorious in its action and itself !
But we, who name ourselves its sovereigns,
   we,
Half dust, half deity, alike unfit   40
To sink or soar, with our mixed essence
   make
A conflict of its elements, and breathe
The breath of degradation and of pride,
Contending with low wants and lofty will,
Till our mortality predominates,
And men are — what they name not to
   themselves,
And trust not to each other. Hark ! the
   note,

   [*The Shepherd's pipe in the distance
        is heard.*]

The natural music of the mountain reed —
For here the patriarchal days are not
A pastoral fable — pipes in the liberal
   air,   50
Mixed with the sweet bells of the saunter-
   ing herd ;
My soul would drink these echoes. Oh,
   that I were
The viewless spirit of a lovely sound,
A living voice, a breathing harmony,
A bodiless enjoyment — born and dying
With the blest tone which made me !

   Enter from below a CHAMOIS HUNTER.
   CHAMOIS HUNTER.   Even so
This way the chamois leapt : her nimble
   feet
Have baffled me ; my gains today will
   scarce

Repay my break-neck travail. — What is
   here ?
Who seems not of my trade, and yet hath
   reached   60
A height which none even of our moun-
   taineers,
Save our best hunters, may attain : his
   garb
Is goodly, his mien manly, and his air
Proud as a free-born peasant's, at this
   distance :
I will approach him nearer.
   MAN. (*not perceiving the other*). To be
   thus —
Gray-haired with anguish, like these blasted
   pines,
Wrecks of a single winter, barkless, branch-
   less,
A blighted trunk upon a cursed root,
Which but supplies a feeling to decay —
And to be thus, eternally but thus,   70
Having been otherwise ! Now furrowed
   o'er
With wrinkles, ploughed by moments, —
   not by years, —
And hours, all tortured into ages — hours
Which I outlive ! — Ye toppling crags of
   ice !
Ye avalanches, whom a breath draws down
In mountainous o'erwhelming, come and
   crush me !
I hear ye momently above, beneath,
Crash with a frequent conflict ; but ye pass,
And only fall on things that still would
   live ;
On the young flourishing forest, or the
   hut   80
And hamlet of the harmless villager.
   C. HUN. The mists begin to rise from up
   the valley ;
I'll warn him to descend, or he may chance
To lose at once his way and life together.
   MAN. The mists boil up around the gla-
   ciers ; clouds
Rise curling fast beneath me, white and
   sulphury,
Like foam from the roused ocean of deep
   hell,
Whose every wave breaks on a living shore,
Heaped with the damned like pebbles. —
   I am giddy.
   C. HUN. I must approach him cautiously ;
   if near,   90
A sudden step will startle him, and he
Seems tottering already.
   MAN.   Mountains have fallen,
Leaving a gap in the clouds, and with the
   shock
Rocking their Alpine brethren ; filling up

The ripe green valleys with destruction's
   splinters;
Damming the rivers with a sudden dash,
Which crushed the waters into mist and
   made
Their fountains find another channel —
   thus,
Thus, in its old age, did Mount Rosen
   berg —
Why stood I not beneath it?   100
   C. HUN.   Friend! have a care,
Your next step may be fatal! — for the love
Of him who made you, stand not on that
   brink!
   MAN. (*not hearing him*). Such would
     have been for me a fitting tomb;
My bones had then been quiet in their
   depth;
They had not then been strewn upon the
   rocks
For the wind's pastime — as thus — thus
   they shall be —
In this one plunge. — Farewell, ye opening
   heavens!
Look not upon me thus reproachfully —
Ye were not meant for me — Earth! take
   these atoms!

[*As* MANFRED *is in act to spring from
the cliff, the* CHAMOIS HUNTER *seizes
and retains him with a sudden grasp.*]

   C. HUN. Hold, madman! — though aweary
     of thy life,   110
Stain not our pure vales with thy guilty
   blood:
Away with me — I will not quit my hold.
   MAN. I am most sick at heart — nay,
     grasp me not —
I am all feebleness — the mountains whirl
Spinning around me — I grow blind —
   What art thou?
   C. HUN. I'll answer that anon. Away with
   me!
The clouds grow thicker — there — now
   lean on me —
Place your foot here — here, take this staff,
   and cling
A moment to that shrub — now give me
   your hand,
And hold fast by my girdle — softly —
   well —   120
The Chalet will be gained within an hour:
Come on, we'll quickly find a surer foot-
   ing,
And something like a pathway, which the
   torrent
Hath washed since winter. — Come, 'tis

bravely done —
You should have been a hunter. — Follow
   me.
[*As they descend the rocks with difficulty,
the scene closes.*]

ACT II

SCENE I

A Cottage amongst the Bernese Alps.

MANFRED *and the* CHAMOIS HUNTER.

   C. HUN. No, no — yet pause — thou must
     not yet go forth:
Thy mind and body are alike unfit
To trust each other, for some hours, at
   least;
When thou art better, I will be thy guide —
But whither?
   MAN.   It imports not: I do know
My route full well, and need no further
   guidance.
   C. HUN. Thy garb and gait bespeak thee
     of high lineage —
One of the many chiefs, whose castled
   crags
Look o'er the lower valleys — which of
   these
May call thee lord? I only know their
   portals;   10
My way of life leads me but rarely down
To bask by the huge hearths of those old
   halls,
Carousing with the vassals; but the paths,
Which step from out our mountains to
   their doors,
I know from childhood — which of these
   is thine?
   MAN. No matter.
   C. HUN.   Well, sir, pardon me
     the question,
And be of better cheer. Come, taste my
   wine;
'Tis of an ancient vintage; many a day
'T has thawed my veins among our gla-
   ciers, now
Let it do thus for thine. Come, pledge me
   fairly.   20
   MAN. Away, away! there's blood upon
     the brim!
Will it then never — never sink in the
   earth?
   C. HUN. What dost thou mean? thy senses
     wander from thee.
   MAN. I say 'tis blood — my blood! the

pure warm stream
Which ran in the veins of my fathers, and
    in ours
When we were in our youth, and had one
    heart,
And loved each other as we should not
    love,
And this was shed : but still it rises up,
Coloring the clouds, that shut me out
    from heaven,
Where thou art not — and I shall never
    be.   30
    C. HUN. Man of strange words, and some
        half-maddening sin,
Which makes thee people vacancy, what-
    e'er
Thy dread and sufferance be, there's com-
    fort yet —
The aid of holy men, and heavenly pa-
    tience —
    MAN. Patience and patience ! Hence —
        that word was made
For brutes of burthen, not for birds of
    prey ;
Preach it to mortals of a dust like thine, —
I am not of thine order.
    C. HUN.   Thanks to heaven !
I would not be of thine for the free fame
Of William Tell ; but whatsoe'er thine
    ill,   40
It must be borne, and these wild starts are
    useless.
    MAN. Do I not bear it ? — Look on me —
        I live.
    C. HUN. This is convulsion, and no
        healthful life.
    MAN. I tell thee, man ! I have lived
        many years,
Many long years, but they are nothing now
To those which I must number : ages —
    ages —
Space and eternity — and consciousness,
With the fierce thirst of death — and still
    unslaked !
    C. HUN. Why, on thy brow the seal of
        middle age
Hath scarce been set ; I am thine elder
    far.   50
    MAN. Think'st thou existence doth de-
        pend on time ?
It doth ; but actions are our epochs : mine
Have made my days and nights imperish-
    able,
Endless, and all alike, as sands on the
    shore,
Innumerable atoms ; and one desert,
Barren and cold, on which the wild waves
    break,

But nothing rests, save carcasses and
    wrecks,
Rocks, and the salt-surf weeds of bitter-
    ness.
    C. HUN. Alas ! he's mad — but yet I must
        not leave him.
    MAN. I would I were — for then the
        things I see   60
Would be but a distempered dream.
    C. HUN.   What is it
That thou dost see, or think thou look'st
    upon ?
    MAN. Myself, and thee — a peasant of
        the Alps —
Thy humble virtues, hospitable home,
And spirit patient, pious, proud, and free ;
Thy self-respect, grafted on innocent
    thoughts ;
Thy days of health, and nights of sleep ;
    thy toils,
By danger dignified, yet guiltless ; hopes
Of cheerful old age and a quiet grave,
With cross and garland over its green
    turf,   70
And thy grandchildren's love for epitaph ;
This do I see — and then I look within —
It matters not — my soul was scorched al-
    ready !
    C. HUN. And wouldst thou then exchange
        thy lot for mine ?
    MAN. No friend ! I would not wrong
        thee, nor exchange
My lot with living being : I can bear —
However wretchedly, 'tis still to bear —
In life what others could not brook to
    dream,
But perish in their slumber.
    C. HUN.   And with this —
This cautious feeling for another's pain, 80
Canst thou be black with evil ? — say not
    so.
Can one of gentle thoughts have wreaked
    revenge
Upon his enemies ?
    MAN.   Oh ! no, no, no !
My injuries came down on those who
    loved me —
On those whom I best loved : I never
    quelled
An enemy, save in my just defence —
But my embrace was fatal.
    C. HUN.   Heaven give thee rest !
And penitence restore thee to thyself ;
My prayers shall be for thee.
    MAN.   I need them not —
But can endure thy pity. I depart —   90
'Tis time — farewell ! — Here's gold, and
    thanks for thee ;

No words — it is thy due. Follow me not —
I know my path — the mountain peril's
     past :
And once again I charge thee, follow not !

[*Exit* MANFRED.]

SCENE II

A lower Valley in the Alps. — A Cataract.

Enter MANFRED.

MAN. It is not noon — the sunbow's rays
     still arch
The torrent with the many hues of heaven,
And roll the sheeted silver's waving col-
     umn
O'er the crag's headlong perpendicular,
And fling its lines of foaming light along
And to and fro, like the pale courser's tail,
The giant steed, to be bestrode by death,
As told in the Apocalypse. No eyes
But mine now drink this sight of loveli-
     ness ;
I should be sole in this sweet solitude,   10
And with the Spirit of the place divide
The homage of these waters. — I will call
     her.
[MANFRED *takes some of the water into
     the palm of his hand, and flings it
     into the air muttering the adjuration.
     After a pause, the* WITCH OF THE ALPS
     *rises beneath the arch of the sunbow
          of the torrent.*]
Beautiful spirit ! with thy hair of light,
And dazzling eyes of glory, in whose form
The charms of earth's least mortal daugh-
     ters grow
To an unearthly stature, in an essence
Of purer elements ; while the hue of
     youth, —
Carnationed like a sleeping infant's cheek,
Rocked by the beating of her mother's
     heart,
Or the rose tints, which summer's twilight
     leaves   20
Upon the lofty glacier's virgin snow,
The blush of earth embracing with her
     heaven, —
Tinge thy celestial aspect, and make tame
The beauties of the sunbow which bends
     o'er thee.
Beautiful Spirit ! in thy calm clear brow,
Wherein is glassed serenity of soul,
Which of itself shows immortality,
I read that thou wilt pardon to a son
Of Earth, whom the abstruser powers per-
     mit

At times to commune with them — if that
     he   30
Avail him of his spells — to call thee thus,
And gaze on thee a moment.
WITCH OF THE ALPS.   Son of Earth !
I know thee, and the powers which give
     thee power ;
I know thee for a man of many thoughts,
And deeds of good and ill, extreme in
     both,
Fatal and fated in thy sufferings.
I have expected this — what wouldst thou
     with me ?
MAN. To look upon thy beauty — noth-
     ing further.
The face of the earth that maddened me,
     and I
Take refuge in her mysteries, and pierce 40
To the abodes of those who govern her —
But they can nothing aid me. I have sought
From them what they could not bestow,
     and now
I search no further.
WITCH.   What could be the quest
Which is not in the power of the most
     powerful,
The rulers of the invisible ?
MAN.   A boon ;
But why should I repeat it ? 'twere in
     vain.
WITCH. I know not that ; let thy lips
     utter it.
MAN. Well, though it torture me, 'tis
     but the same ;
My pangs shall find a voice. From my
     youth upwards   50
My spirit walked not with the souls of
     men,
Nor looked upon the earth with human
     eyes ;
The thirst of their ambition was not mine,
The aim of their existence was not mine ;
My joys, my griefs, my passions, and my
     powers,
Made me a stranger ; though I wore the
     form
I had no sympathy with breathing flesh,
Nor midst the creatures of clay that girded
     me
Was there but one who — but of her anon.
I said with men, and with the thoughts
     of men,   60
I held but slight communion ; but instead,
My joy was in the wilderness, — to breathe
The difficult air of the iced mountain's
     top,
Where the birds dare not build, nor in-
     sect's wing
Flit o'er the herbless granite ; or to plunge

Into the torrent, and to roll along
On the swift whirl of the new-breaking
    wave
Of river-stream, or ocean, in their flow.
In these my early strength exulted ; or
To follow through the night the moving
    moon,   70
The stars and their development ; or catch
The dazzling lightnings till my eyes grew
    dim ;
Or to look, list'ning, on the scattered
    leaves,
While autumn winds were at their evening
    song.
These were my pastimes, and to be alone ;
For if the beings, of whom I was one, —
Hating to be so, — crossed me in my path,
I felt myself degraded back to them,
And was all clay again. And then I dived,
In my lone wanderings, to the caves of
    death,   80
Searching its cause in its effect ; and drew
From withered bones, and skulls, and
    heaped up dust,
Conclusions most forbidden. Then I passed
The nights of years in sciences untaught,
Save in the old time ; and with time and
    toil,
And terrible ordeal, and such penance
As in itself hath power upon the air,
And spirits that do compass air and earth,
Space, and the peopled infinite, I made
Mine eyes familiar with Eternity,   90
Such as, before me, did the Magi, and
He who from out their fountain dwellings
    raised
Eros and Anteros, at Gadara,
As I do thee ; — and with my knowledge
    grew
The thirst of knowledge, and the power
    and joy
Of this most bright intelligence, until —
  WITCH. Proceed.
    MAN. Oh ! I but thus prolonged my
    words,
Boasting these idle attributes, because
As I approach the core of my heart's
    grief —   100
But to my task. I have not named to thee
Father, or mother, mistress, friend, or
    being,
With whom I wore the chain of human
    ties ;
If I had such, they seemed not such to me ;
Yet there was one —
    WITCH.   Spare not thyself — proceed.
    MAN. She was like me in lineaments ;
    her eyes,
Her hair, her features, all, to the very tone

Even of her voice, they said were like to
    mine ;
But softened all, and tempered into
    beauty :
She had the same lone thoughts and wan-
    derings,   110
The quest of hidden knowledge, and a
    mind
To comprehend the universe : nor these
Alone, but with them gentler powers than
    mine,
Pity, and smiles, and tears — which I had
    not ;
And tenderness — but that I had for her ;
Humility — and that I never had.
Her faults were mine — her virtues were
    her own —
I loved her, and destroyed her !
  WITCH.   With thy hand ?
  MAN. Not with my hand, but heart —
    which broke her heart ;
It gazed on mine, and withered. I have
    shed   120
Blood, but not hers — and yet her blood
    was shed ;
I saw — and could not stanch it.
  WITCH.   And for this —
A being of the race thou dost despise,
The order, which thine own would rise
    above,
Mingling with us and ours, — thou dost
    forego
The gifts of our great knowledge, and
    shrink'st back
In recreant mortality — Away !
    MAN. Daughter of air ! I tell thee, since
    that hour —
But words are breath — look on me in my
    sleep,
Or watch my watchings — Come and sit
    by me !   130
My solitude is solitude no more,
But peopled with the furies ; — I have
    gnashed
My teeth in darkness till returning morn,
Then cursed myself till sunset ; — I have
    prayed
For madness as a blessing — 'tis denied me.
I have affronted death — but in the war
Of elements the waters shrunk from me,
And fatal things passed harmless ; the cold
    hand
Of an all-pitiless demon held me back,
Back by a single hair, which would not
    break.   140
In fantasy, imagination, all
The affluence of my soul — which one day
    was
A Crœsus in creation — I plunged deep,

But, like an ebbing wave, it dashed me
    back
Into the gulf of my unfathomed thought.
I plunged amidst mankind — Forgetfulness
I sought in all, save where 'tis to be found,
And that I have to learn ; my sciences,
My long-pursued and superhuman art,
Is mortal here : I dwell in my despair — 150
And live — and live forever.
    WITCH.   It may be
That I can aid thee.
    MAN.   To do this thy power
Must wake the dead, or lay me low with
    them.
Do so — in any shape — in any hour —
With any torture — so it be the last.
    WITCH. That is not in my province ; but
    if thou
Wilt swear obedience to my will, and do
My bidding, it may help thee to thy
    wishes.
    MAN. I will not swear — Obey ! and
    whom ? the spirits
Whose presence I command, and be the
    slave   160
Of those who served me — Never !
    WITCH.   Is this all ?
Hast thou no gentler answer ? — Yet be-
    think thee,
And pause ere thou rejectest.
    MAN.   I have said it.
    WITCH. Enough ! I may retire then —
    say !
    MAN.   Retire !

[*The* WITCH *disappears.*]

    MAN. (*alone*). We are the fools of time
    and terror. Days
Steal on us, and steal from us ; yet we live,
Loathing our life, and dreading still to die.
In all the days of this detested yoke —
This vital weight upon the struggling
    heart,
Which sinks with sorrow, or beats quick
    with pain,   170
Or joy that ends in agony or faintness —
In all the days of past and future, for
In life there is no present, we can number
How few — how less than few — wherein
    the soul
Forbears to pant for death, and yet draws
    back
As from a stream in winter, though the
    chill
Be but a moment's. I have one resource
Still in my science — I can call the dead,
And ask them what it is we dread to be :

The sternest answer can but be the
    grave,   180
And that is nothing. If they answer not —
The buried prophet answered to the Hag
Of Endor ; and the Spartan Monarch drew
From the Byzantine maid's unsleeping
    spirit
An answer and his destiny — he slew
That which he loved, unknowing what he
    slew,
And died unpardoned — though he called
    in aid
The Phyxian Jove, and in Phigalia roused
The Arcadian Evocators to compel
The indignant shadow to depose her
    wrath,   190
Or fix her term of vengeance — she replied
In words of dubious import, but fulfilled.
If I had never lived, that which I love
Had still been living ; had I never loved,
That which I love would still be beau-
    tiful,
Happy and giving happiness. What is she ?
What is she now ? — a sufferer for my
    sins —
A thing I dare not think upon — or noth-
    ing.
Within few hours I shall not call in vain —
Yet in this hour I dread the thing I
    dare :   200
Until this hour I never shrunk to gaze
On spirit, good or evil — now I tremble,
And feel a strange cold thaw upon my
    heart.
But I can act even what I most abhor,
And champion human fears. — The night
    approaches.
         [*Exit.*]

SCENE III

The Summit of the Jungfrau Mountain.

Enter FIRST DESTINY.
    FIRST DESTINY. The moon is rising broad,
    and round, and bright ;
And here on snows, where never human
    foot
Of common mortal trod, we nightly tread,
And leave no traces : o'er the savage sea,
The glassy ocean of the mountain ice,
We skim its rugged breakers, which put on
The aspect of a tumbling tempest's foam,
Frozen in a moment — a dead whirlpool's
    image :
And this most steep fantastic pinnacle,
The fretwork of some earthquake — where
    the clouds   10

Pause to repose themselves in passing
  by —
Is sacred to our revels, or our vigils ;
Here do I wait my sisters, on our way
To the Hall of Arimanes, for tonight
Is our great festival — 'tis strange they
  come not.

A VOICE *without, singing*

The captive usurper,
  Hurled down from the throne,
Lay buried in torpor,
  Forgotten and lone ;
I broke through his slumbers,   20
  I shivered his chain,
I leagued him with numbers —
  He's tyrant again !
With the blood of a million he'll answer
  my care,
With a nation's destruction — his flight
  and despair.

SECOND VOICE, *without*

The ship sailed on, the ship sailed fast,
But I left not a sail, and I left not a mast ;
There is not a plank of the hull or the
  deck,
And there is not a wretch to lament o'er
  his wreck ;
Save one, whom I held, as he swam, by
  the hair,   30
And he was a subject, well worthy my
  care ;
A traitor on land, and a pirate at sea —
But I saved him to wreak further havoc
  for me !

FIRST DESTINY, *answering*

The city lies sleeping ;
  The morn, to deplore it,
May dawn on it weeping :
  Sullenly, slowly,
The black plague flew o'er it —
  Thousands lie lowly ;
Tens of thousands shall perish ;   40
  The living shall fly from
The sick they should cherish ;
  But nothing can vanquish
The touch that they die from.
  Sorrow and anguish,
And evil and dread,
  Envelop a nation ;
The blest are the dead,
  Who see not the sight
Of their own desolation ;   50

This work of a night —
This wreck of a realm — this deed of my
  doing —
For ages I've done, and shall still be re-
  newing !

Enter the SECOND *and* THIRD DESTINIES.

THE THREE

Our hands contain the hearts of men,
  Our footsteps are their graves ;
We only give to take again
  The spirits of our slaves !

FIRST DESTINY.   Welcome ! — Where's
  Nemesis ?
SECOND DESTINY.   At
  some great work ;
But what I know not, for my hands were
  full.
THIRD DESTINY. Behold she cometh.   60

Enter NEMESIS.

FIRST DES. Say, where hast thou been ?
My sisters and thyself are slow tonight.
  NEMESIS. I was detained repairing shat-
    tered thrones,
Marrying fools, restoring dynasties,
Avenging men upon their enemies,
And making them repent their own re-
  venge ;
Goading the wise to madness ; from the
  dull
Shaping out oracles to rule the world
Afresh, for they were waxing out of date,
And mortals dared to ponder for them-
  selves,   70
To weigh kings in the balance, and to
  speak
Of freedom, the forbidden fruit. — Away !
We have outstayed the hour — mount we
  our clouds.

[Exeunt.]

SCENE IV

The Hall of ARIMANES. ARIMANES *on his
Throne, a Globe of Fire, surrounded by
the* SPIRITS.

Hymn of the SPIRITS

Hail to our Master ! — Prince of earth and
  air !

Who walks the clouds and waters — in
  his hand
The sceptre of the elements, which tear
  Themselves to chaos at his high com-
    mand !
He breatheth — and a tempest shakes the
  sea ;
  He speaketh — and the clouds reply in
    thunder ;
He gazeth — from his glance the sunbeams
  flee ;
  He moveth — earthquakes rend the world
    asunder.
Beneath his footsteps the volcanoes rise ;
His shadow is the pestilence ; his path   10
The comets herald through the crackling
  skies ;
  And planets turn to ashes at his wrath.
To him war offers daily sacrifice ;
  To him death pays his tribute ; life is
    his,
With all its infinite of agonies —
And his the spirit of whatever is !

Enter the DESTINIES *and* NEMESIS.

FIRST DES. Glory to Arimanes ! on the
  earth
His power increaseth — both my sisters did
His bidding, nor did I neglect my duty !
  SECOND DES. Glory to Arimanes ! we who
    bow   20
The necks of men, bow down before his
  throne !
  THIRD DES. Glory to Arimanes ! we await
    His nod !
  NEM. Sovereign of sovereigns ! we are
    thine,
And all that liveth, more or less, is ours,
And most things wholly so ; still to in-
  crease
Our power, increasing thine, demands our
  care,
And we are vigilant. Thy late commands
Have been fulfilled to the utmost.

Enter MANFRED.

A SPIRIT.   What is here ?
A mortal ! — Thou most rash and fatal
  wretch,
Bow down and worship !   30
  SECOND SPIRIT.   I do know the man —
A magian of great power, and fearful
  skill !
  THIRD SPIRIT. Bow down and worship,
    slave ! — What, know'st thou not
Thine and our sovereign ? — Tremble, and

obey !
  ALL THE SPIRITS.   Prostrate thyself, and
    thy condemned clay,
Child of the earth ! or dread the worst.
  MAN.   I know it ;
And yet ye see I kneel not.
  FOURTH SPIRIT.   'Twill be taught thee.
  MAN. 'Tis taught already ; — many a
    night on the earth,
On the bare ground, have I bowed down
  my face,
And strewed my head with ashes ; I have
  known   40
The fullness of humiliation, for
I sunk before my vain despair, and knelt
To my own desolation.
  FIFTH SPIRIT.   Dost thou dare
Refuse to Arimanes on his throne
What the whole earth accords, beholding
  not
The terror of his glory ? — Crouch, I say.
  MAN. Bid *him* bow down to that which
    is above him,
The overruling Infinite — the Maker
Who made him not for worship — let him
  kneel,
And we will kneel together.
  THE SPIRITS.   Crush the worm ! 50
Tear him to pieces ! —
  FIRST DES. Hence ! avaunt ! — he's mine.
Prince of the powers invisible ! This man
Is of no common order, as his port
And presence here denote ; his sufferings
Have been of an immortal nature, like
Our own ; his knowledge, and his powers
  and will,
As far as is compatible with clay,
Which clogs the ethereal essence, have
  been such
As clay hath seldom borne ; his aspirations
Have been beyond the dwellers of the
  earth,   60
And they have only taught him what we
  know —
That knowledge is not happiness, and
  science
But an exchange of ignorance for that
Which is another kind of ignorance.
This is not all — the passions, attributes
Of earth and heaven, from which no
  power, nor being,
Nor breath from the worm upwards is
  exempt,
Have pierced his heart, and in their con-
  sequence
Made him a thing which I, who pity not,
Yet pardon those who pity. He is mine, 70
And thine, it may be ; be it so, or not,
No other spirit in this region hath

A soul like his — or power upon his soul.
NEM. What doth he here then ?
FIRST DES.   Let him answer
    that.
MAN. Ye know what I have known ; and
    without power
I could not be amongst ye : but there are
Powers deeper still beyond — I come in
    quest
Of such, to answer unto what I seek.
NEM. What wouldst thou ?
MAN.   Thou canst not reply
    to me.
Call up the dead — my question is for
    them.   80
NEM. Great Arimanes, doth thy will
    avouch
The wishes of this mortal ?
ARIMANES.   Yea.
NEM.   Whom wouldst
    thou
Uncharnel ?
MAN.   One without a tomb — call up
Astarte.

Shadow ! or spirit !
    Whatever thou art,
Which still doth inherit
    The whole or a part
Of the form of thy birth,
    Of the mould of thy clay,   90
Which returned to the earth, —
    Reappear to the day !
Bear what thou borest,
    The heart and the form,
And the aspect thou worest
    Redeem from the worm.
Appear ! — Appear ! — Appear !
Who sent thee there requires thee here !

[*The* PHANTOM OF ASTARTE *rises and stands
    in the midst.*]

MAN. Can this be death ? there's bloom
    upon her cheek ;
But now I see it is no living hue,   100
But a strange hectic — like the unnatural
    red
Which autumn plants upon the perished
    leaf.
It is the same ! Oh, God ! that I should
    dread
To look upon the same — Astarte ! — No,
I cannot speak to her — but bid her
    speak —
Forgive me or condemn me.

NEMESIS

By the power which hath broken
    The grave which enthralled thee,
Speak to him who hath spoken,
    Or those who have called thee !
MAN.   She is silent, 110
And in that silence I am more than an-
    swered.
NEM. My power extends no further.
    Prince of Air !
It rests with thee alone — command her
    voice.
ARI. Spirit — obey this sceptre !
NEM.   Silent still !
She is not of our order, but belongs
To the other powers. Mortal ! thy quest
    is vain,
And we are baffled also.
MAN.   Hear me, hear me —
Astarte ! my beloved ! speak to me :
I have so much endured — so much en-
    dure —
Look on me ! the grave hath not changed
    thee more   120
Than I am changed for thee. Thou lovedst
    me
Too much, as I loved thee : we were not
    made
To torture thus each other, though it were
The deadliest sin to love as we have loved.
Say that thou loath'st me not — that I do
    bear
This punishment for both — that thou wilt
    be
One of the blessed — and that I shall die ;
For hitherto all hateful things conspire
To bind me in existence — in a life
Which makes me shrink from immortal-
    ity —   130
A future like the past. I cannot rest.
I know not what I ask, nor what I seek :
I feel but what thou art, and what I am ;
And I would hear yet once before I perish
The voice which was my music — Speak
    to me !
For I have called on thee in the still
    night,
Startled the slumbering birds from the
    hushed boughs,
And woke the mountain wolves, and made
    the caves
Acquainted with thy vainly echoed name,
Which answered me — many things an-
    swered me —   140
Spirits and men — but thou wert silent
    all.
Yet speak to me ! I have outwatched the
    stars,

And gazed o'er heaven in vain in search
    of thee.
Speak to me ! I have wandered o'er the
    earth,
And never found thy likeness — Speak to
    me !
Look on the fiends around — they feel for
    me :
I fear them not, and feel for thee alone —
Speak to me ! though it be in wrath ; —
    but say —
I reck not what — but let me hear thee
    once —
This once — once more !
    PHANTOM OF ASTARTE. Manfred !
    MAN.   Say on, say on —
I live but in the sound — it is thy voice ! 151
    PHAN. Manfred ! Tomorrow ends thine
      earthly ills.
Farewell !
    MAN. Yet one word more — am I for-
      given ?
    PHAN. Farewell !
    MAN.   Say, shall we meet again ?
    PHAN. Farewell !
    MAN.   One word for mercy !
Say, thou lovest me.
    PHAN. Manfred !

[*The* SPIRIT OF ASTARTE *disappears.*]

    NEM. She's gone, and will not be re-
    called ;
Her words will be fulfilled. Return to the
    earth.
    A SPIRIT. He is convulsed. — This is to be
    a mortal
And seek the things beyond mortality. 160
    ANOTHER SPIRIT. Yet, see, he mastereth
    himself, and makes
His torture tributary to his will.
Had he been one of us, he would have
    made
An awful spirit.
    NEM.   Hast thou further question
Of our great sovereign, or his worship-
    pers ?
    MAN. None.
    NEM.   Then for a time farewell.
    MAN. We meet then ! Where ? On the
    earth ? —
Even as thou wilt : and for the grace
    accorded
I now depart a debtor. Fare ye well !
        [*Exit* MANFRED.]

       (*Scene closes.*)

ACT III

SCENE I

A Hall in the Castle of MANFRED

MANFRED *and* HERMAN.

    MAN. What is the hour ?
    HERMAN.   It wants but one till sun-
    set,
And promises a lovely twilight.
    MAN.   Say,
Are all things so disposed of in the tower
As I directed ?
    HER.   All, my lord, are ready :
Here is the key and casket.
    MAN.   It is well :
Thou may'st retire.

    [*Exit* HERMAN.]

    MAN. (*alone*). There is a calm upon
    me —
Inexplicable stillness ! which till now,
Did not belong to what I knew of life.
If that I did not know philosophy
To be of all our vanities the motliest, 10
The merest word that ever fooled the ear
From out the schoolman's jargon, I should
    deem
The golden secret, the sought "Kalon,"
    found,
And seated in my soul. It will not last,
But it is well to have known it, though
    but once :
It hath enlarged my thoughts with a new
    sense,
And I within my tables would note down
That there is such a feeling. Who is there ?

    Re-enter HERMAN.

    HER. My lord, the abbot of St. Maurice
    craves
To greet your presence.

    Enter the ABBOT OF ST. MAURICE.

    ABBOT.   Peace be with Count Man-
    fred !   20
    MAN. Thanks, holy father ! welcome to
    these walls ;
Thy presence honors them, and blesseth
    those
Who dwell within them.
    ABBOT.   Would it were so, Count !—
But I would fain confer with thee alone.
    MAN. Herman, retire — What would my
    reverend guest ?

ABBOT. Thus, without prelude : — Age and zeal, my office,
And good intent, must plead my privilege ;
Our near, though not acquainted neighborhood,
May also be my herald. Rumors strange,
And of unholy nature, are abroad,   30
And busy with thy name ; a noble name
For centuries : may he who bears it now
Transmit it unimpaired !

MAN.   Proceed, — I listen.

ABBOT. 'Tis said thou holdest converse with the things
Which are forbidden to the search of man ;
That with the dwellers of the dark abodes,
The many evil and unheavenly spirits
Which walk the valley of the shade of death,
Thou communest. I know that with mankind,
Thy fellows in creation, thou dost rarely 40
Exchange thy thoughts, and that thy solitude
Is as an anchorite's, were it but holy.

MAN. And what are they who do avouch these things ?

ABBOT. My pious brethren — the sacred peasantry —
Even thy own vassals — who do look on thee
With most unquiet eyes. Thy life's in peril.

MAN. Take it.

ABBOT. I come to save, and not destroy :
I would not pry into thy secret soul ;
But if these things be sooth, there still is time
For penitence and pity : reconcile thee 50
With the true church, and through the church to heaven.

MAN. I hear thee. This is my reply : whate'er
I may have been, or am, doth rest between
Heaven and myself. I shall not choose a mortal
To be my mediator. Have I sinned
Against your ordinances ? prove and punish !

ABBOT. My son ! I did not speak of punishment,
But penitence and pardon ; — with thyself
The choice of such remains — and for the last,
Our institutions and our strong belief   60
Have given me power to smooth the path from sin
To higher hope and better thoughts ; the first
I leave to heaven, — "Vengeance is mine alone !"
So saith the Lord, and with all humbleness
His servant echoes back the awful word.

MAN. Old man ! there is no power in holy men,
Nor charm in prayer, nor purifying form
Of penitence, nor outward look, nor fast,
Nor agony — nor, greater than all these,
The innate tortures of that deep despair,   70
Which is remorse without the fear of hell,
But all in all sufficient to itself
Would make a hell of heaven — can exorcise
From out the unbounded spirit the quick sense
Of its own sins, wrongs, sufferance, and revenge
Upon itself ; there is no future pang
Can deal that justice on the self-condemned
He deals on his own soul.

ABBOT.   All this is well ;
For this will pass away, and be succeeded
By an auspicious hope, which shall look up   80
With calm assurance to that blessed place,
Which all who seek may win, whatever be
Their earthly errors, so they be atoned :
And the commencement of atonement is
The sense of its necessity. Say on —
And all our church can teach thee shall be taught ;
And all we can absolve thee shall be pardoned.

MAN. When Rome's sixth emperor was near his last,
The victim of a self-inflicted wound,
To shun the torments of a public death 90
From senates once his slaves, a certain soldier,
With show of loyal pity, would have stanched
The gushing throat with his officious robe ;
The dying Roman thrust him back, and said —
Some empire still in his expiring glance —
"It is too late — is this fidelity ?"

ABBOT. And what of this ?

MAN.   I answer with the Roman —
"It is too late !"

ABBOT.   It never can be so,
To reconcile thyself with thy own soul,
And thy own soul with heaven. Hast thou no hope ?   100

'Tis strange — even those who do despair
above,
Yet shape themselves some fantasy on
earth,
To which frail twig they cling, like drown-
ing men.
   MAN. Ay — father! I have had those
earthly visions,
And noble aspirations in my youth,
To make my own the mind of other men,
The enlightener of nations ; and to rise
I knew not whither — it might be to fall ;
But fall, even as the mountain-cataract,
Which, having leapt from its more daz-
zling height,   110
Even in the foaming strength of its
abyss
(Which casts up misty columns that be-
come
Clouds raining from the re-ascended skies),
Lies low but mighty still. — But this is
past,
My thoughts mistook themselves.
   ABBOT.   And wherefore so ?
   MAN. I could not tame my nature down ;
for he
Must serve who fain would sway ; and
soothe, and sue,
And watch all time, and pry into all place,
And be a living lie, who would become
A mighty thing amongst the mean, and
such   120
The mass are ; I disdained to mingle with
A herd, though to be leader — and of
wolves.
The lion is alone, and so am I.
   ABBOT. And why not live and act with
other men ?
   MAN. Because my nature was averse from
life ;
And yet not cruel ; for I would not make,
But find a desolation. Like the wind,
The red-hot breath of the most lone
simoom,
Which dwells but in the desert, and sweeps
o'er
The barren sands which bear no shrubs
to blast,   130
And revels o'er their wild and arid waves,
And seeketh not, so that it is not sought,
But being met is deadly, — such hath been
The course of my existence ; but there
came
Things in my path which are no more.
   ABBOT.   Alas !
I 'gin to fear that thou art past all aid
From me and from my calling ; yet so
young,
I still would —

   MAN.   Look on me ! there is an order
Of mortals on the earth, who do become
Old in their youth, and die ere middle
age,   140
Without the violence of warlike death ;
Some perishing of pleasure, some of study,
Some worn with toil, some of mere weari-
ness,
Some of disease, and some insanity,
And some of withered or of broken hearts ;
For this last is a malady which slays
More than are numbered in the lists of
fate,
Taking all shapes, and bearing many
names.
Look upon me ! for even of all these things
Have I partaken ; and of all these
things,   150
One were enough ; then wonder not that I
Am what I am, but that I ever was,
Or having been, that I am still on earth.
   ABBOT. Yet, hear me still —
   MAN.   Old man ! I do re-
spect
Thine order, and revere thine years ; I
deem
Thy purpose pious, but it is in vain :
Think me not churlish ; I would spare
thyself,
Far more than me, in shunning at this
time
All further colloquy ; and so — farewell.
          [*Exit* MANFRED.]

   ABBOT. This should have been a noble
creature : he   160
Hath all the energy which would have
made
A goodly frame of glorious elements,
Had they been wisely mingled ; as it is,
It is an awful chaos — light and darkness,
And mind and dust, and passions and
pure thoughts
Mixed, and contending without end or
order, —
All dormant or destructive ; he will perish,
And yet he must not ; I will try once
more.
For such are worth redemption ; and my
duty
Is to dare all things for a righteous
end.   170
I'll follow him — but cautiously, though
surely.
          [*Exit* ABBOT.]

SCENE II

Another Chamber.

MANFRED *and* HERMAN.

HER. My lord, you bade me wait on you
    at sunset :
He sinks behind the mountain.
    MAN.   Doth he so ?
I will look on him.
    [MANFRED *advances to the Window of*
        the Hall.]
        Glorious orb ! the idol
Of early nature, and the vigorous race
Of undiseased mankind, the giant sons
Of the embrace of angels, with a sex
More beautiful than they, which did draw
    down
The erring spirits who can ne'er return. —
Most glorious orb ! that wert a worship,
    ere
The mystery of thy making was re-
    vealed !   10
Thou earliest minister of the Almighty,
-Which gladdened, on their mountain tops,
    the hearts
Of the Chaldean shepherds, till they
    poured
Themselves in orisons ! Thou material
    God !
And representative of the unknown —
Who chose thee for his shadow ! Thou
    chief star !
Center of many stars ! which mak'st our
    earth
Endurable, and temperest the hues
And hearts of all who walk within thy
    rays !
Sire of the seasons ! Monarch of the
    climes,   20
And those who dwell in them ! for near
    or far,
Our inborn spirits have a tint of thee
Even as our outward aspects ; — thou dost
    rise,
And shine, and set in glory. Fare thee
    well !
I ne'er shall see thee more. As my first
    glance
Of love and wonder was for thee, then
    take
My latest look ; thou wilt not beam on
    one
To whom the gifts of life and warmth
    have been
Of a more fatal nature. He is gone :
I follow.   30
    [*Exit* MANFRED.]

SCENE III

The Mountains — The Castle of MAN-
FRED *at some distance — A Terrace
before a Tower. — Time, Twilight.*

HERMAN, MANUEL, *and other Dependants
of* MANFRED.

HER. 'Tis strange enough ; night after
    night, for years,
He hath pursued long vigils in this tower,
Without a witness. I have been within it, —
So have we all been ofttimes ; but from it,
Or its contents, it were impossible
To draw conclusions absolute, of aught
His studies tend to. To be sure, there is
One chamber where none enter : I would
    give
The fee of what I have to come these
    three years,
To pore upon its mysteries.
    MANUEL.   'Twere dangerous :   10
Content thyself with what thou know'st
    already.
    HER. Ah ! Manuel ! thou art elderly and
    wise,
And couldst say much ; thou hast dwelt
    within the castle —
How many years is 't ?
    MANUEL.   Ere Count Manfred's birth,
I served his father, whom he nought re-
    sembles.
    HER. There be more sons in like pre-
    dicament.
But wherein do they differ ?
    MANUEL.   I speak not
Of features or of form, but mind and
    habits ;
Count Sigismund was proud, but gay and
    free, —
A warrior and a reveller ; he dwelt not 20
With books and solitude, nor made the
    night
A gloomy vigil, but a festal time,
Merrier than day ; he did not walk the
    rocks
And forests like a wolf, nor turn aside
From men and their delights.
    HER.   Beshrew the hour,
But those were jocund times ! I would that
    such
Would visit the old walls again ; they look
As if they had forgotten them.
    MANUEL.   These walls
Must change their chieftain first. Oh ! I
    have seen
Some strange things in them, Herman.
    HER.   Come, be
    friendly,   30
Relate me some to while away our watch :
I've heard thee darkly of an event

Which happened hereabouts, by this same
    tower.
    MANUEL.   That was a night indeed ! I
    do remember
'Twas twilight, as it may be now, and such
Another evening ; — yon red cloud, which
    rests
On Eigher's pinnacle, so rested then,—
So like that it might be the same ; the
    wind
Was faint and gusty, and the mountain
    snows
Began to glitter with the climbing
    moon ;   40
Count Manfred was, as now, within his
    tower, —
How occupied, we knew not, but with him
The sole companion of his wanderings
And watchings — her, whom of all earthly
    things
That lived, the only thing he seemed to
    love, —
As he, indeed, by blood was bound to do,
The lady Astarte, his —
               Hush ! who comes here ?

Enter the ABBOT.

    ABBOT. Where is your master ?
    HER.   Yonder in the
    tower.
    ABBOT. I must speak with him.
    MANUEL.   'T is impossible ;
He is most private, and must not be
    thus   50
Intruded on.
    ABBOT.   Upon myself I take
The forfeit of my fault, if fault there be —
But I must see him.
    HER.   Thou hast seen him once
This eve already.
    ABBOT.   Herman ! I command thee,
Knock, and apprize the Count of my ap-
    proach.
    HER. We dare not.
    ABBOT.   Then it seems I must be
    herald
Of my own purpose.
    MANUEL.   Reverend father stop —
I pray you pause.
    ABBOT.   Why so ?
    MANUEL.   But step this way,
And I will tell you further.

[Exeunt.]

SCENE IV

Interior of the Tower.

MANFRED *alone*

    MAN. The stars are forth, the moon
    above the tops
Of the snow-shining mountains. — Beauti-
    ful !
I linger yet with nature, for the night
Hath been to me a more familiar face
Than that of man ; and in her starry shade
Of dim and solitary loveliness,
I learned the language of another world.
I do remember me, that in my youth,
When I was wandering, — upon such a
    night
I stood within the Coliseum's wall,   10
'Midst the chief relics of almighty Rome ;
The trees which grew along the broken
    arches
Waved dark in the blue midnight, and
    the stars
Shone through the rents of ruin ; from
    afar
The watch-dog bayed beyond the Tiber ;
    and
More near from out the Caesar's palace
    came
The owl's long cry, and, interruptedly,
Of distant sentinels the fitful song
Begun and died upon the gentle wind.
Some cypresses beyond the time-worn
    breach   20
Appeared to skirt the horizon, yet they
    stood
Within a bowshot. Where the Caesars
    dwelt,
And dwell the tuneless birds of night,
    amidst
A grove which springs through levelled
    battlements,
And twines its roots with the imperial
    hearths,
Ivy usurps the laurel's place of growth ;
But the gladiator's bloody Circus stands,
A noble wreck in ruinous perfection,
While Caesar's chambers, and the Augus-
    tan halls,
Grovel on earth in indistinct decay.   30
And thou didst shine, thou rolling moon,
    upon
All this, and cast a wide and tender light,
Which softened down the hoar austerity
Of rugged desolation, and filled up,
As 't were anew, the gaps of centuries ;
Leaving that beautiful which still was so,
And making that which was not, till the
    place
Became religion, and the heart ran o'er
With silent worship of the great of old, —

The dead but sceptred sovereigns, who
   still rule   40
Our spirits from their urns.
               'Twas such a night !
'Tis strange that I recall it at this time ;
But I have found our thoughts take
   wildest flight
Even at the moment when they should
   array
Themselves in pensive order.

        Enter the ABBOT

ABBOT.   My good lord !
I crave a second grace for this approach ;
But yet let not my humble zeal offend
By its abruptness — all it hath of ill
Recoils on me ; its good in the effect
May light upon your head — could I say
   heart —   50
Could I touch *that,* with words or prayers,
   I should
Recall a noble spirit which hath wan-
   dered ;
But is not yet all lost.
   MAN.   Thou know'st me not ;
My days are numbered, and my deeds
   recorded ;
Retire, or 't will be dangerous — Away !
   ABBOT. Thou dost not mean to menace
   me ?
   MAN.   Not I ;
I simply tell thee peril is at hand,
And would preserve thee.
   ABBOT.   What dost thou mean ?
   MAN.   Look there !
What dost thou see?
   ABBOT.   Nothing.
   MAN.   Look there, I say,
And steadfastly ; — now tell me what thou
   seest.   60
   ABBOT. That which should shake me, but
   I fear it not :
I see a dusk and awful figure rise,
Like an infernal god, from out the
   earth ;
His face wrapt in a mantle, and his form
Robed as with angry clouds : he stands
   between
Thyself and me — but I do fear him not.
   MAN. Thou hast no cause ; he shall not
   harm thee, but
His sight may shock thine old limbs into
   palsy.
I say to thee — Retire !
   ABBOT.   And I reply —
Never — till I have battled with this
   fiend : —   70
What doth he here ?

   MAN.   Why — ay — what doth he here ?
I did not send for him, — he is unbidden.
   ABBOT. Alas ! lost mortal ! what with
   guests like these
Hast thou to do ? I tremble for thy sake :
Why doth he gaze on thee, and thou on
   him ?
Ah ! he unveils his aspect : on his brow
The thunder-scars are graven : from his
   eye
Glares forth the immortality of hell —
Avaunt ! —
   MAN. Pronounce — what is thy mission ?
   SPIRIT.   Come !
   ABBOT. What art thou, unknown being ?
   answer ! — speak !   80
   SPIRIT.   The genius of this mortal. —
   Come ! 'tis time.
   MAN. I am prepared for all things, but
   deny
The power which summons me. Who sent
   thee here ?
   SPIRIT. Thou 'lt know anon — Come !
   come !
   MAN.   I have
   commanded
Things of an essence greater far than
   thine,
And striven with thy masters. Get thee
   hence !
   SPIRIT. Mortal ! thine hour is come —
   Away ! I say.
   MAN. I knew, and know my hour is
   come, but not
To render up my soul to such as thee :
Away ! I'll die as I have lived — alone. 90
   SPIRIT. Then I must summon up my
   brethren. —
   Rise !

       [*Other* SPIRITS *rise up.*]

   ABBOT. Avaunt ! ye evil ones ! — Avaunt !
   I say ;
Ye have no power where piety hath power,
And I do charge ye in the name —
   SPIRIT.   Old man !
We know ourselves, our mission, and
   thine order ;
Waste not thy holy words on idle uses,
It were in vain : this man is forfeited.
Once more I summon him — Away ! Away !
   MAN. I do defy ye, — though I feel my
   soul
Is ebbing from me, yet I do defy ye ; 100
Nor will I hence, while I have earthly
   breath
To breathe my scorn upon ye — earthly

strength
To wrestle, though with spirits ; what ye
    take
Shall be ta'en limb by limb.
    SPIRIT.   Reluctant mortal !
Is this the Magian who would so pervade
The world invisible, and make himself
Almost our equal ? Can it be that thou
Art thus in love with life ? the very life
Which made thee wretched !
    MAN.   Thou false fiend, thou
    liest !
My life is in its last hour, — *that* I
    know,   110
Nor would redeem a moment of that
    hour ;
I do not combat against death, but thee
And thy surrounding angels ; my past
    power,
Was purchased by no compact with thy
    crew,
But by superior science — penance, daring,
And length of watching, strength of mind,
    and skill
In knowledge of our fathers — when the
    earth
Saw men and spirits walking side by side,
And gave ye no supremacy : I stand
Upon my strength — I do defy — deny — 120
Spurn back, and scorn ye ! —
    SPIRIT.   But thy many crimes
Have made thee —
    MAN.   What are they to such as thee ?
Must crimes be punished but by other
    crimes,
And greater criminals ? — Back to thy hell !
Thou hast no power upon me, *that* I feel ;
Thou never shalt possess me, *that* I know :
What I have done is done ; I bear within
A torture which could nothing gain from
    thine :
The mind which is immortal makes itself
Requital for its good or evil thoughts, — 130
Is its own origin of ill and end
And its own place and time ; its innate
    sense,

When stripped of this mortality, derives
No color from the fleeting things without,
But is absorbed in sufferance or in joy,
Born from the knowledge of its own
    desert.
Thou didst not tempt me, and thou couldst
    not tempt me ;
I have not been thy dupe, nor am thy
    prey —
But was my own destroyer, and will be
My own hereafter. — Back, ye baffled
    fiends ! —   140
The hand of death is on me — but not
    yours.

[*The* DEMONS *disappear.*]

ABBOT. Alas ! how pale thou art — thy
    lips are white —
And thy breast heaves — and in thy gasp-
    ing throat
The accents rattle : Give thy prayers to
    heaven —
Pray — albeit but in thought, — but die
    not thus.
    MAN. 'Tis over — my dull eyes can fix
    thee not ;
But all things swim around me, and the
    earth
Heaves as it were beneath me. Fare thee
    well !
Give me thy hand.
    ABBOT.   Cold — cold — even to the
    heart —
But yet one prayer — Alas ! how fares it
    with thee ?   150
    MAN. Old man ! 'tis not so difficult to
    die.

[MANFRED *expires.*]

ABBOT. He's gone — his soul hath ta'en
    its earthless flight ;
Whither ? I dread to think — but he is
    gone.

1816–17 (1817)

4

PERCY BYSSHE SHELLEY'S *THE CENCI*

Condemned as unactable, too horrible, too derivative from the Elizabethans—especially Shakespeare, structurally deficient, and, by F. R. Leavis, as simply "very bad," Shelley's *The Cenci* is nevertheless a compelling and enduring drama. Its validity as drama has been continually verified by favorable audience reactions since its first, private performance in 1886.[1] A successful three-month series of performances at Old Vic in 1959 established its credentials in a way in which no radio production or college performance had previously achieved. The only work by Shelley to be published in a second edition during his lifetime, *The Cenci* received high praise from his contemporaries. Wordsworth called it "the greatest tragedy of the age"; Byron thought it "perhaps the best tragedy modern times have produced," and thought it "a play,—not a poem." Leigh Hunt, to whom it is dedicated, was characteristically ecstatic, unlike his young friend John Keats, who advised Shelley to "curb your magnanimity, and be more of an artist, and load every rift of your subject with ore." This criticism must have particularly stung Shelley, who is quoted by Mary as saying "I have been cautious to avoid introducing the faults of youthful composition: diffuseness, a profusion of inapplicable imagery, vagueness, generality, and, as Hamlet says, *words, words.*"

Shelley's attempt to present in dramatic form, and in "the real language of men in general," a story he was certain would appeal to the "multitude" must be conceded the most successful of such attempts made by the chief Romantic poets. Despite the success of Coleridge's *Remorse* on the stage at the time of its composition, its subsequent history has not shown a sustained interest either by theater groups or by students of the period. *The Cenci* is a major part of the Shelley canon in a way that *Remorse* is not of Coleridge's.

The merits of *The Cenci* as a stage play have been argued extensively during this century, but Shaw's 1886 comments[2] maintain a significance that transcends questions of taste and opinions about theatricality. Shaw, thinking the play "at one or two points unendurably horrible," found it "a failure in the sense in which we call an experiment with negative results a failure." But he immediately continued by stating that "the powers called forth by it were so extraordinary that many generations of audiences will probably submit to have the experiment repeated on them, in spite of the incidental tedium."

Those who find structural flaws in the drama are no less correct in their

1. For details of performances and critical reception see K. N. Cameron and Horst Frenz, "The Stage History of Shelley's *The Cenci*," *PMLA* 60 (1945): 1080–1105; Bert O. States, Jr., "Addendum: The Stage History of Shelley's *The Cenci*," *PMLA* 72 (1957): 633–44; and Marcel Kessel and Bert O. States, Jr., "*The Cenci* as a Stage Play," *PMLA* 75 (1960): 147–49.

2. Quoted by States, *PMLA* 75 (1960): 148.

analyses because of the play's continuing success. The sudden and unexplained entrance of Savella with the Pope's warrant for Cenci is undoubtedly contrived and melodramatic; Desmond King-Hele may be correct in thinking that Shelley "dithers in Act II";[3] Ellsworth Barnard's belief that "after the Count's death the reader almost feels that he is beginning a new play"[4] may be equally correct. Barnard also objects to the opening scene of Act V which, like most of Act II, scene ii, he finds "one of the great weaknesses of the play: because of Shelley's interest in psychological analysis, he allows the main action to lag while two relatively unimportant characters (Orsino and Giacomo) reveal themselves in conversation."[5]

Yet the power of which Shaw wrote triumphs over these defects. Some of this power may reside in the story itself. Though some agree with Woodberry that "Cenci's motive is hate rather than lust; his aim is to win his daughter's consent and thereby destroy her soul,"[6] the incest theme, with all its archetypal resonance, must still account for much of the continuing success of the drama. Shelley, in his excellent Preface, describes how "this national and universal interest which the story produces and has produced for two centuries and among all ranks of people in a great city, where the imagination is kept forever active and awake, first suggested to me the conception of its fitness for a dramatic purpose." And though the incest theme is handled delicately, as Shelley intended, and is not invested with the symbolic significance it bears in Byron's *Manfred*, it undoubtedly accounts for many of the hostile reactions to the play.

But Shelley's intention was not merely to dramatize a gothic tale of incest and murder; he intended to tell the story so as "to make apparent some of the most dark and secret caverns of the human heart." In "A Defense of Poetry" Shelley asserts that "a man, to be greatly good, must imagine intensely and comprehensively; he must put himself in the place of another and of many others; the pains and pleasures of his species must become his own."

Commentators have long assumed that the flawed but profoundly fascinating hearts of the Count and his daughter were the hearts Shelley was attempting to illuminate, and there has been much valuable discussion of their characters. But I believe that Shelley's goal was a more comprehensive one: that his concern was with those secret places in all our hearts where we attempt to forge emotionally and logically acceptable links between the inner and outer worlds of reality. This larger theme, the object of much of Shelley's attention in the drama, is best seen in precisely those characters and scenes which critics have felt to be obstacles to the dramatic success of the play. By demonstrating their importance to the drama we may seem to be strengthening the argument of those who insist that *The Cenci* is most profitably considered, and most successful as, a closet-drama. Yet, if the importance of these characters and scenes is understood, we may be able to endure them on the stage with less of what Shaw called "incidental tedium," and the play itself may become less "temporarily fatiguing to witness."

As Savella says,

> Strange thoughts beget strange deeds; and here are both;
> I judge thee not.
>
> IV.iv.139–40

In these lines lies concealed much of the thematic content of this play. Savella's response to Beatrice's admission—that she desired her father's death, that it had

---

3. Desmond King-Hele, *Shelley: The Man and The Poet* (New York, 1960), p. 127.
4. Ellsworth Barnard, ed., *Shelley: Selected Poems, Essays, and Letters* (New York, 1944), p. 248.
5. *Ibid.*, p. 253.
6. *Ibid.*, p. 237, where Barnard cites G. S. Woodberry's comments in the Centenary Edition.

occurred as strangely and as suddenly as she had believed (hoped, prayed, and knew), and that, it being accomplished, she was given rest on earth and hope in heaven—also posits an attitude for us to adopt toward her actions. Unlike the inquisitorial court before which Beatrice defends herself, posterity struggles to understand, not to judge, the strange thoughts and strange deeds which led her there.

It is with the connections between thoughts and deeds, the relationships between appearance and reality, that *The Cenci* is concerned. Those characters to whom words are the moral equivalents of deeds; who tease their thoughts into action; to whom their reputation, their "fame," is as important as the knowledge of their own motivations; who, unlike Cenci, are not *hardened* to the point where the intensity and apparent moral ugliness of their own conceptions do not inhibit action or provoke remorse—those characters are the centers of interest in this play.

Like so many other great literary achievements of the English Romantics, *The Cenci* explores the delicate and tenuous bonds of the inner life with quotidian reality. Familiar Shelleyean and Romantic themes abound in the play, including an exploration of the relationships between the oppressor and the oppressed, the tyranny of organized religion, of the state and of the parent, and the assertion of the primacy of the truth of one's own perceptions over those of collective or conventional wisdom. More importantly, this play examines the ways in which we mortals, frustrated by our inability fully to understand, analyze, justify, or rationalize our conflicting motives and desires—and fully understanding that the *feeling* of our personal situations can never adequately be communicated to, or understood by, others—act in ways which we hope will bring us relief from intolerable pressures without bringing the world to judgment or punishment.

Act II, scene ii begins to weave together the many strands of this theme. As "scorpions ringed with fire," Giacomo tells Orsino that if he or Beatrice should act against the brutal tyrannies inflicted upon them by Cenci, they would

> but strike ourselves to death
> For he who is our murderous persecutor
> Is shielded by a father's holy name.
> II.ii.70, 71–73

The world, and especially the Pope, to whom paternal power is the shadow of his own, values and gives credence to what should be, rather than what is; we assume that fathers possess the paternal virtues of wisdom, tolerance, gentleness, and so on—especially when such assumptions fill our treasuries.

Were it not for this shield, Giacomo would—would act, but he cannot say precisely what he would do. Orsino, in a fine ironic summary of the roles he and others will enact in this drama, says:

> What? Fear not to speak your thought.
> Words are but holy as the deeds they cover;
> A priest who has forsworn the God he serves,
> A judge who makes Truth weep at his decree,
> A friend who should weave counsel, as I now,
> But as the mantle of some selfish guile,
> A father who is all a tyrant seems,—
> Were the profaner for his sacred name.
> II.ii.74–81

Giacomo's response describes his struggle to conceal from himself and from others the awful power and significance of his less-than-conscious wishes. He describes how he is afraid to put into words or in any way to frame precisely his repressed desires, lest he be tempted to action or forced to recognize that part of his personality he is trying to keep out of the light.

> Ask me not what I think; the unwilling brain
> Feigns often what it would not; and we trust
> Imagination with such fantasies
> As the tongue dares not fashion into words—
> Which have no words, their horror makes them dim
> To the mind's eye. My heart denies itself
> To think what you demand.
>
> II.ii.82–88

It is not only Giacomo who is paralyzed by self-analysis; earlier, Cenci has needed wine to bolster a sagging intention:

> I would not drink this evening, but I must;
> For, strange to say, I feel my spirits fail
> With thinking what I have decreed to do.
>
> I.iii.170–72

Orsino hopes to benefit from his knowledge of the family tendency to self-scrutiny, for he has found that thinking "unthinkable" thoughts leads to acting them out.

>   'tis a trick of this same family
> To analyze their own and other minds.
> Such self-anatomy shall teach the will
> Dangerous secrets; for it tempts our powers,
> Knowing what must be thought, and may be done,
> Into the depth of darkest purposes.
> So Cenci fell into the pit; even I
> Since Beatrice unveiled me to myself,
> And made me shrink from what I cannot shun,
> Show a poor figure to my own esteem,
> To which I grow half-reconciled.
>
> II.ii.108–18

In Act III, Beatrice, half mad from what has befallen her, speaks the truth that

> Horrible things have been in this wild world,
> Prodigious mixtures, and confusions strange
> Of good and ill; and worse have been conceived
> Than ever there was found a heart to do.
> But never fancy imaged such a deed
> As—
>
> III.i.51–56

And, having recovered her balance, Beatrice tells her mother that she is not concealing her sufferings, but rather they are so remote from "all words / That minister to mortal intercourse" (III.i.111–12) that they are nameless. Beatrice is unable even to feign an image in her mind of the deeds that have transformed her. To Orsino she reiterates that "there are deeds / Which have no form, sufferings which have no tongue" (III.i.141–42). There is no word that will be therapeutic and will convince the world that she herself is blameless.

The power and the powerlessness of words continue to paralyze Giacomo:

> That word, parricide,
> Although I am resolved, haunts me like fear.
>
> III.i.340–41

But Orsino cleverly retorts that

> It must be fear itself, for the bare word
> Is hollow mockery.
>
> III.i.342–43

Cenci's speech cursing Beatrice points up the accuracy of Orsino's observation about the psychology of the Cenci family. Not only does the Count comment on the power of public scorn, but he argues that such scorn often seems to us justified because it is a recognition of the secret longings we have labored to repress from consciousness and action. Still, he is unable to name his offence against his daughter.

> She shall stand shelterless in the broad noon
> Of public scorn, for acts blazoned abroad,
> One among which shall be—what? canst thou guess?
> She shall become (for what she most abhors
> Shall have a fascination to entrap
> Her loathing will) to her own conscious self
> All she appears to others . . .
> Her name shall be the terror of the earth.
>
> IV.i.82–88, 92

Giacomo too confirms Orsino's analysis and rationalizes in an attempt to absolve himself of some blame. But Orsino is not prepared to see himself as a catalyst, though he has earlier said he would do "as little mischief as I can" in order to "fee the accuser conscience" (II.ii.119–20). Orsino describes how we disguise our fear of shame as remorse. Giacomo's guilt revealed will occasion retribution; the peril he is in occasions his remorse—not for what he has done, but as an emotion which will conceal the shame of having been discovered and exposed to punishment.

> Giacomo: Oh had I never
> Found in thy smooth and ready countenance
> The mirror of my darkest thoughts; hadst thou
> Never with hints and questions made me look
> Upon the monster of my thought, until
> It grew familiar to desire—
> Orsino: 'Tis thus
> Men cast the blame of their unprosperous acts
> Upon the abettors of their own resolve;
> Or anything but their weak, guilty selves.
> And yet, confess the truth, it is the peril
> In which you stand that gives you this pale sickness
> Of penitance; confess 'tis fear disguised
> From its own shame that takes the mantle now
> Of thin remorse. What if we yet were safe?
>
> V.i.19–32

When Orsino, having betrayed Giacomo, prepares his departure, he again soliloquizes on these themes we have been tracing. He is aware that most of us assume a correspondence between the clothes and the man, the name (father, Pope) and the character of the person. Beatrice has earlier spoken of a name as "the life of life" (IV.iv.142); she continues her plea to Savella reminding him of the importance and potency of public esteem:

> the breath
> Of accusation kills an innocent name,
> And leaves for lame acquittal the poor life
> Which is a mask without it.
> IV.iv.142–45

Orsino, hearing the crowd shout his name, resolves to escape by disguising himself. As he imagines the life he will lead in a new home, he recognizes that he cannot escape self-reproach. After attempting to argue himself out of his fear of mere words, he departs with the knowledge we all bear: that what we can perhaps conceal from others we cannot hide from ourselves.

> But I will pass, wrapped in a vile disguise,
> Rags on my back and a false innocence
> Upon my face, through the misdeeming crowd
> Which judges by what seems. 'Tis easy then
> For a new name and for a country new,
> And a new life fashioned on old desires,
> To change the honors of abandoned Rome.
> And these must be the masks of that within,
> Which must remain unaltered.—Oh, I fear
> That what is past will never let me rest!
> Why, when none else is conscious, but myself,
> Of my misdeeds, should my own heart's contempt
> Trouble me? Have I not the power to fly
> My own reproaches? Shall I be the slave
> Of—what? A word? which those of this false world
> Employ against each other, not themselves,
> As men wear daggers not for self-offence
> But if I am mistaken, where shall I
> Find the disguise to hide me from myself,
> As now I skulk from every other eye?
> V.ii.85–104

It is appropriate that we see no more of Orsino. The ambivalence in which he is left is fully consonant with the doubts he has raised, within the other characters and within us, about the mind's ability to dupe itself. His anatomizing of his own and others' psychology has revealed many complexities; it has explored the shadowy realms of word and deed and has helped us define and feel the prison of personality. This in itself is no mean dramatic achievement.

The themes uncovered and explored through Orsino continue to occupy us after his departure. In Beatrice's long speech to Marzio, the speech that leads him to recant his accusation, she reminds him that "worse than a bloody hand is a hard heart" (V.ii.133), and she tells him he will have to confess to his Maker that with his words he killed her who endured

> what never any
> Guilty or innocent, endured before,
> Because her wrongs could not be told or thought.
> V.ii.139–41

Beatrice, who describes man as

> Cruel, cold, formal man; righteous in words
> In deeds a Cain . . .
>
> V.iv.108–9

knows that it is her brow and her brother's innocent brow that will be stamped with the mark of Cain.

Perhaps because of this knowledge, her heart has become cold to the consolations of religion proffered by her mother. Beatrice, who will lose "light, and life, and love in youth's sweet prime" (V.iv.86) has been hardened by the world, much in the way that Cenci claimed to Camillo that he was hardened because his excesses caused him no misery, and in the way that Giacomo believed he could harden himself against remorse (III.ii.46). Beatrice is able to awaken Marzio to the higher truth of her innocence, although now that she is hardened, martyrdom offers her no solace. At the end, her highmindedness deserts her, leading many commentators to assert that she is not the same Beatrice we encounter in the first four acts.

Yet her love of life needs to be understood in conjunction with the justification of the higher morality to which she pledges devotion. This union of mundane and supra-terrestrial motives should not surprise a reader who has been sensitive to the struggle between inner and outer perceptions of reality that has dominated the play. Man's tangled motives, his repressions, his superstitions about the magical power of words and wishes: this thicket of personality is Shelley's great theme in *The Cenci*.[7] Cenci, Beatrice, Orsino, and the reader have had a steady look at the demons, which, as Paul West says of Byron's plays, heals better than any exorcizing homily.[8] Beatrice is not so much a Cain as an unreconstructed Prometheus. We are asked not to judge her but to understand her, as Savella's brief lines tell us. That such was Shelley's intent is clear from the prefatory comment partially quoted earlier.

> Such a story, if told so as to present to the reader all the feelings of those who once acted it, their hopes and fears, their confidences and misgivings, their various interests, passions and opinions, acting upon and with each other yet all conspiring to one tremendous end, would be as a light to make apparent some of the most dark and secret caverns of the human heart.

I believe Shelley has been successful in this attempt, and I believe he was successful in his endeavor "as nearly as possible to represent the characters as they probably were." He has avoided actuating them by his own "conceptions of right and wrong, false and true," a hope expressed in his Preface, and has, I believe, achieved the purpose so eloquently stated there:

> The highest moral purpose aimed at in the highest species of the drama is the teaching the human heart, through its sympathies and antipathies, the knowledge of itself.

G.B.K.

---

7. Milton Wilson, in *Shelley's Later Poetry* (New York, 1959), pp. 78–92, finds that Shelley's theme is the "centripetal pressures of the ingrown soul," and does a splendid job of relating *The Cenci* to the themes of self-love and self-contempt as they exist in other works in Shelley's canon. Professor Wilson analyzes many of the same passages as are discussed above, but his aims and conclusions are generally different from mine.

8. See above, p. 104.

Other studies of importance are that by Carlos Barker, which carefully analyzes characterization, and that of James Rieger, which explores the theological implications of the drama.

The Cenci

A TRAGEDY IN FIVE ACTS

PREFACE

A manuscript was communicated to me during my travels in Italy, which was copied from the archives of the Cenci Palace at Rome, and contains a detailed account of the horrors which ended in the extinction of one of the noblest and richest families of that city, during the Pontificate of Clement VIII, in the year 1599. The story is, that an old man, having spent his life in debauchery and wickedness, conceived at length an implacable hatred towards his children; which showed itself towards one daughter under the form of an incestuous passion, aggravated by every circumstance of cruelty and violence. This daughter, after long and vain attempts to escape from what she considered a perpetual contamination both of body and mind, at length plotted with her mother-in-law and brother to murder their common tyrant. The young maiden, who was urged to this tremendous deed by an impulse which overpowered its horror, was evidently a most gentle and amiable being, a creature formed to adorn and be admired, and thus violently thwarted from her nature by the necessity of circumstance and opinion. The deed was quickly discovered, and in spite of the most earnest prayers made to the Pope by the highest persons in Rome, the criminals were put to death. The old man had, during his life, repeatedly bought his pardon from the Pope for capital crimes of the most enormous and unspeakable kind, at the price of a hundred thousand crowns; the death therefore of his victims can scarcely be accounted for by the love

of justice. The Pope, among other motives for severity, probably felt that whoever killed the Count Cenci deprived his treasury of a certain and copious source of revenue. Such a story, if told so as to present to the reader all the feelings of those who once acted it, their hopes and fears, their confidences and misgivings, their various interests, passions, and opinions, acting upon and with each other, yet all conspiring to one tremendous end, would be as a light to make apparent some of the most dark and secret caverns of the human heart.

On my arrival at Rome, I found that the story of the Cenci was a subject not to be mentioned in Italian society without awakening a deep and breathless interest; and that the feelings of the company never failed to incline to a romantic pity for the wrongs, and a passionate exculpation of the horrible deed to which they urged her, who has been mingled two centuries with the common dust. All ranks of people knew the outlines of this history, and participated in the overwhelming interest which it seems to have the magic of exciting in the human heart. I had a copy of Guido's picture of Beatrice which is preserved in the Colonna Palace, and my servant instantly recognized it as the portrait of *La Cenci*.

This national and universal interest which the story produces and has produced for two centuries, and among all ranks of people in a great City, where the imagination is kept for ever active and awake, first suggested to me the conception of its fitness for a dramatic purpose. In fact it is a tragedy which has already received, from its capacity of awakening and sustaining the sympathy of men, approbation and success. Nothing remained, as I imagined, but to clothe it to the apprehensions of my countrymen in such language and action as would bring it home to their hearts. The deepest and the sublimest tragic compositions, *King Lear,* and the two plays in which the tale of Œdipus is told, were stories which already existed in tradition, as matters of popular belief and interest, before Shakespeare and Sophocles made them familiar to the sympathy of all succeeding generations of mankind.

This story of the Cenci is indeed eminently fearful and monstrous: anything like a dry exhibition of it on the stage would be insupportable. The person who would treat such a subject must increase the ideal, and diminish the actual horror of the events, so that the pleasure which arises from the poetry which exists in these tempestuous sufferings and crimes, may mitigate the pain of the contemplation of the moral deformity from which they spring. There must also be nothing attempted to make the exhibition subservient to what is vulgarly termed a moral purpose. The highest moral purpose aimed at in the highest species of the drama, is the teaching the human heart, through its sympathies and antipathies, the knowledge of itself; in proportion to the possession of which knowledge, every human being is wise, just, sincere, tolerant, and kind. If dogmas can do more, it is well: but a drama is no fit place for the enforcement of them. Undoubtedly no person can be truly dishonoured by the act of another; and the fit return to make to the most enormous injuries is kindness and forbearance, and a resolution to convert the injurer from his dark passions by peace and love. Revenge, retaliation, atonement, are pernicious mistakes. If Beatrice had thought in this manner she would have been wiser and better; but she would never have been a tragic character: the few whom such an exhibition would have interested, could never have been sufficiently interested for a dramatic purpose, from the want of finding sympathy in their interest among the mass who surround them. It is in the restless and anatomising casuistry with which men seek the justification of Beatrice, yet feel that she has done what needs justification; it is in the superstitious horror with which they contemplate alike her wrongs and their revenge, that the dramatic character of what she did and suffered, consists.

I have endeavoured as nearly as possible to represent the characters as they probably were, and have sought to avoid the error of making them actuated by my own conceptions of right or wrong, false or true: thus under a thin veil converting names and actions of the sixteenth century into cold impersonations of my own mind. They are represented as Catholics, and as Catholics deeply tinged with religion. To a Protestant apprehension there will appear something unnatural in the earnest and perpetual sentiment of the relations between God and man which pervade the tragedy of the Cenci. It will especially be startled at the combination of an undoubting persuasion of the truth of the popular religion with a cool and determined perseverance in enormous guilt. But religion in Italy is not, as in Protestant countries, a cloak to be worn on particular days; or a passport which those who do not wish to be railed at carry with them to exhibit; or a gloomy passion for penetrating the impenetrable mysteries of our being, which terrifies its possessor at the darkness of the abyss to the brink of which it has conducted him. Religion coexists, as it were, in the mind of an Italian Catholic, with a faith in that of which all men have the most certain knowledge. It is interwoven with the whole fabric of life. It is adoration, faith, submission, penitence, blind admiration; not a rule for moral conduct. It has no necessary connexion with any one virtue. The most atrocious villain may be rigidly devout, and, without any shock to established faith, confess himself to be so. Religion pervades intensely the whole frame of society, and is, according to the temper of the mind which it inhabits, a passion, a persuasion, an excuse, a refuge; never a check. Cenci himself built a chapel in the court of his palace, and dedicated it to St. Thomas the Apostle, and established masses for the peace of his soul. Thus in the first scene of the fourth act Lucretia's design in exposing herself to the consequences of an expostulation with Cenci after having administered the opiate, was to induce him by a feigned tale to confess himself before death; this being esteemed by Catholics as essential to salvation; and she only relinquishes her purpose when she perceives that her perseverance would expose Beatrice to new outrages.

I have avoided with great care in writing this play the introduction of what is commonly called mere poetry, and I imagine there will scarcely be found a detached simile or a single isolated description, unless Beatrice's description of the chasm appointed for her father's murder should be judged to be of that nature.

In a dramatic composition the imagery and the passion should interpenetrate one another, the former being reserved simply for the full development and illustration of the latter. Imagination is as the immortal God which should assume flesh for the redemption of mortal passion. It is thus that the most remote and the most familiar imagery may alike be fit for dramatic purposes when employed in the illustration of strong feeling, which raises what is low, and levels to the apprehension that which is lofty, casting over all the shadow of its own greatness. In other respects I have written more carelessly; that is, without an over-fastidious and learned choice of words. In this respect, I entirely agree with those modern critics who assert that in order to move men to true sympathy we must use the familiar language of men, and that our great ancestors the ancient English poets are the writers, a study of whom might incite us to do that for our own age which they have done for theirs. But it must be the real language of men in general, and not that of any particular class to whose society the writer happens to belong. So much for what I have attempted; I need not be assured that success is a very different matter; particularly for one whose attention has but newly been awakened to the study of dramatic literature.

I endeavoured whilst at Rome to observe such monuments of this story as might be accessible to a stranger. The portrait of Beatrice at the Colonna Palace is admirable as a work of art: it was taken by Guido during her confinement in prison. But it is most interesting as a just representation of one of the loveliest specimens of the workmanship of Nature. There is a fixed and pale composure upon the features: she seems sad and stricken down in spirit, yet the despair thus expressed is lightened by the patience of gentleness. Her head is bound with folds of white drapery, from which the yellow strings of her golden hair escape, and fall about her neck. The moulding of her face is exquisitely delicate; the eye-brows are distinct and arched: the lips have that permanent meaning of imagination and sensibility which suffering has not repressed and which it seems as if death scarcely could extinguish. Her forehead is large and clear; her eyes, which we are told were remarkable for their vivacity, are swollen with weeping and lustreless, but beautifully tender and serene. In the whole mien there is a simplicity and dignity which united with her exquisite loveliness and deep sorrow are inexpressibly pathetic. Beatrice Cenci appears to have been one of those rare persons in whom energy and gentleness dwell together without destroying one another: her nature was simple and profound. The crimes and miseries in which she was an actor and a sufferer are as the mask and the mantle in which circumstances clothed her for her impersonation on the scene of the world.

The Cenci Palace is of great extent; and, though in part modernized, there yet remains a vast and gloomy pile of feudal architecture in the same state as during the dreadful scenes which are the subject of this tragedy. The palace is situated in an obscure corner of Rome, near the quarter of the Jews, and from the upper windows you see the immense ruins of Mount Palatine half hidden under their profuse overgrowth of trees. There is a court in one part of the palace (perhaps that in which Cenci built the chapel to St. Thomas), supported by granite columns and adorned with antique friezes of fine workmanship, and built up, according to the ancient Italian fashion, with balcony over balcony of open work. One of the gates of the palace, formed of immense stones, and leading through a passage dark and lofty, and opening into gloomy subterranean chambers, struck me particularly.

Of the Castle of Petrella, I could obtain no further information than that which is to be found in the manuscript.

The Cenci

DRAMATIS PERSONÆ

COUNT FRANCESCO CENCI
GIACOMO, ⎫
BERNARDO, ⎬ *his Sons*
CARDINAL CAMILLO

PRINCE COLONNA
ORSINO, *a Prelate*
SAVELLA, *the Pope's Legate*
OLIMPIO, ⎫
MARZIO, ⎭ *Assassins*
ANDREA, *Servant to Cenci*
Nobles, Judges, Guards, Servants
LUCRETIA, *Wife of* CENCI, *and step-mother
  of his children*
BEATRICE, *his Daughter*

The SCENE *lies principally in Rome, but
changes during the Fourth Act to Petrella,
a castle among the Apulian Apennines.*

TIME. *During the Pontificate of
    Clement VIII.*

ACT I

SCENE I.—*An Apartment in the* CENCI
  Palace. Enter COUNT CENCI, *and*
            CARDINAL CAMILLO.

Camillo. That matter of the murder is
    hushed up
If you consent to yield his Holiness
Your fief that lies beyond the Pincian gate.
It needed all my interest in the conclave
To bend him to this point : he said that
    you
Bought perilous impunity with your gold ;
That crimes like yours if once or twice
    compounded
Enriched the Church, and respited from
    hell
An erring soul which might repent and
    live ;
But that the glory and the interest   10
Of the high throne he fills, little consist
With making it a daily mart of guilt
As manifold and hideous as the deeds
Which you scarce hide from men's re-
    volted eyes.
    Cenci. The third of my possessions —let
    it go !
Ay, I once heard the nephew of the Pope
Had sent his architect to view the ground,
Meaning to build a villa on my vines
The next time I compounded with his
    uncle :
I little thought he should outwit me so ! 20
Henceforth no witness — not the lamp —
    shall see
That which the vassal threatened to di-
    vulge,
Whose throat is choked with dust for his
    reward

The deed he saw could not have rated
    higher
Than his most worthless life : — it angers
    me !
Respited me from Hell ! — So may the
    Devil
Respite their souls from Heaven. No
    doubt Pope Clement,
And his most charitable nephews, pray
That the Apostle Peter and the saints
Will grant for their sake that I long en-
    joy   30
Strength, wealth, and pride, and lust, and
    length of days
Wherein to act the deeds which are the
    stewards
Of their revenue. — But much yet remains
To which they show no title.
    Camillo.   Oh, Count Cenci !
So much that thou mightst honourably live
And reconcile thyself with thine own heart
And with thy God, and with the offended
    world.
How hideously looks deeds of lust and
    blood
Through those snow white and venerable
    hairs !
Your children should be sitting round you
    now,   40
But that you fear to read upon their
    looks
The shame and misery you have written
    there.
Where is your wife ? Where is your gentle
    daughter ?
Methinks her sweet looks, which make all
    things else
Beauteous and glad, might kill the fiend
    within you.
Why is she barred from all society
But her own strange and uncomplaining
    wrongs ?
Talk with me, Count, — you know I mean
    you well.
I stood beside your dark and fiery youth
Watching its bold and bad career, as
    men   50
Watch meteors, but it vanished not : I
    marked
Your desperate and remorseless manhood ;
    now
Do I behold you, in dishonoured age,
Charged with a thousand unrepented
    crimes.
Yet I have ever hoped you would amend,
And in that hope have saved your life
    three times.
    Cenci. For which Aldobrandino owes
    you now

My fief beyond the Pincian. Cardinal,
One thing, I pray you, recollect henceforth,
And so we shall converse with less restraint.   60
A man you knew spoke of my wife and daughter :
He was accustomed to frequent my house ;
So the next day *his* wife and daughter came
And asked if I had seen him ; and I smiled :
I think they never saw him any more.
     Camillo. Thou execrable man, beware ! —
     Cenci.   Of thee ?
Nay this is idle : We should know each other.
As to my character for what men call crime,
Seeing I please my senses as I list,
And vindicate that right with force or guile,   70
It is a public matter, and I care not
If I discuss it with you. I may speak
Alike to you and my own conscious heart ;
For you give out that you have half reformed me,
Therefore strong vanity will keep you silent
If fear should not ; both will, I do not doubt.
All men delight in sensual luxury,
All men enjoy revenge ; and most exult
Over the tortures they can never feel ;
Flattering their secret peace with others' pain.   80
But I delight in nothing else. I love
The sight of agony, and the sense of joy,
When this shall be another's, and that mine.
And I have no remorse, and little fear,
Which are, I think, the checks of other men.
This mood has grown upon me, until now
Any design my captious fancy makes
The picture of its wish, and it forms none
But such as men like you would start to know,
Is as my natural food and rest debarred ⁹⁰
Until it be accomplished.
     Camillo.   Art thou not
Most miserable ?
     Cenci.   Why miserable ? —
No. I am what your theologians call
Hardened ; which they must be in impudence,
So to revile a man's peculiar taste.
True, I was happier than I am, while yet

Manhood remained to act the thing I thought ;
While lust was sweeter than revenge ; and now
Invention palls : ay, we must all grow old :
And but that there yet remains a deed to act   100
Whose horror might make sharp an appetite
Duller than mine — I'd do — I know not what.
When I was young I thought of nothing else
But pleasure ; and I fed on honey sweets :
Men, by St. Thomas ! cannot live like bees,
And I grew tired : yet, till I killed a foe,
And heard his groans, and heard his children's groans,
Knew I not what delight was else on earth,
Which now delights me little. I the rather
Look on such pangs as terror ill conceals,   110
The dry, fixed eye-ball ; the pale, quivering lip,
Which tell me that the spirit weeps within
Tears bitterer than the bloody sweat of Christ.
I rarely kill the body, which preserves,
Like a strong prison, the soul within my power,
Wherein I feed it with the breath of fear
For hourly pain.
     Camillo   Hell's most abandoned fiend
Did never, in the drunkenness of guilt,
Speak to his heart as now you speak to me ;
I thank my God that I believe you not. ¹²⁰
[*Enter* ANDREA.]
     Andrea. My Lord, a gentleman from Salamanca
Would speak with you.
     Cenci.   Bid him attend me in
The grand saloon.
                         [*Exit* ANDREA.]
     Camillo.   Farewell ; and I will pray
Almighty God that thy false, impious words
Tempt not his spirit to abandon thee.

                         [*Exit* CAMILLO.]
     Cenci. The third of my possessions ! I must use
Close husbandry, or gold, the old man's sword,
Falls from my withered hand. But yesterday
There came an order from the Pope to make
Fourfold provision for my cursed sons ; ¹³⁰

Whom I had sent from Rome to Sala-
    manca,
Hoping some accident might cut them off ;
And meaning, if I could, to starve them
    there.
I pray thee, God, send some quick death
    upon them !
Bernardo and my wife could not be worse
If dead and damned : then, as to Bea-
    trice —
        [*Looking around him suspiciously.*]
I think they cannot hear me at that door ;
What if they should ? And yet I need not
    speak
Though the heart triumphs with itself in
    words.
O, thou most silent air, that shalt not
    hear   140
What now I think ! Thou, pavement,
    which I tread
Towards her chamber, — let your echoes
    talk
Of my imperious step, scorning surprise,
But not of my intent ! — Andrea !
[*Enter* ANDREA.]
    Andrea   My lord !
    Cenci. Bid Beatrice attend me in her
    chamber
This evening : — no, at midnight, and
    alone.   [*Exeunt.*]

SCENE 2. — *A Garden of the Cenci Palace.
Enter* BEATRICE *and* ORSINO, *as in conversation.*

    Beatrice. Pervert not truth,
Orsino. You remember where we held
That conversation ;— nay, we see the spot
Even from this cypress ; — two long years
    are past
Since, on an April midnight, underneath
The moon-light ruins of Mount Palatine,
I did confess to you my secret mind.
    Orsino. You said you loved me then.
    Beatrice.   You are a priest :
Speak to me not of love.
    Orsino.   I may obtain
The dispensation of the Pope to marry. 10
Because I am a priest do you believe
Your image, as the hunter some struck
    deer,
Follows me not whether I wake or sleep ?
    Beatrice. As I have said, speak to me
    not of love ;
Had you a dispensation I have not ;
Nor will I leave this home of misery
Whilst my poor Bernard, and that gentle
    lady
To whom I owe life and these virtuous

thoughts,
Must suffer what I still have strength to
    share.
Alas, Orsino ! All the love that once   20
I felt for you, is turned to bitter pain.
Ours was a youthful contract, which you
    first
Broke, by assuming vows no Pope will
    loose.
And thus I love you still, but holily,
Even as a sister or a spirit might;
And so I swear a cold fidelity.
And it is well perhaps we shall not marry.
You have a sly, equivocating vein
That suits me not. Ah, wretched that I
    am !
Where shall I turn ? Even now you look
    on me   30
As you were not my friend, and as if you
Discovered that I thought so, with false
    smiles
Making my true suspicion seem your
    wrong.
Ah ! No, forgive me ; sorrow makes me
    seem
Sterner than else my nature might have
    been ;
I have a weight of melancholy thoughts,
And they forbode, — but what can they
    forbode
Worse than I now endure ?
    Orsino.   All will be well.
Is the petition yet prepared ? You know
My zeal for all you wish, sweet Bea-
    trice ;   40
Doubt not but I will use my utmost skill
So that the Pope attend to your complaint.
    Beatrice. Your zeal for all I wish ? Ah
    me, you are cold !
Your utmost skill — speak but one word —
    (aside) Alas !
Weak and deserted creature that I am,
Here I stand bickering with my only
    friend !   [*To* ORSINO.]
This night my father gives a sumptuous
    feast,
Orsino ; he has heard some happy news
From Salamanca, from my brothers there,
And with this outward shew of love he
    mocks   50
His inward hate. 'Tis bold hypocrisy,
For he would gladlier celebrate their
    deaths,
Which I have heard him pray for on his
    knees :
Great God : that such a father should be
    mine !
But there is mighty preparation made,
And all our kin, the Cenci, will be there,

And all the chief nobility of Rome.
And he has bidden me and my pale
    mother
Attire ourselves in festival array.
Poor lady! She expects some happy
    change   60
In his dark spirit from this act; I none.
At supper I will give you the petition:
Till when — farewell.
 Orsino.   Farewell
       [*Exit* BEATRICE.]
I know the Pope
Will ne'er absolve me from my priestly
    vow
But by absolving me from the revenue
Of many a wealthy see; and, Beatrice,
I think to win thee at an easier rate.
Nor shall he read her eloquent petition:
He might bestow her on some poor re-
    lation   70
Of his sixth cousin, as he did her sister,
And I should be debarred from all access.
Then as to what she suffers from her
    father,
In all this there is much exaggeration:
Old men are testy and will have their
    way;
A man may stab his enemy, or his vassal,
And live a free life as to wine or women,
And with a peevish temper may return
To a dull home, and rate his wife and
    children;
Daughters and wives call this foul tyr-
    anny.   80
I shall be well content if on my conscience
There rest no heavier sin than what they
    suffer
From the devices of my love — A net
From which she shall escape not. Yet I
    fear
Her subtle mind, her awe-inspiring gaze,
Whose beams anatomize me, nerve by
    nerve,
And lay me bare, and make me blush to
    see
My hidden thoughts. — Ah, not a friend-
    less girl
Who clings to me, as to her only hope: —
I were a fool, not less than if a panther 90
Were panic-stricken by the antelope's eye,
If she escapes me.   [*Exit.*]

SCENE 3. — *A Magnificent Hall in the
Cenci Palace. A Banquet. Enter* CENCI,
LUCRETIA, BEATRICE, ORSINO, PRINCE CO-
LONNA, CAMILLO, NOBLES.

 Cenci. Welcome, my friends and kinsmen; welcome ye

Princes and Cardinals, pillars of the
    church,
Whose presence honours our festivity.
I have too long lived like an anchorite,
And, in my absence from your merry
    meetings,
An evil word is gone abroad of me:
But I do hope that you, my noble friends,
When you have shared the entertainment
    here,
And heard the pious cause for which 'tis
    given,
And we have pledged a health or two
    together,   10
Will think me flesh and blood as well as
    you;
Sinful indeed, for Adam made all so,
But tender-hearted, meek and pitiful.
 First Guest. In truth, my lord, you seem
  too light of heart,
Too sprightly and companionable a man,
To act the deeds that rumour pins on you.
[*To his companion.*] I never saw such
    blithe and open cheer
In any eye!
 Second Guest. Some most desired event,
In which we all demand a common joy,
Has brought us hither; let us hear it,
    Count.   20
 Cenci. It is indeed a most desired event.
If, when a parent, from a parent's heart
Lifts from this earth to the great father
    of all
A prayer, both when he lays him down to
    sleep
And when he rises up from dreaming it;
One supplication, one desire, one hope,
That he would grant a wish for his two
    sons,
Even all that he demands in their re-
    gard, —
And suddenly, beyond his dearest hope,
It is accomplished, he should then re-
    joice,   30
And call his friends and kinsmen to a
    feast,
And task their love to grace his merriment,
Then honour me thus far — for I am he.
 Beatrice [*to* LUCRETIA]. Great God! How
  horrible! Some dreadful ill
Must have befallen my brothers.
 Lucretia.   Fear not, child,
He speaks too frankly.
 Beatrice. Ah! My blood runs cold.
I fear that wicked laughter round his eye,
Which wrinkles up the skin even to the
    hair.
 Cenci. Here are the letters brought from
  Salamanca;

Beatrice, read them to your mother. God, ⁴⁰
I thank thee ! In one night didst thou perform,
By ways inscrutable, the thing I sought.
My disobedient and rebellious sons
Are dead ! — Why dead ! — What means this change of cheer ?
You hear me not, I tell you they are dead ;
And they will need no food or raiment more :
The tapers that did light them the dark way
Are their last cost. The Pope, I think, will not
Expect I should maintain them in their coffins.
Rejoice with me — my heart is wondrous glad. ⁵⁰

[LUCRETIA *sinks, half fainting ;* BEATRICE *supports her.*]

Beatrice. It is not true ! — Dear lady, pray look up.
Had it been true, there is a God in Heaven,
He would not live to boast of such a boon.
Unnatural man, thou knowest that it is false.

Cenci. Ay, as the word of God ; whom here I call
To witness that I speak the sober truth ;
And whose most favouring providence was shewn
Even in the manner of their deaths. For Rocco
Was kneeling at the mass, with sixteen others,
When the church fell and crushed him to a mummy ; ⁶⁰
The rest escaped unhurt. Cristofano
Was stabbed in error by a jealous man,
Whilst she he loved was sleeping with his rival ;
All in the self-same hour of the same night ;
Which shows that Heaven has special care of me.
I beg those friends who love me, that they mark
The day a feast upon their calendars.
It was the twenty-seventh of December :
Ay, read the letters if you doubt my oath.

[*The assembly appears confused ; several of the guests rise.*]

First Guest. Oh, horrible ! I will depart. —
Second Guest.　　　　And I. —
Third Guest.　　　　No, stay ! ⁷⁰
I do believe it is some jest ; though faith,

'Tis mocking us somewhat too solemnly.
I think his son has married the Infanta,
Or found a mine of gold in El Dorado ;
'Tis but to season some such news ; stay, stay !
I see 'tis only raillery by his smile.

Cenci [*filling a bowl of wine, and lifting it up*]. Oh, thou bright wine, whose purple splendour leaps
And bubbles gaily in this golden bowl
Under the lamp-light, as my spirits do,
To hear the death of my accursed sons ! ⁸⁰
Could I believe thou wert their mingled blood,
Then would I taste thee like a sacrament,
And pledge with thee the mighty Devil in Hell,
Who, if a father's curses, as men say,
Climb with swift wings after their children's souls,
And drag them from the very throne of Heaven,
Now triumphs in my triumph ! — But thou art
Superfluous ; I have drunken deep of joy,
And I will taste no other wine to-night.
Here, Andrea ! Bear the bowl around.

A Guest [*rising*].　　　Thou wretch ! ⁹⁰
Will none among this noble company
Check the abandoned villain ?
Camillo.　　　For God's sake
Let me dismiss the guests ! You are insane,
Some ill will come of this.
Second Guest.　　　Seize, silence him !
First Guest. I will !
Third Guest.　　　And I !

Cenci [*addressing those who rise with a threatening gesture*].
　Who moves ? Who speaks ?
　[*turning to the Company*]
　　　　'Tis nothing.
Enjoy yourselves. — Beware ! For my revenge
Is as the sealed commission of a king,
That kills, and none dare name the murderer.

[*The Banquet is broken up ; several of the Guests are departing.*]

Beatrice. I do entreat you, go not, noble guests ;
What, although tyranny and impious hate ¹⁰⁰
Stand sheltered by a father's hoary hair ?
What, if 'tis he who clothed us in these limbs
Who tortures them, and triumphs ? What, if we,
The desolate and the dead, were his own

flesh,
His children and his wife, whom he is
    bound
To love and shelter? Shall we therefore
    find
No refuge in the merciless wide world?
Oh, think what deep wrongs must have
    blotted out
First love, then reverence in a child's
    prone mind,
Till it thus vanquish shame and fear!
    Oh, think!   110
I have borne much, and kissed the sacred
    hand
Which crushed us to the earth, and
    thought its stroke
Was perhaps some paternal chastisement!
Have excused much, doubted; and when
    no doubt
Remained, have sought by patience, love
    and tears
To soften him; and when this could not
    be,
I have knelt down through the long sleep-
    less nights,
And lifted up to God, the father of all,
Passionate prayers: and when these were
    not heard
I have still borne; — until I meet you
    here,   120
Princes and kinsmen, at this hideous feast
Given at my brothers' deaths. Two yet
    remain,
His wife remains and I, whom if ye save
    not,
Ye may soon share such merriment again
As fathers make over their children's
    graves.
O! Prince Colonna, thou art our near
    kinsman;
Cardinal, thou art the Pope's chamber-
    lain;
Camillo, thou art chief justiciary;
Take us away!
    Cenci. [*He has been conversing with*
CAMILLO *during the first part of* BEATRICE'S
*speech; he hears the conclusion, and now
advances.*]
    I hope my good friends here
Will think of their own daughters — or
    perhaps   130
Of their own throats — before they lend
    an ear
To this wild girl.
    Beatrice [*not noticing the words of*
CENCI]. Dare no one look on me?
None answer? Can one tyrant overbear
The sense of many best and wisest men?
Or is it that I sue not in some form

Of scrupulous law, that ye deny my suit?
Oh, God! that I were buried with my
    brothers!
And that the flowers of this departed
    spring
Were fading on my grave! And that my
    father
Were celebrating now one feast for all! 140
    Camillo. A bitter wish for one so young
        and gentle;
Can we do nothing? —
    Colonna.   Nothing that I see.
Count Cenci were a dangerous enemy:
Yet I would second any one.
    A Cardinal.   And I.
    Cenci. Retire to your chamber, insolent
        girl!
    Beatrice. Retire thou, impious man! Ay,
        hide thyself
Where never eye can look upon thee
    more!
Wouldst thou have honour and obedience
Who art a torturer? Father, never dream,
Though thou mayst overbear this com-
    pany,   150
But ill must come of ill. — Frown not on
    me!
Haste, hide thyself, lest with avenging
    looks
My brothers' ghosts should hunt thee from
    thy seat!
Cover thy face from every living eye,
And start if thou but hear a human step:
Seek out some dark and silent corner,
    there
Bow thy white head before offended God,
And we will kneel around, and fervently
Pray that he pity both ourselves and thee.
    Cenci. My friends, I do lament this in-
        sane girl   160
Has spoilt the mirth of our festivity.
Good night, farewell; I will not make you
    longer
Spectators of our dull domestic quarrels.
Another time. —
    [*Exeunt all but* CENCI *and* BEATRICE.]
    My brain is swimming round;
Give me a bowl of wine!
                [*To* BEATRICE.]
            Thou painted viper!
Beast that thou art! Fair and yet terrible!
I know a charm shall make thee meek and
    tame,
Now get thee from my sight!
                [*Exit* BEATRICE.]
            Here, Andrea,
Fill up this goblet with Greek wine. I said
I would not drink this evening; but I
    must;   170

For, strange to say, I feel my spirits fail
With thinking what I have decreed to do.
                    [*Drinking the wine.*]
Be thou the resolution of quick youth
Within my veins, and manhood's purpose
    stern,
And age's firm, cold, subtle villainy ;
As if thou wert indeed my children's blood
Which I did thirst to drink. The charm
    works well ;
It must be done ; it shall be done, I swear !
                    [*Exit.*]

ACT II

SCENE I.—*An Apartment in the Cenci
Palace. Enter* LUCRETIA *and* BERNARDO.

Lucretia. Weep not, my gentle boy ; he
    struck but me,
Who have borne deeper wrongs. In truth,
    if he
Had killed me, he had done a kinder deed.
Oh, God Almighty, do thou look upon us,
We have no other friend but only thee !
Yet weep not ; though I love you as my
    own,
I am not your true mother.
    Bernardo.   Oh, more, more
Than ever mother was to any child,
That have you been to me ! Had he not
    been
My father, do you think that I should
    weep ?   10
    Lucretia. Alas ! poor boy, what else
    couldst thou have done !
[*Enter* BEATRICE.]
    Beatrice [*in a hurried voice*]. Did he pass
    this way ? Have you seen
    him, brother?
Ah ! no, that is his step upon the stairs ;
'Tis nearer now ; his hand is on the door ;
Mother, if I to thee have ever been
A duteous child, now save me ! Thou,
    great God,
Whose image upon earth a father is,
Dost thou indeed abandon me ? He
    comes ;
The door is opening now ; I see his face ;
He frowns on others, but he smiles on
    me,   20
Even as he did after the feast last night.
[*Enter a Servant.*]
Almighty God, how merciful thou art !
'Tis but Orsino's servant. — Well, what
    news ?
    Servant. My master bids me say, the
    Holy Father

Has sent back your petition thus un-
    opened.   [*Giving a paper.*]

And he demands at what hour 'twere
    secure
To visit you again?
    Lucretia.   At the Ave Mary.
                    [*Exit Servant.*]
So, daughter, our last hope has failed ; ah
    me,
How pale you look ! you tremble, and you
    stand
Wrapped in some fixed and fearful medi-
    tation,   30
As if one thought were over strong for
    you :
Your eyes have a chill glare ; O, dearest
    child !
Are you gone mad ? If not, pray speak to
    me.
    Beatrice. You see I am not mad : I speak
    to you.
    Lucretia. You talked of something that
    your father did
After that dreadful feast ? Could it be
    worse
Than when he smiled, and cried, My sons
    are dead !
And every one looked in his neighbour's
    face
To see if others were as white as he ?
At the first word he spoke I felt the
    blood   40
Rush to my heart, and fell into a trance ;
And when it passed I sat all weak and
    wild ;
Whilst you alone stood up, and with strong
    words
Checked his unnatural pride ; and I could
    see
The devil was rebuked that lives in him.
Until this hour thus have you ever stood
Between us and your father's moody wrath
Like a protecting presence : your firm
    mind
Has been our only refuge and defence :
What can have thus subdued it ? What can
    now   50
Have given you that cold melancholy look,
Succeeding to your unaccustomed fear ?
    Beatrice. What is it that you say ? I was
    just thinking
'Twere better not to struggle any more.
Men, like my father, have been dark and
    bloody,
Yet never — O ! before worse comes of it,
'Twere wise to die : it ends in that at last.
    Lucretia. Oh, talk not so, dear child !
    Tell me at once

What did your father do or say to you?
He stayed not after that accursed feast   60
One moment in your chamber. — Speak to
    me.
    Bernardo. Oh, sister, sister, prithee,
    speak to us!
    Beatrice [speaking very slowly with a
    forced calmness]. It was one word,
    mother, one little word;
One look, one smile. [Wildly.] Oh! he has
    trampled me
Under his feet, and made the blood stream
    down
My pallid cheeks. And he has given us all
Ditch-water, and the fever-stricken flesh
Of buffaloes, and bade us eat or starve,
And we have eaten. He has made me look
On my beloved Bernardo, when the rust   70
Of heavy chains has gangrened his sweet
    limbs,
And I have never yet despaired — but
    now!
What would I say?   [Recovering herself.]
              Ah, No! 'tis nothing new.
The sufferings we all share have made me
    wild:
He only struck and cursed me as he
    passed;
He said, he looked, he did, — nothing at
    all
Beyond his wont, yet it disordered me.
Alas! I am forgetful of my duty,
I should preserve my senses for your sake.
    Lucretia. Nay, Beatrice; have courage,
    my sweet girl.   80
If any one despairs it should be I
Who loved him once, and now must live
    with him
Till God in pity call for him or me.
For you may, like your sister, find some
    husband,
And smile, years hence, with children
    round your knees;
Whilst I, then dead, and all this hideous
    coil,
Shall be remembered only as a dream.
    Beatrice. Talk not to me, dear lady, of a
    husband.
Did you not nurse me when my mother
    died?
Did you not shield me and that dearest
    boy?   90
And had we any other friend but you
In infancy, with gentle words and looks,
To win our father not to murder us?
And shall I now desert you? May the ghost
Of my dead mother plead against my soul,
If I abandon her who filled the place
She left, with more, even, than a mother's

love!
    Bernardo. And I am of my sister's mind.
    Indeed
I would not leave you in this wretchedness,
Even though the Pope should make me
    free to live   100
In some blithe place, like others of my age,
With sports, and delicate food, and the
    fresh air.
Oh, never think that I will leave you,
    mother!
    Lucretia. My dear, dear children!
[Enter CENCI, suddenly.]
    Cenci.   What, Beatrice here!
Come hither! [She shrinks back, and cov-
    ers her face.]
              Nay, hide not your face, 'tis fair;
Look up! Why, yesternight you dared to
    look
With disobedient insolence upon me,
Bending a stern and an inquiring brow
On what I meant; whilst I then sought to
    hide
That which I came to tell you — but in
    vain.   110
    Beatrice [wildly, staggering towards the
    door]. Oh, that the earth
              would gape. Hide me, oh God!
    Cenci. Then it was I whose inarticulate
    words
Fell from my lips, and who with tottering
    steps
Fled from your presence, as you now from
    mine.
Stay, I command you: From this day and
    hour
Never again, I think, with fearless eye,
And brow superior, and unaltered cheek,
And that lip made for tenderness or scorn,
Shalt thou strike dumb the meanest of
    mankind;
Me least of all. Now get thee to thy cham-
    ber,   120
Thou too, loathed image of thy cursed
    mother,   [To BERNARDO.]
Thy milky, meek face makes me sick with
    hate!
        [Exeunt BEATRICE and BERNARDO.]
    [Aside.] So much has passed between us
    as must make
Me bold, her fearful. 'Tis an awful thing
To touch such mischief as I now conceive:
So men sit shivering on the dewy bank
And try the chill stream with their feet;
    once in —
How the delighted spirit pants for joy!
    Lucretia [advancing timidly towards
    him]. Oh, husband! Pray forgive poor
    Beatrice.

She meant not any ill.

Cenci.   Nor you perhaps ?   130
Nor that young imp, whom you have
     taught by rote
Parricide with his alphabet ? Nor Gia-
     como ?
Nor those two most unnatural sons, who
     stirred
Enmity up against me with the Pope ?
Whom in one night merciful God cut off :
Innocent lambs ! They thought not any ill.
You were not here conspiring ? You said
     nothing
Of how I might be dungeoned as a mad-
     man ;
Or be condemned to death for some
     offence,
And you would be the witnesses ? — This
     failing,   140
How just it were to hire assassins, or
Put sudden poison in my evening drink ?
Or smother me when overcome by wine ?
Seeing we had no other judge but God,
And he had sentenced me, and there were
     none
But you to be the executioners
Of his decree enregistered in heaven ?
Oh, no ! You said not this ?

Lucretia.   So help me God,
I never thought the things you charge me
     with !

Cenci. If you dare speak that wicked lie
     again,   150
I'll kill you. What ! It was not by your
     counsel
That Beatrice disturbed the feast last
     night ?
You did not hope to stir some enemies
Against me, and escape, and laugh to scorn
What every nerve of you now trembles at ?
You judged that men were bolder than
     they are :
Few dare to stand between their grave
     and me.

Lucretia. Look not so dreadfully ! By my
     salvation
I knew not aught that Beatrice designed ;
Nor do I think she designed any thing 160
Until she heard you talk of her dead
     brothers.

Cenci. Blaspheming liar ! You are
     damned for this !
But I will take you where you may per-
     suade
The stones you tread on to deliver you :
For men shall there be none but those
     who dare
All things ; not question that which I com-
     mand.

On Wednesday next I shall set out : you
     know
That savage rock, the Castle of Petrella ?
'Tis safely walled, and moated round
     about :
Its dungeons under-ground, and its thick
     towers   170
Never told tales ; though they have heard
     and seen
What might make dumb things speak.
     Why do you linger ?
Make speediest preparation for the jour-
     ney !

                         [*Exit* LUCRETIA.]

The all-beholding sun yet shines ; I hear
A busy stir of men about the streets ;
I see the bright sky through the window
     panes :
It is a garish, broad, and peering day ;
Loud, light, suspicious, full of eyes and
     ears ;
And every little corner, nook, and hole
Is penetrated with the insolent light.   180
Come, darkness ! Yet, what is the day to
     me ?
And wherefore should I wish for night,
     who do
A deed which shall confound both night
     and day ?
'Tis she shall grope through a bewildering
     mist
Of horror : if there be a sun in heaven
She shall not dare to look upon its beams,
Nor feel its warmth. Let her then wish for
     night ;
The act I think shall soon extinguish all
For me : I bear a darker deadlier gloom
Than the earth's shade, or interlunar
     air,   190
Or constellations quenched in murkiest
     cloud,
In which I walk secure and unbeheld
Towards my purpose. — Would that it
     were done !   [*Exit.*]

SCENE 2. — *A Chamber in the Vatican.*
Enter CAMILLO *and* GIACOMO, *in conversation.*

Camillo. There is an obsolete and
     doubtful law
By which you might obtain a bare provi-
     sion
Of food and clothing —

Giacomo.   Nothing more ? Alas !
Bare must be the provision which strict
     law
Awards, and aged sullen avarice pays.
Why did my father not apprentice me

To some mechanic trade? I should have
     then
Been trained in no high-born necessities
Which I could meet not by my daily toil.
The eldest son of a rich nobleman   10
Is heir to all his incapacities;
He has wide wants, and narrow powers. If
     you,
Cardinal Camillo, were reduced at once
From thrice-driven beds of down, and del-
     icate food,
An hundred servants, and six palaces,
To that which nature doth indeed re-
     quire? —
     Camillo. Nay, there is reason in your
          plea; 'twere hard.
     Giacomo. 'Tis hard for a firm man to
          bear: but I
Have a dear wife, a lady of high birth,
Whose dowry in ill hour I lent my
     father,   20
Without a bond or witness to the deed:
And children, who inherit her fine senses,
The fairest creatures in this breathing
     world;
And she and they reproach me not. Cardi-
     nal,
Do you not think the Pope would inter-
     pose,
And stretch authority beyond the law?
     Camillo. Though your peculiar case is
          hard, I know
The Pope will not divert the course of
     law.
After that impious feast the other night
I spoke with him, and urged him then to
     check   30
Your father's cruel hand; he frowned, and
     said,
"Children are disobedient, and they sting
Their fathers' hearts to madness and de-
     spair,
Requiting years of care with contumely.
I pity the Count Cenci from my heart;
His outraged love perhaps awakened hate,
And thus he is exasperated to ill.
In the great war between the old and
     young,
I, who have white hairs and a tottering
     body,
Will keep at least blameless neutrality." 40
[*Enter* ORSINO.]
You, my good Lord Orsino, heard those
     words.
     Orsino. What words?
     Giacomo.   Alas, repeat them not
          again!
There then is no redress for me; at least

None but that which I may achieve myself,
Since I am driven to the brink. But, say,
My innocent sister and my only brother
Are dying underneath my father's eye.
The memorable torturers of this land,
Galeaz Visconti, Borgia, Ezzelin,
Never inflicted on the meanest slave   50
What these endure; shall they have no
     protection?
     Camillo. Why, if they would petition
          to the Pope,
I see not how he could refuse it — yet
He holds it of most dangerous example
In aught to weaken the paternal power,
Being, as 'twere, the shadow of his own.
I pray you now excuse me. I have business
That will not bear delay.
                              [*Exit* CAMILLO.]

     Giacomo.   But you, Orsino,
Have the petition: wherefore not present
     it?
     Orsino. I have presented it, and backed
          it with   60
My earnest prayers, and urgent interest;
It was returned unanswered. I doubt not
But that the strange and execrable deeds
Alleged in it (in truth they might well
     baffle
Any belief) have turned the Pope's dis-
     pleasure
Upon the accusers from the criminal:
So I should guess from what Camillo said.
     Giacomo. My friend, that palace-walking
          devil, Gold,
Has whispered silence to his Holiness:
And we are left, — as scorpions ringed with
     fire,   70
What should we do but strike ourselves to
     death?
For he who is our murderous persecutor
Is shielded by a father's holy name,
Or I would —   [*Stops abruptly.*]

     Orsino.   What? Fear not to speak
          your thought.
Words are but holy as the deeds they
     cover:
A priest who has forsworn the God he
     serves;
A judge who makes truth weep at his de-
     cree;
A friend who should weave counsel, as I
     now,
But as the mantle of some selfish guile;
A father who is all a tyrant seems,   80
Were the profaner for his sacred name.
     Giacomo. Ask me not what I think; the
          unwilling brain

Feigns often what it would not; and we
trust
Imagination with such fantasies
As the tongue dares not fashion into
words;
Which have no words, their horror makes
them dim
To the mind's eye. My heart denies itself
To think what you demand.
   Orsino.   But a friend's bosom
Is as the inmost cave of our own mind
Where we sit shut from the wide gaze of
day,   90
And from the all-communicating air.
You look what I suspected:
   Giacomo.   Spare me now!
I am as one lost in a midnight wood,
Who dares not ask some harmless pas-
senger
The path across the wilderness, lest he,
As my thoughts are, should be — a mur-
derer.
I know you are my friend, and all I dare
Speak to my soul, that will I trust with
thee.
But now my heart is heavy, and would
take
Lone counsel from a night of sleepless
care.   100
Pardon me, that I say farewell — farewell!
I would that to my own suspected self
I could address a word so full of peace.
   Orsino. Farewell! — Be your thoughts
better or more bold.
                     [*Exit* GIACOMO.]
I had disposed the Cardinal Camillo
To feed his hope with cold encourage-
ment:
It fortunately serves my close designs
That 'tis a trick of this same family
To analyse their own and other minds.
Such self-anatomy shall teach the will 110
Dangerous secrets: for it tempts our
powers,
Knowing what must be thought, and may
be done,
Into the depth of darkest purposes:
So Cenci fell into the pit; even I,
Since Beatrice unveiled me to myself,
And made me shrink from what I cannot
shun,
Show a poor figure to my own esteem,
To which I grow half reconciled. I'll do
As little mischief as I can; that thought
Shall fee the accuser conscience.
   [*After a pause.*] Now what harm 120
If Cenci should be murdered? — Yet, if
murdered,

Wherefore by me? And what if I could
take
The profit, yet omit the sin and peril
In such an action? Of all earthly things
I fear a man whose blows outspeed his
words;
And such is Cenci: and while Cenci lives
His daughter's dowry were a secret grave
If a priest wins her. — Oh, fair Beatrice!
Would that I loved thee not, or loving
thee
Could but despise danger and gold, and
all   130
That frowns between my wish and its
effect,
Or smiles beyond it! There is no escape:
Her bright form kneels beside me at the
altar,
And follows me to the resort of men,
And fills my slumber with tumultuous
dreams,
So, when I wake, my blood seems liquid
fire;
And if I strike my damp and dizzy head,
My hot palm scorches it: her very name,
But spoken by a stranger, makes my heart
Sicken and pant; and thus unprofit-
ably   140
I clasp the phantom of unfelt delights,
Till weak imagination half possesses
The self-created shadow. Yet much longer
Will I not nurse this life of feverous
hours:
From the unravelled hopes of Giacomo
I must work out my own dear purposes.
I see, as from a tower, the end of all:
Her father dead; her brother bound to me
By a dark secret, surer than the grave;
Her mother scared and unexpostulat-
ing   150
From the dread manner of her wish
achieved:
And she! — Once more take courage, my
faint heart;
What dares a friendless maiden matched
with thee?
I have such foresight as assures success:
Some unbeheld divinity doth ever,
When dread events are near, stir up men's
minds
To black suggestions; and he prospers
best,
Not who becomes the instrument of ill,
But who can flatter the dark spirit, that
makes
Its empire and its prey of other hearts 160
Till it become his slave — as I will do.
                       [*Exit.*]

ACT III

SCENE 1. — *An Apartment in the Cenci Palace.* LUCRETIA ; *to her enter* BEATRICE.

Beatrice. [*She enters staggering, and speaks wildly.*] Reach me that
    handkerchief ! — My brain is hurt ;
My eyes are full of blood ; just wipe them
    for me —
I see but indistinctly : —
    Lucretia.   My sweet child,
You have no wound ; 'tis only a cold dew
That starts from your dear brow — Alas !
    alas !
What has befallen ?
    Beatrice. How comes this hair undone ?
Its wandering strings must be what blind
    me so,
And yet I tied it fast. — O, horrible !
The pavement sinks under my feet ! The
    walls
Spin round ! I see a woman weeping
    there,   10
And standing calm and motionless, whilst
    I
Slide giddily as the world reels — My God !
The beautiful blue heaven is flecked with
    blood !
The sunshine on the floor is black ! The
    air
Is changed to vapours such as the dead
    breathe
In charnel pits ! Pah ! I am choked ! There
    creeps
A clinging, black, contaminating mist
About me — 'tis substantial, heavy, thick ;
I cannot pluck it from me, for it glues
My fingers and my limbs to one another, 20
And eats into my sinews, and dissolves
My flesh to a pollution, poisoning
The subtle, pure, and inmost spirit of life !
My God ! I never knew what the mad felt
Before ; for I am mad beyond all doubt !
[*More wildly.*] No, I am dead ! These pu-
    trefying limbs
Shut round and sepulchre the panting soul
Which would burst forth into the wander-
    ing air ! [*A pause.*]
What hideous thought was that I had even
    now ?
'Tis gone ; and yet its burthen remains
    here   30
O'er these dull eyes — upon this weary
    heart !
O, world ! O, life ! O, day ! O, misery !
    Lucretia. What ails thee, my poor child ?
She answers not :
Her spirit apprehends the sense of pain,

But not its cause ; suffering has dried
    away
The source from which it sprung.
    Beatrice [*franticly*].   Like parricide —
Misery has killed its father : yet its father
Never like mine — O, God ! What thing
    am I ?
    Lucretia. My dearest child, what has
    your father done ?
    Beatrice [*doubtfully*]. Who art thou,
    questioner ? I have no father.   40
She is the madhouse nurse who tends on
    me,
It is a piteous office.   [*To* LUCRETIA, *in
    a slow, subdued voice.*]
                    Do you know
I thought I was that wretched Beatrice
Men speak of, whom her father sometimes
    hales
From hall to hall by the entangled hair ;
At others, pens up naked in damp cells
Where scaly reptiles crawl, and starves her
    there,
Till she will eat strange flesh. This woful
    story
So did I overact in my sick dreams,
That I imagined — no, it cannot be !   50
Horrible things have been in this wide
    world,
Prodigious mixtures, and confusions
    strange
Of good and ill ; and worse have been
    conceived
Than ever there was found a heart to do.
But never fancy imaged such a deed
As —   [*Pauses, suddenly recol-
    lecting herself.*]
        Who art thou ? Swear to me, ere I
    die
With fearful expectation, that indeed
Thou art not what thou seemest —
    Mother !
    Lucretia. Oh !
            My sweet child, know you —
    Beatrice.   Yet speak it not :
For then if this be truth, that other too   60
Must be a truth, a firm enduring truth,
Linked with each lasting circumstance of
    life,
Never to change, never to pass away.
Why so it is. This is the Cenci Palace ;
Thou art Lucretia ; I am Beatrice.
I have talked some wild words, but will
    no more.
Mother, come near me : from this point of
    time,
I am —   [*Her voice dies away
    faintly.*]
    Lucretia. Alas ! What has befallen thee,

child ?
What has thy father done ?
 Beatrice.   What have I done ?
Am I not innocent ? Is it my crime   70
That one with white hair, and imperious
   brow,
Who tortured me from my forgotten years,
As parents only dare, should call himself
My father, yet should be ! — Oh, what am
   I ?
What name, what place, what memory
   shall be mine ?
What retrospects, outliving even despair ?
 Lucretia. He is a violent tyrant, surely,
   child :
We know that death alone can make us
   free ;
His death or ours. But what can he have
   done
Of deadlier outrage or worse injury ?   80
Thou art unlike thyself ; thine eyes shoot
   forth
A wandering and strange spirit. Speak to
   me,
Unlock those pallid hands whose fingers
   twine
With one another.
 Beatrice.   'Tis the restless life
Tortured within them. If I try to speak
I shall go mad. Ay, something must be
   done ;
What, yet I know not — something which
   shall make
The thing that I have suffered but a
   shadow
In the dread lightning which avenges it ;
Brief, rapid, irreversible, destroying   90
The consequence of what it cannot cure.
Some such thing is to be endured or done :
When I know what, I shall be still and
   calm,
And never anything will move me more.
But now ! — Oh blood, which art my fa-
   ther's blood,
Circling through these contaminated veins,
If thou, poured forth on the polluted
   earth,
Could wash away the crime, and punish-
   ment
By which I suffer — no, that cannot be !
Many might doubt there were a God
   above   100
Who sees and permits evil, and so die :
That faith no agony shall obscure in me.
 Lucretia. It must indeed have been some
   bitter wrong ;
Yet what, I dare not guess. Oh ! my lost
   child,
Hide not in proud impenetrable grief

Thy sufferings from my fear.
 Beatrice.   I hide them not.
What are the words which you would have
   me speak ?
I, who can feign no image in my mind
Of that which has transformed me : I,
   whose thought
Is like a ghost shrouded and folded up 110
In its own formless horror : of all words,
That minister to mortal intercourse,
Which wouldst thou hear ? For there is
   none to tell
My misery : if another ever knew
Aught like to it, she died as I will die,
And left it, as I must, without a name.
Death ! Death ! Our law and our religion
   call thee
A punishment and a reward. — Oh, which
Have I deserved ?
 Lucretia.   The peace of innocence ;
Till in your season you be called to
   heaven.   120
Whate'er you may have suffered, you have
   done
No evil. Death must be the punishment
Of crime, or the reward of trampling down
The thorns which God has strewed upon
   the path
Which leads to immortality.
 Beatrice.   Ay, death —
The punishment of crime. I pray thee,
   God,
Let me not be bewildered while I judge.
If I must live day after day, and keep
These limbs, the unworthy temple of thy
   spirit,
As a foul den from which what thou
   abhorrest   130
May mock thee, unavenged — it shall not
   be !
Self-murder — no, that might be no escape,
For Thy decree yawns like a Hell between
Our will and it. O ! In this mortal world
There is no vindication and no law
Which can adjudge and execute the doom
Of that through which I suffer.
[*Enter* ORSINO.]
[*She approaches him solemnly.*] Welcome,
   friend !
I have to tell you that, since last we met,
I have endured a wrong so great and
   strange,
That neither life nor death can give me
   rest.   140
Ask me not what it is, for there are deeds
Which have no form, sufferings which
   have no tongue.
 Orsino. And what is he who has thus
   injured you ?

Beatrice. The man they call my father :
a dread name.

Orsino. It cannot be —

Beatrice.   What it can be, or not,
Forbear to think. It is, and it has been ;
Advise me how it shall not be again.
I thought to die, but a religious awe
Restrains me, and the dread lest death
itself
Might be no refuge from the conscious-
ness   150
Of what is yet unexpiated. Oh, speak !

Orsino. Accuse him of the deed, and let
the law
Avenge thee.

Beatrice. Oh, ice-hearted counsellor !
If I could find a word that might make
known
The crime of my destroyer ; and that
done,
My tongue should, like a knife tear out
the secret
Which cankers my heart's core ; ay, lay
all bare,
So that my unpolluted fame should be
With vilest gossips a stale mouthed story ;
A mock, a by-word, an astonishment : — 160
If this were done, which never shall be
done,
Think of the offender's gold, his dreaded
hate,
And the strange horror of the accuser's
tale,
Baffling belief, and overpowering speech :
Scarce whispered, unimaginable, wrapt
In hideous hints — Oh, most assured re-
dress !

Orsino. You will endure it then ?

Beatrice.   Endure ! Orsino,
It seems your counsel is small profit.
        [*Turns from him, and speaks
                half to herself.*]
                Ay,
All must be suddenly resolved and done.
What is this undistinguishable mist   170
Of thoughts, which rise, like shadow after
shadow,
Darkening each other ?

Orsino.   Should the offender live ?
Triumph in his misdeed ? and make, by
use,
His crime, whate'er it is, dreadful no
doubt,
Thine element ; until thou mayst become
Utterly lost ; subdued even to the hue
Of that which thou permittest ?

Beatrice [*to herself*].   Mighty death !
Thou double-visaged shadow ! Only judge !
Rightfullest arbiter ! [*She retires absorbed*

in thought.]

Lucretia.   If the lightning
Of God has e'er descended to avenge — 180

Orsino. Blaspheme not ! His high Provi-
dence commits
Its glory on this earth, and their own
wrongs
Into the hands of men ; if they neglect
To punish crime —

Lucretia. But if one, like this wretch,
Should mock, with gold, opinion, law, and
power ?
If there be no appeal to that which makes
The guiltiest tremble ? If, because our
wrongs,
For that they are unnatural, strange, and
monstrous,
Exceed all measure of belief ? Oh, God !
If, for the very reasons which should
make   190
Redress most swift and sure, our injurer
triumphs ?
And we, the victims, bear worse punish-
ment
Than that appointed for their torturer ?

Orsino.   Think not
But that there is redress where there is
wrong,
So we be bold enough to seize it.

Lucretia.   How ?
If there were any way to make all sure,
I know not — but I think it might be good
To —

Orsino. Why, his late outrage to Bea-
trice ;
For it is such, as I but faintly guess,
As makes remorse dishonour, and leaves
her   200
Only one duty, how she may avenge :
You, but one refuge from ills ill endured :
Me, but one counsel —

Lucretia.   For we cannot hope
That aid, or retribution, or resource
Will arise thence, where every other one
Might find them with less need. [BEATRICE
advances.]

Orsino.   Then —

Beatrice.   Peace, Orsino !
And, honoured Lady, while I speak, I pray,
That you put off, as garments overworn,
Forbearance and respect, remorse and fear,
And all the fit restraints of daily life,   210
Which have been borne from childhood,
but which now
Would be a mockery to my holier plea.
As I have said, I have endured a wrong,
Which, though it be expressionless, is
such
As asks atonement, both for what is past,

And lest I be reserved, day after day,
To load with crimes an overburthened soul,
And be — what ye can dream not. I have prayed
To God, and I have talked with my own heart,
And have unravelled my entangled will, 220
And have at length determined what is right.
Art thou my friend, Orsino? False or true?
Pledge thy salvation ere I speak.
Orsino. I swear
To dedicate my cunning, and my strength,
My silence, and whatever else is mine,
To thy commands.
Lucretia. You think we should devise His death?
Beatrice. And execute what is devised,
And suddenly. We must be brief and bold.
Osino. And yet most cautious.
Lucretia. For the jealous laws
Would punish us with death and in-
famy 230
For that which it became themselves to do.
Beatrice. Be cautious as ye may, but prompt. Orsino,
What are the means?
Orsino. I know two dull, fierce outlaws,
Who think man's spirit as a worm's, and they
Would trample out, for any slight caprice,
The meanest or the noblest life. This mood
Is marketable here in Rome. They sell
What we now want.
Lucretia. To-morrow, before dawn,
Cenci will take us to that lonely rock,
Petrella, in the Apulian Apennines. 240
If he arrive there —
Beatrice. He must not arrive.
Orsino. Will it be dark before you reach the tower?
Lucretia. The sun will scarce be set.
Beatrice. But I remember
Two miles on this side of the fort, the road
Crosses a deep ravine; 'tis rough and nar-
row,
And winds with short turns down the precipice;
And in its depth there is a mighty rock,
Which has, from unimaginable years,
Sustained itself with terror and with toil
Over a gulph, and with the agony 250
With which it clings seems slowly coming down;
Even as a wretched soul hour after hour,
Clings to the mass of life; yet, clinging, leans;
And, leaning, makes more dark the dread abyss
In which it fears to fall : beneath this crag,
Huge as despair, as if in weariness,
The melancholy mountain yawns; below,
You hear but see not an impetuous torrent
Raging among the caverns, and a bridge
Crosses the chasm; and high above there grow, 260
With intersecting trunks, from crag to crag,
Cedars, and yews, and pines; whose tangled hair
Is matted in one solid roof of shade
By the dark ivy's twine. At noon-day here
'Tis twilight, and at sunset blackest night.
Orsino. Before you reach that bridge make some excuse
For spurring on your mules, or loitering Until —
Beatrice. What sound is that?
Lucretia. Hark! No, it cannot be a servant's step;
It must be Cenci, unexpectedly 270
Returned — Make some excuse for being here.
Beatrice. [*To* ORSINO, *as she goes out.*]
That step we hear approach must never pass
The bridge of which we spoke.
[*Exeunt* LUCRETIA *and* BEATRICE.]
Orsino. What shall I do?
Cenci must find me here, and I must bear
The imperious inquisition of his looks
As to what brought me hither: let me mask
Mine own in some inane and vacant smile.
[*Enter* GIACOMO, *in a hurried manner.*]
How! Have you ventured hither? Know you then
That Cenci is from home?
Giacomo. I sought him here;
And now must wait till he returns.
Orsino. Great God! 280
Weigh you the danger of this rashness?
Giacomo. Ay!
Does my destroyer know his danger? We
Are now no more, as once, parent and child,
But man to man; the oppressor to the oppressed;
The slanderer to the slandered; foe to foe.
He has cast Nature off, which was his shield,
And Nature casts him off, who is her shame;
And I spurn both. Is it a father's throat
Which I will shake, and say, I ask not

gold ;
I ask not happy years ; nor memories   290
Of tranquil childhood ; nor home-sheltered
    love ;
Though all these hast thou torn from me,
    and more ;
But only my fair fame ; only one hoard
Of peace, which I thought hidden from
    thy hate,
Under the penury heaped on me by thee ;
Or I will — God can understand and par-
    don.
Why should I speak with man ?
    Orsino.   Be calm, dear friend.
    Giacomo. Well, I will calmly tell you
      what he did.
This old Francesco Cenci, as you know,
Borrowed the dowry of my wife from
    me,   300
And then denied the loan ; and left me so
In poverty, the which I sought to mend
By holding a poor office in the state.
It had been promised to me, and already
I bought new clothing for my ragged
    babes,
And my wife smiled ; and my heart knew
    repose ;
When Cenci's intercession, as I found,
Conferred this office on a wretch, whom
    thus
He paid for vilest service. I returned
With this ill news, and we sate sad
    together   310
Solacing our despondency with tears
Of such affection and unbroken faith
As temper life's worst bitterness ; when he,
As he is wont, came to upbraid and curse,
Mocking our poverty, and telling us
Such was God's scourge for disobedient
    sons.
And then, that I might strike him dumb
    with shame,
I spoke of my wife's dowry ; but he coined
A brief yet specious tale, how I had wasted
The sum in secret riot ; and he saw   320
My wife was touched, and he went smiling
    forth.
And when I knew the impression he had
    made,
And felt my wife insult with silent scorn
My ardent truth, and look averse and cold,
I went forth too : but soon returned again ;
Yet not so soon but that my wife had
    taught
My children her harsh thoughts, and they
    all cried,
"Give us clothes, father ! Give us better
    food !
What you in one night squander were

enough
For months !" I looked, and saw that home
    was hell ;   330
And to that hell will I return no more
Until mine enemy has rendered up
Atonement, or, as he gave life to me
I will, reversing nature's law —
    Orsino.   Trust me,
The compensation which thou seekest here
Will be denied.
    Giacomo.   Then — Are you not my
      friend ?
Did you not hint at the alternative,
Upon the brink of which you see I stand,
The other day when we conversed to-
    gether ?
My wrongs were then less. That word
    parricide,   340
Although I am resolved, haunts me like
    fear.
    Orsino. It must be fear itself, for the
      bare word
Is hollow mockery. Mark, how wisest God
Draws to one point the threads of a just
    doom,
So sanctifying it : what you devise
Is, as it were, accomplished.
    Giacomo.   Is he dead ?
    Orsino. His grave is ready. Know that
      since we met
Cenci has done an outrage to his daughter.
    Giacomo. What outrage ?
    Orsino.   That she speaks not, but
      you may
Conceive such half conjectures as I do, 350
From her fixed paleness, and the lofty
    grief
Of her stern brow, bent on the idle air,
And her severe unmodulated voice,
Drowning both tenderness and dread ; and
    last
From this ; that whilst her step-mother
    and I,
Bewildered in our horror, talked together
With obscure hints ; both self-misunder-
    stood
And darkly guessing, stumbling, in our
    talk,
Over the truth, and yet to its revenge,
She interrupted us, and with a look   360
Which told, before she spoke it, he must
    die : —
    Giacomo. It is enough. My doubts are
      well appeased ;
There is a higher reason for the act
Than mine ; there is a holier judge than
    me,
A more unblamed avenger. Beatrice,
Who in the gentleness of thy sweet youth

Hast never trodden on a worm, or bruised
A living flower, but thou hast pitied it
With needless tears! Fair sister, thou in
   whom
Men wondered how such loveliness and
   wisdom   370
Did not destroy each other! Is there made
Ravage of thee? O, heart, I ask no more
Justification! Shall I wait, Orsino,
Till he return, and stab him at the door?
   Orsino. Not so; some accident might
     interpose
To rescue him from what is now most
   sure;
And you are unprovided where to fly,
How to excuse or to conceal. Nay, listen:
All is contrived; success is so assured
That—
   [*Enter* BEATRICE.]
   Beatrice. 'Tis my brother's voice! You
     know me not?   380
   Giacomo. My sister, my lost sister!
   Beatrice.   Lost indeed!
I see Orsino has talked with you, and
That you conjecture things too horrible
To speak, yet far less than the truth. Now,
   stay not,
He might return: yet kiss me; I shall
   know
That then thou hast consented to his
   death.
Farewell, farewell! Let piety to God,
Brotherly love, justice, and clemency,
And all things that make tender hardest
   hearts,
Make thine hard, brother. Answer not:
   farewell.   390
            [*Exeunt severally.*]

SCENE 2.—*A mean Apartment in* GIA-
COMO's *House.* GIACOMO *alone.*

   Giacomo. 'Tis midnight, and Orsino
     comes not yet.
   [*Thunder, and the sound of a storm.*]
What! can the everlasting elements
Feel with a worm like man? If so, the
   shaft
Of mercy-winged lightning would not fall
On stones and trees. My wife and children
   sleep:
They are now living in unmeaning
   dreams:
But I must wake, still doubting if that
   deed
Be just which is most necessary. O,
Thou unreplenished lamp! whose narrow
   fire
Is shaken by the wind, and on whose
   edge   10

Devouring darkness hovers! Thou small
   flame,
Which, as a dying pulse rises and falls,
Still flickerest up and down, how very
   soon,
Did I not feed thee, wouldst thou fail, and
   be
As thou hadst never been! So wastes and
   sinks
Even now, perhaps, the life that kindled
   mine:
But that no power can fill with vital oil
That broken lamp of flesh. Ha! 'tis the
   blood
Which fed these veins that ebbs till all is
   cold:
It is the form that moulded mine, that
   sinks   20
Into the white and yellow spasms of
   death:
It is the soul by which mine was arrayed
In God's immortal likeness which now
   stands
Naked before Heaven's judgment-seat!
           [*A bell strikes.*]
           One! Two!
The hours crawl on; and when my hairs
   are white,
My son will then perhaps be waiting thus,
Tortured between just hate and vain re-
   morse;
Chiding the tardy messenger of news
Like those which I expect. I almost wish
He be not dead, although my wrongs are
   great;   30
Yet—'tis Orsino's step—
   [*Enter* ORSINO.]
               Speak!
   Orsino.   I am come
To say he has escaped.
   Giacomo.   Escaped!
   Orsino.   And safe
Within Petrella. He passed by the spot
Appointed for the deed an hour too soon.
   Giacomo. Are we the fools of such con-
     tingencies?
And do we waste in blind misgivings thus
The hours when we should act? Then
   wind and thunder,
Which seemed to howl his knell, is the
   loud laughter
With which Heaven mocks our weakness!
   I henceforth
Will ne'er repent of aught, designed or
   done,   40
But my repentance.
   Orsino.   See, the lamp is out.
   Giacomo. If no remorse is ours when the
     dim air

Has drunk this innocent flame, why should
  we quail
When Cenci's life, that light by which ill
  spirits
See the worst deeds they prompt, shall sink
  for ever ?
No, I am hardened.
    Orsino.   Why, what need of this ?
Who feared the pale intrusion of remorse
In a just deed ? Although our first plan
  failed,
Doubt not but he will soon be laid to rest.
But light the lamp ; let us not talk i' the
  dark.   50
  Giacomo [*lighting the lamp*] And yet,
    once quenched, I cannot
    thus relume
My father's life : do you not think his
  ghost
Might plead that argument with God ?
  Orsino.   Once gone,
You cannot now recall your sister's peace ;
Your own extinguished years of youth and
  hope ;
Nor your wife's bitter words ; nor all the
  taunts
Which, from the prosperous, weak mis-
  fortune takes ;
Nor your dead mother ; nor —
  Giacomo.   O, speak no more !
I am resolved, although this very hand
Must quench the life that animated it.   60
  Orsino. There is no need of that. Lis-
    ten : you know
Olimpio, the castellan of Petrella
In old Colonna's time ; him whom your
  father
Degraded from his post ? And Marzio,
That desperate wretch, whom he deprived
  last year
Of a reward of blood, well earned and
  due ?
  Giacomo. I know Olimpio ; and they
    say he hated
Old Cenci so, that in his silent rage
His lips grew white only to see him pass.
Of Marzio I know nothing.
  Orsino.   Marzio's hate   70
Matches Olimpio's. I have sent these men,
But in your name, and as at your request,
To talk with Beatrice and Lucretia.
  Giacomo. Only to talk ?
  Orsino.   The moments which even
    now
Pass onward to to-morrow's midnight hour,
May memorise their flight with death : ere
  then
They must have talked, and may perhaps

have done,
And made an end.
  Giacomo.   Listen ! What sound is
    that ?
  Orsino. The house-dog moans, and the
    beams crack : nought else.
  Giacomo. It is my wife complaining in
    her sleep :   80
I doubt not she is saying bitter things
Of me ; and all my children round her
  dreaming
That I deny them sustenance.
  Orsino.   Whilst he
Who truly took it from them, and who
  fills
Their hungry rest with bitterness, now
  sleeps
Lapped in bad pleasures, and trium-
  phantly
Mocks thee in visions of successful hate
Too like the truth of day.
  Giacomo.   If e'er he wakes
Again, I will not trust to hireling hands —
  Orsino. Why, that were well. I must be
    gone ; good night !   90
When next we meet may all be done !
  Giacomo.   And all
Forgotten : Oh, that I had never been !
             [*Exeunt.*]

ACT IV

SCENE 1. — *An Apartment in the Castle
of Petrella. Enter* CENCI.

  Cenci. She comes not ; yet I left her
    even now
Vanquished and faint. She knows the pen-
  alty
Of her delay : yet what if threats are vain ?
Am I not now within Petrella's moat ?
Or fear I still the eyes and ears of Rome ?
Might I not drag her by the golden hair ?
Stamp on her ? Keep her sleepless till her
  brain
Be overworn ? Tame her with chains and
  famine ?
Less would suffice. Yet so to leave undone
What I most seek ! No, 'tis her stubborn
  will   10
Which, by its own consent, shall stoop as
  low
As that which drags it down.
[*Enter* LUCRETIA.]
            Thou loathed wretch !
Hide thee from my abhorrence : fly, be-
  gone !
Yet stay ! Bid Beatrice come hither.

Lucretia.   Oh,
Husband ! I pray, for thine own wretched
    sake,
Heed what thou dost. A man who walks
    like thee
Through crimes, and through the danger
    of his crimes,
Each hour may stumble o'er a sudden
    grave.
And thou art old ; thy hairs are hoary
    grey ;
As thou wouldst save thyself from death
    and hell,   20
Pity thy daughter ; give her to some
    friend
In marriage : so that she may tempt thee
    not
To hatred, or worse thoughts, if worse
    there be.
    Cenci. What ! like her sister who has
        found a home
To mock my hate from with prosperity ?
Strange ruin shall destroy both her and
    thee,
And all that yet remain. My death may be
Rapid, her destiny outspeeds it. Go,
Bid her come hither, and before my mood
Be changed, lest I should drag her by the
    hair.   30
    Lucretia. She sent me to thee, husband.
        At thy presence
She fell, as thou dost know, into a trance ;
And in that trance she heard a voice which
    said,
"Cenci must die ! let him confess himself !
Even now the accusing angel waits to hear
If God, to punish his enormous crimes,
Harden his dying heart !"
    Cenci.   Why — such things are :
No doubt divine revealings may be made.
'Tis plain I have been favoured from
    above,
For when I cursed my sons they died. —
    Ay — so —   40
As to the right or wrong, that's talk —
    repentance —
Repentance is an easy moment's work,
And more depends on God than me.
    Well — well —
I must give up the greater point, which
    was
To poison and corrupt her soul.
        [*A pause ;* LUCRETIA *approaches
            anxiously, and then shrinks
            back as he speaks.*]
            One, two ;
Ay — Rocco and Cristofano my curse
Strangled : and Giacomo, I think, will find

Life a worse Hell than that beyond the
    grave :
Beatrice shall, if there be skill in hate,
Die in despair, blaspheming : to Ber-
    nardo,   50
He is so innocent, I will bequeath
The memory of these deeds, and make his
    youth
The sepulchre of hope, where evil thoughts
Shall grow like weeds on a neglected tomb.
When all is done, out in the wide Cam-
    pagna
I will pile up my silver and my gold ;
My costly robes, paintings, and tapestries ;
My parchments and all records of my
    wealth ;
And make a bonfire in my joy, and leave
Of my possessions nothing but my
    name ;   60
Which shall be an inheritance to strip
Its wearer bare as infamy. That done,
My soul, which is a scourge, will I resign
Into the hands of him who wielded it ;
Be it for its own punishment or theirs,
He will not ask it of me till the lash
Be broken in its last and deepest wound ;
Until its hate be all inflicted. Yet,
Lest death outspeed my purpose, let me
    make
Short work and sure —   [*Going.*]
    Lucretia. [*Stops him.*] Oh, stay ! It was a
        feint :   70
She had no vision, and she heard no voice.
I said it but to awe thee.
    Cenci.   That is well.
Vile palterer with the sacred truth of God,
Be thy soul choked with that blaspheming
    lie !
For Beatrice, worse terrors are in store,
To bend her to my will.
    Lucretia.   Oh ! to what will ?
What cruel sufferings more than she has
    known,
Canst thou inflict ?
    Cenci.   Andrea ! go call my daughter,
And if she comes not, tell her that I come.
What sufferings ? I will drag her, step by
    step,   80
Through infamies unheard of among
    men :
She shall stand shelterless in the broad
    noon
Of public scorn, for acts blazoned abroad,
One among which shall be — What ?
    Canst thou guess ?
She shall become (for what she most ab-
    hors
Shall have a fascination to entrap

Her loathing will) to her own conscious
self
All she appears to others ; and when dead,
As she shall die unshrived and unfor-
given,
A rebel to her father and her God,   90
Her corpse shall be abandoned to the
hounds ;
Her name shall be the terror of the earth ;
Her spirit shall approach the throne of
God
Plague-spotted with my curses. I will make
Body and soul a monstrous lump of ruin.
[*Enter* ANDREA.]
    Andrea. The Lady Beatrice —
    Cenci.   Speak, pale slave ! What
Said she ?
    Andrea. My Lord, 'twas what she
looked ; she said :
"Go tell my father that I see the gulph
Of Hell between us two, which he may
pass,
I will not."
                    [*Exit* ANDREA.]
    Cenci. Go thou quick, Lucretia,   100
Tell her to come ; yet let her understand
Her coming is consent : and say, more-
over,
That if she come not I will curse her.
                  [*Exit* LUCRETIA.]
                  Ha !
With what but with a father's curse doth
God
Panic-strike armed victory, and make pale
Cities in their prosperity ? The world's
Father
Must grant a parent's prayer against his
child,
Be he who asks even what men call me.
Will not the deaths of her rebellious
brothers
Awe her before I speak ? For I on them 110
Did imprecate quick ruin, and it came.
[*Enter* LUCRETIA.]
Well ; what ? Speak, wretch !
    Lucretia. She said, "I cannot come ;
Go tell my father that I see a torrent
Of his own blood raging between us."
    Cenci [*kneeling*].   God !
Hear me ! If this most specious mass of
flesh,
Which thou hast made my daughter ; this
my blood,
This particle of my divided being ;
Or rather, this my bane and my disease,
Whose sight infects and poisons me ; this
devil,
Which sprung from me as from a hell, was
meant   120

To aught good use ; if her bright loveli-
ness
Was kindled to illumine this dark world ;
If nursed by thy selectest dew of love,
Such virtues blossom in her as should make
The peace of life, I pray thee for my sake,
As thou the common God and Father art
Of her, and me, and all ; reverse that
doom !
Earth, in the name of God, let her food be
Poison, until she be encrusted round
With leprous stains ! Heaven, rain upon
her head   130
The blistering drops of the Maremma's
dew,
Till she be speckled like a toad ; parch up
Those love-enkindled lips, warp those fine
limbs
To loathed lameness ! All-beholding sun,
Strike in thine envy those life-darting
eyes
With thine own blinding beams !
    Lucretia.   Peace ! peace !
For thine own sake unsay those dreadful
words.
When high God grants, he punishes such
prayers.
    Cenci [*leaping up, and throwing his
    right hand towards Heaven*]. He does
    his will, I mine ! This in addition,
That if she have a child —
    Lucretia.   Horrible thought !   140
    Cenci. That if she ever have a child ;
and thou,
Quick Nature ! I adjure thee by thy God,
That thou be fruitful in her, and increase
And multiply, fulfilling his command,
And my deep imprecation ! May it be
A hideous likeness of herself, that, as
From a distorting mirror, she may see
Her image mixed with what she most ab-
hors,
Smiling upon her from her nursing breast.
And that the child may from its in-
fancy   150
Grow, day by day, more wicked and de-
formed,
Turning her mother's love to misery :
And that both she and it may live until
It shall repay her care and pain with hate,
Or what may else be more unnatural.
So he may hunt her through the clamorous
scoffs
Of the loud world to a dishonoured grave.
Shall I revoke this curse ? Go, bid her
come,
Before my words are chronicled in heaven.
                [*Exit* LUCRETIA.]
I do not feel as if I were a man,   160

But like a fiend appointed to chastise
The offences of some unremembered
  world.
My blood is running up and down my
  veins !
A fearful pleasure makes it prick and
  tingle :
I feel a giddy sickness of strange awe :
My heart is beating with an expectation
Of horrid joy.
[*Enter* LUCRETIA.]
                    What ? Speak !
  Lucretia.   She bids thee curse;
And if thy curses, as they cannot do,
Could kill her soul —
  Cenci.   She would not come.
  'Tis well,
I can do both : first take what I de-
  mand,   170
And then extort concession. To thy cham-
  ber !
Fly ere I spurn thee : and beware this
  night
That thou cross not my footsteps. It were
  safer
To come between the tiger and his prey.
                    [*Exit* LUCRETIA.]
It must be late ; mine eyes grow weary
  dim
With unaccustomed heaviness of sleep.
Conscience ! Oh, thou most insolent of
  lies !
They say that sleep, that healing dew of
  heaven,
Steeps not in balm the foldings of the
  brain
Which thinks thee an impostor. I will
  go,   180
First to belie thee with an hour of rest,
Which will be deep and calm, I feel ; and
  then —
O, multitudinous Hell, the fiends will
  shake
Thine arches with the laughter of their
  joy !
There shall be lamentation heard in
  Heaven
As o'er an angel fallen ; and upon Earth
All good shall droop and sicken, and ill
  things
Shall, with a spirit of unnatural life,
Stir and be quickened ; even as I am now.
                              [*Exit.*]

SCENE 2. — *Before the Castle of Petrella.*
Enter BEATRICE *and* LUCRETIA *above on the*
Ramparts.

Beatrice. They come not yet.

  Lucretia.   'Tis scarce midnight.
  Beatrice.   How slow
Behind the course of thought, even sick
  with speed,
Lags leaden-footed time !
  Lucretia.   The minutes pass —
If he should wake before the deed is
  done ?
  Beatrice. O, Mother ! He must never
  wake again.
What thou hast said persuades me that
  our act
Will but dislodge a spirit of deep hell
Out of a human form.
  Lucretia.   'Tis true he spoke
Of death and judgment with strange confi-
  dence
For one so wicked ; as a man believing   10
In God, yet recking not of good or ill.
And yet to die without confession !
  Beatrice.   Oh !
Believe that Heaven is merciful and just,
And will not add our dread necessity
To the amount of his offences.
[*Enter* OLIMPIO AND MARZIO, *below.*]
  Lucretia.   See,
They come.
  Beatrice. All mortal things must hasten
  thus
To their dark end. Let us go down.
    [*Exeunt* LUCRETIA *and* BEATRICE *from*
                              above.]
  Olimpio. How feel you to this work ?
  Marzio.   As one who thinks
A thousand crowns excellent market price
For an old murderer's life. Your cheeks
  are pale.   20
  Olimpio. It is the white reflection of
  your own,
Which you call pale.
  Marzio. Is that their natural hue?
  Olimpio. Or 'tis my hate, and the de-
  ferred desire
To wreak it, which extinguishes their
  blood.
  Marzio. You are inclined then to this
  business?
  Olimpio.   Ay,
If one should bribe me with a thousand
  crowns
To kill a serpent which had stung my
  child,
I could not be more willing.
[*Enter* BEATRICE *and* LUCRETIA, *below.*]
                    Noble ladies !
  Beatrice. Are ye resolved ?
  Olimpio.   Is he asleep ?
  Marzio.   Is all
Quiet ?

Lucretia. I mixed an opiate with his
　　drink :　　　　　　　　　　　　30
He sleeps so soundly —
　Beatrice.　　　That his death will be
But as a change of sin-chastising dreams,
A dark continuance of the Hell within
　　him,
Which God extinguish ! But ye are re-
　　solved ?
Ye know it is a high and holy deed ?
　Olimpio. We are resolved.
　Marzio.　　As to the how of this act
Be warranted, it rests with you.
　Beatrice.　　　Well, follow !
　Olimpio. Hush ! Hark ! What noise is
　　that ?
　Marzio.　　　　Ha ! some one comes !
　Beatrice. Ye conscience-stricken cravens,
　　rock to rest
Your baby hearts. It is the iron gate,　40
Which ye left open, swinging to the wind,
That enters whistling as in scorn. Come,
　　follow !
And be your steps like mine, light, quick
　　and bold.
　　　　　　　　　　　　[Exeunt.]

SCENE 3. — *An Apartment in the Castle.*
Enter BEATRICE *and* LUCRETIA.

　Lucretia. They are about it now.
　Beatrice.　　　　Nay, it is done.
　Lucretia. I have not heard him groan.
　Beatrice.　　　　He will not groan.
　Lucretia. What sound is that ?
　Beatrice.　　List ! 'tis the tread of feet
About his bed.
　Lucretia.　　My God !
If he be now a cold stiff corpse.
　Beatrice.　　　O, fear not
What may be done, but what is left un-
　　done :
The act seals all.
[*Enter* OLIMPIO *and* MARZIO.]
　　　Is it accomplished ?
　Marzio.　　　　　　What ?
　Olimpio Did you not call ?
　Beatrice.　　　　When ?
　Olimpio.　　　　　　Now.
　Beatrice.　　　I ask if all is over ?
　Olimpio. We dare not kill an old and
　　sleeping man ;
His thin gray hair, his stern and reverend
　　brow,　　　　　　　　　　　　10
His veined hands crossed on his heaving
　　breast,
And the calm innocent sleep in which he
　　lay,
Quelled me. Indeed, indeed, I cannot do

　　it.
　Marzio. But I was bolder ; for I chid
　　Olimpio,
And bade him bear his wrongs to his own
　　grave,
And leave me the reward. And now my
　　knife
Touched the loose wrinkled throat, when
　　the old man
Stirred in his sleep, and said, "God ! hear,
　　O hear,
A father's curse ! What, art thou not our
　　father ?"
And then he laughed. I knew it was the
　　ghost　　　　　　　　　　　　20
Of my dead father speaking through his
　　lips,
And could not kill him.
　Beatrice.　　　Miserable slaves !
Where, if ye dare not kill a sleeping man,
Found ye the boldness to return to me
With such a deed undone ? Base palterers !
Cowards and traitors ! Why, the very con-
　　science
Which ye would sell for gold and for
　　revenge
Is an equivocation : it sleeps over
A thousand daily acts disgracing men ;
And when a deed where mercy insults
　　Heaven —　　　　　　　　　　30
Why do I talk ? [*Snatching a dagger from
　　one of them and raising it.*]
　　　Hadst thou a tongue to say,
She murdered her own father, I must do
　　it !
But never dream ye shall outlive him
　　long !
　Olimpio. Stop, for God's sake !
　Marzio.　　I will go back and kill him.
　Olimpio. Give me the weapon, we must
　　do thy will.
　Beatrice. Take it ! Depart ! Return !
　　　　[*Exeunt* OLIMPIO *and* MARZIO.]
　　　　How pale thou art !
We do but that which 'twere a deadly
　　crime
To leave undone.
　Lucretia.　　Would it were done !
　Beatrice.　　　　Even whilst
That doubt is passing through your mind,
　　the world
Is conscious of a change. Darkness and
　　hell　　　　　　　　　　　　40
Have swallowed up the vapour they sent
　　forth
To blacken the sweet light of life. My
　　breath
Comes, methinks, lighter, and the jellied
　　blood

Runs freely through my veins. Hark !
[*Enter* OLIMPIO *and* MARZIO.]
         He is —
Olimpio.   Dead !
Marzio. We strangled him that there
  might be no blood ;
And then we threw his heavy corpse i' the
  garden
Under the balcony ; 'twill seem it fell.
  Beatrice [*giving them a bag of coin*].
  Here, take this gold, and hasten to
  your homes.
And, Marzio, because thou wast only awed
By that which made me tremble, wear
  thou this !   50
    [*Clothes him in a rich mantle.*]
It was the mantle which my grandfather
Wore in his high prosperity, and men
Envied his state : so may they envy thine.
Thou wert a weapon in the hand of God
To a just use. Live long and thrive ! And,
  mark,
If thou hast crimes, repent : this deed is
  none. [*A horn is sounded.*]
  Lucretia. Hark, 'tis the castle horn ; my
  God ! it sounds
Like the last trump.
  Beatrice. Some tedious guest is coming.
  Lucretia. The drawbridge is let down ;
  there is a tramp
Of horses in the court ; fly, hide your-
  selves !   60
    [*Exeunt* OLIMPIO *and* MARZIO.]
  Beatrice. Let us retire to counterfeit
  deep rest ;
I scarcely need to counterfeit it now :
The spirit which doth reign within these
  limbs
Seems strangely undisturbed. I could even
  sleep
Fearless and calm : all ill is surely past.
         [*Exeunt.*]

SCENE 4. — *Another Apartment in the
Castle. Enter on one side the Legate* SA-
VELLA, *introduced by a Servant, and on the
other* LUCRETIA *and* BERNARDO.

  Savella. Lady, my duty to his Holiness
Be my excuse that thus unseasonably
I break upon your rest. I must speak with
Count Cenci ; doth he sleep ?
  Lucretia [*in a hurried and confused
  manner*]. I think he sleeps ;
Yet, wake him not, I pray, spare me
  awhile,
He is a wicked and wrathful man ;
Should he be roused out of his sleep to-
  night,

Which is, I know, a hell of angry dreams,
It were not well ; indeed it were not well.
Wait till day break, — [*aside*] O, I am
  deadly sick !   10
  Savella. I grieve thus to distress you, but
  the Count
Must answer charges of the gravest import,
And suddenly ; such my commission is.
  Lucretia [*with increased agitation*]. I
  dare not rouse him, I know none
  who dare ;
'Twere perilous ; — you might as safely
  waken
A serpent ; or a corpse in which some
  fiend
Were laid to sleep.
  Savella. Lady, my moments here
Are counted. I must rouse him from his
  sleep,
Since none else dare.
  Lucretia [*aside*]. O, terror ! O, despair !
[*To* BERNARDO.] Bernardo, conduct you the
  Lord Legate to   20
Your father's chamber.
    [*Exeunt* SAVELLA *and* BERNARDO.]
[*Enter* BEATRICE.]
  Beatrice.   'Tis a messenger
Come to arrest the culprit who now stands
Before the throne of unappealable God.
Both Earth and Heaven, consenting arbi-
  ters,
Acquit our deed.
  Lucretia. Oh, agony of fear !
Would that he yet might live ! Even now
  I heard
The legate's followers whisper as they
  passed
They had a warrant for his instant death.
All was prepared by unforbidden means,
Which we must pay so dearly, having
  done.   30
Even now they search the tower, and find
  the body ;
Now they suspect the truth ; now they
  consult,
Before they come to tax us with the fact :
O horrible, 'tis all discovered !
  Beatrice.   Mother,
What is done wisely, is done well. Be bold
As thou art just. 'Tis like a truant child,
To fear that others know what thou hast
  done,
Even from thine own strong consciousness,
  and thus
Write on unsteady eyes and altered cheeks
All thou wouldst hide. Be faithful to thy-
  self,   40
And fear no other witness but thy fear.
For if, as cannot be, some circumstance

Should arise in accusation, we can blind
Suspicion with such cheap astonishment,
Or overbear it with such guiltless pride,
As murderers cannot feign. The deed is done,
And what may follow now regards not me.
I am as universal as the light ;
Free as the earth-surrounding air ; as firm
As the world's centre. Consequence, to
   me,   50
Is as the wind which strikes the solid rock,
But shakes it not.   [*A cry within and
                tumult.*]
    Voices.   Murder ! Murder ! Murder !
[*Enter* BERNARDO *and* SAVELLA.]
    Savella [*to his followers*]. Go search the
    castle round ; sound the alarm ;
Look to the gates that none escape !
    Beatrice.   What now ?
    Bernardo. I know not what to say : my
    father's dead.
    Beatrice. How ? dead ? he only sleeps :
    you mistake, brother.
His sleep is very calm, very like death ;
'Tis wonderful how well a tyrant sleeps.
He is not *dead*?
    Bernardo.   Dead ; murdered.
    Lucretia [*with extreme agitation*]. Oh,
    no, no,
He is not murdered though he may be
    dead ;   60
I have alone the keys of those apartments.
    Savella. Ha ! Is it so ?
    Beatrice.   My lord, I pray excuse us ;
We will retire ; my mother is not well ;
She seems quite overcome with this strange
    horror.
        [*Exeunt* LUCRETIA *and* BEATRICE.]
    Savella. Can you suspect who may have
    murdered him ?
    Bernardo. I know not what to think.
    Savella.   Can you name any
Who had an interest in his death ?
    Bernardo.   Alas !
I can name none who had not, and those
    most
Who most lament that such a deed is
    done ;
My mother, and my sister, and myself.   70
    Savella. 'Tis strange ! There were clear
    marks of violence.
I found the old man's body in the moon-
    light,
Hanging beneath the window of his
    chamber
Among the branches of a pine : he could
    not
Have fallen there, for all his limbs lay
    heaped

And effortless ; 'tis true there was no
    blood.
Favour me, Sir, (it much imports your
    house
That all should be made clear) to tell the
    ladies
That I request their presence.
             [*Exit* BERNARDO.]
[*Enter Guards, bringing in* MARZIO.]
    Guard.   We have one.
    Officer. My lord, we found this ruffian
    and another   80
Lurking among the rocks ; there is no
    doubt
But that they are the murderers of Count
    Cenci :
Each had a bag of coin ; this fellow wore
A gold-inwoven robe, which, shining
    bright
Under the dark rocks to the glimmering
    moon,
Betrayed them to our notice : the other
    fell
Desperately fighting.
    Savella.   What does he confess ?
    Officer. He keeps firm silence ; but these
    lines found on him
May speak.
    Savella. Their language is at least sin-
    cere.   [*Reads.*]
"To the Lady Beatrice.   90
  "That the atonement of what my nature
sickens to conjecture may soon arrive, I
send thee, at thy brother's desire, those
who will speak and do more than I dare
write —
        "Thy devoted servant, Orsino."
[*Enter* LUCRETIA, BEATRICE, *and* BERNARDO.]
Knowest thou this writing, Lady ?
    Beatrice.   No.
    Savella.   Nor thou ?
    Lucretia. [*Her conduct throughout the
    scene is marked by extreme agita-
    tion.*] Where was it found ? What
    is it ? It should be
Orsino's hand ! It speaks of that strange
    horror
Which never yet found utterance, but
    which made
Between that hapless child and her dead
    father
A gulf of obscure hatred.
    Savella.   Is it so ?   100
Is it true, lady, that thy father did
Such outrages as to awaken in thee
Unfilial hate ?
    Beatrice.   Not hate, 'twas more than
    hate :
This is most true, yet wherefore question

me ?

Savella. There is a deed demanding
    question done ;
Thou hast a secret which will answer not.
    Beatrice. What sayest ? My Lord, your
    words are bold and rash.
    Savella. I do arrest all present in the
    name
Of the Pope's Holiness. You must to
    Rome.
    Lucretia. O, not to Rome ! Indeed we
    are not guilty.   110
    Beatrice. Guilty ! Who dares talk of
    guilt ? My Lord,
I am more innocent of parricide
Than is a child born fatherless. Dear
    mother,
Your gentleness and patience are no shield
For this keen-judging world, this two-
    edged lie,
Which seems, but is not. What ! will
    human laws,
Rather will ye who are their ministers,
Bar all access to retribution first,
And then, when heaven doth interpose to
    do
What ye neglect, arming familiar things 120
To the redress of an unwonted crime,
Make ye the victims who demanded it
Culprits ? 'Tis ye are culprits ! That poor
    wretch
Who stands so pale, and trembling, and
    amazed,
If it be true he murdered Cenci, was
A sword in the right hand of justest God.
Wherefore should I have wielded it ? Un-
    less
The crimes which mortal tongue dare
    never name
God therefore scruples to avenge.
    Savella.   You own
That you desired his death ?
    Beatrice.   It would have been 130
A crime no less than his, if, for one
    moment
That fierce desire had faded in my heart.
'Tis true I did believe, and hope, and
    pray,
Ay, I even knew — for God is wise and
    just,
That some strange sudden death hung
    over him.
'Tis true that this did happen, and most
    true
There was no other rest for me on earth,
No other hope in Heaven ; now what of
    this ?
    Savella. Strange thoughts beget strange
    deeds ; and here are both :

I judge thee not.
    Beatrice. And yet, if you arrest me, 140
You are the judge and executioner
Of that which is the life of life : the
    breath
Of accusation kills an innocent name,
And leaves for lame acquittal the poor
    life,
Which is a mask without it. 'Tis most false
That I am guilty of foul parricide ;
Although I must rejoice, for justest cause,
That other hands have sent my father's
    soul
To ask the mercy he denied to me.
Now leave us free : stain not a noble
    house   150
With vague surmises of rejected crime ;
Add to our sufferings and your own neglect
No heavier sum ; let them have been
    enough :
Leave us the wreck we have.
    Savella.   I dare not, Lady.
I pray that you prepare yourselves for
    Rome :
There the Pope's further pleasure will be
    known.
    Lucretia. O, not to Rome ! O, take us
    not to Rome !
    Beatrice. Why not to Rome, dear
    mother ? There, as here,
Our innocence is an armed heel
To trample accusation. God is there, 160
As here, and with his shadow ever clothes
The innocent, the injured and the weak ;
And such are we. Cheer up, dear lady !
    lean
On me ; collect your wandering thoughts.
    My lord,
As soon as you have taken some refresh-
    ment,
And had all such examinations made
Upon the spot, as may be necessary
To the full understanding of this matter,
We shall be ready. Mother, will you come ?
    Lucretia. Ha ! they will bind us to the
    rack, and wrest   170
Self-accusation from our agony !
Will Giacomo be there ? Orsino ? Marzio ?
All present ; all confronted ; all demand-
    ing
Each from the other's countenance the
    thing
Which is in every heart ! O, misery !
            [*She faints, and is borne out.*]
    Savella. She faints : an ill appearance
    this.
    Beatrice.   My lord,
She knows not yet the uses of the world.
She fears that power is as a beast which

grasps
And loosens not : a snake whose look
　　transmutes
All things to guilt which is its nutri-
　　ment ;　　　　　　　　　　180
She cannot know how well the supine
　　slaves
Of blind authority read the truth of things
When written on a brow of guilelessness :
She sees not yet triumphant Innocence
Stand at the judgment-seat of mortal man,
A judge and an accuser of the wrong
Which drags it there. Prepare yourself, my
　　lord ;
Our suite will join yours in the court
　　below　　　　　　　　[*Exeunt.*]

ACT V

SCENE 1. — *An Apartment in* ORSINO'S
Palace. Enter ORSINO *and* GIACOMO.

Giacomo. Do evil deeds thus quickly
　　come to end ?
O, that the vain remorse which must chas-
　　tise
Crimes done, had but as loud a voice to
　　warn
As its keen sting is mortal to avenge !
O, that the hour when present had cast off
The mantle of its mystery, and shewn
The ghastly form with which it now re-
　　turns
When its scared game is roused, cheering
　　the hounds
Of conscience to their prey ! Alas, alas !
It was a wicked thought, a piteous deed, 10
To kill an old and hoary-headed father.
　　Orsino. It has turned out unluckily, in
　　truth.
　　Giacomo. To violate the sacred doors of
　　sleep ;
To cheat kind Nature of the placid death
Which she prepares for over-wearied age ;
To drag from Heaven an unrepentant soul
Which might have quenched in reconcil-
　　ing prayers
A life of burning crimes —
　　Orsino.　　　　You cannot say
I urged you to the deed.
　　Giacomo.　　　O, had I never
Found in thy smooth and ready counten-
　　ance　　　　　　　　　　20
The mirror of my darkest thoughts ; hadst
　　thou
Never with hints and questions made me
　　look
Upon the monster of my thought, until

It grew familiar to desire —
　　Orsino.　　　　'Tis thus
Men cast the blame of their unprosperous
　　acts
Upon the abettors of their own resolve ;
Or any thing but their weak, guilty selves.
And yet, confess the truth, it is the peril
In which you stand that gives you this pale
　　sickness
Of penitence ; confess, 'tis fear disguised 30
From its own shame that takes the mantle
　　now
Of thin remorse. What if we yet were safe ?
　　Giacomo. How can that be ? Already
　　Beatrice,
Lucretia, and the murderer, are in prison.
I doubt not officers are, whilst we speak,
Sent to arrest us.
　　Orsino.　　　I have all prepared
For instant flight. We can escape even
　　now,
So we take fleet occasion by the hair.
　　Giacomo. Rather expire in tortures, as
　　I may.
What ! will you cast by self-accusing
　　flight　　　　　　　　　　40
Assured conviction upon Beatrice ?
She, who alone in this unnatural work,
Stands like God's angel ministered upon
By fiends ; avenging such a nameless wrong
As turns black parricide to piety ;
Whilst we for basest ends — I fear, Orsino,
While I consider all your words and looks,
Comparing them with your proposal now,
That you must be a villain. For what end
Could you engage in such a perilous
　　crime,　　　　　　　　　　50
Training me on with hints, and signs, and
　　smiles,
Even to this gulph ? Thou art no liar ? No,
Thou art a lie ! Traitor and murderer !
Coward and slave ! But, no, defend thy-
　　self ;　　　　　　　　[*Drawing.*]
Let the sword speak what the indignant
　　tongue
Disdains to brand thee with.
　　Orsino.　　　　Put up your weapon.
Is it the desperation of your fear
Makes you thus rash and sudden with a
　　friend,
Now ruined for your sake ? If honest anger
Have moved you, know, that what I just
　　proposed　　　　　　　　　60
Was but to try you. As for me, I think
Thankless affection led me to this point,
From which, if my firm temper could
　　repent,
I cannot now recede. Even whilst we speak
The ministers of justice wait below :

They grant me these brief moments. Now if you
Have any word of melancholy comfort
To speak to your pale wife, 'twere best to pass
Out at the postern, and avoid them so.
  Giacomo. O, generous friend ! How canst thou pardon me ?   70
Would that my life could purchase thine !
  Orsino.   That wish
Now comes a day too late. Haste ; fare thee well !
Hear'st thou not steps along the corridor ?
                    [*Exit* GIACOMO.]

I'm sorry for it ; but the guards are waiting
At his own gate, and such was my contrivance
That I might rid me both of him and them.
I thought to act a solemn comedy
Upon the painted scene of this new world,
And to attain my own peculiar ends
By some such plot of mingled good and ill   80
As others weave ; but there arose a Power
Which graspt and snapped the threads of my device.
And turned it to a net of ruin — Ha !
                    [*A shout is heard.*]
Is that my name I hear proclaimed abroad ?
But I will pass, wrapped in a vile disguise ;
Rags on my back, and a false innocence
Upon my face, through the misdeeming crowd
Which judges by what seems. 'Tis easy then,
For a new name and for a country new,
And a new life, fashioned on old desires,   90
To change the honours of abandoned Rome.
And these must be the masks of that within,
Which must remain unaltered. Oh, I fear
That what is past will never let me rest !
Why, when none else is conscious, but myself,
Of my misdeeds, should my own heart's contempt
Trouble me ? Have I not the power to fly
My own reproaches ? Shall I be the slave
Of — what ? A word ? which those of this false world
Employ against each other, not themselves ;   100
As men wear daggers not for self-offence.
But if I am mistaken, where shall I

Find the disguise to hide me from myself,
As now I skulk from every other eye ?
                    [*Exit.*]

SCENE 2.— *A Hall of Justice.* CAMILLO, JUDGES, &c., *are discovered seated ;* MARZIO *is led in.*

  First Judge. Accused, do you persist in your denial ?
I ask you, are you innocent, or guilty ?
I demand who were the participators
In your offence ? Speak truth and the whole truth.
  Marzio. My God ! I did not kill him ; I know nothing ;
Olimpio sold the robe to me from which
You would infer my guilt.
  Second Judge.   Away with him !
  First Judge. Dare you, with lips yet white from the rack's kiss,
Speak false ? Is it so soft a questioner,
That you would bandy lover's talk with it   10
Till it wind out your life and soul ? Away !
  Marzio. Spare me ! O, spare ! I will confess.
  First Judge.   Then speak.
  Marzio. I strangled him in his sleep.
  First Judge.   Who urged you to it ?
  Marzio. His own son Giacomo, and the young prelate
Orsino sent me to Petrella ; there
The ladies Beatrice and Lucretia
Tempted me with a thousand crowns, and I
And my companion forthwith murdered him.
Now let me die.
  First Judge. This sounds as bad as truth. Guards, there,
Lead forth the prisoners !
[*Enter* LUCRETIA, BEATRICE, *and* GIACOMO, *guarded.*]
                Look upon this man ;   20
When did you see him last ?
  Beatrice.   We never saw him.
  Marzio. You know me too well, Lady Beatrice.
  Beatrice. I know thee ! How ? where ? when ?
  Marzio.   You know 'twas I
Whom you did urge with menaces and bribes
To kill your father. When the thing was done
You clothed me in a robe of woven gold
And bade me thrive : how I have thriven, you see.

You, my Lord Giacomo, Lady Lucretia,
You know that what I speak is true.
[BEATRICE *advances towards him ; he covers
his face, and shrinks back.*]
                Oh, dart
The terrible resentment of those eyes   30
On the dead earth ! Turn them away from
   me !
They wound : 'twas torture forced the
   truth. My Lords,
Having said this, let me be led to death.
   Beatrice. Poor wretch, I pity thee : yet
     stay awhile.
   Camillo. Guards, lead him not away.
   Beatrice.   Cardinal Camillo,
You have a good repute for gentleness
And wisdom : can it be that you sit here
To countenance a wicked farce like this ?
When some obscure and trembling slave is
   dragged
From sufferings which might shake the
   sternest heart,   40
And bade to answer, not as he believes,
But as those may suspect or do desire,
Whose questions thence suggest their own
   reply ;
And that in peril of such hideous torments
As merciful God spares even the damned.
   Speak now
The thing you surely know, which is, that
   you
If your fine frame were stretched upon
   that wheel,
And you were told : "Confess that you did
   poison
Your little nephew ; that fair blue-eyed
   child
Who was the lodestar of your life :" — and
   though   50
All see, since his most swift and piteous
   death,
That day and night, and heaven and
   earth, and time,
And all the things hoped for or done
   therein
Are changed to you, through your exceed-
   ing grief,
Yet you would say, "I confess anything :"
And beg from your tormentors, like that
   slave,
The refuge of dishonourable death.
I pray thee, Cardinal, that thou assert
My innocence.
   Camillo [*much moved*]. What shall we
     think, my Lords ?
Shame on these tears ! I thought the heart
   was frozen   60
Which is their fountain. I would pledge
   my soul

That she is guiltless.
   Judge.   Yet she must be tortured.
   Camillo. I would as soon have tortured
     mine own nephew
(If he now lived, he would be just her
   age ;
His hair, too, was her colour, and his eyes
Like hers in shape, but blue, and not so
   deep)
As that most perfect image of God's love
That ever came sorrowing upon the earth.
She is as pure as speechless infancy !
   Judge. Well, be her purity on your
    head, my Lord,   70
If you forbid the rack. His Holiness
Enjoined us to pursue this monstrous
   crime
By the severest forms of law ; nay, even
To stretch a point against the criminals.
The prisoners stand accused of parricide,
Upon such evidence as justifies
Torture.
   Beatrice. What evidence ? This man's ?
   Judge.   Even so.
   Beatrice [to MARZIO]. Come near. And
    who art thou thus chosen forth
Out of the multitude of living men
To kill the innocent ?
   Marzio.   I am Marzio,   80
Thy father's vassal.
   Beatrice.   Fix thine eyes on mine ;
Answer to what I ask.   [*Turning to the
                  Judges.*]
            I prithee mark
His countenance : unlike bold calumny,
Which sometimes dares not speak the
   thing it looks,
He dares not look the thing he speaks, but
   bends
His gaze on the blind earth.
[*To* MARZIO.]   What ! wilt thou say
That I did murder my own father ?
   Marzio.   Oh !
Spare me ! My brain swims round — I can-
   not speak —
It was that horrid torture forced the truth.
Take me away ! Let her not look on
   me !   90
I am a guilty, miserable wretch ;
I have said all I know ; now, let me die !
   Beatrice. My lords, if by nature I had
    been
So stern, as to have planned the crime
   alleged,
Which your suspicions dictate to this slave,
And the rack makes him utter, do you
   think
I should have left this two-edged instru-
   ment

Of my misdeed ; this man ; this bloody
  knife
With my own name engraven on the heft,
Lying unsheathed amid a world of foes, 100
For my own death ? That with such hor-
  rible need
For deepest silence, I should have ne-
  glected
So trivial a precaution, as the making
His tomb the keeper of a secret written
On a thief's memory ? What is his poor
  life ?
What are a thousand lives ? A parricide
Had trampled them like dust ; and see,
  he lives !
[*Turning to* MARZIO.] And thou —
  Marzio.   Oh, spare me ! Speak to me
  no more !
That stern yet piteous look, those solemn
  tones,
Wound worse than torture.
  [*To the Judges.*] I have told it all ; 110
For pity's sake lead me away to death.
  Camillo. Guards, lead him nearer the
  Lady Beatrice,
He shrinks from her regard like autumn's
  leaf
From the keen breath of the serenest
  north.
  Beatrice. Oh, thou who tremblest on the
  giddy verge
Of life and death, pause ere thou answer-
  est me ;
So mayst thou answer God with less dis-
  may :
What evil have we done thee ? I, alas !
Have lived but on this earth a few sad
  years
And so my lot was ordered, that a fa-
  ther   120
First turned the moments of awakening
  life
To drops, each poisoning youth's sweet
  hope ; and then
Stabbed with one blow my everlasting
  soul ;
And my untainted fame ; and even that
  peace
Which sleeps within the core of the heart's
  heart.
But the wound was not mortal ; so my
  hate
Became the only worship I could lift
To our great father, who in pity and love,
Armed thee, as thou dost say, to cut him
  off ;
And thus his wrong becomes my accu-
  sation ;   130
And art thou the accuser ? If thou hopest

Mercy in heaven, show justice upon earth :
Worse than a bloody hand is a hard heart.
If thou hast done murders, made thy life's
  path
Over the trampled laws of God and man,
Rush not before thy Judge, and say : "My
  Maker,
I have done this and more ; for there was
  one
Who was most pure and innocent on
  earth ;
And because she endured what never any
Guilty or innocent endured before ;   140
Because her wrongs could not be told, not
  thought ;
Because thy hand at length did rescue
  her ;
I with my words killed her and all her
  kin."
Think, I adjure you, what it is to slay
The reverence living in the minds of men
Towards our ancient house, and stainless
  fame !
Think what it is to strangle infant pity.
Cradled in the belief of guileless looks,
Till it become a crime to suffer. Think
What 'tis to blot with infamy and blood 150
All that which shows like innocence, and
  is,
Hear me, great God ! I swear, most in-
  nocent,
So that the world lose all discrimination
Between the sly, fierce, wild regard of
  guilt,
And that which now compels thee to reply
To what I ask : Am I, or am I not
A parricide ?
  Marzio. Thou art not !
  Judge.   What is this ?
  Marzio. I here declare those whom I
  did accuse
Are innocent. 'Tis I alone am guilty.
  Judge. Drag him away to torments ; let
  them be   160
Subtle and long drawn out, to tear the
  folds
Of the heart's inmost cell. Unbind him
  not
Till he confess.
  Marzio.   Torture me as ye will :
A keener pang has wrung a higher truth
From my last breath. She is most inno-
  cent !
Bloodhounds, not men, glut yourselves well
  with me ;
I will not give you that fine piece of
  nature
To rend and ruin.
                   [*Exit* MARZIO, *guarded.*]

Camillo.   What say ye now, my Lords?

Judge. Let tortures strain the truth till it
    be white

As snow thrice-sifted by the frozen wind. 170

Camillo. Yet stained with blood.

Judge [to BEATRICE].   Know you this
    paper, Lady?

Beatrice. Entrap me not with questions.
    Who stands here

As my accuser? Ha! wilt thou be he,

Who art my judge? Accuser, witness,
    judge,

What, all in one? Here is Orsino's name:

Where is Orsino? Let his eye meet mine.

What means this scrawl? Alas! ye know
    not what,

And therefore on the chance that it may
    be

Some evil, will ye kill us?

[*Enter an Officer.*]

Officer.   Marzio's dead.

Judge. What did he say?

Officer.   Nothing. As soon as we   180

Had bound him on the wheel, he smiled
    on us,

As one who baffles a deep adversary;

And holding his breath, died.

Judge.   There remains nothing

But to apply the question to those prison-
    ers,

Who yet remain stubborn.

Camillo.   I overrule

Further proceedings, and in the behalf

Of these most innocent and noble persons

Will use my interest with the Holy Father.

Judge. Let the Pope's pleasure then be
    done. Meanwhile

Conduct these culprits each to separate
    cells;   190

And be the engines ready: for this night,

If the Pope's resolution be as grave,

Pious, and just as once, I'll wring the truth

Out of those nerves and sinews, groan by
    groan.

                [*Exeunt.*]

SCENE 3. — *The Cell of a Prison.* BEATRICE
is discovered asleep on a couch. Enter BER-
NARDO.

Bernardo. How gently slumber rests upon
    her face,

Like the last thoughts of some day sweetly
    spent

Closing in night and dreams, and so pro-
    longed.

After such torments as she bore last night,

How light and soft her breathing comes.

Ay, me!

Methinks that I shall never sleep again.

But I must shake the heavenly dew of rest

From this sweet folded flower, thus —
    wake! awake!

What, sister, canst thou sleep?

Beatrice [awaking]. I was just dreaming

That we were all in Paradise. Thou
    knowest   10

This cell seems like a kind of Paradise

After our father's presence.

Bernardo.   Dear, dear sister,

Would that thy dream were not a dream!
    O God!

How shall I tell?

Beatrice. What wouldst thou tell, sweet
    brother?

Bernardo. Look not so calm and happy,
    or even whilst

I stand considering what I have to say

My heart will break.

Beatrice. See now, thou mak'st me weep:

How very friendless thou wouldst be, dear
    child,

If I were dead. Say what thou hast to say.

Bernardo. They have confessed; they
    could endure no more   20

The tortures —

Beatrice. Ha! What was there to con-
    fess?

They must have told some weak and
    wicked lie

To flatter their tormentors. Have they said

That they were guilty? O white innocence,

That thou shouldst wear the mask of guilt
    to hide

Thine awful and serenest countenance

From those who know thee not!

[*Enter* JUDGE, *with* LUCRETIA *and* GIACOMO,
    guarded.]

           Ignoble hearts!

For some brief spasms of pain, which are
    at least

As mortal as the limbs through which they
    pass,

Are centuries of high splendour laid in
    dust?   30

And that eternal honour which should
    live

Sun-like, above the reek of mortal fame,

Changed to a mockery and a bye-word?
    What!

Will you give up these bodies to be
    dragged

At horses' heels, so that our hair should
    sweep

The footsteps of the vain and senseless
    crowd,

Who, that they may make our calamity
Their worship and their spectacle, will
    leave
The churches and the theatres as void
As their own hearts ? Shall the light multi-
    tude   40
Fling, at their choice, curses or faded pity,
Sad funeral flowers to deck a living corpse,
Upon us as we pass, to pass away,
And leave — what memory of our having
    been ?
Infamy, blood, terror, despair ? O thou,
Who wert a mother to the parentless,
Kill not thy child ! Let not her wrongs kill
    thee !
Brother, lie down with me upon the rack,
And let us each be silent as a corpse ;
It soon will be as soft as any grave.   50
'Tis but the falsehood it can wring from
    fear
Makes the rack cruel.
    Giacomo.   They will tear the truth
Even from thee at last, those cruel pains :
For pity's sake say thou art guilty now.
    Lucretia. O, speak the truth ! Let us all
        quickly die ;
And after death, God is our judge, not
    they ;
He will have mercy on us.
    Bernardo.   If indeed
It can be true, say so, dear sister mine ;
And then the Pope will surely pardon you,
And all be well.
    Judge.   Confess, or I will warp   60
Your limbs with such keen tortures —
    Beatrice.   Tortures ! Turn
The rack henceforth into a spinning-
    wheel !
Torture your dog, that he may tell when
    last
He lapped the blood his master shed —
    not me !
My pangs are of the mind, and of the
    heart,
And of the soul ; ay, of the inmost soul,
Which weeps within tears as of burning
    gall
To see, in this ill world where none are
    true,
My kindred false to their deserted selves.
And with considering all the wretched
    life   70
Which I have lived, and its now wretched
    end,
And the small justice shown by Heaven
    and Earth
To me or mine ; and what a tyrant thou
    art,

And what slaves these ; and what a world
    we make,
The oppressor and the oppressed — such
    pangs compel
My answer. What is it thou wouldst with
    me ?
    Judge. Art thou not guilty of thy father's
        death ?
    Beatrice. Or wilt thou rather tax high-
        judging God
That he permitted such an act as that
Which I have suffered, and which he be-
    held ;   80
Made it unutterable, and took from it
All refuge, all revenge, all consequence,
But that which thou hast called my father's
    death ?
Which is or is not what men call a crime,
Which either I have done, or have not
    done ;
Say what ye will. I shall deny no more.
If ye desire it thus, thus let it be,
And so an end of all. Now do your will ;
No other pains shall force another word.
    Judge. She is convicted, but has not con-
        fessed.   90
Be it enough. Until their final sentence
Let none have converse with them. You,
    young lord,
Linger not here !
    Beatrice.   Oh, tear him not away !
    Judge. Guards, do your duty.
    Bernardo [*embracing* BEATRICE].   Oh !
        would ye divide
Body from soul ?
    Officer. That is the headsman's business.
        [*Exeunt all but* LUCRETIA, BEA-
        TRICE, *and* GIACOMO.
    Giacomo. Have I confessed ? Is it all
        over now ?
No hope ? No refuge ! O weak, wicked
    tongue,
Which hast destroyed me, would that thou
    hadst been
Cut out and thrown to dogs first ! To have
    killed
My father first, and then betrayed my
    sister ;   100
Ay, thee ! the one thing innocent and pure
In this black guilty world, to that which I
So well deserve ! My wife ! my little ones !
Destitute, helpless ; and I — Father ! God !
Canst thou forgive even the unforgiving,
When their full hearts break thus, thus !
        [*Covers his face and weeps.*]
    Lucretia.   O, my child !
To what a dreadful end are we all come !
Why did I yield ? Why did I not sustain

Those torments? Oh, that I were all dis-
    solved
Into these fast and unavailing tears,   110
Which flow and feel not!
   Beatrice.   What 'twas weak to do,
'Tis weaker to lament, once being done;
Take cheer! The God who knew my
    wrong, and made
Our speedy act the angel of his wrath,
Seems, and but seems to have abandoned
    us.
Let us not think that we shall die for this.
Brother, sit near me; give me your firm
    hand,
You had a manly heart. Bear up! bear
    up!
Oh! dearest Lady, put your gentle head
Upon my lap, and try to sleep awhile: 120
Your eyes look pale, hollow, and overworn,
With heaviness of watching and slow grief.
Come, I will sing you some low, sleepy
    tune,
Not cheerful, nor yet sad; some dull old
    thing,
Some outworn and unused monotony,
Such as our country gossips sing and spin,
Till they almost forget they live; lie
    down!
So, that will do. Have I forgot the words?
Faith! they are sadder than I thought they
    were.

SONG

False friend, wilt thou smile or weep   130
When my life is laid asleep?
Little cares for a smile or a tear,
The clay-cold corpse upon the bier!
      Farewell! Heigh ho!
      What is this whispers low?
There is a snake in thy smile, my dear;
And bitter poison within thy tear.

Sweet sleep, were death like to thee,
Or if thou couldst mortal be,
I would close these eyes of pain;   140
When to wake? Never again.
      O World! Farewell!
      Listen to the passing bell!
It says, thou and I must part,
With a light and a heavy heart.
                [*The scene closes.*]

SCENE 4. — *A Hall of the Prison. Enter*
CAMILLO *and* BERNARDO.

   Camillo. The Pope is stern; not to be
    moved or bent.
He looked as calm and keen as is the
engine
Which tortures and which kills, exempt
    itself
From aught that it inflicts; a marble form,
A rite, a law, a custom: not a man.
He frowned, as if to frown had been the
    trick
Of his machinery, on the advocates
Presenting the defences, which he tore
And threw behind, muttering with hoarse,
    harsh voice:
"Which among ye defended their old
    father,   10
Killed in his sleep?" Then to another:
    "Thou
Dost this in virtue of thy place; 'tis well."
He turned to me then, looking depreca-
    tion,
And said these three words, coldly: "They
    must die."
   Bernardo. And yet you left him not?
   Camillo.   I urged him still;
Pleading, as I could guess, the devilish
    wrong
Which prompted your unnatural parent's
    death.
And he replied: "Paolo Santa Croce
Murdered his mother yester evening,
And he is fled. Parricide grows so rife,   20
That soon, for some just cause no doubt,
    the young
Will strangle us all, dozing in our chairs.
Authority, and power, and hoary hair
Are grown crimes capital. You are my
    nephew,
You come to ask their pardon; stay a
    moment;
Here is their sentence; never see me more
Till, to the letter, it be all fulfilled."
   Bernardo. O God, not so! I did believe
    indeed
That all you said was but sad preparation
For happy news. O, there are words and
    looks   30
To bend the sternest purpose! Once I
    knew them,
Now I forget them at my dearest need.
What think you if I seek him out, and
    bathe
His feet and robe with hot and bitter
    tears?
Importune him with prayers, vexing his
    brain
With my perpetual cries, until in rage
He strike me with his pastoral cross, and
    trample
Upon my prostrate head, so that my blood
May stain the senseless dust on which he
    treads,

And remorse waken mercy? I will do
   it !   40
O, wait till I return !   [*Rushes out.*]
   Camillo.   Alas ! poor boy !
A wreck-devoted seaman thus might pray
To the deaf sea.
[*Enter* LUCRETIA, BEATRICE, *and* GIACOMO,
   guarded.]
   Beatrice.   I hardly dare to fear
That thou bring'st other news than a just
   pardon.
   Camillo. May God in heaven be less in-
   exorable
To the Pope's prayers, than he has been to
   mine.
Here is the sentence and the warrant.
   Beatrice [*wildly*].   Oh,
My God ! Can it be possible I have
To die so suddenly ? So young to go
Under the obscure, cold, rotting, wormy
   ground !   50
To be nailed down into a narrow place ;
To see no more sweet sunshine ; hear no
   more
Blithe voice of living thing ; muse not
   again
Upon familiar thoughts, sad, yet thus lost !
How fearful ! to be nothing ! Or to be—
What ? O, where am I ? Let me not go
   mad !
Sweet Heaven, forgive weak thoughts ! If
   there should be
No God, no Heaven, no Earth in the void
   world ;
The wide, grey, lampless, deep, unpeopled
   world !
If all things then should be — my father's
   spirit,   60
His eye, his voice, his touch surrounding
   me ;
The atmosphere and breath of my dead
   life !
If sometimes, as a shape more like himself,
Even the form which tortured me on
   earth,
Masked in grey hairs and wrinkles, he
   should come
And wind me in his hellish arms, and fix
His eyes on mine, and drag me down,
   down, down !
For was he not alone omnipotent
On Earth, and ever present ? even tho'
   dead,
Does not his spirit live in all that
   breathe,   70
And work for me and mine still the same
   ruin,
Scorn, pain, despair ? Who ever yet re-
   turned

To teach the laws of death's untrodden
   realm ?
Unjust perhaps as those which drive us
   now,
O, whither, whither ?
   Lucretia.   Trust in God's sweet love,
The tender promises of Christ : ere night,
Think, we shall be in Paradise.
   Beatrice.   'Tis past !
Whatever comes, my heart shall sink no
   more.
And yet, I know not why, your words
   strike chill :
How tedious, false, and cold seem all
   things. I   80
Have met with much injustice in this
   world ;
No difference has been made by God or
   man,
Or any power moulding my wretched lot,
'Twixt good or evil, as regarded me.
I am cut off from the only world I know,
From light, and life, and love, in youth's
   sweet prime.
You do well telling me to trust in God,
I hope I do trust in him. In whom else
Can any trust ? And yet my heart is cold.
   [*During the latter speeches* GIACOMO *has*
   retired conversing with CAMILLO, *who*
   now goes out ; GIACOMO *advances.*]
   Giacomo. Know you not, mother — sis-
   ter, know you not ?   90
Bernardo even now is gone to implore
The Pope to grant our pardon.
   Lucretia.   Child, perhaps
It will be granted. We may all then live
To make these woes a tale for distant
   years :
O, what a thought ! It gushes to my heart
Like the warm blood.
   Beatrice.   Yet both will soon be cold.
O, trample out that thought ! Worse than
   despair,
Worse than the bitterness of death, is
   hope :
It is the only ill which can find place
Upon the giddy, sharp and narrow
   hour   100
Tottering beneath us. Plead with the swift
   frost
That it should spare the eldest flower of
   spring :
Plead with awakening earthquake, o'er
   whose couch
Even now a city stands, strong, fair, and
   free ;
Now stench and blackness yawn, like
   death. O, plead
With famine, or wind-walking pestilence,

Blind lightning, or the deaf sea, not with
　　man !
Cruel, cold, formal man ; righteous in
　　words,
In deeds a Cain. No, mother, we must die :
Since such is the reward of innocent
　　lives ;　　　　　　　　　　　　110
Such the alleviation of worst wrongs.
And whilst our murderers live, and hard,
　　cold men,
Smiling and slow, walk through a world of
　　tears
To death as to life's sleep ; 'twere just the
　　grave
Were some strange joy for us. Come, ob-
　　scure Death,
And wind me in thine all-embracing arms !
Like a fond mother hide me in thy bosom,
And rock me to the sleep from which none
　　wake.
Live ye, who live, subject to one another
As we were once, who now —
[BERNARDO *rushes in.*]
　　Bernardo.　　　　　　O, horrible !　120
That tears, that looks, that hope poured
　　forth in prayer,
Even till the heart is vacant and despairs,
Should all be vain ! The ministers of death
Are waiting round the doors. I thought I
　　saw
Blood on the face of one — what if 'twere
　　fancy ?
Soon the heart's blood of all I love on
　　earth
Will sprinkle him, and he will wipe it off
As if 'twere only rain. O life ! O world !
Cover me ! let me be no more ! To see
That perfect mirror of pure innocence　130
Wherein I gazed, and grew happy and
　　good,
Shivered to dust ! To see thee, Beatrice,
Who made all lovely thou didst look
　　upon —
Thee, light of life — dead, dark ! while I
　　say, sister,
To hear I have no sister ; and thou,
　　Mother,
Whose love was as a bond to all our
　　loves —

Dead ! The sweet bond broken !
[*Enter* CAMILLO *and* GUARDS.]
　　　　　　　　　　They come ! Let me
Kiss those warm lips before their crimson
　　leaves
Are blighted — white — cold. Say farewell,
　　before
Death chokes that gentle voice ! O, let me
　　hear　　　　　　　　　　　　140
You speak !
　　Beatrice. Farewell, my tender brother.
　　Think
Of our sad fate with gentleness, as now :
And let mild, pitying thoughts lighten
　　for thee
Thy sorrow's load. Err not in harsh de-
　　spair,
But tears and patience. One thing more,
　　my child,
For thine own sake be constant to the love
Thou bearest us ; and to the faith that I,
Though wrapped in a strange cloud of
　　crime and shame,
Lived ever holy and unstained. And
　　though
Ill tongues shall wound me, and our com-
　　mon name　　　　　　　　　　150
Be as a mark stamped on thine innocent
　　brow
For men to point at as they pass, do thou
Forbear, and never think a thought un-
　　kind
Of those who perhaps love thee in their
　　graves.
So mayest thou die as I do ; fear and pain
Being subdued. Farewell ! farewell ! fare-
　　well !
　　Bernardo. I cannot say, farewell !
　　Camillo.　　　　　O, Lady Beatrice !
　　Beatrice. Give yourself no unnecessary
　　pain,
My dear Lord Cardinal. Here, Mother, tie
My girdle for me, and bind up this hair　160
In any simple knot ; ay, that does well.
And yours I see is coming down. How
　　often
Have we done this for one another ; now
We shall not do it any more. My Lord,
We are quite ready. Well, 'tis very well.

5

JOHN KEATS'S *OTHO THE GREAT*

Much critical ink has been spilt (and much squandered) in speculation about what Keats might have accomplished had he lived more than twenty-five years. A good deal of this conjecturing has been grounded in estimates of his abilities as a dramatist, and not without good reason. Bernice Slote has convincingly demonstrated the dramatic qualities of Keats's mind, the increasing dramatic objectivity of his poems, and the extent to which he was imbued with the actual theater of his day.[1] And elsewhere I have tried to show that the poetry, considered as a whole, reveals many dramatic clashes of attitude and idea between poem and poem.[2]

Most of the speculation, however, is based on Keats's own comments on the importance of the dramatic element in poetry, on the nature of drama, on his three newspaper reviews of particular performances, on his admiration for the acting of Edmund Kean, and on his profound veneration of Shakespeare. The examination of Keats's own statements must be conducted warily, for they often bear contradictory implications.

The most significant of Keats's statements about the dramatic are those which, taken together, reveal his definition of "the poetical character," whose unique ability it is to perform two related acts. First, he must be able to be content with half-knowledge and not reach irritably after fact and reason. Second, he must be able to free himself of his personal identity and be able intuitively to assume the identities of others. This Eliotian impersonality of the poet, described forever by Keats as "negative capability," is traced extremely well by Slote.

No matter how crucial it is for a dramatist to possess "negative capability," it must not detract from his ability to be what George Bernard Shaw called an "artist-philosopher." Not a tub-thumper, the artist-philosopher is one whose concerns are with the unities of the world, not its diversities. (See the extended discussion in the "Epistle Dedicatory" to *Man and Superman*.) Keats, who many critics still think rejected a life of thought for a life of sensation, falls between two stools in *Otho*; his "negative capability" was not sufficiently intense for him to create characters of more than two dimensions, and his lack of a plan, what Shaw would call "something to assert," are both reasons for the drama's lack of greatness.

There is even more evidence in Keats's letters that points to a mind divided about the nature of drama, and this division unfortunately complements the one just discussed. Despite his ambitions "to make as great a revolution in modern

---

1. *Keats and the Dramatic Principle* (Nebraska, 1958).
2. *The Other Poetry of Keats* (Rutherford, Madison, Teaneck, N.J., 1969).

dramatic writing as Kean has done in acting" and to write a "few fine plays," he confesses a few lines after the first statement, "I look upon fine Phrases like a Lover." This cannot but remind us of his earlier statement to Bailey that "the Lovers of Poetry like to have a little Region to wander in where they may pick and choose, and in which the images are so numerous that many are forgotten and found new in a second Reading." This lack of awareness of the need for dramatic tension must be set against our recognition that Keats realized very early that his "chief attempt in the drama" would be marked by "the playing of different Natures with Joy and Sorrow."

Given this set of critical attitudes, we should not be surprised to find Keats's theatrical criticism more concerned with the acting than with the drama. The most passionate and memorable parts of the reviews are those in which Keats describes Kean's "negative capability": "there is an incredible *gusto* in his voice, by which we feel that the utterer is thinking of the past and future while speaking of the instant." And again, "Kean delivers himself up to the instant of feeling, without a shadow of a thought about anything else." These statements are not contradictory; both reveal the depth and intensity of Kean's understanding of a character—an understanding so complete and complex as to seem fully intuitive and empathetic.

I wrote earlier that *Otho* has nothing to assert. Of course, this weakness is not all Keats's fault. The conditions of his collaboration with Charles Brown must be remembered. During the summer of 1819, during the composition of *Otho*, Keats was also composing *Lamia,* one of his best and most important poems, and revising (and in many respects improving) *Hyperion.* Fresh from the composition of his greatest poems, the magnificent Odes of May and June, he was at the height of his poetical powers. Yet he was tormented by the fear that he was nothing more than "a pet lamb in a sentimental farce." Suffering from a severe sore throat, and tortured by his guardian's dark hints about a lawsuit and by his brother George's requests for money, Keats himself was unable to afford to take a coach to visit his sister. Exacerbating these frustrations was his separation from Fanny Brawne. Now in the midst of this emotional turmoil Keats and his friend Charles Brown were attempting to compose a successful drama in the following "curious" way:

> I [writes Brown] engaged to furnish him with the fable, characters, and dramatic conduct of a tragedy, and he was to embody it into poetry. The progress of this work was curious; for while I sat opposite to him, he caught my description of each scene, *entered into* the characters to be brought forward, the events, and everything connected with it. Thus he went on, scene after scene, never knowing nor inquiring into the scene which was to follow until four acts were completed. It was then he required to know, at once, all the events which were to occupy the fifth act. I explained them to him; but after patient hearing and some thought, he insisted on it that my incidents were too numerous, and, as he termed them, too melodramatic. He wrote the fifth act in accordance with his own view.
>
> [my italics]

Even the timetable of composition is amazing. Between July 22 and August 23 they completed writing and copying the play. On July 31 Keats wrote: "Brown and I are pretty well harnessed again to our dog-cart. I mean the tragedy, which goes on sinkingly." By August 12 they had written nearly a thousand lines of the finished play—or four acts. But by August 16 he writes to Fanny Brawne, "I have been caught in the claws, like a Serpent in an Eagle's, of the last act of our tragedy." Slote takes this as confirmation that Keats was successful in "getting an artist's hold on playwriting" and that he "*was* in the grip of a creative urge so intense and complete that he actually had no other self." But I do not believe that Keats's statement can be so taken. That he was imaginatively caught up in the play is possible, but that he was caught up in it with the hope that he would make £200 is very clear. Writing *Otho* was a way to salvation on earth, not in heaven.

Another problem presented itself to Keats in the historicity of the material. In a review no longer attributed to Keats, but whose ideas—though belonging to his close friend John Hamilton Reynolds—are close to what we have seen Keats writing, the restrictions of historical dramas are identified.

> They are written with infinite vigour, but their regularity tied the hand of Shakespeare. Particular facts kept him in the high road, and would not suffer him to turn down leafy and winding lanes, or to break wildly and at once into the breathing fields. The poetry is for the most part ironed and manacled with a chain of facts, and cannot get free; it cannot escape from the prison house of history, nor often move without our being disturbed by the clanking of its fetters.

Of course, this attitude, no matter how close to Keats's own, cannot excuse the weaknesses of *Otho,* any more than can the other exigencies of its composition. Nevertheless, they are difficulties worth making clear, for understanding them may make us wonder that the play is no worse than it is.

A further drawback to the composition of an excellent tragedy was the idea, nearly the passion, that only Kean could play the role of Ludolph. The effects of the star system are seldom seen so clearly as in this play, but it is important to remember that not all of them were meretricious. Keats's writing for Kean may well be what prompted him, especially in the fifth act, to concentrate more and more on the character of Ludolph. This is all to the good, for one of the weaknesses of the early acts of the play is that our sympathies are not clearly focused anywhere. As a hindrance to the play its effects are more easily seen in the play's fortunes in the world. Keats was alarmed by a rumor that Kean was going to America for the season, but he was away from Drury Lane only during the early weeks. The completed play was sent to Elliston, the manager, early in October. Though it was accepted, it was with the stipulation that it would not be acted until the season of 1820–21. The delay seemed intolerable for many reasons, and Macready's recent successes at Covent Garden determined the authors to send it there. It was speedily returned, apparently unread. (Bernice Slote gives a fine account of the difficulties both theaters were experiencing at the time. See her chapter 7 for a detailed account of their financial and artistic straits.)

Still, this drama is one of the few in this collection that is not only fit for the stage but was accepted by a theater manager. *Otho* was not performed until 1950, but at that time it was relatively successful.[3]

It is time now to turn to the play itself and account for its partial successes and equally partial failures. In fact, there may be one overriding reason accounting for both. The play quite clearly lacks focus. There is neither a strong central character with whose fate and personality we are involved, nor a clear and vigorous plot whose outcome is a matter of doubt and interest. There are, however, so many characters and plots constantly being brought into the light and then submerged that our interest is kept alive by tantalization if nothing else.

The possibilities for plot are numerous. We begin with—and sustain rather weakly through Act IV—the possibilities of political intrigue. Conrad may indeed be plotting to otherthrow Otho by destroying Ludolph and counting on his own recent, calculated shows of loyalty to make him the favorite. The intrigue never gets fully explained, but it is continually present. Ultimately, it is so weak that

---

3. See Dorothy Hewlett, "Otho The Great," *KSMB* 4 (1952) .

it does not even become a counterplot. Conrad is credible primarily because we
are familiar with characters like him from other melodramas (and the device of
the supposedly destroyed letter in Act I is pure melodrama) .

But the conflict between traitorous rebel and benevolent establishment remains
undeveloped. Even in Act I it is (apparently) replaced by the conflict between
Otho and Ludolph—the classic oedipal, generational conflict. Ludolph wants not
only his father's love as a son but also his respect as a man. Precisely, this conflict
is revealed in scene 3 of Act I—an act, by the way, extremely well balanced from
the point of view of bringing to our attention the three conflicting parties and
their motivations. Ludolph confides to Sigifred the reasons for his ambivalence:

> S. What made you then, with such an anxious love,
> Hover round that life whose bitter days
> You vext with bad revolt?
>
> (ll. 32–34)

Ludolph replies in part:

>   twas not to make
> A father his son's debtor, or to heal
> His deep heart-sickness for a rebel child.
> Twas done in memory of my boyish days,
> Poor cancel for his kindness to my youth,
> For all his calming of my childish griefs,
> And all his smiles upon my merriment.
> No, not a thousand foughten fields could sponge
> Those days paternal from my memory,
> Though now upon my head he heaps disgrace.
>
> (ll. 37–46)

But he also demands that the relationship cannot continue to exist as it once
did. Ludolph does not want his father's pity, he wants that kind of equality and
love that should, he thinks, exist between two grown men. Ludolph will go to
his father

> And parlay with him, as a son should do
> Who doubly loaths a father's tyranny;
> Tell him how feeble is that tyranny;
> How the relationship of father and son
> Is no more valid than a silken leash
> Where lions tug adverse, if love grow not
> From interchanged love through many years.
>
> (ll. 95–101)

Here is promising material for a mature psychological drama. Yet, when the
men confront each other (Act II, scene 2) , Otho, who had demonstrated con-
siderable political sagacity and human warmth, rails at his son and threatens him.
He'll cage him up and choose as a jailor Auranthe—the woman with whom
Ludolph is in love. This dreadfully juvenile trick of Otho's completely and in
a twinkling melts Ludolph's heart, and all the tension is drained from the conflict.

Thus we are left with a love story as material for the plot. Ludolph had once
loved Erminia, Otho's niece, but Conrad and his sister Auranthe have conspired
to make it appear that Erminia's honor has been compromised. We find her a
prisoner in the camp of the enemy, and we may be tempted to think of her as
a Cressida in the moments when we think we have a political story being played

before us. But Erminia's character is so undeveloped that it is a good thing that her role in the plot is not more prominent, that she does not win back the love of Ludolph. We are drawn to her not because of her own personality but because she is unlike Auranthe and because she is defended by Ethelbert, whose warmth and generosity are evident early in Act I, scene 2. Between the establishment of Erminia's innocence in Act III and her reconciliation with Otho in Act V, she is not on stage at all, and it would be disastrous for her to play a more active role in a plot of love.

One more plot possibility is raised in the play and must be discussed before we look at the love of Ludolph and Auranthe. Albert, whose loyalty is divided between Erminia and Auranthe, is for a time the center of our attention. Albert has promised Erminia that he will deliver to Otho the letter proving the treachery of Conrad and Auranthe. Yet he is all too aware of his own deep implication in the plot against Erminia, and of the hold Conrad has over him as a result. After his refusal to divulge the letter during the highly dramatic encounter of Act III, scene 2, Albert swears he'll triumph over Conrad. But because he loves Auranthe he tries to devise an escape from the country. Albert's failure to choose removes another character from the center of dramatic interest.

For lack of anything else, we are left with Ludolph and Auranthe as the focus of attention. But even here there is no clear plot. Most of the time we are convinced of Auranthe's capacity for evil, but there are two considerations that intervene in the story of a good man in love with a treacherous woman.

First, though Auranthe's love for Ludolph may seem to be politically motivated, there are frequent suggestions that her actions and motives are not so plain as they seem. For example, early in Act I we learn that she and Conrad have not always agreed; did she perhaps try to thwart his ignoble designs? We learn that she has a sin-worn cheek. Is she perhaps a female Byronic hero? She swears she'll not be perjured in her love for Albert—but yes, she will, though she'll not see him suffer any wrong. Her welcome to Otho is a very gracious speech—but perhaps it is merely a stratagem; her behavior is reminiscent of Lady Macbeth's. She is shrewd enough to recognize that, as Queen, she will have power over her brother, who will try to take advantage of her position. She is called "bewitching," and perhaps she does possess those magic love philtres spoken of in Act III, scene 2. There the confrontation of the six major characters is highly dramatic, and much like the one in *Lamia* wherein Apollonius (Ethelbert) tries to show Lycius (Ludolph) the evil nature of his lover, Lamia (Auranthe).

The second consideration detracting from the progress of the plot develops from this identification with *Lamia*. In Auranthe's long speech in Act IV, scene 1, she expresses her fear that she will "melt in the visionary air" before her wishes can be attained. (Lamia, we are told, vanishes.) There is regret and remorse in her character, but there is none evident in Conrad's. Knowing that Keats was composing *Lamia* at the same time he was at work on *Otho*, one might think that Auranthe was indeed a bewitching, possibly evil, spirit. She can "make the forest hiss" and is called a cockatrice, so that, like Lamia, she has, at least in part, a serpent-like nature. We do not know whether Lamia was originally an evil spirit, and there exists in *Otho* a similar problem: we do not know why Auranthe commits suicide. Does she repent? Does she realize that the world is lost? No matter, we have here an enigma that prevents us from thinking of the plot as involving merely the struggles of a good man and an evil woman. And as yet I have not even commented on the character of Ludolph, except to comment on his sudden change of heart toward Otho. His father calls Ludolph a man of extremes, and it is impossible to find in him enough depth or complexity to hold our interest as a tragic hero. Evidently he is merely a man of action, for when in Act V, scene 1 he hears a "glorious clamour" he begins to "live again." Why he goes mad and why he dies—or how he could die of a broken heart—are unexplained by his characterization in the play.

Therefore, despite what Keats had learned about what Slote calls "the oil of dramatic action," the play is not a success. Yet it was performed successfully. In part this was possible because there is some good poetry in the speeches and a lack of awkwardness in the staging. And in part it may be attributable to some reminiscences of Shakespeare, not only in the lines but in the themes. The arrival of Otho at Conrad's Castle bodes Macbethian action, especially in view of Auranthe's speech (I, 2, 24 ff) and Otho's Duncanesque humanity. Constant references to minds diseased reinforce this motif. Ludolph's relations with his father threaten to lead down a Henry IV path. Gersa seems to function like Fortinbras, Ludolph's madness is akin to Hamlet's, and there is even some Shakespearian rhetoric (see, for example, I, 3, 70 ff).

Imparting even more significance to the play are echoes of familiar Keatsian themes, and their resonance may also account for some of *Otho's* success and power. Aileen Ward writes that the parallel between *Lamia* and *Otho*

is striking: in both the play and the poem there is a father figure who tries to win the infatuated lover back to the truth; in both the woman deceives her lover and is punished by death; and in both the man dies on his wedding night, broken-hearted at the exposure of his bride's falsity.[4]

Otho speaks of the love of Ludolph for Auranthe as "wizard-woven," and as like that in "old Romances," which by this point in his career Keats had rejected. The "wizard-woven" description strengthens the parallel with *Lamia*.

Moreover, we must look at what Ludolph sacrifices by choosing "this earth, this palace, this room, Auranthe."

> Though heaven's choir
> Should in a vast circumference descend
> And sing for my delight, I'd stop my ears!
> Though bright Apollo's car stood burning here,
> And he put out an arm to bid me mount,
> His touch an immortality, Not I!
>
> (III. ii. 38–43)

Ludolph would seem to be in the position of an Endymion who chooses the "real" maiden rather than the "ideal" one, but in this case the real maiden is, at best, the victim of an evil spell, not a beneficent one.

Furthermore, when Ludolph enters the banquet hall he describes a palace of art that he cannot attain as a mortal. But he has become aware, in his madness, of the malignant nature of the real hall which, like Lamia's purple-lined palace, is the scene of his marriage celebration. He becomes aware of a finer and more real hall located in a skyey realm, compared to which earthly splendor is dark. Ludolph, at the end of the play, is like many of Keats's would-be heroes, striving to attain, not reject, the realm of the visionary imagination.

Despite the weaknesses analyzed above, and despite the fact that the plot was not Keats's choice, we have some powerful verse combined with important Keatsian themes, which together may account for some of the play's success and for the power it still possesses.

G.B.K.

---

4. *John Keats.* (New York, 1963), p. 308.

Otho The Great

DRAMATIS PERSONAE

OTHO THE GREAT, *Emperor of Germany.*
LUDOLPH, *his Son.*
CONRAD, *Duke of Franconia.*
ALBERT, *a Knight, favoured by* OTHO
SIGIFRED, *an Officer, friend of Ludolph.*
THEODORE,⎫
GONFRED, ⎭ *Officers.*
ETHELBERT, *an Abbot.*
GERSA, *Prince of Hungary.*
An Hungarian Captain.
Physician.
Page.
Nobles, Knights, Attendants, and Soldiers.

ERMINIA, *Niece of Otho.*
AURANTHE, *Conrad's Sister.*
Ladies and Attendants.
SCENE. — *The Castle of Friedburg, its vicinity, and the Hungarian Camp.*
TIME. — *One Day.*

ACT I

SCENE I. — *An Apartment in the Castle.*
Enter CONRAD.

Conrad. So, I am safe emerged from these broils !
Amid the wreck of thousands I am whole ;
For every crime I have a laurel-wreath,
For every lie a lordship. Nor yet has
My ship of fortune furl'd her silken sails, —
Let her glide on ! This danger'd neck is saved,
By dexterous policy, from the rebel's axe ;
And of my ducal palace not one stone
Is bruised by the Hungarian petards.
Toil hard, ye slaves, and from the miser-
earth   10
Bring forth once more my bullion, treas-
ured deep,
With all my jewell'd salvers, silver and
gold,
And precious goblets that make rich the
wine.
But why do I stand babbling to myself ?
Where is Auranthe ? I have news for her
Shall —

Enter AURANTHE.

Auranthe. Conrad ! what tidings ? Good,
if I may guess
From your alert eyes and high-lifted brows.
What tidings of the battle ? Albert ? Lu-
dolph ? Otho ?
Conrad. You guess aright. And, sister,
slurring o'er
Our by-gone quarrels, I confess my
heart   20
Is beating with a child's anxiety,
To make our golden fortune known to
you.
Auranthe. So serious ?
Conrad.   Yes, so serious, that before
I utter even the shadow of a hint
Concerning what will make that sin-worn
cheek
Blush joyous blood through every linea-
ment,
You must make here a solemn vow to me.
Auranthe. I pr'ythee, Conrad, do not
overact
The hypocrite. What vow would you im-
pose ?
Conrad. Trust me for once. That you
may be assured   30
'Tis not confiding in a broken reed,
A poor court-bankrupt, outwitted and lost,
Revolve these facts in your acutest mood,
In such a mood as now you listen to me :
A few days since, I was an open rebel, —

175

Against the Emperor had suborn'd his
    son, —
Drawn off his nobles to revolt, — and
    shown
Contented fools causes for discontent,
Fresh hatch'd in my ambition's eagle-nest ;
So thrived I as a rebel, — and, behold   40
How I am Otho's favourite, his dear
    friend,
His right hand, his brave Conrad !
    Auranthe.   I confess
You have intrigued with these unsteady
    times
To admiration. But to be a favourite !
    Conrad. I saw my moment. The Hun-
        garians,
Collected silently in holes and corners,
Appear'd, a sudden host, in the open day.
I should have perish'd in our empire's
    wreck,
But, calling interest loyalty, swore faith
To most believing Otho ; and so help'd   50
His blood-stain'd ensigns to the victory
In yesterday's hard fight, that it has turn'd
The edge of his sharp wrath to eager kind-
    ness.
    Auranthe. So far yourself. But what is
        this to me
More than that I am glad ? I gratulate
    you.
    Conrad. Yes, sister, but it does regard
        you greatly,
Nearly, momentously, — aye, painfully !
Make me this vow —
    Auranthe. Concerning whom or what ?
    Conrad. Albert !
    Auranthe.   I would inquire somewhat
        of him :
You had a letter from me touching
    him ?   60
No treason 'gainst his head in deed or
    word !
Surely you spared him at my earnest
    prayer ?
Give me the letter — it should not exist !
    Conrad. At one pernicious charge of the
        enemy,
I, for a moment-whiles, was prisoner ta'en
And rifled, — stuff ! the horses' hoofs have
    minced it!
    Auranthe. He is alive ?
    Conrad.   He is ! but here make oath
To alienate him from your scheming
    brain,
Divorce him from your solitary thoughts,
And cloud him in such utter banish-
    ment,   70
That when his person meets again your
    eye,

Your vision shall quite lose its memory,
And wander past him as through vacancy.
    Auranthe. I'll not be perjured.
    Conrad.   No, nor great, nor mighty ;
You would not wear a crown, or rule a
    kingdom.
To you it is indifferent.
    Auranthe.   What means this ?
    Conrad. You'll not be perjured ! Go to
        Albert then,
That camp-mushroom — dishonour of our
    house.
Go, page his dusty heels upon a march,
Furbish his jingling baldric while he
    sleeps,   80
And share his mouldy ration in a siege.
Yet stay, — perhaps a charm may call you
    back,
And make the widening circlets of your eyes
Sparkle with healthy fevers. — The Emperor
Hath given consent that you should marry
    Ludolph !
    Auranthe. Can it be, brother ? For a
        golden crown
With a queen's awful lips I doubly thank
    you !
This is to wake in Paradise ! Farewell
Thou clod of yesterday — 'twas not myself !
Not till this moment did I ever feel   90
My spirit's faculties ! I'll flatter you
For this, and be you ever proud of it ;
Thou, Jove-like, struck'dst thy forehead,
And from the teeming marrow of thy brain
I spring complete Minerva ! But the
    prince —
His highness Ludolph — where is he ?
    Conrad.   I know not :
When, lackeying my counsel at a beck,
The rebel lords, on bended knees, received
The Emperor's pardon, Ludolph kept aloof,
Sole, in a stiff, fool-hardy, sulky pride ; 100
Yet, for all this, I never saw a father
In such a sickly longing for his son.
We shall soon see him, for the Emperor
He will be here this morning.
    Auranthe.   That I heard
Among the midnight rumours from the
    camp.
    Conrad. You give up Albert to me ?
    Auranthe.   Harm him not !
E'en for his highness Ludolph's sceptry
    hand,
I would not Albert suffer any wrong.
    Conrad. Have I not laboured, plotted — ?
    Auranthe.   See you spare him :
Nor be pathetic, my kind benefactor !   110
On all the many bounties of your hand, —
'Twas for yourself you laboured — not for
    me !

Do you not count, when I am queen, to
take
Advantage of your chance discoveries
Of my poor secrets, and so hold a rod
Over my life?
   Conrad. Let not this slave — this villain —
Be cause of feud between us. See! he
comes!
Look, woman, look your Albert is quite
safe!
In haste it seems. Now shall I be in the way,
And wish'd with silent curses in my
grave,   120
Or side by side with 'whelmed mariners.
           Enter ALBERT.
   Albert. Fair on your graces fall this early
morrow!
So it is like to do, without my prayers,
For your right noble names, like favourite
tunes,
Have fallen full frequent from our Em-
peror's lips,
High commented with smiles.
   Auranthe.   Noble Albert!
   Conrad (*aside*).   Noble!
   Auranthe. Such salutation argues a glad
heart
In our prosperity. We thank you, sir.
   Albert.   Lady!
O, would to Heaven your poor servant
Could do you better service than mere
words!   130
But I have other greeting than mine own,
From no less man than Otho, who has sent
This ring as pledge of dearest amity;
'Tis chosen I hear from Hymen's jewel'ry,
And you will prize it, lady, I doubt not,
Before all pleasures past, and all to come.
To you great duke —
   Conrad.   To me! What of me, ha?
   Albert. What pleased your grace to say?
   Conrad.   Your message, sir!
   Albert. You mean not this to me?
   Conrad.   Sister, this way;
For there shall be no 'gentle Alberts' now,
             [*Aside.* 140
No 'sweet Auranthes!'
      [*Exeunt* CONRAD *and* AURANTHE.
   Albert (*solus*). The duke is out of tem-
per; if he knows
More than a brother of a sister ought,
I should not quarrel with his peevishness.
Auranthe — Heaven preserve her always
fair! —
Is in the heady, proud, ambitious vein;
I bicker not with her, — bid her farewell!
She has taken flight from me, then let her
soar, —
He is a fool who stands at pining gaze!

But for poor Ludolph, he is food for sor-
row: 150
No levelling bluster of my licensed
thoughts,
No military swagger of my mind,
Can smother from myself the wrong I've
done him, —
Without design, indeed, — yet it is so, —
And opiate for the conscience have I
none!   [*Exit.*

SCENE II. — *The Court-yard of the Castle*

Martial Music. Enter, from the outer gate,
OTHO, *Nobles, Knights, and Attendants.*
The Soldiers halt at the gate, with Ban-
ners in sight.
   Otho. Where is my noble Herald?
[*Enter* CONRAD, *from the Castle, attended*
by two Knights and Servants. ALBERT
following.
               Well, hast told
Auranthe our intent imperial?
Lest our rent banners, too o' the sudden
shown,
Should fright her silken casements, and
dismay
Her household to our lack of entertain-
ment.
A victory!
   Conrad. God save imperial Otho!
   Otho. Aye, Conrad, it will pluck out all
grey hairs;
It is the best physician for the spleen;
The courtliest inviter to a feast;
The subtelest excuser of small faults; 10
And a nice judge in the age and smack of
wine.
[*Enter, from the Castle,* AURANTHE, *fol-*
lowed by Pages holding up her robes,
and a train of Women. She kneels.
Hail my sweet hostess! I do thank the
stars,
Or my good soldiers, or their ladies' eyes,
That, after such a merry battle fought,
I can, all safe in body and in soul,
Kiss your fair hand and lady fortune's too.
My ring! now, on my life, it doth rejoice
These lips to feel't on this soft ivory!
Keep it, my brightest daughter; it may
prove
The little prologue to a line of kings.   20
I strove against thee and my hot-blood son,
Dull blockhead that I was to be so blind.
But now my sight is clear — forgive me,
Lady.
   Auranthe. My lord, I was a vassal to
your frown,
And now your favour makes me but more

humble ;
In wintry winds the simple snow is safe,
But fadeth at the greeting of the sun :
Unto thine anger I might well have
    spoken,
Taking on me a woman's privilege,
But this so sudden kindness makes me
    dumb.   30
    Otho. What need of this? Enough, if
    you will be
A potent tutoress to my wayward boy,
And teach him, what it seems his nurse
    could not,
To say, for once, I thank you. Sigifred !
    Albert. He has not yet return'd, my
    gracious liege.
    Otho. What then ! No tidings of my
    friendly Arab ?
    Conrad. None, mighty Otho.
        [*To one of his Knights, who goes out.*]
                    Send forth instantly
An hundred horsemen from my honoured
    gates,
To scour the plains and search the cot-
    tages.
Cry a reward, to him who shall first
    bring   40
News of that vanished Arabian,
A full-heap'd helmet of the purest gold.
    Otho. More thanks, good Conrad ; for,
    except my son's,
There is no face I rather would behold
Than that same quick-eyed pagan's. By
    the saints,
This coming night of banquets must not
    light
Her dazzling torches ; nor the music
    breathe
Smooth, without clashing cymbal, tones of
    peace
And in-door melodies ; nor the ruddy wine
Ebb spouting to the lees ; if I pledge
    not,   50
In my first cup, that Arab !
    Albert.   Mighty Caesar,
I wonder not this stranger's victor-deeds
So hang upon your spirit. Twice in the
    fight
It was my chance to meet his olive brow.
Triumphant in the enemy's shatter'd
    rhomb ;
And, to say truth, in any Christian arm
I never saw such prowess.
    Otho.   Did you ever?
O, 'tis a noble boy ! — tut ! — what do I
    say ?
I mean a triple Saladin, whose eyes,
When in the glorious scuffle they met
    mine,   60

Seem'd to say — 'Sleep, old man, in safety
    sleep ;
I am the victory !'
    Conrad.   Pity he's not here.
    Otho. And my son too, pity he is not
    here.
Lady Auranthe I would not make you
    blush,
But can you give a guess where Ludolph
    is ?
Know you not of him ?
    Auranthe.   Indeed, my liege, no
    secret —
    Otho. Nay, nay, without more words,
    dost know of him ?
    Auranthe. I would I were so over-for-
    tunate,
Both for his sake and mine, and to make
    glad
A father's ears with tidings of his son.   70
    Otho. I see 'tis like to be a tedious day.
Were Theodore and Gonfred and the rest
Sent forth with my commands ?
    Albert.   Aye, my lord.
    Otho. And no news ! No news ! 'Faith !
    'tis very strange
He thus avoids us. Lady, is't not strange ?
Will he be truant to you too ? It is a
    shame.
    Conrad. Will't please your highness en-
    ter, and accept
The unworthy welcome of your servant's
    house ?
Leaving your cares to one whose diligence
May in few hours make pleasures of them
    all.   80
    Otho. Not so tedious, Conrad. No, no,
    no, no, —
I must see Ludolph or the — What's that
    shout ?
    Voices without. Huzza ! huzza ! Long
    live the Emperor !
    Other Voices. Fall back ! Away there !
    Otho.   Say what noise is that ?
[ALBERT *advancing from the back of the
    Stage, whither he had hastened on
    hearing the cheers of the soldiery.*
    Albert. It is young Gersa, the Hungarian
    prince,
Pick'd like a red stag from the fallow herd
Of prisoners. Poor prince, forlorn he steps,
Slow in the demure proudness of despair.
If I may judge by his so tragic bearing,
His eye not downcast, and his folded
    arm,   90
He doth this moment wish himself asleep
Among his fallen captains on yon plains.
    [*Enter* GERSA, *in chains, and guarded.*]
    Otho. Well said, Sir Albert.

Gersa.   Not a word of greeting,
No welcome to a princely visitor,
Most mighty Otho ? Will not my great host
Vouchsafe a syllable, before he bids
His gentlemen conduct me with all care
To some securest lodging — cold perhaps !
   Otho. What mood is this ? Hath fortune
    touch'd thy brain ?
   Gersa. O kings and princes of this
    fev'rous world,   100
What abject things, what mockeries must
   ye be,
What nerveless minions of safe palaces !
When here, a monarch, whose proud foot
   is used
To fallen princes' necks, as to his stirrup,
Must needs exclaim that I am mad for-
   sooth,
Because I cannot flatter with bent knees
My conqueror !
   Otho.   Gersa, I think you wrong me :
I think I have a better fame abroad.
   Gersa. I pr'ythee mock me not with
    gentle speech,
But, as a favour, bid me from thy pres-
   ence ;   110
Let me no longer be the wondering food
Of all these eyes ; pr'ythee command me
   hence !
   Otho. Do not mistake me, Gersa. That
    you may not,
Come, fair Auranthe, try if your soft hands
Can manage those hard rivets to set free
So brave a prince and soldier.
   Auranthe (sets him free). Welcome task !
   Gersa. I am wound up in deep astonish-
    ment !
Thank you, fair lady. Otho ! emperor !
You rob me of myself ; my dignity
Is now your infant ; I am a weak child. 120
   Otho. Give me your hand, and let this
    kindly grasp
Live in our memories.
   Gersa.   In mine it will.
I blush to think of my unchasten'd
   tongue ;
But I was haunted by the monstrous ghost
Of all our slain battalions. Sire, reflect,
And pardon you will grant, that, at this
   hour,
The bruised remnants of our stricken
   camp
Are huddling undistinguished, my dear
   friends,
With common thousands, into shallow
   graves.
   Otho. Enough, most noble Gersa. You
    are free   130
To cheer the brave remainder of your host

By your own healing presence, and that
   too,
Not as their leader merely, but their king ;
For, as I hear, your wily enemy,
Who eased the crownet from your infant
   brows,
Bloody Taraxa, is among the dead.
   Gersa. Then I retire, so generous Caesar
   please,
Bearing with me a weight of benefits
Too heavy to be borne.
   Otho.   It is not so ;
Still understand me, King of Hungary, 140
Nor judge my open purposes awry.
Though I did hold you high in my esteem
For your self's sake, I do not personate
The stage-play emperor to entrap applause,
To set the silly sort o' the world agape,
And make the politic smile ; no, I have
   heard
How in the Council you condemn'd this
   war,
Urging the perfidy of broken faith, —
For that I am your friend.
   Gersa.   If ever, sire,
You are my enemy, I dare here swear 150
'Twill not be Gersa's fault. Otho, farewell !
   Otho. Will you return, Prince, to our
    banqueting ?
   Gersa. As to my father's board I will
    return.
   Otho. Conrad, with all due ceremony,
    give
The prince a regal escort to his camp ;
Albert, go thou and bear him company.
Gersa, farewell !
   Gersa.   All happiness attend you !
   Otho. Return with what good speed you
    may ; for soon
We must consult upon our terms of peace.
   [Exeunt GERSA *and* ALBERT *with others.*
And thus a marble column do I build 160
To prop my empire's dome. Conrad, in
   thee
I have another stedfast one, to uphold
The portals of my state ; and, for my own
Pre-eminence and safety, I will strive
To keep thy strength upon its pedestal.
For, without thee, this day I might have
   been
A show-monster about the streets of
   Prague,
In chains, as just now stood that noble
   prince :
And then to me no mercy had been shown,
For when the conquer'd lion is once dun-
   geon'd,   170
Who lets him forth again ? or dares to
   give

An old lion sugar-cates of mild reprieve ?
Not to thine ear alone I make confession,
But to all here, as, by experience,
I know how the great basement of all
   power
Is frankness, and a true tongue to the
   world ;
And how intriguing secrecy is proof
Of fear and weakness, and a hollow state.
Conrad, I owe thee much.
   Conrad. To [kneel and] kiss that hand,
My emperor, is ample recompense,   180
For a mere act of duty.
   Otho.   Thou art wrong,
For what can any man on earth do more ?
We will make trial of your house's wel-
   come,
My bright Auranthe !
   Conrad.   How is Friedburg honoured !
       Enter ETHELBERT *and six Monks.*
   Ethelbert. The benison of heaven on
   your head,
Imperial Otho !
   Otho.   Who stays me ? Speak ! Quick !
   Ethelbert. Pause but one moment,
   mighty conqueror !
Upon the threshold of this house of joy.
   Otho. Pray, do not prose, good Ethel-
   bert, but speak
What is your purpose.   190
   Ethelbert. The restoration of some cap-
   tive maids,
Devoted to Heaven's pious ministries,
Who, being driven [forth] from their re-
   ligious cells,
And kept in thraldom by our enemy,
When late this province was a lawless
   spoil,
Still weep amid the wild Hungarian camp,
Though hemm'd around by thy victorious
   arms.
   Otho. Demand the holy sisterhood in
   our name
From Gersa's tents. Farewell, old Ethelbert.
   Ethelbert. The saints will bless you for
   this pious care   200
   Otho. Daughter, your hand ; Ludolph's
   would fit it best.
   Conrad. Ho ! let the music sound !
     [*Music,* ETHELBERT *raises his hands,*
     as in benediction of Otho. Exeunt
     severally. The scene closes on them.

   SCENE *III. — The Country, with the Cas-*
tle in the distance

     Enter LUDOLPH *and* SIGIFRED.

   Ludolph. You have my secret ; let it not
   be breath'd.
   Sigifred. Still give me leave to wonder
   that my Prince
Ludolph, and the swift Arab are the same ;
Still to rejoice that 'twas a German arm
Death doing in a turban'd masquerade.
   Ludolph. The Emperor must not know
   it, Sigifred.
   Sigifred. I prythee, why ? What happier
   hour of time
Could thy pleased star point down upon
   from heaven
With silver index, bidding thee make
   peace ?
   Ludolph. Still it must not be known,
   good Sigifred ;   10
The star may point oblique.
   Sigifred.   If Otho knew
His son to be that unknown Mussulman
After whose spurring heels he sent me
   forth,
With one of his well-pleased Olympian
   oaths,
The charters of man's greatness, at this
   hour
He would be watching round the castle
   walls,
And, like an anxious warder, strain his
   sight
For the first glimpse of such a son re-
   turn'd —
Ludolph, that blast of the Hungarians,
That Saracenic meteor of the fight,   20
That silent fury, whose fell scymitar
Kept danger all aloof from Otho's head,
And left him space for wonder.
   Ludolph.   Say no more.
Not as a swordsman would I pardon claim,
But as a son. The bronzed centurion,
Long toil'd in foreign wars, and whose
   high deeds
Are shaded in a forest of tall spears,
Known only to his troop, hath greater plea
Of favour with my sire than I can have.
   Sigifred. My lord, forgive me that I
   cannot see   30
How this proud temper with clear reason
   squares.
What made you then, with such an anx-
   ious love,
Hover around that life, whose bitter days
You vext with bad revolt ? Was't opium,
Or the mad-fumed wine ? Nay, do not
   frown,
I rather would grieve with you than up-
   braid.
   Ludolph. I do believe you. No, 'twas not
   to make
A father his son's debtor, or to heal

His deep heart-sickness for a rebel child.
'Twas done in memory of my boyish
        days,   40
Poor cancel for his kindness to my youth,
For all his calming of my childish griefs,
And all his smiles upon my merriment.
No, not a thousand foughten fields could
        sponge
Those days paternal from my memory,
Though now upon my head he heaps
        disgrace.
    Sigifred. My Prince, you think too
        harshly —
    Ludolph.   Can I so?
Hath he not gall'd my spirit to the quick?
And with a sullen rigour obstinate
Pour'd out a phial of wrath upon my
        faults?   50
Hunted me as a Tartar does the boar,
Driven me to the very edge of the world,
And almost put a price upon my head?
    Sigifred. Remember how he spared the
        rebel lords.
    Ludolph. Yes, yes, I know he hath a
        noble nature
That cannot trample on the fall'n. But his
Is not the only proud heart in his realm.
He hath wrong'd me, and I have done him
        wrong;
He hath lov'd me, and I have shown him
        kindness;
We should be almost equal.
    Sigifred.   Yet, for all this,   60
I would you had appear'd among those
        lords,
And ta'en his favour.
    Ludolph.   Ha! till now I thought
My friend had held poor Ludolph's hon-
        our dear.
What! would you have me sue before his
        throne
And kiss the courtier's missal, its silk
        steps?
Or hug the golden housings of his steed,
Amid a camp, whose steeled swarms I
        dared
But yesterday? And, at the trumpet sound,
Bow like some unknown mercenary's flag,
And lick the soiled grass? No, no, my
        friend,   70
I would not, I, be pardon'd in the heap,
And bless indemnity with all that scum, —
Those men I mean, who on my shoulders
        propp'd
Their weak rebellion, winning me with
        lies,
And pitying forsooth my many wrongs;
Poor self-deceived wretches, who must
        think

Each one himself a king in embryo,
Because some dozen vassals cry'd — my
        lord!
Cowards, who never knew their little
        hearts,
Till flurried Danger held the mirror up, 80
And then they own'd themselves without
        a blush,
Curling, like spaniels, round my father's
        feet.
Such things deserted me and are forgiven,
While I, least guilty, am an outcast still,
And will be, for I love such fair disgrace.
    Sigifred. I know the clear truth; so
        would Otho see,
For he is just and noble. Fain would I
Be pleader for you —
    Ludolph.   He'll hear none of it;
You know his temper, hot, proud, ob-
        stinate;
Endanger not yourself so uselessly.   90
I will encounter his thwart spleen myself,
To-day, at the Duke Conrad's, where he
        keeps
His crowded state after the victory,
There will I be, a most unwelcome guest,
And parley with him, as a son should do,
Who doubly loathes a father's tyranny;
Tell him how feeble is that tyranny;
How the relationship of father and son
Is no more valid than a silken leash
Where lions tug adverse, if love grow
        not   100
From interchanged love through many
        years.
Ay, and those turreted Franconian walls,
Like to a jealous casket, hold my pearl —
My fair Auranthe! Yes, I will be there.
    Sigifred. Be not so rash; wait till his
        wrath shall pass,
Until his royal spirit softly ebbs
Self-influenced; then, in his morning
        dreams
He will forgive thee, and awake in grief
To have not thy good morrow.
    Ludolph.   Yes, to-day
I must be there, while her young pulses
        beat   110
Among the new-plum'd minions of the
        war.
Have you seen her of late? No? Auranthe,
Franconia's fair sister, 'tis I mean.
She should be paler for my troublous
        days —
And there it is — my father's iron lips
Have sworn divorcement 'twixt me and my
        right.
    Sigifred (aside). Auranthe! I had hoped
        this whim had pass'd.

Ludolph. And, Sigfred, with all his love
   of justice,
When will he take that grandchild in his
   arms,
That, by my love I swear, (shall) soon be
   his ?   120
This reconcilement is impossible,
For see — but who are these ?
   Sigifred.   They are messengers
From our great emperor ; to you I doubt
   not,
For couriers are abroad to seek you out.
   Enter THEODORE *and* GONFRED.
   Theodore. Seeing so many vigilant eyes
   explore
The province to invite your highness back
To your high dignities, we are too happy.
   Gonfred. We have no eloquence to col-
   our justly
The emperor's anxious wishes.
   Ludolph.   Go. I follow you.
        [Exeunt THEODORE *and* GONFRED.
I play the prude : it is but venturing — 130
Why should he be so earnest ? Come, my
   friend,
Let us to Friedburg castle.

ACT II

SCENE I. — *An Ante-chamber in the Castle*

Enter LUDOLPH *and* SIGIFRED.

Ludolph. No more advices, no more cau-
   tioning ;
I leave it all to fate — to any thing !
I cannot square my conduct to time, place,
Or circumstance ; to me 'tis all a mist !
   Sigifred. I say no more.
   Ludolph.   It seems I am to wait
Here in the ante-room ; — that may be a
   trifle.
You see now how I dance attendance here,
Without that tyrant temper, you so blame,
Snapping the rein. You have medicin'd me
With good advices ; and I here remain, 10
In this most honourable ante-room,
Your patient scholar.
   Sigifred.   Do not wrong me, Prince.
By Heavens, I'd rather kiss Duke Conrad's
   slipper,
When in the morning he doth yawn with
   pride,
Than see you humbled but a half-degree !
Truth is, the Emperor would fain dismiss
The Nobles ere he sees you.
   Enter GONFRED, *from the Council-room.*

Ludolph.   Well, sir ! what !
   Gonfred. Great honour to the Prince !
   The Emperor,
Hearing that his brave son had re-
   appeared,
Instant dismiss'd the Council from his
   sight,   20
As Jove fans off the clouds. Even now they
   pass.   *[Exit.*
Enter the Nobles from the Council-room.
   They cross the stage, bowing with
   respect to LUDOLPH, *he frowning on*
   them. CONRAD *follows. Exeunt No-*
   bles.
   Ludolph. Not the discoloured poisons of
   a fen,
Which he, who breathes, feels warning of
   his death,
Could taste so nauseous in the bodily
   sense,
As these prodigious sycophants disgust
The soul's fine palate.
   Conrad.   Princely Ludolph, hail !
Welcome, thou younger sceptre to the
   realm !
Strength to thy virgin crownet's golden
   buds,
That they, against the winter of thy sire,
May burst, and swell, and flourish round
   thy brows,   30
Maturing to a weighty diadem !
Yet be that hour far off ; and may he live,
Who waits for thee, as the chapp'd earth
   for rain.
Set my life's star ! I have lived long
   enough,
Since under my glad roof, propitiously,
Father and son each other re-possess.
   Ludolph. Fine wording, Duke ! but words
   could never yet
Forestall the fates ; have you not learnt
   that yet ?
Let me look well : your features are the
   same ;
Your gait the same ; your hair of the same
   shade ;   40
As one I knew some passed weeks ago,
Who sung far different notes into mine
   ears.
I have mine own particular comments
   on 't ;
You have your own perhaps.
   Conrad.   My gracious Prince,
All men may err. In truth I was deceived
In your great father's nature, as you were.
Had I known that of him I have since
   known,
And what you soon will learn, I would
   have turn'd

My sword to my own throat, rather than
    held
Its threatening edge against a good King's
    quiet :   50
Or with one word fever'd you, gentle
    Prince,
Who seem'd to me, as rugged times then
    went,
Indeed too much oppress'd. May I be bold
To tell the Emperor you will haste to
    him ?
    Ludolph. Your Dukedom's privilege will
    grant so much.
                                    [*Exit* CONRAD.
He 's very close to Otho, Sigifred
Your hand — I go. Ha ! here the thunder
    comes
Sullen against the wind ! If in two angry
    brows
My safety lies, then Sigifred, I'm safe.
            Enter OTHO *and* CONRAD.
    Otho. Will you make Titan play the
    lackey-page   60
To chattering pigmies ? I would have you
    know
That such neglect of our high Majesty
Annuls all feel of kindred. What is son, —
Or friend, — or brother,— or all ties of
    blood, —
When the whole kingdom, centred in our-
    self,
Is rudely slighted ? Who am I to wait ?
By Peter's chair ! I have upon my tongue
A word to fright the proudest spirit
    here ! —
Death ! — and slow tortures to the hardy
    fool,
Who dares take such large charter from
    our smiles !   70
Conrad, we would be private. Sigifred !
Off ! And none pass this way on pain of
    death !
                [*Exeunt* CONRAD *and* SIGIFRED.
    Ludolph. This was but half expected,
    my good sire,
Yet I am griev'd at it, to the full height,
As though my hopes of favour had been
    whole.
    Otho. How you indulge yourself ! What
    can you hope for ?
    Ludolph. Nothing, my liege, I have to
    hope for nothing.
I come to greet you as a loving son,
And then depart, if I may be so free,
Seeing that blood of yours in my warm
    veins   80
Has not yet mitigated into milk.
    Otho. What would you, sir ?
    Ludolph.   A lenient banishment ;

So please you let me unmolested pass
This Conrad's gates, to the wide air again.
I want no more. A rebel wants no more.
    Otho. And shall I let a rebel loose again
To muster kites and eagles 'gainst my
    head ?
No, obstinate boy, you shall be kept caged
    up,
Served with harsh food, with scum for
    Sunday-drink.
    Ludolph. Indeed !
    Otho. And chains too heavy for your
    life :   90
I'll choose a jailor, whose swart monstrous
    face
Shall be a hell to look upon, and she —
    Ludolph.   Ha !
    Otho. Shall be your fair Auranthe.
    Ludolph.   Amaze ! Amaze !
    Otho. To-day you marry her.
    Ludolph.   This is a sharp jest !
    Otho. No None at all. When have I
    said a lie ?
    Ludolph. If I sleep not, I am a waking
    wretch.
    Otho. Not one word more. Let me em-
    brace my child.
    Ludolph. I dare not. 'Twould pollute so
    good a father !
O heavy crime ! that your son's blinded
    eyes
Could not see all his parent's love
    aright,   100
As now I see it. Be not kind to me —
Punish me not with favour.
    Otho.   Are you sure,
Ludolph, you have no saving plea in
    store ?
    Ludolph. My father, none !
    Otho.   Then you astonish me.
    Ludolph. No, I have no plea. Disobe-
    dience,
Rebellion, obstinacy, blasphemy,
Are all my counsellors. If they can make
My crooked deed show good and plausible,
Then grant me loving pardon, but not
    else,
Good Gods ! not else, in any way, my
    liege !   110
    Otho. You are a most perplexing, noble
    boy.
    Ludolph. You not less a perplexing no-
    ble father.
    Otho. Well, you shall have free passport
    through the gates.
Farewell !
    Ludolph. Farewell ! and by these tears
    believe,
And still remember, I repent in pain

All my misdeeds !
    Otho.   Ludolph, I will ! I will !
But, Ludolph, ere you go, I would enquire
If you, in all your wandering, ever met
A certain Arab haunting in these parts.
    Ludolph. No, my good lord, I cannot
    say I did.   120
    Otho. Make not your father blind be-
fore his time ;
Nor let these arms paternal hunger more
For an embrace, to dull the appetite
Of my great love for thee, my supreme
child !
Come near, and let me breathe into thine
ear.
I knew you through disguise. You are the
Arab !
You can't deny it.   [*Embracing him.*
    Ludolph.   Happiest of days !
    Otho. We'll make it so.
    Ludolph.   'Stead of one fatted calf
Ten hecatombs shall bellow out their last,
Smote 'twixt the horns by the death stun-
    ning mace   130
Of Mars, and all the soldiery shall feast
Nobly as Nimrod's masons, when the
towers
Of Nineveh new kiss'd the parted clouds !
    Otho. Large as a God speak out, where
all is thine.
    Ludolph. Aye, father, but the fire in my
sad breast
Is quench'd with inward tears ! I must
rejoice
For you, whose wings so shadow over me
In tender victory, but for myself
I still must mourn. The fair Auranthe
mine !
Too great a boon ! I pr'ythee let me
    ask   140
What more than I know of could so have
changed
Your purpose touching her.
    Otho.   At a word, this :
In no deed did you give me more offence
Than your rejection of Erminia.
To my appalling, I saw too good proof
Of your keen-eyed suspicion, — she is
naught !
    Ludolph. You are convinc'd ?
    Otho.   Ay, spite of her sweet looks.
O, that my brother's daughter should so
fall !
Her fame has pass'd into the grosser lips
Of soldiers in their cups.
    Ludolph.   'Tis very sad.   150
    Otho. No more of her. Auranthe — Lu-
dolph, come !
This marriage be the bond of endless

peace !   [*Exeunt.*

SCENE II. — *The Entrance of* GERSA'S *Tent
in the Hungarian Camp*

Enter ERMINIA.

    Erminia. Where ! where ! where shall I
find a messenger ?
A trusty soul ? A good man in the camp ?
Shall I go myself ? Monstrous wickedness !
O cursed Conrad ! devilish Auranthe !
Here is proof palpable as the bright sun !
O for a voice to reach the Emperor's ears !
            [*Shouts in the Camp.*
          Enter an HUNGARIAN CAPTAIN.
    Captain. Fair prisoner, hear you those
joyous shouts ?
The king — aye, now our king,— but still
your slave,
Young Gersa, from a short captivity
Has just return'd. He bids me say, bright
Dame,   10
That even the homage of his ranged chiefs
Cures not his hot impatience to behold
Such beauty once again. What ails you,
lady ?
    Erminia. Say, is not that a German, yon-
der ? There !
    Captain. Methinks by his stout bearing
he should be —
Yes — 'tis one Albert ; a brave German
knight,
And much in the emperor's favour.
    Erminia.   I would fain
Enquire of friends and kinsfolk ; how they
fared
In these rough times. Brave soldier, as you
pass
To royal Gersa with my humble thanks, 20
Will you send yonder knight to me ?
    Captain.   I will.   [*Exit.*
    Erminia. Yes, he was ever known to be
a man
Frank, open, generous ; Albert I may trust.
O proof ! proof ! proof ! Albert's an honest
man ;
Not Ethelbert the monk, if he were here,
Would I hold more trustworthy. Now !

Enter ALBERT.

    Albert.   Good Gods !
Lady Erminia ! are you prisoner
In this beleaguer'd camp ? Or are you here
Of your own will ? You pleas'd to send
for me.
By Venus, 'tis a pity I knew not   30

Your plight before, and, by her Son, I
  swear
To do you every service you can ask.
What would the fairest — ?
  Erminia.   Albert, will you swear ?
  Albert. I have. Well !
  Erminia. Albert, you have fame to lose.
If men, in court and camp, lie not out-
  right,
You should be, from a thousand, chosen
  forth
To do an honest deed. Shall I confide — ?
  Albert. Aye, anything to me, fair crea-
    ture. Do,
Dictate my task. Sweet woman, —
  Erminia.   Truce with that.
You understand me not ; and, in your
  speech,   40
I see how far the slander is abroad.
Without proof could you think me inno-
  cent ?
  Albert. Lady, I should rejoice to know
    you so.
  Erminia. If you have any pity for a
    maid,
Suffering a daily death from evil tongues ;
Any compassion for that Emperor's niece,
Who, for your bright sword and clear
  honesty,
Lifted you from the crowd of common
  men
Into the lap of honour ; — save me,
  knight !
  Albert. How ? Make it clear ; if it be
    possible,   50
I by the banner of Saint Maurice swear
To right you.
  Erminia. Possible ! — Easy. O my heart !
This letter's not so soil'd but you may
  read it ; —
Possible ! There — that letter ! Read —
  read it.
                  [Gives him a letter.
  Albert (reading). 'To the Duke Conrad.
— Forget the threat you made at parting,
and I will forget to send the Emperor let-
ters and papers of your's I have become
possessed of. His life is no trifle to me ; his
death you shall find none to yourself.'
(Speaks to himself.) 'Tis me — my life
that's pleaded for ! *(Reads.)* 'He, for his
own sake, will be dumb as the grave. Erminia has my shame fix'd upon her, sure
as a wen. We are safe.
                AURANTHE.'
A she-devil ! A dragon ! and I her imp !
Fire of Hell ! Auranthe — lewd demon !
Where got you this ? Where ? When ?
  Erminia. I found it here in the tent,

  among some spoils
Which, being noble, fell to Gersa's lot.
Come in, and see.   *[They go in and
  return.*
  Albert.   Villainy ! Villainy !
Conrad's sword, his corslet, and his helm,
And his letter. Caitiff, he shall feel —   70
  Erminia. I see you are thunderstruck.
    Haste, haste away !
  Albert. O I am tortured by this villainy.
  Erminia. You needs must be. Carry it
    swift to Otho ;
Tell him, moreover, I am prisoner
Here in this camp, where all the sister-
  hood,
Forc'd from their quiet cells, are parcell'd
  out
For slaves among these Huns. Away !
  Away !
  Albert. I am gone.
  Erminia.   Swift be your steed ! Within
    this hour
The Emperor will see it.
  Albert.   Ere I sleep :
That I can swear.   *[Hurries out.*
  Gersa (without). Brave captains ! thanks.
    Enough   80
Of loyal homage now !
            Enter GERSA.
  Erminia.   Hail, royal Hun !
  Gersa. What ails you, fair one ? Why in
    such alarm ?
Who was it hurried by me so distract ?
It seem'd you were in deep discourse to-
  gether ;
Your doctrine has not been so harsh to
  him
As to my poor deserts. Come, come, be
  plain.
I am no jealous fool to kill you both,
Or, for such trifles, rob the adorned world
Of such a beauteous vestal.
  Erminia.   I grieve, my Lord,
To hear you condescend to ribald
  phrase.   90
  Gersa. This is too much ! Hearken, my
    lady pure !
  Erminia. Silence ! and hear the magic of
    a name —
Erminia ! I am she, — the Emperor's niece !
Prais'd be the Heavens, I now dare own
  myself !
  Gersa. Erminia ! Indeed ! I've heard of
    her.
Pr'ythee, fair lady, what chance brought
  you here ?
  Erminia. Ask your own soldiers.
  Gersa.   And you dare own your name.
For loveliness you may — and for the rest

My vein is not censorious.
   Erminia.   Alas ! poor me !
'Tis false indeed.
   Gersa.   Indeed you are too fair :   100
The swan, soft leaning on her fledgy
   breast,
When to the stream she launches, looks
   not back
With such a tender grace ; nor are her
   wings
So white as your soul is, if that but be
Twin-picture to your face. Erminia !
To-day, for the first day, I am a king,
Yet would I give my unworn crown away
To know you spotless.
   Erminia.   Trust me one day more,
Generously, without more certain guaran-
   tee,
Than this poor face you deign to praise so
   much ;   110
After that, say and do whate'er you please.
If I have any knowledge of you, sir,
I think, nay I am sure you will grieve
   much
To hear my story. O be gentle to me,
For I am sick and faint with many wrongs,
Tired out, and weary-worn with contu-
   melies.
   Gersa. Poor lady !
          Enter ETHELBERT.
   Erminia. Gentle Prince, 'tis false indeed.
Good morrow, holy father ! I have had
Your prayers, though I look'd for you in
   vain.
   Ethelbert. Blessings upon you, daughter !
   Sure you look   120
Too cheerful for these foul pernicious
   days.
Young man, you heard this virgin say
   'twas false, —
'Tis false I say. What ! can you not employ
Your temper elsewhere, 'mong these burly
   tents,
But you must taunt this dove, for she hath
   lost
The Eagle Otho to beat off assault.
Fie ! fie ! But I will be her guard myself ;
In the Emperor's name, I here demand of
   you
Herself, and all her sisterhood. She false !
   Gersa. Peace ! peace, old man ! I cannot
   think she is.   130
   Ethelbert. Whom I have known from
   her first infancy,
Baptiz'd her in the bosom of the Church,
Watch'd her, as anxious husbandmen the
   grain,
From the first shoot till the unripe mid-
   May,

Then to the tender ear of her June days,
Which, lifting sweet abroad its timid
   green,
Is blighted by the touch of calumny ;
You cannot credit such a monstrous tale.
   Gersa. I cannot. Take her. Fair Erminia,
I follow you to Friedburg, — is't not
   so ?   140
   Erminia. Aye, so we purpose.
   Ethelbert.   Daughter, do you so ?
How's this ? I marvel ! Yet you look not
   mad.
   Erminia. I have good news to tell you,
   Ethelbert.
   Gersa. Ho ! ho, there ! Guards !
Your blessing, father ! Sweet Erminia,
Believe me, I am well nigh sure —
   Erminia.   Farewell !
Short time will show.   [*Enter Chiefs.*
         Yes, father Ethelbert,
I have news precious as we pass along.
   Ethelbert. Dear daughter, you shall guide
   me.
   Erminia.   To no ill.
   Gersa. Command an escort to the Fried-
   burg lines.   150
         [*Exeunt Chiefs.*
Pray let me lead. Fair lady, forget not
Gersa, how he believed you innocent.
I follow you to Friedburg with all speed.
         [*Exeunt.*

ACT III

SCENE I. — *The Country*
Enter ALBERT.

   Albert. O that the earth were empty, as
   when Cain
Had no perplexity to hide his head !
Or that the sword of some brave enemy
Had put a sudden stop to my hot breath,
And hurl'd me down the illimitable gulph
Of times past, unremember'd ! Better so
Than thus fast-limed in a cursed snare,
The limbo of a wanton. This the end
Of an aspiring life ! My boyhood past
In feud with wolves and bears, when no
   eye saw   10
The solitary warfare, fought for love
Of honour 'mid the growling wilderness —
My sturdier youth, maturing to the sword,
Won by the syren-trumpets, and the ring
Of shields upon the pavement, when
   bright mail'd
Henry the Fowler pass'd the streets of
   Prague.
Was't to this end I louted and became
The menial of Mars, and held a spear

Sway'd by command, as corn is by the
wind ?
Is it for this, I now am lifted up   20
By a well-judging Emperor, to see
My honour be my executioner, —
My love of fame, my prided honesty
Put to the torture for confessional ?
Then the damn'd crime of blurting to the
world
A woman's secret — though a fiend she be,
Too tender of my ignominious life ;
But then to wrong the generous Emperor
In such a searching point, were to give up
My soul for foot-ball at Hell's holiday ! 30
I must confess, — and cut my throat, — to-
day ?
To-morrow ? Ho ! some wine !

> *Enter* SIGIFRED.

Sigifred.   A fine humour —
Albert. Who goes there ? Count Sigi-
fred ? Ha ! Ha ! Ha !
Sigifred. What, man, do you mistake the
hollow sky
For a throng'd tavern, — and these stubbed
trees
For old serge hangings, — me, your humble
friend,
For a poor waiter ? Why, man, how you
stare !
What gipsies have you been carousing
with ?
No, no more wine ; methinks you've had
enough.
Albert. You well may laugh and banter.
What a fool   40
An injury may make of a staid man !
You shall know all anon.
Sigifred.   Albert ! a tavern brawl ?
Albert. 'Twas with some people of high
consequence ;
Revenge is difficult.
Sigifred.   I am your friend ;
We meet again to-day, and can confer
Upon it. For the present I'm in haste.
Albert. Whither ?
Sigifred.   To fetch King Gersa to the
feast.
The Emperor on this marriage is so hot,
Pray Heaven it end not in apoplexy !
The very porters, as I pass'd the doors, 50
Heard his loud laugh, and answer'd in full
choir.
I marvel, Albert, you delay so long
From those bright revelries ; go, show
yourself,
You may be made a duke.
Albert.   Ay, very like :
Pray, what day has his Highness fix'd
upon ?

Sigifred. For what ?
Albert.   The marriage. What else can
I mean ?
Sigifred. To-day ! O, I forgot, you could
not know ;
The news is scarce a minute old with me.
Albert. Married to-day ! To-day ! You
did not say so ?
Sigifred. Now, while I speak to you, their
comley heads   60
Are bow'd before the mitre.
Albert.   O ! monstrous !
Sigifred. What is this ?
Albert.   Nothing, Sigifred. Farewell !
We'll meet upon our subject. Farewell,
count !   [*Exit.*
Sigifred. Is this clear-headed Albert ?
He brain-turn'd !
'Tis as portentous as a meteor.   [*Exit.*

SCENE II. — *An Apartment in the Castle*
   Enter as from the Marriage, OTHO,
   LUDOLPH, AURANTHE, CONRAD, *Nobles,*
   Knights, Ladies, &c. &c. &c. Music.

Otho. Now, Ludolph ! Now Auranthe !
Daughter fair !
What can I find to grace your nuptial day
More than my love, and these wide realms
in fee ?
Ludolph. I have too much.
Auranthe.   And I, my liege, by far.
Ludolph. Auranthe ! I have ! O, my
bride, my love !
Not all the gaze upon us can restrain
My eyes, too long poor exiles from thy
face,
From adoration, and my foolish tongue
From uttering soft responses to the love
I see in thy mute beauty beaming forth ! 10
Fair creature, bless me with a single word !
All mine !
Auranthe. Spare, spare me, my Lord ; I
swoon else.
Ludolph. Soft beauty ! by to-morrow I
should die,
Wert thou not mine.   [*They talk apart.*
First Lady. How deep she has bewitch'd
him !
First Knight. Ask you for her receipt for
her love philtres.
Second Lady. They hold the Emperor
in admiration.
Otho. If ever king was happy, that am I !
Devoted, made a slave to this day's joy,
What are the cities 'yond the Alps to me,
The provinces about the Danube's mouth,
The promise of fair soil beyond the
Rhone ;   20
Or routing out of Hyperborean hordes,

To these fair children, stars of a new age ?
Unless perchance I might rejoice to win
This little ball of earth, and chuck it
    them
To play with !
  Auranthe. Nay, my Lord, I do not know.
  Ludolph. Let me not famish.
  Otho (to Conrad).   Good Franconia,
You heard what oath I sware, as the sun
    rose,
That unless Heaven would send me back
    my son,
My Arab, — no soft music should enrich
The cool wine, kiss'd off with a soldier's
    smack ;   30
Now all my empire, barter'd for one feast,
Seems poverty.
  Conrad.   Upon the neighbour-plain
The heralds have prepar'd a royal lists ;
Your knights, found war-proof in the
    bloody field,
Speed to the game.
  Otho.   Well, Ludolph, what say you ?
  Ludolph. My Lord !
  Otho.   A tourney ?
  Conrad.   Or, if't please you best —
  Ludolph. I want no more !
  First Lady.   He soars !
  Second Lady.   Past all reason.
  Ludolph. Though heaven's choir
Should in a vast circumference descend,
And sing for my delight, I'd stop my
    ears !   40
Though bright Apollo's car stood burning
    here,
And he put out an arm to bid me mount,
His touch an immortality, not I !
This earth, this palace, this room, Au-
    ranthe !
  Otho. This is a little painful ; just too
    much.
Conrad, if he flames longer in this wise,
I shall believe in wizard-woven loves
And old romances ; but I'll break the
    spell.
Ludolph !
  Conrad. He will be calm, anon.
  Ludolph.   You call'd !
  Otho. Come, come, a little sober reason,
    Ludolph.
  Ludolph. Yes, yes, yes, I offend. You
    must forgive me ;   50
Not being quite recover'd from the stun
Of your large bounties. A tourney, is it
    not ?
              [*A senet heard faintly.*
  Conrad. The trumpets reach us.
  Ethelbert (without). On your peril, sirs,

Detain us !
  First Voice (without). Let not the abbot
    pass.
  Second Voice (without).   No,
On your lives !
  First Voice (without). Holy father, you
    must not.
  Ethelbert (without). Otho !
  Otho.   Who calls on Otho ?
  Ethelbert (without).   Ethelbert !
  Otho. Let him come in.
    [*Enter* ETHELBERT *leading in* ERMINIA.
             Thou cursed abbot, why
Hast brought pollution to our holy rites ?
Hast thou no fear of hangman, or the
    faggot ?
Mad Churchman, would'st thou be impal'd
    alive ?
  Ludolph. What portent — what strange
    prodigy is this ?   60
  Conrad. Away !
  Ethelbert.   You, Duke ?
  Erminia.   Albert has surely fail'd me !
Look at the Emperor's brow upon me
    bent !
  Ethelbert. A sad delay !
  Conrad.   Away, thou guilty thing !
  Ethelbert. You again, Duke ? Justice,
    most mighty Otho !
You — go to your sister there and plot
    again,
A quick plot, swift as thought to save your
    heads ;
For lo ! the toils are spread around your
    den,
The world is all agape to see dragg'd
    forth
Two ugly monsters.
  Ludolph.   What means he, my lord ?
  Conrad. I cannot guess.
  Ethelbert.   Best ask your lady sister, 70
Whether the riddle puzzles her beyond
The power of utterance.
  Conrad.   Foul barbarian, cease ;
The Princess faints !
  Ludolph.   Stab him ! O, sweetest wife !
    [*Attendants bear off* AURANTHE.
  Erminia. Alas !
  Ethelbert.   Your wife !
  Ludolph. Aye, Satan ! does that yerk ye ?
  Ethelbert. Wife ! so soon !
  Ludolph.   Aye, wife ! Oh, impudence !
Thou bitter mischief ! Venomous mad
    priest !
How durst thou lift those beetle brows at
    me ?
Me — the prince Ludolph, in this presence
    here,

Upon my marriage-day, and scandalize
My joys with such opprobrious sur-
prise ?   80
Wife ! Why dost linger on that syllable,
As if it were some demon's name pro-
nounc'd
To summon harmful lightning, and make
roar
The sleepy thunder ? Hast no sense of
fear ?
No ounce of man in thy mortality ?
Tremble ! for, at my nod, the sharpen'd
axe
Will make thy bold tongue quiver to the
roots,
Those grey lids wink, and thou not know
it, Monk !
  Ethelbert. O, poor deceived Prince ! I
pity thee !
Great Otho ! I claim justice —
  Ludolph.   Thou shalt have 't !   90
Thine arms from forth a pulpit of hot fire
Shall sprawl distracted ! O that that dull
cowl
Were some most sensitive portion of thy
life,
That I might give it to my hounds to
tear !
Thy girdle some fine zealous-pained nerve
To girth my saddle ! And those devil's
beads
Each one a life, that I might, every day,
Crush one with Vulcan's hammer !
  Otho.   Peace, my son ;
You far outstrip my spleen in this affair.
Let us be calm, and hear the abbot's
plea   100
For this intrusion.
  Ludolph.   I am silent, sire.
  Otho. Conrad, see all depart not wanted
here.

            [Exeunt Knights, Ladies, &c.
Ludolph, be calm. Ethelbert, peace awhile.
This mystery demands an audience
Of a just judge, and that will Otho be.
  Ludolph. Why has he time to breathe
another word ?
  Otho. Ludolph, old Ethelbert, be sure,
comes not
To beard us for no cause ; he's not the
man
To cry himself up an ambassador
Without credentials.
  Ludolph.   I'll chain up myself.   110
  Otho. Old Abbot, stand here forth.
Lady Erminia,
Sit. And now, Abbot ! what have you to
say ?

Our ear is open. First we here denounce
Hard penalties against thee, if't be found
The cause for which you have disturb'd
us here,
Making our bright hours muddy, be a
thing
Of little moment.
  Ethelbert.   See this innocent !
Otho ! thou father of the people call'd,
Is her life nothing ? Her fair honour
nothing ?
Her tears from matins until even-song 120
Nothing ? Her burst heart nothing ? Em-
peror !
Is this your gentle niece — the simplest
flower
Of the world's herbal — this fair lily
blanch'd
Still with the dews of piety, this meek lady
Here sitting like an angel newly-shent,
Who veils its snowy wings and grows all
pale, —
Is she nothing ?
  Otho. What more to the purpose, abbot ?
  Ludolph. Whither is he winding ?
  Conrad.   No clue yet !
  Ethelbert. You have heard, my Liege,
and so, no doubt, all here,
Foul, poisonous, malignant whisper-
ings ;   130
Nay open speech, rude mockery grown
common,
Against the spotless nature and clear fame
Of the princess Erminia, your niece.
I have intruded here thus suddenly,
Because I hold those base weeds with tight
hand
Which now disfigure her fair growing
stem,
Waiting but for your sign to pull them up
By the dark roots, and leave her palpable,
To all men's sight, a Lady innocent.
The ignominy of that whisper'd tale   140
About a midnight gallant, seen to climb
A window to her chamber neighbour'd
near,
I will from her turn off, and put the load
On the right shoulders ; on that wretch's
head,
Who, by close stratagems, did save herself,
Chiefly by shifting to this lady's room
A rope-ladder for false witness.
  Ludolph.   Most atrocious !
  Otho. Ethelbert, proceed.
  Ethelbert.   With sad lips I shall :
For, in the healing of one wound, I fear
To make a greater. His young highness
here   150

To-day was married.
   Ludolph.   Good.
   Ethelbert.   Would it were good !
Yet why do I delay to spread abroad
The names of those two vipers, from
    whose jaws
A deadly breath went forth to taint and
    blast
This guileless lady ?
   Otho.   Abbot, speak their names.
   Ethelbert. A minute first. It cannot be —
    but may
I ask, great judge, if you to-day have put
A letter by unread ?
   Otho.   Does't end in this ?
   Conrad. Out with their names !
   Ethelbert.   Bold sinner, say you so ?
   Ludolph. Out, tedious monk !
   Otho.   Confess, or by the wheel —   160
   Ethelbert. My evidence cannot be far
    away ;
And, though it never come, be on my
    head
The crime of passing an attaint upon
The slanderers of this virgin.
   Ludolph.   Speak aloud !
   Ethelbert. Auranthe, and her brother
    there.
   Conrad.   Amaze !
   Ludolph. Throw them from the win-
    dows !
   Otho. Do what you will !
   Ludolph.   What shall I do with them ?
Something of quick dispatch, for should
    she hear,
My soft Auranthe, her sweet mercy would
Prevail against my fury. Damned
    priest !   170
What swift death wilt thou die ? As to
    the lady
I touch her not.
   Ethelbert.   Illustrious Otho, stay !
An ample store of misery thou hast,
Choak not the granary of thy noble mind
With more bad bitter grain, too difficult
A cud for the repentance of a man
Grey-growing. To thee only I appeal,
Not to thy noble son, whose yeasting
    youth
Will clear itself, and crystal turn again.
A young man's heart, by Heaven's bless-
    ing, is   180
A wide world, where a thousand new-born
    hopes
Empurple fresh the melancholy blood :
But an old man's is narrow, tenantless
Of hopes, and stuff'd with many memories,
Which, being pleasant, ease the heavy
    pulse —

Painful, clog up and stagnate. Weigh this
    matter
Even as a miser balances his coin ;
And, in the name of mercy, give command
That your knight Albert be brought here
    before you.
He will expound this riddle ; he will
    show   190
A noon-day proof of bad Auranthe's guilt.
   Otho. Let Albert straight be summon'd.
                    [*Exit one of the Nobles.*
   Ludolph.   Impossible !
I cannot doubt — I will not — no — to
    doubt
Is to be ashes ! — wither'd up to death !
   Otho. My gentle Ludolph, harbour not
    a fear ;
You do yourself much wrong.
   Ludolph.   O, wretched dolt !
Now, when my foot is almost on thy neck,
Wilt thou infuriate me ? Proof ! Thou
    fool !
Why wilt thou tease impossibility
With such a thick-skull'd persevering
    suit ?   200
Fanatic obstinacy ! Prodigy !
Monster of folly ! Ghost of a turn'd brain !
You puzzle me, — you haunt me, — when
    I dream
Of you my brain will split ! Bald sorcerer !
Juggler ! May I come near you ? On my
    soul
I know not whether to pity, curse, or
    laugh.
    Enter ALBERT, *and the Nobleman.*
Here, Albert, this old phantom wants a
    proof !
Give him his proof ! A camel's load of
    proofs !
   Otho. Albert, I speak to you as to a man
Whose words once utter'd pass like cur-
    rent gold ;   210
And therefore fit to calmly put a close
To this brief tempest. Do you stand
    possess'd
Of any proof against the honourableness
Of Lady Auranthe, our new-spoused
    daughter ?
   Albert. You chill me with astonishment.
    How's this ?
My Liege, what proof should I have
    'gainst a fame
Impossible of slur ?   [OTHO *rises.*
   Erminia.   O wickedness !
   Ethelbert. Deluded monarch, 'tis a cruel
    lie.
   Otho. Peace, rebel-priest !
   Conrad.   Insult beyond credence !
   Erminia. Almost a dream !

Ludolph. We have awaken'd from ! 220
A foolish dream that from my brow has
    wrung
A wrathful dew. O folly ! why did I
So act the lion with this silly gnat ?
Let them depart. Lady Erminia !
I ever griev'd for you, as who did not ?
But now you have, with such a brazen
    front,
So most maliciously, most madly striven
To dazzle the soft moon, when tenderest
    clouds
Should be unloop'd around to curtain
    her ;
I leave you to the desert of the world 230
Almost with pleasure. Let them be set free
For me ! I take no personal revenge
More than against a nightmare, which a
    man
Forgets in the new dawn. [*Exit* LUDOLPH.
    Otho. Still in extremes ! No, they must
        not be loose.
    Ethelbert. Albert, I must suspect thee of
        a crime
So fiendish —
    Otho. Fear'st thou not my fury, monk ?
Conrad, be they in your sure custody
Till we determine some fit punishment.
It is so mad a deed, I must reflect   240
And question them in private ; for per-
    haps,
By patient scrutiny, we may discover
Whether they merit death, or should be
    placed
In care of the physicians.
        [*Exeunt* OTHO *and Nobles,* ALBERT
        following.
    Conrad. My guards, ho !
    Erminia. Albert, will you follow there ?
Will you creep dastardly behind his back,
And slink away from a weak woman's eye ?
Turn, thou court-Janus ! thou forget'st
    thyself ;
Here is the duke, waiting with open arms,
        [*Enter Guards.*
To thank thee ; here congratulate each
    other ;   250
Wring hands ; embrace ; and swear how
    lucky 'twas
That I, by happy chance, hit the right
    man
Of all the world to trust in.
    Albert.   Trust ! to me !
    Conrad (*aside*). He is the sole one in
        this mystery.
    Erminia. Well, I give up, and save my
        prayers for Heaven !
You, who could do this deed, would ne'er
    relent,

Though, at my words, the hollow prison-
    vaults
Would groan for pity.
    Conrad.   Manacle them both !
    Ethelbert. I know it — it must be — I
        see it all !
Albert, thou art the minion !
    Erminia.   Ah ! too plain —   260
    Conrad. Silence ! Gag up their mouths !
        I cannot bear
More of this brawling. That the Emperor
Had plac'd you in some other custody !
Bring them away. [*Exeunt all but* ALBERT.
    Albert. Though my name perish from
        the book of honour,
Almost before the recent ink is dry,
And be no more remember'd after death,
Than any drummer's in the muster-roll ;
Yet shall I season high my sudden fall
With triumph o'er that evil-witted
    duke !   270
He shall feel what it is to have the hand
Of a man drowning, on his hateful throat.
Erminia ! dream to night of better days
Tomorrow makes them real — once more
    good morrow.

Enter GERSA *and* SIGIFRED.
    Sigifred. What discord is at ferment in
        this house ?
    Gersa. We are without conjecture ; not
        a soul
We met could answer any certainty.
    Sigifred. Young Ludolph, like a fiery
        arrow, shot
By us.
    Gersa. The Emperor, with cross'd arms,
        in thought.
    Sigifred. In one room music, in another
        sadness,
Perplexity every where !
    Albert.   A trifle mere !
Follow ; your presences will much avail 280
To tune our jarred spirits. I'll explain.
        [*Exeunt.*

ACT IV

SCENE I. — AURANTHE'S *Apartment*

AURANTHE *and* CONRAD *discovered.*

    Conrad. Well, well, I know what ugly
        jeopardy
We are caged in ; you need not pester that
Into my ears. Prythee, let me be spared
A foolish tongue, that I may bethink me
Of remedies with some deliberation.

You cannot doubt but 'tis in Albert's
    power
To crush or save us ?
    Auranthe.   No, I cannot doubt.
He has, assure yourself, by some strange
    means,
My secret ; which I ever hid from him,
Knowing his mawkish honesty.
    Conrad.   Cursed slave !   10
    Auranthe. Ay, I could almost curse him
        now myself.
Wretched impediment ! Evil genius !
A glue upon my wings, that cannot spread,
When they should span the provinces ! A
    snake,
A scorpion, sprawling on the first gold
    step,
Conducting to the throne high canopied.
    Conrad. You would not hear my coun-
        sel, when his life
Might have been trodden out, all sure and
    hush'd ;
Now the dull animal forsooth must be
Intreated, managed ! When can you con-
    trive   20
The interview he demands ?
    Auranthe.   As speedily
It must be done as my bribed woman can
Unseen conduct him to me ; but I fear
'Twill be impossible, while the broad day
Comes through the panes with persecuting
    glare.
Methinks, if 't now were night I could
    intrigue
With darkness, bring the stars to second
    me,
And settle all this trouble.
    Conrad.   Nonsense ! Child !
See him immediately ; why not now ?
    Auranthe. Do you forget that even the
        senseless door-posts   30
Are on the watch and gape through all the
    house ;
How many whisperers there are about,
Hungry for evidence to ruin me :
Men I have spurn'd, and women I have
    taunted ?
Besides, the foolish prince sends, minute
    whiles,
His pages — so they tell me — to inquire
After my health, entreating, if I please,
To see me.
    Conrad. Well, suppose this Albert here ;
What is your power with him ?
    Auranthe.   He should be
My echo, my taught parrot ! but I fear ⁴⁰
He will be cur enough to bark at me ;
Have his own say ; read me some silly
    creed

'Bout shame and pity.
    Conrad.   What will you do then ?
    Auranthe. What I shall do, I know not ;
        what I would
Cannot be done ; for see, this chamber-
    floor
Will not yield to the pick-axe and the
    spade, —
Here is no quiet depth of hollow ground.
    Conrad. Sister, you have grown sensible
        and wise,
Seconding, ere I speak it, what is now,
I hope, resolv'd between us.
    Auranthe.   Say, what is 't ?   50
    Conrad. You need not be his sexton
        too : a man
May carry that with him shall make him
    die
Elsewhere, — give that to him ; pretend the
    while
You will to-morrow succumb to his wishes,
Be what they may, and send him from the
    Castle
On some fool's errand ; let his latest groan
Frighten the wolves !
    Auranthe.   Alas ! he must not die !
    Conrad. Would you were both hearsed
        up in stifling lead !
Detested —
    Auranthe. Conrad, hold ! I would not
        bear
The little thunder of your fretful
    tongue,   60
Tho' I alone were taken in these toils,
And you could free me ; but remember, sir,
You live alone in my security :
So keep your wits at work, for your own
    sake,
Not mine, and be more mannerly.
    Conrad.   Thou wasp !
If my domains were emptied of these folk,
And I had thee to starve —
    Auranthe.   O, marvellous !
But Conrad, now be gone ; the Host is
    look'd for ;
Cringe to the Emperor, entertain the no-
    bles,
And, do ye mind, above all things, pro-
    claim   70
My sickness, with a brother's sadden'd eye,
Condoling with Prince Ludolph. In fit
    time
Return to me.
    Conrad. I leave you to your thoughts.
                    [*Exit.*
    Auranthe (sola). Down, down, proud
        temper ! down, Auranthe's pride !
Why do I anger him when I should kneel ?
Conrad ! Albert ! help ! help ! What can

I do?
O wretched woman! lost, wreck'd, swallow'd up,
Accursed, blasted! O, thou golden Crown,
Orbing along the serene firmament
Of a wide empire, like a glowing moon; 80
And thou, bright sceptre! lustrous in my
        eyes, —
There — as the fabled fair Hesperian tree,
Bearing a fruit more precious! graceful
        thing,
Delicate, godlike, magic! must I leave
Thee to melt in the visionary air,
Ere, by one grasp, this common hand is
        made
Imperial? I do not know the time
When I have wept for sorrow; but methinks
I could now sit upon the ground, and
        shed
Tears, tears of misery. O, the heavy day! 90
How shall I bear my life till Albert comes?
Ludolph! Erminia! Proofs! O heavy day!
Bring me some mourning weeds, that I
        may 'tire
Myself, as fits one wailing her own death:
Cut off these curls, and brand this lily
        hand,
And throw these jewels from my loathing
        sight, —
Fetch me a missal, and a string of beads, —
A cup of bitter'd water, and a crust, —
I will confess, O holy father! — How!
What is this? Auranthe! thou fool,
        dolt,   100
Whimpering idiot! up! up! act and
        quell!
I'm safe! Coward! why am I in fear?
Albert! he cannot stickle, chew the cud
In such a fine extreme, — impossible!
Who knocks?   [*Goes to the door, listens,
        and opens it.*

Enter ALBERT.

Albert, I have been waiting for you here
With such an aching heart, such swooning
        throbs
On my poor brain, such cruel — cruel sorrow,
That I should claim your pity! Art not
        well?
    Albert. Yes, lady, well.
    Auranthe.   You look not so, alas! 110
But pale, as if you brought some heavy
        news.
    Albert. You know full well what makes
        me look so pale.
    Auranthe. No! Do I? Surely I am still
to learn
Some horror; all I know, this present, is
I am near hustled to a dangerous gulph,
Which you can save me from, — and therefore safe,
So trusting in thy love; that should not
        make
Thee pale, my Albert.
    Albert.   It does make me freeze.
    Auranthe. Why should it, love?
    Albert.   You should not ask me that,
But make your own heart monitor, and
        save   120
Me the great pain of telling. You must
        know.
    Auranthe. Something has vext you, Albert. There are times
When simplest things put on a sombre
        cast;
A melancholy mood will haunt a man,
Until most easy matters take the shape
Of unachievable tasks; small rivulets
Then seem impassable.
    Albert.   Do not cheat yourself
With hope that gloss of words, or suppliant action,
Or tears, or ravings, or self-threaten'd
        death,
Can alter my resolve.
    Auranthe. You make me tremble; 130
Not so much at your threats, as at your
        voice,
Untun'd, and harsh, and barren of all
        love.
    Albert. You suffocate me! Stop this
        devil's parley,
And listen to me; know me once for all.
    Auranthe. I thought I did. Alas! I am
        deceived.
    Albert. No, you are not deceived. You
        took me for
A man detesting all inhuman crime;
And therefore kept from me your demon's
        plot
Against Erminia. Silent? Be so still;
For ever! Speak no more; but hear my
        words,   140
Thy fate. To-day you are safe
I have told a lie for you which in the
        dawn
I'll expiate with truth.
    Auranthe.   O cruel traitor!
    Albert. For I would not set eyes upon
        thy shame;
I would not see thee dragg'd to death by
        the hair,
Penanced, and taunted on a scaffolding!
To-night, upon the skirts of the blind
        wood

That blackens northward of these horrid towers,
I wait for you with horses. Choose your fate.
Farewell !

Auranthe. Albert, you jest ; I'm sure you must.   150
You, an ambitious Soldier ! I, a Queen,
One who could say, — Here, rule these Provinces !
Take tribute from those cities for thyself !
Empty these armouries, these treasuries,
Muster thy warlike thousands at a nod !
Go ! conquer Italy !

Albert.   Auranthe, you have made
The whole world chaff to me. Your doom is fix'd.

Auranthe. Out, villain ! dastard !

Albert.   Look there to the door !
Who is it ?

Auranthe. Conrad, traitor !

Albert.   Let him in.   [*Enter* CONRAD.
Do not affect amazement, hypocrite,   160
At seeing me in this chamber.

Conrad.   Auranthe ?

Albert. Talk not with eyes, but speak your curses out
Against me, who would sooner crush and grind
A brace of toads, than league with them to oppress
An innocent lady, gull an Emperor,
More generous to me than autumn's sun
To ripening harvests.

Auranthe.   No more insult, sir !

Albert. Ay, clutch your scabbard ; but, for prudence' sake,
Draw not the sword ; 'twould make an uproar, Duke,
You would not hear the end of. At night-fall   170
Your lady sister, if I guess aright,
Will leave this busy castle. You had best
Take farewell too of worldly vanities.

Conrad. Vassal !

Albert. To-morrow, when the Emperor sends
For loving Conrad, see you fawn on him.
Good even !

Auranthe. You'll be seen !

Albert.   See the coast clear then.

Auranthe (as he goes). Remorseless Albert ! Cruel, cruel wretch !
                    [*She lets him out.*

Conrad. So, we must lick the dust ?

Auranthe.   I follow him.

Conrad. How ? Where ? The plan of your escape ?

Auranthe.   He waits

For me with horses by the forest-side,   180
Northward.

Conrad. Good, good ; he dies. You go, say you ?

Auranthe. Perforce.

Conrad.   Be speedy darkness ! Till that comes,
Fiends keep you company !   [*Exit.*

Auranthe.   And you ! And you !
And all men ! Vanish ! Oh ! Oh ! Oh !
          [*Retires to an inner apartment.*

SCENE II. — *An Apartment in the Castle.*

Enter LUDOLPH *and* Page.

Page. Still very sick, my lord ; but now I went,
Knowing my duty to so good a Prince ;
And there her women, in a mournful throng,
Stood in the passage whispering ; if any
Moved, 'twas with careful steps, and hush'd as death :
They bade me stop.

Ludolph.   Good fellow, once again
Make soft inquiry ; prythee, be not stay'd
By any hindrance, but with gentlest force
Break through her weeping servants, till thou com'st
E'en to her chamber door, and there, fair boy, —   10
If with thy mother's milk thou hast suck'd in
Any diviner eloquence, — woo her ears
With plaints for me, more tender than the voice
Of dying Echo, echoed.

Page.   Kindest master !
To know thee sad thus, will unloose my tongue
In mournful syllables. Let but my words reach
Her ears, and she shall take them coupled with
Moans from my heart, and sighs not counterfeit.
May I speed better !   [*Exit Page.*

Ludolph (solus). Auranthe ! My life !
Long have I lov'd thee, yet till now not lov'd :   20
Remembering, as I do, hard-hearted times
When I had heard e'en of thy death perhaps,
And thoughtless ! — suffered thee to pass alone
Into Elysium ! — now I follow thee,
A substance or a shadow, wheresoe'er
Thou leadest me, — whether thy white feet

press,
With pleasant weight, the amorous-aching
    earth,
Or thro' the air thou pioneerest me,
A shade! Yet sadly I predestinate!
O, unbenignest Love, why wilt thou let   30
Darkness steal out upon the sleepy world
So wearily, as if night's chariot-wheels
Were clog'd in some thick cloud? O,
    changeful Love,
Let not her steeds with drowsy-footed pace
Pass the high stars, before sweet embas-
    sage
Comes from the pillow'd beauty of that
    fair
Completion of all delicate nature's wit!
Pout her faint lips anew with rubious
    health;
And, with thine infant fingers, lift the
    fringe
Of her sick eye-lids; that those eyes may
    glow   40
With wooing light upon me, ere the morn
Peers with disrelish, grey, barren, and
    cold!

Enter GERSA *and Courtiers.*

Otho calls me his Lion, — should I blush
To be so tam'd? so ——
  Gersa.   Do me the courtesy,
Gentlemen, to pass on.
  Courtier.   We are your servants.
                [*Exeunt Courtiers.*
  Ludolph. It seems then, sir, you have
    found out the man
You would confer with; — me?
  Gersa.   If I break not
Too much upon your thoughtful mood, I
    will
Claim a brief while your patience.
  Ludolph.   For what cause
Soe'er, I shall be honour'd.
  Gersa.   I not less.   50
  Ludolph. What may it be? No trifle can
    take place
Of such deliberate prologue, serious
    'haviour.
But, be it what it may, I cannot fail
To listen with no common interest;
For though so new your presence is to me,
I have a soldier's friendship for your fame.
Please you explain.
  Gersa.   As thus: — for, pardon me,
I cannot, in plain terms, grossly assault
A noble nature; and would faintly sketch
What your quick apprehension will fill
    up;   60
So finely I esteem you.

  Ludolph.   I attend.
  Gersa. Your generous father, most illus-
    trious Otho,
Sits in the banquet-room among his chiefs;
His wine is bitter, for you are not there;
His eyes are fix'd still on the open doors,
And every passer in he frowns upon,
Seeing no Ludolph comes.
  Ludolph.   I do neglect.
  Gersa. And for your absence, may I
    guess the cause?
  Ludolph. Stay there! no — guess? More
    princely you must be
Than to make guesses at me. 'Tis
    enough.   70
I'm sorry I can hear no more.
  Gersa.   And I
As griev'd to force it on you so abrupt;
Yet, one day, you must know a grief, whose
    sting
Will sharpen more the longer 'tis con-
    ceal'd.
  Ludolph. Say it at once, sir! dead —
    dead — is she dead?
  Gersa. Mine is a cruel task: she is not
    dead,
And would, for your sake, she were inno-
    cent.
  Ludolph. Hungarian! thou amazest me
    beyond
All scope of thought, convulsest my heart's
    blood
To deadly churning! Gersa, you are
    young,   80
As I am; let me observe you, face to face:
Not grey-brow'd like the poisonous Ethel-
    bert,
No rheumed eyes, no furrowing of age,
No wrinkles, where all vices nestle in
Like crannied vermin, — no! but fresh,
    and young,
And hopeful featur'd. Ha! by heaven you
    weep!
Tears, human tears! Do you repent you
    then
Of a curs'd torturer's office? Why shouldst
    join, —
Tell me, — the league of devils? Confess
    — confess —
The lie!
  Gersa.   Lie! — but begone all cere-
    monious points   90
Of honour battailous! I could not turn
My wrath against thee for the orbed world.
  Ludolph. Your wrath, weak boy? Trem-
    ble at mine, unless
Retraction follow close upon the heels
Of that late 'stounding insult! Why has
    my sword

Not done already a sheer judgment on
    thee ?
Despair, or eat thy words ! Why, thou wast
    nigh
Whimpering away my reason ! Hark ye,
    Sir,
It is no secret, that Erminia,
Erminia, Sir, was hidden in your tent, —   100
O bless'd asylum ! Comfortable home !
Begone ! I pity thee ; thou art a gull,
Erminia's fresh puppet !
    Gersa.   Furious fire !
Thou mak'st me boil as hot as thou canst
    flame !
And in thy teeth I give thee back the lie !
Thou liest ! Thou, Auranthe's fool ! A
    wittol !
    Ludolph. Look ! look at this bright
    sword ;
There is no part of it, to the very hilt,
But shall indulge itself about thine heart !
Draw ! but remember thou must cower
    thy plumes,   110
As yesterday the Arab made thee stoop.
    Gersa. Patience ! not here ; I would not
    spill thy blood
Here, underneath this roof where Otho
    breathes, —
Thy father, — almost mine.
    Ludolph.   O faltering coward !
    Re-enter Page.
Stay, stay ; here is one I have half a word
    with.
Well ? What ails thee, child ?
    Page.   My lord !
    Ludolph.   What wouldst say ?
    Page. They are fled !
    Ludolph.   They ! Who ?
    Page.   When anxiously
I hasten'd back, your grieving messenger,
I found the stairs all dark, the lamps ex-
    tinct,
And not a foot or whisper to be heard. 120
I thought her dead, and on the lowest step
Sat listening ; when presently came by
Two muffled up, — one sighing heavily,
The other cursing low, whose voice I knew
For the Duke Conrad's. Close I follow'd
    them
Thro' the dark ways they chose to the
    open air ;
And, as I follow'd, heard my lady speak.
    Ludolph. Thy life answer the truth !
    Page.   The chamber's empty !
    Ludolph. As I will be of mercy ! So, at
    last,
This nail is in my temples !
    Gersa.   Be calm in this. 130
    Ludolph. I am.

Gersa. And Albert too has disappear'd ;
Ere I met you, I sought him everywhere ;
You would not hearken.
    Ludolph.   Which way went they, boy ?
Gersa. I'll hunt with you.
    Ludolph.   No, no, no. My senses are
Still whole. I have surviv'd. My arm is
    strong,
My appetite sharp — for revenge ! I'll no
    sharer
In my feast ; my injury is all my own,
And so is my revenge, my lawful chattels !
Jackall, lead on : the lion preys to-
    night.
Terrier, ferret them out ! Burn — burn the
    witch !
Trace me their footsteps ! Away !   140
                              [*Exeunt.*

ACT V

SCENE I. — *A part of the Forest*

Enter CONRAD *and* AURANTHE.

Auranthe. Go no further ; not a step
    more. Thou art
A master-plague in the midst of miseries.
Go, — I fear thee ! I tremble every limb,
Who never shook before. There 's moody
    death
In thy resolved looks ! Yes, I could kneel
To pray thee far away ! Conrad, go ! go ! —
There ! yonder underneath the boughs I
    see
Our horses !
    Conrad. Ay, and a man.
    Auranthe.   Yes, he is there !
Go go, — no blood ! no blood ! — go, gentle
    Conrad !
    Conrad. Farewell !
    Auranthe.   Farewell ! For this
    Heaven pardon you !   10
                              [*Exit* AURANTHE.
    Conrad. If he escape me, may I die a
    death
Of unimagined tortures, or breathe through
A long life in the foulest sink of the
    world !
He dies ! 'Tis well she do not advertise
The caitiff of the cold steel at his back.
                              [*Exit* CONRAD.
    Enter LUDOLPH *and Page.*

Ludolph. Miss'd the way, boy ? Say not
    that on your peril !
Page. Indeed, indeed I cannot trace
    them further.

Ludolph. Must I stop here ? Here solitary die ?
Stifled beneath the thick oppressive shade
Of these dull boughs, — this oven of dark
    thickets, —   20
Silent, — without revenge ? — pshaw ! — bitter end, —
A bitter death, — a suffocating death, —
A gnawing — silent — deadly-quiet death !
Escap'd — fled — vanish'd — melted into
    air —
She's gone — I cannot catch her ! no revenge !
A muffled death, ensnared in horrid silence !
Suck'd to my grave amid a dreary calm !
O, where is that illustrious noise of war,
To smother up this sound of labouring
    breath,
This rustle of the trees !
       [AURANTHE *shrieks at a distance.*
Page.   My lord, a noise !   30
This way — hark !
Ludolph. Yes, yes ! A hope ! A music !
A glorious clamour ! Now I live again !
                   [*Exeunt.*

SCENE II. — *Another part of the Forest*

Enter ALBERT (*wounded*) .

Albert. O ! for enough life to support
    me on
To Otho's feet !
        Enter LUDOLPH.
Ludolph. Thrice villainous, stay there !
Tell me where that detested woman is,
Or this is through you !
Albert.   My good Prince, with me
The sword has done its worst ; not without worst
Done to another, — Conrad has it home !
I see you know it all !
Ludolph.   Where is his sister ?
    AURANTHE *rushes in.*
Auranthe. Albert !
Ludolph.   Ha ! There ! there ! —
He is the paramour ! —
There — hug him — dying ! O, thou innocence,
Shrive him and comfort him at his last
    gasp,   10
Kiss down his eyelids ! Was he not thy
    love ?
Wilt thou forsake him at his latest hour ?
Keep fearful and aloof from his last gaze,
His most uneasy moments, when cold
    death

Stands with the door ajar to let him in ?
    Albert. O that that door with hollow
        slam would close
Upon me sudden ! for I cannot meet,
In all the unknown chambers of the dead,
Such horrors !
    Ludolph. Auranthe ! what can he mean ?
What horrors ? Is it not a joyous time ? 20
Am I not married to a paragon
'Of personal beauty and untainted soul' ?
A blushing fair-eyed purity ! A sylph,
Whose snowy timid hand has never sin'd
Beyond a flower pluck'd, mild as itself ?
Albert, you do insult my bride — your
    mistress —
To talk of horrors on our wedding-night !
    Albert. Alas ! poor Prince, I would you
        knew my heart !
'Tis not so guilty —
    Ludolph.   Hear you, he pleads not
        guilty !
You are not ? or, if so, what matters it ? 30
You have escap'd me, free as the dusk air,
Hid in the forest, safe from my revenge ;
I cannot catch you ! You should laugh at
    me,
Poor cheated Ludolph ! Make the forest
    hiss
With jeers at me ! You tremble — faint at
    once,
You will come to again. O cockatrice,
I have you ! Whither wander those fair
    eyes
To entice the devil to your help, that he
May change you to a spider, so to crawl
Into some cranny to escape my wrath ? 40
    Albert. Sometimes the counsel of a dying
        man
Doth operate quietly when his breath is
    gone :
Disjoin those hands — part — part — do
    not destroy
Each other — forget her ! — Our miseries
Are [almost] equal shar'd, and mercy is —
    Ludolph.   A boon
When one can compass it. Auranthe, try
Your oratory ; your breath is not so
    hitch'd.
Aye, stare for help !
               [ALBERT *groans and dies.*
            There goes a spotted soul
Howling in vain along the hollow night !
Hear him ! He calls you — Sweet Auranthe,
    come !   50
    Auranthe. Kill me !
    Ludolph.   No ! What ? upon our
    marriage-night ?
The earth would shudder at so foul a
    deed !

A fair bride ! A sweet bride ! An innocent
    bride !
No ! we must revel it, as 'tis in use
In times of delicate brilliant ceremony :
Come, let me lead you to our halls again !
Nay, linger not ; make no resistance,
    sweet : —
Will you ? Ah, wretch, thou canst not, for
    I have
The strength of twenty lions 'gainst a
    lamb !
Now — one   adieu   for   Albert ! — Come
    away !   60
                  [*Exeunt.*

SCENE III. — *An inner Court of the Castle.*

Enter SIGIFRED, GONFRED, *and*
THEODORE, *meeting.*

Theodore. Was ever such a night ?
Sigifred.   What horrors more ?
Things unbelieved one hour, so strange
    they are,
The next hour stamps with credit.
  Theodore.   Your last news ?
Gonfred. After the page's story of the
    death
Of Albert and Duke Conrad ?
  Sigifred.   And the return
Of Ludolph with the Princess.
  Gonfred.   No more, save
Prince Gersa's freeing Abbot Ethelbert,
And the sweet lady, fair Erminia,
From prison.
  Theodore. Where are they now ? Hast
    yet heard ?
Gonfred. With the sad Emperor they
    are closeted ;   10
I saw the three pass slowly up the stairs,
The lady weeping, the old abbot cowl'd.
  Sigifred. What next ?
  Theodore.   I ache to think on 't.
  Gonfred.   'Tis with fate.
  Theodore. One while these proud tow-
    ers are hush'd as death.
  Gonfred. The next our poor Prince fills
    the arched rooms
With ghastly ravings.
  Sigifred.   I do fear his brain.
  Gonfred. I will see more. Bear you so
    stout a heart ?
              [*Exeunt into the Castle.*

SCENE IV. — *A Cabinet, opening towards*
a Terrace

OTHO, ERMINIA, ETHELBERT, *and a*
Physician, discovered.
Otho. O, my poor boy ! my son ! my

son ! my Ludolph !
Have ye no comfort for me, ye physicians
Of the weak body and soul ?
  Ethelbert.   'Tis not the medicine,
Either of heaven or earth, can cure, unless
Fit time be chosen to administer.
  Otho. A kind forbearance, holy Abbot.
    Come,
Erminia ; here, sit by me, gentle Girl ;
Give me thy hand ; hast thou forgiven me ?
  Erminia. Would I were with the saints
    to pray for you !
  Otho. Why will ye keep me from my
    darling child ?   10
  Physician. Forgive me, but he must not
    see thy face.
  Otho. Is then a father's countenance a
    Gorgon ?
Hath it not comfort in it ? Would it not
Console my poor boy, cheer him, heal his
    spirits ?
Let me embrace him ; let me speak to
    him ;
I will ! Who hinders me ? Who 's Em-
    peror ?
  Physician. You may not, Sire ; 'twould
    overwhelm him quite,
He is so full of grief and passionate wrath ;
Too heavy a sigh would kill him, or do
    worse.
He must be sav'd by fine contrivances ; 20
And, most especially, we must keep clear
Out of his sight a father whom he loves ;
His heart is full, it can contain no more,
And do its ruddy office.
  Ethelbert.   Sage advice ;
We must endeavour how to ease and
    slacken
The tight-wound energies of his despair,
Not make them tenser.
  Otho.   Enough ! I hear, I hear.
Yet you were about to advise more, — I
    listen.
  Ethelbert. This learned doctor will agree
    with me,
That not in the smallest point should he
    be thwarted,   30
Or gainsaid by one word ; his very mo-
    tions,
Nods, becks, and hints, should be obey'd
    with care,
Even on the moment ; so his troubled mind
May cure itself.
  Physician.   There is no other means.
  Otho. Open the door ; let 's hear if all
    is quiet.
  Physician. Beseech you, Sire, forbear.
  Erminia.   Do, do.
  Otho.   I command !

Open it straight ; — Sh ! — quiet ! — my
    lost boy !
My miserable Child !
   Ludolph (indistinctly without). Fill full
My goblet — here, a health !
   Erminia.   O, close the door !
   Otho. Let, let me hear his voice ; this
    cannot last ;   40
And fain would I catch up his dying
    words,
Though my own knell they be ! This can-
    not last !
O let me catch his voice — for lo ! I hear
This silence whisper me that he is dead !
It is so ! Gersa ?
          Enter GERSA.
   Physician. Say, how fares the prince ?
   Gersa. More calm ; his features are less
    wild and flush'd ;
Once he complain'd of weariness.
   Physician.   Indeed !
'Tis good, — 'tis good ; let him but fall
    asleep,
That saves him.
   Otho.   Gersa, watch him like a child ;
Ward him from harm, — and bring me
    better news !   50
   Physician. Humour him to the height.
    I fear to go ;
For should he catch a glimpse of my dull
    garb,
It might affright him, fill him with sus-
    picion
That we believe him sick, which must not
    be.
   Gersa. I will invent what soothing means
    I can.   [*Exit* GERSA.
   Physician. This should cheer up your
    Highness ; weariness
Is a good symptom, and most favourable ;
It gives me pleasant hopes. Please you,
    walk forth
Onto the terrace ; the refreshing air
Will blow one half of your sad doubts
    away.   60
                  [*Exeunt.*

SCENE V. — *A Banqueting Hall, brilliantly
   illuminated, and set forth with all
   costly magnificence, with Supper-
   tables, laden with services of Gold and
   Silver. A door in the back scene,
   guarded by two Soldiers. Lords, La-
   dies, Knights, Gentlemen, &c., whis-
   pering sadly, and ranging themselves;
   part entering and part discovered*
   First Knight. Grievously are we tanta-
    liz'd, one and all ;
Sway'd here and there, commanded to
    and fro,
As though we were the shadows of a
    dream,
And link'd to a sleeping fancy. What do
    we here ?
   Gonfred. I am no seer ; you know we
    must obey
The prince from A to Z, though it should
    be
To set the place in flames. I pray, hast
    heard
Where the most wicked Princess is ?
   First Knight.   There, sir,
In the next room ; have you remark'd
    those two
Stout soldiers posted at the door ?
   Gonfred.   For what ? 10
                  [*They whisper.*
   First Lady. How ghast a train !
   Second Lady. Sure this should be some
    splendid burial.
   First Lady. What fearful whispering !
    See, see, — Gersa there !
          Enter GERSA.
   Gersa. Put on your brightest looks ;
    smile if you can ;
Behave as all were happy ; keep your eyes
From the least watch upon him ; if he
    speaks
To any one, answer, collectedly,
Without surprise, his questions, howe'er
    strange.
Do this to the utmost, — though, alas !
    with me
The remedy grows hopeless ! Here he
    comes, —   20
Observe what I have said, — show no sur-
    prise.
     Enter LUDOLPH, *followed by*
       SIGIFRED *and Page.*
   Ludolph. A splendid company ! rare
    beauties here !
I should have Orphean lips, and Plato's
    fancy,
Amphion's utterance, toned with his lyre,
Or the deep key of Jove's sonorous mouth,
To give fit salutation. Methought I heard,
As I came in, some whispers, — what of
    that ?
'Tis natural men should whisper ; at the
    kiss
Of Psyche given by Love, there was a buzz
Among the gods ! — and silence is as natu-
    ral.   30
These draperies are fine, and, being a
    mortal,
I should desire no better ; yet, in truth,
There must be some superior costliness,
Some wider-domed high magnificence !

I would have, as a mortal I may not,
Hanging of heaven's clouds, purple and
    gold,
Slung from the spheres; gauzes of silver
    mist,
Loop'd up with cords of twisted wreathed
    light,
And tassell'd round with weeping meteors !
These pendent lamps and chandeliers are
    bright   40
As earthly fires from dull dross can be
    cleansed ;
Yet could my eyes drink up intenser beams
Undazzled, — this is darkness, — when I
    close
These lids, I see far fiercer brilliances, —
Skies full of splendid moons, and shooting
    stars,
And spouting exhalations, diamond fires,
And panting fountains quivering with
    deep glows !
Yes — this is dark — is it not dark ?
    Sigifred.   My Lord,
'Tis late ; the lights of festival are ever
Quench'd in the morn.
    Ludolph.   'Tis not to-morrow then ? 50
    Sigifred. 'Tis early dawn.
    Gersa.   Indeed full time we slept ;
Say you so, Prince ?
    Ludolph.   I say I quarrell'd with you ;
We did not tilt each other, — that's a
    blessing, —
Good gods ! no innocent blood upon my
    head !
    Sigifred. Retire, Gersa !
    Ludolph.   There should be three more
    here :
For two of them, they stay away perhaps,
Being gloomy-minded, haters of fair
    revels, —
They know their own thoughts best.
                        As for the third,
We'll have her presently ; ay, you shall
    see her,
And wonder at her, friends, she is so
    fair ;   60
Deep blue eyes, semi-shaded in white lids,
Finish'd with lashes fine for more soft
    shade,
Completed by her twin-arch'd ebon brows ;
White temples, of exactest elegance,
Of even mould, felicitous and smooth ;
Cheeks fashion'd tenderly on either side,
So perfect, so divine, that our poor eyes
Are dazzled with the sweet proportioning,
And wonder that 'tis so, — the magic
    chance !
Her nostrils, small, fragrant, faery-deli-
    cate ;   70

Her lips — I swear no human bones e'er
    wore
So taking a disguise ; — you shall behold
    her !
She is the world's chief jewel, and, by
    heaven
She's mine by right of marriage ! — she is
    mine !
Patience, good people. In fit time I send
A summoner, — she will obey my call,
Being a wife most mild and dutiful.
First I would hear what music is prepared
To herald and receive her ; let me hear !
    Sigifred. Bid the musicians soothe him
        tenderly.   80
        [*A soft strain of Music.*
    Ludolph. Ye have none better ? No, I
        am content ;
'Tis a rich sobbing melody, with reliefs
Full and majestic ; it is well enough,
And will be sweeter, when ye see her pace
Sweeping into this presence, glisten'd o'er
With emptied caskets, and her train up-
    held
By ladies, habited in robes of lawn,
Sprinkled with golden crescents, others
    bright
In silks, with spangles shower'd, and bow'd
    to
By Duchesses and pearled Margravines ! 90
Sad, that the fairest creature of the earth —
I pray you mind me not — 'tis sad, I say,
That the extremest beauty of the world
Should so entrench herself away from me,
Behind a barrier of engender'd guilt !
    Second Lady. Ah ! what a moan !
    First Knight.   Most piteous indeed !
    Ludolph. She shall be brought before
        this company,
And then — then —
    First Lady.   He muses.
    Gersa. O, Fortune, where will this end ?
    Sigifred. I guess his purpose ! Indeed
        he must not have
That pestilence brought in, — that cannot
    be,   100
There we must stop him.
    Gersa.   I am lost ! Hush, hush !
He is about to rave again.
    Ludolph. A barrier of guilt ! I was the
        fool,
She was the cheater ! Who's the cheater
    now,
And who the fool ? The entrapp'd, the
    caged fool,
The bird-limed raven ? She shall croak to
    death
Secure ! Methinks I have her in my fist,
To crush her with my heel ! Wait, wait !

I marvel
My father keeps away. Good friend — ah,
   Sigifred !
Do bring him to me, — and Erminia   110
I fain would see before I sleep — and
   [holy] Ethelbert
That he may bless me, as I know he will,
Though I have curs'd him.
   Sigifred.   Rather suffer me
To lead you to them.
   Ludolph.   No, excuse me, — no !
The day is not quite done. Go, bring
   them hither.
                 [*Exit* SIGIFRED.
Certes, a father's smile should, like sun
   light,
Slant on my sheafed harvest of ripe bliss.
Besides, I thirst to pledge my lovely bride
In a deep goblet : let me see — what wine ?
The strong Iberian juice, or mellow
   Greek ?   120
Or pale Calabrian ? Or the Tuscan grape ?
Or of old Ætna's pulpy wine-presses,
Black stain'd with the fat vintage, as it
   were
The purple slaughter-house, where Bac-
   chus' self
Prick'd his own swollen veins ! Where is
   my page ?
   Page.   Here, here !
   Ludolph. Be ready to obey me ; anon
   thou shalt
Bear a soft message for me ; for the hour
Draws near when I must make a winding
   up
Of bridal mysteries. A fine-spun ven-
   geance !
Carve it on my tomb, that, when I rest
   beneath,   130
Men shall confess, this Prince was gull'd
   and cheated,
But from the ashes of disgrace he rose
More than a fiery dragon, and did burn
His ignominy up in purging fires !
Did I not send, sir, but a moment past,
For my father ?
   Gersa.   You did.
   Ludolph.   Perhaps 'twould be
Much better he came not.
   Gersa.   He enters now !
   Enter OTHO, ERMINIA, ETHELBERT, SIGI-
      FRED, *and Physician.*
   Ludolph. O ! thou good man, against
   whose sacred head
I was a mad conspirator, chiefly too
For the sake of my fair newly wedded
   wife,   140
Now to be punish'd ! — do not look so
   sad !

Those charitable eyes will thaw my heart,
Those tears will wash away a just resolve,
A verdict ten times sworn ! Awake —
   awake —
Put on a judge's brow, and use a tongue
Made iron-stern by habit ! Thou shalt see
A deed to be applauded, 'scribed in gold !
Join a loud voice to mine, and so de-
   nounce
What I alone will execute !
   Otho.   Dear son,
What is it ? By your father's love, I sue 150
That it be nothing merciless !
   Ludolph.   To that demon ?
Not so ! No ! She is in temple-stall
Being garnish'd for the sacrifice, and I,
The Priest of Justice, will immolate her
Upon the altar of wrath ! She stings me
   through ! —
Even as the worm doth feed upon the nut,
So she, a scorpion, preys upon my brain !
I feel her gnawing here ! Let her but
   vanish,
Then, father, I will lead your legions
   forth,
Compact in steeled squares, and speared
   files,   160
And bid our trumpets speak a fell rebuke
To nations drowsed in peace !
   Otho.   To-morrow, son,
Be your word law ; forget to-day —
   Ludolph.   I will
When I have finish'd it ! Now, — now, I'm
   pight,
Tight-footed for the deed !
   Erminia.   Alas ! Alas !
   Ludolph. What angel's voice is that ?
   Erminia !
Ah ! gentlest creature, whose sweet inno-
   cence
Was almost murder'd ; I am penitent,
Wilt thou forgive me ? And thou, holy
   man,
Good Ethelbert, shall I die in peace with
   you ?   170
   Erminia. Die, my lord !
   Ludolph.   I feel it possible.
   Otho.   Physician ?
   Physician. I fear me he is past my skill.
   Otho.   Not so !
   Ludolph. I see it — I see it — I have
   been wandering !
Half-mad — not right here — I forget my
   purpose.
Bestir — bestir — Auranthe ! Ha ! ha ! ha !
Youngster ! Page ! go bid them drag her
   to me !
Obey ! This shall finish it !
                 [*Draws a dagger.*

Otho.   O, my son ! my son !
Sigifred. This must not be — stop there !
Ludolph.   Am I obey'd ?
A little talk with her — no harm — haste !
    haste !   [*Exit Page.*
Set her before me — never fear I can
    strike.   180
Several Voices. My Lord ! My Lord !
Gersa.   Good Prince !
Ludolph. Why do ye trouble me ? out
    — out — out away !
There she is ! take that ! and that ! no no,
That 's not well done. — Where is she ?
    [*The doors open. Enter Page. Several
    women are seen grouped about Au-
    ranthe in the inner room.*
Page. Alas ! My Lord, my Lord ! they
    cannot move her !

Her arms are stiff, — her fingers clench'd.
    and cold !
Ludolph. She's dead !
    [*Staggers and falls into their arms.*
Ethelbert.   Take away the dagger.
Gersa.   Softly ; so !
Otho. Thank God for that !
Sigifred.   I fear it could not harm him.
Gersa. No ! — brief be his anguish !
Ludolph. She 's gone ! I am content —
    Nobles, good night !   190
We are all weary — faint — set ope the
    doors —
I will to bed ! — To-morrow —   [*Dies.*
Where is your hand — father, what sultry
    air !

THE CURTAIN FALLS

6

MATTHEW ARNOLD'S *EMPEDOCLES ON ETNA*

Empedocles on Etna is without doubt, I think, a central poem in the Arnold canon. Despite his famous rejection of it in the "Preface" to the 1853 *Poems*, the work remains fundamental to an understanding of Arnold's poetic practice and of his thought. It is, moreover, one of those works (W. Stacy Johnson compares it, for example, to *Sartor Resartus*[1]) that express a conflict central to the Victorian imagination—"the dialogue of the mind with itself," Arnold termed it. But it is not simply this self-consciousness that marks *Empedocles on Etna* as being characteristically Arnoldian or Victorian: it is the nature of the forces involved in the conflict, as well as Arnold's eventual inability to resolve that conflict, that makes the poem archetypical. For the dialogue in which Empedocles engages with himself is an attempt to preserve the nobility of the human spirit in an indifferent, if not actively hostile, material universe. The "solution" at which Empedocles arrives—self-destruction—was no solution at all for most Victorians, and certainly not for Arnold himself. Yet the anguish that Empedocles feels, and the various possibilities for life that his dialogue suggests, are attitudes to which every Victorian, at one time or another, must have been heir.

It is not, however, only because of its ideational content that *Empedocles on Etna* is important; the poem is clearly poetry of thought, but its form, an essentially dramatic one, is a key to the complexity of that thought. *Empedocles* was Arnold's first major experiment with Greek "dramatic" form. Only once again did he attempt anything so closely resembling Greek tragedy, and in *Merope* (1858) he failed roundly. *Merope* is more nearly dramatically perfect than *Empedocles,* but it is also, as Lionel Trilling has pointed out, subject matter of less moment—it is simply not very interesting.[2] *Empedocles,* on the other hand, with a crucially interesting thematic problem, is dramatically imperfect. Though the conflict is clear, and though aspects of it are embodied in various characters, the characters themselves, as G. Robert Stange indicates, are not "brought into significant relation with each other." In this respect, Stange goes on, *Empedocles on Etna* is characteristic of Arnold's practice: many of his poems are dramatic insofar as they have a fable and characters, and a definite setting in place and time; but "in Arnold's practice generally . . . the characters do not act upon each other; place and time, rigidly limited by the unities, are static and assume an entirely symbolic significance."[3] This form is one that Arnold used repeatedly—Stange makes reference to such diverse works as "The Strayed Reveller," "Resig-

1. W. Stacy Johnson, *The Voices of Matthew Arnold* (New Haven, 1961), p. 7.
2. Lionel Trilling, *Matthew Arnold* (New York, 1949), p. 142.
3. G. Robert Stange, *Matthew Arnold: The Poet as Humanist* (Princeton, 1967), p. 17.

nation," and even "Stanzas from the Grande Chartreuse"—and it is a form that is sometimes varied, "but never transcended."

The importance to Arnold of dramatic or pseudo-dramatic form is implied throughout his literary criticism, but the remarks perhaps most relevant to the present purpose are those in the "Preface" to the 1853 *Poems* and the "Preface" to *Merope*. In both, Arnold spends some time justifying his choice of plot. What is wrong with *Empedocles on Etna* is not, certainly, the fact that Empedocles is not (at least apparently) a Victorian Englishman. In fact, "tradition is a great matter to a poet; . . . it gives him the feeling that he is treading on solid ground."[4] Moreover, classical art has still attached to it, even in these dark days, "a nameless hope and interest."[5] That interest, though part of Arnold probably realized that it was simply romantic Hellenism, was, he hoped, also the result of an unconscious attraction to what he apparently saw as most fundamentally Greek, perfection of form, a perfection that he identified with a certain moral and/or intellectual stance. (In the 1853 "Preface" Arnold speaks of the characteristics of "the great monuments of early Greek genius": "calm, cheerfulness . . . disinterested objectivity.") [6]

Of all literary forms, too, the drama was the most nearly perfect. Given the physical conditions of the Greek theater, Arnold points out, these artists found what was necessary: their effects had to be broad and simple, yet intense. "Unity of plan in the action, and symmetry in the treatment of it, were indispensable."[7] Whatever "rules" existed were not dogmatically insisted on to the exclusion of other modes of expression, but they had nevertheless a practical advantage: they were *"prophecies of the improbability of dramatic success under other conditions."* (Arnold's emphasis). Those prophecies may be, Arnold suggests, as useful for the modern as the ancient; they satisfy the human spirit's simultaneous needs for variety and for "depth and concentration."[8] If we naturally delight in imitation or representation, it is nevertheless desirable that the imitation not be "vaguely conceived and loosely drawn."[9] Precision, then, is of the utmost importance; it is the responsibility upon which is contingent the freedom allowed the author of dramatic works. (And certainly it was that freedom, that appearance of utter impersonality, that attracted Arnold to the drama.)

In *Merope*, Arnold stuck very carefully to the prescription, and failed. *Empedocles on Etna* is constructed with greater freedom, and although Arnold violated the "rules," he produced a great work, great not only by virtue of the superior importance of its matter, but at least in part because of the particular form in which it is cast. Arnold tells us that *Empedocles* is a failure because in it "suffering finds no vent in action." There is, apparently, in the view with which the poem leaves us, no room for that "joy," that inspirational insight, that Arnold prized so highly. A more recent criticism has it that, although Arnold set out to produce a poetry of thought, he "merely produced a poetry of the diseases of thought."[10] Agreement seems in fact to be general that the poem is great but seriously flawed—another of those magnificent attempts. Yet the fact that Arnold allowed himself to be persuaded to reprint the poem in the *New Poems* of 1867 ought to indicate that despite his very strong statements against *Empedocles on Etna*, he retained some fondness and, no doubt, respect, for it. (Interestingly enough, the songs of Callicles crept back into the "official" canon rather quickly, in 1855.)

---

4. "Preface" to *Merope, On the Classical Tradition*, vol. 1 of *The Complete Prose Works of Matthew Arnold*, ed. R. H. Super (Ann Arbor, Mich., 1960), p. 53.

5. *Ibid.*, p. 38.

6. "Preface" to *Poems* (1853), *On the Classical Tradition*, p. 1.

7. "Preface" to *Merope*, p. 57.

8. *Ibid.*, p. 58.

9. "Preface" to *Poems* (1853), p. 2.

10. E. K. Brown, *Matthew Arnold: A Study in Conflict* (Chicago, 1948), p. 44.

Nevertheless, the chief difficulty with the poem—that its conflict is, finally, impossible to resolve—is major, and must be taken into account in any assessment.

Given the character of Empedocles, there can be no action that will approach a satisfactory resolution. We must not, in the first place, make the mistake of confusing Arnold with his creation. Empedocles may, as Dwight Culler suggests, write Arnoldian poetry,[11] but he is a rather clearly realized persona, and not a simple projection of Matthew Arnold. Arnold shows us not the Empedocles of history, and not his alter ego, but another personality, a mid-nineteenth century man weakened by life. If the universe is indifferent, man is thrust back upon himself, and the conflict is thus internalized. It is Empedocles' failure to find internal resource that leads to his suicide: self-destruction is the necessary outcome of his emotional and intellectual exhaustion. He often gives Arnoldian advice: "Because thou must not dream, thou need'st not then despair!" (I. ii. 426) ; but he cannot himself act on it. Throwing oneself into a volcano is an action, but one that ends despair and does not resolve the problem that has caused it. If we take Empedocles as Arnold's only spokesman in the poem, we too are likely to feel the joylessness of man's existence. But Arnold would not have chosen dramatic form unless he wanted us to distance ourselves from Empedocles. Empedocles' answer is not a workable one, and the poem does not show that it is the only solution. Empedocles sees life neither steadily nor wholly; he has been, he fears, the "slave of thought"—and, though he quickly shoves the notion aside, he seeks death as salvation from the "mists of despondency and gloom" that are the consequence of slavery to the power of the mind. Suicide is an escape, not meaningful action; it is without the inspiration and the "joyful emotion" that "make moral action perfect."[12]

And Empedocles' death is not the note on which the poem closes. Callicles' final song perfects the tonal quality of the poem; it is impossible for Empedocles to live, but there is possible another vision, a balance of thought and sense—poise:

> What will be forever;
> What was from of old .
> The day in his hotness,
> The strife with the palm;
> The night in her silence,
> The stars in their calm.
>
> (II. 459–68)

Callicles' words underscore with grim irony the futility of Empedocles' suicide, yet they also convey a sense of the ultimate peace of resignation.

Lest it appear that this one song of Callicles is too fragile for the weight that Arnold seems to put on it, the pattern of the poem as a whole demonstrates the need for it. The circumstance of the poem is, initially, a convenience to allow Empedocles to speak his mind at great length. Both Pausanias and Callicles serve as foils against which to play off Empedocles' attitudes, and it is important that there be a clear difference between the two, and that Empedocles confront only one of them directly. Callicles thus serves a double function in the poem: he is both character and lyric chorus, causal to the action and apart from it, experiencing and commenting.

The initial exchange between Pausanias and Callicles sets the scene for the scant action of the play. It introduces the two, and hints at the conflict by involving them in a dialogue on Empedocles' spiritual and physical health. The con-

---

11. A. Dwight Culler, *Imaginative Reason* (New Haven, 1966) , p. 161.
12. "Marcus Aurelius," *Lectures and Essays in Criticism*, vol. 3 of *The Complete Prose Works* (Ann Arbor, Mich., 1962) , p. 134.

versation also makes clear some differences between them. Pausanias, though Callicles initially calls him Empedocles' "sage friend," proves less intelligent than credulous. He is an old friend, yet his chief motive for accompanying Empedocles is apparently not to cure his friend's restless gloom, but to discover the secret whereby Empedocles raised Pantheia from the dead. Pausanias' belief in "spells" causes Callicles and the audience to change their minds about him—he becomes "simple Pausanias," and Callicles begins to see, too, that Pausanias lacks insight and true sympathy:

> . . . thou art no company for him!
> Thou art as cross, as sour'd as himself. . . .
> (I.i.140–41)

Callicles senses the real truth about Empedocles ("There is some root of suffering in himself" I. i. 151) and begs Pausanias not to pester him with talk of miracles; it is that pestering that leads to Empedocles' long disquisition in scene ii. Empedocles tells himself (after delivering to Pausanias one long speech of some 392 lines) that he has paid his debt to his old friend, that if Pausanias heeds the lesson he

> May bravelier front his life, and in himself
> Find henceforth energy and heart.
> (II. 9–10)

But he knows that for himself it is too late, and his conviction may be strengthened —as, in effect, is ours—by the suspicion that Pausanias has not accurately understood him. And Callicles' songs, as Empedocles listens to them throughout the course of the play, emphasize Empedocles' distance from others and from himself. Repeatedly, Callicles' songs create in Empedocles, despite the fact that he "never fail'd to love his lyre," a consciousness of what he has not done, what he can no longer do. (His long speech in Act I, the attempt to enlighten Pausanias, follows Callicles' lyric narrating the story of Chiron's advice to Achilles—how he taught him "all the wisdom of his race.") And his songs also serve to comment, usually indirectly, on Empedocles' speeches. (At the end of the same long speech to Pausanias, Callicles sings of Cadmus and Harmonia, who escaped the curse of Thebes—that of human existence—by being changed into snakes:

> Placed safely in changed forms, the pair
> Wholly forget their first sad life, and home,
> And all that Theban woe, and stray
> For ever through the glens, placid and dumb.
> (I.ii.457–60)

Or, as Empedocles says, after hearing Callicles on Typho, "He fables, yet speaks truth" (II. 89). It is precisely because the truths are not intentionally addressed to the subject of Empedocles' monologue that he feels their truth as keenly as he does. Callicles must remain apart from Empedocles as a sort of haunting consciousness of other possibilities, and just as important as the "truths" of his fables is the voice in which he utters them. The form of Callicles' songs is as true—perhaps, indeed, truer. While the "moral truth" gives point, the poetic truth provides relief.

In the "Preface" to *Merope*, Arnold comments on his agreement with Schlegel that in Greek tragedy the chorus is the ideal spectator, "designed to enable the actual spectator to feel his own impressions more distinctly and more deeply."[13]

---

13. "Preface" to *Merope*, p. 60.

The chorus gives relief, not in mere buffoonery, but in lyrical song. Further, "the noble and natural relief from the emotion produced by tragic events is in the transition to the emotion produced by lyric poetry, not in the contrast and shock of a totally opposite order of feelings."[14]

It is possible—necessary, I feel, to an adequate understanding of the poem—to regard Callicles' function in the poem as primarily a choric one. The business of the chorus is not, assuredly, the substantive business of the drama, but it may provide the element necessary to restore some measure of balance.

Dwight Culler comments that

[Callicles] is the kind of artist who does not realize that poems have a content as well as a form. Empedocles, on the other hand, is the kind of artist who does not realize that poems have a form as well as a content. And so one sings to the other songs whose form is designed to cure him, while the other listens to their content and is moved by them to the edge of destruction.[15]

Empedocles is moved by Callicles' songs to the edge of destruction, but not because Callicles thinks that songs have only form and not content. His last song, in fact, makes it very clear that he is aware of the content of his (and of all) poetry. One of the points that must be made is that Callicles' voice—the rhythmic, irregularly rhymed iambic tetrameter that dominates the songs—is the "being" of their content. His songs fail, finally, but not because Empedocles is weary of the lyre and the laurel. For him poetry can fence out the profane:

> Thou fencest him from the multitude—
> Who will fence him from himself?
> (II. 211–12)

Apparently Empedocles' understanding of poetry is not, then, entire. It, too, has succumbed to that disease of will that tortures him. There was a time, he can still recall, when he had "fulness of life and power of feeling." Poetry might oppress the brain, but it could be eased by, because seen as one with, "the delightful commerce of the world." In his present state, little wonder that Callicles' songs drive him to the edge of destruction: "I alone," he says, "am dead to life and joy, therefore I read / In all things my own deadness" (II. 320–23).

It is the gloom of that deadness that is balanced by Callicles' final song. It does not alter the fact of Empedocles' final despair, but it does alter the echo of that act in the mind of the reader. *Empedocles on Etna* may be imperfect dramatically, but clearly the dramatic elements in it are important to its success.

G. C. S.

---

14. *Ibid.*, p. 61.
15. Culler, p. 176.

Empedocles On Etna

A DRAMATIC POEM

PERSONS

EMPEDOCLES.
PAUSANIAS, *a Physician.*
CALLICLES, *a young Harp-player.*

*The Scene of the Poem is on Mount Etna;
at first in the forest region, afterwards on
the summit of the mountain.*

ACT I. SCENE I.

*Morning. A Pass in the forest region
of Etna.*

CALLICLES.
(Alone, resting on a rock by the path.)

The mules, I think, will not be here this
    hour ;
They feel the cool wet turf under their
    feet
By the stream-side, after the dusty lanes
In which they have toil'd all night from
    Catana,
And scarcely will they budge a yard. O
    Pan,   5
How gracious is the mountain at this
    hour !
A thousand times have I been here alone,
Or with the revellers from the mountain-
    towns,
But never on so fair a morn ; — the sun
Is shining on the brilliant mountain-
    crests,   10
And on the highest pines ; but farther
    down,
Here in the valley, is in shade ; the sward
Is dark, and on the stream the mist still
    hangs ;

One sees one's footprints crush'd in the
    wet grass,
One's breath curls in the air ; and on
    these pines   15
That climb from the stream's edge, the
    long grey tufts,
Which the goats love, are jewell'd thick
    with dew.
Here will I stay till the slow litter comes.
I have my harp too — that is well. —
    Apollo !
What mortal could be sick or sorry
    here ?   20
I know not in what mind Empedocles,
Whose mules I follow'd, may be coming
    up,
But if, as most men say, he is half mad
With exile, and with brooding on his
    wrongs,
Pausanias, his sage friend, who mounts
    with him,   25
Could scarce have lighted on a lovelier
    cure.
The mules must be below, far down. I hear
Their tinkling bells, mix'd with the song
    of birds,
Rise faintly to me — now it stops ! — Who's
    here ?
Pausanias ! and on foot ? alone ?

Pausanias

                And thou, then ?   30
I left thee supping with Peisianax,
With thy head full of wine, and thy hair
    crown'd,
Touching thy harp as the whim came on
    thee,
And praised and spoil'd by master and by
    guests

208

Almost as much as the new dancing-girl. 35
Why hast thou follow'd us?

Callicles

                        The night was hot,
And the feast past its prime; so we
    slipp'd out,
Some of us, to the portico to breathe; —
Peisianax, thou know'st, drinks late; —
    and then,
As I was lifting my soil'd garland off,   40
I saw the mules and litter in the court,
And in the litter sate Empedocles;
Thou, too, wast with him. Straightway I
    sped home;
I saddled my white mule, and all night
    long
Through the cool lovely country follow'd
    you,   45
Pass'd you a little since as morning
    dawn'd,
And have this hour sate by the torrent
    here,
Till the slow mules should climb in sight
    again.
And now?

Pausanias

    And now, back to the town with speed!
Crouch in the wood first, till the mules
    have pass'd;   50
They do but halt, they will be here anon.
Thou must be viewless to Empedocles;
Save mine, he must not meet a human eye.
One of his moods is on him that thou
    know'st;
I think, thou wouldst not vex him.

Callicles

                        No — and yet 55
I would fain stay, and help thee tend
    him. Once
He knew me well, and would oft notice
    me;
And still, I know not how, he draws me
    to him,
And I could watch him with his proud
    sad face,
His flowing locks and gold-encircled
    brow   60
And kingly gait, for ever; such a spell
In his severe looks, such a majesty
As drew of old the people after him,
In Agrigentum and Olympia,
When his star reign'd, before his banish-
    ment,   65

Is potent still on me in his decline.
But oh! Pausanias, he is changed of late;
There is a settled trouble in his air
Admits no momentary brightening now,
And when he comes among his friends
    at feasts,   70
'Tis as an orphan among prosperous boys.
Thou know'st of old he loved this harp
    of mine,
When first he sojourn'd with Peisianax;
He is now always moody, and I fear him;
But I would serve him, soothe him, if I
    could,   75
Dared one but try.

Pausanias

                    Thou wast a kind child ever!
He loves thee, but he must not see thee
    now.
Thou hast indeed a rare touch on thy
    harp,
He loves that in thee, too; — there was
    a time
(But that is pass'd), he would have paid
    thy strain   80
With music to have drawn the stars from
    heaven.
He hath his harp and laurel with him still,
But he has laid the use of music by,
And all which might relax his settled
    gloom.
Yet thou may'st try thy playing, if thou
    wilt —   85
But thou must keep unseen; follow us on,
But at a distance! in these solitudes,
In this clear mountain-air, a voice will rise,
Though from afar, distinctly; it may
    soothe him.
Play when we halt, and, when the evening
    comes   90
And I must leave him (for his pleasure is
To be left musing these soft nights alone
In the high unfrequented mountain-spots),
Then watch him, for he ranges swift and
    far,
Sometimes to Etna's top, and to the
    cone;   95
But hide thee in the rocks a great way
    down,
And try thy noblest strains, my Callicles,
With the sweet night to help thy har-
    mony!
Thou wilt earn my thanks sure, and per-
    haps his.

Callicles

More than a day and night, Pausanias,   100

Of this fair summer-weather, on these hills,
Would I bestow to help Empedocles.
That needs no thanks ; one is far better
   here
Than in the broiling city in these heats.
But tell me, how hast thou persuaded
   him   105
In this his present fierce, man-hating mood,
To bring thee out with him alone on
   Etna ?

Pausanias

Thou hast heard all men speaking of
   Pantheia
The woman who at Agrigentum lay
Thirty long days in a cold trance of
   death,   110
And whom Empedocles call'd back to life.
Thou art too young to note it, but his
   power
Swells with the swelling evil of this time,
And holds men mute to see where it will
   rise.
He could stay swift diseases in old days, 115
Chain madmen by the music of his lyre,
Cleanse to sweet airs the breath of poison-
   ous streams,
And in the mountain-chinks inter the
   winds.
This he could do of old ; but now, since all
Clouds and grows daily worse in Sicily, 120
Since broils tear us in twain, since this
   new swarm
Of sophists has got empire in our schools
Where he was paramount, since he is
   banish'd
And lives a lonely man in triple gloom —
He grasps the very reins of life and
   death.   125
I ask'd him of Pantheia yesterday,
When we were gather'd with Peisianax,
And he made answer, I should come at
   night
On Etna here, and be alone with him,
And he would tell me, as his old, tried
   friend,   130
Who still was faithful, what might profit
   me ;
That is, the secret of this miracle.

Callicles

Bah ! Thou a doctor ! Thou art super-
   stitious.
Simple Pausanias, 'twas no miracle !
Pantheia, for I know her kinsmen well, 135
Was subject to these trances from a girl.
Empedocles would say so, did he deign ;

But he still lets the people, whom he
   scorns,
Gape and cry *wizard* at him, if they list.
But thou, thou art no company for
   him !   140
Thou art as cross, as sour'd as himself !
Thou hast some wrong from thine own
   citizens,
And then thy friend is banish'd, and on
   that,
Straightway thou fallest to arraign the
   times,
As if the sky was impious not to fall.   145
The sophists are no enemies of his ;
I hear, Gorgias, their chief, speaks nobly
   of him,
As of his gifted master, and once friend.
He is too scornful, too high-wrought, too
   bitter.
'Tis not the times, 'tis not the sophists vex
   him ;   150
There is some root of suffering in himself,
Some secret and unfollow'd vein of woe,
Which makes the time look black and sad
   to him.
Pester him not in this his sombre mood
With questionings about an idle tale,   155
But lead him through the lovely mountain-
   paths,
And keep his mind from preying on itself,
And talk to him of things at hand and
   common,
Not miracles ! thou art a learned man,
But credulous of fables as a girl.   160

Pausanias

And thou, a boy whose tongue outruns
   his knowledge,
And on whose lightness blame is thrown
   away.
Enough of this ! I see the litter wind
Up by the torrent-side, under the pines.
I must rejoin Empedocles. Do thou   165
Crouch in the brushwood till the mules
   have pass'd ;
Then play thy kind part well. Farewell till
   night !

SCENE II

*Noon. A Glen on the highest skirts of the
woody region of Etna.*

EMPEDOCLES — PAUSANIAS

Pausanias

The noon is hot. When we have cross'd
   the stream,

We shall have left the woody tract, and
　　come
Upon the open shoulder of the hill.
See how the giant spires of yellow bloom
Of the sun-loving gentian, in the heat,　5
Are shining on those naked slopes like
　　flame!
Let us rest here; and now, Empedocles,
Pantheia's history!
　　　　　[A harp-note below is heard.

Empedocles

Hark! what sound was that
Rose from below? If it were possible,
And we were not so far from human
　　haunt,　10
I should have said that some one touch'd
　　a harp.
Hark! there again!

Pausanias
'Tis the boy Callicles,
The sweetest harp-player in Catana.
He is for ever coming on these hills,
In summer, to all country-festivals,　15
With a gay revelling band; he breaks from
　　them
Sometimes, and wanders far among the
　　glens.
But heed him not, he will not mount to
　　us;
I spoke with him this morning. Once more,
　　therefore,
Instruct me of Pantheia's story, Master,　20
As I have pray'd thee.

Empedocles

That? and to what end?

Pausanias

It is enough that all men speak of it.
But I will also say, that when the Gods
Visit us as they do with sign and plague,
To know those spells of thine which stay
　　their hand　25
Were to live free from terror.

Empedocles

Spells? Mistrust them!
Mind is the spell which governs earth and
　　heaven.
Man has a mind with which to plan his
　　safety;
Know that, and help thyself!

Pausanias

But thine own words?
'The wit and counsel of man was never
　　clear,　30
Troubles confound the little wit he has.'
Mind is a light which the Gods mock us
　　with,
To lead those false who trust it.
　　　　　[The harp sounds again.

Empedocles

Hist! once more!
Listen, Pausanias! — Ay, 'tis Callicles;
I know these notes among a thousand.
　　Hark!　35

Callicles

(Sings unseen, from below)

The track winds down to the clear stream,
To cross the sparkling shallows; there
The cattle love to gather, on their way
To the high mountain-pastures, and to
　　stay,
Till the rough cow-herds drive them
　　past,　40
Knee-deep in the cool ford; for 'tis the
　　last
Of all the woody, high, well-water'd dells
On Etna; and the beam
Of noon is broken there by chestnut-
　　boughs
Down its steep verdant sides; the air　45
Is freshen'd by the leaping stream, which
　　throws
Eternal showers of spray on the moss'd
　　roots
Of trees, and veins of turf, and long dark
　　shoots
Of ivy-plants, and fragrant hanging bells
Of hyacinths, and on late anemonies,　50
That muffle its wet banks; but glade,
And stream, and sward, and chestnut-
　　trees,
End here; Etna beyond, in the broad glare
Of the hot noon, without a shade,
Slope behind slope, up to the peak, lies
　　bare;　55
The peak, round which the white clouds
　　play.

In such a glen, on such a day,
On Pelion, on the grassy ground,
Chiron, the aged Centaur lay,
The young Achilles standing by.　60
The Centaur taught him to explore

The mountains; where the glens are
    dry
And the tired Centaurs come to rest,
And where the soaking springs abound
And the straight ashes grow for
    spears,   65
And where the hill-goats come to feed,
And the sea-eagles build their nest.
He show'd him Phthia far away,
And said : O boy, I taught this lore
To Peleus, in long distant years !   70
He told him of the Gods, the stars,
The tides ; — and then of mortal wars,
And of the life which heroes lead
Before they reach the Elysian place
And rest in the immortal mead ;   75
And all the wisdom of his race.

The music below ceases, and EMPEDOCLES
speaks, accompanying himself in a
solemn manner on his harp.

The out-spread world to span
A cord the Gods first slung,
And then the soul of man
There, like a mirror, hung,   80
And bade the winds through space impel
    the gusty toy.

Hither and thither spins
The wind-borne, mirroring soul,
A thousand glimpses wins,
And never sees a whole ;   85
Looks once, and drives elsewhere, and
    leaves its last employ.

The Gods laugh in their sleeve
To watch man doubt and fear,
Who knows not what to believe
Since he sees nothing clear,   90
And dares stamp nothing false where he
    finds nothing sure.

Is this, Pausanias, so ?
And can our souls not strive,
But with the winds must go,
And hurry where they drive ?   95
Is fate indeed so strong, man's strength
    indeed so poor ?

I will not judge. That man,
Howbeit, I judge as lost,
Whose mind allows a plan,
Which would degrade it
    most ;   100
And he treats doubt the best who tries to
    see least ill.

Be not, then, fear's blind slave !

Thou art my friend ; to thee,
All knowledge that I have,
All skill I wield, are free.   105
Ask not the latest news of the last miracle,

Ask not what days and nights
In trance Pantheia lay,
But ask how thou such sights
May'st see without dismay ;   110
Ask what most helps when known, thou
    son of Anchitus !

What ? hate, and awe, and shame
Fill thee to see our time ;
Thou feelest thy soul's frame
Shaken and out of chime ?   115
What ? life and chance go hard with thee
    too, as with us ;

Thy citizens, 'tis said,
Envy thee and oppress,
Thy goodness no men aid,
All strive to make it less ;   120
Tyranny, pride, and lust, fill Sicily's
    abodes ;

Heaven is with earth at strife,
Signs make thy soul afraid,
The dead return to life,
Rivers are dried, winds stay'd ; 125
Scarce can one think in calm, so threaten-
    ing are the Gods ;

And we feel, day and night,
The burden of ourselves —
Well, then, the wiser wight
In his own bosom delves,   130
And asks what ails him so, and gets what
    cure he can.

The sophist sneers : Fool, take
Thy pleasure, right or wrong.
The pious wail : Forsake
A world these sophists throng. 135
Be neither saint nor sophist-led, but be a
    man !

These hundred doctors try
To preach thee to their school.
We have the truth ! they cry ;
And yet their oracle,   140
Trumpet it as they will, is but the same as
    thine.

Once read thy own breast right,
And thou hast done with fears ;
Man gets no other light,
Search he a thousand years.   145

Sink in thyself ! there ask what ails thee,
    at that shrine !

    What makes thee struggle and
      rave ?
    Why are men ill at ease ? —
    'Tis that the lot they have
    Fails their own will to please ; 150
For man would make no murmuring,
    were his will obey'd.

    And why is it, that still
    Man with his lot thus fights ? —
    'Tis that he makes this *will*
    The measure of his *rights*,   155
And believes Nature outraged if his will 's
    gainsaid.

    Couldst thou, Pausanias, learn
    How deep a fault is this ;
    Couldst thou but once discern
    Thou hast no *right* to bliss,   160
No title from the Gods to welfare and re-
    pose ;

    Then thou wouldst look less
      mazed
    Whene'er of bliss debarr'd,
    Nor think the Gods were crazed
    When thy own lot went hard. 165
But we are all the same — the fools of
    our own woes !

    For, from the first faint morn
    Of life, the thirst for bliss
    Deep in man's heart is born ;
    And, sceptic as he is,   170
He fails not to judge clear if this be
    quench'd or no.

    Nor is the thirst to blame.
    Man errs not that he deems
    His welfare his true aim,
    He errs because he dreams   175
The world does but exist that welfare to
    bestow.

    We mortals are no kings
    For each of whom to sway
    A new-made world up-springs,
    Meant merely for his play ;   180
No, we are strangers here ; the world is
    from of old.

    In vain our pent wills fret,
    And would the world subdue.
    Limits we did not set
    Condition all we do :   185

Born into life we are, and life must be our
    mould.

    Born into life ! — man grows
    Forth from his parents' stem,
    And blends their bloods, as those
    Of theirs are blent in them ;   190
So each new man strikes root into a far
    fore-time.

    Born into life ! — we bring
    A bias with us here,
    And, when here, each new thing
    Affects us we come near ;   195
To tunes we did not call our being must
    keep chime.

    Born into life ! — in vain,
    Opinions, those or these,
    Unalter'd to retain
    The obstinate mind decrees ;   200
Experience, like a sea, soaks all-effacing in.

    Born into life ! — who lists
    May what is false hold dear,
    And for himself make mists
    Through which to see less
      clear ;   205
The world is what it is, for all our dust
    and din.

    Born into life ! — 'tis we,
    And not the world, are new ;
    Our cry for bliss, our plea,
    Others have urged it too —   210
Our wants have all been felt, our errors
    made before.

    No eye could be too sound
    To observe a world so vast,
    No patience too profound
    To sort what 's here amass'd ; 215
How man may here best live no care too
    great to explore.

    But we — as some rude guest
    Would change, where'er he roam,
    The manners there profess'd
    To those he brings from
      home —   220
We mark not the world's course, but
    would have *it* take *ours*.

    The world's course proves the
      terms
    On which man wins content ;
    Reason the proof confirms —
    We spurn it, and invent   225

A false course for the world, and for ourselves, false powers.

    Riches we wish to get,
    Yet remain spendthrifts still ;
    We would have health, and yet
    Still use our bodies ill ;   230
Bafflers of our own prayers, from youth
    to life's last scenes.

    We would have inward peace,
    Yet will not look within ;
    We would have misery cease,
    Yet will not cease from sin ;   235
We want all pleasant ends, but will use no
    harsh means ;

    We do not what we ought,
    What we ought not, we do,
    And lean upon the thought
    That chance will bring us
        through ;   240
But our own acts, for good or ill, are
    mightier powers.

    Yet, even when man forsakes
    All sin, — is just, is pure,
    Abandons all which makes
    His welfare insecure, —   245
Other existences there are, that clash with
    ours.

    Like us, the lightning-fires
    Love to have scope and play ;
    The stream, like us, desires
    An unimpeded way ;   250
Like us, the Libyan wind delights to roam
    at large.

    Streams will not curb their pride
    The just man not to entomb,
    Nor lightnings go aside
    To give his virtues room ;   255
Nor is that wind less rough which blows a
    good man's barge.

    Nature, with equal mind,
    Sees all her sons at play ;
    Sees man control the wind,
    The wind sweep man away ;   260
Allows the proudly-riding and the founder-
    ing bark.

    And, lastly, though of ours
    No weakness spoil our lot,
    Though the non-human powers
    Of Nature harm us not,   265
The ill deeds of other men make often *our*
    life dark.

    What were the wise man's
        plan ? —
    Through this sharp, toil-set life,
    To work as best he can,
    And win what 's won by
        strife. —   270
But we an easier way to cheat our pains
    have found.

    Scratch'd by a fall, with moans
    As children of weak age
    Lend life to the dumb stones
    Whereon to vent their rage,   275
And bend their little fists, and rate the
    senseless ground ;

    So, loath to suffer mute,
    We, peopling the void air,
    Make Gods to whom to impute
    The ills we ought to bear ;   280
With God and Fate to rail at, suffering
    easily.

    Yet grant — as sense long miss'd
    Things that are now perceived,
    And much may still exist
    Which is not yet believed —   285
Grant that the world were full of Gods
    we cannot see ;

    All things the world which fill
    Of but one stuff are spun,
    That we who rail are still,
    With what we rail at, one ;   290
One with the o'erlabour'd Power that
    through the breadth and length

    Of earth, and air, and sea,
    In men, and plants, and stones,
    Hath toil perpetually,
    And travails, pants, and
        moans ;   295
Fain would do all things well, but some-
    times fails in strength.

    And patiently exact
    This universal God
    Alike to any act
    Proceeds at any nod,   300
And quietly declaims the cursings of him-
    self.

    This is not what man hates,
    Yet he can curse but this.
    Harsh Gods and hostile Fates
    Are dreams ! this only *is* —   305
Is everywhere ; sustains the wise, the fool-
    ish elf.

Nor only, in the intent
To attach blame elsewhere,
Do we at will invent
Stern Powers who make their
    care   310
To embitter human life, malignant Dei-
   ties ;

But, next, we would reverse
The scheme ourselves have spun,
And what we made to curse
We now would lean upon,   315
And feign kind Gods who perfect what
   man vainly tries.

Look, the world tempts our eye,
And we would know it all !
We map the starry sky,
We mine this earthen ball,   320
We measure the sea-tides, we number the
   sea-sands ;

We scrutinise the dates
Of long-past human things,
The bounds of effaced states,
The lines of deceased kings ; 325
We search out dead men's words, and
   works of dead men's hands ;

We shut our eyes, and muse
How our own minds are made,
What springs of thought they use,
How righten'd, how betray'd — 330
And spend our wit to name what most
   employ unnamed.

But still, as we proceed
The mass swells more and more
Of volumes yet to read,
Of secrets yet to explore.   335
Our hair grows grey, our eyes are dimm'd,
   our heat is tamed ;

We rest our faculties,
And thus address the Gods :
'True science if there is,
It stays in your abodes !   340
Man's measures cannot mete the im-
   measurable All.

'You only can take in
The world's immense design.
Our desperate search was sin,
Which henceforth we resign,   345
Sure only that your mind sees all things
   which befal.'

Fools ! That in man's brief term
He cannot all things view,

Affords no ground to affirm
That there are Gods who do ;   350
Nor does being weary prove that he has
   where to rest.

Again. — Our youthful blood
Claims rapture as its right ;
The world, a rolling flood
Of newness and delight,   355
Draws in the enamour'd gazer to its shin-
   ing breast ;

Pleasure, to our hot grasp,
Gives flowers after flowers ;
With passionate warmth we clasp
Hand after hand in ours ;   360
Now do we soon perceive how fast our
   youth is spent.

At once our eyes grow clear !
We see, in blank dismay,
Year posting after year,
Sense after sense decay ;   365
Our shivering heart is mined by secret
   discontent ;

Yet still, in spite of truth,
In spite of hopes entomb'd,
That longing of our youth
Burns ever unconsumed,   370
Still hungrier for delight as delights grow
   more rare.

We pause ; we hush our heart,
And thus address the Gods :
'The world hath fail'd to impart
The joy our youth forebodes,   375
Fail'd to fill up the void which in our
   breasts we bear.

'Changeful till now, we still
Look'd on to something new ;
Let us, with changeless will,
Henceforth look on to you,   380
To find with you the joy we in vain here
   require !'

Fools ! That so often here
Happiness mock'd our prayer,
I think, might make us fear
A like event elsewhere ;   385
Make us, not fly to dreams, but moderate
   desire.

And yet, for those who know
Themselves, who wisely take
Their way through life, and bow
To what they cannot break,   390

Why should I say that life need yield but
   moderate bliss ?

     Shall we, with temper spoil'd,
     Health sapp'd by living ill,
     And judgment all embroil'd
     By sadness and self-will,   395
Shall *we* judge what for man is not true
   bliss or is ?

     Is it so small a thing
     To have enjoy'd the sun,
     To have lived light in the spring,
     To have loved, to have thought,
       to have done ;   400
To have advanced true friends, and beat
   down baffling foes —

     That we must feign a bliss
     Of doubtful future date,
     And, while we dream on this,
     Lose all our present state,   405
And relegate to worlds yet distant our repose ?

     Not much, I know, you prize
     What pleasures may be had,
     Who look on life with eyes
     Estranged, like mine, and
       sad ;   410
And yet the village-churl feels the truth
   more than you,

     Who's loath to leave this life
     Which to him little yields —
     His hard-task'd sunburnt wife,
     His often-labour'd fields,   415
The boors with whom he talk'd, the coun-
   try-spots he knew.

     But thou, because thou hear'st
     Men scoff at Heaven and Fate,
     Because the Gods thou fear'st
     Fail to make blest thy state,   420
Tremblest, and wilt not dare to trust the
   joys there are !

     I say : Fear not ! Life still
     Leaves human effort scope.
     But, since life teems with ill,
     Nurse no extravagant hope ;   425
Because thou must not dream, thou need'st
   not then despair !

*A long pause. At the end of it the notes of
  a harp below are again heard, and*
CALLICLES *sings :—*

Far, far from here,

The Adriatic breaks in a warm bay
Among the green Illyrian hills ; and there
The sunshine in the happy glens is fair,   430
And by the sea, and in the brakes.
The grass is cool, the sea-side air
Buoyant and fresh, the mountain flowers
More virginal and sweet than ours.
And there, they say, two bright and aged
   snakes,   435
Who once were Cadmus and Harmonia,
Bask in the glens or on the warm sea-shore,
In breathless quiet, after all their ills ;
Nor do they see their country, nor the
   place
Where the Sphinx lived among the frown-
   ing hills,   440
Nor the unhappy palace of their race,
Nor Thebes, nor the Ismenus, any more.

     There those two live, far in the Illyrian
     brakes !
They had stay'd long enough to see,
In Thebes, the billow of calamity   445
Over their own dear children roll'd,
Curse upon curse, pang upon pang,
For years, they sitting helpless in their
   home,
A grey old man and woman ; yet of old
The Gods had to their marriage come,   450
And at the banquet all the Muses sang.

Therefore they did not end their days
In sight of blood ; but were rapt, far away,
To where the west-wind plays,
And murmurs of the Adriatic come   455
To those untrodden mountain-lawns ; and
   there
Placed safely in changed forms, the pair
Wholly forget their first sad life, and home,
And all that Theban woe, and stray
For ever through the glens, placid and
   dumb.   460

          Empedocles

That was my harp-player again ! — where
   is he ?
Down by the stream ?

          Pausanias

     Yes, Master, in the wood.

          Empedocles

He ever loved the Theban story well !
But the day wears. Go now, Pausanias,
For I must be alone. Leave me one
   mule ;   465

Take down with thee the rest to Catana.
And for young Callicles, thank him from
   me ;
Tell him, I never fail'd to love his lyre —
But he must follow me no more to-night.

Pausanias

Thou wilt return to-morrow to the
   city ?   470

Empedocles

Either to-morrow or some other day,
In the sure revolutions of the world,
Good friend, I shall revisit Catana.
I have seen many cities in my time,
Till mine eyes ache with the long spec-
   tacle,   475
And I shall doubtless see them all again ;
Thou know'st me for a wanderer from of
   old.
Meanwhile, stay me not now. Farewell,
   Pausanias !
He departs on his way up the mountain.

Pausanias (alone)

I dare not urge him further — he must go ;
But he is strangely wrought ! — I will speed
   back   480
And bring Peisianax to him from the city ;
His counsel could once soothe him. But,
   Apollo !
How his brow lighten'd as the music rose !
Callicles must wait here, and play to him ;
I saw him through the chestnuts far be-
   low,   485
Just since, down at the stream. — Ho !
   Callicles !
He descends, calling.

ACT II

Evening. The Summit of Etna.

EMPEDOCLES

                Alone ! —
On this charr'd, blacken'd, melancholy
   waste,
Crown'd by the awful peak, Etna's great
   mouth.
Round which the sullen vapour rolls —
   alone !
Pausanias is far hence, and that is well, 5
For I must henceforth speak no more with
   man.

He hath his lesson too, and that debt's
   paid ;
And the good, learned, friendly, quiet man
May bravelier front his life, and in himself
Find henceforth energy and heart. But
   I —   10
The weary man, the banish'd citizen,
Whose banishment is not his greatest ill,
Whose weariness no energy can reach,
And for whose hurt courage is not the
   cure —
What should I do with life and living
   more ?   15

   No, thou art come too late, Empedocles !
And the world hath the day, and must
   break thee,
Not thou the world. With men thou canst
   not live,
Their thoughts, their ways, their wishes,
   are not thine ;
And being lonely thou art miserable, 20
For something has impair'd thy spirit's
   strength,
And dried its self-sufficing fount of joy.
Thou canst not live with men nor with
   thyself —
O sage ! O sage ! — Take then the one way
   left ;
And turn thee to the elements, thy
   friends,   25
Thy well-tried friends, thy willing minis-
   ters,
And say : Ye helpers, hear Empedocles,
Who asks this final service at your hands !
Before the sophist-brood hath overlaid
The last spark of man's consciousness with
   words —   30
Ere quite the being of man, ere quite the
   world
Be disarray'd of their divinity —
Before the soul lose all her solemn joys,
And awe be dead, and hope impossible,
And the soul's deep eternal night come
   on —   35
Receive me, hide me, quench me, take me
   home !
He advances to the edge of the crater.
Smoke and fire break forth with a loud
noise, and CALLICLES *is heard below*
singing : —

The lyre's voice is lovely everywhere ;
In the court of Gods, in the city of men,
And in the lonely rock-strewn mountain-
   glen,
In the still mountain air.   40

Only to Typho it sounds hatefully ;

To Typho only, the rebel o'erthrown,
Through whose heart Etna drives her
    roots of stone
To imbed them in the sea.

Wherefore dost thou groan so loud ?   45
Wherefore do thy nostrils flash,
Through the dark night, suddenly,
Typho, such red jets of flame ? —
Is thy tortured heart still proud ?
Is thy fire-scathed arm still rash ?   50
Still alert thy stone-crush'd frame ?
Doth thy fierce soul still deplore
Thine ancient rout by the Cilician hills,
And that curst treachery on the Mount of
    Gore ?
Do thy bloodshot eyes still weep   55
The fight which crown'd thine ills,
Thy last mischance on this Sicilian deep ?
Hast thou sworn, in thy sad lair,
Where erst the strong sea-currents suck'd
    thee down,
Never to cease to writhe, and try to
    rest,   60
Letting the sea-stream wander through thy
    hair ?
That thy groans, like thunder prest,
Begin to roll, and almost drown
The sweet notes whose lulling spell
Gods and the race of mortals love so
    well,   65
When through thy caves thou hearest music
    swell ?

But an awful pleasure bland
Spreading o'er the Thunderer's face,
When the sound climbs near his seat,
The Olympian council sees ;   70
As he lets his lax right hand,
Which the lightnings doth embrace,
Sink upon his mighty knees.
And the eagle, at the beck
Of the appeasing, gracious harmony,   75
Droops all his sheeny, brown, deep-
    feather'd neck,
Nestling nearer to Jove's feet ;
While o'er his sovran eye
The curtains of the blue films slowly meet
And the white Olympus-peaks   80
Rosily brighten, and the soothed Gods
    smile
At one another from their golden chairs,
And no one round the charmed circle
    speaks.
Only the loved Hebe bears
The cup about, whose draughts beguile   85
Pain and care, with a dark store
Of fresh-pull'd violets wreathed and nod-
    ding o'er ;

And her flush'd feet glow on the marble
    floor.

Empedocles

He fables, yet speaks truth !
The brave, impetuous heart yields every-
    where   90
To the subtle, contriving head ;
Great qualities are trodden down,
And littleness united
Is become invincible.

These rumblings are not Typho's groans,
    I know !   95
These angry smoke-bursts
Are not the passionate breath
Of the mountain-crush'd, tortured, intrac-
    table Titan king —
But over all the world
What suffering is there not seen   100
Of plainness oppress'd by cunning,
As the well-counsell'd Zeus oppress'd
That self-helping son of earth !
What anguish of greatness,
Rail'd and hunted from the world,   105
Because its simplicity rebukes
This envious, miserable age !

I am weary of it.
— Lie there, ye ensigns
Of my unloved preëminence   110
In an age like this !
Among a people of children,
Who throng'd me in their cities,
Who worshipp'd me in their houses,
And ask'd, not wisdom,   115
But drugs to charm with,
But spells to mutter —
All the fool's-armoury of magic ! — Lie
    there,
My golden circlet,
My purple robe !   120

Callicles (from below) .

As the sky-brightening south-wind clears
    the day,
And makes the mass'd clouds roll,
The music of the lyre blows away
The clouds which wrap the soul.

Oh ! that Fate had let me see   125
That triumph of the sweet persuasive lyre,
That famous, final victory,
When jealous Pan with Marsyas did con-
    spire ;
When, from far Parnassus' side,
Young Apollo, all the pride   130

Of the Phrygian flutes to tame,
To the Phrygian highlands came ;
Where the long green reed-beds sway
In the rippled waters grey
Of that solitary lake   135
Where Mæander's springs are born ;
Whence the ridged pine-wooded roots
Of Messogis westward break,
Mounting westward, high and higher.
There was held the famous strife ;   140
There the Phrygian brought his flutes,
And Apollo brought his lyre ;
And, when now the westering sun
Touch'd the hills, the strife was done,
And the attentive Muses said :   145
'Marsyas, thou art vanquished !'
Then Apollo's minister
Hang'd upon a branching fir
Marsyas, the unhappy Faun,
And began to whet his knife.   150
But the Mænads, who were there,
Left their friend, and with robes flowing
In the wind, and loose dark hair
O'er their polish'd bosoms blowing,
Each her ribbon'd tambourine   155
Flinging on the mountain-sod,
With a lovely frighten'd mien
Came about the youthful God.
But he turn'd his beauteous face
Haughtily another way,   160
From the grassy sun-warm'd place
Where in proud repose he lay,
With one arm over his head,
Watching how the whetting sped.

But aloof, on the lake-strand,   165
Did the young Olympus stand,
Weeping at his master's end ;
For the Faun had been his friend.
For he taught him how to sing,
And he taught him flute-playing.   170
Many a morning had they gone
To the glimmering mountain-lakes,
And had torn up by the roots
The tall crested water-reeds
With long plumes and soft brown seeds,   175
And had carved them into flutes,
Sitting on a tabled stone
Where the shoreward ripple breaks.
And he taught him how to please
The red-snooded Phrygian girls,   180
Whom the summer evening sees
Flashing in the dance's whirls
Underneath the starlit trees
In the mountain-villages.
Therefore now Olympus stands,   185
At his master's piteous cries
Pressing fast with both his hands
His white garment to his eyes,

Not to see Apollo's scorn ; —
Ah, poor Faun, poor Faun ! ah, poor
    Faun !   190

Empedocles

And lie thou there,
My laurel bough !
Scornful Apollo's ensign, lie thou there !
Though thou hast been my shade in the
    world's heat —
Though I have loved thee, lived in hon-
    ouring thee —   195
Yet lie thou there,
My laurel bough !

I am weary of thee.
I am weary of the solitude
Where he who bears thee must abide — 200
Of the rocks of Parnassus,
Of the gorge of Delphi,
Of the moonlit peaks, and the caves.
Thou guardest them, Apollo !
Over the grave of the slain Pytho,   205
Though young, intolerably severe !
Thou keepest aloof the profane,
But the solitude oppresses thy votary !
The jars of men reach him not in thy
    valley —
But can life reach him ?   210
Thou fencest him from the multitude —
Who will fence him from himself ?
He hears nothing but the cry of the tor-
    rents,
And the beating of his own heart.
The air is thin, the veins swell,   215
The temples tighten and throb there —
Air ! air !

Take thy bough, set me free from my
    solitude ;
I have been enough alone !

Where shall thy votary fly then ? back to
    men ? —   220
But they will gladly welcome him once
    more,
And help him to unbend his too tense
    thought,
And rid him of the presence of himself,
And keep their friendly chatter at his ear,
And haunt him, till the absence from
    himself,   225
That other torment, grow unbearable ;
And he will fly to solitude again,
And he will find its air too keen for him,
And so change back ; and many thousand
    times
Be miserably bandied to and fro   230

Like a sea-wave, betwixt the world and
    thee,
Thou young, implacable God ! and only
    death
Can cut his oscillations short, and so
Bring him to poise. There is no other way.

And yet what days were those, Parmeni-
    des !   235
When we were young, when we could
    number friends
In all the Italian cities like ourselves,
When with elated hearts we join'd your
    train,
Ye Sun-born Virgins ! on the road of truth.
Then we could still enjoy, then neither
    thought   240
Nor outward things were closed and dead
    to us ;
But we received the shock of mighty
    thoughts
On simple minds with a pure natural joy ;
And if the sacred load oppress'd our brain,
We had the power to feel the pressure
    eased,   245
The brow unbound, the thoughts flow
    free again,
In the delightful commerce of the world.
We had not lost our balance then, nor
    grown
Thought's slaves, and dead to every natural
    joy.
The smallest thing could give us pleasure
    then —   250
The sports of the country-people,
A flute-note from the woods,
Sunset over the sea ;
Seed-time and harvest,
The reapers in the corn,   255
The vinedresser in his vineyard,
The village-girl at her wheel.

Fulness of life and power of feeling, ye
Are for the happy, for the souls at ease,
Who dwell on a firm basis of content ! 260
But he, who has outlived his prosperous
    days —
But he, whose youth fell on a different
    world
From that on which his exiled age is
    thrown —
Whose mind was fed on other food, was
    train'd
By other rules than are in vogue to-
    day —   265
Whose habit of thought is fix'd, who will
    not change,
But, in a world he loves not, must subsist

In ceaseless opposition, be the guard
Of his own breast, fetter'd to what he
    guards,
That the world win no mastery over
    him —   270
Who has no friend, no fellow left, not
    one ;
Who has no minute's breathing space
    allow'd
To nurse his dwindling faculty of joy —
Joy and the outward world must die to
    him,
As they are dead to me.   275
    A long pause, during which EMPEDOCLES
    *remains motionless, plunged in
    thought. The night deepens. He
    moves forward and gazes round him,
    and proceeds : —*
And you, ye stars,
Who slowly begin to marshal,
As of old, in the fields of heaven,
Your distant, melancholy lines !
Have you, too, survived yourselves ?   280
Are you, too, what I fear to become ?
You, too, once lived ;
You, too, moved joyfully
Among august companions,
In an older world, peopled by Gods,   285
In a mightier order,
The radiant, rejoicing, intelligent Sons of
    Heaven.
But now, ye kindle
Your lonely, cold-shining lights,
Unwilling lingerers   290
In the heavenly wilderness,
For a younger, ignoble world ;
And renew, by necessity,
Night after night your courses,
In echoing, unnear'd silence,   295
Above a race you know not —
Uncaring and undelighted,
Without friend and without home ;
Weary like us, though not
Weary with our weariness.   300

No, no, ye stars ! there is no death with
    you,
No languor, no decay ! languor and death,
They are with me, not you ! ye are alive —
Ye, and the pure dark ether where ye ride
Brilliant above me ! And thou, fiery
    world,   305
That sapp'st the vitals of this terrible
    mount
Upon whose charr'd and quaking crust
    I stand —
Thou, too, brimmest with life ! — the sea
    of cloud,

That heaves its white and billowy vapours
up
To moat this isle of ashes from the
world,   310
Lives ; and that other fainter sea, far down,
O'er whose lit floor a road of moonbeams
leads
To Etna's Liparëan sister-fires
And the long dusky line of Italy —
That mild and luminous floor of waters
lives,   315
With held-in joy swelling its heart ; I only,
Whose spring of hope is dried, whose
spirit has fail'd,
I, who have not, like these, in solitude
Maintain'd courage and force, and in my-
self
Nursed an immortal vigour — I alone   320
Am dead to life and joy, therefore I read
In all things my own deadness.
                     A long silence. He continues : —
Oh, that I could glow like this mountain !
Oh, that my heart bounded with the swell
of the sea !
Oh, that my soul were full of light as the
stars !   325
Oh, that it brooded over the world like
the air !

But no, this heart will glow no more ;
thou art
A living man no more, Empedocles !
Nothing but a devouring flame of
thought —
But a naked, eternally restless mind !   330
                     After a pause : —
To the elements it came from
Everything will return —
Our bodies to earth,
Our blood to water,
Heat to fire,   335
Breath to air.
They were well born, they will be well
entomb'd —
But mind ? . . .

And we might gladly share the fruitful stir
Down in our mother earth's miraculous
womb ;   340
Well would it be
With what roll'd of us in the stormy main ;
We might have joy, blent with the all-
bathing air,
Or with the nimble, radiant life of fire.

But mind, but thought —   345
If these have been the master part of us —
Where will *they* find their parent ele-
ment ?
What will receive *them,* who will call *them*
home ?
But we shall still be in them, and they
in us,
And we shall be the strangers of the
world,   350
And they will be our lords, as they are
now ;
And keep us prisoners of our conscious-
ness,
And never let us clasp and feel the All
But through their forms, and modes, and
stifling veils.
And we shall be unsatisfied as now ;   355
And we shall feel the agony of thirst,
The ineffable longing for the life of life
Baffled for ever ; and still thought and
mind
Will hurry us with them on their home-
less march,
Over the unallied unopening earth,   360
Over the unrecognising sea ; while air
Will blow us fiercely back to sea and earth,
And fire repel us from its living waves.
And then we shall unwillingly return
Back to this meadow of calamity,   365
This uncongenial place, this human life ;
And in our individual human state
Go through the sad probation all again,
To see if we will poise our life at last,
To see if we will now at last be true   370
To our own only true, deep-buried selves,
Being one with which we are one with the
whole world ;
Or whether we will once more fall away
Into some bondage of the flesh or mind,
Some slough of sense, or some fantastic
maze   375
Forged by the imperious lonely thinking-
power.
And each succeeding age in which we are
born
Will have more peril for us than the last ;
Will goad our senses with a sharper spur,
Will fret our minds to an intenser play, 380
Will make ourselves harder to be discern'd.
And we shall struggle awhile, gasp and
rebel —
And we shall fly for refuge to past times,
Their soul of unworn youth, their breath
of greatness ;
And the reality will pluck us back,   385
Knead us in its hot hand, and change our
nature
And we shall feel our powers of effort flag,
And rally them for one last fight — and
fail ;

And we shall sink in the impossible strife,
And be astray for ever.

Slave of sense   390
I have in no wise been ; — but slave of
    thought ? . . .
And who can say : I have been always free,
Lived ever in the light of my own soul ? —
I cannot ; I have lived in wrath and gloom,
Fierce, disputatious, ever at war with
    man,   395
Far from my own soul, far from warmth
    and light.
But I have not grown easy in these
    bonds —
But I have not denied what bonds these
    were.
Yea, I take myself to witness,
That I have loved no darkness,   400
Sophisticated no truth,
Nursed no delusion,
Allow'd no fear !

And therefore, O ye elements ! I know —
Ye know it too — it hath been granted
    me   405
Not to die wholly, not to be all enslaved.
I feel it in this hour. The numbing cloud
Mounts off my soul ; I feel it, I breathe
    free.

Is it but for a moment ?
— Ah, boil up, ye vapours !   410
Leap and roar, thou sea of fire !
My soul glows to meet you.
Ere it flag, ere the mists
Of despondency and gloom
Rush over it again,   415
Receive me, save me !
          [He plunges into the crater.

Callicles

(from below)

Through the black, rushing smoke-
    bursts,
Thick breaks the red flame ;
All Etna heaves fiercely
Her forest-clothed frame.   420

Not here, O Apollo !
Are haunts meet for thee.
But, where Helicon breaks down
In cliff to the sea,

Where the moon-silver'd inlets   425
Send far their light voice
Up the still vale of Thisbe,
O speed, and rejoice !

On the sward at the cliff-top
Lie strewn the white flocks,   430
On the cliff-side the pigeons
Roost deep in the rocks.

In the moonlight the shepherds,
Soft lull'd by the rills,
Lie wrapt in their blankets   435
Asleep on the hills.

— What forms are these coming
So white through the gloom ?
What garments out-glistening
The gold-flower'd broom ?   440

What sweet-breathing presence
Out-perfumes the thyme ?
What voices enrapture
The night's balmy prime ? —

'Tis Apollo comes leading   445
His choir, the Nine.
— The leader is fairest,
But all are divine.

They are lost in the hollows !
They stream up again !   450
What seeks on this mountain
The glorified train ? —

They bathe on this mountain,
In the spring by their road ;
Then on to Olympus,   455
Their endless abode.

— Whose praise do they mention ?
Of what is it told ? —
What will be for ever ;
What was from of old.   460

First hymn they the Father
Of all things ; and then,
The rest of immortals,
The action of men.

The day in his hotness,   465
The strife with the palm ;
The night in her silence,
The stars in their calm.

7

ROBERT BROWNING'S *KING VICTOR AND KING CHARLES*

King Victor and King Charles is perhaps the least known of all Browning's plays, and most critics have agreed that the play's obscurity is well deserved. Yet the work that the distinguished actor Macready called "a *great mistake*" has much to recommend it to our attention; with all its defects, *King Victor and King Charles* suggests clearly some of the lines of development that culminate in the great dramatic monologues.

In the heyday of the Browning Societies it was conventional to admire Browning's plays as highly as the lyrics and dramatic monologues. Indeed, Browning himself, his most recent biographer points out, characteristically over-rated "all his bad plays,"[1] and he could hardly help doing so when his admirers were comparing him to Shakespeare. *King Victor and King Charles* was originally composed for Macready and given to him in the late summer of 1839, when the friendship between the two men had already begun to cool. Macready's low opinion of the play did not, however, dissuade Browning from writing for the stage, nor did it, evidently, affect Browning's opinion of *King Victor*. Although when he was forced to replace *A Blot i' the Scutcheon* with *King Victor* as the second number of *Bells and Pomegranates* he called it a "very indifferent sub-stitute," he nevertheless retained the play among his works in all editions published during his lifetime. In contrast, *Strafford*, in which Macready had earlier starred, was omitted from both *Bells and Pomegranates* and the collected edition in 1849. After its first appearance in 1842, *King Victor and King Charles* not only appeared in all editions of the collected works, but was each time revised by Browning, even in the 16-volume *Works* published just before his death.

The play has never, it seems, been performed. DeVane calls it "probably the most neglected of all Browning's works";[2] whether that neglect is just is not a moot point, despite the low esteem in which the play has been held by commentators.

A balanced, though negative, view is that expressed by Park Honan, one of the best of Browning's modern critics:

There is no possible way to justify *King Victor* in its own right; eliminating the seething, character-obscuring action of his first play [*Strafford*], abandoning any serious attempt to create pathos or striking situations, and, instead, concentrating on the depiction of character through realistic, "unpoetic" conversation in blank verse, Browning wrote a drama that dismayed Macready at first glance.[3]

The failure of the play, according to Honan, is in Browning's inability to establish

1. Maisie Ward, *Robert Browning and His World*, (New York, 1967), p. 70.
2. W. C. DeVane, *A Browning Handbook*, (New York, 1955), p. 101.
3. Park Honan, *Browning's Characters*, (New Haven, 1961), p. 62.

a vital connection between the characters and the events in which they are involved. The emphasis is not on the event, but on the nature of the characters, and because the event is underplayed the characters, despite the clarity of the individual portraits, are never fully developed.[4]

Browning's preface to *Strafford* had claimed that he was to dwell upon "Action in Character rather than Character in Action"; the preface to *King Victor* tells us that the tragedy is the "first artistic consequence of what Voltaire termed 'a terrible event without consequences.'" The "terrible event" of which Voltaire spoke was the attempt of Victor to recapture the throne he had abdicated, and Charles's imprisonment of his father for his attempt.

Significantly, Browning alters history; the conclusion of his play has Charles handing over his crown to Victor, only to have Victor die as he once again grasps all that he had spent his life to attain. Browning's refusal to accept the historical truth, his substitution for it of an obviously concocted melodramatic scene, underscores his interest in the characters rather than the events. Browning's Charles, whose personality the playwright has been at pains to develop, is incapable, finally, of taking the step that history records. Insofar as Browning changes "fact," then, he is clearly attempting to establish a vital connection between the characters and the events in which they are involved. The primacy for Browning of the "truth" of character over the supposed truth of events may be made clear in his remark in the preface that his "statement (combining as it does what appears correct in Voltaire and plausible in Condorcet) [is] more true to person and thing" than any other he had encountered.

The same is true of the only other event of any magnitude in the play, Victor's abdication. At the opening of the play, Charles is entirely unaware of his father's plans, and, when he is called before the king, looks forward rather to a life of retirement with his wife, Polyxena, than to a kingship. Only with difficulty can Victor make it clear that Charles is to have the throne, which he finally accepts with trepidation but with no less resolve to govern wisely and firmly. The critical event thus serves to help outline Charles's character for us—it is not gratuitous action. These two incidents are Browning's attempts to give us "Action in Character." The uncertainty of Charles as he accepts the throne becomes, later, his willingness to return it to his father. Surprisingly enough, despite a rule that we are told is successful, a rule in which Charles proves himself truly royal, he is willing to hand over all he has gained, not from weakness but out of love.

The difficulty with the play is not that there is not a significant relationship between the characters and the action, but that neither action in character nor character in action is sufficient to make Charles a credible character. Ultimately he is a figure of rather flimsy cardboard, played upon alternately by his father and his wife. In narrowing the action as he does, Browning provides too little room for expansion of character. We are told of Charles's kingcraft; we do not see it practiced. We are told, too, of his other needs and aspirations, but are told by Polyxena, who is, unfortunately, a peculiarly unsympathetic person. Charles himself simply does not convince—by thought, word, or deed.

It is fair to take the brief sketch given of the characters in the preface as approximating Browning's understanding of what he had wrought. Charles is there described as a man of "extreme and painful sensibility . . . earnest good purpose and vacillating will"—not, it would seem on the face of it, a character ripe with dramatic possibility. Victor, of "fiery and audacious temper," is much more likely to interest an audience, and so it turns out. Both Victor and D'Ormea, the Machiavellian minister, strike us immediately as the vital characters of the play. Even Polyxena, for all her "right woman's manliness," has a sort of life

---

4. Honan, p. 58.

that Charles never attains. Charles is weak, not because of his vacillating will but because there is no tension in his vacillation. Macready had been carried away by the "truth of character" in *Strafford;*[5] it is not surprising, therefore, that he objected strenuously to *King Victor and King Charles,* in which Charles, despite the title and format of the play, is clearly the hero.

Everything in the play is subordinated to the characters. T. R. Lounsbury long ago expressed his surprise that "Browning of all men should have been the only great writer of our day, at all events of our race, to deliver himself of his own accord into the bondage of the unities."[6] The point is, of course, that the unities are not an "antiquated superstition," as Lounsbury calls them, but the best means that Browning has for focusing our attention on the characters. The play is indeed cast into two large sections, each of which takes place in one day, something short of a year apart. But this division, and the further division of each of the parts ("King Victor" and "King Charles") into two parts, have almost nothing to do with the fact that one day's action is given in each. Every playwright concentrates time, and it is dramatic time with which every play and every member of the audience must finally deal. The unity of the play is not at all false, but very real, and it has a most important purpose beyond truth to itself. The four sections of the play are simply acts, with a time lapse between the second and third. In each the plot is advanced by the development of conflict.

Certainly there is sufficient evidence that for Browning the important conflicts are internal. That, after we have done quibbling over the ways in which "Character in Action" best reveals "Action in Character," seems to have been what he had in mind. His remark in the preface to *Sordello* that he wished to lay stress on "incidents in the development of a soul: little else is worth study" should warn us that it is less than fruitful to discuss his practice in light of any theory other than his own. The difference between *King Victor and King Charles* and Browning's dramatic monologues, lies, respectively, in the nature of the conflict and in the ways in which the conflict is rendered.

H. B. Charlton, who thought little of Browning's plays and least of *King Victor and King Charles,* claimed that perhaps the chief problem of the play is that while its plot is political its theme is not.[7] An outline of the plot suggests the truth of that assertion, but also raises the problem of character and the relationship between character and theme. The clash between Victor and Charles is a clash between father and son, between a lack of paternal love and what seems an excess of filial devotion—and, only finally, between a repressive, strong-minded king and an apparently weak but open-hearted, liberal, and progressive monarch. Some evidence suggests that it was the liberalism of Charles's regime that first drew Browning's attention to the story.[8] The play itself is, however, hardly a monument in the fight for liberalism. Charles makes peace and eases the oppressive tax burden of his people, but the events take place offstage, and become important only in the final confrontation between Charles and his father, where they help to create sympathy for Charles. But more important as an explanation for our sympathy with him is our understanding of the character of Victor. Charles wins, ultimately, by default. That he is the one with whom we sympathize is rather a negative achievement on Browning's part.

More than once in the last section of the play Browning attempts to portray the conflict politically. As Charles, after he has sent D'Ormea to capture Victor, paces the room, he muses on Victor's motives: And why

5. Ward, p. 69.

6. T. R. Lounsbury, *The Early Literary Career of Robert Browning,* (New York, 1966), p. 153.

7. H. B. Charlton, "Browning as Dramatist," *Bulletin of the John Rylands Library* 23 (1939): 47–48.

8. DeVane, pp. 100–101.

> Does Victor come? to undo all that's done,
> Restore the past, prevent the future! Seat
> His mistress in your seat, and place in mine
> . . . Oh, my own people, whom will you find there,
> To ask of, to consult with, to care for,
> To hold up with your hands? Whom? One that's false—
> False—from the head's crown to the foot's sole, false!

But immediately after, he repents for having sent D'Ormea to tear

> My father from his bed; to old hands feel
> For one who is not, but who should be there . . .

Polyxena in turn urges on him his duty, "to live and rule," but when Victor is brought before him Charles yields his crown to him *as his father,* and despite the political implications of his action:

> No doubt, my people think
> I am their King still . . . but I cannot strive!
> Take it!

Throughout, the conflict is, for Charles, personal; the issue is not justice versus tyranny, but the unloved son striving to earn his father's respect. Victor sees the conflict in political terms; he points out that his heart has been broken by the belief that Charles would deny him. Even in the last hours of the play, when he tells us he is at last learning to know his son, his thoughts turn to his kingship, which he knows is shortly to pass once again to his son.

The fact that the conflict is within Charles, and is not objectified in significant action, places particular strain on Browning's craft. The speaker of the typical dramatic monologue reveals to the reader his personality and his conflicts by means of Browning's subtle manipulations of rhythm, syntax, and imagery. Dramatic tension is maintained by irony: we see the speaker revealing things he does not know he is letting slip, and frequently they are things that even he does not "know" about himself. But this sort of dramatic irony is different from that operating in *King Victor and King Charles.* Here we have in advance information unavailable to Charles, as in the cases of the abdication and Victor's return. Our interest lies in seeing Charles's response—in the instance of Victor's return, how he will meet the threat to his throne. We know his character, but we know, too, what response is proper to the situation. When he fails to react appropriately or naturally, and when his vacillation is unconvincing, he becomes the goat of the irony.

Having been warned, for example, that Victor is returning from his retreat to regain the throne, Charles's response to discovering his father in the throne room is fearful, and he rationalizes:

> You are returned for . . . true, your health declines;
> True, Chambery's a bleak unkindly spot;
> You'd choose one fitter for your final lodge—
> Veneria or Moncaglier—ay, that's close
> And I concede it.

This is, we may concede, a natural reaction: the son refusing to face the purpose of his father's visit. So, too, perhaps, is the momentary cynicism and bitterness in his replies to Victor's protestations of innocence. When the truth of Victor's purpose begins to emerge, Charles draws himself up to deliver the ultimatum:

> Keep within your sphere and mine!
> It is God's province we usurp on, else.
> Here, blindfold through the maze of things we walk
> By a slight due of false, true, right and wrong;
> All else is rambling and presumption. I
> Have sworn to keep this kingdom: there's my truth.

As much force as Charles can muster is in these lines, but they are not convincing. He means to retain the throne, how or why we may guess, but the language does not tell us with any force.

In contrast, Victor's plea to Charles makes clear a number of the reasons why he desires the throne. What if, he asks Charles, your father

> . . . said he could not die
> Deprived of baubles he had put aside,
> He deemed, for ever—of the Crown that binds
> Your brain up, whole, sound, and impregnable,
> Creating kingliness—the Sceptre too,
> Whose mere wind, should you wave it, back would beat
> Invaders—and the golden Ball which throbs
> As if you grasped the palpitating heart
> Indeed o' the realm, to mould as choose you may!

In point of fact, we know that Victor is lying, that he has all along planned this return as soon as affairs have settled sufficiently. Yet, in the quality of the imagery, the real force of the relationship between Victor and the kingship becomes apparent. There is more than a little in Victor that reminds us, from time to time, of Browning's Duke of Ferrara, or of the bishop ordering his tomb. Clearly Victor is not so powerfully realized as either of the latter, but there are nevertheless moments when Browning's future techniques are to be seen in a more-than-minimal stage of development.

Park Honan has suggested that in *King Victor and King Charles* we see Browning feeling his way toward imagery "springing from the imagined mental condition and past experiences of character itself."[9] But Victor, not Charles, is the one with a distinctive voice. In the dramatic monologues, the putative audience—the Count's emissary in "My Last Duchess," the watch in "Fra Lippo Lippi"—serves to draw out the speaker, to objectify somehow attitudes and ideas of which he is not himself aware. In *King Victor and King Charles,* the opinions of those who surround Charles do not reflect back into his character, though they represent the various attitudes that it would be possible for him to adopt. Near the conclusion of the play, Polyxena tells Victor that he had all along served as a model for Charles:

> He reigned at first through setting up yourself
> As pattern . . . he acted you—
> Ne'er for an instant did I think it real,
> Nor look for any other than this end.
> I hold him worlds the worse on that account;
> But so it was.

Unfortunately, she has been the only one privy to the information.

---

9. Honan, p. 62.

A sensitive reading of *King Victor and King Charles* will not convince one that it is a play of great intrinsic worth. It should, however, enable one to see that there is life in the play and that its characters, often imperfectly realized, are nevertheless real. Moreover, it will show Browning working his way toward a poetic means of rendering "Action in Character," a means which came ultimately to a point of development which shows that "the dramatic" need hardly include movement on a stage. Indeed, a dramatic monologue is a playlet with one character always on center stage.

G. C. S.

King Victor and King Charles,

A TRAGEDY

1842.

NOTE.

So far as I know, this Tragedy is the first artistic consequence of what Voltaire termed "a terrible event without consequences"; and although it professes to be historical, I have taken more pains to arrive at the history than most readers would thank me for particularizing: since acquainted, as I will hope them to be, with the chief circumstances of Victor's remarkable European career—nor quite ignorant of the sad and surprising facts I am about to reproduce (a tolerable account of which is to be found, for instance, in Abbé Roman's *Récit*, or even the fifth of Lord Orrery's *Letters from Italy*)—I cannot expect them to be versed, nor desirous of becoming so, in all the detail of the memoirs, correspondence, and relations of the time. From these only may be obtained a knowledge of the fiery and audacious temper, unscrupulous selfishness, profound dissimulation, and singular fertility in resources, of Victor—the extreme and painful sensibility, prolonged immaturity of powers, earnest good purpose and vacillating will of Charles—the noble and right woman's manliness of his wife—and the ill-considered rascality and subsequent better-advised rectitude of D'Ormea. When I say, therefore, that I cannot but believe my statement (combining as it does what appears correct in Voltaire and plausible in Condorcet) more true to person and thing than any it has hitherto been my fortune to meet with, no doubt my word will be taken, and my evidence spared as readily.   R.B.
LONDON: 1842.

KING VICTOR AND KING CHARLES.

PERSONS.

VICTOR AMADEUS, *first King of Sardinia.*
CHARLES EMMANUEL, *his son, Prince of Piedmont.*
POLYXENA, *wife of Charles.*
D'ORMEA, *minister.*

SCENE. — *The Council Chamber of Rivoli Palace, near Turin, communicating with a Hall at the back, an Apartment to the left, and another to the right of the stage.*

TIME, 1730–1731.

FIRST YEAR, 1730. — KING VICTOR.

PART I.

CHARLES, POLYXENA.

Charles. You think so? Well, I do not.
Polyxena.   My beloved,
All must clear up; we shall be happy yet:
This cannot last for ever — oh, may change
To-day or any day!
Charles.   — May change? Ah yes —
May change!
Polyxena. Endure it, then.

Charles.   No doubt, a life
Like this drags on, now better and now
    worse.
My father may . . . may take to loving
    me ;
And he may take D'Ormea closer yet
To counsel him ; — may even cast off her
— That bad Sebastian ; but he also may
. . . Or no, Polyxena, my only friend,
He may not force you from me ?
    Polyxena.   Now, force me
From you ! — me, close by you as if there
    gloomed
No Sebastians, no D'Ormeas on our path —
At Rivoli or Turin, still at hand,
Arch-counsellor, prime confidant . . . force
    me !
    Charles. Because I felt as sure, as I feel
    sure
We clasp hands now, of being happy once.
Young was I, quite neglected, nor con-
    cerned
By the world's business that engrossed so
    much
My father and my brother : if I peered
From out my privacy, — amid the crash
And blaze of nations, domineered those
    two.
'Twas war, peace — France our foe, now —
    England, friend —
In love with Spain — at feud with Austria !
    Well —
I wondered, laughed a moment's laugh for
    pride
In the chivalrous couple, then let drop
My curtain — "I am out of it," I said —
When . . .
    Polyxena. You have told me, Charles.
    Charles.   Polyxena —
When suddenly, — a warm March day, just
    that !
Just so much sunshine as the cottage child
Basks in delighted, while the cottager
Takes off his bonnet, as he ceases work,
To catch the more of it — and it must fall
Heavily on my brother ! Had you seen
Philip — the lion-featured ! not like me !
    Polyxena. I know —
    Charles.   And Philip's mouth
    yet fast to mine,
His dead cheek on my cheek, his arm
    still round
My neck, — they bade me rise, "for I was
    heir
"To the Duke," they said, "the right hand
    of the Duke :"
Till then he was my father, not the Duke.
So . . . let me finish .   the whole intri-
    cate

World's-business their dead boy was born
    to, I
Must conquer, — ay, the brilliant thing he
    was,
I, of a sudden must be : my faults, my
    follies,
— All bitter truths were told me, all at
    once,
To end the sooner. What I simply styled
Their overlooking me, had been contempt :
How should the Duke employ himself, for-
    sooth,
With such an one, while lordly Philip rode
By him their Turin through ? But he
    was punished,
And must put up with — me ! 'Twas sad
    enough
To learn my future portion and submit.
And then the wear and worry, blame on
    blame !
For, spring-sounds in my ears, spring-
    smells about,
How could I but grow dizzy in their pent
Dim palace-rooms at first ? My mother's
    look
As they discussed my insignificance,
She and my father, and I sitting by, —
I bore ; I knew how brave a son they
    missed :
Philip had gaily run state-papers through,
While Charles was spelling at them pain-
    fully !
But Victor was my father spite of that.
"Duke Victor's entire life has been," I said,
"Innumerable efforts to one end :
"And on the point now of that end's suc-
    cess,
"Our Ducal turning to a Kingly crown,
"Where's time to be reminded 'tis his
    child
"He spurns ?" And so I suffered — scarcely
    suffered,
Since I had you at length !
    Polyxena.   — To serve in place
Of monarch, minister, and mistress,
    Charles.
    Charles. But, once that crown obtained,
    then was't not like
Our lot would alter? "When he rests,
    takes breath,
"Glances around, sees who there's left to
    love —
"Now that my mother's dead, sees I am
    left —
"Is it not like he'll love me at the last ?"
Well, Savoy turns Sardinia ; the Duke's
    King :
Could I — precisely then — could you ex-
    pect

His harshness to redouble? These few months
Have been . . . have been . . . Polyxena, do you
And God conduct me, or I lose myself!
What would he have? What is't they want with me?
Him with this mistress and this minister,
— You see me and you hear him; judge us both!
Pronounce what I should do, Polyxena!
   Polyxena. Endure, endure, beloved! Say you not
He is your father? All's so incident
To novel sway! Beside, our life must change:
Or you'll acquire his kingcraft, or he'll find
Harshness a sorry way of teaching it.
I bear this — not that there's so much to bear.
   Charles. You bear? Do not I know that you, tho' bound
To silence for my sake, are perishing
Piecemeal beside me? And how otherwise
When every creephole from the hideous Court
Is stopped: the Minister to dog me, here —
The Mistress posted to entrap you, there!
And thus shall we grow old in such a life;
Not careless, never estranged, — but old: to alter
Our life, there is so much to alter!
   Polyxena. Come —
Is it agreed that we forego complaint
Even at Turin, yet complain we here
At Rivoli? 'Twere wiser you announced
Our presence to the King. What's now afoot
I wonder? Not that any more's to dread
Than every day's embarrassment: but guess
For me, why train so fast succeeded train
On the high-road, each gayer still than each!
I noticed your Archbishop's pursuivant,
The sable cloak and silver cross; such pomp
Bodes . . . what now, Charles? Can you conceive?
   Charles. Not I.
   Polyxena. A matter of some moment.
   Charles. There's our life!
Which of the group of loiterers that stare
From the lime-avenue, divines that I —
About to figure presently, he thinks,
In face of all assembled — am the one
Who knows precisely least about it?
   Polyxena. Tush!

D'Ormea's contrivance!
   Charles. Ay, how otherwise
Should the young Prince serve for the old King's foil?
— So that the simplest courtier may remark
'Twere idle raising parties for a Prince
Content to linger the Court's laughing-stock.
Something, 'tis like, about that weary business
   [*Pointing to papers he has laid down, and which* POLYXENA *examines.*
— Not that I comprehend three words, of course,
After all last night's study.
   Polyxena. The faint heart!
Why, as we rode and you rehearsed just now
Its substance . . . (that's the folded speech I mean,
Concerning the Reduction of the Fiefs)
— What would you have? — I fancied while you spoke,
Some tones were just your father's.
   Charles. Flattery!
   Polyxena. I fancied so: — and here lurks, sure enough,
My note upon the Spanish Claims! You've mastered
The fief-speech thoroughly: this other, mind,
Is an opinion you deliver, — stay,
Best read it slowly over once to me;
Read — there's bare time; you read it firmly — loud
— Rather loud, looking in his face, — don't sink
Your eye once — ay, thus! "If Spain claims . . ." begin
— Just as you look at me!
   Charles. At you! Oh truly,
You have I seen, say, marshalling your troops,
Dismissing councils, or, through doors ajar,
Head sunk on hand, devoured by slow chagrins
— Then radiant, for a crown had all at once
Seemed possible again! I can behold
Him, whose least whisper ties my spirit fast,
In this sweet brow, nought could divert me from
Save objects like Sebastian's shameless lip,
Or worse, the clipped grey hair and dead white face
And dwindling eye as if it ached with

guile,
D'Ormea wears . . .
    [*As he kisses her, enter from the
      KING's apartment* D'ORMEA.
          I said he would divert
My kisses from your brow!
    D'Ormea [*aside*].   Here! So, King
    Victor
Spoke truth for once : and who's ordained,
    but I
To make that memorable? Both in call,
As he declared. Were't better gnash the
    teeth,
Or laugh outright now?
    Charles [*to* POLYXENA]. What's his visit
    for?
    D'Ormea [*aside*]. I question if they even
    speak to me.
    Polyxena [*to* CHARLES]. Face the man!
    He'll suppose you fear him, else.
    [*Aloud.*] The Marquis bears the King's
    command, no doubt?
    D'Ormea [*aside*]. Precisely! — If I threat-
    ened him, perhaps?
Well, this at least is punishment enough!
Men used to promise punishment would
    come.
    Charles. Deliver the King's message,
    Marquis!
    D'Ormea [*aside*].   Ah —
So anxious for his fate? [*Aloud.*] A word,
    my Prince,
Before you see your father — just one
    word
Of counsel!
    Charles. Oh, your counsel certainly!
Polyxena, the Marquis counsels us!
Well, sir? Be brief, however!
    D'Ormea.   What?   You know
As much as I? — preceded me, most like,
In knowledge! So! ('Tis in his eye, be-
    side —
His voice : he knows it, and his heart's on
    flame
Already.) You surmise why you, myself,
Del Borgo, Spava, fifty nobles more,
Are summoned thus?
    Charles.   Is the Prince used to know,
At any time, the pleasure of the King,
Before his minister? — Polyxena,
Stay here till I conclude my task : I feel
Your presence (smile not) through the
    walls, and take
Fresh heart. The King's within that cham-
    ber?
    D'Ormea [*passing the table whereon a
    paper lies, exclaims, as he glances at
    it*].   "Spain!"
    Polyxena [*aside to* CHARLES]. Tarry
    awhile : what ails the minister?

    D'Ormea. Madam, I do not often
    trouble you.
The Prince loathes, and you scorn me —
    let that pass!
But since it touches him and you, not me,
Bid the Prince listen!
    Polyxena [*to* CHARLES].   Surely you will
    listen!
— Deceit? — those fingers crumpling up his
    vest?
    Charles. Deceitful to the very fingers'
    ends!
    D'Ormea [*who has approached them,
    overlooks the other paper* CHARLES
    continues to hold]. My project for
    the Fiefs! As I supposed!
Sir, I must give you light upon those
    measures
— For this is mine, and that I spied of
    Spain,
Mine too!
    Charles. Release me! Do you gloze on
    me
Who bear in the world's face (that is,
    the world
You make for me at Turin) your con-
    tempt?
— Your measures? — When was not a hate-
    ful task
D'Ormea's imposition? Leave my robe!
What post can I bestow, what grant con-
    cede?
Or do you take me for the King?
    D'Ormea.   Not I!
Not yet for King, — not for, as yet, thank
    God,
One who in . . . shall I say a year, a
    month?
Ay! — shall be wretcheder than e'er was
    slave
In his Sardinia. — Europe's spectacle
And the world's bye-word! What? The
    Prince aggrieved
That I excluded him our counsels? Here
    [*Touching the paper in* CHARLES's *hand.*
Accept a method of extorting gold
From Savoy's nobles, who must wring its
    worth
In silver first from tillers of the soil,
Whose hinds again have to contribute brass
To make up the amount : there's counsel,
    sir,
My counsel, one year old ; and the fruit,
    this —
Savoy's become a mass of misery
And wrath, which one man has to meet —
    the King :
You're not the King! Another counsel,
    sir!
Spain entertains a project (here it lies)

Which, guessed, makes Austria offer that
    same King
Thus much to baffle Spain ; he promises ;
Then comes Spain, breathless lest she be
    forestalled,
Her offer follows ; and he promises . . .
  Charles. — Promises, sir, when he has just
    agreed
To Austria's offer ?
  D'Ormea.   That's a counsel, Prince !
But past our foresight, Spain and Austria
    (choosing
To make their quarrel up between them-
    selves
Without the intervention of a friend)
Produce both treaties, and both prom-
    ises . . .
  Charles. How ?
  D'Ormea.   Prince, a counsel ! And
    the fruit of that ?
Both parties covenant afresh, to fall
Together on their friend, blot out his
    name,
Abolish him from Europe. So, take note,
Here's Austria and here's Spain to fight
    against :
And what sustains the King but Savoy
    here,
A miserable people mad with wrongs ?
You're not the King !
  Charles.   Polyxena, you said
All would clear up : all does clear up to
    me.
  D'Ormea. Clear up ! 'Tis no such thing
    to envy, then ?
You see the King's state in its length and
    breadth ?
You blame me now for keeping you aloof
From counsels and the fruit of counsels ?
    Wait
Till I explain this morning's business !
  Charles [*aside*].   No —
Stoop to my father, yes, — D' Ormea, no :
— The King's son, not to the King's coun-
    sellor !
I will do something, but at least retain
The credit of my deed. [*Aloud.*] Then it is
    this
You now expressly come to tell me ?
  D'Ormea.   This
To tell ! You apprehended me ?
  Charles.   Perfectly.
Further, D'Ormea, you have shown your-
    self,
For the first time these many weeks and
    months,
Disposed to do my bidding ?
  D'Ormea.   From the heart !
  Charles. Acquaint my father, first, I wait
    his pleasure :

Next . . . or, I'll tell you at a fitter time.
Acquaint the King !
  D'Ormea [*aside*]. If I 'scape Victor yet !
First, to prevent this stroke at me : if
    not, —
Then, to avenge it ! [*To* CHARLES.] Gra-
    cious sir, I go.   [*Goes.*
  Charles. God, I forbore ! Which more
    offends, that man
Or that man's master ? Is it come to this ?
Have they supposed (the sharpest insult
    yet)
I needed e'en his intervention ? No !
No — dull am I, conceded, — but so dull,
Scarcely ! Their step decides me.
  Polyxena.   How decides ?
  Charles. You would be freed D'Ormea's
    eye and hers ?
— Could fly the court with me and live
    content ?
So, this it is for which the knights assem-
    ble !
The whispers and the closeting of late,
The savageness and insolence of old,
— For this !
  Polyxena. What mean you ?
  Charles.   How ? You fail to catch
Their clever plot ? I missed it, but could
    you ?
These last two months of care to inculate
How dull I am, — D'Ormea's present visit
To prove that, being dull, I might be
    worse
Where I a King — as wretched as now
    dull —
You recognize in it no winding up
Of a long plot ?
  Polyxena. Why should there be a plot ?
  Charles. The crown's secure now ; I
    should shame the crown —
An old complaint : the point is, how to
    gain
My place for one, more fit in Victor's eyes,
His mistress the Sebastian's child.
  Polyxena.   In truth ?
  Charles. They dare not quite dethrone
    Sardinia's Prince :
But they may descant on my dulness till
They sting me into even praying them
Grant leave to hide my head, resign my
    state,
And end the coil. Not see now ? In a word,
They'd have me tender them myself my
    rights
As one incapable ; — some cause for that,
Since I delayed thus long to see their drift !
I shall apprise the King he may resume
My rights this moment.
  Polyxena.   Pause ! I dare not think
So ill of Victor.

Charles.   Think no ill of him !

Polyxena. — Nor think him, then, so
        shallow as to suffer

His purpose be divined thus easily.

And yet — you are the last of a great line ;

There's a great heritage at stake ; new
        days

Seemed to await this newest of the realms

Of Europe : — Charles, you must withstand
        this !

Charles.   Ah —

You dare not then renounce the splendid
        Court

For one whom all the world despises ?
        Speak !

Polyxena. My gentle husband, speak I
        will, and truth.

Were this as you believe, and I once sure

Your duty lay in so renouncing rule,

I could . . . could ? Oh what happiness it
        were —

To live, my Charles, and die, alone with
        you !

Charles. I grieve I asked you. To the
        presence, then !

By this, D'Ormea acquaints the King, no
        doubt,

He fears I am too simple for mere hints,

And that no less will serve than Victor's
        mouth

Demonstrating in council what I am.

I have not breathed, I think, these many
        years !

Polyxena. Why, it may be ! — if he desire
        to wed

That woman, call legitimate her child.

Charles. You see as much ? Oh, let his
        will have way !

You'll not repent confiding in me, love ?

There's many a brighter spot in Piedmont,
        far,

Than Rivoli. I'll seek him : or, suppose

You hear first how I mean to speak my
        mind ?

— Loudly and firmly both, this time, be
        sure !

I yet may see your Rhine-land, who can
        tell ?

Once away, ever then away ! I breathe.

Polyxena. And I too breathe.

Charles.   Come, my Polyxena !

KING VICTOR

PART II.

Enter King Victor, *bearing the Regalia on
a cushion, from his apartment. He*

calls loudly.

Victor. D'Ormea ! — for patience fails
        me, treading thus

Among the obscure trains I have laid, —
        my knights

Safe in the hall here — in that anteroom,

My son, — D'Ormea, where ? Of this, one
        touch —   [*Laying down the crown.*

This fireball to these mute black cold
        trains — then

Outbreak enough !

[*Contemplating it.*] To lose all, after all !

This, glancing o'er my house for ages —
        shaped,

Brave meteor, like the crown of Cyprus
        now,

Jerusalem, Spain, England, every change

The braver, — and when I have clutched
        a prize

My ancestry died wan with watching for,

To lose it ! — by a slip, a fault, a trick

Learnt to advantage once and not un-
        learned

When past the use, — " just this once
        more " (I thought)

" Use it with Spain and Austria happily,

" And then away with trick ! " An over-
        sight

I'd have repaired thrice over, any time

These fifty years, must happen now !
        There's peace

At length ; and I, to make the most of
        peace,

Ventured my project on our people here,

As needing not their help : which Europe
        knows,

And means, cold-blooded, to dispose her-
        self

(Apart from plausibilities of war)

To crush the new-made King — who ne'er
        till now

Feared her. As Duke, I lost each foot of
        earth

And laughed at her : my name was left,
        my sword

Left, all was left ! But she can take, she
        knows,

This crown, herself conceded . . . That's
        to try,

Kind Europe ! My career's not closed as
        yet !

This boy was ever subject to my will,

Timid and tame — the fitter ! D'Ormea,
        too —

What if the sovereign also rid himself

Of thee, his prime of parasites ? — I delay !

D'Ormea !   [*As* D'ORMEA *enters, the*
                        KING *seats himself.*

My son, the Prince — attends he?

D'Ormea.   Sir,
He does attend. The crown prepared! —
it seems
That you persist in your resolve.

   Victor.   Who's come?
The chancellor and the chamberlain? My
   knights?

   D'Ormea. The whole Annunziata. If,
   my liege,
Your fortune had not tottered worse than
   now . . .

   Victor. Del Borgo has drawn up the
   schedules? mine —
My son's, too? Excellent! Only, beware
Of the least blunder, or we look but fools.
First, you read the Annulment of the
   Oaths;
Del Borgo follows . . . no, the Prince shall
   sign;
Then let Del Borgo read the Instrument:
On which, I enter.

   D'Ormea.   Sir, this may be truth;
You, sir, may do as you affect — may break
Your engine, me, to pieces: try at least
If not a spring remain worth saving! Take
My counsel as I've counselled many times!
What if the Spaniard and the Austrian
   threat?
There's England, Holland, Venice — which
   ally
Select you?

   Victor. Aha! Come, D'Ormea, —
   " truth "
Was on your lip a minute since. Allies?
I've broken faith with Venice, Holland,
   England
— As who knows if not you?

   D'Ormea.   But why with me
Break faith — with one ally, your best,
   break faith?

   Victor. When first I stumbled on you,
   Marquis — 'twas
At Mondovi — a little lawyer's clerk . . .

   D'Ormea. Therefore your soul's ally! —
   who brought you through
Your quarrel with the Pope, at pains
   enough —
Who simply echoed you in these affairs —
On whom you cannot therefore visit these
Affairs' ill-fortune — whom you trust to
   guide
You safe (yes, on my soul) through these
   affairs!

   Victor. I was about to notice, had you
   not
Prevented me, that since that great town
   kept
With its chicane D'Ormea's satchel stuffed

And D'Ormea's self sufficiently recluse,
He missed a sight, — my naval armament
When I burned Toulon. How the skiff
   exults
Upon the galliot's wave! — rises its height,
O'ertops it even; but the great wave
   bursts,
And hell-deep in the horrible profound
Buries itself the galliot: shall the skiff
Think to escape the sea's black trough in
   turn?
Apply this: you have been my minister
— Next me, above me possibly; — sad post,
Huge care, abundant lack of peace of
   mind;
Who would desiderate the eminence?
You gave your soul to get it; you'd yet give
Your soul to keep it, as I mean you shall,
D'Ormea! What if the wave ebbed with
   me?
Whereas it cants you to another crest;
I toss you to my son; ride out your ride!

   D'Ormea. Ah, you so much despise me?

   Victor.   You, D'Ormea?
Nowise: and I'll inform you why. A king
Must in his time have many ministers,
And I've been rash enough to part with
   mine
When I thought proper. Of the tribe, not
   one
(. . . Or wait, did Pianezze? — ah, just the
   same!)
Not one of them, ere his remonstrance
   reached
The length of yours, but has assured me
   (commonly
Standing much as you stand, — or nearer,
   say,
The door to make his exit on his speech)
— I should repent of what I did. D'Ormea,
Be candid, you approached it when I bade
   you
Prepare the schedules! But you stopped
   in time,
You have not so assured me: how should
   I
Despise you then?

          Enter CHARLES.

   Victor [*changing his tone*]. Are you instructed? Do
My order, point by point! About it, sir!

   D'Ormea. You so despise me! [*Aside.*]
   One last stay remains —
The boy's discretion there.

       [*To* CHARLES.] For your sake, Prince,
I pleaded, wholly in your interest,
To save you from this fate!

Charles [*aside*]   Must I be told
The Prince was supplicated for — by him ?
  Victor [*to* D'ORMEA]. Apprise Del Borgo,
    Spava, and the rest,
Our son attends them ; then return.
  D'Ormea.   One word !
  Charles [*aside*]. A moment's pause and
    they would drive me hence.
I do believe !
  D'Ormea [*aside*]. Let but the boy be
    firm !
  Victor. You disobey ?
  Charles [*to* D'ORMEA]. You do not dis-
    obey
Me, at least ? Did you promise that or no ?
  D'Ormea. Sir, I am yours : what would
    you ? Yours am I !
  Charles. When I have said what I shall
    say, 'tis like
Your face will ne'er again disgust me. Go !
Through you, as through a breast of glass,
  I see,
And for your conduct, from my youth till
  now,
Take my contempt ! You might have
  spared me much,
Secured me somewhat, nor so harmed
  yourself :
That's over now. Go, ne'er to come again !
  D'Ormea. As son, the father — father
    as, the son !
My wits ! My wits !   [*Goes.*
  Victor [*seated*]. And you, what meant
    you, pray,
Speaking thus to D'Ormea ?
  Charles.   Let us not
Waste words upon D'Ormea ! Those I
  spent
Have half unsettled what I came to say.
His presence vexes to my very soul.
  Victor. One called to manage a kingdom,
    Charles, needs heart
To bear up under worse annoyances
Than seems D'Ormea — to me, at least.
  Charles [*aside*].   Ah, good !
He keeps me to the point. Then be it so.
[*Aloud.*] Last night, sir, brought me cer-
  tain papers — these —
To be reported on, — your way of late.
Is it last night's result that you demand ?
  Victor. For God's sake, what has night
    brought forth ? Pronounce
The . . . what's your word ? — result !
  Charles.   Sir, that had proved
Quite worthy of your sneer, no doubt : —
  a few
Lame thoughts, regard for you alone could
  wring,
Lame as they are, from brains like mine,

believe !
As 'tis, sir, I am spared both toil and sneer.
These are the papers
  Victor.   Well, sir ? I suppose
You hardly burned them. Now for your
  result !
  Charles. I never should have done great
    things of course,
But . . . oh my father, had you loved me
  more !
  Victor. Loved ? [*Aside.*] Has D'Ormea
    played me false, I wonder ?
[*Aloud.*] Why, Charles, a king's love is
  diffused — yourself
May overlook, perchance, your part in it.
Our monarchy is absolutest now
In Europe, or my trouble's thrown away.
I love, my mode, that subjects each and all
May have the power of loving, all and
  each,
Their mode : I doubt not, many have
  their sons
To trifle with, talk soft to, all day long :
I have that crown, this chair, D'Ormea,
  Charles !
  Charles. 'Tis well I am a subject then,
    not you.
  Victor [*aside*]. D'Ormea has told him
    everything.
        [*Aloud.*] Aha !
I apprehend you : when all's said, you take
Your private station to be prized beyond
My own, for instance ?
  Charles.   — Do and ever did
So take it : 'tis the method you pursue
That grieves . . .
  Victor.   These words ! Let me
    express, my friend,
Your thoughts. You penetrate what I sup-
  posed
Secret. D'Ormea plies his trade betimes !
I purpose to resign my crown to you.
  Charles. To me ?
  Victor. Now, — in that chamber.
  Charles.   You resign
The crown to me ?
  Victor.   And time enough, Charles,
    sure ?
Confess with me, at four-and-sixty years
A crown's a load. I covet quiet once
Before I die, and summoned you for that.
  Charles. 'Tis I will speak : you ever
    hated me.
I bore it, — have insulted me, borne too —
Now you insult yourself ; and I remember
What I believed you, what you really are,
And cannot bear it. What ! My life has
  passed
Under your eye, tormented as you know, —

Your whole sagacities, one after one,
At leisure brought to play on me — to
    prove me
A fool, I thought and I submitted ; now
You'd prove . . . what would you prove
    me ?
    Victor.   This to me ?
I hardly know you !
    Charles.   Know me ?   Oh indeed
You do not ! Wait till I complain next
    time
Of my simplicity ! — for here's a sage
Knows the world well, is not to be de-
    ceived,
And his experience and his Macchiavels,
D'Ormeas, teach him — what ? — that I this
    while
Have envied him his crown ! He has not
    smiled,
I warrant, — has not eaten, drunk, nor
    slept,
For I was plotting with my Princess yon-
    der !
Who knows what we might do or might
    not do ?
Go now, be politic, astound the world !
That sentry in the antechamber — nay,
The varlet who disposed this precious trap
          [*Pointing to the crown.*
That was to take me — ask them if they
    think
Their own sons envy them their posts !
    — Know me !
    Victor. But you know me, it seems : so,
    learn in brief,
My pleasure. This assembly is convened . . .
    Charles. Tell me, that woman put it in
    your head !
You were not sole contriver of the scheme,
My father !
    Victor.   Now observe me, sir !   I jest
Seldom — on these points, never. Here, I
    say,
The knights assemble to see me concede,
And you accept, Sardinia's crown.
    Charles.   Farewell !
'Twere vain to hope to change this : I can
    end it.
Not that I cease from being yours, when
    sunk
Into obscurity : I'll die for you,
But not annoy you with my presence. Sir,
Farewell ! Farewell !

Enter D'ORMEA.

    D'Ormea [*aside*]. Ha, sure he's changed
    again —
Means not to fall into the cunning trap !

Then Victor, I shall yet escape you, Vic-
    tor !
    Victor [*suddenly placing the crown upon
    the head of* CHARLES]. D'Ormea,
    your King !
        [*To* CHARLES.] My son, obey me !
Charles,
Your father, clearer-sighted than yourself,
Decides it must be so. 'Faith, this looks
    real !
My reasons after ; reason upon reason
After : but now, obey me ! Trust in me !
By this, you save Sardinia, you save me !
Why, the boy swoons ! [*To* D'ORMEA.]
    Come this side !
    D'Ormea [*as* CHARLES *turns from him to*
    VICTOR].   You persist ?
    Victor. Yes, I conceive the gesture's
    meaning. 'Faith,
He almost seems to hate you : how is that ?
Be re-assured, my Charles ! Is't over now ?
Then, Marquis, tell the new King what
    remains
To do ! A moment's work. Del Borgo
    reads
The Act of Abdication out, you sign it,
Then I sign ; after that, come back to me.
    D'Ormea. Sir, for the last time, pause !
    Victor.   Five minutes longer
I am your sovereign, Marquis. Hesitate —
And I'll so turn those minutes to account
That . . . Ay, you recollect me ! [*Aside.*]
    Could I bring
My foolish mind to undergo the reading
That Act of Abdication !
        [*As* CHARLES *motions* D'ORMEA
                to precede him.
        Thanks, dear Charles !
        [CHARLES *and* D'ORMEA *retire.*
    Victor. A novel feature in the boy, —
    indeed
Just what I feared he wanted most. Quite
    right,
This earnest tone : your truth, now, for
    effect !
It answers every purpose : with that look,
That voice, — I hear him : "I began no
    treaty,"
(He speaks to Spain) , "nor ever dreamed
    of this
"You show me ; this I from my soul re-
    gret ;
"But if my father signed it, bid not me
"Dishonour him — who gave me all, be-
    side :"
And, "True," says Spain, " 'twere harsh to
    visit that
"Upon the Prince." Then come the nobles
    trooping :

"I grieve at these exactions — I had cut
"This hand off ere impose them ; but
    shall I
"Undo my father's deed ?" — and they con-
    fer :
"Doubtless he was no party, after all ;
"Give the Prince time !"
              Ay, give us time, but time !
Only, he must not, when the dark day
    comes,
Refer our friends to me and frustrate all.
We'll have no child's play, no desponding
    fits,
No Charles at each cross turn entreating
    Victor
To take his crown again. Guard against
    that !

Enter D'ORMEA.

Long live King Charles !
          No — Charles's counsellor !
Well, is it over, Marquis ? Did I jest ?
   D'Ormea. "King Charles !" What then
    may you be ?
   Victor.   Anything !
A country gentleman that, cured of bustle,
Now beats a quick retreat toward Cham-
    bery,
Would hunt and hawk and leave you noisy
    folk
To drive your trade without him. I'm
    Count Remont —
Count Tende — any little place's Count !
   D'Ormea. Then Victor, Captain against
    Catinat
At Staffarde, where the French beat you ;
    and Duke
At Turin, where you beat the French ;
    King late
Of Savoy, Piedmont, Montferrat, Sardinia,
— Now, "any little place's Count" —
   Victor.   Proceed !
   D'Ormea. Breaker of vows to God, who
    crowned you first ;
Breaker of vows to man, who kept you
    since ;
Most profligate to me who outraged God
And man to serve you, and am made pay
    crimes
I was but privy to, by passing thus
To your imbecile son — who, well you
    know,
Must — (when the people here, and na-
    tions there,
Clamour for you the main delinquent,
    slipped
From King to — "Count of any little
    place")

Must needs surrender me, all in his
    reach, —
I, sir, forgive you : for I see the end —
See you on your return — (you will re-
    turn) —
To him you trust, a moment . . .
   Victor.   Trust him ? How ?
My poor man, merely a prime-minister,
Make me know where my trust errs !
   D'Ormea.   In his fear,
His love, his — — but discover for yourself
What you are weakest, trusting in !
   Victor.   Aha,
D'Ormea, not a shrewder scheme than this
In your repertory ? You know old Victor —
Vain, choleric, inconstant, rash — (I've
    heard
Talkers who little thought the King so
    close)
Felicitous now, were't not, to provoke him
To clean forget, one minute afterward,
His solemn act, and call the nobles back
And pray them give again the very power
He has abjured ? — for the dear sake of
    what ?
Vengeance on you, D'Ormea ! No : such
    am I,
Count Tende or Count anything you
    please,
— Only, the same that did the things you
    say,
And, among other things you say not, used
Your finest fibre, meanest muscle, — you
I used, and now, since you will have it so,
Leave to your fate — mere lumber in the
    midst,
You and your works. Why, what on earth
    beside
Are you made for, you sort of ministers ?
   D'Ormea. Not left, though, to my fate !
    Your witless son
Has more wit than to load himself with
    lumber :
He foils you that way, and I follow you.
   Victor. Stay with my son — protect the
    weaker side !
   D'Ormea. Ay, to be tossed the people
    like a rag,
And flung by them for Spain and Austria's
    sport,
Abolishing the record of your part
In all this perfidy !
   Victor.   Prevent, beside,
My own return !
   D'Ormea.   That's half prevented now !
'Twill go hard but you find a wondrous
    charm
In exile, to discredit me. The Alps,
Silk-mills to watch, vines asking vigilance —

Hounds open for the stag, your hawk's
    a-wing —
Brave days that wait the Louis of the
    South,
Italy's Janus!
    Victor.   So, the lawyer's clerk
Won't tell me that I shall repent!
    D'Ormea.   You give me
Full leave to ask if you repent?
    Victor.   Whene'er
Sufficient time's elapsed for that, you
    judge!
        [*Shouts inside* "King CHARLES!"
    D'Ormea. Do you repent?
    Victor [*after a slight pause*]. . . . I've
    kept them waiting? Yes!
Come in, complete the Abdication, sir!
               [*They go out.*

Enter POLYXENA.

Polyxena. A shout! The sycophants are
    free of Charles!
Oh is not this like Italy? No fruit
Of his or my distempered fancy, this,
But just an ordinary fact! Beside,
Here they've set forms for such proceed-
    ings; Victor
Imprisoned his own mother: he should
    know,
If any, how a son's to be deprived
Of a son's right. Our duty's palpable.
Ne'er was my husband for the wily king
And the unworthy subjects: be it so!
Come you safe out of them, my Charles!
    Our life
Grows not the broad and dazzling life, I
    dreamed
Might prove your lot; for strength was
    shut in you
None guessed but I — strength which, un-
    tramelled once,
Had little shamed your vaunted ancestry —
Patience and self-devotion, fortitude,
Simplicity and utter truthfulness
— All which, they shout to lose!
               So, now my work
Begins — to save him from regret. Save
    Charles
Regret? — the noble nature! He's not
    made
Like these Italians: 'tis a German soul.

CHARLES *enters crowned.*

Oh, where's the King's heir? Gone! —
    the Crown Prince? Gone! —
Where's Savoy? Gone! — Sardinia? Gone!
    But Charles

Is left! And when my Rhine-land bowers
    arrive,
If he looked almost handsome yester-
    twilight
As his grey eyes seemed widening into
    black
Because I praised him, then how will he
    look?
Farewell, you stripped and whited mul-
    berry-trees
Bound each to each by lazy ropes of vine!
Now I'll teach you my language: I'm not
    forced
To speak Italian now, Charles?
    [*She sees the crown.*] What is this?
Answer me — who has done this? Answer!
    Charles.   He!
I am King now.
    Polyxena. Oh worst, worst, worst of all!
Tell me! What, Victor? He has made you
    King?
What's he then? What's to follow this?
    You, King?
    Charles. Have I done wrong? Yes, for
    you were not by!
    Polyxena. Tell me from first to last.
    Charles.   Hush — a new world
Brightens before me; he is moved away
— The dark form that eclipsed it, he sub-
    sides
Into a shape supporting me like you,
And I, alone, tend upward, more and
    more
Tend upward: I am grown Sardinia's
    King.
    Polyxena. Now stop: was not this Vic-
    tor, Duke of Savoy
At ten years old?
    Charles.   He was.
    Polyxena.   And the Duke spent
Since then, just four-and-fifty years in toil
To be — what?
    Charles.   King.
    Polyxena.   Then why unking himself?
    Charles. Those years are cause enough.
    Polyxena.   The only cause?
    Charles. Some new perplexities.
    Polyxena.   Which you can solve
Although he cannot?
    Charles.   He assures me so.
    Polyxena. And this he means shall last
    — how long?
    Charles.   How long?
Think you I fear the perils I confront?
He's praising me before the people's face —
My people!
    Polyxena. Then he's changed — grown
    kind, the King?
Where can the trap be?

Charles.   Heart and soul I pledge !
My father, could I guard the crown you
     gained,
Transmit as I received it, — all good else
Would I surrender !
     Polyxena.   Ah, it opens then
Before you, all you dreaded formerly ?
You are rejoiced to be a king, my Charles ?
     Charles. So much to dare ? The better ;
     — much to dread ?
The better. I'll adventure though alone.
Triumph or die, there's Victor still to wit-
     ness
Who dies or triumphs — either way, alone !
     Polyxena. Once I had found my share
     in triumph, Charles,
Or death.
     Charles.   But you are I ! But you I call
To take, Heaven's proxy, vows I tendered
     Heaven
A moment since. I will deserve the crown !
     Polyxena. You will. [*Aside.*] No doubt
     it were a glorious thing
For any people, if a heart like his
Ruled over it. I would I saw the trap.

Enter VICTOR.

'Tis he must show me.
     Victor.   So, the mask falls off
An old man's foolish love at last. Spare
     thanks !
I know you, and Polyxena I know.
Here's Charles — I am his guest now —
     does he bid me
Be seated ? And my light-haired blue-eyed
     child
Must not forget the old man far away
At Chambery, who dozes while she reigns.
     Polyxena. Most grateful shall we now
     be, talking least
Of gratitude — indeed of anything
That hinders what yourself must need to
     say
To Charles.
     Charles.   Pray speak, sir !
     Victor.   'Faith, not much to say :
Only what shows itself, you once i' the
     point
Of sight. You're now the King : you'll
     comprehend
Much you may oft have wondered at —
     the shifts,
Dissimulation, wiliness I showed.
For what's our post ? Here's Savoy and
     here's Piedmont,
Here's Montferrat — a breadth here, a
     space there —
To o'ersweep all these, what's one weapon

worth ?
I often think of how they fought in
     Greece :
(Or Rome, which was it ? You're the
     scholar, Charles !)
You made a front-thrust ? But if your
     shield too
Were not adroitly planted, some shrewd
     knave
Reached you behind ; and him foiled,
     straight if thong
And handle of that shield were not cast
     loose,
And you enabled to outstrip the wind,
Fresh foes assailed you, either side : 'scape
     these,
And reach your place of refuge — e'en
     then, odds
If the gate opened unless breath enough
Were left in you to make its lord a speech.
Oh, you will see !
     Charles.   No : straight on shall I go,
Truth helping ; win with it or die with it.
     Victor. 'Faith, Charles, you're not made
     Europe's fighting-man !
The barrier-guarder, if you please. You
     clutch
Hold and consolidate, with envious France
This side, with Austria that, the territory
I held — ay, and will hold . . . which *you*
     shall hold
Despite the couple ! But I've surely earned
Exemption from these weary politics,
— The privilege to prattle with my son
And daughter here, though Europe wait
     the while.
     Polyxena. Nay, sir, — at Chambery, away
     for ever,
As soon you will be, 'tis farewell we bid
     you :
Turn these few fleeting moments to ac-
     count !
'Tis just as though it were a death.
     Victor.   Indeed !
     Polyxena [*aside*]. Is the trap there ?
     Charles. Ay, call this parting — death !
The sacreder your memory becomes.
If I misrule Sardinia, how bring back
My father ?
     Victor.   I mean . . .
     Polyxena [*who watches* VICTOR *narrowly
     this while*]. Your father does not
     mean
You should be ruling for your father's
     sake :
It is your people must concern you wholly
Instead of him. You mean this, sir ? (He
     drops
My hand !)

Charles. That people is now part of me.

Victor. About the people! I took certain measures
Some short time since . . . Oh, I know well, you know
But little of my measures! These affect
The nobles; we've resumed some grants, imposed
A tax or two: prepare yourself, in short,
For clamour on that score. Mark me: you yield
No jot of aught entrusted you!

Polyxena.   No jot
You yield!

Charles. My father, when I took the oath,
Although my eye might stray in search of yours,
I heard it, understood it, promised God
What you require. Till from this eminence
He move me,' here I keep, nor shall concede
The meanest of my rights.

Victor [*aside*].   The boy's a fool!
— Or rather, I'm a fool: for, what's wrong here?
To-day the sweets of reigning: let to-morrow
Be ready with its bitters.

Enter D'ORMEA.

                    There's beside
Somewhat to press upon your notice first.

Charles. Then why delay it for an instant, sir?
That Spanish claim perchance? And, now you speak,
— This morning, my opinion was mature,
Which, boy-like, I was bashful in producing
To one I ne'er am like to fear in future!
My thought is formed upon that Spanish claim.

Victor. Betimes indeed. Not now, Charles! You require
A host of papers on it.

D'Ormea [*coming forward*]. Here they are. [*To* CHARLES.] I, sir, was minister and much beside
Of the late monarch; to say little, him
I served: on you I have, to say e'en less,
No claim. This case contains those papers: with them
I tender you my office.

Victor [*hastily*].   Keep him, Charles!
There's reason for it — many reasons: you
Distrust him, nor are so far wrong there,

— but
He's mixed up in this matter — he'll desire
To quit you, for occasions known to me:
Do not accept those reasons: have him stay!

Polyxena [*aside*]. His minister thrust on us!

Charles [*to* D'ORMEA].   Sir, believe,
In justice to myself, you do not need
E'en this commending: howsoe'er might seem
My feelings toward you, as a private man,
They quit me in the vast and untried field
Of action. Though I shall myself (as late
In your own hearing I engaged to do)
Preside o'er my Sardinia, yet your help
Is necessary. Think the past forgotten
And serve me now!

D'Ormea.   I did not offer you
My service — would that I could serve you, sir!
As for the Spanish matter . . .

Victor.   But despatch
At least the dead, in my good daughter's phrase,
Before the living! Help to house me safe
Ere with D'Ormea you set the world a-gape!
Here is a paper — will you overlook
What I propose reserving for my needs?
I get as far from you as possible:
Here's what I reckon my expenditure.

Charles [*reading*]. A miserable fifty thousand crowns —

Victor. Oh, quite enough for country gentlemen!
Beside the exchequer happens . . . but find out
All that, yourself!

Charles [*still reading*]. "Count Tende"
— what means this?

Victor. Me: you were but an infant when I burst
Through the defile of Tende upon France.
Had only my allies kept true to me!
No matter. Tende's, then, a name I take
Just as . . .

D'Ormea. — The Marchioness Sebastian takes
The name of Spigno.

Charles.   How, sir?

Victor [*to* D'ORMEA].   Fool! All that
Was for my own detailing. [*To* CHARLES.]
That anon!

Charles [*to* D'ORMEA]. Explain what you have said, sir!

D'Ormea.   I supposed
The marriage of the King to her I named,

Profoundly kept a secret these few weeks,
Was not to be one, now he's Count.

Polyxena [*aside*].　　　　With us
The minister — with him the mistress !

Charles [*to* VICTOR].　　　　No —
Tell me you have not taken her — that
　woman
To live with, past recall !

Victor.　　　And where's the crime . . .

Polyxena [*to* CHARLES]. True, sir, this is
　a matter past recall
And past your cognizance. A day before,
And you had been compelled to note this :
　now, —
Why note it ? The King saved his House
　from shame :
What the Count did, is no concern of
　yours.

Charles [*after a pause*].　　The Spanish
　claim, D'Ormea !

Victor.　　　　Why, my son,
I took some ill-advised . . . one's age, in
　fact,
Spoils everything : though I was over-
　reached,
A younger brain, we'll trust, may extricate
Sardinia readily. To-morrow, D'Ormea,
Inform the King !

D'Ormea [*without regarding* VICTOR, *and
　leisurely*]. Thus stands the case with
　Spain :
When first the Infant Carlos claimed his
　proper
Succession to the throne of Tuscany . . .

Victor. I tell you, that stands over ! Let
　that rest !
There is the policy !

Charles [*to* D'ORMEA].　Thus much I
　know,
And more — too much : the remedy ?

D'Ormea.　　　　Of course !
No glimpse of one.

Victor.　　　No remedy at all !
It makes the remedy itself — time makes it.

D'Ormea [*to* CHARLES]. But if . . .

Victor [*still more hastily*].　In fine, I
　shall take care of that :
And, with another project that I have . . .

D'Ormea [*turning on him*]. Oh, since
　Count Tende means to take again
King Victor's crown ! —

Polyxena [*throwing herself at* VICTOR'S
　feet].　　E'en now retake it, sir !
Oh speak ! We are your subjects both, once
　more !
Say it — a word effects it ! You meant not,
Nor do mean now, to take it : but you
　must !

'Tis in you — in your nature — and the
　shame's
Not half the shame 'twould grow to after-
　wards !

Charles. Polyxena !

Polyxena. A word recalls the knights —
Say it ! What's promising and what's the
　past ?
Say you are still King Victor !

D'Ormea.　　　　Better say
The Count repents, in brief !

　　　　　　　　　　[VICTOR *rises.*

Charles.　　　With such a crime
I have not charged you, sir !

Polyxena.　　(Charles turns from me !)

SECOND YEAR, — 1731.
KING CHARLES.

PART I.

Enter Queen POLYXENA *and* D'ORMEA.—
　A pause.

Polyxena. And now, sir, what have you
　to say ?

D'Ormea.　　　Count Tende . . .

Polyxena. Affirm not I betrayed you ;
　you resolve
On uttering this strange intelligence
— Nay, post yourself to find me ere I reach
The capital, because you know King
　Charles
Tarries a day or two at Evian baths
Behind me : — but take warning, — here
　and thus [*Seating herself in the
　royal seat.*
I listen, if I listen — not your friend.
Explicitly the statement, if you still
Persist to urge it on me, must proceed :
I am not made for aught else.

D'Ormea.　　Good ! Count Tende . . .

Polyxena. I, who mistrust you, shall
　acquaint King Charles
Who even more mistrusts you.

D'Ormea.　　　Does he so ?

Polyxena. Why should he not ?

D'Ormea.　　　Ay, why not ?
　Motives, seek
You virtuous people, motives ! Say, I serve
God at the devil's bidding — will that do ?
I'm proud : our people have been pacified,
Really I know not how —

Polyxena.　　　By truthfulness.

D'Ormea. Exactly ; that shows I had
　nought to do
With pacifying them. Our foreign perils

Also exceed my means to stay: but here
'Tis otherwise, and my pride's piqued.
    Count Tende
Completes a full year's absence: would
    you, madam,
Have the old monarch back, his mistress
    back,
His measures back? I pray you, act upon
My counsel, or they will be.
    Polyxena.   When?
    D'Ormea.   Let's think.
Home-matters settled — Victor's coming
    now;
Let foreign matters settle — Victor's here
Unless I stop him; as I will, this way.
    Polyxena [*reading the papers he pre-*
        sents]. If this should prove a plot
    'twixt you and Victor?
You seek annoyances to give the pretext
For what you say you fear.
    D'Ormea.   Oh, possibly!
I go for nothing. Only show King Charles
That thus Count Tende purposes return,
And style me his inviter, if you please!
    Polyxena. Half of your tale is true;
    most like, the Count
Seeks to return: but why stay you with us?
To aid in such emergencies.
    D'Ormea.   Keep safe
Those papers; or, to serve me, leave no
    proof
I thus have counselled! When the Count
    returns,
And the King abdicates, 'twill stead me
    little
To have thus counselled.
    Polyxena.   The King abdicate!
    D'Ormea. He's good, we knew long since
    — wise, we discover —
Firm, let us hope: — but I'd have gone to
    work
With him away. Well!
    [CHARLES *without*]. In the Council
    Chamber?
    D'Ormea. All's lost!
    Polyxena.   Oh, surely not King
    Charles! He's changed —
That's not this year's care-burthened voice
    and step:
'Tis last year's step, the Prince's voice!
    D'Ormea.   I know.

    [*Enter* CHARLES : — D'ORMEA
        retiring a little.

    Charles. Now wish me joy, Polyxena!
    Wish it me
The old way!   [*She embraces him.*

There was too much cause for that!
But I have found myself again. What news
At Turin? Oh, if you but felt the load
I'm free of — free! I said this year would
    end
Or it, or me — but I am free, thank God!
    Polyxena. How, Charles?
    Charles.   You do not
    guess? The day I found
Sardinia's hideous coil, at home, abroad,
And how my father was involved in it, —
Of course, I vowed to rest and smile no
    more
Until I cleared his name from obloquy.
We did the people right — 'twas much to
    gain
That point, redress our nobles' grievance,
    too —
But that took place here, was no crying
    shame:
All must be done abroad, — if I abroad
Appeased the justly-angered Powers, de-
    stroyed
The scandal, took down Victor's name at
    last
From a bad eminence, I then might breathe
And rest! No moment was to lose. Behold
The proud result — a Treaty, Austria,
    Spain
Agree to —
    D'Ormea [*aside*]. I shall merely stipulate
For an experienced headsman.
    Charles.   Not a soul
Is compromised: the blotted past's a
    blank:
Even D'Ormea escapes unquestioned. See!
It reached me from Vienna; I remained
At Evian to despatch the Count his news;
'Tis gone to Chambery a week ago —
And here am I: do I deserve to feel
Your warm white arms around me?
    D'Ormea [*coming forward*]. He knows
    that?
    Charles. What, in Heaven's name, means
    this?
    D'Ormea.   He knows that matters
Are settled at Vienna? Not too late!
Plainly, unless you post this very hour
Some man you trust (say, me) to Cham-
    bery
And take precautions I acquaint you with,
Your father will return here.
    Charles.   Are you crazed,
D'Ormea? Here? For what? As well re-
    turn
To take his crown!
    D'Ormea.   He will return for that.
    Charles [*to* POLYXENA]. You have not

listened to this man?

Polyxena.   He spoke
About your safety — and I listened.
   [*He disengages himself from her arms.*
Charles [*to* D'ORMEA].   What
Apprised you of the Count's intentions?
   D'Ormea.   Me?
His heart, sir: you may not be used to
   read
Such evidence however; therefore read
     [*Pointing to* POLYXENA'S *papers.*
My evidence.
   Charles [*to* POLYXENA]. Oh, worthy this
   of you!
And of your speech I never have forgotten,
Though I professed forgetfulness; which
   haunts me
As if I did not know how false it was;
Which made me toil unconsciously thus
   long
That there might be no least occasion left
For aught of its prediction coming true!
And now, when there is left no least
   occasion
To instigate my father to such crime —
When I might venture to forget (I hoped)
That speech and recognize Polyxena —
Oh worthy, to revive, and tenfold worse,
That plague! D'Ormea at your ear, his
   slanders
Still in your hand! Silent?
   Polyxena.   As the wronged are.
   Charles. And you, D'Ormea, since when
   have you presumed
To spy upon my father? I conceive
What that wise paper shows, and easily.
Since when?
   D'Ormea.   The when and where and
   how belong
To me. 'Tis sad work, but I deal in such.
You ofttimes serve yourself; I'd serve you
   here:
Use makes me not so squeamish. In a word,
Since the first hour he went to Chambery,
Of his seven servants, five have I sub-
   orned.
   Charles. You hate my father?
   D'Ormea.   Oh, just as you will!
     [*Looking at* POLYXENA.
A minute since, I loved him — hate him,
   now!
What matter? — if you ponder just one
   thing:
Has he that treaty? — he is setting for-
   ward
Already. Are your guards here?
   Charles.   Well for you
They are not! [*To* POLYXENA]. Him I
   knew of old, but you —

To hear that pickthank, further his de-
   signs!
             [*To* D'ORMEA.
Guards? — were they here, I'd bid them,
   for your trouble,
Arrest you.
   D'Ormea. Guards you shall not want.
   I lived
The servant of your choice, not of your
   need.
You never greatly needed me till now
That you discard me. This is my arrest.
Again I tender you my charge — its duty
Would bid me press you read those docu-
   ments.
Here, sir!   [*Offering his badge of office.*
   Charles [*taking it*]. The papers also!
   Do you think
I dare not read them?
   Polyxena.   Read them, sir!
   Charles.   They prove,
My father, still a month within the year
Since he so solemnly consigned it me,
Means to resume his crown? They shall
   prove that,
Or my best dungeon . . .
   D'Ormea.   Even say, Chambery!
'Tis vacant, I surmise, by this.
   Charles.   You prove
Your words or pay their forfeit, sir. Go
   there!
Polyxena, one chance to rend the veil
Thickening and blackening 'twixt us two!
   Do say,
You'll see the falsehood of the charges
   proved!
Do say, at least, you wish to see them
   proved
False charges — my heart's love of other
   times!
   Polyxena. Ah, Charles!
   Charles [*to* D'ORMEA]. Precede me, sir!
   D'Ormea.   And I'm at length
A martyr for the truth! No end, they say,
Of miracles. My conscious innocence!
   [*As they go out, enter — by the middle
     door, at which he pauses —* VICTOR.
Victor. Sure I heard voices? No. Well,
   I do best
To make at once for this, the heart o' the
   place.
The old room! Nothing changed! So near
   my seat,
D'Ormea?   [*Pushing away the stool
     which is by the* KING'S *chair.*
   I want that meeting over first,
I know not why. Tush, he, D'Ormea,
   slow
To hearten me, the supple knave? That

burst
Of spite so eased him! He'll inform
    me . . .
                          What?
Why come I hither? All's in rough: let all
Remain rough. There's full time to draw
    back — nay,
There's nought to draw back from, as yet;
    whereas,
If reason should be, to arrest a course
Of error — reason good, to interpose
And save, as I have saved so many times,
Our House, admonish my son's giddy
    youth,
Relieve him of a weight that proves too
    much —
Now is the time, — or now, or never.
                        'Faith,
This kind of step is pitiful, not due
To Charles, this stealing back — hither,
    because
He's from his capital! Oh Victor! Victor!
But thus it is. The age of crafty men
Is loathsome; youth contrives to carry off
Dissimulation; we may intersperse
Extenuating passages of strength,
Ardour, vivacity, and wit — may turn
E'en guile into a voluntary grace:
But one's old age, when graces drop away
And leave guile the pure staple of our
    lives —
Ah, loathsome!
           Not so — or why pause I? Turin
Is mine to have, were I so minded, for
The asking; all the army's mine — I've
    witnessed
Each private fight beneath me; all the
    Court's
Mine too; and, best of all, D'Ormea's still
D'Ormea and mine. There's some grace
    clinging yet.
Had I decided on this step, ere midnight
I'd take the crown.
              No. Just this step to rise
Exhausts me. Here am I arrived: the rest
Must be done for me. Would I could sit
    here
And let things right themselves, the
    masque unmasque
Of the old King, crownless, grey hair and
    hot blood, —
The young King, crowned, but calm be-
    fore his time,
They say, — the eager mistress with her
    taunts, —
And the sad earnest wife who motions me
Away — ay, there she knelt to me! E'en yet
I can return and sleep at Chambery
A dream out.

            Rather shake it off at Turin,
King Victor! Say: to Turin — yes, or no?
'Tis this relentless noonday-lighted
    chamber,
Lighted like life but silent as the grave,
That disconcerts me. That's the change
    must strike.
No silence last year! Some one flung doors
    wide
(Those two great doors which scrutinize
    me now)
And out I went 'mid crowds of men —
    men talking,
Men watching if my lip fell or brow knit,
Men saw me safe forth, put me on my
    road:
That makes the misery of this return.
Oh had a battle done it! Had I dropped
Haling some battle, three entire days old,
Hither and thither by the forehead —
    dropped
In Spain, in Austria, best of all, in
    France —
Spurned on its horns or underneath its
    hooves,
When the spent monster went upon its
    knees
To pad and pash the prostrate wretch —
    I, Victor,
Sole to have stood up against France, beat
    down
By inches, brayed to pieces finally
In some vast unimaginable charge,
A flying hell of horse and foot and guns
Over me, and all's lost, for ever lost,
There's no more Victor when the world
    wakes up!
Then silence, as of a raw battle-field,
Throughout the world. Then after (as
    whole days
After, you catch at intervals faint noise
Through the stiff crust of frozen blood) —
    there creeps
A rumour forth, so faint, no noise at all,
That a strange old man, with face out-
    worn for wounds,
Is stumbling on from frontier town to
    town,
Begging a pittance that may help him find
His Turin out; what scorn and laughter
    follow
The coin you fling into his cap! And last,
Some bright morn, how men crowd about
    the midst
O' the market-place, where takes the old
    king breath
Ere with his crutch he strike the palace-
    gate
Wide ope!

To Turin, yes or no — or no ?

Re-enter CHARLES *with papers.*

Charles. Just as I thought ! A miserable
falsehood
Of hirelings discontented with their pay
And longing for enfranchisement ! A few
Testy expressions of old age that thinks
To keep alive its dignity o'er slaves
By means that suit their natures !
    [*Tearing them.*] Thus they shake
My faith in Victor !
     [*Turning, he discovers* VICTOR.
Victor [*after a pause*]. Not at Evian,
Charles ?
What's this ? Why do you run to close the
doors ?
No welcome for your father ?
Charles [*aside*].   Not his voice !
What would I give for one imperious tone
Of the old sort ! That's gone for ever.
Victor.   Must
I ask once more . . .
Charles.   No — I concede it, sir !
You are returned for . . . true, your
health declines ;
True, Chambery's a bleak unkindly spot ;
You'd choose one fitter for your final
lodge —
Veneria, or Moncaglier — ay, that's close
And I concede it.
Victor.   I received advices
Of the conclusion of the Spanish matter,
Dated from Evian Baths . . .
Charles.   And you forbore
To visit me at Evian, satisfied
The work I had to do would fully task
The little wit I have, and that your pres-
ence
Would only disconcert me —
Victor.   Charles ?
Charles.   — Me, set
For ever in a foreign course to yours,
And . . .
Sir, this way of wile were good to catch,
But I have not the sleight of it. The
truth !
Though I sink under it ! What brings you
here ?
Victor. Not hope of this reception, cer-
tainly,
From one who'd scarce assume a stranger
mode
Of speech, did I return to bring about
Some awfulest calamity !
Charles.   — You mean,
Did you require your crown again ! Oh,
yes,

I should speak otherwise ! But turn not
that
To jesting ! Sir, the truth ! Your health
declines ?
Is aught deficient in your equipage ?
Wisely you seek myself to make complaint,
And foil the malice of the world which
laughs
At petty discontents ; but I shall care
That not a soul knows of this visit. Speak !
Victor [*aside*]. Here is the grateful much-
professing son
Prepared to worship me, for whose sole
sake
I think to waive my plans of public good !
[*Aloud.*] Nay, Charles, if I did seek to take
once more
My crown, were so disposed to plague my-
self,
What would be warrant for this bitter-
ness ?
I gave it — grant I would resume it — well ?
Charles. I should say simply — leaving
out the why
And how — you made me swear to keep
that crown :
And as you then intended . . .
Victor.   Fool ! What way
Could I intend or not intend ? As man,
With a man's will, when I say "I intend,"
I can intend up to a certain point,
No farther. I intended to preserve
The crown of Savoy and Sardinia whole :
And if events arise demonstrating
The way, I hoped should guard it, rather
like
To lose it . . .
Charles. Keep within your sphere
and mine !
It is God's province we usurp on, else.
Here, blindfold through the maze of
things we walk
By a slight clue of false, true, right and
wrong ;
All else is rambling and presumption. I
Have sworn to keep this kingdom : there's
my truth.
Victor. Truth, boy, is here, within my
breast ; and in
Your recognition of it, truth is, too ;
And in the effect of all this tortuous deal-
ing
With falsehood, used to carry out the
truth,
— In its success, this falsehood turns,
again,
Truth for the world. But you are right :
these themes
Are over-subtle. I should rather say

In such a case, frankly, — it fails, my
    scheme :
I hoped to see you bring about, yourself,
What I must bring about. I interpose
On your behalf — with my son's good in
    sight —
To hold what he is nearly letting go,
Confirm his title, add a grace perhaps.
There's Sicily, for instance, — granted me
And taken back, some years since : till I
    give
That island with the rest, my work's half
    done.
For his sake, therefore, as of those he
    rules . . .
    Charles. Our sakes are one ; and that,
      you could not say,
Because my answer would present itself
Forthwith : — a year has wrought an age's
    change.
This people's not the people now, you
    once
Could benefit ; nor is my policy
Your policy.
    Victor [*with an outburst*]. I know it !
      You undo
All I have done — my life of toil and care !
I left you this the absolutest rule
In Europe : do you think I sit and smile,
Bid you throw power to the populace —
See my Sardinia, that has kept apart,
Join in the mad and democratic whirl
Whereto I see all Europe haste full tide ?
England casts off her kings ; France mimics
    England :
This realm I hoped was safe. Yet here
    I talk,
When I can save it, not by force alone,
But bidding plagues, which follow sons
    like you,
Fasten upon my disobedient . . .
        [*Recollecting himself.*] Surely
I could say this — if minded so — my son ?
    Charles. You could not. Bitterer curses
      than your curse
Have I long since denounced upon myself
If I misused my power. In fear of these
I entered on those measures — will abide
By them : so, I should say, Count
    Tende . . .
    Victor.   No !
But no ! But if, my Charles, your — more
    than old —
Half-foolish father urged these arguments,
And then confessed them futile, but said
    plainly
That he forgot his promise, found his
    strength
Fail him, had thought at savage Chambery

Too much of brilliant Turin, Rivoli here,
And Susa, and Veneria, and Superga —
Pined for the pleasant places he had built
When he was fortunate and young —
    Charles.   My father !
    Victor. Stay yet ! — and if he said he
      could not die
Deprived of baubles he had put aside,
He deemed, for ever — of the Crown that
    binds
Your brain up, whole, sound and impreg-
    nable,
Creating kingliness — the Sceptre too,
Whose mere wind, should you wave it,
    back would beat
Invaders — and the golden Ball which
    throbs
As if you grasped the palpitating heart
Indeed o' the realm, to mould as choose
    you may !
— If I must totter up and down the streets
My sires built, where myself have intro-
    duced
And fostered laws and letters, sciences,
The civil and the military arts !
Stay, Charles ! I see you letting me pretend
To live my former self once more — King
    Victor,
The venturous yet politic : they style me
Again, the Father of the Prince : friends
    wink
Good-humouredly at the delusion you
So sedulously guard from all rough truths
That else would break upon my dotage ! —
    You —
Whom now I see preventing my old
    shame —
I tell not, point by cruel point, my tale —
For is't not in your breast my brow is hid ?
Is not your hand extended ? Say you
    not . . .

Enter D'ORMEA, *leading in* POLYXENA.

Polyxena [*advancing and withdrawing*
    CHARLES — *to* VICTOR]. In this con-
    juncture even, he would say
(Though with a moistened eye and quiv-
    ering lip)
The suppliant is my father. I must save
A great man from himself, nor see him
    fling
His well-earned fame away : there must
    not follow
Ruin so utter, a break-down of worth
So absolute : no enemy shall learn,
He thrust his child 'twixt danger and
    himself,
And, when that child somehow stood

danger out,
Stole back with serpent wiles to ruin
    Charles
— Body, that's much, — and soul, that's
    more — and realm,
That's most of all! No enemy shall
    say . . .
    D'Ormea. Do you repent, sir?
    Victor [*resuming himself*]. D'Ormea?
    This is well!
Worthily done, King Charles, craftily
    done!
Judiciously you post these, to o'erhear
The little your importunate father thrusts
Himself on you to say! — Ah, they'll cor-
    rect
The amiable blind facility
You show in answering his peevish suit.
What can he need to sue for? Thanks,
    D'Ormea!
You have fulfilled your office: but for you,
The old Count might have drawn some
    few more livres
To swell his income! Had you, lady,
    missed
The moment, a permission might be
    granted
To buttress up my ruinous old pile!
But you remember properly the list
Of wise precautions I took when I gave
Nearly as much away — to reap the fruits
I should have looked for!
    Charles.   Thanks, sir: degrade me.
So you remain yourself! Adieu!
    Victor.   I'll not
Forget it for the future, nor presume
Next time to slight such mediators! Nay —
Had I first moved them both to intercede,
I might secure a chamber in Moncaglier
— Who knows?
    Charles.   Adieu!
    Victor.   You bid me this adieu
With the old spirit?
    Charles.   Adieu!
    Victor.   Charles — Charles!
    Charles.   Adieu!
                [VICTOR *goes.*
    Charles. You were mistaken, Marquis, as
    you hear.
'Twas for another purpose the Count
    came.
The Count desires Moncaglier. Give the
    order!
    D'Ormea [*leisurely*]. Your minister has
    lost your confidence,
Asserting late, for his own purposes,
Count Tende would . . .
    Charles [*flinging his badge back*]. Be
    still the minister!

And give a loose to your insulting joy;
It irks me more thus stifled than ex-
    pressed:
Loose it!
    D'Ormea.   There's none to loose,
    alas! I see
I never am to die a martyr.
    Polyxena.   Charles!
    Charles. No praise, at least, Polyxena —
    no praise!

KING CHARLES.

PART II.

D'ORMEA, *seated, folding papers he has
    been examining.*

This at the last effects it: now, King
    Charles
Or else King Victor — that's a balance:
    but now,
D'Ormea the arch-culprit, either turn
O' the scale, — that's sure enough. A point
    to solve,
My masters, moralists, whate'er your style!
When you discover why I push myself
Into a pitfall you'd pass safely by,
Impart to me among the rest! No matter.
Prompt are the righteous ever with their
    rede
To us the wrongful; lesson them this
    once!
For safe among the wicked are you set,
D'Ormea! We lament life's brevity,
Yet quarter e'en the threescore years and
    ten,
Nor stick to call the quarter roundly
    "life."
D'Ormea was wicked, say, some twenty
    years;
A tree so long was stunted; afterward,
What if it grew, continued growing, till
No fellow of the forest equalled it?
'Twas a stump then; a stump it still must
    be:
While forward saplings, at the outset
    checked,
In virtue of that first sprout keep their
    style
Amid the forest's green fraternity.
Thus I shoot up to surely get lopped
    down
And bound up for the burning. Now for
    it!

Enter CHARLES *and* POLYXENA *with*
Attendants.

D'Ormea [*rises*]. Sir, in the due dis-
    charge of this my office —
This enforced summons of yourself from
    Turin,
And the disclosure I am bound to make
To-night, — there must already be, I feel,
So much that wounds . . .
Charles.   Well, sir ?
D'Ormea.   — That I, perchance,
May utter also what, another time,
Would irk much, — it may prove less irk-
    some now.
Charles. What would you utter ?
D'Ormea.   That I from my soul
Grieve at to-night's event : for you I grieve,
E'en grieve for . . .
Charles. Tush, another time for talk !
My kingdom is in imminent danger ?
D'Ormea.   Let
The Count communicate with France —
    its King,
His grandson, will have Fleury's aid for
    this,
Though for no other war.
Charles.   First for the levies :
What forces can I muster presently ?
            [D'ORMEA *delivers papers which*
                    CHARLES *inspects.*
Charles. Good — very good. Montorio . . .
    how is this ?
— Equips me double the old complement
Of soldiers ?
D'Ormea. Since his land has been re-
    lieved
From double imposts, this he manages :
But under the late monarch . . .
Charles.   Peace ! I know.
Count Spava has omitted mentioning
What proxy is to head these troops of his.
D'Ormea. Count Spava means to head
    his troops himself.
Something to fight for now ; "Whereas,"
    says he,
"Under the sovereign's father" . . .
Charles.   It would seem
That all my people love me.
D'Ormea.   Yes.
        [*To* POLYXENA *while* CHARLES *con-
            tinues to inspect the papers.*
                        A temper
Like Victor's may avail to keep a state ;
He terrifies men and they fall not off ;
Good to restrain : best, if restraint were
    all.
But, with the silent circle round him, ends
Such sway : our King's begins precisely
    there.
For to suggest, impel and set at work,
Is quite another function. Men may slight,

In time of peace, the King who brought
    them peace :
In war, — his voice, his eyes, help more
    than fear.
They love you, sir !
    Charles [*to* Attendants]. Bring the rega-
        lia forth !
Quit the room ! And now, Marquis, an-
    swer me !
Why should the King of France invade my
    realm ?
    D'Ormea. Why ? Did I not acquaint
        your Majesty
An hour ago ?
    Charles. I choose to hear again
What then I heard.
    D'Ormea.   Because, sir, as I said,
Your father is resolved to have his crown
At any risk ; and, as I judge, calls in
The foreigner to aid him.
    Charles.   And your reason
For saying this ?
    D'Ormea [*aside*]. Ay, just his father's
        way !
[*To* CHARLES.] The Count wrote yesterday
    to your forces' Chief,
Rhebinder — made demand of help —
    Charles.   To try
Rhebinder — he's of alien blood : aught
    else ?
    D'Ormea. Receiving a refusal, — some
        hours after,
The Count called on Del Borgo to deliver
The Act of Abdication : he refusing,
Or hesitating, rather —
    Charles.   What ensued ?
    D'Ormea. At midnight, only two hours
        since, at Turin,
He rode in person to the citadel
With one attendant, to Soccorso gate,
And bade the governor, San Remi, open —
Admit him.
    Charles. For a purpose I divine.
These three were faithful, then ?
    D'Ormea.   They told it me.
And I —
    Charles. Most faithful —
    D'Ormea.   Tell it you — with this
Moreover of my own : if, an hour hence,
You have not interposed, the Count will
    be.
O' the road to France for succour.
    Charles.   Very good !
You do your duty now to me your
    monarch
Fully, I warrant ? — have, that is, your
    project
For saving both of us disgrace, no doubt ?
    D'Ormea. I give my counsel, — and the

only one.
A month since, I besought you to employ
Restraints which had prevented many a
     pang :
But now the harsher course must be pur-
     sued.
These papers, made for the emergency,
Will pain you to subscribe : this is a list
Of those suspected merely — men to
     watch ;
This — of the few of the Count's very
     household
You must, however reluctantly, arrest ;
While here's a method of remonstrance —
     sure
Not stronger than the case demands — to
     take
With the Count's self.
    Charles.   Deliver those three papers.
    Polyxena [*while* CHARLES *inspects them
     — to* D'ORMEA]. Your measures are
     not over-harsh, sir : France
Will hardly be deterred from her intents
By these.
    D'Ormea. If who proposes might
     dispose,
I could soon satisfy you.   Even these,
Hear what he'll say at my presenting !
    Charles [*who has signed them*].   There !
About the warrants ! You've my signature.
What turns you pale ? I do my duty by you
In acting boldly thus on your advice.
    D'Ormea [*reading them separately*]. Ar-
     rest the people I suspected merely ?
    Charles. Did you suspect them ?
    D'Ormea.   Doubtless : but — but — sir,
This Forquieri's governor of Turin,
And Rivarol and he have influence over
Half of the capital !   Rabella, too ?
Why, sir —
    Charles. Oh, leave the fear to me !
    D'Ormea [*still reading*].   You bid me
Incarcerate the people on this list ?
Sir —
    Charles. But you never bade arrest those
     men,
So close related to my father too,
On trifling grounds ?
    D'Ormea.   Oh, as for that, St. George,
President of Chambery's senators,
Is hatching treason ! still —
    [*More troubled.*] Sir, Count Cumiane
Is brother to your father's wife !   What's
     here ?
Arrest the wife herself ?
    Charles.   You seem to think
A venial crime this plot against me. Well ?
    D'Ormea [*who has read the last paper*].
     Wherefore am I thus ruined ?   Why

not take
My life at once ? This poor formality
Is, let me say, unworthy you ! Prevent it
You, madam ! I have served you, am pre-
     pared
For all disgraces : only, let disgrace
Be plain, be proper — proper for the world
To pass its judgment on 'twixt you and
     me !
Take back your warrant, I will none of it !
    Charles. Here is a man to talk of fickle-
     ness !
He stakes his life upon my father's false-
     hood ;
I bid him . . .
    D'Ormea.   Not you !   Were he trebly
     false,
You do not bid me . . .
    Charles.   Is't not written there ?
I thought so : give — I'll set it right.
    D'Ormea.   Is it there ?
Oh yes, and plain — arrest him now — drag
     here
Your father ! And were all six times as
     plain,
Do you suppose I trust it ?
    Charles.   Just one word !
You bring him, taken in the act of flight,
Or else your life is forfeit.
    D'Ormea.   Ay, to Turin
I bring him, and to-morrow ?
    Charles.   Here and now !
The whole thing is a lie, a hateful lie,
As I believed and as my father said.
I knew it from the first, but was compelled
To circumvent you ; and the great
     D'Ormea,
That baffled Alberoni and tricked Coscia,
The miserable sower of such discord
'Twixt sire and son, is in the toils at last.
Oh I see ! you arrive — this plan of yours,
Weak as it is, torments sufficiently
A sick old peevish man — wrings hasty
     speech,
An ill-considered threat from him ; that's
     noted ;
Then out you ferret papers, his amuse-
     ment
In lonely hours of lassitude — examine
The day-by-day report of your paid spies —
And back you come : all was not ripe, you
     find,
And, as you hope, may keep from ripening
     yet,
But you were in bare time ! Only, 'twere
     best
I never saw my father — these old men
Are potent in excuses : and meanwhile,
D'Ormea's the man I cannot do without !

Polyxena.   Charles —
Charles.   Ah, no question !
You against me too !
You'd have me eat and drink and sleep,
    live, die
With this lie coiled about me, choking me !
No, no, D'Ormea ! You venture life, you
    say,
Upon my father's perfidy : and I
Have, on the whole, no right to disregard
The chains of testimony you thus wind
About me ; though I do — do from my
    soul
Discredit them : still I must authorize
These measures, and I will.   Perugia !
    [*Many* Officers *enter.*]   Count —
You and Solar, with all the force you have,
Stand at the Marquis' orders : what he
    bids,
Implicitly perform !   You are to bring
A traitor here ; the man that's likest one
At present, fronts me ; you are at his beck
For a full hour ! he undertakes to show
A fouler than himself, — but, failing that,
Return with him, and, as my father lives,
He dies this night ! The clemency you
    blame
So oft, shall be revoked — rights exercised,
Too long abjured.
    [*To* D'ORMEA.] Now sir, about the
    work !
To save your king and country ! Take the
    warrant !
    D'Ormea. You hear the sovereign's man-
    date, Count Perugia ?
Obey me ! As your diligence, expect
Reward ! All follow to Moncaglier !
    Charles [*in great anguish*]. D'Ormea !
                    [*D'Ormea goes.*
He goes, lit up with that appalling smile !
            [*To* POLYXENA, *after a pause.*
At least you understand all this ?
    Polyxena.   These means
Of our defence — these measures of pre-
    caution ?
    Charles. It must be the best way ; I
    should have else
Withered beneath his scorn.
    Polyxena.   What would you say ?
    Charles. Why, do you think I mean to
    keep the crown,
Polyxena ?
    Polyxena. You then believe the story
In spite of all — that Victor comes ?
    Charles.   Believe it ?
I know that he is coming — feel the
    strength
That has upheld me leave me at his com-
    ing !

'Twas mine, and now he takes his own
    again.
Some kinds of strength are well enough to
    have ;
But who's to have that strength ? Let my
    crown go !
I meant to keep it ; but I cannot —
    cannot !
Only, he shall not taunt me — he, the
    first . . .
See if he would not be the first to taunt
    me
With having left his kingdom at a word.
With letting it be conquered without
    stroke,
With . . . no — no — 'tis no worse than
    when he left !
I've just to bid him take it, and, that over,
We'll fly away — fly, for I loathe this
    Turin,
This Rivoli, all titles loathe, all state.
We'd best go to your country — unless God
Send I die now !
    Polyxena.   Charles, hear me !
    Charles.   And again
Shall you be my Polyxena — you'll take me
Out of this woe ! Yes, do speak, and keep
    speaking !
I would not let you speak just now, for
    fear
You'd counsel me against him : but talk,
    now,
As we two used to talk in blessed times :
Bid me endure all his caprices ; take me
From this mad post above him !
    Polyxena.   I believe
We are undone, but from a different cause,
All your resources, down to the least
    guard,
Are at D'Ormea's beck. What if, the while,
He act in concert with your father ? We
Indeed were lost. This lonely Rivoli —
Where find a better place for them ?
    Charles [*pacing the room*]. And why
Does Victor come ? To undo all that's
    done,
Restore the past, prevent the future ! Seat
His mistress in your seat, and place in
    mine
. . . Oh, my own people, whom will you
    find there,
To ask of, to consult with, to care for,
To hold up with your hands ? Whom ?
    One that's false —
False — from the head's crown to the foot's
    sole, false !
The best is, that I knew it in my heart
From the beginning, and expected this,
And hated you, Polyxena, because

You saw thro' him, though I too saw thro
    him,
Saw that he meant this while he crowned
    me, while
He prayed for me, — nay, while he kissed
    my brow,
I saw ——
    Polyxena. But if your measures take
    effect,
D'Ormea true to you ?
    Charles.   Then worst of all !
I shall have loosed that callous wretch on
    him !
Well may the woman taunt him with his
    child —
I, eating here his bread, clothed in his
    clothes,
Seated upon his seat, let slip D'Ormea
To outrage him ! We talk — perchance he
    tears
My father from his bed ; the old hands
    feel
For one who is not, but who should be
    there,
He finds D'Ormea ! D'Ormea too finds
    him !
The crowded chamber when the lights go
    out —
Closed doors — the horrid scuffle in the
    dark —
The accursed prompting of the minute !
    My guards !
To horse — and after, with me — and pre-
    vent !
    Polyxena [*seizing his hand*]. King
    Charles !
    Pause here upon this strip of time
Allotted you out of eternity !
Crowns are from God : you in his name
    hold yours.
Your life's no least thing, were it fit your
    life
Should be abjured along with rule ; but
    now,
Keep both ! Your duty is to live and
    rule —
You, who would vulgarly look fine enough
In the world's eye, describing your soul's
    charge, —
Ay, you would have men's praise, this
    Rivoli
Would be illumined ! While, as 'tis, no
    doubt,
Something of stain will ever rest on you ;
No one will rightly know why you refused
To abdicate ; they'll talk of deeds you
    could
Have done, no doubt, — nor do I much
    expect

Future achievement will blot out the past,
Envelope it in haze — nor shall we two
Live happy any more. 'Twill be, I feel,
Only in moments that the duty's seen
As palpably as now : the months, the years
Of painful indistinctness are to come,
While daily must we tread these palace-
    rooms
Pregnant with memories of the past : your
    eye
May turn to mine and find no comfort
    there,
Through fancies that beset me, as yourself,
Of other courses, with far other issues,
We might have taken this great night :
    such bear,
As I will bear ! What matters happiness ?
Duty ! There's man's one moment : this is
    yours !
    [*Putting the crown on his head, and
    the sceptre in his hand, she places
    him on his seat : a long pause and
    silence.*

Enter D'ORMEA *and* VICTOR, *with* Guards.

    Victor. At last I speak ; but once — that
    once, to you !
'Tis you I ask, not these your varletry,
Who's King of us ?
    Charles [*from his seat*].   Count
    Tende . . .
    Victor.   What your spies
Assert I ponder in my soul, I say —
Here to your face, amid your guards ! I
    choose
To take again the crown whose shadow I
    gave —
For still its potency surrounds the weak
White locks their felon hands have discom-
    posed.
Or I'll not ask who's King, but simply,
    who
Withholds the crown I claim ? Deliver it !
I have no friend in the wide world : nor
    France
Nor England cares for me : you see the
    sum
Of what I can avail. Deliver it !
    Charles. Take it, my father !
               And now say in turn,
Was it done well, my father — sure not
    well,
To try me thus ! I might have seen much
    cause
For keeping it — too easily seen cause !
But, from that moment, e'en more woe-
    fully
My life had pined away, than pine it will.

Already you have much to answer for.
My life to pine is nothing, — her sunk eyes
Were happy once ! No doubt, my people
think
I am their King still . . . but I cannot
strive !
Take it !
   Victor [*one hand on the crown* CHARLES
     offers, the other on his neck]. So few
     years give it quietly,
My son ! It will drop from me. See you
not ?
A crown's unlike a sword to give away —
That, let a strong hand to a weak hand
give !
But crowns should slip from palsied brows
to heads
Young as this head : yet mine is weak
enough,
E'en weaker than I knew. I seek for
phrases
To vindicate my right. 'Tis of a piece !
All is alike gone by with me — who beat
Once D'Orleans in his lines — his very
lines !
To have been Eugene's comrade, Louis's
rival,
And now . . .
   Charles [*putting the crown on him, to
     the rest*]. The King speaks, yet
     none kneels, I think !
   Victor. I am then King ! As I became a
     King
Despite the nations, kept myself a King,
So I die King, with Kingship dying too
Around me. I have lasted Europe's time.
What wants my story of completion ?
Where
Must needs the damning break show ? who
mistrusts
My children here — tell they of any break
'Twixt my day's sunrise and its fiery fall ?
And who were by me when I died but
they ?
D'Ormea there !
   Charles.   What means he ?
   Victor.   Ever there !
Charles — how to save your story ! Mine
must go.
Say — say that you refused the crown to
me !
Charles, yours shall be my story ! You im-
mured
Me, say, at Rivoli. A single year

I spend without a sight of you, then die.
That will serve every purpose — tell that
tale
The world !
   Charles. Mistrust me ? Help !
   Victor.   Past help, past reach !
'Tis in the heart — you cannot reach the
heart :
This broke mine, that I did believe, you,
Charles,
Would have denied me and disgraced me.
   Polyxena.   Charles
Has never ceased to be your subject, sir !
He reigned at first through setting up
yourself
As pattern : if he e'er seemed harsh to you,
'Twas from a too intense appreciation
Of your own character : he acted you —
Ne'er for an instant did I think it real,
Nor look for any other than this end.
I hold him worlds the worse on that ac-
count ;
But so it was.
   Charles. [*to* POLYXENA]. I love you now
     indeed.
[*To* VICTOR.] You never knew me.
   Victor.   Hardly till this moment,
When I seem learning many other things
Because the time for using them is past.
If 'twere to do again ! That's idly wished.
Truthfulness might prove policy as good
As guile. Is this my daughter's forehead ?
Yes :
I've made it fitter now to be a queen's
Than formerly : I've ploughed the deep
lines there
Which keep too well a crown from slip-
ping off.
No matter. Guile has made me King
again.
Louis — 'twas in King Victor's time : — *long
   since,*
*When Louis reigned and, also, Victor
   reigned.*
How the world talks already of us two !
God of eclipse and each discoloured star,
Why do I linger then ?
          Ha ! Where lurks he ?
D'Ormea ! Nearer to your King ! Now
stand !
   [*Collecting his strength as* D'ORMEA
               approaches.
You lied, D'Ormea ! I do not repent.
                     [*Dies.*

8

ALFRED, LORD TENNYSON'S *BECKET*

Of all the plays in this anthology, Tennyson's *Becket* was in its day perhaps the most admired. Sir Henry Irving, who first produced the play in 1893, claimed that it was one of the most successful plays he had staged at the Lyceum.[1] He is said to have played the title role some 380 times in his career,[2] a fact that clearly establishes the popularity of the play with late nineteenth-century audiences. It is likely that a share of that popularity was the result of Irving's talents as an actor and producer; no doubt, too, the fact that Tennyson died only four months before the first performance stimulated interest and made the play a sort of sentimental favorite. Yet, without assuming that popular approval signifies real merit, one can claim, on several bases, that *Becket* is a play worth serious attention. J. H. Buckley notes that, after Irving's success, "Becket has more and more been relegated to the low dusty shelves where it awaits the very few readers of arm-chair literary drama."[3] The truth of that remark does not require us to assent to the implied proposition that *Becket* must therefore be, at best, a mediocre play.

Becket, like the rest of Tennyson's plays, has elicited very little serious critical response. The best criticism, and one which must be taken into account in any discussion of the play, is Buckley's in *Tennyson: the Growth of a Poet. Becket*, he says, "is a loose chronicle with several striking characters and ably framed separate scenes but no real coherence of total action."[4] The lack of coherence is compounded by the mere melodrama of the Rosamund subplot and the lack of credibility in the characters of Rosamund and Eleanor, and the play suffers, Buckley says, by the inevitable comparison with T. S. Eliot's treatment of the same material in *Murder in the Cathedral*, with its "narrowed concentration on theme and its deft use of the anonymous interpretive Chorus of Women."[5] Buckley's conclusion is that Tennyson was embarrassed both by his raw material—his need to remain faithful to history—and by the demands of a dead theatrical convention.

That the Victorians found themselves trapped in the Elizabethan mold is a frequent motif of criticism of their verse drama, and it is a sort of catch-all that covers everything from poetic language to plot construction. Very often one finds the charge made in connection with their choice of historical plots from either English or classical sources (as exemplified in the Victorian drama in this anthology). One may not be stretching too far to claim that they chose to deal

---

1. Hallam Tennyson, *Alfred, Lord Tennyson: A Memoir* (New York, 1897), vol. 2, p. 195.
2. Cornelia Japikse, *The Dramas of Alfred, Lord Tennyson* (New York, 1966), p. 78.
3. Jerome H. Buckley, *Tennyson: the Growth of a Poet* (Cambridge, Mass., 1960), p. 207.
4. *Ibid.*, p. 206.
5. *Ibid.*, p. 207.

with historical material, not simply because Shakespeare, or some other antecedent, had done so, but because they found it as significant and useful, for a variety of purposes, as their predecessors had. Certainly in *Becket* Tennyson was conscious of the problem of dealing with history. His research was careful, as was the composition itself; Hallam Tennyson tells us that his father "bestowed infinite trouble on his dramas."

Becket was begun in 1876, and first set in proof in 1879, but not published until 1884.[6] Tennyson's hesitation was certainly due at least in part to his concern for the play's artistic integrity; he did not delay out of simple diffidence. And when the play was to be staged, Tennyson, on Irving's advice, revised again with great care. In his plays, Hallam also tells, Tennyson sought to complete the line of Shakespeare's histories.[7] And, like Shakespeare, he seems to have been conscious of the contemporaneity of his work. Tennyson was interested, for example, in the effect of *Becket* on Roman Catholics[8]—a fact that would seem to indicate not that he was embarrassed by the raw materials of history, but that he thought the historical fact had important application to his own time. (One need not make Becket an exclusively Catholic hero to recognize in the religious and political conflicts of the nineteenth century countless echoes of his struggle.)

There had been, in the fifty years preceding Tennyson's play, at least three dramatic treatments of the martyrdom of Becket. Tennyson must have been conscious that in its outlines the material was threadbare, and he must, too, have been confident of the depth of his insight and of his ability to make the problem of the play dramatically interesting. (This, despite the perennial unpopularity of his plays.) The central issue of the play is the struggle for power, and although the struggle is between church and state, and ultimately between king and people, these two forces are embodied in characters whose complexity does not allow us to make easy judgments, to interpret the conflict as one simply of might against right. Tennyson's achievement in the play is his ability to render these characters credible and alive, and in light of that achievement the play's faults are perhaps more obviously defects, but also less important in our judgment of the whole. Tennyson is determined that we see in Thomas Becket and in Henry Plantagenet human beings with various motives, some noble and some contemptible. He wants us to see, too, that though in each case character is fate, each man is also an instrument of larger forces. He bears responsibility for what he does, whether he betrays his friendship or disobeys man's law or God's; but each character is to be understood, not judged. If the play may be said to express any theory—about history in general or the English past in particular—it is that events move, apparently through some purposeful inner will, to an unstated and imperfectly understood goal. (It would not be unfair to suggest that Tennyson sees that as a "far-off, divine event.") The movement of history calls forth men (much like Carlyle's heroes) to express its will. Both Becket and Henry II are such men, though in Tennyson's interpretation they have flaws that Carlyle would not have admitted in his heroes.

The game of chess that opens the play perfectly expresses Tennyson's conception of their characters. Each player moves as the rules of the game dictate he must, Becket with his bishop moving, as events allow, toward checkmate of Henry's king. As in the play, each move controls to some extent the moves that come after, and the train of events gathers force and becomes inexorable. Always a piece is limited by its nature: bishops move only in a predetermined pattern. Within that pattern there is freedom: Henry moves so "wildly" that he allows Becket to check him. And without the pattern there is no game—as when Henry, in a rage

6. *Memoir*, vol. 2, p. 193.
7. *Ibid.*, p. 174.
8. *Ibid.*, p. 193.

at losing, knocks over the board entirely: "down go bishop and king together."
Each is a victim of the rules, and the question of rules is amplified in the drama in
various ways. The rules of the game of chess are also roles that each man plays:
Henry as king, politician, or lover; Becket as the son of a merchant, or as Lord
Chancellor, is a different person from, yet the same as, the Archbishop of Canterbury who must be martyred. And the roles that they play raise questions of
law—of legal right and of moral right: the king's justice and God's. One of the
guises that the issue assumes is that of the "customs of the realm," which is introduced in the dialogue skillfully woven around the chess game in the prologue.
It is these customs that Becket will not, finally, yield to; as Archbishop he has
other promises to keep, and he is as much trapped by his mitre as Henry is by his
crown. Yet, in this early scene, the justice of Henry's complaints against the
Church is clear (as is his stubborn determination to maintain absolute power).
"The Church," Henry says,

> Hath climbed the throne and almost clutched the crown;
> But by the royal customs of our realm
> The Church should hold her baronies of me, . . .
> Like other lords amenable to law.

At this point, Henry insists on the identity of the law of the realm and true
justice. (He has just commented on the fact that clerics accused of atrocious
crimes are lightly treated by the ecclesiastical courts.) Becket, still Lord Chancellor,
is not allowed to comment, beyond moving his bishop, though Tennyson shortly
thereafter has him say (only half-jokingly) that if he were Henry's confessor he
"should beat/Thy kingship as my bishop hath beaten it."

The scene acts as a microcosm of the whole, introducing the major theme and
implying its complexity, as it does that of the characters who are to act it out.
The Prologue introduces, in a scale of descending importance, those who are to
play minor roles as well—Rosamund, then Eleanor, then Fitzurse, who is the
leader of those who will wield the knives at Becket's martyrdom. But despite the
firm initial structure of the conflict, and the clear inevitability of its issue, it may
well seem that other elements of the play—the Rosamund plot, for example—are
distracting and unnecessary.

When Irving produced the play he cut it by nearly one-third of its original
length, and when he did so it was objected that the play had become only a series
of episodes. Among his cuts were the whole of Walter Map's part and the com-
pression of portions of the Rosamund plot (Henry's two visits to Rosamund were
merged into one).[9] Neither of these is clearly a loss, and that such is the case may
demonstrate the faultiness of Tennyson's dramatic sense. Map has, indeed, a choric
function, but his fascination for Tennyson, who wanted the role spared in Irving's
editing, seems to have been on other grounds. (Map is as fond of a quibble as any
three or four together of Shakespeare's punsters.) Further, the choric function is
fulfilled as well by other characters, primarily by Herbert, John of Salisbury, and
Rosamund. But the play would suffer from any further alteration of the Rosamund plot, which is not at all a melodramatic distraction, but a part carefully
integrated into the whole—a series of events providing us with an important
example of the quality of the relationship between Henry and Becket in their
various roles as friends, as king and obedient subject, and as representatives of the
secular and spiritual. (Becket enunciates Rosamund's role in this connection
when he comments on the meaning of her name.)

The subject of Rosamund is introduced in the Prologue, when Henry solicits
Becket's promise to watch over her bower. Henry gains the promise because of

---

9. Japikse, p. 82.

Becket's loyalty to him, both as Lord Chancellor and as a friend. Becket swears, but not, he says, "to please myself." He swears, too, despite whatever may come between the two of them. (Tennyson leaves ambiguous throughout the play the nature of Henry's relationship to Rosamund. Married or not, she is, Henry says, "my true heart-wife.") Thus Rosamund becomes the real link between Henry and Becket, a link that is to bind them when they are most at odds. Essentially innocent, she serves as a measure of the worth of both men. Becket is made to feel the reality of her love for Henry, and he sees it as a type of "this love, this mother [that] runs thro' all/The world God made" (V. ii. 130–31). Rosamund's love for Henry is an echo of Becket's own, the love that kept him from excommunicating Henry. John of Salisbury tells Rosamund, when she accuses Becket,

> . . . once in France the King had been so harsh,
> He thought to excommunicate him — Thomas,
> You could not — old affection master'd you,
> You falter'd into tears.
>
> (V.ii.72–75) .

Becket defends himself against the charge only weakly. He does not, he says, want to be made into a woman; but his excuse, that the king was "sick and almost unto death," has at its core that same love. Yet when Rosamund objects that Henry is not cruel—"it is the law, not he;/The customs of the realm"—Becket cannot accept that Henry, like himself, is a victim of the role he must play. As Lord Chancellor, Becket says, he was as cruel as the King. Now, as Archbishop, he represents God, and he speaks for him and for the people against the King.

But Becket as Archbishop implies Becket as martyr, and that is so because of that quality of character (Tennyson called it "rashness") that keeps him from understanding Henry even as he retains his old affection for the King. Becket is a fatalist, too: it is part of his mission not to bend, and nowhere is this clearer than when he is threatened by the knights:

> Ye think to scare me from my loyalty
> To God and to the Holy Father. No!
> Tho' all the swords in England flash'd above me
> Ready to fall at Henry's word or yours—
> Tho' all the loud-lung'd trumpets upon earth
> Blared from the heights of all the thrones of her kings.
> Blowing the world against me, I would stand
> Clothed with the full authority of Rome,
> Mail'd in the perfect panoply of faith,
> First of the foremost of their files who die
> For God.
>
> (V.ii.259–69)

To bend is, for Becket, to violate the charge given by God; it is also quite simply out of character. Repeatedly John of Salisbury comments on Becket's inability to listen to advice, or to moderate rather than heat the anger of his enemies. But Becket takes counsel only of God; conscience will not heed mere reason. He must, therefore, die, and Tennyson's treatment foreshadows the way in which Eliot was later to deal with the theme. Is Becket's martyrdom truly selfless? Is this the right deed for the wrong reason? He will not seek refuge, and he will not relent; neither course is in Becket the man. Yet, as John says, "We must not force the crown of martyrdom" (V. iii. 16) .

Finally, Becket does not force that crown, though he is very ready to receive it. One of the knights comments, when Becket warns them not to touch him, "How the good priest gods himself!" (V. iii. 77). Becket, fortunately, is always aware of a key distinction: it is for and to God that he offers himself, and if that appears *as* God to his murderers, their crime is so much the greater.

The thunderstorm that breaks over the cathedral as Becket dies seems at first an obvious theatrical device: it was perhaps for this reason that Tennyson foot-noted it, in embarrassed fashion, as a historical occurrence. One wonders whether in the theater it would fail of its effect as clearly as it seems to do in reading. But if Tennyson was a man who sought to avoid the dramatic gesture, Irving was not. Every one of the cuts he made in *Becket* clearly strengthens the leading role, and sometimes at the expense of the literary design of the work. (It has been suggested, in fact, that the dominance of the actor-manager is one reason for the inferior literary value of much nineteenth-century drama: people like Irving wanted pri-marily plays that showed them in a strong starring role.) [10] There was plenty of opportunity for Irving in *Becket,* for essentially the meaning of the play is in his actions as the key to a heroic personality. The facts of his conflict with Henry, and of his martyrdom, are known to us from history; but his personality, what he was as a man, can never be known without the sympathetic insight of created literature. Fully to reveal that personality meant, for Tennyson, to reveal selectively those people and events that illuminate personality. If the plot of *Becket*—either before or after Irving's editing—is episodic, it must still be said that the common thread uniting those episodes is a strong one. The play coheres around the revela-tion of Becket's character, and every bit of the action is somehow related to it. Even the apparently irrelevant scenes in Rosamund's bower, by exemplifying for us the relationship between Henry and Rosamund; or the scenes between Eleanor, Fitzurse, and Becket, by clarifying Eleanor's attitude toward Rosamund, toward Henry, and ultimately toward political power—all reflect, finally, on Becket. The subplot is not intended to relieve "the often rather arid debate between church and crown"[11] but to expose and exemplify the human issues involved in that debate. Unless we understand that, the conflict loses its complexity, and Becket's victory is robbed of its real force and meaning. Even Eleanor's role, in connecting the supremacy of the crown with the basest of human motives, is essential to Tennyson's conception of Becket's character. That she is a type is unimportant if Tennyson succeeds in making Becket complex.

We should hardly expect *Becket* to meet the standards of late nineteenth-century dramatic realism. It may be that Tennyson wrote poetic drama because, like the other authors in this anthology, he could conceive of nothing else. To reproach him with standards he had no intention of meeting is inappropriate. Surely it is patronizing on our part to insist that Tennyson write *Murder in the Cathedral.* But, even measured against Eliot's achievement, *Becket* is still impressive, still effective.

G. C. S.

---

10. Edith Batho and Bonamy Dobrée, *The Victorians and After* (New York, 1938), p. 122.
11. Buckley, p. 206.

Becket

To the Lord Chancellor,

The Right Honorable Earl of Selborne.

My dear Selborne, — To you, the honored Chancellor of our own day, I dedicate this dramatic memorial of your great predecessor ; — which, altho' not intended in its present form to meet the exigencies of our modern theatre, has nevertheless — for so you have assured me — won your approbation.   Ever yours,

Tennyson.

DRAMATIS PERSONÆ

Henry II. (*son of the Earl of Anjou*).
Thomas Becket, *Chancellor of England, afterwards Archbishop of Canterbury.*
Gilbert Foliot, *Bishop of London.*
Roger, *Archbishop of York.*
Bishop of Hereford.
Hilary, *Bishop of Chichester.*
Jocelyn, *Bishop of Salisbury.*
John of Salisbury ⎱
Herbert of Bosham ⎰ *friends of Becket.*
Walter Map, *reputed author of 'Golias,' Latin poems against the priesthood.*
King Louis of France.
Geoffrey, *son of Rosamund and Henry.*
Grim, *a monk of Cambridge.*
Sir Reginald Fitzurse,
Sir Richard de Brito,
Sir William de Tracy,
Sir Hugh de Morville,
     (*the four knights of the king's household, enemies of Becket.*)
De Broc of Saltwood Castle.
Lord Leicester.
Philip de Eleemosyna.

Two Knight Templars.
John of Oxford (*called the Swearer*).
Eleanor of Aquitaine, *Queen of England (divorced from Louis of France).*
Rosamund de Clifford.
Margery.

     Knights, Monks, Beggars, etc.

PROLOGUE

A Castle in Normandy. Interior of the
     Hall. Roofs of a City seen thro'
     Windows

Henry *and* Becket *at chess.*

Henry. So then our good Archbishop
     Theobald
Lies dying.
     Becket. I am grieved to know as much.
Henry. But we must have a mightier
     man than he
For his successor.
     Becket.   Have you thought of one ?
Henry. A cleric lately poison'd his own
     mother,
And being brought before the courts of
     the Church,
They but degraded him. I hope they
     whipt him.
I would have hang'd him.
     Becket.   It is your move.
Henry.   Well — there. [*Moves.*
The Church in the pell-mell of Stephen's
     time
Hath climb'd the throne and almost
     clutch'd the crown ;   10
But by the royal customs of our realm
The Church should hold her baronies of
     me,
Like other lords amenable to law.

I 'll have them written down and made the law.

Becket. My liege, I move my bishop.

Henry. And if I live,
No man without my leave shall excommunicate
My tenants or my household.

Becket. Look to your king.

Henry. No man without my leave shall cross the seas
To set the Pope against me — I pray your pardon. 19

Becket. Well — will you move ?

Henry. There. [*Moves.*

Becket. Check — you move so wildly.

Henry. There then ! [*Moves.*

Becket. Why — there then, for you see my bishop
Hath brought your king to a standstill. You are beaten.

Henry (*kicks over the board*). Why, there then — down go bishop and king together.
I loathe being beaten ; had I fixt my fancy
Upon the game I should have beaten thee,
But that was vagabond.

Becket. Where, my liege ? With Phryne,
Or Lais, or thy Rosamund, or another ?

Henry. My Rosamund is no Lais, Thomas Becket ;
And yet she plagues me too — no fault in her —
But that I fear the Queen would have her life. 30

Becket. Put her away, put her away, my liege !
Put her away into a nunnery !
Safe enough there from her to whom thou art bound
By Holy Church. And wherefore should she seek
The life of Rosamund de Clifford more
Than that of other paramours of thine ?

Henry. How dost thou know I am not wedded to her ?

Becket. How should I know ?

Henry. That is my secret, Thomas.

Becket. State secrets should be patent to the statesman
Who serves and loves his king, and whom the king 40
Loves not as statesman, but true lover and friend.

Henry. Come, come, thou art but deacon, not yet bishop,
No, nor archbishop, nor my confessor yet.
I would to God thou wert, for I should find
An easy father confessor in thee.

Becket. Saint Denis, that thou shouldst not. I should beat
Thy kingship as my bishop hath beaten it.

Henry. Hell take thy bishop then, and my kingship too !
Come, come, I love thee and I know thee, I know thee,
A doter on white pheasant-flesh at feasts, 50
A sauce-deviser for thy days of fish,
A dish-designer, and most amorous
Of good old red sound liberal Gascon wine.
Will not thy body rebel, man, if thou flatter it ?

Becket. That palate is insane which cannot tell
A good dish from a bad, new wine from old.

Henry. Well, who loves wine loves woman.

Becket. So I do.
Men are God's trees, and women are God's flowers ;
And when the Gascon wine mounts to my head,
The trees are all the statelier, and the flowers 60
Are all the fairer.

Henry. And thy thoughts, thy fancies ?

Becket. Good dogs, my liege, well train'd, and easily call'd
Off from the game.

Henry. Save for some once or twice,
When they ran down the game and worried it.

Becket. No, my liege, no ! — not once — in God's name, no !

Henry. Nay, then, I take thee at thy word — believe thee
The veriest Galahad of old Arthur's hall.
And so this Rosamund, my true heart-wife,
Not Eleanor — she whom I love indeed
As a woman should be loved — Why dost thou smile 70
So dolorously ?

Becket. My good liege, if a man
Wastes himself among women, how should he love
A woman as a woman should be loved ?

Henry. How shouldst thou know that never hast loved one ?
Come, I would give her to thy care in England
When I am out in Normandy or Anjou.

Becket. My lord, I am your subject, not your —

Henry. Pander.
God's eyes ! I know all that — not my purveyor

Of pleasures, but to save a life — her life ;
Ay, and the soul of Eleanor from hell-fire.
I have built a secret bower in England,
    Thomas,   81
A nest in a bush.
    Becket.   And where, my liege ?
    Henry (whispers).   Thine ear.
    Becket. That 's lone enough.
    Henry (laying paper on table). This
    chart here mark'd 'Her Bower,'
Take, keep it, friend. See, first, a circling
    wood,
A hundred pathways running everyway,
And then a brook, a bridge ; and after that
This labyrinthine brickwork maze in maze,
And then another wood, and in the midst
A garden and my Rosamund. Look, this
    line —
The rest you see is color'd green — but
    this   90
Draws thro' the chart to her.
    Becket.   This blood-red line ?
    Henry. Ay ! blood, perchance, except
    thou see to her.
    Becket. And where is she ? There in her
    English nest ?
    Henry. Would God she were ! — no, here
    within the city.
We take her from her secret bower in
    Anjou
And pass her to her secret bower in
    England.
She is ignorant of all but that I love her.
    Becket. My liege, I pray thee let me
    hence ; a widow
And orphan child, whom one of thy wild
    barons —
    Henry. Ay, ay, but swear to see to her
    in England.   100
    Becket. Well, well, I swear, but not to
    please myself.
    Henry. Whatever come between us ?
    Becket.   What should come
Between us, Henry ?
    Henry.   Nay — I know not, Thomas.
    Becket. What need then ? Well — what-
    ever come between us.   [*Going.*
    Henry. A moment ! thou didst help me
    to my throne
In Theobald's time, and after by thy
    wisdom
Hast kept it firm from shaking ; but now I,
For my realm's sake, myself must be the
    wizard
To raise that tempest which will set it
    trembling
Only to base it deeper. I, true son   110
Of Holy Church — no croucher to the
    Gregories

That tread the kings their children under-
    heel —
Must curb her ; and the Holy Father,
    while
This Barbarossa butts him from his chair,
Will need my help — be facile to my hands.
Now is my time. Yet — lest there should
    be flashes
And fulminations from the side of Rome,
An interdict on England — I will have
My young son Henry crown'd the King of
    England,
That so the Papal bolt may pass by
    England,   120
As seeming his, not mine, and fall abroad.
I'll have it done — and now.
    Becket.   Surely too young
Even for this shadow of a crown ; and tho'
I love him heartily, I can spy already
A strain of hard and headstrong in him.
    Say,
The Queen should play his kingship
    against thine !
    Henry. I will not think so, Thomas.
    Who shall crown him ?
Canterbury is dying.
    Becket.   The next Canterbury.
    Henry. And who shall he be, my friend
    Thomas ? Who ?   129
    Becket. Name him ; the Holy Father
    will confirm him.
    Henry (lays his hand on Becket's *shoul-
    der).* Here !
    Becket. Mock me not. I am not even
    a monk.
Thy jest — no more. Why — look — is this
    a sleeve
For an archbishop ?
    Henry.   But the arm within
Is Becket's, who hath beaten down my
    foes.
    Becket. A soldier's, not a spiritual arm.
    Henry. I lack a spiritual soldier,
    Thomas —
A man of this world and the next to boot.
    Becket. There 's Gilbert Foliot.
    Henry.   He ! too thin, too thin.
Thou art the man to fill out the Church
    robe ;
Your Foliot fasts and fawns too much for
    me.   140
    Becket. Roger of York.
    Henry.   Roger is Roger of York ;
King, Church, and State to him but foils
    wherein
To set that precious jewel, Roger of York.
No.
    Becket. Henry of Winchester ?
    Henry.   Him who crown'd Stephen —

King Stephen's brother! No; too royal
for me.
And I'll have no more Anselms.

Becket. Sire, the business
Of thy whole kingdom waits me; let me
go.

Henry. Answer me first.

Becket. Then for thy barren jest
Take thou mine answer in bare common-
place —
Nolo episcopari.

Henry. Ay, but *Nolo
Archiepiscopari*, my good friend, 151
Is quite another matter.

Becket. A more awful one.
Make *me* archbishop! Why, my liege, I
know
Some three or four poor priests a thousand times
Fitter for this grand function. *Me* archbishop!
God's favor and king's favor might so
clash
That thou and I — That were a jest indeed!

Henry. Thou angerest me, man; I do
not jest.

Enter ELEANOR *and* SIR REGINALD
FITZURSE.

ELEANOR *(singing)*.

Over! the sweet summer closes,
The reign of the roses is done — 160

Henry (to Becket, *who is going).* Thou
shalt not go. I have not ended with
thee.

Eleanor (seeing chart on table). This
chart with the red line! her bower! whose
bower?

Henry. The chart is not mine, but
Becket's; take it, Thomas.

Eleanor. Becket! O, — ay — and these
chessmen on the floor — the king's crown
broken! Becket hath beaten thee again —
and thou hast kicked down the board. I
know thee of old. 171

Henry. True enough, my mind was set
upon other matters.

Eleanor. What matters? State matters?
love matters?

Henry. My love for thee, and thine for
me.

ELEANOR.

Over! the sweet summer closes,

The reign of the roses is done;
Over and gone with the roses, 180
And over and gone with the sun.

Here; but our sun in Aquitaine lasts
longer. I would I were in Aquitaine again
— your North chills me.

Over! the sweet summer closes,
And never a flower at the close;
Over and gone with the roses,
And winter again and the snows.

That was not the way I ended it first —
but unsymmetrically, preposterously, illogi-
cally, out of passion, without art — like a
song of the people. Will you have it? The
last Parthian shaft of a forlorn Cupid at
the King's left breast, and all left-handed-
ness and under-handedness.

And never a flower at the close;
Over and gone with the roses,
Not over and gone with the rose. 198

True, one rose will outblossom the rest,
one rose in a bower. I speak after my
fancies, for I am a Troubadour, you know,
and won the violet at Toulouse; but my
voice is harsh here, not in tune, a nightingale out of season; for marriage, rose or
no rose, has killed the golden violet.

Becket. Madam, you do ill to scorn
wedded love. 207

Eleanor. So I do. Louis of France
loved me, and I dreamed that I loved
Louis of France: and I loved Henry of
England, and Henry of England dreamed
that he loved me; but the marriage-gar-
land withers even with the putting on, the
bright link rusts with the breath of the
first after-marriage kiss, the harvest moon
is the ripening of the harvest, and the
honey-moon is the gall of Love; he dies of
his honey-moon. I could pity this poor
world myself that it is no better ordered.

Henry. Dead is he, my Queen? What,
altogether? Let me swear nay to that by
this cross on thy neck. God's eyes! what
a lovely cross! what jewels! 228

Eleanor. Doth it please you? Take it
and wear it on that hard heart of yours —
there. [*Gives it to him.*

Henry (puts it on). On this left breast
before so hard a heart,
To hide the scar left by thy Parthian dart.

Eleanor. Has my simple song set you
jingling? Nay, if I took and translated
that hard heart into our Provençal facili-

ties, I could so play about it with the
rhyme —   233

Henry. That the heart were lost in the
rhyme, and the matter in the metre. May
we not pray you, madam, to spare us the
hardness of your facility?

Eleanor. The wells of Castaly are not
wasted upon the desert. We did but jest.

Henry. There's no jest on the brows of
Herbert there. What is it, Herbert?   241

Enter HERBERT OF BOSHAM.

Herbert. My liege, the good archbishop
    is no more.

Henry. Peace to his soul!

Herbert. I left him with peace on his
face, — that sweet other-world smile, which
will be reflected in the spiritual body
among the angels. But he longed much to
see your Grace and the Chancellor ere he
past, and his last words were a commenda-
tion of Thomas Becket to your Grace as
his successor in the archbishopric.   251

Henry. Ha, Becket! thou rememberest
    our talk!

Becket. My heart is full of tears — I have
    no answer.

Henry. Well, well, old men must die, or
the world would grow mouldy, would only
breed the past again. Come to me to-morrow. Thou hast but to hold out thy hand.
Meanwhile the revenues are mine. A-hawking, a-hawking! If I sit, I grow fat.
            [*Leaps over the table, and exit.*

Becket. He did prefer me to the chancel-
    lorship,   260
Believing I should ever aid the Church —
But have I done it? He commends me now
From out his grave to this archbishopric.

Herbert. A dead man's dying wish
    should be of weight.

Becket. His should. Come with me. Let
    me learn at full
The manner of his death, and all he said.
            [*Exeunt* Herbert *and* Becket.

Eleanor. Fitzurse, that chart with the
red line — thou sawest it — her bower.

Fitzurse. Rosamund's?

Eleanor. Ay — there lies the secret of
her whereabouts, and the King gave it to
his Chancellor.   272

Fitzurse. To this son of a London merchant — how your Grace must hate him!

Eleanor. Hate him? as brave a soldier
as Henry and a goodlier man: but thou
— dost thou love this Chancellor, that
thou hast sworn a voluntary allegiance to
him?

Fitzurse. Not for my love toward him,
but because he had the love of the King.
How should a baron love a beggar on
horseback, with the retinue of three kings
behind him, out-royalling royalty? Besides,
he holp the King to break down our
castles, for the which I hate him.

Eleanor. For the which I honor him.
Statesman, not Churchman, he. A great
and sound policy that; I could embrace
him for it: you could not see the King for
the kinglings.   291

Fitzurse. Ay, but he speaks to a noble
as tho' he were a churl, and to a churl as
if he were a noble.

Eleanor. Pride of the plebeian!

Fitzurse. And this plebeian like to be
Archbishop!

Eleanor. True, and I have an inherited
loathing of these black sheep of the Papacy. Archbishop? I can see further into
a man than our hot-headed Henry, and if
there ever come feud between Church and
Crown, and I do not then charm this
secret out of our loyal Thomas, I am not
Eleanor.   305

Fitzurse. Last night I followed a woman
in the city here. Her face was veiled, but
the back methought was Rosamund — his
paramour, thy rival. I can feel for thee.

Eleanor. Thou feel for me! — paramour
— rival! King Louis had no paramours,
and I loved him none the more. Henry
had many, and I loved him none the less
— now neither more nor less — not at all;
the cup's empty. I would she were but his
paramour, for men tire of their fancies;
but I fear this one fancy hath taken root,
and borne blossom too, and she, whom the
King loves indeed, is a power in the State.
Rival! — ay, and when the King passes,
there may come a crash and embroilment
as in Stephen's time; and her children —
canst thou not — that secret matter which
would heat the King against thee (*whispers him and he starts*). Nay, that is safe
with me as with thyself; but canst thou not
— thou art drowned in debt — thou shalt
have our love, our silence, and our gold —
canst thou not — if thou light upon her —
free me from her?   330

Fitzurse. Well, Madam, I have loved
her in my time.

Eleanor. No, my bear, thou hast not.
My Courts of Love would have held thee
guiltless of love — the fine attractions and
repulses, the delicacies, the subtleties.

Fitzurse. Madam, I loved according to
the main purpose the intent of nature.

Eleanor. I warrant thee ! thou wouldst hug thy Cupid till his ribs cracked — enough of this. Follow me this Rosamund day and night, whithersoever she goes ; track her, if thou canst, even into the King's lodging, that I may (*clenches her fist*) — may at least have my cry against him and her, — and thou in thy way shouldst be jealous of the King, for thou in thy way didst once, what shall I call it, affect her thine own self.   349

Fitzurse. Ay, but the young colt winced and whinnied and flung up her heels ; and then the King came honeying about her, and this Becket, her father's friend, like enough stayed us from her.

Eleanor. Us !

Fitzurse. Yea, by the Blessed Virgin ! There were more than I buzzing round the blossom — De Tracy — even that flint De Brito.

Eleanor. Carry her off among you ; run in upon her and devour her, one and all of you ; make her as hateful to herself and to the King as she is to me.   363

Fitzurse. I and all would be glad to wreak our spite on the rose-faced minion of the King, and bring her to the level of the dust, so that the King —

Eleanor. Let her eat it like the serpent, and be driven out of her paradise.

ACT I

SCENE I. — BECKET'S HOUSE IN LONDON

Chamber barely furnished. BECKET *unrobing.* HERBERT OF BOSHAM *and* SERVANT.

Servant. Shall I not help your lordship to your rest ?

Becket. Friend, am I so much better than thyself
That thou shouldst help me ? Thou art wearied out
With this day's work ; get thee to thine own bed.
Leave me with Herbert, friend.

          [*Exit* Servant.

Help me off, Herbert, with this — and this.

Herbert. Was not the people's blessing as we passed
Heart-comfort and a balsam to thy blood ?

Becket. The people know their Church a tower of strength,
A bulwark against Throne and Baronage.
Too heavy for me, this ; off with it, Herbert !   10

Herbert. Is it so much heavier than thy Chancellor's robe ?

Becket. No ; but the Chancellor's and the Archbishop's
Together more than mortal man can bear.

Herbert. Not heavier than thine armor at Toulouse ?

Becket. O Herbert, Herbert, in my chancellorship
I more than once have gone against the Church.

Herbert. To please the King ?

Becket.   Ay, and the King of kings,
Or justice ; for it seem'd to me but just
The Church should pay her scutage like the lords.   20
But hast thou heard this cry of Gilbert Foliot
That I am not the man to be your primate,
For Henry could not work a miracle —
Make an archbishop of a soldier ?

Herbert.   Ay,
For Gilbert Foliot held himself the man.

Becket. Am I the man ? My mother, ere she bore me,
Dream'd that twelve stars fell glittering out of heaven
Into her bosom.

Herbert.   Ay, the fire, the light,
The spirit of the twelve Apostles enter'd
Into thy making.

Becket.   And when I was a child,
The Virgin, in a vision of my sleep,   31
Gave me the golden keys of Paradise. Dream,
Or prophecy, that ?

Herbert. Well, dream and prophecy both.

Becket. And when I was of Theobald's household, once —
The good old man would sometimes have his jest —
He took his mitre off, and set it on me,
And said, 'My young archbishop — thou wouldst make
A stately archbishop !' Jest or prophecy there ?

Herbert. Both, Thomas, both.

Becket.   Am I the man ? That rang
Within my head last night, and when I slept   40
Methought I stood in Canterbury Minster,
And spake to the Lord God, and said, 'O Lord,
I have been a lover of wines, and delicate meats,
And secular splendors, and a favorer
Of players, and a courtier, and a feeder

Of dogs and hawks, and apes, and lions,
and lynxes.
Am *I* the man?' And the Lord answer'd
me,
'Thou art the man, and all the more the
man.'
And then I asked again, 'O Lord my God,
Henry the King hath been my friend, my
brother,   50
And mine uplifter in this world, and
chosen me
For this thy great archbishopric, believing
That I should go against the Church with
him,
And I shall go against him with the
Church,
And I have said no word of this to him.
Am *I* the man?' And the Lord answer'd
me,
'Thou art the man, and all the more the
man.'
And thereupon, methought, He drew
toward me,
And smote me down upon the minster
floor.   59
I fell.
    Herbert. God make not thee, but thy
foes, fall!
    Becket. I fell. Why fall? Why did He
smite me? What?
Shall I fall off — to please the King once
more?
Not fight — tho' somehow traitor to the
King —
My truest and mine utmost for the
Church?
    Herbert. Thou canst not fall that way.
Let traitor be;
For how have fought thine utmost for the
Church,
Save from the throne of thine archbishop-
ric?
And how been made archbishop hadst
thou told him,
'I mean to fight mine utmost for the
Church,   69
Against the King'?
    Becket.   But dost thou think the King
Forced mine election?
    Herbert.   I do think the King
Was potent in the election, and why not?
Why should not Heaven have so inspired
the King?
Be comforted. Thou art the man — be
thou
A mightier Anselm.
    Becket. I do believe thee, then. I am
the man.

And yet I seem appall'd — on such a sud-
den
At such an eagle-height I stand and see
The rift that runs between me and the
King.
I served our Theobald well when I was
with him;   80
I served King Henry well as Chancellor;
I am his no more, and I must serve the
Church.
This Canterbury is only less than Rome,
And all my doubts I fling from me like
dust,
Winnow and scatter all scruples to the
wind,
And all the puissance of the warrior,
And all the wisdom of the Chancellor,
And all the heap'd experiences of life,
I cast upon the side of Canterbury —
Our holy mother Canterbury, who sits   90
With tatter'd robes. Laics and barons
thro'
The random gifts of careless kings, have
graspt
Her livings, her advowsons, granges,
farms,
And goodly acres — we will make her
whole;
Not one rood lost. And for these Royal
customs,
These ancient Royal customs — they *are*
Royal,
Not of the Church — and let them be
anathema.
And all that speak for them anathema.
    Herbert. Thomas, thou art moved too
much.
    Becket.   O Herbert, here
I gash myself asunder from the King,   100
Tho' leaving each, a wound; mine own,
a grief
To show the scar for ever — his, a hate
Not ever to be heal'd.

Enter ROSAMUND DE CLIFFORD, *flying from*
SIR REGINALD FITZURSE. *Drops her veil.*

    Becket.   Rosamund de Clifford!
    Rosamund. Save me, father, hide me —
they follow me —and I must not be known.
    Becket. Pass in with Herbert there.
        [*Exeunt* Rosamund *and* Herbert *by*
side door.

Enter FITZURSE.

Fitzurse. The archbishop!

Becket. Ay! what wouldst thou, Reginald?

Fitzurse. Why — why, my lord, I follow'd — follow'd one —

Becket. And then what follows? Let me follow thee.

Fitzurse. It much imports me I should know her name. 110

Becket. What her?

Fitzurse. The woman that I follow'd hither.

Becket. Perhaps it may import her all as much

Not to be known.

Fitzurse. And what care I for that?

Come, come, my lord archbishop; I saw that door

Close even now upon the woman.

Becket. Well?

Fitzurse (making for the door). Nay, let me pass, my lord, for I must know.

Becket. Back, man!

Fitzurse. Then tell me who and what she is.

Becket. Art thou so sure thou followedst anything?

Go home, and sleep thy wine off, for thine eyes

Glare stupid-wild with wine.

Fitzurse (making to the door). I must and will.

I care not for thy new archbishopric. 121

Becket. Back, man, I tell thee! What!

Shall I forget my new archbishopric

And smite thee with my crozier on the skull?

'Fore God, I am a mightier man than thou.

Fitzurse. It well befits thy new archbishopric

To take the vagabond woman of the street

Into thine arms!

Becket. O drunken ribaldry!

Out, beast! out, bear!

Fitzurse. I shall remember this.

Becket. Do, and begone!

[*Exit* Fitzurse.

[*Going to the door, sees* De Tracy.

Tracy, what dost thou here?

De Tracy. My lord, I follow'd Reginald Fitzurse. 131

Becket. Follow him out!

De Tracy. I shall remember this

Discourtesy. [*Exit.*

Becket. Do. These be those baron-brutes

That havock'd all the land in Stephen's day.

Rosamund de Clifford!

Re-enter ROSAMUND *and* HERBERT.

Rosamund. Here am I.

Becket. Why here?

We gave thee to the charge of John of Salisbury,

To pass thee to thy secret bower to-morrow.

Wast thou not told to keep thyself from sight?

Rosamund. Poor bird of passage! so I was; but, father,

They say that you are wise in winged things, 140

And know the ways of Nature. Bar the bird

From following the fled summer — a chink — he's out,

Gone! And there stole into the city a breath

Full of the meadows, and it minded me

Of the sweet woods of Clifford, and the walks

Where I could move at pleasure, and I thought

'Lo! I must out or die.'

Becket. Or out *and* die.

And what hast thou to do with this Fitzurse?

Rosamund. Nothing. He sued my hand. I shook at him.

He found me once alone. Nay — nay — I cannot 150

Tell you. My father drove him and his friends,

De Tracy and De Brito, from our castle.

I was but fourteen and an April then.

I heard him swear revenge.

Becket. Why will you court it

By self-exposure? flutter out at night?

Make it so hard to save a moth from the fire?

Rosamund. I have saved many of 'em. You catch 'em, so,

Softly, and fling them out to the free air.

They burn themselves *within*-door.

Becket. Our good John

Must speed you to your bower at once. The child 160

Is there already.

Rosamund. Yes — the child — the child —

O, rare, a whole long day of open field!

Becket. Ay, but you go disguised.

Rosamund. O, rare again!

We'll baffle them, I warrant. What shall it be?

I'll go as a nun.

Becket. No.

Rosamund.   What, not good enough
Even to play at nun ?
    Becket.   Dan John with a nun,
That Map and these new railers at the
        Church
May plaister his clean name with scurri-
        lous rhymes !
No !   169
Go like a monk, cowling and clouding up
That fatal star, thy beauty, from the squint
Of lust and glare of malice. Good-night !
        good-night !
    Rosamund. Father, I am so tender to all
        hardness !
Nay, father, first thy blessing.
    Becket.   Wedded ?
    Rosamund.   Father !
    Becket. Well, well ! I ask no more.
        Heaven bless thee ! hence !
    Rosamund. O holy father, when thou
        seest him next,
Commend me to thy friend.
    Becket.   What friend ?
    Rosamund.   The King.
    Becket. Herbert, take out a score of
        armed men
To guard this bird of passage to her cage ;
And watch Fitzurse, and if he follow thee,
Make him thy prisoner. I am Chancellor
        yet.   181
            [*Exeunt* Herbert *and* Rosamund.
Poor soul ! poor soul !
My friend, the King ! — O thou Great Seal
        of England,
Given me by my dear friend, the King of
        England —
We long have wrought together, thou and
        I —
Now must I send thee as a common friend
To tell the King, my friend, I am against
        him.
We are friends no more ; he will say that,
        not I.
The worldly bond between us is dissolved,
Not yet the love. Can I be under him   190
As Chancellor ? as Archbishop over him ?
Go therefore like a friend slighted by one
That hath climb'd up to nobler company.
Not slighted — all but moan'd for. Thou
        must go.
I have not dishonor'd thee — I trust I have
        not —
Not mangled justice. May the hand that
        next
Inherits thee be but as true to thee
As mine hath been ! O, my dear friend,
        the King !
O brother ! — I may come to martyrdom.
I am martyr in myself already. — Herbert !

Herbert (re-entering). My lord, the
        town is quiet, and the moon   201
Divides the whole long street with light
        and shade.
No footfall — no Fitzurse. We have seen
        her home.
    Becket. The hog hath tumbled himself
        into some corner,
Some ditch, to snore away his drunkenness
Into the sober headache, — Nature's moral
Against excess. Let the Great Seal be sent
Back to the King to-morrow.
    Herbert.   Must that be ?
The King may rend the bearer limb from
        limb.
Think on it again.
    Becket.   Against the moral excess
No physical ache, but failure it may be [211]
Of all we aim'd at. John of Salisbury
Hath often laid a cold hand on my heats.
And Herbert hath rebuked me even now.
I will be wise and wary, not the soldier
As Foliot swears it. — John, and out of
        breath !

Enter JOHN OF SALISBURY.

John of Salisbury. Thomas, thou wast
        not happy taking charge
Of this wild Rosamund to please the King,
Nor am I happy having charge of her —
The included Danaë has escaped again
Her tower and her Acrisius — where to
        seek ?   221
I have been about the city.
    Becket.   Thou wilt find her
Back in her lodging. Go with her — at
        once —
To-night — my men will guard you to the
        gates.
Be sweet to her, she has many enemies.
Send the Great Seal by daybreak. Both,
        good-night !

SCENE II

STREET IN NORTHAMPTON LEADING TO
            THE CASTLE

ELEANOR'S RETAINERS *and* BECKET'S RE-
    TAINERS *fighting. Enter* ELEANOR *and*
    BECKET *from opposite streets.*

Eleanor. Peace, fools !
Becket. Peace, friends ! what idle brawl
        is this ?
Retainer of Becket. They said — her
        Grace's people — thou wast found —

Liars ! I shame to quote 'em — caught, my
  lord,
With a wanton in thy lodging — Hell re-
  quite 'em !
  Retainer of Eleanor. My liege, the Lord
    Fitzurse reported this
In passing to the Castle even now.
  Retainer of Becket. And then they
    mock'd us and we fell upon 'em,
For we would live and die for thee, my
  lord,
However kings and queens may frown on
  thee.   9
  Becket to his Retainers. Go, go — no
    more of this !
  Eleanor to her Retainers. Away ! —
    (*Exeunt* Retainers.)   Fitzurse —
  Becket. Nay, let him be.
  Eleanor. No, no, my lord archbishop,
'T is known you are midwinter to all
  women,
But often in your chancellorship you
  served
The follies of the King.
  Becket.   No, not these follies !
  Eleanor. My lord, Fitzurse beheld her
    in your lodging.
  Becket. Whom ?
  Eleanor. Well — you know — the minion,
    Rosamund.
  Becket. He had good eyes !
  Eleanor.   Then hidden in the street
He watch'd her pass with John of Salis-
  bury,
And heard her cry, 'Where is this bower
  of mine ?'   19
  Becket. Good ears too !
  Eleanor.   You are going to the Castle,
Will you subscribe the customs ?
  Becket.   I leave that,
Knowing how much you reverence Holy
  Church,
My liege, to your conjecture.
  Eleanor.   I and mine —
And many a baron holds along with me —
Are not so much at feud with Holy Church
But we might take your side against the
  customs —
So that you grant me one slight favor.
  Becket.   What ?
  Eleanor. A sight of that same chart
    which Henry gave you
With the red line — 'her bower.'
  Becket.   And to what end ?
  Eleanor. That Church must scorn her-
    self whose fearful priest   30
Sits winking at the license of a king,
Altho' we grant when kings are dangerous
The Church must play into the hands of
  kings ;
Look ! I would move this wanton from
  his sight
And take the Church's danger on myself.
  Becket. For which she should be duly
    grateful.
  Eleanor.   True !
Tho' she that binds the bond, herself
  should see
That kings are faithful to their marriage
  vow.
  Becket. Ay, madam, and queens also.
  Eleanor.   And queens also !
What is your drift ?
  Becket.   My drift is to the Castle,
Where I shall meet the barons and my
  King.   [*Exit.*

DE BROC, DE TRACY, DE BRITO, DE
  MORVILLE (*passing*).

  Eleanor. To the Castle ?
  De Broc.   Ay !
  Eleanor. Stir up the King, the lords !
Set all on fire against him !
  De Brito.   Ay, good madam !
                                      [*Exeunt.*
  Eleanor. Fool ! I will make thee hateful
    to thy King.
Churl ! I will have thee frighted into
  France,
And I shall live to trample on thy grave.

SCENE III
THE HALL IN NORTHAMPTON CASTLE

*On one side of the stage the doors of an
inner Council-chamber, half-open. At the
bottom, the great doors of the Hall.*
ROGER ARCHBISHOP OF YORK, FOLIOT
BISHOP OF LONDON, HILARY OF CHI-
CHESTER, BISHOP OF HEREFORD, RICHARD
DE HASTINGS (*Grand Prior of Tem-
plars*), PHILIP DE ELEEMOSYNA (*the
Pope's Almoner*), *and others.* DE BROC,
FITZURSE, DE BRITO, DE MORVILLE, DE
TRACY, *and other* BARONS *assembled —
a table before them.* JOHN OF OXFORD,
President of the Council.

Enter BECKET *and* HERBERT OF BOSHAM.

  Becket. Where is the King ?
  Roger of York. Gone hawking on the
    Nene,
His heart so gall'd with thine ingratitude,
He will not see thy face till thou hast
  sign'd

These ancient laws and customs of the realm.

Thy sending back the Great Seal madden'd him;

He all but pluck'd the bearer's eyes away.

Take heed lest he destroy thee utterly.

Becket. Then shalt thou step into my place and sign.

Roger of York. Didst thou not promise Henry to obey

These ancient laws and customs of the realm ?   10

Becket. Saving the honor of my order — ay.

Customs, traditions, — clouds that come and go ;

The customs of the Church are Peter's rock.

Roger of York. Saving thine order ! But King Henry sware

That, saving his King's kingship, he would grant thee

The crown itself. Saving thine order, Thomas,

Is black and white at once, and comes to nought.

O bolster'd up with stubbornness and pride,

Wilt thou destroy the Church in fighting for it,

And bring us all to shame ?

Becket.   Roger of York,

When I and thou were youths in Theobald's house,   21

Twice did thy malice and thy calumnies

Exile me from the face of Theobald.

Now I am Canterbury, and thou art York.

Roger of York. And is not York the peer of Canterbury ?

Did not Great Gregory bid Saint Austin here

Found two archbishoprics, London and York ?

Becket. What came of that ? The first archbishop fled,

And York lay barren for a hundred years.

Why, by this rule, Foliot may claim the pall   30

For London too.

Foliot.   And with good reason too,

For London had a temple and a priest

When Canterbury hardly bore a name.

Becket. The pagan temple of a pagan Rome !

The heathen priesthood of a heathen creed !

Thou goest beyond thyself in petulancy !

Who made thee London ? Who, but Can-

terbury ?

John of Oxford. Peace, peace, my lords ! these customs are no longer

As Canterbury calls them, wandering clouds,

But by the King's command are written down,   40

And by the King's command I, John of Oxford,

The President of this Council, read them.

Becket.   Read !

John of Oxford (reads). 'All causes of advowsons and presentations, whether between laymen or clerics, shall be tried in the King's court.'

Becket. But that I cannot sign ; for that would drag

The cleric before the civil judgment-seat,

And on a matter wholly spiritual.   49

John of Oxford. 'If any cleric be accused of felony, the Church shall not protect him ; but he shall answer to the summons of the King's court to be tried therein.'

Becket. And that I cannot sign.

Is not the Church the visible Lord on earth ?

Shall hands that do create the Lord be bound

Behind the back like laymen-criminals ?

The Lord be judged again by Pilate ? No !   59

John of Oxford. 'When a bishopric falls vacant, the King, till another be appointed, shall receive the revenues thereof.'

Becket. And that I cannot sign. Is the King's treasury

A fit place for the moneys of the Church,

That be the patrimony of the poor ?

John of Oxford. 'And when the vacancy is to be filled up, the King shall summon the chapter of that church to court, and the election shall be made in the Chapel Royal, with the consent of our lord the King, and by the advice of his Government.   71

Becket. And that I cannot sign ; for that would make

Our island-Church a schism from Christendom,

And weight down all free choice beneath the throne.

Foliot. And was thine own election so canonical,

Good father ?

Becket. If it were not, Gilbert Foliot,

I mean to cross the sea to France, and lay

My crozier in the Holy Father's hands,

And bid him re-create me, Gilbert Foliot.

Foliot. Nay ; by another of these customs
   thou   80
Wilt not be suffer'd so to cross the seas
Without the license of our lord the King.

Becket. That, too, I cannot sign.

DE BROC, DE BRITO, DE TRACY, FITZURSE,
   DE MORVILLE, *start up — a clash of*
   swords.
                 Sign and obey !

Becket. My lords, is this a combat or a
   council ?
Are ye my masters, or my lord the King ?
Ye make this clashing for no love o' the
   customs
Or constitutions, or whate'er ye call them,
But that there be among you those that
   hold
Lands reft from Canterbury.

De Broc.   And mean to keep them,
In spite of thee !

Lords (shouting). Sign, and obey the
   crown !   90

Becket. The crown ? Shall I do less for
   Canterbury
Than Henry for the crown ? King Ste-
   phen gave
Many of the crown lands to those that
   helpt him ;
So did Matilda, the King's mother. Mark,
When Henry came into his own again,
Then he took back not only Stephen's
   gifts,
But his own mother's, lest the crown
   should be
Shorn of ancestral splendor. This did
   Henry.
Shall I do less for mine own Canterbury ?
And thou, De Broc, that holdest Saltwood
   Castle —   100

De Broc. And mean to hold it, or —

Becket.   To have my life.

De Broc. The King is quick to anger ;
   if thou anger him,
We wait but the King's word to strike thee
   dead.

Becket. Strike, and I die the death of
   martyrdom ;
Strike, and ye set these customs by my
   death
Ringing their own death-knell thro' all the
   realm.

Herbert. And I can tell you, lords, ye
   are all as like
To lodge a fear in Thomas Becket's heart
As find a hare's form in a lion's cave.

John of Oxford. Ay, sheathe your swords,
   ye will displease the King.   110

De Broc. Why, down then thou ! but an
   he come to Saltwood,
By God's death, thou shalt stick him like
   a calf !   [*Sheathing his sword.*

Hilary. O my good lord, I do entreat
   thee — sign.
Save the King's honor here before his
   barons.
He hath sworn that thou shouldst sign,
   and now but shuns
The semblance of defeat ; I have heard
   him say
He means no more ; so if thou sign, my
   lord,
That were but as the shadow of an assent.

Becket. 'T would seem too like the substance, if I sign'd.

Philip de Eleemosyna. My lord, thine
   ear ! I have the ear of the Pope.
As thou hast honor for the Pope our mas-
   ter,   121
Have pity on him, sorely prest upon
By the fierce Emperor and his Antipope.
Thou knowest he was forced to fly to
   France ;
He pray'd me to pray thee to pacify
Thy King ; for if thou go against thy King,
Then must he likewise go against thy King,
And then thy King might join the Anti-
   pope,
And that would shake the Papacy as it
   stands.
Besides, thy King swore to our cardinals
He meant no harm nor damage to the
   Church.   131
Smoothe thou his pride — thy signing is
   but form ;
Nay, and should harm come of it, it is the
   Pope
Will be to blame — not thou. Over and
   over
He told me thou shouldst pacify the King,
Lest there be battle between Heaven and
   Earth,
And Earth should get the better — for the
   time.
Cannot the Pope absolve thee if thou
   sign ?

Becket. Have I the orders of the Holy
   Father ?

Philip de Eleemosyna. Orders, my lord
   — why, no ; for what am I ?   140
The secret whisper of the Holy Father.
Thou, that hast been a statesman, couldst
   thou always
Blurt thy free mind to the air ?

Becket. If Rome be feeble, then should
   I be firm.

Philip. Take it not that way — balk not the Pope's will.

When he hath shaken off the Emperor,
He heads the Church against the King
    with thee.
    Richard de Hastings (kneeling). Becket,
        I am the oldest of the Templars;
I knew thy father; he would be mine age
Had he lived now; think of me as thy father!   150
Behold thy father kneeling to thee, Becket.
Submit; I promise thee on my salvation
That thou wilt hear no more o' the customs.
    Becket   What!
Hath Henry told thee? hast thou talk'd
    with him?
    Another Templar (kneeling). Father, I
        am the youngest of the Templars,
Look on me as I were thy bodily son,
For, like a son, I lift my hands to thee.
    Philip. Wilt thou hold out for ever,
        Thomas Becket?
Dost thou not hear?
    Becket (signs). Why — there   then —
        there — I sign,
And swear to obey the customs.
    Foliot.   Is it thy will,
My lord archbishop, that we too should
    sign?   161
    Becket. O, ay, by that canonical obedience
Thou still hast owed thy father, Gilbert
    Foliot.
    Foliot. Loyally and with good faith, my
        lord archbishop?
    Becket. O, ay, with all that loyalty and
        good faith
Thou still hast shown thy primate, Gilbert
    Foliot.
        [Becket *draws apart with* Herbert.
Herbert, Herbert, have I betray'd the
    Church?
I'll have the paper back — blot out my
    name.
    Herbert. Too late, my lord : you see they
        are signing there.
    Becket. False to myself — it is the will
        of God   170
To break me, prove me nothing of myself!
This almoner hath tasted Henry's gold.
The cardinals have finger'd Henry's gold.
And Rome is venal even to rottenness.
I see it, I see it.
I am no soldier, as he said — at least
No leader. Herbert, till I hear from the
    Pope
I will suspend myself from all my functions.

If fast and prayer, the lacerating scourge —
    Foliot (from the table). My lord archbishop, thou hast yet to seal.   180
    Becket. First, Foliot, let me see what I
        have sign'd.   [*Goes to the table.*
What, this! and this! — what! new and
    old together!
Seal? If a seraph shouted from the sun,
And bade me seal against the rights of the
    Church,
I would anathematize him. I will not seal.
        [*Exit with* Herbert.

        Enter KING HENRY.

    Henry. Where's Thomas? hath he
        signed? show me the papers!
Sign'd and not seal'd! How's that?
    John of Oxford. He would not seal.
And when he sign'd, his face was stormyred —
Shame, wrath, I know not what. He sat
    down there
And dropt it in his hands, and then a paleness,   190
Like the wan twilight after sunset, crept
Up even to the tonsure, and he groan'd,
'False to myself! It is the will of God!'
    Henry. God's will be what it will, the
        man shall seal,
Or I will seal his doom. My burgher's
    son —
Nay, if I cannot break him as the prelate,
I'll crush him as the subject. Send for
    him back.   [*Sits on his throne.*
Barons and bishops of our realm of England,
After the nineteen winters of King Stephen —
A reign which was no reign, when none
    could sit   200
By his own hearth in peace; when murder
    common
As nature's death, like Egypt's plague, had
    fill'd
All things with blood; when every doorway blush'd,
Dash'd red with that unhallow'd passover;
When every baron ground his blade in
    blood;
The household dough was kneaded up
    with blood;
The mill-wheel turn'd in blood; the wholesome plow
Lay rusting in the furrow's yellow weeds,
Till famine dwarft the race — I came, your
    King!

Nor dwelt alone, like a soft lord of the
   East,   210
In mine own hall, and sucking thro' fools'
   ears
The flatteries of corruption — went abroad
Thro' all my counties, spied my people's
   ways ;
Yea, heard the churl against the baron —
   yea,
And did him justice ; sat in mine own
   courts
Judging my judges, that had found a King
Who ranged confusions, made the twilight
   day,
And struck a shape from out the vague,
   and law
From madness. And the event — our fal-
   lows till'd,   219
Much corn, repeopled towns, a realm
   again.
So far my course, albeit not glassy-smooth,
Had prosper'd in the main, but suddenly
Jarr'd on this rock. A cleric violated
The daughter of his host, and murder'd
   him.
Bishops — York, London, Chichester, West-
   minster —
Ye haled this tonsured devil into your
   courts ;
But since your canon will not let you take
Life for a life, ye but degraded him
Where I had hang'd him. What doth hard
   murder care   229
For degradation ? and that made me muse,
Being bounden by my coronation oath
To do men justice. Look to it, your own
   selves !
Say that a cleric murder'd an archbishop,
What could ye do ? Degrade, imprison
   him —
Not death for death.
   John of Oxford. But I, my liege, could
     swear,
To death for death.
   Henry.   And, looking thro' my reign,
I found a hundred ghastly murders done
By men, the scum and offal of the Church ;
Then, glancing thro' the story of this
   realm,
I came on certain wholesome usages,   240
Lost in desuetude, of my grandsire's day,
Good royal customs — had them written
   fair
For John of Oxford here to read to you.
   John of Oxford. And I can easily swear
     to these as being
The King's will and God's will and jus-
     tice ; yet
I could but read a part to-day, because —

Fitzurse. Because my lord of Canter-
   bury —
   De Tracy.   Ay,
This lord of Canterbury —
   De Brito.   As is his wont
Too much of late whene'er your royal
   rights   249
Are mooted in our councils —
   Fitzurse.   — made an uproar.
   Henry. And Becket had my bosom on all
   this ;
If ever man by bonds of gratefulness —
I raised him from the puddle of the gut-
   ter,
I made him porcelain from the clay of the
   city —
Thought that I knew him, err'd thro' love
   of him,
Hoped, were he chosen archbishop, Church
   and Crown,
Two sisters gliding in an equal dance,
Two rivers gently flowing side by side —
But no !
The bird that moults sings the same song
   again,   260
The snake that sloughs comes out a snake
   again.
Snake — ay, but he that lookt a fangless
   one
Issues a venomous adder.
For he, when having dofft the Chancellor's
   robe —
Flung the Great Seal of England in my
   face —
Claim'd some of our crown lands for Can-
   terbury —
My comrade, boon companion, my co-rev-
   eller,
The master of his master, the King's
   king. —
God's eyes ! I had meant to make him all
   but king.
Chancellor-Archbishop, he might well have
   sway'd   270
All England under Henry, the young King,
When I was hence. What did the traitor
   say ?
False to himself, but ten-fold false to
   me !
The will of God — why, then it is my
   will —
Is he coming ?
   Messenger (entering). With a crowd of
     worshippers,
And holds his cross before him thro' the
   crowd,
As one that puts himself in sanctuary.
   Henry. His cross !
   Roger of York. His cross ! I'll front

him, cross to cross.
                    [*Exit* Roger of York.
Henry. His cross! it is the traitor that
    imputes
Treachery to his King!   280
It is not safe for me to look upon him.
Away — with me!
    [*Goes in with his* Barons *to the Council-*
    Chamber, the door of which is left
    open.
Enter BECKET, *holding his cross of silver*
    before him. The BISHOPS *come round*
    him.
    Hereford. The King will not abide thee
        with thy cross.
Permit me, my good lord, to bear it for
    thee,
Being thy chaplain.
    Becket.   No; it must protect me.
    Herbert. As once he bore the standard
        of the Angles,
So now he bears the standard
        of the angels.
    Foliot. I am the dean of the province;
        let me bear it.
Make not thy King a traitorous murderer.
    Becket. Did not your barons draw their
        swords against me?   290

Enter ROGER OF YORK, *with his cross, ad-*
    vancing to BECKET.

    Becket. Wherefore dost thou presume to
        bear thy cross,
Against the solemn ordinance from Rome,
Out of thy province?
    Roger of York. Why dost thou presume,
Arm'd with thy cross, to come before the
    King?
If Canterbury bring his cross to court,
Let York bear his to mate with Canter-
    bury.
    Foliot. (seizing hold of Becket's *cross)*,
Nay, nay, my lord, thou must not
    brave the King.
Nay, let me have it. I will have it!
    Becket.   Away!
                    [*Flinging him off.*
    Foliot. He fasts, they say, this mitred
        Hercules!
He fast! is that an arm of fast? My
    lord,   300
Hadst thou not sign'd, I had gone along
    with thee;
But thou the shepherd hast betray'd the
    sheep,
And thou art perjured, and thou wilt not
    seal.

As Chancellor thou wast against the
    Church,
Now as archbishop goest against the King;
For, like a fool, thou know'st no middle
    way.
Ay, ay! but art thou stronger than the
    King?
    Becket. Strong — not in mine own self,
        but Heaven; true   308
To either function, holding it; and thou
Fast, scourge thyself, and mortify thy
    flesh,
Not spirit — thou remainest Gilbert Foliot,
A worldly follower of the worldly strong.
I, bearing this great ensign, make it clear
Under what prince I fight.
    Foliot.   My lord of York,
Let us go in to the Council, where our
    bishops
And our great lords will sit in judgment
    on him.
    Becket. Sons sit in judgment on their
        father! — then
The spire of Holy Church may prick the
    graves —
Her crypt among the stars. Sign? seal?
    I promised
The King to obey these customs, not yet
    written,   320
Saving mine order; true, too, that when
    written
I sign'd them — being a fool, as Foliot
    call'd me.
I hold not by my signing. Get ye hence,
Tell what I say to the King.
    [*Exeunt* Hereford, Foliot, *and other*
    Bishops.
Roger of York. The Church will hate
    thee.   [*Exit.*
    Becket. Serve my best friend and make
        him my worst foe;
Fight for the Church, and set the Church
    against me!
    Herbert. To be honest is to set all
        knaves against thee.
Ah, Thomas, excommunicate them all!
    Hereford (re-entering). I cannot brook
        the turmoil thou hast raised.
I would, my lord Thomas of Canterbury,
Thou wert plain Thomas and not Canter-
    bury,   331
Or that thou wouldst deliver Canterbury
To our King's hands again, and be at
    peace.
    Hilary (re-entering). For hath not thine
        ambition set the Church
This day between the hammer and the an-
    vil —

Fealty to the King, obedience to thyself?

Herbert. What say the bishops?

Hilary. Some have pleaded for him,
But the King rages — most are with the
King;
And some are reeds, that one time sway to
the current,
And to the wind another. But we hold
Thou art forsworn; and no forsworn arch-
bishop   341
Shall helm the Church. We therefore place
ourselves
Under the shield and safeguard of the
Pope,
And cite thee to appear before the Pope,
And answer thine accusers. — Art thou
deaf?

Becket. I hear you.   [*Clash of arms.*

Hilary. Dost thou hear those others?

Becket.   Ay!

Roger of York (re-entering). The King's
'God's eyes!' come now so thick
and fast
We fear that he may reave thee of thine
own.
Come on, come on! it is not fit for us
To see the proud archbishop mutilated.
Say that he blind thee and tear out thy
tongue.   351

Becket. So be it. He begins at top with
me;
They crucified Saint Peter downward.

Roger of York.   Nay,
But for their sake who stagger betwixt
thine
Appeal and Henry's anger, yield.

Becket.   Hence, Satan!
                    [*Exit* Roger of York.

Fitzurse (re-entering). My lord, the
King demands three hundred marks,
Due from his castles of Berkhamstead and
Eye
When thou thereof wast warden.

Becket.   Tell the King
I spent thrice that in fortifying his castles.

De Tracy (re-entering). My lord, the
King demands seven hundred
marks,
Lent at the siege of Toulouse by the
King.   361

Becket. I led seven hundred knights and
fought his wars.

De Brito (re-entering). My lord, the
King demands five hundred marks,
Advanced thee at his instance by the Jews,
For which the King was bound security.

Becket. I thought it was a gift; I
thought it was a gift.

Enter LORD LEICESTER *(followed by*
BARONS *and* BISHOPS).

Leicester. My lord, I come unwillingly.
The King
Demands a strict account of all those reve-
nues
From all the vacant sees and abbacies,
Which came into thy hands when Chan-
cellor.   370

Becket. How much might that amount
to, my lord Leicester?

Leicester. Some thirty — forty thousand
silver marks.

Becket. Are these your customs? O my
good lord Leicester,
The King and I were brothers. All I
had
I lavish'd for the glory of the King;
I shone from him, for him, his glory, his
Reflection. Now the glory of the Church
Hath swallow'd up the glory of the King;
I am his no more, but hers. Grant me one
day   379
To ponder these demands.

Leicester.   Hear first thy sentence!
The King and all his lords —

Becket.   Son, first hear *me*!

Leicester. Nay, nay, canst thou, that
holdest thine estates
In fee and barony of the King, decline
The judgment of the King?

Becket.   The King! I hold
Nothing in fee and barony of the King.
Whatever the Church owns — she holds it
in
Free and perpetual alms, unsubject to
One earthly sceptre.

Leicester. Nay, but hear thy judgment.
The King and all his barons —

Becket.   Judgment! Barons!
Who but the bridegroom dares to judge
the bride,   390
Or he the bridegroom may appoint?
Not he
That is not of the house, but from the
street
Stain'd with the mire thereof.
                        I had been so true
To Henry and mine office that the King
Would throne me in the great archbishop-
ric;
And I, that knew mine own infirmity,
For the King's pleasure rather than God's
cause
Took it upon me — err'd thro' love of him.
Now therefore God from me withdraws
Himself,
And the King too.

What! forty thousand marks!
Why, thou, the King, the Pope, the Saints,
   the world,   401
Know that when made archbishop I was
   freed,
Before the Prince and chief justiciary,
From every bond and debt and obligation
Incurr'd as Chancellor.
                 Hear me, son. As gold
Outvalues dross, light darkness, Abel Cain,
The soul the body, and the Church the
   Throne,
I charge thee, upon pain of mine anath-
   ema,
That thou obey, not me, but God in me,
Rather than Henry. I refuse to stand
By the King's censure, make my cry to the
   Pope,   411
By whom I will be judged; refer myself,
The King, these customs, all the Church,
   to him,
And under his authority — I depart.
                  [*Going.*
   [Leicester *looks at him doubtingly.*
Am I a prisoner?
   Leicester.   By Saint Lazarus, no!
I am confounded by thee. Go in peace.
   De Broc. In peace now — but after.
Take that for earnest.
   [*Flings a bone at him from the
   rushes.*
   De Brito, Fitzurse, De Tracy, and Others
(*flinging wisps of rushes*). Ay, go in peace,
caitiff, caitiff! And that too, perjured
prelate — and that, turncoat shaveling!
There, there, there! traitor, traitor,
   traitor!
   Becket. Mannerless wolves!
            [*Turning and facing them.*
   Herbert.   Enough, my lord, enough!
   Becket. Barons of England and of Nor-
   mandy,
When what ye shake at doth but seem to
   fly,
True test of coward, ye follow with a yell.
But I that threw the mightiest knight of
   France,
Sir Engelram de Trie, —
   Herbert.   Enough, my lord.
   Becket. More than enough. I play the
   fool again.

             Enter HERALD.

   Herald. The King commands you, upon
   pain of death,
That none should wrong or injure your
   archbishop.   430
   Foliot. Deal gently with the young man

Absalom.
   [*Great doors of the Hall at the back
      open, and discover a crowd.
                They shout:*
Blessed is he that cometh in the name of
   the Lord!

             SCENE IV

   REFECTORY OF THE MONASTERY AT
            NORTHAMPTON

   A Banquet on the Tables.

   Enter BECKET. BECKET'S RETAINERS.

   First Retainer. Do thou speak first.
   Second Retainer. Nay, thou! Nay, thou!
Hast not thou drawn the short straw?
   First Retainer. My lord archbishop, wilt
thou permit us —
   Becket. To speak without stammering
and like a free man? Ay.
   First Retainer. My lord, permit us then
to leave thy service.
   Becket. When?   10
   First Retainer. Now.
   Becket. To-night?
   First Retainer. To-night, my lord.
   Becket. And why?
   First Retainer. My lord, we leave thee
not without tears.
   Becket. Tears? Why not stay with me
then?
   First Retainer. My lord, we cannot yield
thee an answer altogether to thy satisfac-
tion.   21
   Becket. I warrant you, or your own
either. Shall I find you one? The King
hath frowned upon me.
   First Retainer. That is not altogether
our answer, my lord.
   Becket. No; yet all but all. Go, go!
Ye have eaten of my dish and drunken of
my cup for a dozen years.
   First Retainer. And so we have. We
mean thee no wrong. Wilt thou not say,
'God bless you,' ere we go?   32
   Becket. God bless you all! God redden
your pale blood! But mine is human-red;
and when ye shall hear it is poured out
upon earth, and see it mounting to heaven,
my 'God bless you,' that seems sweet to
you now, will blast and blind you like a
curse.
   First Retainer. We hope not, my lord.
Our humblest thanks for your blessing.
Farewell!   [*Exeunt* Retainers.

Becket. Farewell, friends! farewell, swallows! I wrong the bird; she leaves only the nest she built, they leave the builder. Why? Am I to be murdered to-night?

[*Knocking at the door.*

Attendant. Here is a missive left at the gate by one from the castle.

Becket. Cornwall's hand or Leicester's; they write marvellously alike. 50

[*Reading.*

'Fly at once to France, to King Louis of France; there be those about our King who would have thy blood.'

Was not my lord of Leicester bidden to our supper?

Attendant. Ay, my lord, and divers other earls and barons. But the hour is past, and our brother, Master Cook, he makes moan that all be a-getting cold. 59

Becket. And I make my moan along with him. Cold after warm, winter after summer, and the golden leaves, these earls and barons, that clung to me, frosted off me by the first cold frown of the King. Cold, but look how the table steams, like a heathen altar; nay, like the altar at Jerusalem. Shall God's good gifts be wasted? None of them here! Call in the poor from the streets, and let them feast. 69

Herbert. That is the parable of our blessed Lord.

Becket. And why should not the parable of our blessed Lord be acted again? Call in the poor! The Church is ever at variance with the kings, and ever at one with the poor. I marked a group of lazars in the marketplace—half-rag, half-sore—beggars, poor rogues (Heaven bless 'em!) who never saw nor dreamed of such a banquet. I will amaze them. Call them in, I say. They shall henceforward be my earls and barons—our lords and masters in Christ Jesus. [*Exit* Herbert.

If the King hold his purpose, I am myself a beggar. Forty thousand marks! forty thousand devils—and these craven bishops! 87

A Poor Man (entering) with his dog. My lord archbishop, may I come in with my poor friend, my dog? The King's verdurer caught him a-hunting in the forest, and cut off his paws. The dog followed his calling, my lord. I ha' carried him ever so many miles in my arms, and he licks my face and moans and cries out against the King.

Becket. Better thy dog than thee. The King's courts would use thee worse than thy dog—they are too bloody. Were the Church king, it would be otherwise. Poor beast! poor beast! set him down. I will bind up his wounds with my napkin. Give him a bone, give him a bone! Who misuses a dog would misuse a child—they cannot speak for themselves. Past help! his paws are past help. God help him!

Enter the BEGGARS *(and seat themselves at the Tables).* BECKET *and* HERBERT *wait upon them.*

First Beggar. Swine, sheep, ox—here's a French supper! When thieves fall out, honest men—

Second Beggar. Is the archbishop a thief who gives thee thy supper? 110

First Beggar. Well, then, how does it go? When honest men fall out, thieves—no, it can't be that.

Second Beggar. Who stole the widow's one sitting hen o' Sunday, when she was at mass?

First Beggar. Come, come! thou hadst thy share on her. Sitting hen! Our Lord Becket's our great sitting-hen cock, and we should n't ha' been sitting here if the barons and bishops had n't been a-sitting on the archbishop. 122

Becket. Ay, the princes sat in judgment against me, and the Lord hath prepared your table—*Sederunt principes, ederunt pauperes.*

A Voice. Becket, beware of the knife!

Becket. Who spoke?

Third Beggar. Nobody, my lord. What's that, my lord? 130

Becket. Venison.

Third Beggar. Venison?

Becket. Buck—deer, as you call it.

Third Beggar. King's meat! By the Lord, won't we pray for your lordship!

Becket. And, my children, your prayers will do more for me in the day of peril that dawns darkly and drearily over the house of God—yea, and in the day of judgment also, than the swords of the craven sycophants would have done had they remained true to me whose bread they have partaken. I must leave you to your banquet. Feed, feast, and be merry. Herbert, for the sake of the Church itself, if not for my own, I must fly to France to-night. Come with me.

[*Exit with* Herbert.

Third Beggar. Here—all of you—my lord's health! *(they drink).* Well—if that is n't goodly wine— 150

First Beggar. Then there is n't a goodly wench to serve him with it; they were

fighting for her to-day in the street.
Third Beggar. Peace !

FIRST BEGGAR.

The black sheep baaed to the miller's
 ewe-lamb,
'The miller 's away for to-night.'
'Black sheep,' quoth she, 'too black a sin
 for me.'

And what said the black sheep, my masters ?

'We can make a black sin white.'

Third Beggar. Peace !   160

FIRST BEGGAR.

'Ewe-lamb, ewe-lamb, I am here by the
 dam.'
But the miller came home that night,
And so dusted his back with the meal in
 his sack,
That he made the black sheep white.

Third Beggar. Be we not of the family ?
be we not a-supping with the head of the
family ? be we not in my lord's own re-
fractory ? Out from among us ; thou art
our black sheep.   169

Enter the four KNIGHTS.

Fitzurse. Sheep, said he ? And sheep
without the shepherd, too. Where is my
lord archbishop ? Thou the lustiest and
lousiest of this Cain's brotherhood, answer.
Third Beggar. With Cain's answer, my
lord. Am I his keeper ? Thou shouldst
call him Cain, not me.
Fitzurse. So I do, for he would murder
his brother the State.
Third Beggar (*rising and advancing*).
No, my lord ; but because the Lord hath
set his mark upon him that no man should
murder him.   182
Fitzurse. Where is he ? where is he ?
Third Beggar. With Cain belike, in the
land of Nod, or in the land of France for
aught I know.
Fitzurse. France ! Ha ! De Morville,
Tracy, Brito — fled is he ? Cross swords,
all of you ! swear to follow him ! Re-
member the Queen !
 [*The four* Knights *cross their swords.*
De Brito. They mock us ; he is here.

 [*All the* Beggars *rise and advance
  upon them.*
Fitzurse. Come, you filthy knaves, let
us pass.   193
Third Beggar. Nay, my lord, let *us* pass.
We be a-going home after our supper in
all humbleness, my lord ; for the archbishop loves humbleness, my lord, and
though we be fifty to four, we dare n't fight
you with our crutches, my lord. There now,
if thou hast not laid hands upon me ! and
my fellows know that I am all one scale
like a fish. I pray God I have n't given
thee my leprosy, my lord.   203
 [*Fitzurse shrinks from him, and another presses upon* De Brito.
De Brito. Away, dog !
Fourth Beggar. And I was bit by a mad
dog o' Friday, an' I be half dog already by
this token, that tho' I can drink wine I
cannot bide water, my lord ; and I want to
bite, I want to bite, and they do say the
very breath catches.   210
De Brito. Insolent clown ! Shall I smite
him with the edge of the sword ?
De Morville. No, nor with the flat of it
either. Smite the shepherd, and the sheep
are scattered. Smite the sheep, and the
shepherd will excommunicate thee.
De Brito. Yet my fingers itch to beat
him into nothing.
Fifth Beggar. So do mine, my lord. I
was born with it, and sulphur won't bring
it out o' me. But for all that the archbishop washed my feet o' Tuesday. He
likes it, my lord.   223
Sixth Beggar. And see here, my lord,
this rag fro' the grangrene i' my leg. It's
humbling — it smells o' human natur'.
Wilt thou smell it, my lord ? for the archbishop likes the smell on it, my lord ; for I
be his lord and master i' Christ, my lord.
De Morville. Faugh ! we shall all be
poisoned. Let us go.   231
 [*They draw back,* Beggars *following.*
Seventh Beggar. My lord, I ha' three
sisters a-dying at home o' the sweating
sickness. They be dead while I be a-supping.
Eighth Beggar. And I ha' nine darters
i' the spital that be dead ten times o'er i'
one day wi' the putrid fever ; and I bring
the taint on it along wi' me, for the archbishop likes it, my lord.   240
 [*Pressing upon the* Knights *till they
  disappear thro' the door.*
Third Beggar. Crutches, and itches, and
leprosies, and ulcers, and gangrenes, and

running sores, praise ye the Lord, for to-
night ye have saved our archbishop !

First Beggar. I 'll go back again. I
hain't half done yet.

Herbert of Bosham (entering). My
friends, the archbishop bids you good-
night. He hath retired to rest, and being in
great jeopardy of his life, he hath made his
bed between the altars, from whence he
sends me to bid you this night pray for him
who hath fed you in the wilderness.   253

Third Beggar. So we will — so we will,
I warrant thee. Becket shall be king, and
the Holy Father shall be king, and the
world shall live by the King's venison and
the bread o' the Lord, and there shall be
no more poor for ever. Hurrah ! Vive le
Roy ! That 's the English of it.

ACT II

SCENE I. — ROSAMUND'S BOWER

*A Garden of Flowers. In the midst a bank
of wild-flowers with a bench before it.*

Voices *heard singing among the trees.*

DUET.

1. Is it the wind of the dawn that I hear
    in the pine overhead ?
2. No ; but the voice of the deep as it
    hollows the cliffs of the land.
1. Is there a voice coming up with the
    voice of the deep from the strand,
    One coming up with a song in the flush
    of the glimmering red ?
2. Love that is born of the deep coming
    up with the sun from the sea.
1. Love that can shape or can shatter a
    life till the life shall have fled ?
2. Nay, let us welcome him, Love that can
    lift up a life from the dead.
1. Keep him away from the lone little isle.
    Let us be, let us be.
2. Nay, let him make it his own, let him
    reign in it — he, it is he,
    Love that is born of the deep coming up
    with the sun from the sea.   10

Enter HENRY *and* ROSAMUND.

Rosamund. Be friends with him again —
    I do beseech thee.
Henry. With Becket ? I have but one
    hour with thee —
Sceptre and crozier clashing, and the mitre

Grappling the crown — and when I flee
    from this
For a gasp of freer air, a breathing-while
To rest upon thy bosom and forget him —
Why thou, my bird, thou pipest 'Becket,
    Becket' —
Yea, thou my golden dream of Love's own
    bower,
Must be the nightmare breaking on my
    peace   19
With 'Becket.'
    Rosamund. O my life's life, not to smile
Is all but death to me. My sun, no cloud !
Let there not be one frown in this one
    hour.
Out of the many thine, let this be mine !
Look rather thou all-royal as when first
I met thee.
    Henry.   Where was that ?
    Rosamund.   Forgetting that
Forgets me too.
    Henry.   Nay, I remember it well.
There on the moors.
    Rosamund.   And in a narrow path.
A plover flew before thee. Then I saw
Thy high black steed among the flaming
    furze,
Like sudden night in the main glare of
    day.
And from that height something was said
    to me,   31
I knew not what.
    Henry.   I ask'd the way.
    Rosamund.   I think so.
So I lost mine.
    Henry. Thou wast too shamed to answer.
    Rosamund. Too scared — so young !
    Henry.   The rosebud of my rose ! —
Well, well, no more of *him* — I have sent
    his folk,
His kin, all his belongings, over-seas ;
Age, orphans, and babe-breasting mothers
    — all
By hundreds to him — there to beg, starve,
    die —
So that the fool King Louis feed them
    not.   39
The man shall feel that I can strike him
    yet.
    Rosamund. Babes, orphans, mothers ! is
    that royal, sire ?
    Henry. And I have been as royal with
    the Church.
He shelter'd in the Abbey of Pontigny,
There wore his time studying the canon
    law
To work it against me. But since he
    cursed

My friends at Veselay, I have let them
    know
That if they keep him longer as their
    guest,
I scatter all their cowls to all the hells.
    Rosamund. And is that altogether royal?
    Henry.   Traitress!
    Rosamund. A faithful traitress to thy
    royal fame.   50
    Henry. Fame! what care I for fame?
    Spite, ignorance, envy,
Yea, honesty too, paint her what way they
    will,
Fame of to-day is infamy to-morrow;
Infamy of to-day is fame to-morrow;
And round and round again. What mat-
    ters? Royal —
I mean to leave the royalty of my crown
Unlessen'd to mine heirs.
    Rosamund.   Still — thy fame too;
I say that should be royal.
    Henry.   And I say,
I care not for thy saying.
    Rosamund.   And I say,   59
I care not for *thy* saying. A greater King
Than thou art, Love, who cares not for
    the word,
Makes 'care not' — care. There have I
    spoken true?
    Henry. Care dwell with me for ever
    when I cease
To care for thee as ever!
    Rosamund.   No need! no need! . . .
There is a bench. Come, wilt thou sit? —
    My bank
Of wild-flowers [*he sits*]. At thy feet!
             [*She sits at his feet.*
    Henry.   I bade them clear
A royal pleasaunce for thee, in the wood,
Not leave these country-folk at court.
    Rosamund.   I brought them
In from the wood, and set them here. I
    love them
More than the garden flowers, that seem
    at most   70
Sweet guests, or foreign cousins, not half
    speaking
The language of the land. I love *them* too,
Yes. But, my liege, I am sure, of all the
    roses —
Shame fall on those who gave it a dog's
    name! —
This wild one (*picking a briar-rose*) —
    nay, I shall not prick myself —
Is sweetest. Do but smell!
    Henry.   Thou rose of the world!
Thou rose of all the roses!   [*Muttering.*
I am not worthy of her — this beast-body
That God has plunged my soul in — I, that

taking
The Fiend's advantage of a throne, so long
Have wander'd among women, — a foul
    stream   81
Thro' fever-breeding levels, — at her side,
Among these happy dales, run clearer,
    drop
The mud I carried, like yon brook, and
    glass
The faithful face of heaven —
    [*Looking at her, and unconsciously aloud,*
               — thine! thine!
    Rosamund.   I know it.
    Henry (*muttering*). Not hers. We have
    but one bond, her hate of Becket.
    Rosamund (*half hearing*). Nay! nay!
    what art thou muttering? *I* hate
    Becket?
    Henry (*muttering*). A sane and natural
    loathing for a soul
Purer, and truer and nobler than herself;
And mine a bitterer illegitimate hate,   90
A bastard hate born of a former love.
    Rosamund. My fault to name him! O,
    let the hand of one
To whom thy voice is all her music stay it
But for a breath!
          [*Puts her hand before his lips.*
          Speak only of thy love.
Why, there — like some loud beggar at
    thy gate —
The happy boldness of this hand hath
    won it
Love's alms, thy kiss (*looking at her hand*)
    — Sacred! I'll kiss it too.
                [*Kissing it.*
There! wherefore dost thou so peruse it?
    Nay,
There may be crosses in my line of life.
    Henry. Not half *her* hand — no hand to
    mate with *her*,   100
If it should come to that.
    Rosamund.   With her? with whom?
    Henry. Life on the hand is naked gipsy-
    stuff;
Life on the face, the brows — clear inno-
    cence!
Vein'd marble — not a furrow yet — and
    hers   [*Muttering.*
Crost and recrost, a venomous spider's
    web —
    Rosamund (*springing up*). Out of the
    cloud, my Sun — out of the eclipse
Narrowing my golden hour!
    Henry.   O Rosamund,
I would be true — would tell thee all —
    and something
I had to say — I love thee none the less —
Which will so vex thee.

Rosamund. Something against *me*?

Henry. No, no, against myself.

Rosamund. I will not hear it.
Come, come, mine hour! I bargain for
    mine hour. 112
I'll call thee little Geoffrey.

Henry. Call him!

Rosamund. Geoffrey!

    Enter GEOFFREY.

Henry. How the boy grows!

Rosamund. Ay, and his brows are thine ;
The mouth is only Clifford, my dear
    father.

Geoffrey. My liege, what hast thou
    brought me?

Henry. Venal imp!
What say'st thou to the Chancellorship of
    England?

Geoffrey. O, yes, my liege.

Henry. 'O, yes, my liege!' He speaks
As if it were a cake of gingerbread. 119
Dost thou know, my boy, what it is to be
Chancellor of England?

Geoffrey. Something good, or thou
wouldst not give it me.

Henry. It is, my boy, to side with the
King when Chancellor, and then to be
made archbishop and go against the King
who made him, and turn the world upside
down.

Geoffrey. I won't have it then. Nay,
but give it me, and I promise thee not to
turn the world upside down. 131

Henry (giving him a ball). Here is a
ball, my boy, thy world, to turn any way
and play with as thou wilt — which is more
than I can do with mine. Go try it, play.
    [*Exit* Geoffrey.
A pretty lusty boy.

Rosamund. So like to thee ;
Like to be liker.

Henry. Not in my chin, I hope!
That threatens double.

Rosamund. Thou art manlike perfect.

Henry. Ay, ay, no doubt; and were I
    humpt behind,
Thou 'dst say as much — the goodly way of
    women 140
Who love, for which I love them. May
    God grant
No ill befall or him or thee when I
Am gone!

Rosamund. Is *he* thy enemy?

Henry. He? who? ay!

Rosamund. Thine enemy knows the se-
    cret of my bower.

Henry. And I could tear him asunder
with wild horses
Before he would betray it. Nay — no fear !
More like is he to excommunicate me.

Rosamund. And I would creep, crawl
    over knife-edge flint
Barefoot, a hundred leagues, to stay his
    hand 149
Before he flash'd the bolt.

Henry. And when he flash'd it
Shrink from me, like a daughter of the
    Church.

Rosamund. Ay, but he will not.

Henry. Ay! but if he did?

Rosamund. O, then! O, then! I almost
    fear to say
That my poor heretic heart would excom-
    municate
His excommunication, clinging to thee
Closer than ever.

Henry (raising Rosamund *and kissing
    her).* My brave-hearted Rose!
Hath he ever been to see thee?

Rosamund. Here? not he.
And it is so lonely here — no confessor.

Henry. Thou shalt confess all thy sweet
    sins to me.

Rosamund. Besides, we came away in
    such a heat, 160
I brought not even my crucifix.

Henry. Take this.
    [*Giving her the Crucifix which* Elea-
    nor *gave him.*

Rosamund. O, beautiful! May I have it
    as mine, till mine
Be mine again?

Henry (throwing it round her neck).
    Thine — as I am — till death!

Rosamund. Death? no! I'll have it with
    me in my shroud,
And wake with it, and show it to all the
    Saints.

Henry. Nay — I must go ; but when thou
    layest thy lip
To this, remembering One who died for
    thee,
Remember also one who lives for thee
Out there in France ; for I must hence to
    brave
The Pope, King Louis, and this turbulent
    priest. 170

Rosamund (kneeling). O, by thy love
    for me, all mine for thee,
Fling not thy soul into the flames of hell!
I kneel to thee — be friends with him
    again.

Henry. Look, look! if little Geoffrey
    have not tost
His ball into the brook! makes after it
    too

To find it. Why, the child will drown
    himself.
Rosamund. Geoffrey ! Geoffrey !
                    [*Exeunt.*

SCENE II

MONTMIRAIL

'*The Meeting of the Kings.*' JOHN OF OX-
FORD *and* HENRY. *Crowd in the distance.*

    John of Oxford. You have not crown'd
      young Henry yet, my liege ?
    Henry. Crown'd ! by God's eyes, we will
      not have him crown'd.
I spoke of late to the boy, he answer'd me,
As if he wore the crown already — No,
We will not have him crown'd.
'T is true what Becket told me, that the
    mother
Would make him play his kingship against
    mine.
    John of Oxford. Not have him crown'd ?
    Henry. Not now — not yet ! and
      Becket —
Becket should crown him were he crown'd
    at all ;
But, since we would be lord of our own
    manor,   10
This Canterbury, like a wounded deer,
Has fled our presence and our feeding-
    grounds.
    John of Oxford. Cannot a smooth
      tongue lick him whole again
To serve your will ?
    Henry.   He hates my will, not me.
    John of Oxford. There 's York, my liege.
    Henry. But England scarce would hold
Young Henry king, if only crown'd by
    York,
And that would stilt up York to twice
    himself.
There is a movement yonder in the
    crowd —
See if our pious — what shall I call him,
    John ? —
Husband-in-law, our smooth-shorn suze-
    rain,   20
Be yet within the field.
    John of Oxford.   I will.   [*Exit.*
    Henry.   Ay ! Ay !
Mince and go back ! his politic Holiness
Hath all but climb'd the Roman perch
    again,
And we shall hear him presently with
    clapt wing
Crow over Barbarossa — at last tongue-
    free

To blast my realms with excommunication
And interdict. I must patch up a peace —
A peace in this long-tugged-at, threadbare-
    worn
Quarrel of Crown and Church — to rend
    again.
His Holiness cannot steer straight thro'
    shoals,   30
Nor I. The citizen's heir hath conquer'd
    me
For the moment. So we make our peace
    with him.

          Enter LOUIS.

Brother of France, what shall be done
    with Becket ?
    Louis. The holy Thomas ! Brother, you
    have traffick'd
Between the Emperor and the Pope, be-
    tween
The Pope and Antipope — a perilous game
For men to play with God.
    Henry.   Ay, ay, good brother,
They call you the Monk-King.
    Louis.   Who calls me ? she
That was my wife, now yours ? You have
    her Duchy,
The point you aim'd at, and pray God she
    prove   40
True wife to you. You have had the bet-
    ter of us
In secular matters.
    Henry.   Come, confess, good brother,
You did your best or worst to keep her
    Duchy,
Only the golden Leopard printed in it
Such hold-fast claws that you perforce
    again
Shrank into France. Tut, tut ! did we
    convene
This conference but to babble of our
    wives ?
They are plagues enough in-door.
    Louis.   We fought in the East
And felt the sun of Antioch scald our
    mail,
And push'd our lances into Saracen hearts.
We never hounded on the State at home 51
To spoil the Church.
    Henry. How should you see this rightly ?
    Louis. Well, well, no more ! I am proud
    of my 'Monk-King,'
Whoever named me ; and, brother, Holy
    Church
May rock, but will not wreck, nor our
    archbishop
Stagger on the slope decks for any rough
    sea

Blown by the breath of kings. We do for-
    give you
For aught you wrought against us.
                [Henry *holds up his hand.*
                        Nay, I pray you,
Do not defend yourself. You will do much
To rake out all old dying heats if you,   60
At my requesting, will but look into
The wrongs you did him, and restore his
    kin,
Reseat him on his throne of Canterbury,
Be, both, the friends you were.
    Henry.   The friends we were !
Co-mates we were, and had our sport to-
    gether.
Co-kings we were, and made the laws to-
    gether.
The world had never seen the like before.
You are too cold to know the fashion of
    it.
Well, well, we will be gentle with him,
    gracious —   69
Most gracious.

Enter BECKET, *after him,* JOHN OF OX-
    FORD, ROGER OF YORK, GILBERT FOLIOT,
    DE BROC, FITZURSE, *etc.*

                Only that the rift he made
May close between us, here I am wholly
    king,
The word should come from him.
    Becket (kneeling). Then, my dear liege,
I here deliver all this controversy
Into your royal hands.
    Henry.   Ah, Thomas, Thomas,
Thou art thyself again, Thomas again.
    Becket (rising). Saving God's honor !
    Henry.   Out upon thee, man !
Saving the devil's honor, his yes and no.
Knights, bishops, earls, this London spawn
    — by Mahound,
I had sooner have been born a Mussul-
    man —
Less clashing with their priests —   80
I am half-way down the slope — will no
    man stay me ?
I dash myself to pieces — I stay myself —
Puff — it is gone. You, Master Becket, you
That owe to me your power over me —
Nay, nay —
Brother of France, you have taken, cher-
    ish'd him
Who thief-like fled from his own church
    by night,
No man pursuing. I would have had him
    back.
Take heed he do not turn and rend you
    too :

For whatsoever may displease him — that
Is clean against God's honor — a shift, a
    trick   91
Whereby to challenge, face me out of all
My regal rights. Yet, yet — that none may
    dream
I go against God's honor — ay, or himself
In any reason, choose
A hundred of the wisest heads from
    England,
A hundred, too, from Normandy and
    Anjou ;
Let these decide on what was customary
In olden days, and all the Church of
    France
Decide on their decision, I am content. 100
More, what the mightiest and the holiest
Of all his predecessors may have done
Even to the least and meanest of my own,
Let him do the same to me — I am content.
    Louis. Ay, ay ! the King humbles him-
    self enough.
    Becket (aside). Words ! he will wriggle
    out of them like an eel
When the time serves. (*Aloud.*) My
    lieges and my lords,
The thanks of Holy Church are due to
    those
That went before us for their work, which
    we   109
Inheriting reap an easier harvest. Yet —
    Louis. My lord, will you be greater than
    the Saints,
More than Saint Peter ? whom — what is it
    you doubt ?
Behold your peace at hand.
    Becket.   I say that those
Who went before us did not wholly clear
The deadly growths of earth, which hell's
    own heat
So dwelt on that they rose and darken'd
    heaven.
Yet they did much. Would God they had
    torn up all
By the hard root, which shoots again ;
    our trial
Had so been less ; but, seeing they were
    men
Defective or excessive, must we follow 120
All that they overdid or underdid ?
Nay, if they were defective as Saint Peter
Denying Christ, who yet defied the tyrant,
We hold by his defiance, not his defect.
O good son Louis, do not counsel me,
No, to suppress God's honor for the sake
Of any king that breathes. No, God for-
    bid !
    Henry. No ! God forbid ! and turn me
    Mussulman !

No God but one, and Mahound is his
    prophet.
But for your Christian, look you, you shall
    have   130
None other God but me — me, Thomas,
    son
Of Gilbert Becket, London merchant.
    Out !
I hear no more.   [*Exit.*
   Louis.   Our brother's anger puts him,
Poor man, beside himself — not wise. My
    lord,
We have claspt your cause, believing that
    our brother
Had wrong'd you ; but this day he prof-
    fer'd peace.
You will have war ; and tho' we grant the
    Church
King over this world's kings, yet, my good
    lord,
We that are kings are something in this
    world,
And so we pray you, draw yourself from
    under   140
The wings of France. We shelter you no
    more.   [*Exit.*
   John of Oxford. I am glad that France
    hath scouted him at last.
I told the Pope what manner of man he
    was.   [*Exit.*
   Roger of York. Yea, since he flouts the
    will of either realm,
Let either cast him away like a dead dog !
                       [*Exit.*
   Foliot. Yea, let a stranger spoil his her-
    itage,
And let another take his bishopric ! [*Exit.*
   De Broc. Our castle, my lord, belongs
    to Canterbury.
I pray you come and take it.   [*Exit.*
   Fitzurse.   When you will.
                        [*Exit.*
   Becket. Cursed be John of Oxford,
    Roger of York,   150
And Gilbert Foliot ! cursed those De Brocs
That hold our Saltwood Castle from our
    see !
Cursed Fitzurse, and all the rest of them
That sow this hate between my lord and
    me !
   Voices from the Crowd. Blessed be the
lord archbishop, who hath withstood two
kings to their faces for the honor of God.
   Becket. Out of the mouths of babes and
    sucklings, praise !
I thank you, sons ; when kings but hold
    by crowns,
The crowd that hungers for a crown in

heaven   160
Is my true king.
   Herbert.   Thy true King bade thee be
A fisher of men ; thou hast them in thy
    net.
   Becket. I am too like the King here ;
    both of us
Too headlong for our office. Better have
    been
A fisherman at Bosham, my good Herbert,
Thy birthplace — the sea-creek — the petty
    rill
That falls into it — the green field — the
    gray church —
The simple lobster-basket, and the mesh —
The more or less of daily labor done —
The pretty gaping bills in the home-
    nest   170
Piping for bread — the daily want sup-
    plied —
The daily pleasure to supply it.
   Herbert.   Ah, Thomas,
You had not borne it, no, not for a day.
   Becket. Well, maybe, no.
   Herbert.   But bear with Walter Map,
For here he comes to comment on the
    time.

              Enter WALTER MAP.

   Walter Map. Pity, my lord, that you
have quenched the warmth of France toward you, tho' His Holiness, after much
smouldering and smoking, be kindled
again upon your quarter.   180
   Becket. Ay, if he do not end in smoke
    again.
   Walter Map. My lord, the fire, when
first kindled, said to the smoke, 'Go up,
my son, straight to heaven.' And the
smoke said, 'I go ;' but anon the North-
east took and turned him Southwest, then
the Southwest turned him Northeast, and
so of the other winds ; but it was in him to
go up straight if the time had been quieter.
Your lordship affects the unwavering perpendicular ; but His Holiness, pushed one
way by the Empire and another by
England, if he move at all — Heaven stay
him ! — is fain to diagonalize.
   Herbert. Diagonalize ! thou art a word-
    monger.
Our Thomas never will diagonalize.
Thou art a jester and a verse-maker.
Diagonalize !   198
   Walter Map. Is the world any the worse
for my verses if the Latin rhymes be rolled
out from a full mouth ? or any harm done

to the people if my jest be in defence of the Truth?

Becket. Ay, if the jest be so done that the people
Delight to wallow in the grossness of it,
Till Truth herself be shamed of her defender.
Non defensoribus istis, Walter Map!

Walter Map. Is that my case? so if the city be sick, and I cannot call the kennel sweet, your lordship would suspend me from verse-writing, as you suspended yourself after sub-writing to the customs. 212

Becket. I pray God pardon mine infirmity!

Walter Map. Nay, my lord, take heart; for tho' you suspended yourself, the Pope let you down again; and tho' you suspend Foliot or another, the Pope will not leave them in suspense, for the Pope himself is always in suspense, like Mahound's coffin hung between heaven and earth — always in suspense, like the scales, till the weight of Germany or the gold of England brings one of them down to the dust — always in suspense, like the tail of the horologe — to and fro — tick-tack — we make the time, we keep the time, ay, and we serve the time; for I have heard say that if you boxed the Pope's ears with a purse, you might stagger him, but he would pocket the purse. No saying of mine — Jocelyn of Salisbury. But the King hath bought half the College of Red-hats. He warmed to you to-day, and you have chilled him again. Yet you both love God. Agree with him quickly again, even for the sake of the Church. My one grain of good counsel which you will not swallow. I hate a split between old friendships as I hate the dirty gap in the face of a Cistercian monk, that will swallow anything. Farewell. *[Exit.*

Becket. Map scoffs at Rome. I all but hold with Map. 242
Save for myself no Rome were left in England,
All had been his. Why should this Rome, this Rome,
Still choose Barabbas rather than the Christ,
Absolve the left-hand thief and damn the right?
Take fees of tyranny, wink at sacrilege,
Which even Peter had not dared? condemn
The blameless exile? —

Herbert. Thee, thou holy Thomas!

I would that thou hadst been the Holy Father. 250

Becket. I would have done my most to keep Rome holy,
I would have made Rome know she still is Rome —
Who stands aghast at her eternal self
And shakes at mortal kings — her vacillation,
Avarice, craft — O God, how many an innocent
Has left his bones upon the way to Rome
Unwept, uncared for! Yea — on mine own self
The King had had no power except for Rome.
'T is not the King who is guilty of mine exile,
But Rome, Rome, Rome!

Herbert. My lord, I see this Louis
Returning, ah! to drive thee from his realm. 261

Becket. He said as much before. Thou art no prophet,
Nor yet a prophet's son.

Herbert. Whatever he say,
Deny not thou God's honor for a king.
The King looks troubled.

Re-enter KING LOUIS.

Louis. My dear lord archbishop,
I learn but now that those poor Poitevins
That in thy cause were stirr'd against King Henry
Have been, despite his kingly promise given
To our own self of pardon, evilly used
And put to pain. I have lost all trust in him. 270
The Church alone hath eyes — and now I see
That I was blind — suffer the phrase — surrendering
God's honor to the pleasure of a man.
Forgive me and absolve me, holy father.
[Kneels.

Becket. Son, I absolve thee in the name of God.

Louis (rising). Return to Sens, where we will care for you.
The wine and wealth of all our France are yours;
Rest in our realm, and be at peace with all. *[Exeunt.*

Voices from the Crowd. Long live the

good King Louis! God bless the great
archbishop!   281

Re-enter HENRY *and* JOHN OF OXFORD.

Henry (*looking after* King Louis *and*
    Becket). Ay, there they go — both
    backs are turn'd to me —
Why, then I strike into my former path
For England, crown young Henry there,
    and make
Our waning Eleanor all but love me!
                                        John,
Thou hast served me heretofore with
    Rome — and well.
They call thee John the Swearer.
John of Oxford.   For this reason,
That, being ever duteous to the King,
I evermore have sworn upon his side, 289
And ever mean to do it.
    Henry (*claps him on the shoulder*).
        Honest John!
To Rome again! the storm begins again.
Spare not thy tongue! be lavish with our
    coins,
Threaten our junction with the Emperor
    — flatter
And fright the Pope — bribe all the cardi-
    nals — leave
Lateran and Vatican in one dust of gold —
Swear and unswear, state and misstate thy
    best!
I go to have young Henry crown'd by
    York.

ACT III

SCENE I. — THE BOWER

HENRY *and* ROSAMUND.

Henry. All that you say is just. I can-
    not answer it
Till better times when I shall put away —
Rosamund. What will you put away?
Henry.   That which you ask me
Till better times. Let it content you now
There is no woman that I love so well.
    Rosamund. No woman but should be
        content with that —
Henry. And one fair child to fondle!
Rosamund.   O, yes, the child
We waited for so long — Heaven's gift at
    last —
And how you doted on him then! To-day
I almost fear'd your kiss was colder —
    yes —   10

But then the child *is* such a child! What
    chance
That he should ever spread into the man
Here in our silence? I have done my best.
I am not learn'd.
    Henry.   I am the King, his father,
And I will look to it. Is our secret ours?
Have you had any alarm? no stranger?
    Rosamund.   No.
The warder of the bower hath given him-
    self
Of late to wine. I sometimes think he
    sleeps
When he should watch; and yet what
    fear? the people
Believe the wood enchanted. No one
    comes,   20
Nor foe nor friend; his fond excess of
    wine
Springs from the loneliness of my poor
    bower,
Which weighs even on me.
    Henry.   Yet these tree-towers,
Their long bird-echoing minster-aisles, —
    the voice
Of the perpetual brook, these golden
    slopes
Of Solomon-shaming flowers — that was
    your saying,
All pleased you so at first.
    Rosamund.   Not now so much.
My Anjou bower was scarce as beautiful.
But you were oftener there. I have none
    but you.
The brook's voice is not yours, and no
    flower, not   30
The sun himself, should he be changed to
    one,
Could shine away the darkness of that gap
Left by the lack of love.
    Henry.   The lack of love!
    Rosamund. Of one we love. Nay, I
        would not be bold,
Yet hoped ere this you might —
                        [*Looks earnestly at him.*
    Henry.   Anything further?
    Rosamond. Only my best bower maiden
        died of late,
And that old priest whom John of Salis-
    bury trusted
Hath sent another.
    Henry.   Secret?
    Rosamund.   I but ask'd her
One question, and she primm'd her mouth
    and put
Her hands together — thus — and said,
    God help her,   40
That she was sworn to silence.
    Henry.   What did you ask her?

Rosamund. Some daily something-nothing.

Henry.   Secret, then ?

Rosamund. I do not love her. Must you go, my liege,
So suddenly ?

Henry.   I came to England suddenly,
And on a great occasion sure to wake
As great a wrath in Becket —

Rosamund.   Always Becket !
He always comes between us.

Henry.   And to meet it
I needs must leave as suddenly. It is raining,
Put on your hood and see me to the bounds.   [*Exeunt.*

MARGERY (*singing behind scene*).

    Babble in bower   50
      Under the rose !
    Bee must n't buzz,
      Whoop — but he knows.

    Kiss me, little one,
      Nobody near !
    Grasshopper, grasshopper,
      Whoop — you can hear.

    Kiss in the bower,
      Tit on the tree !
    Bird must n't tell,   60
      Whoop — he can see.

Enter MARGERY.

I ha' been but a week here and I ha' seen what I ha' seen, for to be sure it 's no more than a week since our old Father Philip that has confessed our mother for twenty years, and she was hard put to it, and to speak truth, nigh at the end of our last crust, and that mouldy, and she cried out on him to put me forth in the world and to make me a woman of the world, and to win my own bread, whereupon he asked our mother if I could keep a quiet tongue i' my head, and not speak till I was spoke to, and I answered for myself that I never spoke more than was needed, and he told me he would advance me to the service of a great lady, and took me ever so far away, and gave me a great pat o' the cheek for a pretty wench, and said it was a pity to blind-fold such eyes as mine, and such to be sure they be, but he blinded 'em for all that, and so brought me no-hows as I may say, and the more shame to him after his promise, into a garden and not into the world, and bade me whatever I saw not to speak one word, an' it 'ud be well for me in the end, for there were great ones who would look after me, and to be sure I ha' seen great ones to-day — and then not to speak one word, for that's the rule o' the garden, tho' to be sure if I had been Eve i' the garden I should n't ha' minded the apple, for what 's an apple, you know, save to a child, and I 'm no child, but more a woman o' the world than my lady here, and I ha' seen what I ha' seen — tho' to be sure if I had n't minded it we should all on us ha' had to go, bless the Saints, wi' bare backs, but the backs 'ud ha' countenanced one another, and belike it 'ud ha' been always summer, and anyhow I am as well-shaped as my lady here, and I ha' seen what I ha' seen, and what 's the good of my talking to myself, for here comes my lady (*enter* Rosamund), and, my lady, tho' I should n't speak one word, I wish you joy o' the King's brother.

Rosamund. What is it you mean ?   108

Margery. I mean your goodman, your husband, my lady, for I saw your ladyship a-parting wi' him even now i' the coppice, when I was a-getting o' bluebells for your ladyship's nose to smell on — and I ha' seen the King once at Oxford, and he 's as like the King as fingernail to fingernail, and I thought at first it was the King, only you know the King 's married, for King Louis —

Rosamund. Married !

Margery. Years and years, my lady, for her husband, King Louis —   121

Rosamund. Hush !

Margery. And I thought if it were the King's brother he had a better bride than the King, for the people do say that his is bad beyond all reckoning, and —

Rosamund. The people lie.   127

Margery. Very like, my lady, but most on 'em know an honest woman and a lady when they see her, and besides they say she makes songs, and that 's against her, for I never knew an honest woman that could make songs, tho' to be sure our mother 'ill sing me old songs by the hour, but then, God help her, she had 'em from her mother, and her mother from her mother back and back for ever so long, but none on 'em ever made songs, and they were all honest.

Rosamund. Go, you shall tell me of her some other time.   141

Margery. There 's none so much to tell

on her, my lady, only she kept the seventh
commandment better than some I know
on, or I could n't look your ladyship i' the
face, and she brew'd the best ale in all
Glo'ster, that is to say in her time when
she had the 'Crown.'

Rosamund. The crown ! who ?

Margery. Mother.   150

Rosamund. I mean her whom you call
— fancy — my husband's brother's wife.

Margery. O, Queen Eleanor. Yes, my
lady ; and tho' I be sworn not to speak a
word, I can tell you all about her, if —

Rosamund. No word now. I am faint
and sleepy. Leave me. Nay — go. What !
will you anger me ?   [*Exit* Margery.
He charged me not to question any of
    those
About me. Have I ? no ! she question'd
    me.   160
Did she not slander *him ?* Should she stay
    here ?
May she not tempt me, being at my side,
To question *her ?* Nay, can I send her
    hence
Without his kingly leave ? I am in the
    dark.
I have lived, poor bird, from cage to cage,
    and known
Nothing but him — happy to know no
    more,
So that he loved me — and he loves me —
    yes,
And bound me by his love to secrecy
Till his own time.
            Eleanor, Eleanor, have I
Not heard ill things of her in France ? O,
    she 's   170
The Queen of France. I see it — some
    confusion,
Some strange mistake. I did not hear
    aright,
Myself confused with parting from the
    King.

MARGERY (*behind scene*).

Bee must n't buzz,
    Whoop — but he knows.

Rosamund. Yet her — what her ? he
    hinted of some her —
When he was here before —
Something that would displease me. Hath
    he stray'd
From love's clear path into the common
    bush,
And, being scratch'd, returns to his true

rose,   180
Who hath not thorn enough to prick him
    for it,
Even with a word ?

MARGERY (*behind scene*).

Bird must n't tell,
    Whoop — he can see.

Rosamund. I would not hear him. Nay
    — there 's more — he frown'd
'No mate for her, if it should come to
    that' —
To that — to what ?

MARGERY (*behind scene*).

Whoop — but he knows,
    Whoop — but he knows.

Rosamund. O God ! some dreadful truth
    is breaking on me —   190
Some dreadful thing is coming on me.

Enter GEOFFREY.

            Geoffrey !
Geoffrey. What are you crying for, when
    the sun shines ?
Rosamund. Hath not thy father left us
    to ourselves ?
Geoffrey. Ay, but he 's taken the rain
with him. I hear Margery : I 'll go play
with her.   [*Exit* Geoffrey

ROSAMUND.

Rainbow, stay,
Gleam upon gloom,
Bright as my dream.
Rainbow, stay !   200

But it passes away,
Gloom upon gleam,
Dark as my doom —
O rainbow, stay !

SCENE II

OUTSIDE THE WOODS NEAR ROSA-
MUND'S BOWER

ELEANOR. FITZURSE.

Eleanor. Up from the salt lips of the
    land we two

Have track'd the King to this dark inland
    wood ;
And somewhere hereabouts he vanish'd.
    Here
His turtle builds ; his exit is our adit.
Watch ! he will out again, and presently,
Seeing he must to Westminster and crown
Young Henry there to-morrow.
    Fitzurse.   We have watch'd
So long in vain, he hath pass'd out again,
And on the other side.
                  [A great horn winded.
                  Hark ! Madam !
    Eleanor.   Ay,
How ghostly sounds that horn in the black
    wood !   *[A countryman flying.*
Whither away, man ? what are you flying
    from ?   11
Countryman. The witch ! the witch ! she
sits naked by a great heap of gold in the
middle of the wood, and when the horn
sounds she comes out as a wolf. Get you
hence ! a man passed in there to-day. I
holla'd to him, but he did n't hear me ;
he 'll never out again, the witch has got
him. I dare n't stay — I dare n't stay !   19
    Eleanor. Kind of the witch to give thee
    warning, tho'.   *[Man flies.*
Is not this wood-witch of the rustic's fear
Our woodland Circe that hath witch'd the
    King ?
        [Horn sounded. Another flying.
Fitzurse. Again ! stay, fool, and tell me
    why thou fliest.
Countryman. Fly thou too. The King
keeps his forest head of game here, and
when that horn sounds a score of wolf-dogs
are let loose that will tear thee piecemeal.
Linger not till the third horn. Fly !
                           [Exit.
    Eleanor. This is the likelier tale. We
    have hit the place.   29
Now let the King's fine game look to itself.
                       [Horn.
Fitzurse. Again ! —
And far on in the dark heart of the wood
I hear the yelping of the hounds of hell.
    Eleanor. I have my dagger here to still
    their throats.
Fitzurse. Nay, madam, not to-night — the
    night is falling.
What can be done to-night ?
    Eleanor.   Well — well — away.

SCENE III

TRAITOR'S MEADOW AT FRÉTEVAL.

PAVILIONS AND TENTS OF THE EN-
GLISH AND FRENCH BARONAGE

BECKET *and* HERBERT OF BOSHAM.

    Becket. See here !
    Herbert.   What 's here ?
    Becket.   A notice from the priest
To whom our John of Salisbury commit-
    ted
The secret of the bower, that our wolf-
    Queen
Is prowling round the fold. I should be
    back
In England even for this.
    Herbert.   These are by-things
In the great cause.
    Becket.   The by-things of the Lord
Are the wrong'd innocences that will cry
From all the hidden by-ways of the world
In the great day against the wronger. I
    know
Thy meaning. Perish she, I all, before   10
The Church should suffer wrong !
    Herbert.   Do you see, my lord,
There is the King talking with Walter
    Map ?
    Becket. He hath the Pope's last letters,
    and they threaten
The immediate thunder-blast of interdict ;
Yet he can scarce be touching upon those,
Or scarce would smile that fashion.
    Herbert.   Winter sunshine !
Beware of opening out thy bosom to it,
Lest thou, myself, and all thy flock should
    catch
An after ague-fit of trembling.   Look !
He bows, he bares his head, he is coming
    hither.   20
Still with a smile.

Enter KING HENRY *and* WALTER MAP.

    Henry. We have had so many hours to-
    gether, Thomas,
So many happy hours alone together,
That I would speak with you once more
    alone.
    Becket. My liege, your will and happi-
    ness are mine.
              [Exeunt King *and* Becket.
    Herbert. The same smile still.
    Walter Map. Do you see that great
black cloud that hath come over the sun
and cast us all into shadow ?
    Herbert. And feel it too.   30
    Walter Map. And see you yon side-beam
that is forced from under it, and sets the

church-tower over there all a-hell-fire as it were ?

Herbert. Ay.

Walter Map. It is this black, bell-silencing, anti-marrying, burial-hindering interdict that hath squeezed out this side-smile upon Canterbury, whereof may come conflagration. Were I Thomas, I would n't trust it. Sudden change is a house on sand ; and tho' I count Henry honest enough, yet when fear creeps in at the front, honesty steals out at the back, and the King at last is fairly scared by this cloud — this interdict. I have been more for the King than the Church in this matter — yea, even for the sake of the Church ; for, truly, as the case stood, you had safelier have slain an arch-bishop than a she-goat. But our recoverer and upholder of customs hath in this crowning of young Henry by York and London so violated the immemorial usage of the Church, that, like the grave-digger's child I have heard of, trying to ring the bell, he hath half-hanged himself in the rope of the Church, or rather pulled all the Church with the Holy Father astride of it down upon his own head.

Herbert. Were you there ?   60

Walter Map. In the church rope ? — no. I was at the crowning, for I have pleasure in the pleasure of crowds, and to read the faces of men at a great show.

Herbert. And how did Roger of York comport himself ?

Walter Map. As magnificently and archiepiscopally as our Thomas would have done : only there was a dare-devil in his eye — I should say a dare - Becket. He thought less of two kings than of one Roger, the king of the occasion. Foliot is the holier man, perhaps the better. Once or twice there ran a twitch across his face, as who should say 'what 's to follow ?' but Salisbury was a calf cowed by Mother Church, and every now and then glancing about him like a thief at night when he hears a door open in the house and thinks 'the master.'   80

Herbert. And the father-king ?

Walter Map. The father's eye was so tender it would have called a goose off the green, and once he strove to hide his face, like the Greek king when his daughter was sacrificed, but he thought better of it. It was but the sacrifice of a kingdom to his son, a smaller matter ; but as to the young crownling himself, he looked so malapert in the eyes, that had I fathered him I had given him more of the rod than the scep-

tre. Then followed the thunder of the captains and the shouting, and so we came on to the banquet, from whence there puffed out such an incense of unctuosity into the nostrils of our Gods of Church and state, that Lucullus or Apicius might have sniffed it in their Hades of heathenism, so that the smell of their own roast had not come across it —   100

Herbert. Map, tho' you make your butt too big, you overshoot it.

Walter Map. For as to the fish, they de-miracled the miraculous draught, and might have sunk a navy —

Herbert. There again, Goliasing and Goliathizing !

Walter Map. And as for the flesh at table, a whole Peter's sheet, with all manner of game, and four-footed things, and fowls —   111

Herbert. And all manner of creeping things too ?

Walter Map. Well, there were abbots — but they did not bring their women ; and so we were dull enough at first, but in the end we flourished out into a merriment ; for the old King would act servitor and hand a dish to his son ; whereupon my Lord of York — his fine-cut face bowing and beaming with all that courtesy which hath less loyalty in it than the backward scrape of the clown's heel — 'great honor,' says he, 'from the King's self to the King's son.' Did you hear the young King's quip ?   125

Herbert. No, what was it ?

Walter Map. Glancing at the days when his father was only Earl of Anjou, he answered, 'Should not an earl's son wait on a king's son ?' And when the cold corners of the King's mouth began to thaw, there was a great motion of laughter among us, part real, part childlike, to be freed from the dulness — part royal, for King and kingling both laughed, and so we could not but laugh, as by a royal necessity — part childlike again — when we felt we had laughed too long and could not stay ourselves — many midriff-shaken even to tears, as springs gush out after earthquakes — but from those, as I said before, there may come a conflagration — tho', to keep the figure moist and make it hold water, I should say rather, the lacrymation of a lamentation ; but look if Thomas have not flung himself at the King's feet. They have made it up again — for the moment.

Herbert. Thanks to the blessed Magdalen, whose day it is !

Re-enter HENRY *and* BECKET. (*During their conference the* BARONS *and* BISHOPS OF FRANCE *and* ENGLAND *come in at back of stage.*)

Becket. Ay, King ! for in thy kingdom, as thou knowest,   150
The spouse of the Great King, thy King, hath fallen —
The daughter of Zion lies beside the way —
The priests of Baal tread her underfoot —
The golden ornaments are stolen from her —
Henry. Have I not promised to restore her, Thomas,
And send thee back again to Canterbury ?
Becket. Send back again those exiles of my kin
Who wander famine-wasted thro' the world.
Henry. Have I not promised, man, to send them back ?
Becket. Yet one thing more. Thou hast broken thro' the pales   160
Of privilege, crowning thy young son by York,
London, and Salisbury — not Canterbury.
Henry. York crown'd the Conqueror — not Canterbury.
Becket. There was no Canterbury in William's time.
Henry. But Hereford, you know, crown'd the first Henry.
Becket. But Anselm crown'd this Henry o'er again.
Henry. And thou shalt crown my Henry o'er again.
Becket. And is it then with thy good-will that I
Proceed against thine evil councillors,
And hurl the dread ban of the Church on those   170
Who made the second mitre play the first,
And acted me ?
Henry. Well, well, then — have thy way !
It may be they were evil councillors.
What more, my lord archbishop ? What more, Thomas ?
I make thee full amends. Say all thy say,
But blaze not out before the Frenchmen here.
Becket. More ? Nothing, so thy promise be thy deed.
Henry (*holding out his hand*). Give me thy hand. My Lords of France and England,
My friend of Canterbury and myself
Are now once more at perfect amity.   180
Unkingly should I be, and most un-
knightly,
Not striving still, however much in vain,
To rival him in Christian charity.
Herbert. All praise to Heaven, and sweet Saint Magdalen !
Henry. And so farewell until we meet in England.
Becket. I fear, my liege, we may not meet in England.
Henry. How, do you make me a traitor ?
Becket.   No, indeed !
That be far from thee.
Henry.   Come, stay with us, then,
Before you part for England.
Becket.   I am bound
For that one hour to stay with good King Louis,   190
Who helpt me when none else.
Herbert.   He said thy life
Was not one hour's worth in England save
King Henry gave thee first the kiss of peace.
Henry. He said so ? Louis, did he ? look you, Herbert,
When I was in mine anger with King Louis.
I sware I would not give the kiss of peace,
Not on French ground, nor any ground but English,
Where his cathedral stands. Mine old friend, Thomas,
I would there were that perfect trust between us,
That health of heart, once ours, ere Pope or King   200
Had come between us ! Even now — who knows ? —
I might deliver all things to thy hand —
If — but I say no more — farewell, my lord.
Becket. Farewell, my liege !
[*Exit* Henry, *then the* Barons *and* Bishops.
Walter Map. There again ! when the full fruit of the royal promise might have dropt into thy mouth hadst thou but opened it to thank him.
Becket. He fenced his royal promise with an *if*.   209
Walter Map. And is the King's *if* too high a stile for your lordship to overstep and come at all things in the next field ?
Becket. Ay, if this *if* be like the devil's '*if*
Thou wilt fall down and worship me.'
Herbert.   O, Thomas,
I could fall down and worship thee, my Thomas,
For thou hast trodden this wine-press alone.

Becket. Nay, of the people there are
  many with me.   217

Walter Map. I am not altogether with
you, my lord, tho' I am none of those that
would raise a storm between you, lest ye
should draw together like two ships in a
calm. You wrong the King : he meant
what he said to-day. Who shall vouch for
his to-morrows ? One word further. Doth
not the *fewness* of anything make the fulness of it in estimation ? Is not virtue
prized mainly for its rarity and great baseness loathed as an exception : for were all,
my lord, as noble as yourself, who would
look up to you ? and were all as base as —
who shall I say ? — Fitzurse and his following — who would look down upon them ?
My lord, you have put so many of the
King's household out of communion, that
they begin to smile at it.   235

Becket. At their peril, at their peril —

Walter Map. For tho' the drop may hollow out the dead stone, doth not the living
skin thicken against perpetual whippings ?
This is the second grain of good counsel I
ever proffered thee, and so cannot suffer
by the rule of frequency. Have I sown it in
salt ? I trust not, for before God I promise you the King hath many more wolves
than he can tame in his woods of England,
and if it suit their purpose to howl for
the King, and you still move against him,
you may have no less than to die for it ;
but God and his free wind grant your
lordship a happy home-return and the
King's kiss of peace in Kent. Farewell ! I
must follow the King.   [*Exit.*

Herbert. Ay, and I warrant the customs.
  Did the King   252
Speak of the customs ?

Becket.   No ! — To die for it —
I live to die for it, I die to live for it.
The State will die, the Church can never
  die.
The King's not like to die for that which
  dies ;
But I must die for that which never dies.
It will be so — my visions in the Lord —
It must be so, my friend ! the wolves of
  England
Must murder her one shepherd, that the
  sheep   260
May feed in peace. False figure, Map
  would say.
Earth's falses are heaven's truths. And
  when my voice
Is martyr'd mute, and this man disappears,
That perfect trust may come again be-
  tween us,

And there, there, there, not here I shall
  rejoice
To find my stray sheep back within the
  fold.
The crowd are scattering, let us move
  away !
And thence to England.   [*Exeunt.*

ACT IV

SCENE I. — THE OUTSKIRTS OF THE BOWER

Geoffrey (*coming out of the wood*).
Light again ! light again ! Margery ? no,
that's a finer thing there. How it glitters !

Eleanor (*entering*). Come to me, little
one. How camest thou hither ?

Geoffrey. On my legs.

Eleanor. And mighty pretty legs too.
Thou art the prettiest child I ever saw.
Wilt thou love me ?

Geoffrey. No ; I only love mother.   10

Eleanor. Ay ; and who is thy mother ?

Geoffrey. They call her — But she lives
secret, you see.

Eleanor. Why ?

Geoffrey. Don't know why.

Eleanor. Ay, but some one comes to see
her now and then. Who is he ?

Geoffrey. Can't tell.

Eleanor. What does she call him ?

Geoffrey. My liege.   20

Eleanor. Pretty one, how camest thou ?

Geoffrey. There was a bit of yellow silk
here and there, and it looked pretty like a
glowworm, and I thought if I followed it
I should find the fairies.

Eleanor. I am the fairy, pretty one, a
good fairy to thy mother. Take me to
her.

Geoffrey. There are good fairies and bad
fairies, and sometimes she cries, and can't
sleep sound o' nights because of the bad
fairies.   32

Eleanor. She shall cry no more ; she
shall sleep sound enough if thou wilt take
me to her. I am her good fairy.

Geoffrey. But you don't look like a good
fairy. Mother does. You are not pretty,
like mother.

Eleanor. We can't all of us be as pretty
as thou art — (*aside*) little bastard ! Come,
here is a golden chain I will give thee if
thou wilt lead me to thy mother.   42

Geoffrey. No — no gold. Mother says gold
spoils all. Love is the only gold.

Eleanor. I love thy mother, my pretty

boy. Show me where thou camest out of
the wood.

Geoffrey. By this tree ; but I don't know
if I can find the way back again.

Eleanor. Where 's the warder ?

Geoffrey. Very bad. Somebody struck
him.   52

Eleanor. Ay ? who was that ?

Geoffrey. Can't tell. But I heard say he
had had a stroke, or you 'd have heard his
horn before now. Come along, then ; we
shall see the silk here and there, and I
want my supper.   [*Exeunt.*

Scene II

Rosamund's Bower

Rosamund. The boy so late ; pray God,
he be not lost !
I sent this Margery, and she comes not
back ;
I sent another, and she comes not back.
I go myself — so many alleys, crossings,
Paths, avenues — nay, if I lost him, now
The folds have fallen from the mystery
And left all naked, I were lost indeed.

Enter GEOFFREY and ELEANOR.

Geoffrey, the pain thou hast put me to !
[*Seeing* Eleanor.
Ha, you !
How came you hither ?

Eleanor. Your own child brought me
hither !   9

Geoffrey. You said you could n't trust
Margery, and I watched her and followed
her into the woods, and I lost her and went
on and on till I found the light and the
lady, and she says she can make you sleep
o' nights.

Rosamund. How dared you ? Know you
not this bower is secret,
Of and belonging to the King of England,
More sacred than his forests for the chase ?
Nay, nay, Heaven help you ; get you hence
in haste   19
Lest worse befall you.

Eleanor.   Child, I am mine own self
Of and belonging to the King. The King
Hath divers ofs and ons, ofs and belong-
ings,
Almost as many as your true Mussulman —
Belongings, paramours, whom it pleases
him
To call his wives ; but so it chances, child,
That I am his main paramour, his sultana.
But since the fondest pair of doves will

jar,
Even in a cage of gold, we had words of
late,
And thereupon he call'd my children bas-
tards.
Do you believe that you are married to
him ?   30

Rosamund. I *should* believe it.

Eleanor.   You must not believe it,
Because I have a wholesome medicine here
Puts that belief asleep. Your answer,
beauty !
Do you believe that you are married to
him ?

Rosamund. Geoffrey, my boy, I saw the
ball you lost in the fork of the great willow over the brook. Go. See that you do
not fall in. Go.   38

Geoffrey. And leave you alone with the
good fairy. She calls you beauty, but I
don't like her looks. Well, you bid me go,
and I 'll have my ball anyhow. Shall I
find you asleep when I come back ?

Rosamund. Go.   [*Exit* Geoffrey.

Eleanor. He is easily found again. *Do*
you believe it ?
I pray you then to take my sleeping-
draught ;
But if you should not care to take it —
see !   [*Draws a dagger.*
What ! have I scared the red rose from
your face
Into your heart ? But this will find it
there,   49
And dig it from the root for ever.

Rosamund.   Help ! help !

Eleanor. They say that walls have ears ;
but these, it seems,
Have none ! and I have none — to pity
thee.

Rosamund. I do beseech you — my child
is so young,
So backward too ; I cannot leave him yet.
I am not so happy I could not die myself,
But the child is so young. You have chil-
dren — his ;
And mine is the King's child ; so, if you
love him —
Nay, if you love him, there is great wrong
done
Somehow ; but if you do not — there are
those   59
Who say you do not love him — let me go
With my young boy, and I will hide my
face,
Blacken and gipsyfy it ; none shall know
me ;
The King shall never hear of me again,
But I will beg my bread along the world

With my young boy, and God will be our
      guide.
I never meant you harm in any way.
See, I can say no more.
      Eleanor. Will you not say you are not
            married to him?
      Rosamund. Ay, madam, I can *say* it, if
            you will.   69
      Eleanor. Then is thy pretty boy a bas-
            tard?
      Rosamund. No.
      Eleanor. And thou thyself a proven
            wanton?
      Rosamund.   No.
I am none such. I never loved but one.
I have heard of such that range from love
      to love,
Like the wild beast — if you can call it
      love.
I have heard of such — yea, even among
      those
Who sit on thrones — I never saw any
      such,
Never knew any such, and howsoever
You do misname me, match'd with any
      such,
I am snow to mud.
      Eleanor.   The more the pity then
That thy true home — the heavens — cry
      out for thee   80
Who art too pure for earth.

                Enter FITZURSE.

      Fitzurse.   Give her to me.
      Eleanor. The Judas-lover of our passion-
            play
Hath track'd us hither.
      Fitzurse.   Well, why not? I follow'd
You and the child: he babbled all the way.
Give her to me to make my honey-moon.
      Eleanor. Ay, as the bears love honey.
            Could you keep her
Indungeon'd from one whisper of the
      wind,
Dark even from a side glance of the moon,
And oublietted in the centre — No!
I follow out my hate and thy revenge. 90
      Fitzurse. You bade me take revenge an-
            other way —
To bring her to the dust. — Come with me,
      love,
And I will love thee. — Madam, let her
      live.
I have a far-off burrow where the King
Would miss her and for ever.
      Eleanor. How sayst thou, sweetheart?
Wilt thou go with him? he will marry
      thee.

      Rosamund. Give me the poison; set me
            free of him!
                [Eleanor *offers the vial.*
No, no! I will not have it.
      Eleanor.   Then this other,
The wiser choice, because my sleeping-
      draught
May bloat thy beauty out of shape, and
      make   100
Thy body loathsome even to thy child;
While this but leaves thee with a broken
      heart,
A doll-face blanch'd and bloodless, over
      which
If pretty Geoffrey do not break his own,
It must be broken for him.
      Rosamund.   O, I see now
Your purpose is to fright me — a trouba-
      dour,
You play with words. You had never used
      so many,
Not if you meant it, I am sure. The child —
No — mercy! No! (*Kneels.*)
      Eleanor.   Play! — that bosom never
Heaved under the King's hand with such
      true passion   110
As at this loveless knife that stirs the riot,
Which it will quench in blood! Slave, if
      he love thee,
Thy life is worth the wrestle for it. Arise,
And dash thyself against me that I may
      slay thee!
The worm! shall I let her go? But ha!
      what's here?
By very God, the cross I gave the King!
His village darling in some lewd caress
Has wheedled it off the King's neck to
      her own.
By thy leave, beauty. Ay, the same! I
      warrant
Thou hast sworn on this my cross a hun-
      dred times   120
Never to leave him — and that merits
      death,
False oath on holy cross — for thou must
      leave him
To-day, but not quite yet. My good Fitz-
      urse,
The running down the chase is kindlier
      sport
Even than the death. Who knows but that
      thy lover
May plead so pitifully, that I may spare
      thee?
Come hither, man; stand there. (*To Rosa-*
      mund.) Take thy one chance;
Catch at the last straw. Kneel to thy
      lord Fitzurse:
Crouch even because thou hatest him;

fawn upon him
For thy life and thy son's.
   Rosamund (rising).   I am a Clifford,
My son a Clifford and Plantagenet.   131
I am to die then, tho' there stand beside
   thee
One who might grapple with thy dagger,
   if he
Had aught of man, or thou of woman;
   or I
Would bow to such a baseness as would
   make me
Most worthy of it. Both of us will die,
And I will fly with my sweet boy to
   heaven,
And shriek to all the saints among the
   stars :
'Eleanor of Aquitaine, Eleanor of England !
Murder'd by that adulteress Eleanor,   140
Whose doings are a horror to the east,
A hissing in the west !' Have we not heard
Raymond of Poitou, thine own uncle —
   nay,
Geoffrey Plantagenet, thine own husband's
   father —
Nay, even the accursed heathen Salad-
   deen —
Strike !
I challenge thee to meet me before God.
Answer me there.
   Eleanor (raising the dagger). This in
   thy bosom, fool,
And after in thy bastard's !

Enter BECKET *from behind. Catches hold
of her arm.*

   Becket.   Murderess !
   [*The dagger falls; they stare at one
   another. After a pause.*
   Eleanor. My lord, we know you proud
   of your fine hand,   150
But having now admired it long enough,
We find that it is mightier than it seems —
At least mine own is frailer ; you are
   laming it.
   Becket. And lamed and maim'd to dis-
   location, better
Than raised to take a life which Henry
   bade me
Guard from the stroke that dooms thee
   after death
To wail in deathless flame.
   Eleanor.   Nor you nor I
Have now to learn, my lord, that our good
   Henry   158
Says many a thing in sudden heats which
   he

Gainsays by next sunrising — often ready
To tear himself for having said as much.
My lord, Fitzurse —
   Becket. He too ! what dost thou here ?
Dares the bear slouch into the lion's den ?
One downward plunge of his paw would
   rend away
Eyesight and manhood, life itself, from
   thee.
Go, lest I blast thee with anathema,
And make thee a world's horror.
   Fitzurse.   My lord, I shall
Remember this.
   Becket.   I *do* remember thee ;
Lest I remember thee to the lion, go.   169
             [*Exit* Fitzurse.
Take up your dagger ; put it in the sheath.
   Eleanor. Might not your courtesy stoop
   to hand it me ?
But crowns must bow when mitres sit so
   high.
Well — well — too costly to be left or lost.
            [*Picks up the dagger.*
I had it from an Arab soldan, who,
When I was there in Antioch, marvell'd at
Our unfamiliar beauties of the west ;
But wonder'd more at my much constancy
To the monk-king, Louis, our former bur-
   then,
From whom, as being too kin, you know,
   my lord,   179
God's grace and Holy Church deliver'd us.
I think, time given, I could have talk'd
   him out of
His ten wives into one. Look at the hilt.
What excellent workmanship ! In our poor
   west
We cannot do it so well.
   Becket.   We can do worse.
Madam, I saw your dagger at her throat ;
I heard your savage cry.
   Eleanor.   Well acted, was it ?
A comedy meant to seem a tragedy —
A feint, a farce. My honest lord, you are
   known
Thro' all the courts of Christendom as one
That mars a cause with over violence.   190
You have wrong'd Fitzurse. I speak not
   of myself.
We thought to scare this minion of the
   King
Back from her churchless commerce with
   the King
To the fond arms of her first love, Fitzurse,
Who swore to marry her. You have spoilt
   the farce.
My savage cry ? Why, she — she — when
   I strove
To work against her license for her good,

Bark'd out at me such monstrous charges
that
The King himself, for love of his own sons,
If hearing, would have spurn'd her; whereupon   200
I menaced her with this, as when we threaten
A yelper with a stick. Nay, I deny not
That I was somewhat anger'd. Do you hear me?
Believe or no, I care not. You have lost
The ear of the King. I have it. — My lord paramount,
Our great High-priest, will not your Holiness
Vouchsafe a gracious answer to your Queen?
  Becket. Rosamund hath not answer'd you one word;
Madam, I will not answer you one word.
Daughter, the world hath trick'd thee.
    Leave it, daughter;   210
Come thou with me to Godstow nunnery,
And live what may be left thee of a life
Saved as by miracle alone with Him
Who gave it.

        Re-enter GEOFFREY.

  Geoffrey. Mother, you told me a great fib; it was n't in the willow.
  Becket. Follow us, my son, and we will find it for thee —
Or something manlier.
    [*Exeunt* Becket, Rosamund, *and* Geoffrey.
  Eleanor. The world hath trick'd her — that's the King; if so,
There was the farce, the feint — not mine.
    And yet   219
I am all but sure my dagger was a feint
Till the worm turn'd — not life shot up in blood,
But death drawn in; — (*looking at the vial*) *this* was no feint, then? no.
But can I swear to that, had she but given
Plain answer to plain query? nay, methinks
Had she but bowed herself to meet the wave
Of humiliation, worshipt whom she loathed,
I should have let her be, scorn'd her too much
To harm her. Henry — Becket tells him this —
To take my life might lose him Aquitaine.
Too politic for that. Imprison me?   230

No, for it came to nothing — only a feint.
Did she not tell me I was playing on her?
I 'll swear to mine own self it was a feint.
Why should I swear, Eleanor, who am, or was,
A sovereign power? The King plucks out their eyes
Who anger him, and shall not I, the Queen,
Tear out her heart — kill, kill with knife or venom
One of his slanderous harlots? 'None of such?'
I love her none the more. Tut, the chance gone,
She lives — but not for him; one point is gain'd.   240
O, I that thro' the Pope divorced King Louis,
Scorning his monkery, — I that wedded Henry,
Honoring his manhood — will he not mock at me,
The jealous fool balk'd of her will — with *him*?
But he and he must never meet again.
Reginald Fitzurse!

        Re-enter FITZURSE.

  Fitzurse. Here, Madam, at your pleasure.
  Eleanor. My pleasure is to have a man about me.
Why did you slink away so like a cur?
  Fitzurse. Madam, I am as much man as the King.
Madam, I fear Church-censures like your King.   250
  Eleanor. He grovels to the Church when he 's black-blooded,
But kinglike fought the proud archbishop, — kinglike
Defied the Pope, and, like his kingly sires,
The Normans, striving still to break or bind
The spiritual giant with our island laws
And customs, made me for the moment proud
Even of that stale Church-bond which link'd me with him
To bear him kingly sons. I am not so sure
But that I love him still. Thou as much man!
No more of that; we will to France and be
Beforehand with the King, and brew from out   261
This Godstow-Becket intermeddling such

A strong hate-philtre as may madden him
— madden
Against his priest beyond all hellebore.

ACT V

SCENE 1. — CASTLE IN NORMANDY
KING'S CHAMBER

HENRY, ROGER OF YORK, FOLIOT, JOCELYN
OF SALISBURY.

Roger of York. Nay, nay, my liege,
He rides abroad with armed followers,
Hath broken all his promises to thyself,
Cursed and anathematized us right and
left,
Stirr'd up a party there against your son —
    Henry. Roger of York, you always hated
him,
Even when you both were boys at Theo-
bald's.
    Roger of York. I always hated bound-
less arrogance.
In mine own cause I strove against him
there,   9
And in thy cause I strive against him now.
    Henry. I cannot think he moves against
my son,
Knowing right well with what a tender-
ness
He loved my son.
    Roger of York.   Before you made him
king.
But Becket ever moves against a king.
The Church is all — the crime to be a
king.
We trust your Royal Grace, lord of more
land
Than any crown in Europe, will not yield
To lay your neck beneath your citizen's
heel.
    Henry. Not to a Gregory of my thron-
ing ! No.
    Foliot. My royal liege, in aiming at your
love,   20
It may be sometimes I have overshot
My duties to our Holy Mother Church.
Tho' all the world allows I fall no inch
Behind this Becket, rather go beyond
In scourgings, macerations, mortifyings,
Fasts, disciplines that clear the spiritual
eye,
And break the soul from earth. Let all
that be.
I boast not ; but you know thro' all this
quarrel

I still have cleaved to the crown, in hope
the crown
Would cleave to me that but obey'd the
crown,   30
Crowning your son ; for which our loyal
service.
And since we likewise swore to obey the
customs,
York and myself, and our good Salisbury
here,
Are push'd from out communion of the
Church.
    Jocelyn of Salisbury. Becket hath trod-
den on us like worms, my liege,
Trodden one half dead ; one half, but half-
alive,
Cries to the King.
    Henry (aside). Take care o' thyself, O
King !
    Jocelyn of Salisbury. Being so crush'd
and so humiliated
We scarcely dare to bless the food we
eat
Because of Becket.
    Henry.   What would ye have me do ?
    Roger of York. Summon your barons ;
        take their counsel ; yet   41
I know — could swear — as long as Becket
breathes,
Your Grace will never have one quiet
hour.
    Henry. What ? — Ay — but pray you do
not work upon me.
I see your drift — it may be so — and yet
You know me easily anger'd. Will you
hence ?
He shall absolve you — you shall have re-
dress.
I have a dizzying headache. Let me rest.
I 'll call you by and by.
    [*Exeunt* Roger of York, Foliot, *and*
        Jocelyn of Salisbury.
Would he were dead ! I have lost all love
for him.   50
If God would take him in some sudden
way —
Would he were dead !   [*Lies down.*
    Page (entering). My liege, the Queen of
England.
    Henry. God's eyes !   [*Starting up.*

Enter ELEANOR.

    Eleanor.   Of England ? Say of Aqui-
taine.
I am no Queen of England. I had dream'd
I was the bride of England, and a queen.
    Henry. And, — while you dream'd you

were the bride of England, —
Stirring her baby-king against me ? ha !
   Eleanor. The brideless Becket is thy
   king and mine ;
I will go live and die in Aquitaine.
   Henry. Except I clap thee into prison
   here,   60
Lest thou shouldst play the wanton there
again.
Ha, you of Aquitaine ! O you of Aqui-
taine !
You were but Aquitaine to Louis — no
wife ;
You are only Aquitaine to me — no wife.
   Eleanor. And why, my lord, should I be
   wife to one
That only wedded me for Aquitaine ?
Yet this no-wife — her six and thirty sail
Of Provence blew you to your English
throne ;
And this no-wife has borne you four brave
sons,
And one of them at least is like to prove 70
Bigger in our small world than thou art.
   Henry.   Ay —
Richard, if he *be* mine — I hope him mine.
But thou art like enough to make him
thine.
   Eleanor. Becket is like enough to make
   all his.
   Henry. Methought I had recover'd of
   the Becket,
That all was planed and bevell'd smooth
again,
Save from some hateful cantrip of thine
own.
   Eleanor. I will go live and die in Aqui-
   taine
I dream'd I was the consort of a king, 79
Not one whose back his priest has broken.
   Henry.   What !
Is the end come ? You, will you crown
my foe
My victor in mid-battle ? I will be
Sole master of my house. The end is mine.
What game, what juggle, what devilry are
you playing ?
Why do you thrust this Becket on me
again ?
   Eleanor. Why ? for I *am* true wife, and
   have my fears
Lest Becket thrust you even from your
throne.
Do you know this cross, my liege ?
   Henry (turning his head). Away ! Not I.
   Eleanor. Not even the central diamond,
   worth, I think,
Half of the Antioch whence I had it.
   Henry.   That ?

   Eleanor. I gave it you, and you your
   paramour ;   91
She sends it back, as being dead to earth,
So dead henceforth to you.
   Henry. Dead ! you have murder'd her,
Found out her secret bower and murder'd
her.
   Eleanor. Your Becket knew the secret
   of your bower.
   Henry (calling out). Ho there ! thy rest
   of life is hopeless prison.
   Eleanor. And what would my own Aqui-
   taine say to that ?
First, free thy captive from *her* hopeless
prison.
   Henry. O devil, can I free her from the
   grave ?
   Eleanor. You are too tragic ; both of us
   are players   100
In such a comedy as our court of Provence
Had laugh'd at. That 's a delicate Latin
lay
Of Walter Map : the lady holds the cleric
Lovelier than any soldier, his poor ton-
sure
A crown of Empire. Will you have it
again ?
(Offering the cross. He dashes it down.)
Saint Cupid, that is too irreverent.
Then mine once more.   *(Puts it on.)*
              Your cleric hath your lady.
Nay, what uncomely faces, could he see
you !
Foam at the mouth because King Thomas,
lord
Not only of your vassals but amours,   110
Thro' chastest honor of the Decalogue
Hath used the full authority of his Church
To put her into Godstow nunnery.
   Henry. To put her into Godstow nun-
   nery !
He dared not — liar ! yet, yet I remem-
ber —
I do remember.
He bade me put her into a nunnery —
Into Godstow, into Hellstow, Devilstow ?
The Church ! the Church !   119
God's eyes ! I would the Church were
down in hell !   [*Exit.*
   Eleanor. Aha !

       Enter the four KNIGHTS.

   Fitzurse. What made the King cry out
   so furiously ?
   Eleanor. Our Becket, who will not ab-
   solve the bishops.
I think ye four have cause to love this
Becket.

Fitzurse. I hate him for his insolence to all.

De Tracy. And I for all his insolence to thee.

De Brito. I hate him for I hate him is my reason,
And yet I hate him for a hypocrite.

De Morville. I do not love him, for he did his best
To break the barons, and now braves the King.   130

Eleanor. Strike, then, at once, the King would have him — See !

Re-enter HENRY.

Henry. No man to love me, honor me, obey me !
Sluggards and fools !
The slave that eat my bread has kick'd his King !
The dog I cramm'd with dainties worried me !
The fellow that on a lame jade came to court,
A ragged cloak for saddle — he, he, he,
To shake my throne, to push into my chamber —
My bed, where even the slave is private — he —
I 'll have her out again, he shall absolve 140
The bishops — they but did my will — not you —
Sluggards and fools, why do you stand and stare ?
You are no King's men — you — you — you are Becket's men.
Down with King Henry ! up with the Archbishop !
Will no man free me from this pestilent priest ?   [*Exit.*
        [*The* Knights *draw their swords.*
Eleanor. Are ye King's men ? I am King's woman, I.
The Knights. King's men ! King's men !

SCENE II

A ROOM IN CANTERBURY MONASTERY

BECKET *and* JOHN OF SALISBURY.

Becket. York said so ?
John of Salisbury. Yes : a man may take good counsel
Even from his foe.
Becket.   York will say anything.
What is he saying now ? gone to the King

And taken our anathema with him. York !
Can the King de-anathematize this York ?
John of Salisbury. Thomas, I would thou hadst return'd to England
Like some wise prince of this world from his wars,
With more of olive-branch and amnesty
For foes at home —thou hast raised the world against thee.
Becket. Why, John, my kingdom is not of this world.   10
John of Salisbury. If it were more of this world it might be
More of the next. A policy of wise pardon
Wins here as well as there. To bless thine enemies —
Becket. Ay, mine, not Heaven's.
John of Salisbury. And may there not be something
Of this world's leaven in thee too, when crying
On Holy Church to thunder out her rights
And thine own wrong so pitilessly ? Ah, Thomas,
The lightnings that we think are only Heaven's
Flash sometimes out of earth against the heavens.   19
The soldier, when he lets his whole self go
Lost in the common good, the common wrong,
Strikes truest even for his own self. I crave
Thy pardon — I have still thy leave to speak.
Thou hast waged God's war against the King ; and yet
We are self-uncertain creatures, and we may,
Yea, even when we know not, mix our spites
And private hates with our defence of Heaven.

Enter EDWARD GRIM.

Becket. Thou art but yesterday from Cambridge, Grim ;
What say ye there of Becket ?
Grim.   *I* believe him
The bravest in our roll of primates down   30
From Austin — there are some — for there are men
Of canker'd judgment everywhere —
Becket.   Who hold
With York, with York against me.
Grim.   Well, my lord,
A stranger monk desires access to you.

Becket. York against Canterbury, York
against God!
I am open to him.   [*Exit* Grim.

Enter ROSAMUND *as a Monk.*

Rosamund.   Can I speak with you
Alone, my father?
    Becket.   Come you to confess?
    Rosamund. Not now.
    Becket. Then speak; this is my other
self,
Who, like my conscience, never lets me be.
    Rosamund (throwing back the cowl). I
        know him, our good John of Salis-
        bury.   40
    Becket. Breaking already from thy no-
        vitiate
To plunge into this bitter world again —
These wells of Marah! I am grieved, my
        daughter.
I thought that I had made a peace for
        thee.
    Rosamund. Small peace was mine in my
        novitiate, father.
Thro' all closed doors a dreadful whisper
        crept
That thou wouldst excommunicate the
        King.
I could not eat, sleep, pray. I had with me
The monk's disguise thou gavest me for
        my bower;   49
I think our abbess knew it and allow'd it.
I fled, and found thy name a charm to
        get me
Food, roof, and rest. I met a robber once:
I told him I was bound to see the arch-
        bishop:
'Pass on,' he said, and in thy name I pass'd
From house to house. In one a son stone-
        blind
Sat by his mother's hearth. He had gone
        too far
Into the King's own woods; and the poor
        mother,
Soon as she learnt I was a friend of thine,
Cried out against the cruelty of the King.
I said it was the King's courts, not the
        King,   60
But she would not believe me, and she
        wish'd
The Church were king; she had seen the
        archbishop once,
So mild, so kind. The people love thee,
        father.
    Becket. Alas! when I was Chancellor to
        the King,
I fear I was as cruel as the King.
    Rosamund. Cruel? O, no — it is the law,

not he;
The customs of the realm.
    Becket.   The customs! customs!
    Rosamund. My lord, you have not ex-
        communicated him?   68
O, if you have, absolve him!
    Becket.   Daughter, daughter,
Deal not with things you know not.
    Rosamund.   I know *him.*
Then you have done it, and I call *you*
        cruel.
    John of Salisbury. No, daughter, you
        mistake our good archbishop;
For once in France the King had been so
        harsh,
He thought to excommunicate him —
        Thomas,
You could not — old affection master'd
        you,
You falter'd into tears.
    Rosamund.   God bless him for it!
    Becket. Nay, make me not a woman,
        John of Salisbury,
Nor make me traitor to my holy office.   78
Did not a man's voice ring along the aisle,
'The King is sick and almost unto death.'
How could I excommunicate him then?
    Rosamund. And wilt thou excommuni-
        cate him now?
    Becket. Daughter, my time is short, I
        shall not do it.
And were it longer — well — I should not
        do it.
    Rosamund. Thanks in this life, and in
        the life to come!
    Becket. Get thee back to thy nunnery
        with all haste;
Let this be thy last trespass. But one
        question —
How fares thy pretty boy, the little Geof-
        frey?
No fever, cough, croup, sickness?
    Rosamund.   No, but saved
From all that by our solitude. The
        plagues   90
That smite the city spare the solitudes.
    Becket. God save him from all sickness
        of the soul!
Thee too, thy solitude among thy nuns,
May that save thee! Doth he remember
        me?
    Rosamund. I warrant him.
    Becket. He is marvellously like thee.
    Rosamund. Liker the King.
    Becket.   No, daughter.
    Rosamund.   Ay, but wait
Till his nose rises; he will be very king.
    Becket. Even so; but think not of the
        King. Farewell!

Rosamund. My lord, the city is full of
    armed men.   99

Becket. Even so. Farewell !

Rosamund.   I will but pass to vespers,
And breathe one prayer for my liege-lord
    the King,
His child and mine own soul, and so
    return.

Becket. Pray for me too ; much need of
    prayer have I.
        [Rosamund *kneels and goes.*
Dan John, how much we lose, we celibates,
Lacking the love of woman and of child !

John of Salisbury. More gain than loss ;
    for of your wives you shall
Find one a slut whose fairest linen seems
Foul as her dust-cloth, if she used it — one
So charged with tongue that every thread
    of thought   109
Is broken ere it joins — a shrew to boot,
Whose evil song far on into the night
Thrills to the topmost tile — no hope but
    death ;
One slow, fat, white, a burthen of the
    hearth ;
And one that being thwarted ever swoons
And weeps herself into the place of power ;
And one an *uxor pauperis Ibyci.*
So rare the household honey-making bee,
Man's help ! but we, we have the Blessed
    Virgin
For worship, and our Mother Church for
    bride ;
And all the souls we saved and father'd
    here   120
Will greet us as our babes in Paradise.
What noise was that ? she told us of arm'd
    men
Here in the city. Will you not withdraw ?

Becket. I once was out with Henry in
    the days
When Henry loved me, and we came upon
A wild-fowl sitting on her nest, so still
I reach'd my hand and touch'd ; she did
    not stir ;
The snow had frozen round her, and she
    sat
Stone-dead upon a heap of ice-cold eggs.
Look ! how this love, this mother, runs
    thro' all   130
The world God made — even the beast —
    the bird !

John of Salisbury. Ay, still a lover of the
    beast and bird ?
But these arm'd men — will you not hide
    yourself ?
Perchance the fierce De Brocs from Salt-
    wood Castle,
To assail our Holy Mother lest she brood

Too long o'er this hard egg, the world,
    and send
Her whole heart's heat into it, till it break
Into young angels. Pray you, hide your-
    self.

Becket. There was a little fair-hair'd
    Norman maid   139
Lived in my mother's house ; if Rosamund
    is
The world's rose, as her name imports her
    — she
Was the world's lily.

John of Salisbury. Ay, and what of her ?

Becket. She died of leprosy.

John of Salisbury.   I know not why
You call these old things back again, my
    lord.

Becket. The drowning man, they say,
    remembers all
The chances of his life, just ere he dies.

John of Salisbury. Ay — but these arm'd
    men — will *you* drown *yourself ?*
He loses half the meed of martyrdom   148
Who will be martyr when he might escape.

Becket. What day of the week ? Tues-
    day ?

John of Salisbury.   Tuesday, my lord.

Becket. On a Tuesday was I born, and
    on a Tuesday
Baptized ; and on a Tuesday did I fly
Forth from Northampton ; on a Tuesday
    pass'd
From England into bitter banishment ;
On a Tuesday at Pontigny came to me
The ghostly warning of my martyrdom ;
On a Tuesday from mine exile I return'd,
And on a Tuesday —

TRACY *enters, then* FITZURSE, DE BRITO,
    and DE MORVILLE. MONKS *following.*
        — on a Tuesday — Tracy !

(*A long silence, broken by* FITZURSE *say-*
    ing, contemptuously,)
God help thee !

John of Salisbury (*aside*). How the good
    archbishop reddens !
He never yet could brook the note of
    scorn.   160

Fitzurse. My lord, we bring a message
    from the King
Beyond the water ; will you have it alone,
Or with these listeners near you ?

Becket.   As you will.

Fitzurse. Nay as *you* will.

Becket.   Nay, as *you* will.

John of Salisbury.   Why, then
Better perhaps to speak with them apart.
Let us withdraw.

[*All go out except the four* Knights *and* Becket.

Fitzurse.   We are all alone with him.
Shall I not smite him with his own cross-
    staff?
    De Morville. No, look! the door is
    open: let him be.
    Fitzurse. The King condemns your ex-
    communicating —
    Becket. This is no secret, but a public
    matter.   170
In here again!

JOHN OF SALISBURY *and* MONKS *return.*

        Now, sirs, the King's commands!
    Fitzurse. The King beyond the water,
    thro' our voices, -
Commands you to be dutiful and leal
To your young King on this side of the
    water,
Not scorn him for the foibles of his youth.
What! you would make his coronation
    void
By cursing those who crown'd him. Out
    upon you!
    Becket. Reginald, all men know I loved
    the prince.
His father gave him to my care, and I
Became his second father. He had his
    faults,   180
For which I would have laid mine own
    life down
To help him from them, since indeed I
    loved him,
And love him next after my lord his
    father.
Rather than dim the splendor of his crown
I fain would treble and quadruple it
With revenues, realms, and golden prov-
    inces
So that were done in equity.
    Fitzurse.   You have broken
Your bond of peace, your treaty with the
    King —
Wakening such brawls and loud disturb-
    ances
In England, that he calls you over-sea 190
To answer for it in his Norman courts.
    Becket. Prate not of bonds, for never,
    O, never again
Shall the waste voice of the bond-breaking
    sea
Divide me from the mother church of
    England,
My Canterbury. Loud disturbances!
O, ay — the bells rang out even to deafen-
    ing,
Organ and pipe, and dulcimer, chants and
    hymns

In all the churches, trumpets in the halls,
Sobs, laughter, cries: they spread their
    raiment down
Before me — would have made my path-
    way flowers,   200
Save that it was midwinter in the street,
But full midsummer in those honest hearts.
    Fitzurse. The King commands you to
    absolve the bishops
Whom you have excommunicated.
    Becket.   I?
Not I, the Pope. Ask *him* for absolution.
    Fitzurse. But you advised the Pope.
    Becket.   And so I did.
They have but to submit.
    The Four Knights. The King commands
    you.
We are all King's men.
    Becket. King's men at least should know
That their own King closed with me last
    July
That I should pass the censures of the
    Church   210
On those that crown'd young Henry in this
    realm,
And trampled on the rights of Canter-
    bury.
    Fitzurse. What! dare you charge the
    King with treachery?
He sanction thee to excommunicate
The prelates whom he chose to crown his
    son!
    Becket. I spake no word of treachery,
    Reginald.
But for the truth of this I make appeal
To all the archbishops, bishops, prelates,
    barons,
Monks, knights, five hundred, that were
    there and heard.
Nay, you yourself were there: you heard
    yourself.   220
    Fitzurse. I was not there.
    Becket.   I saw you there.
    Fitzurse.   I was not.
    Becket. You were. I never forget any-
    thing.
    Fitzurse. He makes the King a traitor,
    me a liar.
How long shall we forbear him?
    John of Salisbury (*drawing* Becket
    aside). O my good lord,
Speak with them privately on this here-
    after.
You see they have been revelling, and I
    fear
Are braced and brazen'd up with Christ-
    mas wines
For any murderous brawl.

Becket.   And yet they prate
Of mine, my brawls, when those that name
    themselves
Of the King's part have broken down our
    barns,   230
Wasted our diocese, outraged our tenants,
Lifted our produce, driven our clerics
    out —
Why they, your friends, those ruffians, the
    De Brocs,
They stood on Dover beach to murder me,
They slew my stags in mine own manor
    here,
Mutilated, poor brute, my sumpter-mule,
Plunder'd the vessel full of Gascon wine,
The old King's present, carried off the
    casks,
Kill'd half the crew, dungeon'd the other
    half   239
In Pevensey Castle —
De Morville.   Why not rather then,
If this be so, complain to your young
    King,
Not punish of your own authority?
Becket. Mine enemies barr'd all access
    to the boy.
They knew he loved me.
Hugh, Hugh, how proudly you exalt your
    head!
Nay, when they seek to overturn our
    rights,
I ask no leave of king, or mortal man,
To set them straight again. Alone I do it.
Give to the King the things that are the
    King's,   249
And those of God to God.
Fitzurse. Threats! threats! ye hear him.
What! will he excommunicate all the
    world?
        [*The* Knights *come round* Becket.
De Tracy. He shall not.
De Brito.   Well, as yet — I should be
    grateful —
He hath not excommunicated *me.*
Becket. Because thou wast *born* excom-
    municate.
I never spied in thee one gleam of grace.
De Brito. Your Christian's Christian
    charity!
Becket.   By Saint Denis —
De Brito. Ay, by Saint Denis, now will
    he flame out,
And lose his head as old Saint Denis did.
Becket. Ye think to scare me from my
    loyalty
To God and to the Holy Father. No! 260
Tho' all the swords in England flash'd
    above me
Ready to fall at Henry's word or yours —

Tho' all the loud-lung'd trumpets upon
    earth
Blared from the heights of all the thrones
    of her kings,
Blowing the world against me, I would
    stand
Clothed with the full authority of Rome,
Mail'd in the perfect panoply of faith,
First of the foremost of their files who die
For God, to people heaven in the great
    day
When God makes up his jewels. Once I
    fled —   270
Never again, and you — I marvel at you —
Ye know what is between us. Ye have
    sworn
Yourselves my men when I was Chan-
    cellor —
My vassals — and yet threaten your arch-
    bishop
In his own house.
Knights.   Nothing can be between us
That goes against our fealty to the King.
Fitzurse. And in his name we charge you
    that ye keep
This traitor from escaping.
Becket.   Rest you easy,
For I am easy to keep. I shall not fly. 279
Here, here, here will you find me.
De Morville.   Know you not
You have spoken to the peril of your life?
Becket. As I shall speak again.
Fitzurse, De Tracy, and De Brito. To
    arms!
        [*They rush out,* De Morville *lingers.*
Becket.   De Morville,
I had thought so well of you; and even
    now
You seem the least assassin of the four.
O, do not damn yourself for company!
Is it too late for me to save your soul?
I pray you for one moment stay and speak.
De Morville. Becket, it *is* too late.
                                        [*Exit.*
Becket.   Is it too late?
Too late on earth may be too soon in
    hell.   289
Knights (*in the distance*). Close the
    great gate — ho, there — upon the
    town!
Becket's Retainers. Shut the hall-doors!
                                    [*A pause.*
Becket.   You hear them, brother John;
Why do you stand so silent, brother John?
John of Salisbury. For I was musing on
    an ancient saw,
Suaviter in modo, fortiter in re;
Is strength less strong when hand-in-hand
    with grace?

Gratior in pulchro corpore virtus. Thomas,
Why should you heat yourself for such as
    these?
    Becket. Methought I answer'd moder-
        ately enough.
    John of Salisbury. As one that blows the
        coal to cool the fire.
My lord, I marvel why you never lean ³⁰⁰
On any man's advising but your own.
    Becket. Is it so, Dan John? well, what
        should I have done?
John of Salisbury. You should have taken
    counsel with your friends
Before these bandits brake into your
    presence.
They seek — you make — occasion for your
    death.
    Becket. My counsel is already taken,
        John.
I am prepared to die.
    John of Salisbury.   We are sinners all,
The best of all not all-prepared to die.
    Becket. God's will be done!
    John of Salisbury. Ay, well, God's will
        be done!
    Grim (re-entering). My lord, the knights
        are arming in the garden   ³¹⁰
Beneath the sycamore.
    Becket.   Good! let them arm.
    Grim. And one of the De Brocs is with
        them, Robert,
The apostate monk that was with Randulf
    here.
He knows the twists and turnings of the
    place.
    Becket. No fear!
    Grim.   No fear, my lord.
        [*Crashes on the hall-doors. The* Monks
        flee.
    Becket (rising).   Our dovecote flown!
I cannot tell why monks should all be
    cowards.
    John of Salisbury. Take refuge in your
        own cathedral, Thomas.
    Becket. Do they not fight the Great
        Fiend day by day?
Valor and holy life should go together. ³¹⁹
Why should all monks be cowards?
    John of Salisbury.   Are they so?
I say, take refuge in your own cathedral.
    Becket. Ay, but I told them I would
        wait them here.
    Grim. May they not say you dared not
        show yourself
In your old place? and vespers are begin-
    ning.
        [*Bell rings for vespers till end of scene.*
You should attend the office, give them
    heart.

They fear you slain; they dread they know
    not what.
    Becket. Ay, monks, not men.
    Grim.   I am a monk, my lord.
Perhaps, my lord, you wrong us.   ³²⁸
Some would stand by you to the death.
    Becket.   Your pardon.
    John of Salisbury. He said, 'Attend the
        office.'
    Becket.   Attend the office?
Why then — the Cross! — who bears my
    Cross before me?
Methought they would have brain'd me
    with it, John.   [Grim *takes it.*
    Grim. I! Would that I could bear thy
        cross indeed!
    Becket. The mitre!
    John of Salisbury. Will you wear it? —
        there!   [Becket *puts on the mitre.*
    Becket.   The pall!
I go to meet my King!   [*Puts on the pall.*
    Grim.   To meet the King?
        [*Crashes on the doors as they go out.*
    John of Salisbury. Why do you move
        with such a stateliness?
Can you not hear them yonder like a
    storm,
Battering the doors, and breaking thro'
    the walls?
    Becket. Why do the heathen rage? My
        two good friends,
What matters murder'd here, or murder'd
    there?   ³⁴⁰
And yet my dream foretold my martyrdom
In mine own church. It is God's will. Go
    on.
Nay, drag me not. We must not seem to
    fly.

SCENE III

NORTH TRANSEPT OF CANTERBURY
CATHEDRAL

*On the right hand a flight of steps leading
to the Choir, another flight on the left,
leading to the North Aisle. Winter after-
noon slowly darkening. Low thunder
now and then of an approaching storm.*
Monks *heard chanting the service.* Rosamund *kneeling.*

    Rosamund. O blessed saint, O glorious
        Benedict, —
These arm'd men in the city, these fierce
    faces —
Thy holy follower founded Canterbury —
Save that dear head which now is Canter-
    bury,

Save him, he saved my life, he saved my
    child,
Save him, his blood would darken Henry's
    name ;
Save him till all as saintly as thyself
He miss the searching flame of purgatory,
And pass at once perfect to Paradise.   9
[*Noise of steps and voices in the cloisters.*
Hark ! Is it they ? Coming ! He is not
    here —
Not yet, thank heaven.   O, save him !
        [*Goes up steps leading to choir.*
Becket (*entering, forced along by* John
    of Salisbury *and* Grim). No, I tell
    you !
I cannot bear a hand upon my person ;
Why do you force me thus against my
    will ?
Grim. My lord, we force you from your
    enemies.
Becket. As you would force a king from
    being crown'd.
John of Salisbury. We must not force
    the crown of martyrdom.
[*Service stops.* Monks *come down from
    the stairs that lead to the choir.*
Monks. Here is the great archbishop !
    He lives ! he lives !
Die with him, and be glorified together.
Becket. Together ? — get you back ! go
    on with the office.   19
Monks. Come, then, with us to vespers.
Becket.   How can I come
When you so block the entry ? Back, I
    say !
Go on with the office. Shall not Heaven
    be served
Tho' earth's last earthquake clash'd the
    minster-bells,
And the great deeps were broken up again,
And hiss'd against the sun ?
                [*Noise in the cloisters.*
Monks.   The murderers, hark !
Let us hide ! let us hide !
Becket.   What do these people fear ?
Monks. Those arm'd men in the cloister.
Becket.   Be not such cravens !
I will go out and meet them.
Grim and Others.   Shut the doors !
We will not have him slain before our
    face.   29
    [*They close the doors of the transept.
    Knocking.*
Fly, fly, my lord, before they burst the
    doors !   [*Knocking.*
Becket. Why, these are our own monks
    who follow'd us !
And will you bolt them out, and have
    them slain ?

Undo the doors ; the church is not a cas-
    tle.
Knock, and it shall be open'd. Are you
    deaf ?
What, have I lost authority among you ?
Stand by, make way !
    [*Opens the doors. Enter* Monks *from
    cloister.*
        Come in, my friends, come in !
Nay, faster, faster !
    Monks.   O, my lord archbishop.
A score of knights all arm'd with swords
    and axes —
To the choir, to the choir !
    [*Monks divide, part flying by the stairs
    on the right, part by those on the
    left. The rush of these last bears*
    Becket *along with them some way
    up the steps, where he is left stand-
    ing alone.*
Becket.   Shall I too pass to the choir,
And die upon the patriarchal throne   40
Of all my predecessors ?
    John of Salisbury.   No, to the crypt !
Twenty steps down. Stumble not in the
    darkness,
Lest they should seize thee.
    Grim.   To the crypt ? no — no,
To the chapel of Saint Blaise beneath the
    roof !
    John of Salisbury (*pointing upward and
    downward*). That way or this ! Save
    thyself either way.
    Becket. O, no, not either way, nor any
    way
Save by that way which leads thro' night
    to light.
Not twenty steps, but one.
And fear not I should stumble in the dark-
    ness,
Not tho' it be their hour, the power of
    darkness,   50
But my hour too, the power of light in
    darkness.
I am not in the darkness but the light,
Seen by the Church in heaven, the Church
    on earth —
The power of life in death to make her
    free !

Enter the four KNIGHTS. JOHN OF SALIS-
BURY *flies to the altar of Saint Benedict.*

    Fitzurse. Here, here, King's men !
    [*Catches hold of the last flying* Monk.
        Where is the traitor Becket ?
    Monk. I am not he ! I am not he, my
    lord.
I am not he indeed !

Fitzurse.   Hence to the fiend !
                    [*Pushes him away.*
Where is this treble traitor to the King ?
De Tracy. Where is the archbishop,
    Thomas Becket ?
Becket.   Here.   59
No traitor to the King, but Priest of God,
Primate of England.
              [*Descending into the transept.*
                I am he ye seek.
What would ye have of me ?
Fitzurse.   Your life.
De Tracy.   Your life.
De Morville. Save that you will absolve
    the bishops.
Becket.   Never, —
Except they make submission to the
    Church.
You had my answer to that cry before.
De Morville. Why, then you are a dead
    man ; flee !
Becket.   I will not.
I am readier to be slain than thou to slay.
Hugh, I know well thou hast but half a
    heart
To bathe this sacred pavement with my
    blood.
God pardon thee and these, but God's full
    curse   71
Shatter you all to pieces if ye harm
One of my flock !
Fitzurse. Was not the great gate shut ?
They are thronging in to vespers — half
    the town.
We shall be overwhelm'd. Seize him and
    carry him !
Come with us — nay — thou art our pris-
    oner — come !
De Morville. Ay, make him prisoner, do
    not harm the man.
[*Fitzurse lays hold of the* Archbishop's
    pall.
Becket. Touch me not !
De Brito. How the good priest gods him-
    self !
He is not yet ascended to the Father.
Fitzurse. I will not only touch, but drag
    thee hence.
Becket. Thou art my man, thou art my
    vassal. Away !   80
[*Flings him off till he reels, almost to
    falling.*
De Tracy (lays hold of the pall). Come ;
    as he said, thou art our prisoner.
Becket.   Down !
              [*Throws him headlong.*
Fitzurse (advances with drawn sword). I
    told thee that I should remember
    thee !

Becket. Profligate pander !
Fitzurse. Do you hear that ? strike,
    strike.
[*Strikes off the* Archbishop's *mitre, and
    wounds him in the forehead.*
Becket (covers his eyes with his hand). I
    do commend my cause to God, the
    Virgin,
Saint Denis of France and Saint Alphege
    of England,
And all the tutelar Saints of Canterbury.
    [Grim *wraps his arms about the* Arch-
    bishop.
Spare this defence, dear brother.
    [*Tracy has arisen, and approaches, hesi-
    tatingly, with his sword raised.*
Fitzurse.   Strike him, Tracy !
*Rosamund (rushing down steps from the
    choir).* No, no, no, no !
Fitzurse. This wanton here. De Mor-
    ville,
Hold her away.
De Morville. I hold her.
Rosamund (held back by De Morville,
    and stretching out her arms).
                Mercy, mercy,
As you would hope for mercy !
Fitzurse.   Strike, I say !
Grim. O God, O noble knights, O sacri-
    lege !   91
Strike our archbishop in his own cathe-
    dral !
The Pope, the King, will curse you — the
    whole world
Abhor you ; ye will die the death of dogs !
Nay, nay, good Tracy.   [*Lifts his arm.*
Fitzurse.   Answer not, but strike.
De Tracy. There is my answer then.
    [*Sword falls on Grim's arm, and glances
    from it, wounding* Becket.
Grim.   Mine arm is sever'd.
I can no more — fight out the good fight —
    die
Conqueror.
    [*Staggers into the chapel of Saint Bene-
    dict.*
Becket (falling on his knees). At the
    right hand of Power —
Power and great glory — for thy Church,
    O Lord —
Into thy hands, O Lord — into thy
    hands ! —   [*Sinks prone.*
De Brito. This last to rid thee of a
    world of brawls ! *(Kills him.)*
The traitor 's dead, and will arise no more.
Fitzurse. Nay, have we still'd him ?
    What ! the great archbishop !
De Tracy. No, Reginald, he is dead.
Does he breathe ? No ?

[*Storm bursts.*

De Morville. Will the earth gape and swallow us?

De Brito.   The deed's done —
Away!

[De Brito, De Tracy, Fitzurse, *rush out, crying 'King's men!'* De Morville *follows slowly. Flashes of lightning thro' the Cathedral.* Rosamund *seen kneeling by the body of* Becket.

9

ALGERNON CHARLES SWINBURNE'S *ATALANTA IN CALYDON*

It is striking that those who have attempted serious criticism of *Atalanta in Calydon* often begin (and sometimes end) by summarizing the action of the play. This approach reflects not on the obtuseness of critics, unfortunately, but on the play itself, and indicates how far *Atalanta* is from drama that could be effectively presented on stage. There seems in *Atalanta* a disjunction between the events and the significance attributed to them, a disjunction reflected in the "Swinburnian" language of the play. The lines sometimes seem to move on their own, a sort of torrent of verse, almost divorced from the dramatic problems of developing and resolving conflict. Yet the play was extremely popular when it was published, and was of primary importance in establishing Swinburne as a significant poet. One of the reasons for its popularity, certainly, was that Swinburne adopted the form of the Greek tragedy.

In describing the recently finished play, Swinburne wrote, "I think it is pure Greek, and the first poem of the sort in modern times, combining lyric and dramatic work on the old principle."[1] But if it is "Greek" in its external aspect—and certainly it imitates the form closely, and often successfully—it is just as true that the lyric so far outweighs the dramatic as to make it often difficult to follow the action. (Critics commonly describe it as "lyric drama" rather than tragedy.) And for all his consciousness of and adherence to Aristotelian principles, Swinburne produced a play that is, finally, unplayable. Harold Nicolson aptly calls *Atalanta* "an event in the mind."[2] There is action, surely, action that is of a certain magnitude, action that has a beginning, middle, and end, and manifests in its progress the good tragic principle that character is fate. The play is in this respect a thing well wrought. But the most important thematic implications of *Atalanta in Calydon* are expressed, not by an imitation of human action, but through the more purely "poetic" action of symbol and image patterns. If the work is to be considered even momentarily as a drama, then the apparent lack of complete articulation between its modes of action and language creates the confusion that criticism has sought to clarify—usually by narrating the plot.

Swinburne might have drawn the legend of *Atalanta* from any or all of several sources, among them Ovid's *Metamorphoses*, the Euripedean fragment *Meleager*, or a brief reference in Book Nine of the *Iliad*. None of these sources, however, treats the matter as Swinburne does. In the older versions, Atalanta and Meleager are the chief characters. In Swinburne's poem, Althæa is obviously the most important; Atalanta and Meleager are simply counters in Althæa's game with fate.

---

1. Cecil Lang, ed., *The Swinburne Letters* (New Haven, 1959), vol. 1, p. 115.
2. Harold Nicolson, *Swinburne* (London, 1926), p. 92.

The conclusion of the play—Meleager's death and Althæa's resignation to silence and suffering—apparently demonstrates the moral that to disobey the gods entails punishment. That Althæa sought to save Meleager by rescuing from the fire the brand which the Fates say is identical with his life only delays his death, and finally makes his agony and hers greater. But Althæa cannot do otherwise, as she cannot keep from throwing the brand back into the fire when her son slays her two brothers. There was never, Althæa says,

> queen of men
> More perfect in her heart toward whom she loved.
> . . . I forget never.

These lines, while giving us the apparent motive for Althæa's revenge, are a crux in the play, for her perfection of heart causes not only her murder of Meleager, but her defiance of love itself in doing so, and ultimately her defiance of the gods.

Given Althæa's character, then, the action demonstrates not the necessity of accepting the will of the gods, but the inevitable human need to protest the apparent malevolence of that will. The gods, Althæa says, leave us but one choice: "to live and do just deeds and die." Since "just" here means the retributive murder of her son, the choice is clearly not a meaningful one:

> . . . madness have ye given us and not health,
> And sins whereof we know not; and for these
> Death, and sudden destruction unaware.

Thus the play that Swinburne called "pure Greek" ("in spite," he added, "of funereal circumstances which I suspect have a little deepened the natural colours of Greek fatalism here and there"[3]) is at heart not Greek at all. (The fact may well account for the great initial popularity of the play. The vitality of Swinburne's attack on God was perhaps reinforced by his use of the Greek form. If one can believe the rumor that Christina Rossetti pasted a blank slip over the phrase "the supreme evil, God," in her copy of the poem, one can also imagine the secret thrill of horror with which she must have lifted the figleaf occasionally.)

The necessity for summary of the action comes, not so much from one's failure to see what happens, but from an inability to understand *why* things happen as they do. Althæa's apparent motivation—her perfection of heart and her long memory—does not give us an adequate explanation of her actions. But what Swinburne is most interested in is not logical explanation, but the emotional quality of intense experience, and this is most clearly conveyed in the play's medium—its poetry.

Althæa dominates the play to the extent that it is difficult to see how Swinburne could avoid naming it for her—though Atalanta is, to be sure, the immediate cause of the conflict about which the play turns. But Althæa is the protagonist (in the literal and figurative senses of the term). She performs the key actions of the drama, and she enunciates (with the chorus) the significance of those actions. Beside her, Atalanta appears pale and cold—emotionless, almost, though she apparently returns Meleager's love. (It may be that Swinburne purposely keeps us at a distance from Atalanta; from one point of view she is *only* an instrument of Diana's vengeance against the royal house of Calydon.) Even Meleager has little life next to the passion of Althæa, though Swinburne tries much harder than with Atalanta to make him heroic. He, at least, shares with Althæa the desire and strength to act. Atalanta has no need to act: she fulfills her function in the drama simply by being.

---

3. *Letters*, vol. 1, p. 115. The "funereal circumstances" were the illness and death of his sister Edith, while he was composing the play.

Because of the intensity of Althæa's character, and the particular quality of her passion, it is fair to suggest that the most important theme of the play is not religious: it is not an attempt to explain the ways of man to God, but an exploration of love as the single most important element of human life. Love is the mainspring of Althæa's being, and of course that love is expressed in reverence for the gods as well as in the perfection of her heart toward her brothers and son. Ideally, the two sorts of love coincide: when they do not, Swinburne would have us choose life. The most striking image patterns of the play express the notion that in varying ways love is the essential human element. "In *Atalanta*," S. C. Chew says, "wrath and woe and death are the offspring of love."[4] But wrath and woe and death are the contraries necessary to life, the sensible proof that we are human.

The first speech in the play, the invocation of Diana by the chief huntsman, identifies the gods as givers of life who also keep the secret of death—"the end, that lies unreached as yet / Between the hands and on the knees of gods." But while Diana is "mother of months," as the chorus announces in the famous "hounds of spring" song, the life she gives is not entirely satisfying. With spring, the "brown bright nightingale amorous" is only "half assuaged for Itylus, / For the Thracian ships and the foreign faces, / The tongueless vigil, and all the pain." There is no answer to the riddle of human life, the necessary condition of which is pain. As Althæa says, in response to the chorus,

> . . . though the spring put back a little while
> Winter, and snows that plague all men for sin,
> And the iron time of cursing, yet I know
> Spring shall be ruined with the rain, and storm
> Eat up like fire the ashen autumn days.

The gods may spare us for a while, but finally "they smite and spare no whit." No reverence is due Diana, Althæa says; having failed to conquer Calydon in war, she has sent the curse of the boar that wastes the land, and now she has prepared a new curse greater than all the rest, the curse of love, in the guise of her maiden Atalanta.

Althæa identifies this curse in terms that express the central image pattern of the play: Diana

> hath lit
> Fire where the old fire went out, and where the wind
> Slackened, hath blown on us with deadlier air.

(Almost the same terms are later used in describing Althæa, when in burning the brand she robs Meleager of life.) Fire here represents power, and the pain of punishment. It is also, however, the central symbol in the play for life, and in the interplay among the various aspects of the symbol Swinburne seeks to define the quality of human existence.

The identification of Diana with the moon is one version of this pattern: while the moon as it waxes and wanes is associated with various life forces, the light it sheds is pale and cold. So Diana and her purest maiden, Atalanta, whatever fire may lie beneath, are chaste and aloof. The moon is "twin-born" with the sun (as are time and death), but while the sun is consistently described in terms of flame or burning, the moon in its light becomes a "flameless shell." Diana is the "lady of light," but her heat—like that of "snowy-souled Atalanta"—is but a moderate one. Her vengeance is paradoxically hot and cold at once. Atalanta "hath no touch of love," the chorus says, and throughout the play Swinburne uses

---

4. Samuel C. Chew, *Swinburne* (Boston, 1929), p. 63.

images of whiteness and lack of warmth to describe her. Meleager describes her as "pure, and a light lit at the hands of gods," and even Atalanta describes her life of dedication to Diana as

> cold and sacred . . .
> far from dances and the back-blowing torch.

But love—the response that Atalanta draws from Meleager, and more particularly the relationship between Althæa and Meleager or Althæa and her brothers—is consistently identified with heat and flame. The chorus calls Aphrodite "the perilous goddess,"

> A fleshly blossom, a flame
> Filling the heavens with heat
> To the cold white ends of the north.

And love excites only to destroy. All of Althæa's foreboding is expressed in one remark early in the play: love "is an evil thing, and turns / Choice words and wisdom into fire and air."

Significantly, it is the chorus, which in the initial interchanges with Althæa protests the justice of the ways of the gods, that comes to state most clearly and fully her darkly pessimistic view of human life. It is God

> Who makes desire, and slays desire with shame;
> Who shakes the heaven as ashes in his hand;
> . . . Bids day waste night as fire devours a brand,
> Smites without sword, and scourges without rod;
> The supreme evil, God.

Every human experience in the play focuses finally on the problem of love, whether between Althæa and Meleager or Atalanta and Meleager. And every human experience is also related to one of the patterns of fire imagery. Meleager (in the plot and in the language of the play) is born to flame, and he must die by flame, because Althæa returns to the fire the brand she had rescued shortly after his birth. The effect of emotion on both Meleager and Althæa is always described as heat: tears are as fire, desire is a fire that blinds; Meleager slays Toxeus and Plexippus "as fire cleaves wood." Finally, the chorus says as it moralizes on Meleager's dying, *life* burns.

Oliver Elton long ago commented that in his poetry generally Swinburne is often best "when the poetic idea is the merest film holding the foambell together."[5] In *Atalanta in Calydon*, the poetic idea is a good deal more than film, is in fact extremely forceful, but the foambell does not hang together completely. On the one hand, the action of the play apparently meshes perfectly with this pattern of images. What is, however, weakly accounted for in the plot, but rendered in extremely vivid imagery, is Althæa's motivation in revenging herself on Meleager. True, she tells us of her perfection of heart toward those she loves, and tries to persuade us that Toxeus and Plexippus, who appear simply boors in the play, earned her love by their kindness to her when she was small. But while this may offer a reasonable excuse, it leaves unaccounted for the intense, irrational jealousy she feels toward Atalanta. Somehow Meleager's infatuation with Atalanta violates the bond between mother and son, and it is that violation that Althæa cannot forgive, and the poem suggests that the most important human experiences cannot be accounted for: the most that the artist can do is attempt to capture them in poetic images. For this reason alone, then, the story as story

---

5. Oliver Elton, *A Survey of English Literature, 1830–1880* (London, 1920) , vol. 2, p. 55.

(or drama) seems incomplete—an unrealized idea lurks behind the action. Whether Swinburne was conscious of this or not is, finally, irrelevant. It is nevertheless hard to resist thinking of the poem as a sort of drama of the author's psyche. The fascination with pain generally, the aloofness of the loved one who both because of and despite her coldness causes great mental and physical anguish, the masculinity of the loved one, all recall motifs of Swinburne's life. (There are, it happens, rather specific parallels between Atalanta and Swinburne's cousin, Mary Gordon, to whom he proposed marriage and by whom he was rejected in a fit of hysterical laughter.) But close (and sometimes illuminating) as such parallels may be, one cannot use them to justify the work, either as poem or as drama.

The kindest of critics must admit that the play fails as drama. Despite the tightness of construction, despite Swinburne's knowledge and use of various devices of the Greek theater, the dramatic idea is not workable. Were the play to be staged (and we have been unable to discover that any attempt has been made to present it), its faults would be all too obvious, since performance would no doubt emphasize the strength of Althæa's passion and her lack of incentive. It might also, we think, obscure even further the characters of Atalanta and Meleager, and lessen the possibility of dramatic conflict. In both cases, the rush of Swinburne's language would overwhelm the most skilled performer. One has to say that a good many of the speeches—mostly Althæa's, but sometimes those of the other characters as well—are simply too long. The speeches reveal a good deal of feeling, and very strong feeling at that, but they detract from, rather than adding to or clarifying, the drama of the incidents described. Swinburne's approach to theme primarily through image and symbol is a bit like thirteen ways of looking at a blackbird, and it requires the sort of reflection that an audience has too little time for.

As poem, however, *Atalanta in Calydon* deserves its fame and more; it is unfortunate that only a few of the choric passages are well known—and those not always the best or most interesting. One finds implicit or explicit in *Atalanta* all the technical skill and virtuosity of Swinburne at his best, and one finds, too, relatively less of fascination with the "foambell" of poetry, the delight in sound and form and color for their own sake. The same ideas that were to enrage critics of *Poems and Ballads* are discernible in *Atalanta*, and some reviewers saw whither the play, and Swinburne's practice, tended, though most were willing nevertheless to recognize Swinburne's great vitality and artistic skill. (Browning, for example, had remarked that the contents of Swinburne's first volume of poems, which preceded *Atalanta*, were "moral mistakes, redeemed by much intellectual ability."[6] Though the attitude is characteristically Browning's, the tone is similar to much of the contemporary criticism of *Atalanta*.)

It was to Swinburne's advantage, certainly, that *Atalanta* was published rather than performed (though, to be sure, he seems never to have envisioned its performance). His consciousness of the Greek model no doubt accounts for some of the restraint he exercised, and it was partly because of that "Greekness" that Landor enthusiastically approved the portion that Swinburne read to him, and allowed Swinburne to dedicate it to him. The "pure Greek" that Swinburne described has also a reciprocal relationship with the fad for Greek drama that was so important a part of Oxbridge life in the late nineteenth century. But finally it is as poetry—Swinburnian poetry, surely—that *Atalanta in Calydon* must be measured. This is perhaps the most obviously "poetic" of all the plays in this anthology, and the very nature of its poetry is one of the reasons why it is least successful as drama.

G. C. S.

---

6. *Letters*, vol. 1, p. 84.

Atalanta in Calydon

THE PERSONS

CHIEF HUNTSMAN
CHORUS
ALTHÆA
MELEAGER
ŒNEUS
ATALANTA
TOXEUS
PLEXIPPUS
HERALD
MESSENGER
SECOND MESSENGER

THE ARGUMENT

ALTHÆA, daughter of Thestius and Eurythemis, queen of Calydon, being with child of Meleager her first-born son, dreamed that she brought forth a brand burning; and upon his birth came the three Fates and prophesied of him three things, namely these; that he should have great strength of his hands, and good fortune in this life, and that he should live no longer when the brand then in the fire were consumed: wherefore his mother plucked it forth and kept it by her. And the child being a man grown sailed with Jason after the fleece of gold, and won himself great praise of all men living; and when the tribes of the north and west made war upon Ætolia, he fought against their army and scattered it. But Artemis, having at the first stirred up these tribes to war against Œneus king of Calydon, because he had offered sacrifice to all the gods saving her alone, but her he had forgotten to honour, was yet more wroth because of the destruction of this army, and sent upon the land of Calydon a wild boar which slew many and wasted all their increase, but him could none slay, and many went against him and perished. Then were all the chief men of Greece gathered together, and among them Atalanta, daughter of Iasius the Arcadian, a virgin; for whose sake Artemis let slay the boar, seeing she favoured the maiden greatly; and Meleager having despatched it gave the spoil thereof to Atalanta, as one beyond measure enamoured of her; but the brethren of Althæa his mother, Toxeus and Plexippus, with such others as misliked that she only should bear off the praise whereas many had borne the labour, laid wait for her to take away her spoil; but Meleager fought against them and slew them: whom when Althæa their sister beheld and knew to be slain of her son, she waxed for wrath and sorrow like as one mad, and taking the brand whereby the measure of her son's life was meted to him, she cast it upon a fire; and with the wasting thereof his life likewise wasted away, that being brought back to his father's house he died in a brief space; and his mother also endured not long after for very sorrow; and this was his end, and the end of that hunting.

CHIEF HUNTSMAN

MAIDEN, and mistress of the months and
    stars
Now folded in the flowerless fields of
    heaven,
Goddess whom all gods love with three-
    fold heart,
Being treble in thy divided deity,
A light for dead men and dark hours, a
    foot

Swift on the hills as morning, and a hand
To all things fierce and fleet that roar and
    range
Mortal, with gentler shafts than snow or
    sleep ;
Hear now and help and lift no violent
    hand,
But favourable and fair as thine eye's
    beam
Hidden and shown in heaven ; for I all
    night
Amid the king's hounds and the hunting
    men
Have wrought and worshipped toward
    thee ; nor shall men
See goodlier hounds or deadlier edge of
    spears ;
But for the end, that lies unreached at yet
Between the hands and on the knees of
    gods.
O fair-faced sun, killing the stars and dews
And dreams and desolation of the night !
Rise up, shine, stretch thine hand out,
    with thy bow
Touch the most dimmest height of trem-
    bling heaven,
And burn and break the dark about thy
    ways,
Shot through and through with arrows :
    let thine hair
Lighten as flame above that flameless shell
Which was the moon, and thine eyes fill
    the world
And thy lips kindle with swift beams ;
    let earth
Laugh, and the long sea fiery from thy feet
Through all the roar and ripple of stream-
    ing springs
And foam in reddening flakes and flying
    flowers
Shaken from hands and blown from lips
    of nymphs
Whose hair or breast divides the wander-
    ing wave
With salt close tresses cleaving lock to
    lock,
All gold, or shuddering and unfurrowed
    snow ;
And all the winds about thee with their
    wings,
And fountain-heads of all the watered
    world ;
Each horn of Acheloüs, and the green
Euenus, wedded with the straitening sea.
For in fair time thou comest ; come also
    thou,
Twin-born with him, and virgin, Artemis,
And give our spears their spoil, the wild
    boar's hide,

Sent in thine anger against us for sin done
And bloodless altars without wine or fire.
Him now consume thou ; for thy sacrifice
With sanguine-shining steam divides the
    dawn,
And one, the maiden rose of all thy maids,
Arcadian Atalanta, snowy-souled,
Fair as the snow and footed as the wind,
From Ladon and well-wooded Mænalus
Over the firm hills and the fleeting sea
Hast thou drawn hither, and many an
    armèd king,
Heroes, the crown of men, like gods in
    fight.
Moreover out of all the Ætolian land,
From the full-flowered Lelantian pasturage
To what of fruitful field the son of Zeus
Won from the roaring river and labouring
    sea
When the wild god shrank in his horn
    and fled
And foamed and lessened through his
    wrathful fords,
Leaving clear lands that steamed with
    sudden sun,
These virgins with the lightening of the
    day
Bring thee fresh wreaths and their own
    sweeter hair,
Luxurious locks and flower-like mixed
    with flowers,
Clean offering, and chaste hymns ; but me
    the time
Divides from these things ; whom do thou
    not less
Help and give honour, and to mine
    hounds good speed,
And edge to spears, and luck to each
    man's hand.

CHORUS

When the hounds of spring are on win-
    ter's traces,
    The mother of months in meadow or
        plain
Fills the shadows and windy places
    With lisp of leaves and ripple of rain ;
And the brown bright nightingale amorous
Is half assuaged for Itylus,
For the Thracian ships and the foreign
    faces,
    The tongueless vigil, and all the pain.

Come with bows bent and with emptying
    of quivers,
    Maiden most perfect, lady of light,
With a noise of winds and many rivers,

With a clamour of waters, and with
　　might ;
Bind on thy sandals, O thou most fleet,
Over the splendour and speed of thy feet ;
For the faint east quickens, the wan west
　　shivers,
　　Round the feet of the day and the feet
　　of the night.

Where shall we find her, how shall we
　　sing to her,
　　Fold our hands round her knees, and
　　cling ?
O that man's heart were as fire and could
　　spring to her,
　　Fire, or the strength of the streams that
　　spring !
For the stars and the winds are unto her
As raiment, as songs of the harp-player ;
For the risen stars and the fallen cling to
　　her,
　　And the southwest-wind and the west-
　　wind sing.

For winter's rains and ruins are over,
　　And all the season of snows and sins ;
The days dividing lover and lover,
　　The light that loses, the night that
　　wins ;
And time remembered is grief forgotten,
And frosts are slain and flowers begotten,
And in green underwood and cover
　　Blossom by blossom the spring begins.

The full streams feed on flower of rushes,
　　Ripe grasses trammel a travelling foot,
The faint fresh flame of the young year
　　flushes
　　From leaf to flower and flower to fruit ;
And fruit and leaf are as gold and fire,
And the oat is heard above the lyre,
And the hoofèd heel of a satyr crushes
　　The chestnut-husk at the chestnut-root.

And Pan by noon and Bacchus by night,
　　Fleeter of foot than the fleet-foot kid,
Follows with dancing and fills with delight
　　The Mænad and the Bassarid ;
And soft as lips that laugh and hide
The laughing leaves of the trees divide,
And screen from seeing and leave in sight
　　The god pursuing, the maiden hid.

The ivy falls with the Bacchanal's hair
　　Over her eyebrows hiding her eyes ;
The wild vine slipping down leaves bare
　　Her bright breast shortening into sighs ;
The wild vine slips with the weight of its
　　leaves,

But the berried ivy catches and cleaves
To the limbs that glitter, the feet that
　　scare
　　The wolf that follows, the fawn that
　　flies.

ALTHÆA

What do ye singing ? what is this ye sing ?

CHORUS

Flowers bring we, and pure lips that please
　　the gods,
And raiment meet for service : lest the day
Turn sharp with all its honey in our lips.

ALTHÆA

Night, a black hound, follows the white
　　fawn day,
Swifter than dreams the white flown feet
　　of sleep ;
Will ye pray back the night with any
　　prayers ?
And though the spring put back a little
　　while
Winter, and snows that plague all men
　　for sin,
And the iron time of cursing, yet I know
Spring shall be ruined with the rain, and
　　storm
Eat up like fire the ashen autumn days.
I marvel what men do with prayers awake
Who dream and die with dreaming ; any
　　god,
Yea the least god of all things called
　　divine,
Is more than sleep and waking ; yet we
　　say,
Perchance by praying a man shall match
　　his god.
For if sleep have no mercy, and man's
　　dreams
Bite to the blood and burn into the bone,
What shall this man do waking ? By the
　　gods,
He shall not pray to dream sweet things
　　to-night,
Having dreamt once more bitter things
　　than death.

CHORUS

Queen, but what is it that hath burnt thine
　　heart ?
For thy speech flickers like a blown-out
　　flame.

ALTHÆA

Look, ye say well, and know not what ye
     say ;
For all my sleep is turned into a fire,
And all my dreams to stuff that kindles it.

CHORUS

Yet one doth well being patient of the
     gods.

ALTHÆA

Yea, lest they smite us with some four-foot
     plague.

CHORUS

But when time spreads find out some herb
     for it.

ALTHÆA

And with their healing herbs infect our
     blood.

CHORUS

What ails thee to be jealous of their ways ?

ALTHÆA

What if they give us poisonous drinks for
     wine ?

CHORUS

They have their will ; much talking mends
     it not.

ALTHÆA

And gall for milk, and cursing for a
     prayer ?

CHORUS

Have they not given life, and the end of
     life ?

ALTHÆA

Lo, where they heal, they help not ; thus
     they do,
They mock us with a little piteousness,
And we say prayers, and weep ; but at the
     last,
Sparing awhile, they smite and spare no
     whit.

CHORUS

Small praise man gets dispraising the high
     gods :
What have they done that thou dishonour-
     est them ?

ALTHÆA

First Artemis for all this harried land
I praise not, and for wasting of the boar
That mars with tooth and tusk and fiery
     feet
Green pasturage and the grace of standing
     corn
And meadow and marsh with springs and
     unblown leaves,
Flocks and swift herds and all that bite
     sweet grass,
I praise her not ; what things are these
     to praise ?

CHORUS

But when the king did sacrifice, and gave
Each god fair dues of wheat and blood and
     wine,
Her not with bloodshed nor burnt-offering
Revered he, nor with salt or cloven cake ;
Wherefore being wroth she plagued the
     land ; but now
Takes off from us fate and her heavy
     things.
Which deed of these twain were not good
     to praise ?
For a just deed looks always either way
With blameless eyes, and mercy is no fault.

ALTHÆA

Yea, but a curse she hath sent above all
     these
To hurt us where she healed us ; and hath
     lit
Fire where the old fire went out, and
     where the wind
Slackened, hath blown on us with deadlier
     air.

CHORUS

What storm is this that tightens all our
     sail ?

ALTHÆA

Love, a thwart sea-wind full of rain and
     foam.

CHORUS

Whence blown, and born under what
    stormier star ?

ALTHÆA

Southward across Euenus from the sea.

CHORUS

Thy speech turns toward Arcadia like
    blown wind.

ALTHÆA

Sharp as the north sets when the snows
    are out.

CHORUS

Nay, for this maiden hath no touch of
    love.

ALTHÆA

I would she had sought in some cold gulf
    of sea
Love, or in dens where strange beasts lurk,
    or fire,
Or snows on the extreme hills, or iron
    land
Where no spring is ; I would she had
    sought therein
And found, or ever love had found her
    here.

CHORUS

She is holier than all holy days or things,
The sprinkled water or fume of perfect
    fire ;
Chaste, dedicated to pure prayers, and
    filled
With higher thoughts than heaven ; a
    maiden clean,
Pure iron, fashioned for a sword ; and
    man
She loves not ; what should one such do
    with love ?

ALTHÆA

Look you, I speak not as one light of wit,
But as a queen speaks, being heart-vexed ;
    for oft
I hear my brothers wrangling in mid hall,
And am not moved ; and my son chiding
    them,

And these things nowise move me, but I
    know
Foolish and wise men must be to the end,
And feed myself with patience ; but this
    most,
This moves me, that for wise men as for
    fools
Love is one thing, an evil thing, and turns
Choice words and wisdom into fire and
    air.
And in the end shall no joy come, but
    grief,
Sharp words and soul's division and fresh
    tears
Flower-wise upon the old root of tears
    brought forth,
Fruit-wise upon the old flower of tears
    sprung up,
Pitiful sighs, and much regrafted pain.
These things are in my presage, and myself
Am part of them and know not ; but in
    dreams
The gods are heavy on me, and all the
    fates
Shed fire across my eyelids mixed with
    night,
And burn me blind, and disilluminate
My sense of seeing, and my perspicuous
    soul
Darken with vision ; seeing I see not, hear
And hearing am not holpen, but mine eyes
Stain many tender broideries in the bed
Drawn up about my face that I may weep
And the king wake not ; and my brows
    and lips
Tremble and sob in sleeping, like swift
    flames
That tremble, or water when it sobs with
    heat
Kindled from under ; and my tears fill my
    breast
And speck the fair dyed pillows round
    the king
With barren showers and salter than the
    sea,
Such dreams divide me dreaming ; for
    long since
I dreamed that out of this my womb had
    sprung
Fire and firebrand ; this was ere my son,
Meleager, a goodly flower in fields of fight,
Felt the light touch him coming forth, and
    wailed
Childlike ; but yet he was not ; and in time
I bare him, and my heart was great ; for
    yet
So royally was never strong man born,
Nor queen so nobly bore as noble a thing
As this my son was : such a birth God sent

And such a grace to bear it. Then came in
Three weaving women, and span each a
     thread,
Saying This for strength and That for
     luck, and one
Saying Till the brand upon the hearth
     burn down,
So long shall this man see good days and
     live.
And I with gathered raiment from the bed
Sprang, and drew forth the brand, and
     cast on it
Water, and trod the flame bare-foot, and
     crushed
With naked hand spark beaten out of
     spark
And blew against and quenched it; for
     I said,
These are the most high Fates that dwell
     with us,
And we find favour a little in their sight,
A little, and more we miss of, and much
     time
Foils us; howbeit they have pitied me, O
     son,
And thee most piteous, thee a tenderer
     thing
Than any flower of fleshly seed alive.
Wherefore I kissed and hid him with my
     hands,
And covered under arms and hair, and
     wept,
And feared to touch him with my tears,
     and laughed;
So light a thing was this man, grown so
     great
Men cast their heads back, seeing against
     the sun
Blaze the armed man carven on his shield,
     and hear
The laughter of little bells along the brace
Ring, as birds singing or flutes blown, and
     watch,
High up, the cloven shadow of either
     plume
Divide the bright light of the brass, and
     make
His helmet as a windy and wintering moon
Seen through blown cloud and plume-like
     drift, when ships
Drive, and men strive with all the sea,
     and oars
Break, and the beaks dip under, drinking
     death;
Yet was he then but a span long, and
     moaned
With inarticulate mouth inseparate words,
And with blind lips and fingers wrung my
     breast

Hard, and thrust out with foolish hands
     and feet,
Murmuring; but those grey women with
     bound hair
Who fright the gods frighted not him: he
     laughed
Seeing them, and pushed out hands to
     feel and haul
Distaff and thread, intangible; but they
Passed, and I hid the brand, and in my
     heart
Laughed likewise, having all my will of
     heaven.
But now I know not if to left or right
The gods have drawn us hither; for again
I dreamt, and saw the black brand burst
     on fire
As a branch bursts in flower, and saw the
     flame
Fade flower-wise, and Death came and
     with dry lips
Blew the charred ash into my breast: and
     Love
Trampled the ember and crushed it with
     swift feet.
This I have also at heart; that not for me,
Not for me only or son of mine, O girls,
The gods have wrought life, and desire
     of life,
Heart's love and heart's division; but for
     all
There shines one sun and one wind blows
     till night.
And when night comes the wind sinks and
     the sun,
And there is no light after, and no storm,
But sleep and much forgetfulness of things.
In such wise I gat knowledge of the gods
Years hence, and heard high sayings of
     one most wise,
Eurythemis my mother, who beheld
With eyes alive and spake with lips of
     these
As one on earth disfleshed and disallied
From breath or blood corruptible; such
     gifts
Time gave her, and an equal soul to these
And equal face to all things; thus she
     said.
But whatsoever intolerable or glad
The swift hours weave and unweave, I go
     hence
Full of mine own soul, perfect of myself,
Toward mine and me sufficient; and what
     chance
The gods cast lots for and shake out on us,
That shall we take, and that much bear
     withal.
And now, before these gather to the hunt,

I will go arm my son and bring him forth,
Lest love or some man's anger work him
    harm.

CHORUS

Before the beginning of years
    There came to the making of man
Time, with a gift of tears ;
    Grief, with a glass that ran ;
Pleasure, with pain for leaven ;
    Summer, with flowers that fell ;
Remembrance fallen from heaven,
    And madness risen from hell ;
Strength without hands to smite ;
Love that endures for a breath :
Night, the shadow of light,
    And life, the shadow of death.
And the high gods took in hand
    Fire, and the falling of tears,
And a measure of sliding sand
    From under the feet of the years :
And froth and drift of the sea ;
    And dust of the labouring earth :
And bodies of things to be
    In the houses of death and of birth ;
And wrought with weeping and laugh-
    ter,
    And fashioned with loathing and love
With life before and after
    And death beneath and above,
For a day and a night and a morrow,
    That his strength might endure for a
    span
With travail and heavy sorrow,
    The holy spirit of man.
From the winds of the north and the
    south
    They gathered as unto strife ;
They breathed upon his mouth,
    They filled his body with life ;
Eyesight and speech they wrought
    For the veils of the soul therein,
A time for labour and thought,
    A time to serve and to sin ;
They gave him light in his ways,
    And love, and a space for delight,
And beauty and length of days,
    And night, and sleep in the night.
His speech is a burning fire ;
    With his lips he travaileth ;
In his heart is a blind desire,
    In his eyes foreknowledge of death ;
He weaves, and is clothed with derision ;
    Sows, and he shall not reap ;
His life is a watch or a vision
    Between a sleep and a sleep.

MELEAGER

O sweet new heaven and air without a
    star,
Fair day, be fair and welcome, as to men
With deeds to do and praise to pluck from
    thee.
Come forth a child, born with clear sound
    and light,
With laughter and swift limbs and pros-
    perous looks ;
That this great hunt with heroes for the
    hounds
May leave thee memorable and us well
    sped.

ALTHÆA

Son, first I praise thy prayer, then bid thee
    speed ;
But the gods hear men's hands before
    their lips,
And heed beyond all crying and sacrifice
Light of things done and noise of labour-
    ing men.
But thou, being armed and perfect for
    the deed,
Abide ; for like rain-flakes in a wind they
    grow,
The men thy fellows, and the choice of
    the world,
Bound to root out the tuskèd plague, and
    leave
Thanks and safe days and peace in Caly-
    don.

MELEAGER

For the whole city and all the low-lying
    land
Flames, and the soft air sounds with them
    that come ;
The gods give all these fruit of all their
    works.

ALTHÆA

Set thine eye thither and fix thy spirit
    and say
Whom there thou knowest ; for sharp
    mixed shadow and wind
Blown up between the morning and the
    mist,
With steam of steeds and flash of bridle or
    wheel,
And fire, and parcels of the broken dawn,
And dust divided by hard light, and spears

That shine and shift as the edge of wild
beasts' eyes,
Smite upon mine ; so fiery their blind edge
Burns, and bright points break up and
baffle day.

MELEAGER

The first, for many I know not, being far
off,
Peleus the Larissæan, couched with whom
Sleeps the white sea-bred wife and silver-
shod,
Fair as fled foam, a goddess ; and their
son
Most swift and splendid of men's children
born,
Most like a god, full of the future fame.

ALTHÆA

Who are these shining like one sundered
star ?

MELEAGER

Thy sister's sons, a double flower of men.

ALTHÆA

O sweetest kin to me in all the world,
O twin-born blood of Leda, gracious heads
Like kindled lights in untempestuous
heaven,
Fair flower-like stars on the iron foam of
fight,
With what glad heart and kindliness of
soul,
Even to the staining of both eyes with
tears
And kindling of warm eyelids with desire,
A great way off I greet you, and rejoice
Seeing you so fair, and moulded like as
gods.
Far off ye come, and least in years of these,
But lordliest, but worth love to look upon.

MELEAGER

Even such (for sailing hither I saw far
hence,
And where Eurotas hollows his moist rock
Nigh Sparta with a strenuous-hearted
stream)
Even such I saw their sisters ; one swan-
white,
The little Helen, and less fair than she
Fair Clytæmnestra, grave as pasturing

fawns
Who feed and fear some arrow : but at
whiles,
As one smitten with love or wrung with
joy,
She laughs and lightens with her eyes,
and then
Weeps ; whereat Helen, having laughed,
weeps too,
And the other chides her, and she being
chid speaks nought,
But cheeks and lips and eyelids kisses her,
Laughing ; so fare they, as in their bloom-
less bud
And full of unblown life, the blood of
gods.

ALTHÆA

Sweet days befall them and good loves
and lords,
And tender and temperate honours of the
hearth,
Peace, and a perfect life and blameless
bed.
But who shows next an eagle wrought in
gold,
That flames and beats broad wings against
the sun
And with void mouth gapes after emptier
prey ?

MELEAGER

Know by that sign the reign of Telamon
Between the fierce mouths of the encoun-
tering brine
On the strait reefs of twice-washed Salamis.

ALTHÆA

For like one great of hand he bears him-
self,
Vine-chapleted, with savours of the sea,
Glittering as wine and moving as a wave.
But who girt round there roughly follows
him ?

MELEAGER

Ancæus, great of hand, an iron bulk,
Two-edged for fight as the axe against his
arm,
Who drives against the surge of stormy
spears
Full-sailed ; him Cepheus follows, his twin-
born,
Chief name next his of all Arcadian men.

ALTHÆA

Praise be with men abroad ; chaste lives
   with us,
Home-keeping days and household rever-
   ences.

MELEAGER

Next by the left unsandalled foot know
   thou
The sail and oar of this Ætolian land,
Thy brethren, Toxeus and the violent-
   souled
Plexippus, over-swift with hand and
   tongue ;
For hands are fruitful, but the ignorant
   mouth
Blows and corrupts their work with barren
   breath.

ALTHÆA

Speech too bears fruit, being worthy ; and
   air blows down
Things poisonous, and high-seated vio-
   lences,
And with charmed words and songs have
   men put out
Wild evil, and the fire of tyrannies.

MELEAGER

Yea, all things have they, save the gods
   and love.

ALTHÆA

Love thou the law and cleave to things
   ordained.

MELEAGER

Law lives upon their lips whom these
   applaud.

ALTHÆA

How sayest thou these ? what god applauds
   new things ?

MELEAGER

Zeus, who hath fear and custom under
   foot.

ALTHÆA

But loves not laws thrown down and lives
awry.

MELEAGER

Yet is not less himself than his own law.

ALTHÆA

Nor shifts and shuffles old things up and
   down.

MELEAGER

But what he will remoulds and discreates.

ALTHÆA

Much, but not this, that each thing live
   its life.

MELEAGER

Nor only live, but lighten and lift up
   higher.

ALTHÆA

Pride breaks itself, and too much gained
   is gone.

MELEAGER

Things gained are gone, but great things
   done endure.

ALTHÆA

Child, if a man serve law through all his
   life
And with his whole heart worship, him
   all gods
Praise ; but who loves it only with his lips,
And not in heart and deed desiring it
Hides a perverse will with obsequious
   words,
Him heaven infatuates and his twin-born
   fate
Tracks, and gains on him, scenting sins
   far off,
And the swift hounds of violent death
   devour.
Be man at once with equal-minded gods,
So shall he prosper ; not through laws
   torn up,
Violated rule and a new face of things.
A woman armed makes war upon herself,
Unwomanlike, and treads down use and
   wont

And the sweet common honour that she
  hath,
Love, and the cry of children, and the
  hand
Trothplight and mutual mouth of mar-
  riages.
This doth she, being unloved ; whom if
  one love,
Not fire nor iron and the wide-mouthed
  wars
Are deadlier than her lips or braided hair.
For of the one comes poison, and a curse
Falls from the other and burns the lives
  of men.
But thou, son, be not filled with evil
  dreams,
Nor with desire of these things ; for with
  time
Blind love burns out ; but if one feed it
  full
Till some discolouring stain dyes all his
  life,
He shall keep nothing praiseworthy, nor
  die
The sweet wise death of old men honour-
  able,
Who have lived out all the length of all
  their years
Blameless, and seen well-pleased the face
  of gods,
And without shame and without fear have
  wrought
Things memorable, and while their days
  held out
In sight of all men and the sun's great
  light
Have gat them glory and given of their
  own praise
To the earth that bare them and the day
  that bred,
Home friends and far-off hospitalities,
And filled with gracious and memorial
  fame
Lands loved of summer washed by violent
  seas,
Towns populous and many unfooted ways,
And alien lips and native with their own.
But when white age and venerable death
Mow down the strength and life within
  their limbs,
Drain out the blood and darken their
  clear eyes,
Immortal honour is on them, having past
Through splendid life and death desirable
To the clear seat and remote throne of
  souls,
Lands indiscoverable in the unheard-of
  west,

Round which the strong stream of a sacred
  sea
Rolls without wind for ever, and the snow
There shows not her white wings and
  windy feet,
Nor thunder nor swift rain saith anything,
Nor the sun burns, but all things rest and
  thrive ;
And these, filled full of days, divine and
  dead,
Sages and singers fiery from the god,
And such as loved their land and all
  things good
And, best beloved of best men, liberty,
Free lives and lips, free hands of men
  free-born,
And whatsoever on earth was honourable
And whosoever of all the ephemeral seed,
Live there a life no liker to the gods
But nearer than their life of terrene days.
Love thou such life and look for such a
  death.
But from the light and fiery dreams of
  love
Spring heavy sorrows and a sleepless life,
Visions not dreams, whose lids no charm
  shall close
Nor song assuage them waking ; and swift
  death
Crushes with sterile feet the unripening
  ear,
Treads out the timeless vintage ; whom
  do thou
Eschewing embrace the luck of this thy
  life,
Not without honour ; and it shall bear
  to thee
Such fruit as men reap from spent hours
  and wear,
Few men, but happy ; of whom be thou,
  O son,
Happiest, if thou submit thy soul to fate,
And set thine eyes and heart on hopes
  high-born
And divine deeds and abstinence divine.
So shalt thou be toward all men all thy
  days
As light and might communicable, and
  burn
From heaven among the stars above the
  hours,
And break not as a man breaks nor burn
  down :
For to whom other of all heroic names
Have the gods given his life in hand as
  thine ?
And gloriously hast thou lived, and made
  thy life

To me that bare thee and to all men born
Thankworthy, a praise for ever ; and hast
    won fame
When wild wars broke all round thy
    father's house,
And the mad people of windy mountain
    ways
Laid spears against us like a sea, and all
Ætolia thundered with Thessalian hoofs ;
Yet these, as wind baffles the foam, and
    beats
Straight back the relaxed ripple, didst
    thou break
And loosen all their lances, till undone
And man from man they fell ; for ye
    twain stood
God against god, Ares and Artemis,
And thou the mightier ; wherefore she
    unleashed
A sharp-toothed curse thou too shalt over-
    come ;
For in the greater blossom of thy life
Ere the full blade caught flower, and when
    time gave
Respite, thou didst not slacken soul nor
    sleep,
But with great hand and heart seek praise
    of men
Out of sharp straits and many a grievous
    thing,
Seeing the strange foam of undivided seas
On channels never sailed in, and by shores
Where the old winds cease not blowing,
    and all the night
Thunders, and day is no delight to men.

CHORUS

Meleager, a noble wisdom and fair words
The gods have given this woman : hear
    thou these.

MELEAGER

O mother, I am not fain to strive in speech
Nor set my mouth against thee, who art
    wise
Even as they say and full of sacred words.
But one thing I know surely, and cleave
    to this ;
That though I be not subtle of wit as thou
Nor womanlike to weave sweet words, and
    melt
Mutable minds of wise men as with fire,
I too, doing justly and reverencing the
    gods,
Shall not want wit to see what things be
    right.

For whom they love and whom reject,
    being gods,
There is no man but seeth, and in good
    time
Submits himself, refraining all his heart.
And I too as thou sayest have seen great
    things ;
Seen otherwhere, but chiefly when the sail
First caught between stretched ropes the
    roaring west,
And all our oars smote eastward, and the
    wind
First flung round faces of seafaring men
White splendid snow-flakes of the sunder-
    ing foam,
And the first furrow in virginal green sea
Followed the plunging ploughshare of
    hewn pine,
And closed, as when deep sleep subdues
    man's breath
Lips close and heart subsides ; and closing,
    shone
Sunlike with many a Nereid's hair, and
    moved
Round many a trembling mouth of doubt-
    ful gods,
Risen out of sunless and sonorous gulfs
Through waning water and into shallow
    light,
That watched us ; and when flying the
    dove was snared
As with men's hands, but we shot after
    and sped
Clear through the irremeable Symplega-
    des ;
And chiefliest when hoar beach and herb-
    less cliff
Stood out ahead from Colchis, and we
    heard
Clefts hoarse with wind, and saw through
    narrowing reefs
The lightning of the intolerable wave
Flash, and the white wet flame of breakers
    burn
Far under a kindling south-wind, as a
    lamp
Burns and bends all its blowing flame one
    way ;
Wild heights untravelled of the wind, and
    vales
Cloven seaward by their violent streams,
    and white
With bitter flowers and bright salt scurf
    of brine ;
Heard sweep their sharp swift gales, and
    bowing birdwise
Shriek with birds' voices, and with furious
    feet

Tread loose the long skirts of a storm :
    and saw
The whole white Euxine clash together
    and fall
Full-mouthed, and thunderous from a
    thousand throats :
Yet we drew thither and won the fleece
    and won
Medea, deadlier than the sea ; but there
Seeing many a wonder and fearful things
    to men
I saw not one thing like this one seen here,
Most fair and fearful, feminine, a god,
Faultless ; whom I that love not, being
    unlike,
Fear, and give honour, and choose from
    all the gods.

ŒNEUS

Lady, the daughter of Thestius, and thou,
    son,
Not ignorant of your strife nor light of
    wit,
Scared with vain dreams and fluttering
    like spent fire,
I come to judge between you, but a king
Full of past days and wise from years
    endured.
Nor thee I praise, who art fain to undo
    things done :
Nor thee, who art swift to esteem them
    overmuch.
For what the hours have given is given,
    and this
Changeless ; howbeit these change, and in
    good time
Devise new things and good, not one thing
    still.
Us have they sent now at our need for
    help
Among men armed a woman, foreign born,
Virgin, not like the natural flower of
    things
That grows and bears and brings forth
    fruit and dies ;
Unlovable, no light for a husband's house,
Espoused ; a glory among unwedded girls,
And chosen of gods who reverence maiden-
    hood.
These too we honour in honouring her ;
    but thou,
Abstain thy feet from following, and thine
    eyes
From amorous touch ; nor set toward hers
    thine heart,
Son, lest hate bear no deadlier fruit than
    love.

ALTHÆA

O king, thou art wise, but wisdom halts ;
    and just,
But the gods love not justice more than
    fate,
And smite the righteous and the violent
    mouth,
And mix with insolent blood the reverent
    man's,
And bruise the holier as the lying lips.
Enough ; for wise words fail me, and my
    heart
Takes fire and trembles flamewise, O my
    son,
O child, for thine head's sake ; mine eyes
    wax thick,
Turning toward thee, so goodly a weap-
    oned man,
So glorious ; and for love of thine own
    eyes
They are darkened, and tears burn them,
    fierce as fire,
And my lips pause and my soul sinks with
    love.
But by thine hand, by thy sweet life and
    eyes,
By thy great heart and these clasped knees,
    O son,
I pray thee that thou slay me not with
    thee.
For there was never a mother woman-born
Loved her sons better ; and never a queen
    of men
More perfect in her heart toward whom
    she loved.
For what lies light on many and they
    forget,
Small things and transitory as a wind o'
    the sea,
I forget never ; I have seen thee all thine
    years
A man in arms, strong and a joy to men,
Seeing thine head glitter and thine hand
    burn its way
Through a heavy and iron furrow of sun-
    dering spears ;
But always also a flower of three suns old,
The small one thing that lying drew down
    my life
To lie with thee and feed thee ; a child
    and weak,
Mine, a delight to no man, sweet to me.
Who then sought to thee ? who gat help ?
    who knew
If thou wert goodly ? nay, no man at all.
Or what sea saw thee, or sounded with
    thine oar,

Child? or what strange land shone with
 war through thee?
But fair for me thou wert, O little life,
Fruitless, the fruit of mine own flesh, and
 blind,
More than much gold, ungrown, a foolish
 flower.
For silver nor bright snow nor feather of
 foam
Was whiter, and no gold yellower than
 thine hair,
O child, my child; and now thou art
 lordlier grown,
Not lovelier, nor a new thing in mine eyes,
I charge thee by thy soul and this my
 breast,
Fear thou the gods and me and thine own
 heart,
Lest all these turn against thee; for who
 knows
What wind upon what wave of altering
 time
Shall speak a storm and blow calamity?
And there is nothing stabile in the world
But the gods break it; yet not less, fair
 son,
If but one thing be stronger, if one endure,
Surely the bitter and the rooted love
That burns between us, going from me
 to thee,
Shall more endure than all things. What
 dost thou,
Following strange loves? why wilt thou
 kill mine heart?
Lo, I talk wild and windy words, and fall
From my clear wits, and seem of mine
 own self
Dethroned, dispraised, disseated; and my
 mind,
That was my crown, breaks, and mine
 heart is gone,
And I am naked of my soul, and stand
Ashamed, as a mean woman; take thou
 thought:
Live if thou wilt, and if thou wilt not,
 look,
The gods have given thee life to lose or
 keep,
Thou shalt not die as men die, but thine
 end
Fallen upon thee shall break me unaware.

MELEAGER

Queen, my whole heart is molten with thy
 tears,
And my limbs yearn with pity of thee, and
 love
Compels with grief mine eyes and labour-
ing breath;
For what thou art I know thee, and this
 thy breast
And thy fair eyes I worship, and am bound
Toward thee in spirit and love thee in all
 my soul.
For there is nothing terribler to men
Than the sweet face of mothers, and the
 might.
But what shall be let be; for us the day
Once only lives a little, and is not found.
Time and the fruitful hour are more than
 we,
And these lay hold upon us; but thou,
 God,
Zeus, the sole steersman of the helm of
 things,
Father, be swift to see us, and as thou wilt
Help: or if adverse, as thou wilt, refrain.

CHORUS

We have seen thee, O Love, thou art fair;
 thou art goodly, O Love;
Thy wings make light in the air as the
 wings of a dove.
Thy feet are as winds that divide the
 stream of the sea;
Earth is thy covering to hide thee, the
 garment of thee.
Thou art swift and subtle and blind as a
 flame of fire;
Before thee the laughter, behind thee the
 tears of desire;
And twain go forth beside thee, a man
 with a maid;
Her eyes are the eyes of a bride whom
 delight makes afraid;
As the breath in the buds that stir is her
 bridal breath:
But Fate is the name of her; and his
 name is Death.

For an evil blossom was born
 Of sea-foam and the frothing of blood,
 Blood-red and bitter of fruit,
  And the seed of it laughter and
  tears,
And the leaves of it madness and scorn;
 A bitter flower from the bud,
  Sprung of the sea without root,
   Sprung without graft from the
   years.

The weft of the world was untorn
 That is woven of the day on the night,
 The hair of the hours was not white
Nor the raiment of time overworn,
 When a wonder, a world's delight,

A perilous goddess was born ;
  And the waves of the sea as she came
Clove, and the foam at her feet,
  Fawning, rejoiced to bring forth
  A fleshly blossom, a flame
Filling the heavens with heat
  To the cold white ends of the north.

And in air the clamorous birds,
  And men upon earth that hear
Sweet articulate words
  Sweetly divided apart,
And in shallow and channel and mere
The rapid and footless herds,
  Rejoiced, being foolish of heart.

For all they said upon earth,
  She is fair, she is white like a dove,
  And the life of the world in her
    breath
Breathes, and is born at her birth ;
  For they knew thee for mother of love,
  And knew thee not mother of death.

What hadst thou to do being born,
  Mother, when winds were at ease,
As a flower of the springtime of corn,
  A flower of the foam of the seas?
For bitter thou wast from thy birth,
  Aphrodite, a mother of strife ;
For before thee some rest was on earth,
  A little respite from tears,
  A little pleasure of life ;
For life was not then as thou art,
  But as one that waxeth in years
Sweet-spoken, a fruitful wife ;
  Earth had no thorn, and desire
No sting, neither death any dart ;
  What hadst thou to do among these,
    Thou, clothed with a burning fire,
Thou, girt with sorrow of heart,
  Thou, sprung of the seed of the seas
As an ear from a seed of corn,
  As a brand plucked forth of a pyre,
As a ray shed forth of the morn,
  For division of soul and disease,
For a dart and a sting and a thorn ?
What ailed thee then to be born ?

Was there not evil enough,
  Mother, and anguish on earth
Born with a man at his birth,
Wastes underfoot, and above,
  Storm out of heaven, and dearth
Shaken down from the shining thereof,
  Wrecks from afar overseas
And peril of shallow and firth,
  And tears that spring and increase
In the barren places of mirth,

That thou, having wings as a dove,
  Being girt with desire for a girth,
    That thou must come after these,
That thou must lay on him love ?

Thou shouldst not so have been born :
  But death should have risen with thee,
  Mother, and visible fear,
    Grief and the wringing of hands,
And noise of many that mourn ;
  The smitten bosom, the knee
    Bowed, and in each man's ear
    A cry as of perishing lands,
A moan as of people in prison,
  A tumult of infinite griefs ;
    And thunder of storm on the
      sands,
    And wailing of waves on the shore :
And under thee newly arisen
  Loud shoals and shipwrecking reefs,
    Fierce air and violent light :
    Sail rent and sundering oar,
    Darkness, and noises of night :
Clashing of streams in the sea,
  Wave against wave as a sword,
    Clamour of currents, and foam ;
    Rains making ruin on earth,
    Winds that wax ravenous and roam
As wolves in a wolfish horde :
Fruits growing faint in the tree,
    And blind things dead in their
      birth ;
    Famine, and blighting of corn,
    When thy time was come to be born.

All these we know of ; but thee
  Who shall discern or declare ?
In the uttermost ends of the sea
  The light of thine eyelids and hair,
    The light of thy bosom as fire
      Between the wheel of the sun
  And the flying flames of the air ?
    Wilt thou turn thee not yet nor
      have pity,
But abide with despair and desire
  And the crying of armies undone,
    Lamentation of one with another
And breaking of city by city ;
  The dividing of friend against friend,
    The severing of brother and
      brother ;
  Wilt thou utterly bring to an end ?
    Have mercy, mother !

For against all men from of old
  Thou hast set thine hand as a curse,
    And cast out gods from their places.
    These things are spoken of thee.
Strong kings and goodly with gold

Thou hast found out arrows to pierce,
    And made their kingdoms and races
      As dust and surf of the sea.
All these, overburdened with woes
    And with length of their days waxen
      weak,
      Thou slewest ; and sentest moreover
      Upon Tyro an evil thing,
Rent hair and a fetter and blows
    Making bloody the flower of the cheek,
      Though she lay by a god as a lover,
        Though fair, and the seed of a
        king.
For of old, being full of thy fire,
    She endured not longer to wear
      On her bosom a saffron vest,
        On her shoulder an ashwood
        quiver ;
Being mixed and made one through
    desire
    With Enipeus, and all her hair
      Made moist with his mouth, and
      her breast
        Filled full of the foam of the
        river.

ATALANTA

Sun, and clear light among green hills,
    and day
Late risen and long sought after, and you
    just gods
Whose hands divide anguish and recom-
    pense,
But first the sun's white sister, a maid in
    heaven,
On earth of all maids worshipped — hail,
    and hear,
And witness with me if not without sign
    sent,
Not without rule and reverence, I a maid
Hallowed, and huntress holy as whom I
    serve,
Here in your sight and eyeshot of these
    men
Stand, girt as they toward hunting, and
    my shafts
Drawn ; wherefore all ye stand up on my
    side,
If I be pure and all ye righteous gods,
Lest one revile me, a woman, yet no wife,
That bear a spear for spindle, and this
    bow strung
For a web woven ; and with pure lips
    salute
Heaven, and the face of all the gods, and
    dawn
Filling with maiden flames and maiden
    flowers
The starless fold o' the stars, and making

    sweet
The warm wan heights of the air, moon-
    trodden ways
And breathless gates and extreme hills of
    heaven.
Whom, having offered water and bloodless
    gifts,
Flowers, and a golden circlet of pure hair,
Next Artemis I bid be favourable
And make this day all golden, hers and
    ours,
Gracious and good and white to the un-
    blamed end.
But thou, O well-beloved, of all my days
Bid it be fruitful, and a crown for all,
To bring forth leaves and bind round all
    my hair
With perfect chaplets woven for thine of
    thee.
For not without the word of thy chaste
    mouth,
For not without law given and clean
    command,
Across the white straits of the running sea
From Elis even to the Acheloian horn,
I with clear winds came hither and gentle
    gods,
Far off my father's house, and left un-
    cheered
Iasius, and uncheered the Arcadian hills
And all their green-haired waters, and all
    woods
Disconsolate, to hear no horn of mine
Blown, and behold no flash of swift white
    feet.

MELEAGER

For thy name's sake and awe toward thy
    chaste head,
O holiest Atalanta, no man dares
Praise thee, though fairer than whom all
    men praise,
And godlike for thy grace of hallowed hair
And holy habit of thine eyes, and feet
That make the blown foam neither swift
    nor white
Though the wind winnow and whirl it ;
    yet we praise
Gods, found because of thee adorable
And for thy sake praiseworthiest from all
    men :
Thee therefore we praise also, thee as
    these,
Pure, and a light lit at the hands of gods.

TOXEUS

How long will ye whet spears with elo-
    quence,

Fight, and kill beasts dry-handed with
 sweet words?
Cease, or talk still and slay thy boars at
 home.

PLEXIPPUS

Why, if she ride among us for a man,
Sit thou for her and spin; a man grown
 girl
Is worth a woman weaponed; sit thou
 here.

MELEAGER

Peace, and be wise; no gods love idle
 speech.

PLEXIPPUS

Nor any man a man's mouth woman-
 tongued.

MELEAGER

For my lips bite not sharper than mine
 hands.

PLEXIPPUS

Nay, both bite soft, but no whit softly
 mine.

MELEAGER

Keep thine hands clean; they have time
 enough to stain.

PLEXIPPUS

For thine shall rest and wax not red to-day.

MELEAGER

Have all thy will of words; talk out thine
 heart.

ALTHÆA

Refrain your lips, O brethren, and my son,
Lest words turn snakes and bite you uttering them.

TOXEUS

Except she give her blood before the gods,
What profit shall a maid be among men?

PLEXIPPUS

Let her come crowned and stretch her
 throat for a knife,
Bleat out her spirit and die, and so shall
 men
Through her too prosper and through
 prosperous gods,
But nowise through her living; shall she
 live
A flower-bud of the flower bed, or sweet
 fruit
For kisses and the honey-making mouth,
And play the shield for strong men and
 the spear?
Then shall the heifer and her mate lock
 horns,
And the bride overbear the groom, and
 men
Gods; for no less division sunders these:
Since all things made are seasonable in
 time,
But if one alter unseasonable are all.
But thou, O Zeus, hear me that I may slay
This beast before thee and no man halve
 with me
Nor woman, lest these mock thee, though
 a god,
Who hast made men strong, and thou
 being wise be held
Foolish; for wise is that thing which en-
 dures.

ATALANTA

Men, and the chosen of all this people,
 and thou,
King, I beseech you a little bear with me.
For if my life be shameful that I live,
Let the gods witness and their wrath; but
 these
Cast no such word against me. Thou, O
 mine,
O holy, O happy goddess, if I sin
Changing the words of women and the
 works
For spears and strange men's faces, hast
 not thou
One shaft of all thy sudden seven that
 pierced
Seven through the bosom or shining throat
 or side,
All couched about one mother's loosening
 knees,
All holy born, engraffed of Tantalus?
But if toward any of you I am overbold
That take thus much upon me, let him
 think
How I, for all my forest holiness,
Fame, and this armed and iron maiden-
 hood,
Pay thus much also; I shall have no man's
 love

For ever, and no face of children born
Or feeding lips upon me or fastening eyes
For ever, nor being dead shall kings my
   sons
Mourn me and bury, and tears on daugh-
   ters' cheeks
Burn ; but a cold and sacred life, but
   strange,
But far from dances and the back-blowing
   torch,
Far off from flowers or any bed of man,
Shall my life be for ever : me the snows
That face the first o' the morning, and
   cold hills
Full of the land-wind and sea-travelling
   storms
And many a wandering wing of noisy
   nights
That know the thunder and hear the
   thickening wolves —
Me the utmost pine and footless frost of
   woods
That talk with many winds and gods, the
   hours
Re-risen, and white divisions of the dawn,
Springs thousand-tongued with the inter-
   mitting reed
And streams that murmur of the mother
   snow —
Me these allure, and know me ; but no
   man
Knows, and my goddess only. Lo now, see
If one of all you these things vex at all.
Would God that any of you had all the
   praise
And I no manner of memory when I die,
So might I show before her perfect eyes
Pure, whom I follow, a maiden to my
   death.
But for the rest let all have all they will ;
For is it a grief to you that I have part,
Being woman merely, in your male might
   and deeds
Done by main strength ? yet in my body is
   throned
As great a heart, and in my spirit, O men,
I have not less of godlike. Evil it were
That one coward should mix with you,
   one hand
Fearful, one eye abase itself ; and these
Well might ye hate and well revile, not me.
For not the difference of the several flesh
Being vile or noble or beautiful or base
Makes praiseworthy, but purer spirit and
   heart
Higher than these meaner mouths and
   limbs, that feed,
Rise, rest, and are and are not ; and for
   me,

What should I say ? but by the gods of the
   world
And this my maiden body, by all oaths
That bind the tongue of men and the
   evil will,
I am not mighty-minded, nor desire
Crowns, nor the spoil of slain things nor
   the fame ;
Feed ye on these, eat and wax fat ; cry out,
Laugh, having eaten, and leap without a
   lyre,
Sing, mix the wind with clamour, smite
   and shake
Sonorous timbrels and tumultuous hair,
And fill the dance up with tempestuous
   feet,
For I will none ; but having prayed my
   prayers
And made thank-offering for prosperities,
I shall go hence and no man see me more.
What thing is this for you to shout me
   down,
What, for a man to grudge me this my
   life
As it were envious of all yours, and I
A thief of reputations ? nay, for now,
If there be any highest in heaven, a god
Above all thrones and thunders of the gods
Throned, and the wheel of the world roll
   under him,
Judge he between me and all of you, and
   see
If I transgress at all : but ye, refrain
Transgressing hands and reinless mouths,
   and keep
Silence, lest by much foam of violent words
And proper poison of your lips ye die.

ŒNEUS

O flower of Tegea, maiden, fleetest foot
And holiest head of women, have good
   cheer
Of thy good words : but ye, depart with
   her
In peace and reverence, each with blameless eye
Following his fate ; exalt your hands and
   hearts,
Strike, cease not, arrow on arrow and
   wound on wound,
And go with gods and with the gods return.

CHORUS

Who hath given man speech ? or who hath
   set therein
A thorn for peril and a snare for sin ?
For in the word his life is and his breath,

And in the word his death,
That madness and the infatuate heart may
  breed
  From the word's womb the deed
And life bring one thing forth ere all
  pass by,
Even one thing which is ours yet cannot
  die —
Death. Hast thou seen him ever anywhere,
Time's twin-born brother, imperishable as
  he
Is perishable and plaintive, clothed with
  care
  And mutable as sand,
But death is strong and full of blood and
  fair
And perdurable and like a lord of land ?
Nay, time thou seest not, death thou wilt
  not see
Till life's right hand be loosened from
  thine hand
  And thy life-days from thee.
For the gods very subtly fashion
  Madness with sadness upon earth :
Not knowing in any wise compassion,
  Nor holding pity of any worth ;
And many things they have given and
  taken,
  And wrought and ruined many things ;
The firm land have they loosed and
  shaken,
  And sealed the sea with all her springs :
They have wearied time with heavy bur-
  dens
  And vexed the lips of life with breath :
Set men to labour and given them guer-
  dons,
  Death, and great darkness after death :
Put moans into the bridal measure
  And on the bridal wools a stain ;
And circled pain about with pleasure,
  And girdled pleasure about with pain ;
And strewed one marriage-bed with tears
  and fire
For extreme loathing and supreme desire.

What shall be done with all these tears
  of ours ?
  Shall they make watersprings in the fair
    heaven
To bathe the brows of morning ? or like
  flowers
Be shed and shine before the starriest
  hours,
  Or made the raiment of the weeping
    Seven ?
Or rather, O our masters, shall they be
Food for the famine of the grievous sea,
  A great well-head of lamentation

Satiating the sad gods ? or fall and flow
Among the years and seasons to and fro,
  And wash their feet with tribulation
And fill them full with grieving ere they
  go ?
  Alas, our lords, and yet alas again,
Seeing all your iron heaven is gilt as gold
  But all we smite thereat in vain ;
Smite the gates barred with groanings
  manifold,
  But all the floors are paven with our
    pain.
Yea, and with weariness of lips and eyes,
With breaking of the bosom, and with
  sighs,
  We labour, and are clad and fed with
    grief
And filled with days we would not fain
  behold
And nights we would not hear of ; we wax
  old,
  All we wax old and wither like a leaf.
We are outcast, strayed between bright
  sun and moon ;
  Our light and darkness are as leaves of
    flowers,
Black flowers and white, that perish ; and
  the noon
  As midnight, and the night as daylight
    hours.
  A little fruit a little while is ours,
    And the worm finds it soon.

But up in heaven the high gods one by
  one
  Lay hands upon the draught that quick-
    eneth,
Fulfilled with all tears shed and all things
  done,
  And stir with soft imperishable breath
  The bubbling bitterness of life and
    death,
And hold it to our lips and laugh ; but
  they
Preserve their lips from tasting night or
  day,
  Lest they too change and sleep, the
    fates that spun,
The lips that made us and the hands that
  slay ;
  Lest all these change, and heaven bow
    down to none,
Change and be subject to the secular sway
  And terrene revolution of the sun.
Therefore they thrust it from them, put-
  ting time away.

I would the wine of time, made sharp and
  sweet

With multitudinous days and nights and
    tears
And many mixing savours of strange
    years,
Were no more trodden of them under
    feet,
    Cast out and spilt about their holy
        places :
That life were given them as a fruit to
    eat
And death to drink as water ; that the
    light
Might ebb, drawn backward from their
    eyes, and night
    Hide for one hour the imperishable
        faces.
That they might rise up sad in heaven,
    and know
Sorrow and sleep, one paler than young
    snow,
    One cold as blight of dew and ruinous
        rain ;
Rise up and rest and suffer a little, and be
Awhile as all things born with us and we,
    And grieve as men, and like slain men
        be slain.

For now we know not of them ; but one
    saith
    The gods are gracious, praising God ;
        and one,
When hast thou seen ? or hast thou felt
    his breath
    Touch, nor consume thine eyelids as the
        sun,
Nor fill thee to the lips with fiery death ?
    None hath beheld him, none
Seen above other gods and shapes of
    things,
Swift without feet and flying without
    wings,
Intolerable, not clad with death or life,
    Insatiable, not known of night or day,
The lord of love and loathing and of
    strife
    Who gives a star and takes a sun away ;
Who shapes the soul, and makes her a
    barren wife
    To the earthly body and grievous
        growth of clay ;
Who turns the large limbs to a little flame
    And binds the great sea with a little
        sand ;
Who makes desire, and slays desire with
    shame ;
    Who shakes the heaven as ashes in his
        hand ;
Who, seeing the light and shadow for the

same,
Bids day waste night as fire devours a
    brand,
Smites without sword, and scourges with-
    out rod ;
    The supreme evil, God.
Yea, with thine hate, O God, thou hast
    covered us,
    One saith, and hidden our eyes away
        from sight,
And made us transitory and hazardous,
    Light things and slight ;
Yet have men praised thee, saying, He
    hath made man thus,
    And he doeth right.
Thou hast kissed us, and hast smitten ;
    thou hast laid
Upon us with thy left hand life, and said,
Live : and again thou hast said, Yield up
    your breath,
And with thy right hand laid upon us
    death.
Thou hast sent us sleep, and stricken sleep
    with dreams,
    Saying, Joy is not, but love of joy shall
        be ;
Thou hast made sweet springs for all the
    pleasant streams,
    In the end thou hast made them bitter
        with the sea.
Thou hast fed one rose with dust of many
    men ;
    Thou hast marred one face with fire of
        many tears ;
Thou hast taken love, and given us sorrow
    again ;
    With pain thou hast filled us full to the
        eyes and ears.
Therefore because thou art strong, our
    father, and we
    Feeble ; and thou art against us, and
        thine hand
Constrains us in the shallows of the sea
    And breaks us at the limits of the land ;
Because thou hast bent thy lightnings as
    a bow,
    And loosed the hours like arrows ; and
        let fall
Sins and wild words and many a wingèd
    woe
    And wars among us, and one end of all ;
Because thou hast made the thunder, and
    thy feet
    Are as a rushing water when the skies
Break, but thy face as an exceeding heat
    And flames of fire the eyelids of thine
        eyes ;
Because thou art over all who are over us ;

Because thy name is life and our name
    death ;
Because thou art cruel and men are
    piteous,
  And our hands labour and thine hand
    scattereth ;
Lo, with hearts rent and knees made
    tremulous,
  Lo, with ephemeral lips and casual
    breath,
    At least we witness of thee ere we die
That these things are not otherwise, but
    thus ;
  That each man in his heart sigheth, and
    saith,
    That all men even as I,
All we are against thee, against thee, O
    God most high.

  But ye, keep ye on earth
  Your lips from over-speech,
Loud words and longing are so little
    worth ;
  And the end is hard to reach.
For silence after grievous things is good,
  And reverence, and the fear that makes
    men whole,
And shame, and righteous governance of
    blood,
    And lordship of the soul.
But from sharp words and wits men pluck
    no fruit,
And gathering thorns they shake the tree
    at root ;
For words divide and rend ;
But silence is most noble till the end.

ALTHÆA

I heard within the house a cry of news
And came forth eastward hither, where
    the dawn
Cheers first these warder gods that face
    the sun
And next our eyes unrisen ; for unaware
Came clashes of swift hoofs and trampling
    feet
And through the windy pillared corridor
Light sharper than the frequent flames of
    day
That daily fill it from the fiery dawn ;
Gleams, and a thunder of people that
    cried out,
And dust and hurrying horsemen ; lo their
    chief,
That rode with Œneus rein by rein, re-
    turned.
What cheer, O herald of my lord the
king ?

HERALD

Lady, good cheer and great ; the boar is
    slain.

CHORUS

Praised be all gods that look toward
    Calydon.

ALTHÆA

Good news and brief ; but by whose
    happier hand ?

HERALD

A maiden's and a prophet's and thy son's.

ALTHÆA

Well fare the spear that severed him and
    life.

HERALD

Thine own, and not an alien, hast thou
    blest.

ALTHÆA

Twice be thou too for my sake blest and
    his.

HERALD

At the king's word I rode afoam for thine.

ALTHÆA

Thou sayest he tarrieth till they bring the
    spoil ?

HERALD

Hard by the quarry, where they breathe,
    O queen.

ALTHÆA

Speak thou their chance ; but some bring
    flowers and crown
These gods and all the lintel, and shed
    wine,
Fetch sacrifice and slay ; for heaven is
    good.

HERALD

Some furlongs northward where the brakes
    begin
West of that narrowing range of warrior
    hills
Whose brooks have bled with battle when
    thy son
Smote Acarnania, there all they made halt,
And with keen eye took note of spear and
    hound,
Royally ranked ; Laertes island-born,
The young Gerenian Nestor, Panopeus,
And Cepheus and Ancæus, mightiest
    thewed,
Arcadians ; next, and evil-eyed of these,
Arcadian Atalanta, with twain hounds
Lengthening the leash, and under nose
    and brow
Glittering with lipless tooth and fire-swift
    eye ;
But from her white braced shoulder the
    plumed shafts
Rang, and the bow shone from her side ;
    next her
Meleager, like a sun in spring that strikes
Branch into leaf and bloom into the
    world,
A glory among men meaner ; Iphicles,
And following him that slew the biform
    bull
Pirithous, and divine Eurytion,
And, bride-bound to the gods, Æacides,
Then Telamon his brother, and Argive-
    born
The seer and sayer of visions and of truth,
Amphiaraus ; and a four-fold strength,
Thine, even thy mother's and thy sister's
    sons.
And recent from the roar of foreign foam
Jason, and Dryas twin-begot with war,
A blossom of bright battle, sword and man
Shining ; and Idas, and the keenest eye
Of Lynceus, and Admetus twice-espoused,
And Hippasus and Hyleus, great in heart.
These having halted bade blow horns, and
    rode
Through woods and waste lands cleft by
    stormy streams,
Past yew-trees and the heavy hair of pines,
And where the dew is thickest under oaks,
This way and that ; but questing up and
    down
They saw no trail nor scented ; and one
    said,
Plexippus, Help, or help not, Artemis,
And we will flay thy boarskin with male
    hands ;
But saying, he ceased and said not that
he would.
Seeing where the green ooze of a sun-
    struck marsh
Shook with a thousand reeds untunable.
And in their moist and multitudinous
    flower
Slept no soft sleep, with violent visions fed.
The blind bulk of the immeasurable
    beast.
And seeing, he shuddered with sharp lust
    of praise
Through all his limbs, and launched a
    double dart.
And missed ; for much desire divided him,
Too hot of spirit and feebler than his will.
That his hand failed, through fervent ;
    and the shaft,
Sundering the rushes, in a tamarisk stem
Shook, and stuck fast ; then all abode save
    one,
The Arcadian Atalanta ; from her side
Sprang her hounds, labouring at the leash,
    and slipped,
And plashed ear-deep with plunging feet ;
    but she
Saying, Speed it as I send it for thy sake,
Goddess, drew bow and loosed ; the sud-
    den string
Rang, and sprang inward, and the waterish
    air
Hissed, and the moist plumes of the song-
    less reeds
Moved as a wave which the wind moves
    no more.
But the boar heaved half out of ooze and
    slime
His tense flank trembling round the
    barbèd wound,
Hateful ; and fiery with invasive eyes
And bristling with intolerable hair
Plunged, and the hounds clung, and green
    flowers and white
Reddened and broke all round them where
    they came.
And charging with sheer tusk he drove,
    and smote
Hyleus ; and sharp death caught his sud-
    den soul,
And violent sleep shed night upon his eyes.
Then Peleus, with strong strain of hand
    and heart,
Shot ; but the sidelong arrow slid, and
    slew
His comrade born and loving countryman,
Under the left arm smitten, as he no less
Poised a like arrow ; and bright blood
    brake afoam,
And falling, and weighted back by clamor-
    ous arms,

Sharp rang the dead limbs of Eurytion.
Then one shot happier, the Cadmean seer,
Amphiaraus; for his sacred shaft
Pierced the red circlet of one ravening eye
Beneath the brute brows of the sanguine
boar,
Now bloodier from one slain; but he so
galled
Sprang straight, and rearing cried no les-
ser cry
Than thunder and the roar of wintering
streams
That mix their own foam with the yel-
lower sea;
And as a tower that falls by fire in fight
With ruin of walls and all its archery,
And breaks the iron flower of war beneath,
Crushing charred limbs and molten arms
of men;
So through crushed branches and the red-
dening brake
Clamoured and crashed the fervour of his
feet,
And trampled, springing sideways from the
tusk,
Too tardy a moving mould of heavy
strength,
Ancæus; and as flakes of weak-winged
snow
Break, all the hard thews of his heaving
limbs
Broke, and rent flesh fell every way, and
blood
Flew, and fierce fragments of no more
a man.
Then all the heroes drew sharp breath,
and gazed,
And smote not; but Meleager, but thy
son,
Right in the wild way of the coming curse
Rock-rooted, fair with fierce and fastened
lips,
Clear eyes, and springing muscle and
shortening limb —
With chin aslant indrawn to a tightening
throat,
Grave, and with gathered sinews, like a
god, —
Aimed on the left side his well-handled
spear
Grasped where the ash was knottiest hewn,
and smote,
And with no missile wound, the monstrous
boar
Right in the hairiest hollow of his hide
Under the last rib, sheer through bulk and
bone,
Deep in; and deeply smitten, and to
death,

The heavy horror with his hanging shafts
Leapt, and fell furiously, and from raging
lips
Foamed out the latest wrath of all his life.
And all they praised the gods with might-
ier heart,
Zeus and all gods, but chiefliest Artemis,
Seeing; but Meleager bade whet knives
and flay,
Strip and stretch out the splendour of the
spoil;
And hot and horrid from the work all
these
Sat, and drew breath and drank and made
great cheer
And washed the hard sweat off their calm-
er brows.
For much sweet grass grew higher than
grew the reed,
And good for slumber, and every holier
herb,
Narcissus, and the low-lying melilote,
And all of goodliest blade and bloom that
springs
Where, hid by heavier hyacinth, violet
buds
Blossom and burn; and fire of yellower
flowers
And light of crescent lilies, and such leaves
As fear the Faun's and know the Dryad's
foot;
Olive and ivy and poplar dedicate,
And many a well-spring overwatched of
these.
There now they rest; but me the king
bade bear
Good tidings to rejoice this town and thee.
Wherefore be glad, and all ye give much
thanks,
For fallen is all the trouble of Calydon.

ALTHÆA

Laud ye the gods; for this they have given
is good,
And what shall be they hide until their
time.
Much good and somewhat grievous hast
thou said,
And either well; but let all sad things be,
Till all have made before the prosperous
gods
Burnt-offering, and poured out the floral
wine.
Look fair, O gods, and favourable; for we
Praise you with no false heart or flattering
mouth,
Being merciful, but with pure souls and
prayer.

HERALD

Thou hast prayed well; for whoso fears
    not these,
But once being prosperous waxes huge of
    heart,
Him shall some new thing unaware de-
    stroy.

CHORUS

O that I now, I too were
By deep wells and water-floods,
Streams of ancient hills, and where
All the wan green places bear
Blossoms cleaving to the sod,
Fruitless fruit, and grasses fair,
Or such darkest ivy-buds
As divide thy yellow hair,
Bacchus, and their leaves that nod
Round thy fawnskin brush the bare
Snow-soft shoulders of a god;
There the year is sweet, and there
Earth is full of secret springs,
And the fervent rose-cheeked hours,
Those that marry dawn and noon,
There are sunless, there look pale
In dim leaves and hidden air,
Pale as grass or latter flowers
Or the wild vine's wan wet rings
Full of dew beneath the moon,
And all day the nightingale
Sleeps, and all night sings;
There in cold remote recesses
That nor alien eyes assail,
Feet, nor imminence of wings,
Nor a wind nor any tune,
Thou, O queen and holiest,
Flower the whitest of all things,
With reluctant lengthening tresses
And with sudden splendid breast
Save of maidens unbeholden,
There art wont to enter, there
Thy divine swift limbs and golden
Maiden growth of unbound hair,
Bathed in waters white,
Shine, and many a maid 's by thee
In moist woodland or the hilly
Flowerless brakes where wells abound
Out of all men's sight;
Or in lower pools that see
All their marges clothed all round
With the innumerable lily,
Whence the golden-girdled bee
Flits through flowering rush to fret
White or duskier violet,
Fair as those that in far years
With their buds left luminous

And their little leaves made wet,
From the warmer dew of tears,
Mother's tears in extreme need,
Hid the limbs of Iamus,
Of thy brother's seed;
For his heart was piteous
Toward him, even as thine heart now
Pitiful toward us;
Thine, O goddess, turning hither
A benignant blameless brow;
Seeing enough of evil done
And lives withered as leaves wither
In the blasting of the sun;
Seeing enough of hunters dead,
Ruin enough of all our year,
Herds and harvests slain and shed,
Herdsmen stricken many an one,
Fruits and flocks consumed together,
And great length of deadly days.
Yet with reverent lips and fear
Turn we toward thee, turn and praise
For this lightening of clear weather
And prosperities begun.
For not seldom, when all air
As bright water without breath
Shines, and when men fear not, fate
Without thunder unaware
Breaks, and brings down death.
Joy with grief ye great gods give,
Good with bad, and overbear
All the pride of us that live,
All the high estate,
As ye long since overbore,
As in old time long before,
Many a strong man and a great,
All that were.
But do thou, sweet, otherwise,
Having heed of all our prayer,
Taking note of all our sighs;
We beseech thee by thy light,
By thy bow, and thy sweet eyes,
And the kingdom of the night,
Be thou favourable and fair;
By thine arrows and thy might
And Orion overthrown;
By the maiden thy delight,
By the indissoluble zone
And the sacred hair.

MESSENGER

Maidens, if ye will sing now, shift your
    song,
Bow down, cry, wail for pity; is this a
    time
For singing? nay, for strewing of dust and
    ash,

Rent raiment, and for bruising of the
  breast.

CHORUS

What new thing wolf-like lurks behind thy
  words?
What snake's tongue in thy lips? what fire
  in the eyes?

MESSENGER

Bring me before the queen and I will
  speak.

CHORUS

Lo, she comes forth as from thank-offering
  made.

MESSENGER

A barren offering for a bitter gift.

ALTHÆA

What are these borne on branches, and
  the face
Covered? no mean men living, but now
  slain
Such honour have they, if any dwell with
  death.

MESSENGER

Queen, thy twain brethren and thy
  mother's sons.

ALTHÆA

Lay down your dead till I behold their
  blood
If it be mine indeed, and I will weep.

MESSENGER

Weep if thou wilt, for these men shall no
  more.

ALTHÆA

O brethren, O my father's sons, of me
Well loved and well reputed, I should
  weep
Tears dearer than the dear blood drawn
  from you
But that I know you not uncomforted
Sleeping no shameful sleep, however slain,

For my son surely hath avenged you dead.

MESSENGER

Nay, should thine own seed slay himself,
  O queen?

ALTHÆA

Thy double word brings forth a double
  death.

MESSENGER

Know this then singly, by one hand they
  fell.

ALTHÆA

What mutterest thou with thine ambiguous mouth?

MESSENGER

Slain by thy son's hand; is that saying so
  hard?

ALTHÆA

Our time is come upon us: it is here.

CHORUS

O miserable, and spoiled at thine own
  hand.

ALTHÆA

Wert thou not called Meleager from this
  womb?

CHORUS

A grievous huntsman hath it bred to thee.

ALTHÆA

Wert thou born fire, and shalt thou not
  devour?

CHORUS

The fire thou madest, will it consume
  even thee?

ALTHÆA

My dreams are fallen upon me; burn thou
  too.

CHORUS

Not without God are visions born and die.

ALTHÆA

The gods are many about me; I am one.

CHORUS

She groans as men wrestling with heavier gods.

ALTHÆA

They rend me, they divide me, they destroy.

CHORUS

Or one labouring in travail of strange births.

ALTHÆA

They are strong, they are strong; I am broken, and these prevail.

CHORUS

The god is great against her; she will die.

ALTHÆA

Yea, but not now; for my heart too is great.
I would I were not here in sight of the sun,
But thou, speak all thou sawest, and I will die.

MESSENGER

O queen, for queenlike hast thou borne thyself,
A little word may hold so great mischance.
For in division of the sanguine spoil
These men thy brethren wrangling bade yield up
The boar's head and the horror of the hide
That this might stand a wonder in Calydon,
Hallowed; and some drew toward them; but thy son
With great hands grasping all that weight of hair
Cast down the dead heap clanging and collapsed

At female feet, saying This thy spoil not mine,
Maiden, thine own hand for thyself hath reaped,
And all this praise God gives thee : she thereat
Laughed, as when dawn touches the sacred night
The sky sees laugh and redden and divide
Dim lips and eyelids virgin of the sun,
Hers, and the warm slow breasts of morning heave,
Fruitful, and flushed with flame from lamp-lit hours,
And maiden undulation of clear hair
Colour the clouds; so laughed she from pure heart,
Lit with a low blush to the braided hair,
And rose-coloured and cold like very dawn,
Golden and godlike, chastely with chaste lips,
A faint grave laugh; and all they held their peace,
And she passed by them. Then one cried Lo now,
Shall not the Arcadian shoot out lips at us,
Saying all we were despoiled by this one girl?
And all they rode against her violently
And cast the fresh crown from her hair, and now
They had rent her spoil away, dishonouring her,
Save that Meleager, as a tame lion chafed,
Bore on them, broke them, and as fire cleaves wood
So clove and drove them, smitten in twain; but she
Smote not nor heaved up hand; and this man first,
Plexippus, crying out This for love's sake, sweet,
Drove at Meleager, who with spear straightening
Pierced his cheek through; then Toxeus made for him,
Dumb, but his spear spake; vain and violent words.
Fruitless; for him too stricken through both sides
The earth felt falling, and his horse's foam
Blanched thy son's face, his slayer; and these being slain,
None moved nor spake; but Œneus bade bear hence
These made of heaven infatuate in their deaths,
Foolish; for these would baffle fate, and fell.

And they passed on, and all men honoured her,
Being honourable, as one revered of
heaven.

ALTHÆA

What say you, women ? is all this not well
done ?

CHORUS

No man doth well but God hath part in
him.

ALTHÆA

But no part here ; for these my brethren
born
Ye have no part in, these ye know not of
As I that was their sister, a sacrifice
Slain in their slaying. I would I had died
for these ;
For this man dead walked with me, child
by child,
And made a weak staff for my feebler feet
With his own tender wrist and hand, and
held
And led me softly and shewed me gold
and steel
And shining shapes of mirror and bright
crown
And all things fair ; and threw light spears,
and brought
Young hounds to huddle at my feet and
thrust
Tame heads against my little maiden
breasts
And please me with great eyes ; and those
days went
And these are bitter and I a barren queen
And sister miserable, a grievous thing
And mother of many curses ; and she too,
My sister Leda, sitting overseas
With fair fruits round her, and her fault-
less lord,
Shall curse me, saying A sorrow and not a
son,
Sister, thou barest, even a burning fire,
A brand consuming thine own soul and
me.
But ye now, sons of Thestius, make good
cheer,
For ye shall have such wood to funeral fire
As no king hath ; and flame that once
burnt down
Oil shall not quicken or breath relume or
wine
Refresh again ; much costlier than fine
gold,

And more than many lives of wandering
men.

CHORUS

O queen, thou hast yet with thee love-
worthy things,
Thine husband, and the great strength
of thy son.

ALTHÆA

Who shall get brothers for me while I
live ?
Who bear them ? who bring forth in lieu
of these ?
Are not our fathers and our brethren one,
And no man like them ? are not mine here
slain ?
Have we not hung together, he and I,
Flowerwise feeding as the feeding bees,
With mother-milk for honey ? and this
man too,
Dead, with my son's spear thrust between
his sides,
Hath he not seen us, later born than he,
Laugh with lips filled, and laughed again
for love ?
There were no sons then in the world, nor
spears,
Nor deadly births of women ; but the gods
Allowed us, and our days were clear of
these.
I would I had died unwedded, and
brought forth
No swords to vex the world ; for these
that spake
Sweet words long since and loved me will
not speak
Nor love nor look upon me ; and all my
life
I shall not hear nor see them living men.
But I too living, how shall I now live ?
What life shall this be with my son, to
know
What hath been and desire what will not
be,
Look for dead eyes and listen for dead
lips,
And kill mine own heart with remember-
ing them,
And with those eyes that see their slayer
alive
Weep, and wring hands that clasp him by
the hand ?
How shall I bear my dreams of them, to
hear
False voices, feel the kisses of false mouths
And footless sound of perished feet, and
then

Wake and hear only it may be their own
    hounds
Whine masterless in miserable sleep,
And see their boar-spears and their beds
    and seats
And all the gear and housings of their lives
And not the men? shall hounds and horses
    mourn,
Pine with strange eyes, and prick up hun-
    gry ears,
Famish and fail at heart for their dear
    lords,
And I not heed at all? and those blind
    things
Fall off from life for love's sake, and I
    live?
Surely some death is better than some life,
Better one death for him and these and me
For if the gods had slain them it may be
I had endured it; if they had fallen by
    war
Or by the nets and knives of privy death
And by hired hands while sleeping, this
    thing too
I had set my soul to suffer; or this hunt,
Had this despatched them, under tusk or
    tooth
Torn, sanguine, trodden, broken; for all
    deaths
Or honourable or with facile feet avenged
And hands of swift gods following, all
    save this,
Are bearable; but not for their sweet land
Fighting, but not a sacrifice, lo these
Dead; for I had not then shed all mine
    heart
Out at mine eyes: then either with good
    speed,
Being just, I had slain their slayer aton-
    ingly,
Or strewn with flowers their fire and on
    their tombs
Hung crowns, and over them a song, and
    seen
Their praise outflame their ashes: for all
    men,
All maidens, had come thither, and from
    pure lips
Shed songs upon them, from heroic eyes
Tears; and their death had been a death-
    less life;
But now, by no man hired nor alien sword,
By their own kindred are they fallen, in
    peace,
After much peril, friendless among friends,
By hateful hands they loved; and how
    shall mine
Touch these returning red and not from
    war,

These fatal from the vintage of men's
    veins,
Dead men my brethren? how shall these
    wash off
No festal stains of undelightful wine,
How mix the blood, my blood on them,
    with me,
Holding mine hand? or how shall I say,
    son,
That am no sister? but by night and day
Shall we not sit and hate each other, and
    think
Things hate-worthy? not live with shame-
    fast eyes,
Brow-beaten, treading soft with fearful
    feet,
Each unupbraided, each without rebuke
Convicted, and without a word reviled
Each of another? and I shall let thee live
And see thee strong and hear men for thy
    sake
Praise me, but these thou wouldest not
    let live
No man shall praise for ever? these shall
    lie
Dead, unbeloved, unholpen, all through
    thee?
Sweet were they toward me living, and
    mine heart
Desired them, but was then well satisfied,
That now is as men hungered; and these
    dead
I shall want always to the day I die.
For all things else and all men may renew;
Yea, son for son the gods may give and
    take,
But never a brother or sister any more.

CHORUS

Nay, for the son lies close about thine
    heart,
Full of thy milk, warm from thy womb,
    and drains
Life and the blood of life and all thy
    fruit,
Eats thee and drinks thee as who breaks
    bread and eats,
Treads wine and drinks, thyself, a sect
    of thee;
And if he feed not, shall not thy flesh
    faint?
Or drink not, are not thy lips dead for
    thirst?
This thing moves more than all things,
    even thy son,
That thou cleave to him; and he shall
    honour thee,

Thy womb that bare him and the breasts
he knew,
Reverencing most for thy sake all his gods.

ALTHÆA

But these the gods too gave me, and these
my son,
Not reverencing his gods nor mine own
heart
Nor the old sweet years nor all venerable
things,
But cruel, and in his ravin like a beast,
Hath taken away to slay them: yea, and
she,
She the strange woman, she the flower,
the sword,
Red from spilt blood, a mortal flower to
men,
Adorable, detestable — even she
Saw with strange eyes and with strange
lips rejoiced,
Seeing these mine own slain of mine own,
and me
Made miserable above all miseries made,
A grief among all women in the world,
A name to be washed out with all men's
tears.

CHORUS

Strengthen thy spirit; is this not also a
god,
Chance, and the wheel of all necessities?
Hard things have fallen upon us from
harsh gods,
Whom lest worse hap rebuke we not for
these.

ALTHÆA

My spirit is strong against itself, and I
For these things' sake cry out on mine own
soul
That it endures outrage, and dolorous
days,
And life, and this inexpiable impotence.
Weak am I, weak and shameful; my breath
drawn
Shames me, and monstrous things and
violent gods.
What shall atone? what heal me? what
bring back
Strength to the foot, light to the face?
what herb
Assuage me? what restore me? what re-
lease?
What strange thing eaten or drunken, O
great gods,

Make me as you or as the beasts that feed,
Slay and divide and cherish their own
hearts?
For these ye show us; and we less than
these
Have not wherewith to live as all these
things
Which all their lives fare after their own
kind
As who doth well rejoicing; but we ill,
Weeping or laughing, we whom eyesight
fails,
Knowledge and light of face and perfect
heart,
And hands we lack, and wit; and all our
days
Sin, and have hunger, and die infatuated.
For madness have ye given us and not
health,
And sins whereof we know not; and for
these
Death, and sudden destruction unaware.
What shall we say now? what thing comes
of us?

CHORUS

Alas, for all this all men undergo.

ALTHÆA

Wherefore I will not that these twain, O
gods,
Die as a dog dies, eaten of creeping things,
Abominable, a loathing; but though dead
Shall they have honour and such funereal
flame
As strews men's ashes in their enemies'
face
And blinds their eyes who hate them: lest
men say,
'Lo how they lie, and living had great kin,
And none of these hath pity of them, and
none
Regards them lying, and none is wrung
at heart,
None moved in spirit for them, naked and
slain,
Abhorred, abased, and no tears comfort
them':
And in the dark this grieve Eurythemis,
Hearing how these her sons come down
to her
Unburied, unavenged, as kinless men,
And had a queen their sister. That were
shame
Worse than this grief. Yet how to atone
at all

I know not ; seeing the love of my born
son,
A new-made mother's new-born love, that
grows
From the soft child to the strong man,
now soft
Now strong as either, and still one sole
same love,
Strives with me, no light thing to strive
withal ;
This love is deep, and natural to man's
blood,
And ineffaceable with many tears.
Yet shall not these rebuke me though I die,
Nor she in that waste world with all her
dead,
My mother, among the pale flocks fallen
as leaves,
Folds of dead people, and alien from the
sun ;
Nor lack some bitter comfort, some poor
praise,
Being queen, to have borne her daughter
like a queen,
Righteous ; and though mine own fire
burn me too,
She shall have honour and these her sons,
though dead.
But all the gods will, all they do, and we
Not all we would, yet somewhat ; and
one choice
We have, to live and do just deeds and
die.

CHORUS

Terrible words she communes with, and
turns
Swift fiery eyes in doubt against herself,
And murmurs as who talks in dreams
with death.

ALTHÆA

For the unjust also dieth, and him all men
Hate, and himself abhors the unrighteous-
ness,
And seeth his own dishonour intolerable.
But I being just, doing right upon myself,
Slay mine own soul, and no man born
shames me.
For none constrains nor shall rebuke,
being done,
What none compelled me doing ; thus
these things fare.
Ah, ah, that such things should so fare ;
ah me,
That I am found to do them and endure,
Chosen and constrained to choose, and

bear myself
Mine own wound through mine own flesh
to the heart
Violently stricken, a spoiler and a spoil,
A ruin ruinous, fallen on mine own son.
Ah, ah, for me too as for these ; alas,
For that is done that shall be, and mine
hand
Full of the deed, and full of blood mine
eyes,
That shall see never nor touch anything
Save blood unstanched and fire unquench-
able.

CHORUS

What wilt thou do ? what ails thee ? for
the house
Shakes ruinously ; wilt thou bring fire
for it ?

ALTHÆA

Fire in the roofs, and on the lintels fire.
Lo ye, who stand and weave, between the
doors,
There ; and blood drips from hand and
thread, and stains
Threshold and raiment and me passing in
Flecked with the sudden sanguine drops of
death.

CHORUS

Alas that time is stronger than strong
men,
Fate than all gods : and these are fallen
on us.

ALTHÆA

A little since and I was glad ; and now
I never shall be glad or sad again.

CHORUS

Between two joys a grief grows unaware.

ALTHÆA

A little while and I shall laugh ; and then
I shall weep never and laugh not any
more.

CHORUS

What shall be said ? for words are thorns
to grief.
Withhold thyself a little and fear the gods.

ALTHÆA

Fear died when these were slain ; and I
am as dead,
And fear is of the living ; these fear none.

CHORUS

Have pity upon all people for their sake.

ALTHÆA

It is done now ; shall I put back my day ?

CHORUS

An end is come, an end ; this is of God.

ALTHÆA

I am fire, and burn myself ; keep clear
of fire.

CHORUS

The house is broken, is broken ; it shall
not stand.

ALTHÆA

Woe, woe for him that breaketh ; and a
rod
Smote it of old, and now the axe is here.

CHORUS

Not as with sundering of the earth
Nor as with cleaving of the sea
Nor fierce foreshadowings of a birth
Nor flying dreams of death to be
Nor loosening of the large world's girth
And quickening of the body of night,
And sound of thunder in men's ears
And fire of lightning in men's sight,
Fate, mother of desires and fears,
Bore unto men the law of tears ;
But sudden, an unfathered flame,
And broken out of night, she shone,
She, without body, without name,
In days forgotten and foregone ;
And heaven rang round her as she came
Like smitten cymbals, and lay bare :
Clouds and great stars, thunders and
snows,
The blue sad fields and folds of air,
The life that breathes, the life that
grows,
All wind, all fire, that burns or blows,
Even all these knew her : for she is
great ;
The daughter of doom, the mother of
death,
The sister of sorrow ; a lifelong weight
That no man's finger lighteneth,
Nor any god can lighten fate ;
A landmark seen across the way
Where one race treads as the other
trod ;
An evil sceptre, an evil stay,
Wrought for a staff, wrought for a rod,
The bitter jealousy of God.

For death is deep as the sea,
And fate as the waves thereof.
Shall the waves take pity on thee
Or the southwind offer thee love ?
Wilt thou take the night for thy day
Or the darkness for light on thy way,
Till thou say in thine heart Enough ?
Behold, thou art over fair, thou art over
wise ;
The sweetness of spring in thine hair, and
the light in thine eyes.
The light of the spring in thine eyes, and
the sound in thine ears ;
Yet thine heart shall wax heavy with sighs
and thine eyelids with tears.
Wilt thou cover thine hair with gold, and
with silver thy feet ?
Hast thou taken the purple to fold thee,
and made thy mouth sweet ?
Behold, when thy face is made bare, he
that loved thee shall hate ;
Thy face shall be no more fair at the fall
of thy fate.
For thy life shall fall as a leaf and be
shed as the rain ;
And the veil of thine head shall be grief :
and the crown shall be pain.

ALTHÆA

Ho, ye that wail, and ye that sing, make
way
Till I be come among you. Hide your
tears,
Ye little weepers, and your laughing lips,
Ye laughers for a little ; lo mine eyes
That outweep heaven at rainiest, and my
mouth
That laughs as gods laugh at us. Fate's
are we,
Yet fate is ours a breathing-space ; yea,
mine,
Fate is made mine for ever ; he is my son,
My bedfellow, my brother. You strong
gods,
Give place unto me ; I am as any of you,

To give life and to take life. Thou, old
    earth,
That hast made man and unmade ; thou
    whose mouth
Looks red from the eaten fruits of thine
    own womb ;
Behold me with what lips upon what food
I feed and fill my body ; even with flesh
Made of my body. Lo, the fire I lit
I burn with fire to quench it ; yea, with
    flame
I burn up even the dust and ash thereof.

CHORUS

Woman, what fire is this thou burnest
    with ?

ALTHÆA

Yea to the bone, yea to the blood and all.

CHORUS

For this thy face and hair are as one fire.

ALTHÆA

A tongue that licks and beats upon the
    dust.

CHORUS

And in thine eyes are hollow light and
    heat.

ALTHÆA

Of flame not fed with hand or frank-
    incense.

CHORUS

I fear thee for the trembling of thine eyes,

ALTHÆA

Neither with love they tremble nor for
    fear.

CHORUS

And thy mouth shuddering like a shot
    bird.

ALTHÆA

Not as the bride's mouth when man kisses
    it.

CHORUS

Nay, but what thing is this thing thou
    hast done ?

ALTHÆA

Look, I am silent, speak your eyes for me.

CHORUS

I see a faint fire lightening from the hall.

ALTHÆA

Gaze, stretch your eyes, strain till the lids
    drop off.

CHORUS

Flushed pillars down the flickering vesti-
    bule.

ALTHÆA

Stretch with your necks like birds : cry,
    chirp as they.

CHORUS

And a long brand that blackens : and
    white dust.

ALTHÆA

O children, what is this ye see ? your eyes
Are blinder than night's face at fall of
    moon.
That is my son, my flesh, my fruit of life,
My travail, and the year's weight of my
    womb.
Meleager, a fire enkindled of mine hands
And of mine hands extinguished : this
    is he.

CHORUS

O gods, what word has flown out at thy
    mouth ?

ALTHÆA

I did this and I say this and I die.

CHORUS

Death stands upon the doorway of thy
    lips,
And in thy mouth has death set up his
    house.

ALTHÆA

O death, a little, a little while, sweet
   death,
Until I see the brand burnt down and die.

CHORUS

She reels as any reed under the wind,
And cleaves unto the ground with staggering feet.

ALTHÆA

Girls, one thing will I say and hold my
   peace.
I that did this will weep not nor cry out,
Cry ye and weep : I will not call on gods,
Call ye on them ; I will not pity man,
Shew ye your pity. I know not if I live ;
Save that I feel the fire upon my face
And on my cheek the burning of a brand.
Yea the smoke bites me, yea I drink the
   steam
With nostril and with eyelid and with lip
Insatiate and intolerant ; and mine hands
Burn, and fire feeds upon mine eyes ; I
   reel
As one made drunk with living, whence he
   draws
Drunken delight ; yet I, though mad for
   joy,
Loathe my long living and am waxen red
As with the shadow of shed blood ; be-
   hold,
I am kindled with the flames that fade in
   him,
I am swollen with subsiding of his veins,
I am flooded with his ebbing ; my lit eyes
Flame with the falling fire that leaves his
   lids
Bloodless ; my cheek is luminous with
   blood
Because his face is ashen. Yet, O child,
Son, first-born, fairest — O sweet mouth,
   sweet eyes,
That drew my life out through my suck-
   ling breast,
That shone and clove mine heart through
   — O soft knees
Clinging, O tender treadings of soft feet,
Cheeks warm with little kissings — O child,
   child,
What have we made each other ? Lo, I felt
Thy weight cleave to me, a burden of
   beauty, O son,
Thy cradled brows and loveliest loving
   lips,
The floral hair, the little lightening eyes,

And all thy goodly glory ; with mine hands
Delicately I fed thee, with my tongue
Tenderly spake, saying, Verily in God's
   time,
For all the little likeness of thy limbs,
Son, I shall make thee a kingly man to
   fight,
A lordly leader ; and hear before I die,
'She bore the goodliest sword of all the
   world.'
Oh ! oh ! For all my life turns round on
   me ;
I am severed from myself, my name is
   gone,
My name that was a healing, it is changed,
My name is a consuming. From this time,
Though mine eyes reach to the end of all
   these things,
My lips shall not unfasten till I die.

SEMICHORUS

She has filled with sighing the city,
   And the ways thereof with tears :
She arose, she girdled her sides,
She set her face as a bride's ;
She wept, and she had no pity ;
   Trembled, and felt no fears.

SEMICHORUS

Her eyes were clear as the sun,
   Her brows were fresh as the day ;
She girdled herself with gold,
Her robes were manifold ;
But the days of her worship are done,
   Her praise is taken away.

SEMICHORUS

For she set her hand to the fire,
   With her mouth she kindled the same ;
As the mouth of a flute-player,
So was the mouth of her ;
With the might of her strong desire
   She blew the breath of the flame.

SEMICHORUS

She set her hand to the wood,
   She took the fire in her hand ;
As one who is nigh to death,
She panted with strange breath ;
She opened her lips unto blood,
   She breathed and kindled the brand.

SEMICHORUS

As a wood-dove newly shot,

She sobbed and lifted her breast ;
She sighed and covered her eyes,
Filling her lips with sighs ;
She sighed, she withdrew herself not,
   She refrained not, taking not rest ;

SEMICHORUS

But as the wind which is drouth,
   And as the air which is death,
As storm that severeth ships,
Her breath severing her lips,
The breath came forth of her mouth
And the fire came forth of her breath.

SECOND MESSENGER

Queen, and you maidens, there is come
   on us
A thing more deadly than the face of
   death ;
Meleager the good lord is as one slain.

SEMICHORUS

Without sword, without sword is he
   stricken ;
   Slain, and slain without hand.

SECOND MESSENGER

For as keen ice divided of the sun
His limbs divide, and as thawed snow the
   flesh
Thaws from off all his body to the hair.

SEMICHORUS

He wastes as the embers quicken ;
   With the brand he fades as a brand.

SECOND MESSENGER

Even while they sang and all drew hither
   and he
Lifted both hands to crown the Arcadian's
   hair
And fix the looser leaves, both hands fell
   down.

SEMICHORUS

With rending of cheek and of hair
   Lament ye, mourn for him, weep.

SECOND MESSENGER

Straightway the crown slid off and smote
   on earth,

First fallen ; and he, grasping his own
   hair, groaned
And cast his raiment round his face and
   fell.

SEMICHORUS

Alas for visions that were,
   And soothsayings spoken in sleep.

SECOND MESSENGER

But the king twitched his reins in and
   leapt down
And caught him, crying out twice 'O
   child' and thrice,
So that men's eyelids thickened with their
   tears.

SEMICHORUS

Lament with a long lamentation,
   Cry, for an end is at hand.

SECOND MESSENGER

O son, he said, son, lift thine eyes, draw
   breath,
Pity me ; but Meleager with sharp lips
Gasped, and his face waxed like as sun-
   burnt grass.

SEMICHORUS

Cry aloud, O thou kingdom, O nation,
   O stricken, a ruinous land.

SECOND MESSENGER

Whereat king Œneus, straightening feeble
   knees,
With feeble hands heaved up a lessening
   weight,
And laid him sadly in strange hands, and
   wept.

SEMICHORUS

Thou art smitten, her lord, her desire,
   Thy dear blood wasted as rain.

SECOND MESSENGER

And they with tears and rendings of the
   beard
Bear hither a breathing body, wept upon
And lightening at each footfall, sick to
   death.

SEMICHORUS

Thou madest thy sword as a fire,
    With fire for a sword thou art slain.

SECOND MESSENGER

And lo, the feast turned funeral, and the
    crowns
Fallen ; and the huntress and the hunter
    trapped ;
And weeping and changed faces and veiled
    hair.

MELEAGER

Let your hands meet
    Round the weight of my head ;
Lift ye my feet
    As the feet of the dead ;
For the flesh of my body is molten, the
    limbs of it molten as lead.

CHORUS

O thy luminous face,
    Thine imperious eyes !
O the grief, O the grace,
    As of day when it dies !
Who is this bending over thee, lord, with
    tears and suppression of sighs ?

MELEAGER

Is a bride so fair ?
    Is a maid so meek ?
With unchapleted hair,
    With unfilleted cheek,
Atalanta, the pure among women, whose
    name is as blessing to speak.

ATALANTA

I would that with feet
    Unsandalled, unshod,
Overbold, overfleet,
    I had swum not nor trod
From Arcadia to Calydon northward, a
    blast of the envy of God.

MELEAGER

Unto each man his fate ;
    Unto each as he saith
In whose fingers the weight
    Of the world is as breath ;
Yet I would that in clamour of battle mine
    hands had laid hold upon death.

CHORUS

Not with cleaving of shields
    And their clash in thine ear,
When the lord of fought fields
    Breaketh spearshaft from spear,
Thou art broken, our lord, thou art bro-
    ken, with travail and labour and
    fear.

MELEAGER

Would God he had found me
    Beneath fresh boughs !
Would God he had bound me
    Unawares in mine house,
With light in mine eyes, and songs in my
    lips, and a crown on my brows !

CHORUS

Whence art thou sent from us ?
    Whither thy goal ?
How art thou rent from us,
    Thou that wert whole,
As with severing of eyelids and eyes, as
    with sundering of body and soul !

MELEAGER

My heart is within me
    As an ash in the fire ;
Whosoever hath seen me,
    Without lute, without lyre,
Shall sing of me grievous things, even
    things that were ill to desire.

CHORUS

Who shall raise thee
    From the house of the dead ?
Or what man praise thee
    That thy praise may be said ?
Alas thy beauty ! alas thy body ! alas thine
    head !

MELEAGER

But thou, O mother,
    The dreamer of dreams,
Wilt thou bring forth another
    To feel the sun's beams
When I move among shadows a shadow,
    and wail by impassable streams ?

ŒNEUS

What thing wilt thou leave me
    Now this thing is done ?

A man wilt thou give me,
A son for my son,
For the light of mine eyes, the desire of
my life, the desirable one ?

CHORUS

Thou wert glad above others,
Yea, fair beyond word ;
Thou wert glad among mothers ;
For each man that heard
Of thee, praise there was added unto thee,
as wings to the feet of a bird.

ŒNEUS

Who shall give back
Thy face of old years,
With travail made black,
Grown grey among fears,
Mother of sorrow, mother of cursing,
mother of tears ?

MELEAGER

Though thou art as fire
Fed with fuel in vain,
My delight, my desire,
Is more chaste than the rain,
More pure than the dewfall, more holy
than stars are that live without stain.

ATALANTA

I would that as water
My life's blood had thawn,
Or as winter's wan daughter
Leaves lowland and lawn
Spring-stricken, or ever mine eyes had be-
held thee made dark in thy dawn.

CHORUS

When thou dravest the men
Of the chosen of Thrace,
None turned him again
Nor endured he thy face
Clothed round with the blush of the battle,
with light from a terrible place.

ŒNEUS

Thou shouldst die as he dies
For whom none sheddeth tears ;
Filling thine eyes
And fulfilling thine ears
With the brilliance of battle, the bloom
and the beauty, the splendour of
spears.

CHORUS

In the ears of the world
It is sung, it is told,
And the light thereof hurled
And the noise thereof rolled
From the Acroceraunian snow to the ford
of the fleece of gold.

MELEAGER

Would God ye could carry me
Forth of all these ;
Heap sand and bury me
By the Chersonese
Where the thundering Bosphorus answers
the thunder of Pontic seas.

ŒNEUS

Dost thou mock at our praise
And the singing begun
And the men of strange days
Praising my son
In the folds of the hills of home, high
places of Calydon ?

MELEAGER

For the dead man no home is ;
Ah, better to be
What the flower of the foam is
In fields of the sea,
That the sea-waves might be as my rai-
ment, the gulf-stream a garment
for me.

CHORUS

Who shall seek thee and bring
And restore thee thy day,
When the dove dipt her wing
And the oars won their way
Where the narrowing Symplegades whit-
ened the straits of Propontis with
spray ?

MELEAGER

Will ye crown me my tomb
Or exalt me my name,
Now my spirits consume,
Now my flesh is a flame ?
Let the sea slake it once, and men speak
of me sleeping to praise me or
shame.

CHORUS

Turn back now, turn thee,

As who turns him to wake ;
Though the life in thee burn thee,
Couldst thou bathe it and slake
Where the sea-ridge of Helle hangs heav-
    ier, and east upon west waters
    break ?

MELEAGER

Would the winds blow me back
Or the waves hurl me home ?
Ah, to touch in the track
Where the pine learnt to roam
Cold girdles and crowns of the sea-gods,
    cool blossoms of water and foam !

CHORUS

The gods may release
    That they made fast ;
Thy soul shall have ease
    In thy limbs at the last ;
But what shall they give thee for life,
    sweet life that is overpast ?

MELEAGER

Not the life of men's veins,
    Not of flesh that conceives ;
But the grace that remains,
    The fair beauty that cleaves
To the life of the rains in the grasses, the
    life of the dews on the leaves.

CHORUS

Thou wert helmsman and chief ;
    Wilt thou turn in an hour,
Thy limbs to the leaf,
    Thy face to the flower,
Thy blood to the water, thy soul to the
    gods who divide and devour ?

MELEAGER

The years are hungry,
    They wail all their days ;
The gods wax angry
    And weary of praise ;
And who shall bridle their lips ? and who
    shall straiten their ways ?

CHORUS

The gods guard over us
    With sword and with rod ;
Weaving shadow to cover us,
    Heaping the sod,
That law may fulfil herself wholly, to
    darken man's face before God.

MELEAGER

O holy head of Œneus, lo thy son
Guiltless, yet red from alien guilt, yet foul
With kinship of contaminated lives,
Lo, for their blood I die ; and mine own
    blood
For bloodshedding of mine is mixed there-
    with,
That death may not discern me from my
    kin.
Yet with clean heart I die and faultless
    hand,
Not shamefully ; thou therefore of thy
    love
Salute me, and bid fare among the dead
Well, as the dead fare ; for the best man
    dead
Fares sadly ; nathless I now faring well
Pass without fear where nothing is to fear
Having thy love about me and thy good-
    will,
O father, among dark places and men
    dead.

ŒNEUS

Child, I salute thee with sad heart and
    tears,
And bid thee comfort, being a perfect man
In fight, and honourable in the house of
    peace.
The gods give thee fair wage and dues
    of death,
And me brief days and ways to come at
    thee.

MELEAGER

Pray thou thy days be long before thy
    death,
And full of ease and kingdom ; seeing in
    death
There is no comfort and none after-
    growth,
Nor shall one thence look up and see day's
    dawn
Nor light upon the land whither I go.
Live thou and take thy fill of days and die
When thy day comes ; and make not much
    of death
Lest ere thy day thou reap an evil thing.
Thou too, the bitter mother and mother-
    plague
Of this my weary body — thou too, queen,
The source and end, the sower and the
    scythe,

The rain that ripens and the drought that
        slays,
The sand that swallows and the spring
        that feeds,
To make me and unmake me — thou, I
        say,
Althæa, since my father's ploughshare,
        drawn
Through fatal seedland of a female field,
Furrowed thy body, whence a wheaten ear
Strong from the sun and fragrant from
        the rains
I sprang and cleft the closure of thy
        womb,
Mother, I dying with unforgetful tongue
Hail thee as holy and worship thee as just
Who art unjust and unholy; and with my
        knees
Would worship, but thy fire and subtlety,
Dissundering them, devour me; for these
        limbs
Are as light dust and crumblings from
        mine urn
Before the fire has touched them; and
        my face
As a dead leaf or dead foot's mark on
        snow,
And all this body a broken barren tree
That was so strong, and all this flower of
        life
Disbranched and desecrated miserably,
And minished all that god-like muscle and
        might
And lesser than a man's: for all my veins
Fail me, and all mine ashen life burns
        down.
I would thou hadst let me live; but gods
        averse,
But fortune, and the fiery feet of change,
And time, these would not, these tread out
        my life,
These and not thou; me too thou hast
        loved, and I
Thee; but this death was mixed with all
        my life,
Mine end with my beginning: and this
        law,
This only, slays me, and not my mother
        at all.
And let no brother or sister grieve too sore,
Nor melt their hearts out on me with
        their tears,
Since extreme love and sorrowing over-
        much
Vex the great gods, and overloving men
Slay and are slain for love's sake; and
        this house
Shall bear much better children; why
        should these

Weep? but in patience let them live their
        lives
And mine pass by forgotten: thou alone,
Mother, thou sole and only, thou not
        these,
Keep me in mind a little when I die
Because I was thy first-born; let thy soul
Pity me, pity even me gone hence and
        dead,
Though thou wert wroth, and though
        thou bear again
Much happier sons, and all men later born
Exceedingly excel me; yet do thou
Forget not, nor think shame; I was thy
        son.
Time was I did not shame thee; and
        time was
I thought to live and make thee honour-
        able
With deeds as great as these men's; but
        they live,
These, and I die; and what thing should
        have been
Surely I know not; yet I charge thee,
        seeing
I am dead already, love me not the less,
Me, O my mother; I charge thee by these
        gods,
My father's, and that holier breast of
        thine,
By these that see me dying, and that which
        nursed,
Love me not less, thy first-born: though
        grief come,
Grief only, of me, and of all these great
        joy,
And shall come always to thee; for thou
        knowest,
O mother, O breasts that bare me, for ye
        know,
O sweet head of my mother, sacred eyes,
Ye know my soul albeit I sinned, ye know
Albeit I kneel not neither touch thy knees,
But with my lips I kneel, and with my
        heart
I fall about thy feet and worship thee.
And ye farewell now, all my friends; and
        ye,
Kinsmen, much younger and glorious more
        than I,
Sons of my mother's sister; and all fare-
        well
That were in Colchis with me, and bare
        down
The waves and wars that met us: and
        though times
Change, and though now I be not any-
        thing,
Forget not me among you, what I did

In my good time; for even by all those
days,
Those days and this, and your own living
souls,
And by the light and luck of you that live,
And by this miserable spoil, and me
Dying, I beseech you, let my name not die.
But thou, dear, touch me with thy rose-
like hands,
And fasten up mine eyelids with thy
mouth,
A bitter kiss; and grasp me with thine
arms,
Printing with heavy lips my light waste
flesh,
Made light and thin by heavy-handed fate,
And with thine holy maiden eyes drop
dew,
Drop tears for dew upon me who am
dead,
Me who have loved thee; seeing without
sin done
I am gone down to the empty weary house
Where no flesh is nor beauty nor swift
eyes
Nor sound of mouth nor might of hands
and feet.
But thou, dear, hide my body with thy
veil,
And with thy raiment cover foot and head,
And stretch thyself upon me and touch
hands
With hands and lips with lips: be pitiful
As thou art maiden perfect; let no man
Defile me to despise me, saying, This man
Died woman-wise, a woman's offering,
slain
Through female fingers in his woof of life,
Dishonourable; for thou hast honoured
me.
And now for God's sake kiss me once and
twice
And let me go; for the night gathers me,
And in the night shall no man gather
fruit.

ATALANTA

Hail thou: but I with heavy face and feet
Turn homeward and am gone out of thine
eyes.

CHORUS

Who shall contend with his lords
    Or cross them or do them wrong?
Who shall bind them as with cords?
    Who shall tame them as with song?
Who shall smite them as with swords?
    For the hands of their kingdom are
    strong.

BIBLIOGRAPHY

Agate, James, ed. *The English Dramatic Critics, 1660–1932: An Anthology.* London, 1932.

Archer, William. *English Dramatists of Today.* London, 1882.

Archer, William, and Lowe, R. W., eds. *Dramatic Essays of George Henry Lewes.* London, 1896.

Archer, William. *W. C. Macready.* London, 1890.

Armstrong, C. F. *From Shakespeare to Shaw.* London, 1913.

Arnold, Matthew. *Letters of an Old Playgoer.* Edited by Brander Matthews. New York, 1919.

Ashley, Leonard R. N., ed. *Nineteenth-Century British Drama.* Glenview, Ill., 1967.

Baker, H. B. *History of the London Stage.* London, 1904.

Baker, W. T. *The Manchester Stage: 1800–1900.* London, 1903.

Bates, Alfred, ed. *The Drama.* 2 vols. London, 1913.

Batho, Edith, and Dobree, Bonamy. *The Victorians and After.* New York, 1938.

Booth, Michael R. *English Melodrama.* London, 1965.

Bradbrook, M. C. *English Dramatic Form: A History of Its Development.* London, 1965.

Brandes, Georg. *Main Currents in Nineteenth Century Literature.* 5 vols. London, 1906.

Brereton, A. *Dramatic Notes.* London, 1881–1882.

Bunn, Alfred. *The Stage.* 3 vols. London, 1840.

Child, H. "Nineteenth-Century Drama," *Cambridge History of English Literature* 13:203–5. London, 1916.

Clark, Barrett H. *A Study of the Modern Drama.* London, 1925.

Cook, Dutton. *On the Stage.* 2 vols. London, 1883.

Darbyshire, A. *The Art of the Victorian Stage.* London, 1907.

Dibdin, J. C. *The Annals of the Edinburgh Stage.* London, 1888.

Donoghue, Dennis. *The Third Voice.* New York, 1966.

Downer, Alan S. *The British Drama: A Handbook and Brief Chronicle.* New York, 1950.

Eldredge, H. J. *'The Stage' Cyclopedia.* London, 1909.

Elton, Oliver. *A Survey of English Literature, 1830–1880.* 2 vols. London, 1920.

Evans, Sir B. Ifor. *A Short History of English Drama.* London, 1948.

Evans, Bertrand. *Gothic Drama from Walpole to Shelley.* Berkeley, Calif., 1947.

Filon, Augustin. *The English Stage, Being an Account of the Victorian Drama.* Translated by Frederic Whyte. London, 1897.

Firkins, Ina Ten Eyck. *Index to Plays, 1800–1926.* New York, 1927.

Fitzgerald, P. H. *A New History of the English Stage (1660–1842).* 2 vols. London, 1882.

Granville-Barker, Harley, ed. *The Eighteen-Seventies.* Cambridge, 1929.

Grein, J. T. *Dramatic Criticism.* 3 vols. London, 1899–1903.

Hartnell, Phyllis, ed. *The Oxford Companion to the Theatre.* London, 1957.

Hazlitt, William. *A View of the English Stage.* Edited by William Archer and R. W. Lowe. London, 1895.

Heilman, Robert B. "Tragedy and Melodrama: Speculations on Generic Form." *Texas Quarterly* 3 (Summer 1960) : 36–50.

Heraud, J. A. *The Present Position of the Dramatic Poet in England.* London, 1841.

Horne, R. H. *A New Spirit of the Age.* 2 vols. London, 1844.

Huneker, James G. *Iconoclasts: A Book of Dramatists.* London, 1905.

Irving, Sir Henry. *The Stage.* London, 1878.

Jones, F. M. *On the Causes of the Decline of the Drama.* Edinburgh, 1834.

Jones, Henry A. *The Renascence of the English Drama.* London, 1895.

Joseph, B. L. *The Tragic Actor . . . from Burbage to Irving.* London, 1959.

Knight, J. *The History of the English Stage During the Reign of Victoria.* London, 1901.

Lennox, William, Lord. *Plays, Players, and Playhouses.* 2 vols. London, 1881.

Lewes, G. H. *On Actors and Acting.* London, 1875.

Lowe, Robert W. *A Bibliographical Account of English Theatrical Literature.* London, 1888.

Lucas, F. L. *Ten Victorian Poets.* 3rd ed. New York, 1966.

Matthews, Brander, and Hutton, Laurence, eds. *Actors and Actresses . . . David Garrick to the Present.* 5 vols. New York, 1886.

Mears, Richard. "Serious Verse Drama in England, 1812–1850." Ph.D. Diss. University of North Carolina, Chapel Hill, 1954.

Montague, C. E. "The Literary Play." *Essays and Studies* 2 (1911) : 71–90.

Nag, U. C. "The English Theatre of the Romantic Revival," *Nineteenth Century* 104 (1928) : 384–98.

Neville, Henry. *The Stage: Its Past and Present in Relation to Fine Art.* London, 1875.

Nicoll, Allardyce. *British Drama.* 4th ed. London, 1947.

Nicoll, Allardyce. *A History of English Drama, 1660–1900.* Rev. ed. 5 vols. See especially vols. 4 and 5. Cambridge, 1959.

Peacock, Ronald. *The Poet in the Theatre.* New York, 1960.

Pearson, Hesketh. *The Last Actor-Managers.* London, 1950.

Pollock, Sir Frederick, ed. *Macready's Reminiscences.* 2 vols. London, 1875.

Reynolds, Ernest. *Early Victorian Drama, 1830–1870.* Cambridge, 1936.

Rowell, George. *The Victorian Theatre.* London, 1956.

Scott, C. W. *The Drama of Yesterday and Today.* 2 vols. London, 1899.

Scrimgeour, Gary J. "Nineteenth-Century Drama." *Victorian Studies* 12 (Sept. 1968) : 91–100.

Shaw, Desmond. *London Nights of Long Ago.* London, 1927.

Thouless, Priscilla. *Modern Poetic Drama.* Oxford, 1934.

Toynbee, William, ed. *The Diaries of William Macready.* 2 vols. London, 1912.

Watson, E. B. *Sheridan to Robertson: A Study of the Nineteenth Century London Stage.* Cambridge, Mass., 1926.

West, E. J. "The London Stage, 1870–1890." *University of Colorado Studies* 2, Series B (1943) : 31–84.

Wynne, A. *The Growth of English Drama.* Oxford, 1914.